Discover

A Better Vocabulary, A Better Way
Second Edition

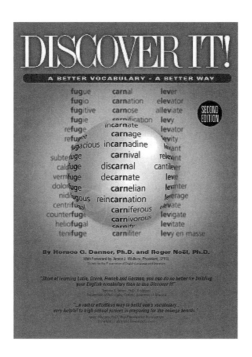

By
Horace G. Danner, Ph.D.
Professor of Communication
University of Maryland University College
Adelphi, Maryland

Roger Noël, Ph.D.
Chairperson, Department of Modern Foreign Languages
Georgia College and State University
Milledgeville, Georgia

Occoquan Books
Occoquan, VA 22125

Discover It!
A Better Vocabulary, A Better Way

Printed in the United States of America

ISBN: 0-937600-04-0 (this permabound edition)
Library of Congress Control Number: 2004092603

ISBN: 0-937600-05-9
(with GBC binding)

ISBN: 0-937600-06-7
(loose-leaf edition licensed for on-site reproduction)

Additional books by the authors
A Thesaurus of Medical Word Roots
A Thesaurus of Word Roots of the English Language
The English Tree of Roots: and Words from around the World

TABLE OF CONTENTS

(Each section is preceded by pretests and posttests on the word clusters
   and wordbuilders.)

Supplemental Section

DEDICATION

Dr. Danner dedicates his efforts in this book
to his six grandchildren,
Nathan, Alissa, Margaret, Donna, Susan, Madelline.

Dr. Noël dedicates his efforts in this book
to his wife,
Cookie.

ACKNOWLEDGMENTS

THIS BOOK IS THE RESULT OF THE COLLABORATIVE EFFORTS OF COLLEGE PROFESSORS, HIGH SCHOOL TEACHERS, PHYSICIANS, LAWYERS, ENGINEERS, COMPUTER SCIENTISTS, MINISTERS, PRIESTS, HOME SCHOOL TEACHERS, AND OTHER PROFESSIONALS who have either read the first edition of this book in its original version, *An Introduction to an Academic Vocabulary*, or portions of the manuscript of later editions. These individuals have made many valuable suggestions; they have indicated the most important words in their particular fields; and they have also added words, as well as the meanings as those words are used in their fields. The book is a more complete learning package because of their combined efforts.

Members of The MITRE Corporation (where Dr. Danner was a technical editor and foreign communications analyst) who contributed to this book are as follows: Malcolm J. Airst and Daniel P. Dunbrack, electrical engineers; Robert T. Garrow, Major, USMC, Retired, Russian linguist; Edward F. Gonzalez, aeronautical engineer, Paul T. Hedeman, theoretical chemist; J. Fredrick Klingener, mechanical engineer; Frank E. Owens, systems engineer; Lucjan J. Rusiecki, Slavic linguist; William A. Tidwell, Brigadier General, USA, Retired, member of the technical staff; and John W. Watson, Ph.D., comparative linguist.

For those educators who have used previous editions of the book and for their helpful comments, the authors are indeed appreciative. In addition to the book being used in colleges and universities, over 200 public and private schools and school systems have used it, from Fairfax County Public Schools, Fairfax, VA, to the American Embassy School in New Delhi, India, to the Military Dependents School at Ankara, Turkey. The book has also been used in the two state universities of Estonia. Bookseller amazon.com lists ten five-star reviews of the previous edition.

To Craig Prall, a computer systems consultant, the authors are deeply appreciative. Craig formatted the first version of the book so that it could be printed in near-typeset quality. The current edition was formatted throughout by Chris Cruz, a student of Dr. Danner. A very special thanks to Chris for aligning and bolding the common elements, which was no easy job. Chris was such a pleasure to work with.

Dr. Danner is especially grateful to The Honorable Dumitru Aldea, First Secretary of the Embassy of Romania, Washington, DC, and to other Embassy personnel, not only for checking the Romanian elements but also for relating fascinating information concerning the history and *romance* of the Romanian language.

Dr. Danner is also grateful to his students at Northern Virginia Community College, Annandale; Manassas; Alexandria campuses; and at Montgomery College, Rockville, Maryland, for their critiquing the book in its developmental stages.

The authors are indebted to Blake Archeleta, Bill Bartelmes, Kevin Clark, Kevin Eaton, and Mike Patrow for reading portions of the manuscript. Dr. Eric Strobel, who holds a Ph.D. in physics, read the entire manuscript and offered many suggestions on terms used in mathematics and physics. Dr. Rebecca Keller, professor of chemistry, University of New Mexico, Albuquerque, was most helpful in identifying words used in chemistry. Thank you, Rebecca. A very special thanks goes to Dr. Patterson Ellis for checking the book from a theological standpoint. His knowledge of Greek and Hebrew, his extensive knowledge of biology, and his impeccable use of grammar added finesse to the book. Kathy Clark, an educator with Prince William County (VA) Public Schools, edited the final version of the manuscript.

For computer expertise and desktop publishing assistance throughout the many recent revisions of this book, including formatting of the front and back matter of the second edition, Dr. Danner would like to thank Ric Clark, of Trinity Rivers Publishing, Manassas, Virginia. He also converted the computer files to the format required for printing and binding by Sheridan Books of Ann Arbor, Michigan. And to the good people at the Fredericksburg office of Sheridan, Dr. Danner would like to recognize them for their patience, understanding, and excellent work: Marcel Southern, Julie Good, and Karlene Browder. In addition, Jane Perry, the receptionist, was always very helpful. The book was printed and bound at Sheridan's headquarters in Ann Arbor, Michigan. Jean Schroeder supervised the final production; her patience and professionalism are appreciated.

Dr. Danner wishes to thank his friend Donald Peabody for researching the background of the Iditarod dog sled race on MSN's Encarta search engine. In addition, retired Navy Captain William (Bill) Carpenter, a survivor of Pearl Harbor, translated the Japanese war cry: Tora! Tora! Tora!

Though James J. Kilpatrick, syndicated wordsmith columnist, doesn't know it, I owe him credit for jogging my memory. I was reading one of his columns called "Writer's Art," where he mentioned the use of idioms. I found that I had not included the root, *idio-*, **one's own**. Consequently, I added that as one of the **wordbuilders**, but had to append it after *zyme*, p. 214. I had already found that I had omitted the prefix *pro-*; therefore, I added it after *idio-*. If I had put the two elements in their respective places, it would have thrown off all the cross-references.

Dr. Danner would also like to express his gratitude to Thomas H. Estes, Ph.D., Professor Emeritus of Reading and former Department Head, University of Virginia, Charlottesville, for his seeing the value of the first edition and adopting it as a textbook at the university. Now retired, Dr. Estes serves as a consultant in reading. You may contact him at the@virginia.edu.

Finally, Dr. Danner wishes to express his appreciation to Steve and Gwynn Fuchs of Lexington Design Group, Arlington, Virginia, for their designing the cover for this edition.

With the extensive cross-references and the multiple indexes, it is quite possible there is an error, or *errors*, in the book. Dr. Danner would appreciate your sending any corrections to book@occoquanbooks.com, or mail them to Occoquan Books, PO Box 614, Occoquan, VA 22125. In addition, you may call him at 703-491-5283.

FOREWORD TO THE SECOND EDITION

Everyone who is able to speak has a vocabulary. Basic vocabularies are built without the expenditure of much labor. Toddlers learn the words for the necessities of life rather effortlessly, simply by listening, absorbing, and repeating. By the time a child reaches adolescence, he or she has acquired enough words needed to survive in a verbal society, all without consciously working at it.

Then comes the hard part. Just as the great pyramids of ancient Egypt were built one massive stone at a time, a good vocabulary is built one new word at a time. For students and adults who see value in developing a strong, professional vocabulary, the authors have performed a great service by giving us *Discover It!*, a volume that facilitates the process immensely.

Dr. Danner, a renowned philologist, and Dr. Noël, a gifted linguist, are both experts in the origins as well as the meanings of words. But users of this book need not fear: You will be able to "discover" and add to your stockpile hundreds of new words without (consciously) memorizing a single Latin or Greek root. You won't need to learn Sanskrit or study Chaucerian English. The authors have found a better way, and this book passes that knowledge along to you.

The best part of the process is that it is exciting and interesting. One can master the method rather quickly. From there, it's a word adventure, a small investment of time and effort that pays real dividends.

Discover It! should be in the hands of every person who wants to have a vocabulary that's useful, professional, precise, and impressive.

James J. Wallace
President
Society for the Preservation of English Language and Literature

FOREWORD TO THE FIRST EDITION

Many years ago as a high school senior, I studied vocabulary from a little blue book under Mrs. Gillespie's disciplining gaze. Twenty-five words a week, five words a day. Every Friday morning, she tested us—on five words total: four from the current week and one from any of the previous. It was, to say the least, grueling.

Memorizing vocabulary out of context is like trying to catch rain in a Kleenex. At best, it frustrates the students who are trying to make meaning of the world they're creating. At worst, it is a means of keeping students down.

Equally frustrating is the sage advice I got from several English professors when I was an undergraduate. "If you want to improve your vocabulary, my son, read, read, read." I was reading—morning, noon, and night—but I still felt deficient in vocabulary, the kind of vocabulary that would enliven and enrich my writing and would inform my writing.

By the time I graduated from college, I had amassed thousands of words in my long-term memory—words which I used well. I was, after all, a fluent native of the English language. I had learned from my parents, peers, teachers, and books. I had learned the way most speakers learn their first language—by hearing and guessing, by stretching and questioning—all within context. It was the total-immersion method at its best.

Unfortunately, we all reach a stage when attempting to learn new words from conversations or reading becomes an activity with diminishing returns. To learn any subject, one has to stop doing and sit down with the theory, the abstract principles derived from practice and research.

Dr. Danner has devised a method that I find immensely productive. It's "learner-centered." That's educationese which means that the person reading this book is in the driver's seat. Horace calls it inductive learning—you scan the words in the cluster list and discover the root meaning. It's like a puzzle—and like a puzzle—it's fun.

Then you go to the *Clavis*, Latin for "key," which defines the words you were guessing about only moments before. Clever fellow, this Horace. He knew I wanted answers at the flip of a page. The Clavis, however, is no ordinary list of definitions. It's juicy—succulent in meanings that grab you where you stand, teetering on the edge of knowing.

This is a deceptive book. It teaches, and you learn while you're having an uproarious time, cavorting in a semantic and etymological field. And because you're having so much fun, you return, time and again. What Mrs. Gillespie could do only with quizzes, Professor Danner has done with structure, meaning, and enjoyment. And Dr. Noël's extensive knowledge in Greek, Latin, French, Spanish, Italian, and German makes this book rich in the classics as well as in expressions in other languages.

This book is a miniature college education and certainly deserves a place in the vocabulary teaching of high school students as they prepare for the college entrance examinations.

No two persons will have the same experience with this book. The words which I focused on in my first reading were not the ones I focused on in my second reading. I found myself raising my level of difficulty, selecting words which I previously found too difficult.

But enough of forewords. This book is meant to be enjoyed. I suspect that even those students for whom this book has been assigned will find it a joy to read, reread, and continue to reread. Let the fun of discovery begin!

Donald R. Gallehr, Ph.D.
Professor of English
Director, Northern Virginia Writing Project
George Mason University
Fairfax, Virginia

PREFACE

There are two principal purposes for writing a book: either there is something that needs to be said, or there is a better, more effective way of saying what has already been said. Certainly, the latter is the main purpose in this work, for there is a plethora of books dealing with etymology and academic and professional vocabulary development.

Though these books have been instructive and informative, not one has employed an inductive, or *discovery*, approach to mastering the art of vocabulary building. In this book, it is hoped that this deficiency will be corrected, for the book has been built around readers discovering the answers for themselves.

More than a compilation of vocabulary exercises, however, this book is a handbook, a thesaurus, a storehouse, a *vade mecum* (Latin for "go with me," or **a handbook**). It is a book you can refer to at odd moments, or one you can diligently study from cover to cover. It is a browsing book or a textbook, depending on your purpose. Teachers in both high school and college, as well as home school teachers, are encouraged to use it either as a basic, or as a supplementary, text.

The format is arranged so that the right-hand page lists the word cluster, or words with a common element. In addition, there are words with disguised roots, which are those words whose forms have changed as the words passed through centuries of use in locales quite apart from ancient Rome or Greece. The histories of some of these words are quite intriguing; if these words spark your interest to research further their etymological background, and thereby lend meaning to your reading and expression, the book will have been worth the effort. That which has taken the authors several decades to learn by memorization, or by saturation in the languages from infancy can now be simply "discovered."

By scanning the words in the Word Cluster where the common element is in bold, you should attempt to determine what the common element means. Simply choose two or three words, the meanings of which are known reasonably well; after defining them in your own words, you will notice a central meaning in all of them. From years of testing this approach, it has been found that almost invariably the deduced meaning will be correct, but you have only to turn the page to check your answer.

In addition to the elements from the Romance languages (French, Romanian, Italian, Portuguese, and Spanish as well as Catalan and Provençal), words from Greek and German as well as from other Indo-European languages have been included. The authors have concentrated on the Romance languages, inasmuch as these have had the greatest impact upon a general academic and professional vocabulary. However, the majority of medical and scientific words are from Greek.

Also on the word cluster page are cognates from the five major Romance languages. This feature alone can help you see the similarities of words within these languages as well as the influence of a particular language on English; this feature can also reinforce your learning of these languages. Since English is basically a Germanic language, having been derived ultimately from the languages of the Angles, the Saxons, and other Germanic tribes who invaded Britain (before it was called Angleland, or England), words from German have been included as well.

Many words in the Word Cluster may prod you to ask what a particular word has to do with the common element under consideration. For example, on p. 85, there are listed *fugitive, refugee, nidifugous,* and *centrifugal,* among others. You can readily surmise that the meaning of the root *fug* has something to do with running away, fleeing, or escaping. But what, you may ask, does *centrifugal* have to do with running away or escaping? Turning the page to the *Clavis,* you will immediately find that *centrifugal* describes a force that *flees from the center*. *Clavis* is Latin for key—that which opens doors; it has come to mean a key to opening or discovering the meanings to words, thus a glossary, or a set of explanatory notes.

Along with the Clavis, the Latin base, as well as the Indo-European root, has been listed. The appendix of roots in the *American Heritage Dictionary*, the cross-referencing of roots in *Webster's New World Dictionary*, and Eric Partridge's *Origins* were indispensable aids in preparing this feature.

It is important to understand that English is set against the background of the Indo-European languages. Since Indo-European is prehistoric, there are no written accounts of the languages. But comparative linguists have long noted the similarities of certain words in such diverse languages as Albanian, Armenian, Celtic, Danish, Dutch, English, German, Greek, Hindi, Latin, Lithuanian, Persian, Polish, Punjabi, Russian, Sanskrit, Urdu, and Welsh. These linguists have concluded that there was once a common language spoken throughout Europe and that this language extended to India, thus the term Indo-European. To gain an even greater benefit from this book, you are encouraged to explore further the Indo-European language. Especially, it is suggested that you explore Grimm's Law, which describes "the great shift" in both vowels and consonants; for example, the *f* in Latin *frater* (brother) in Latin becomes *b* of *brother* in English and *Bruder* in German (all nouns in German are capitalized). Throughout the book, references to the Indo-European language are indicated by IE.

There was often not enough space for developing many of the ideas. Consequently, we have often been assertive rather than expository; however, it is anticipated that the serious student will corroborate the authors' assertions. Such corroboration can be an enriched learning experience, regardless if you are a high school or college student, a home-schooled student, or a seasoned professional.

Unlike many other vocabulary books, there are no roots to memorize; the breakthrough of the book is that you capitalize on your reservoir of knowledge. Further, it is not expected, nor is it suggested, that the definitions of individual words be memorized.

The underlying principle of this book is to guide in bonding the words and word elements. After you have worked through the book, with its one hundred Latin and Greek word families, related words from German, other Indo-European languages, as well as words from non-Indo-European languages, e.g., Arabic, Chinese, Hindi, Japanese, Korean, hundreds, even thousands, of academic and professional words will be permanently established in your memory. Probably more important than this knowledge will be the habit of automatically grouping words and seeing their similar forms, and hence their similar meanings. For instance, the root *spec* is not included as a cluster in this book, but it will immediately be seen that *spectator, spectacle, speculate, aspect, circumspect, inspect, introspect, respect, retrospect*, and *suspect* are in this family. As you study this particular word family further, you will discover that *despise, despicable, conspicuous, respite, especial, frontispiece*, and *auspice* are also in this family.

Where there was room on the word cluster page, we have included the features **wordextra** and **wordbuilder**, which we have found to be beneficial in building an extensive vocabulary; we have also indicated words derived from the names of people, places, as well as from classical mythology, legends, and history. Mottoes of colleges, universities, countries, and movements have also been included. These features will reward the reader's diligence and will provide a wealth of expertise in using a mature, professional vocabulary. In this revised edition, writing tips have been interspersed throughout the book.

The practical aspect of this book is that you can immediately discern the meaning of an unfamiliar word from your reading or lectures, or a standardized test, such as a college entrance examination. For instance, if *nidifugous* (previously referred to) is encountered in the sentence: "Nidifugous birds are not dependent on their parents for sustenance," you can more easily discern the meaning of at least part of the word; added to this knowledge is the context of the sentence in the paragraph in which the sentence occurs. Even if you are not aware that *nidi* is from Latin *nidus*, meaning "nest," you would still be able to infer some of the meaning, and given the context, might surely be able to discern the entire meaning: describing a bird that flees the nest shortly after being hatched, the best example of which is a chicken, unlike arboreal birds, such as the robin, which must be fed by their parents. The counterpart of *nidifugous* is *nidicolous*, where *col* comes from *colere*, meaning "to dwell."

The exercises are designed to produce optimum results: you should immediately notice an increased awareness in your reading, listening, and thinking, and a greater ease of expression in your writing and speaking. In addition, this book should aid in gaining a fuller appreciation of the vast influence of the Greek and Roman civilizations upon present-day society. These influences are especially evident in architecture, music, law, the military, engineering, drama, rhetoric, philosophy, as well as in language and literature.

The ancient Greeks were the first to develop a democratic way of life, albeit not a benefit they extended to the enslaved victims of their conquests. They also produced the Western world's first great dramatists, historians, orators, philosophers, and poets. They were also the first to study botany, geometry, medicine, physics, and zoology on a scientific basis.

When Rome conquered Greece before the time of Christ, the Romans assimilated not only much of Greek mythology, philosophy, drama, and rhetoric, but also adopted many Greek words for which there were no Latin counterparts. As an example, Greek *perimeter* literally means "the distance around (any object)." Since the Romans already used *circumference* to refer to the same concept, they adopted *perimeter* to means "the distance around a sided

object," and retained *circumference* to refer only to "the distance around a circle." Thus, the rather sparse and concrete Latin language was enhanced by the subtle nuances of Greek. In addition, some of the wealthier Roman young men were sent to Athens to study philosophy and rhetoric. There is no doubt that this influence helped produce Cicero, Horace, Ovid, and Virgil, to mention only a few of the Roman literati whose works are referenced in this book.

Thus, the classical languages of Latin and Greek, as well as German, form the foundation of this book. The following categories illustrate some Latin elements that have been absorbed into English. First, there are words which have entered English without so much as change of letter, e.g., *impetus, bonus, onus, opus, datum, exit*; there are possibly more than a hundred words in this category. Second, there are Latin words which English has anglicized with only a minor change, e.g., *alien, antique, arbitrate, auction, brevity, mandate, opinion*. Next, there are words that have been derived through one of the Romance languages. For example, *journal* is French, but comes from Latin *diurnalis*, **daily**; *piano* is Italian and means "soft" in music, but ultimately comes from Latin *planus*, which means "smooth," or "flat," and which also yields *plane* and *plain*, known as doublets.

There is also a host of Latin phrases and expressions in both academic and general use, such as *alma mater, modus operandi, habeas corpus, semper fidelis, sine qua non*, and *persona non grata*, to mention only a few. Space does not permit detailing the rationale for the montaging of this vast array of words in English, a Germanic language. Instead, it is suggested that you explore the history of English; you might begin by reading the entry on "English language" in an encyclopedia or on the Internet. Other works that may of interest are included in the *List of Works* of this book (p. 225).

Practical use has been made of both Latin and Greek in science and technology. Inventions, discoveries, and commercial products as well as scientific classifications of plants utilize Latin worldwide. For example, Bon Ami, a cleaning compound, and French for "good friend," may convey the idea that the product is a good friend to the cleaning person, whose job will be made lighter by using this particular product. The claim that "it hasn't scratched yet" may also convey the idea that the cleaner will be a "good friend" to the object being cleaned. Scientific classifications, e.g., Juglans Regis—Walnut king—is the scientific classification for the California walnut, more commonly known as the English walnut, or the soft-shelled walnut.

So that the value of the book can continue to be verified empirically, sectional tests have been provided; these tests may be used as both pretests and posttests. Altogether, there are 100 word cluster questions, one for each word cluster in the book. These questions have been placed before each section of ten word clusters. Simply take the test, listing answers in the left column; after a section has been completed, take the same test as a posttest, listing the answers in the right column. Answers may be checked by noting the meanings of the common elements on the even-numbered pages of the book. After the book has been completely finished, take the composite test found in Appendix A, p. 215; the answer key to Appendix A is found in Appendix C, p. 221. A pretest on the **wordbuilders** has been included as well; the answers to this test are found within the **wordbuilders** themselves. As with the test on word clusters, this test may also be taken as a posttest. A composite **wordbuilders** test is found in Appendix B, p. 218; the answers to the composite tests are found in Appendix D, p. 221.

Suggestions for improving the book are solicited; your ideas will be beneficial in structuring future editions. Correspondence should be sent to Horace G. Danner, Occoquan Books, PO Box 614, Occoquan, Virginia 22125, or email to danner@occoquanbooks.com.

In a book of this scope and with so many cross-references, it is possible that errors may have crept in. You are encouraged to send these as well as any other errors that may exist. Your help will be appreciated.

A NOTE ON THE TESTS

A test of the word clusters as well as of the wordbuilders is placed before each 20-page section. These tests should be taken before working through the exercises in each section; the answers are revealed as one works through the particular section. The answers for the word clusters are found on the verso, or the page after the recto (the right-hand page); the answers to the wordbuilders are found in the wordbuilders themselves. After completing a section, it is recommended that the reader retake the tests. For a final check on the word clusters, take the composite test (Appendix A, p. 215); the answer key is found in Appendix C (p. 221). The composite wordbuilder post-test is found in Appendix B (p. 218); the answer key is found in Appendix D (p. 223).

Word Cluster Presection Scores

Section 1_____Section 2_____Section 3_____Section 4_____Section 5_____

Section 6_____Section 7_____Section 8_____Section 9_____Section 10_____

Total Presection Score _____

Record this score below.

Word Cluster Postsection Scores

Section 1_____Section 2_____Section 3_____Section 4_____Section 5_____

Section 6_____Section 7_____Section 8_____Section 9_____Section 10_____

Total Postsection Score _____

Record this score below.

Total Presection score_____ Total Postsection score_____

Difference in Score _____

Wordbuilder Presection Scores

Section 1_____Section 2_____Section 3_____Section 4_____Section 5_____

Section 6_____Section 7_____Section 8_____Section 9_____Section 10_____

Wordbuilder Postsection Scores

Section 1_____Section 2_____Section 3_____Section 4_____Section 5_____

Section 6_____Section 7_____Section 8_____Section 9_____Section 10_____

Supplemental Wordbuilder Presection Scores

Section 1_____Section 2_____Section 3_____Section 4_____Section 5_____

Section 6_____Section 7_____Section 8_____Section 9_____Section 10_____

Supplemental Wordbuilder Postsection Scores

Section 1_____Section 2_____Section 3_____Section 4_____Section 5_____

Section 6_____Section 7_____Section 8_____Section 9_____Section 10_____

Total Presection score_____ Total Postsection score_____

Difference in score _____

SUMMARY OF INSTRUCTIONS FOR USING BOOK

1. Take the test on both the word clusters and the wordbuilders before each section. (Do not look up the answers, as the answers will be "discovered" throughout the exercises.)

2. Read over the columned words for the particular cluster.

3. Notice the similarities of the words, that is, the columned common elements.

4. Select two or three words with which you are most familiar and define them in your own words.

5. From the recurring common meaning of the definitions, select the most likely meaning of the common element(s).

6. Write the meaning(s) in the blank provided, or to conserve the further use of the book, write the answer on a separate sheet of paper.

7. Turn the page and check the correctness of your answer(s).

8. Read over the Clavis notes to form a solid bond of the meaning of the common elements.

9. Turn back to the front page and read the additional material, that is, the information which follows the spaces for writing the answer(s). *The reader may wish to work through the entire book, skipping the additional material until a second reading.*

10. For those interested in how the common element is spelled in each of the primary Romance languages, see the Romance Cognates feature. This feature gives the form of the common element in French, Romanian, Italian, Portuguese, and Spanish.

11. Note the Greek cognate words or Greek words with similar meaning.

12. Note the German words and phrases.

13. Note the words or concepts to explore further.

14. As a bonus, read the wordbuilders and word wordextras, as well as additional information concerning origins of words, e.g., words from Greek and Roman mythology, words from persons' names.

15. After finishing a section, retake the test that precedes the section. Check the correctness of the answers. Record the score in the space provided.

16. Continue this procedure throughout the ten sections. After completing the entire book, take the composite word cluster postsection test (Appendix A, p. 215) as well the composite wordbuilder postsection test (Appendix B, p. 218). Then, check your answers using the keys for these two tests: use Appendix C, p. 221, for Appendix A; use Appendix D, p. 223, for Appendix B.

17. Record these final scores in the spaces provided on pp. xiii-xiv.

18. Refer to the book periodically to add words encountered in your reading and in lectures. These may be written in the blank pages at the end of the book. You may also wish to add particular words not listed in the index.

Have a pleasant and rewarding experience *exploring* (and *discovering*!) the English language.

Sectional Word Cluster Test

INSTRUCTIONS: For each set of words from Latin and Greek (and sometimes, French, Spanish, and German), write the common meaning in the blank. Follow these instructions for each of ten lessons (20 pages).

Example: **hypo**tenuse, **hypo**thesis, **sub**ject   <u>under</u>

		Presection Answer	Postsection Answer
1.	**alb**ino, **alb**umin, **leuk**emia, edel**weiss**	_____	_____
2.	**alti**meter, **alti**tude, contr**alto**, **acro**phobia	_____	_____
3.	**amb**le, **amb**ition, pre**amb**le, somn**amb**ulist	_____	_____
4.	**ann**uity, **ann**ual, super**ann**uated, cent**enn**ial	_____	_____
5.	**ante**bellum, **ante**cedent, **ante**diluvian, penny **ante**	_____	_____
6.	**arm**ada, **arm**adillo, **arm**ature, **arm**istice	_____	_____
7.	**aud**it, **aud**ition, **aud**itor, **aud**itorium	_____	_____
8.	a**bat**ement, a**bat**toir, com**bat**, de**bate**	_____	_____
9.	cui **bono**?, de**bon**air, **bene**fit, **eu**logy, **eu**phony	_____	_____
10.	**bi**ceps, **bi**cycle, **bi**gamy, **bi**valve, **ba**lance	_____	_____

_____ _____
Presection Score   Postsection Score

Note: Enter scores for this test and the following ones after completing this section; then, enter them on p. xvii.

The answers to each set of clusters are found within the material presented.

Sectional Wordbuilder Test

Throughout the book and as a supplement, there are wordbuilders; these wordbuilders are designed to help you build a family of words from a single root.

	Presection Answer	Postsection Answer
1. What is the meaning of *cur-* as in **cur**riculum, re**cur**?	_____	_____
2. What is the meaning of *all-* as in par**all**el, **allo**gamy?	_____	_____
3. What is the meaning of *pachy-* as in **pachy**derm, **pachy**cephalic?	_____	_____
4. What is the meaning of *alter-* as in **alter**cation, **alter**nate?	_____	_____
5. What is the meaning of *clam-* as in **clam**ant, ex**clam**ation ?	_____	_____
6. What is the meaning of *exo-* as in **exo**biology, **exo**gamy?	_____	_____
7. What is the meaning of *vest-* as in di**vest**, in**vest**?	_____	_____

_____   _____
Presection Score   Postsection Score

Note: Enter scores for this test and the following ones after completing this section; then, enter them on p. xviii.
The answers to each set of wordbuilders are found within the material presented.

```
alb        albus       albino      albatross     albumin       albescent
alba       albite      albedo      album         albumen       albuminuria
```

Common elements_____**Inferred Meaning**_____

Romance Cognates*	French	Romanian	Italian	Portuguese	Spanish
	alb-, aub-	alb-	alb-	alb-	alb-

Words with disguised Latin roots: abele, aubade, Alps, daub

Latin phrases: *alba firma, alba tunica, albus liber; terra alba, album graecum* (for last two phrases, see **Clavis**)

Frankish *blanc*, **brilliant**, superseded *albus*, resulting in *blanc, blanco, bianco*. For example, there is a *blanc-bec*, literally, **white beak**, meaning **beardless youth**, or **greenhorn**; also, *carte blanche; arme blanche*, **white arms**, said of non-firing weapons, such as swords and lances (see p. 11); also, **point-blank**, with the verb *point*, the *white* mark in the center of a target; often heard in the phrase *at point-blank range*; **straightforward, plain**, as *a point-blank answer*.

Placenames: Blanca, Colorado; Blanco, Casa Blanca (**White House**); both in New Mexico

NB*: *Albacore*, Arabic for **the young camel**, indicating a particular type of *tuna*, is not in this family.

*See p. 134, for **Cognate** as used in this book; see p. 18 for **NB** so used.

Latin *candere*, **to shine**, yields **can**escent; **cand**ela, **cand**elabrum, **cand**escent; **candid, candid**ate (see p. 175), **candl**e, **cand**or; in**cand**escent; **cand**ida Pax. Like *blank*, this root conveys the idea of **brilliant, shining**, as though **white**.

Greek: *leukos*, **white**: **leuk**emia,** **leuk**odontia, **leuk**oma; **leuk**oblast, **leuk**ocyte, **leuk**ocythemia, **leuk**ocytosis, **leuk**odermia, **leuk**openia, **leuk**oplakia, **leuk**oplasia, **leuk**orrhea; *leuco*: **leuc**oplast, **leuc**opoiesis. **–emia**, **abnormal blood condition**: e.g., acid**emia**, an**emia**, chol**emia**, glyc**emia**, hypoglyc**emia**, py**emia**, sapr**emia**, tox**emia**, ur**emia**.

Germanic: elf, edelweiss, eldritch, erlking

Indo-European (IE) *albho-*, **white**: **luc**arne, **dormer window**; **luc**ent, **luc**id, **luc**iferous, **Luc**ite®, e**luc**idate, trans-**luc**ent; **lun**ar, **lun**atic (see pp. 53, 187), cis**lun**ar; **light** (one meaning). Review background on IE languages, p. viii.

wordbuilder #1
Latin *currere*, **to run**, yields **cur**rency, **curr**ent, **curr**icle, **curr**iculum, curriculum vitae; con**cur**, in**cur**, oc**cur**, re**cur**; con**curr**ent; extra**curr**icular; **curse, curs**ive, **curs**or, **curs**orial; dis**curs**ion, ex**curs**ion; pre**curs**or; **course**, con-**course**, dis**course**, inter**course**, re**course**; **corr**al, **corr**ida, **corr**idor; **cors**air; **cour**ante, **cour**ier; suc**cor***. *Cursorial legs*, as of certain birds—or people—are those adapted for running. *Cursory*, **hasty, superficial**, describes that which is "done on the run." **Succor, aid, help**, is *secours* in French; hence, Bon Secour, Alabama (see p. 17).

Word from a person's name: *silhouette*: from *Étienne Silhouette* (1709-67), French Minister of Finance, in derogatory reference to his fiscal policies and to such amateur portraits by him, both regarded as inept.

wordextras
Republic, literally, **matter of the people**, from Latin *res*, **matter** + *publica*, **of the people**, is a state in which the supreme power rests in the body of citizens entitled to vote, exercised by representatives chosen directly or indirectly by the citizens. There is *Republic*, AL, and *Republican City*, NE. See p. 65, under **Greek cognates**.

French *aperçu*, past participle of *apercevoir*, **to perceive**, is "a discerning perception"; an insight; also, a short outline or summary; a brief digest or survey. English pronunciation: AP er SOO.

French *étagère* is a free-standing set of open shelves for displaying art objects, ornaments, etc. Pronounced: ay tah ZHER. Such shelves as well as a rack or bookcase is *estante* in Spanish. See *bric-a-brac*, p. 3.

Originally WWII slang, **boondocks**, from Tagalog *bundok*, **mountain**, is any remote rural or provincial region. Of the more than 250 dialects on only the main island of Luzon, the four major languages of the Philippines are Tagalog, English, Filipino, and Spanish. The Philippines was once a part of New Spain. See p. 159, under *Albuquerque*.

Ophicleide, from Greek *ophis*, **snake** + *kleis*, **key**, was an early brass instrument containing a long tube doubled back on itself, with keys for fingering. Other words from *ophis* include **ophi**dian, **ophi**tic (designating a texture of rock in which long, flat, narrow crystals are embedded), **ophi**olatry (see p. 62), **ophi**olite, **ophi**ology; **ophidio**phobia.

Common element base: albus   **Meaning**: white; also, blank
IE base: *albho-*, **white**; **Greek**: *alphos*; therefore, *alphosis*, lack of skin pigmentation, or **albinism**

Clavis

alba:	from *albus*, **whitening**, or **dawning** of the day; a Provençal lament over the parting of lovers at the break of day; medieval *albas* were inspired by Ovid (43 B.C.-A.D. 77), a Roman poet. Compare French *aubades*, **morning songs**, which are joyous; *aubade* also designates a lyric love poem; compare *serenades*, **evening love songs**, which are also joyous. See also *alborado*, next entry.
alborado:	Spanish; an instrumental serenade usually played on a bagpipe or oboe to the accompaniment of a small drum. Compare *aubades*, under *alba*, above. See more on *serenade*, p. 177.
albatross:	probably influenced by *albus*; from Arabic *al qadus*, **white-tailed** sea eagle. From the poem "The Rime of the Ancient Mariner," by Samuel Taylor Coleridge (1772-1834), *albatross* has figuratively come to mean "an encumbrance, a burden," as *to have an albatross around one's neck*.
albino:	Portuguese; a person with deficient pigmentation, exhibited by milky or translucent skin, **white** or colorless hair, and eyes with pink or blue iris and deep-red pupil; birds and animals, as well as plants, known for their striking colors, may also be abnormally lacking in color.
album:	**white book**; originally, a tablet on which edicts or registrations were written; extended to mean **blank**, e.g., a photograph *album* has *blank* pages upon which to affix snapshots; an *album* can also designate **an anthology**.
terra alba:	**white earth**; finely pulverized gypsum used in making paints.
daub:	Old French *dauber*, **to whiten**, from *de-*, **intensifier** + *albus*; thus, **to whitewash**; **plaster**; **smear on**; thus, as a *noun*, **a poorly painted picture**, as though smeared with oils.
Albion:	**poetic name of England**; not from this root, but understood as such, since the cliffs of southern England are **white**, e.g., the White Cliffs of Dover. Aristotle referred to Britain, as it was then called, as *Albion* almost 300 years before Caesar's invasion in 55 B.C.
incandescent:	*in-*, **intensifier**; therefore, **glowing with intense heat**; **red**-hot or **white**-hot; very bright; brilliant; gleaming, as *an incandescent light bulb*.
carte blanche:	French, **white** or **blank card**; permission to act freely; unconditional authority.
album graecum:	literally, **Greek white**; the dung of dogs and hyenas that becomes **white** when dry; used to dress leather and was formerly used in medicine.
leukemia:	*-em-*, short for *hemo*, **blood**; the condition of unrestrained growth of **white** corpuscles, or leukocytes; in medical terms, the suffix *-ia* often indicates an abnormal or diseased condition, e.g., *amentia, anemia, hypoglycemia, pneumonia, leukopenia* (see next entry).
leukopenia:	Greek *penia*, **poverty**, **lack**, **deficiency**; an abnormally low number of leukocytes: **white** or colorless blood cells. Some other words with *-penia*: baso**penia**, cyto**penia**, eosino**penia**, granulo**penia**.
eldritch:	probably from Middle English *elve*, **elf** + *rice*, **realm**, means **strange**, **unearthly**, **weird**, **eerie**.

wordextras

Orangutan, Malay for **man of the forest**, is from *oran*, **man** + *utan*, **forest**. An *orangutan* is an arboreal (**tree-living**) anthropoid (**similar to man**) ape, found only in the coastal jungles Borneo and Sumatra. The orangutan has a shaggy reddish-brown coat, very long arms, no tail, and a hairless face. Also spelled *orang̲o̲utang*.

Machete, from Spanish *macho*, **hammer**, **ax**, and further from Latin *marcus*, **hammer**, is a large, heavy-bladed knife used for cutting down sugar cane, dense underbrush, etc., especially in Central and South America.

Daunt, **to make fearful**, **to intimidate**, is from Latin *domitare*, **to tame**; ***undaunted***: **to not be afraid**. See *damsel*, p. 125.

Latin ***bacterium***, **a rod-shaped organism**, is from Greek *baktron*, **rod**; the plural of *bacterium* is **bacteria**.

A Writing Tip: *Unique* is an absolute; it can't be qualified by *unusually*, *very* or *more*. If something is *unique*, it is **unparalleled**, **nonpareil**, **without equal**, **incomparable**, e.g., the Smithsonian Institution, in Washington, DC, is a *unique* museum. There is nothing else like it! See p. 92 for more on the *Smithsonian*.

```
                        Word Cluster No. 2

altar              altimeter           altithermal          altocumulus
altazimuth         altiplanation       altitude             contralto
alticamelus        altiplano           exalted              alto
```

Common elements_____Inferred Meaning_____

Romance Cognates	French	Romanian	Italian	Portuguese	Spanish
	haut	înalt	alto	alto	alto

Words with disguised Latin roots: enhance, haughty, oboe

Placenames: Altadena, CA (from *Pasadena*, CA, but at a higher plane); Alta Loma (CA, TX); Altamont, MO; Altavista (IA, VA); Altitude, MS; Altus, OK; Mont Alto, PA; Terre Haute, IN (see p. 192). There is an *Alto* in each of the following states: IN, LA, NM, TN, TX. In Maine, there is *Isle au Haut*, the name of the island itself as well as one of its villages; so named for the high cliffs on the island.

Romance words and phrases: *alteza, altissimo, altezza, altocumulus undulatus, altocumulus castellanus, alto-relievo* vs. *basso-relievo, de monte alto*: **from a high mountain**: punning motto of the De Montalt family in Ireland.

French phrases: *de haute lutte*: **with a high hand**; by main force; *à haute voix*: **in a loud voice**; *haute cuisine; haute couture; haute école* (**high school**)*; haut monde; à haute voix*

Motto of the University of Cincinnati: *Juncta juvant: Alta petit.* **Union is strength. It seeks the heights.** See p. 107.

Greek *akros*, **high**, **at the point**: acromion (*omos*, **shoulder**), acronym (*onym*, **name**); acrobat, acrocarpous, acrocentric (see p. 36), acrocephaly, acrodome, acrogen, acrolith, acromegaly (enlargement of the extremities: the head, hands, and feet), acronical (*nyx*, **night**; happening at night, as the rising of a star), acropetal, acrophobia, acropolis, the Acropolis, acrospire, acrostic (*stichos*, **line of verse**). Akron: AL, CO, IN, IA, NY, PA.

German: *hoch*, **high**, as in *Hochachtung, Hochdeutsch, Hochsommer, Hochzeit, Hochamt*, **High Mass**.

wordextras

Delicatessen appears to come from French *délicat* + German *essen*, **to eat**. More likely, it is from Latin *delicates*, from which both *delicious* and *delicate* are derived.

Scotland Yard, made famous by detective story writers, was so called because it is on the site of a palace where the Scottish kings once lived when they visited England.

Janizary, from Turkish *yenicheri*, **new troops** (*yeni*, **new** + *cheri*, **soldiery**), meant a Turkish soldier (originally, a slave) in the Turkish sultan's guard, established in the 14th century and abolished in 1826; now, any very loyal or submissive follower or supporter; also spelled *janissary*. See *sycophant*, p. 42.

Alacrity, from Latin *alacer*, **lively**, denotes an eager willingness or readiness, often manifested by quick, lively action; **celerity**. *Alacrity* is the only known word in English coming from *alacer*. See *celerity*, p. 71.

School, from Dutch *scole*, is a **multitude**, thus *a school of fish*. The Dutch word is related to Old English *shoal*, **a large group, mass, crowd**, as *a shoal of fish*. As an intransitive verb, *shoal* means "to come together in or move about as a shoal or school." See another *school*, an educational institution, p. 12.

Bric-a-brac, from French *bric-à-brac*, and further from the phrase *de bric et de brat*, **by hook or by crook**, designates small, rare, or artistic objects placed about a room for decoration; curios, knickknacks; gimcracks. See *étagère*, p. 1.

Nabob, from Urdu *nawwab*, but originally from Arabic, designates **a very rich or important man**.

Ensiform, **sword-shaped**, describes an iris or gladiolus leaf; xiphoid. See *xiph-*, **sword**, p. 214; *glad-*, **sword**, p. 206.

Word named for a place: *solecism*, substandard error in speech; from *Soloi* in Cilicia, whose dialect was a corrupt form of Attic, speech spoken in Athens.

an aphorism: A *burnt child dreads the fire.* **A person who has been exposed to danger tries to avoid it in the future.** (See p. 132 for meaning of *aphorism* as used in this book.)

A Writing Tip: *Via* means **by way of**, not **by means of**. Therefore, Gerald drove to Alabama *via Interstate 85*, *not* Gerald drove to Alabama *via car*.

Common element base: altus   **Meaning**: high, height

IE base: *al*, **to grow**, **nourish**, which also yields Latin *alere*, **to nourish**, which itself yields *adolescent, alimentary* (as in *alimentary canal*), *alma mater* (**nourishing mother**), and *alimony* (see p. 100, under *intestine*)

Clavis

alto: originally, the **highest** male part in choral music; now the *lowest* female part in four-part harmony, which previously was *contralto*, or *contra alto*, or the voice *opposite* the alto. See *contralto*, p. 46.

altar: authorities are divided on whether *altar* is from *altus* or from *adolere*, **to burn up**. If it is from *altus*, it might be so inferred because *altars* are generally regarded as **raised** structures. If from *adolere*, it is probably because of the burnt sacrifices made upon *altars* in primitive times.

exalt: *ex-*, **out**, **up**; **to raise on high**. From this basic definition, *exalt* means "to raise in status, power, honor, wealth," as well as "to praise, glorify, extol."

exaltation: **an exalting or being exalted**; a feeling of great joy, pride, power, etc.; elation; rapture.

altazimuth: a mounting for astronomical telescopes that permits both horizontal and vertical rotation, and that measures both the *altitude* and *azimuth* of celestial bodies.

altimeter: *metiri*, **to measure**; an instrument for measuring the *altitude* or **height** above a given reference level, as the sea or ground: in aircraft, designates either an aneroid* barometer or an instrument using radar. The aneroid barometer contains gas, which has fluid properties. [*aneroid: *a-*, **negative** + *neros*, **fluid**; using no fluid] Other words with -*meter*: baro**meter**, dia**meter**, para**meter**, peri**meter**. Dozens of others.

altiplano: Spanish: **high plane**, or plateau, as in Bolivia, named after Simón Bolívar, the George Washington of South America. See p. 47 for the vow of Simón Bolívar.

enhance: from Anglo-French *enhauncer*; **to increase or make greater**, or **higher**, as in cost, value, attractiveness, or reputation. SYNONYMS: advance, augment, elevate, heighten, intensify.

haughty: Old French; originally, **noble**, **high-minded**, **lofty**; the latter meaning is preserved in such phrases as "the haughty cathedral," or "the haughty mountains"; has come to mean **arrogant**, **proud**, **disdainful**.

oboe: Italian: a double-reed musical instrument known in French as *hautbois*, or **high wood**, and pronounced the same as *oboe* in English; with a range of almost three octaves, the *oboe* has a high, shrill, penetrating, melancholy tone. The oboe is related to the *English horn*, which is larger and pitched a fifth lower. See *English horn*, p. 95; for more on *oboe*, see p. 42, under *clarinet*.

acronym: *akros*, **high**, **end**, **topmost** + *onym*, **name**, a word formed from the first or few letters of a series of words, as in *radar*, from <u>ra</u>dio <u>d</u>etection <u>a</u>nd <u>r</u>anging, and in *scuba*, from <u>s</u>elf-<u>c</u>ontained <u>u</u>nderwater <u>b</u>reathing <u>a</u>pparatus. Abbreviations pronounced using the letters' names and not phonetically produced, such as IBM, TRW, are properly called *initialisms*. *Akros* can also mean **extremities**, as in <u>acro</u>megaly, the abnormal enlargement of the head, hands, and feet.

Acropolis: *polis*, **city**; **upper city**; in lowercase, the fortified *height* or citadel of an ancient Greek city; in capitals, *the citadel of Athens*. French *citadelle* is from Italian *cittadella*, a diminutive of Latin *civitas*, **city**. There is *The Citadel*, a military university built in the manner of a fort, in Charleston, SC.

Word from the name of an imaginary place: *utopia*: a place or state of ideal perfection; from Sir Thomas More's novel *Utopia* (1516), meaning literally **not a place**. *Utopia* is from Greek *ou*, **not** + *topos*, **place**. There is a *Utopia* in each of the following states: FL, IL, KS, NY, OH, TX.

There are at least 21 -*gamy* words in the English language: allo**gamy** (*allo-*, **other**), apo**gamy** (*apo-*, **away**), auto**gamy** (*auto-*, **self**), bi**gamy** (*bi-*, **two**), cleisto**gamy** (*cleisto-*, **closed**), deutero**gamy** (*deutero-*, **second**), dicho**gamy** (*dicho-*, **in two**, **asunder**), di**gamy** (*di-*, **two**), endo**gamy** (*endo-*, **within**), exo**gamy** (*exo-*, **outside**), hetero**gamy** (*hetero-*, **other**), homo**gamy** (*homo-*, **same**), hyper**gamy** (*hyper-*, **beyond**), iso**gamy** (*iso-*, **equal**), miso**gamy** (*miso-*, **hatred of**), mono**gamy** (*mono-*, **one**, **alone**), oo**gamy** (*oo-*, **egg**), opsi**gamy** (*opsi-*, **late**; see p. 165), poly**gamy** (*poly-*, **many**), syn**gamy** (*syn-*, **with**, **together**), and xeno**gamy** (*xeno-*, **stranger**). With -*gamy* meaning "pertaining to marriage or sexual reproduction," try to determine the words' meanings—with the help of the prefixes' definitions—and then confirm your answer by looking them up in a college-edition or unabridged dictionary. Or email book@occoquanbooks.com. See **wordbuilder #23**, p. 44.

Word Cluster No. 3

ambulant	ambulate	circumambulate	somnambulant
ambulance	ambulatory	noctambulate	perambulator
ambulacrum	amble	preamble	praeambulum

Common elements_____**Inferred Meaning**_____

Romance Cognates	French	Romanian	Italian	Portuguese	Spanish
	ambler	umbla	andare	andar	andar

Words with disguised Latin roots: alley, purlieu, exile, andante, andamento; possibly, ramble

Related *ambi-*, **around, both, on both sides**: **amb**ient, **amb**ition, **amb**iguity, **amb**iguous; **ambi**dextrous, **ambi**valent, **ambi**sexual, **ambi**version; **amp**utate, **amb**assador, **emb**assy; also, Greek *amphi-*, with the same meaning as in Latin, and yielding **amp**hora (*amphi-* + *phorein*, **to bear**: a tall jar with a narrow neck and base and two handles, used by the ancient Greeks and Romans); **amphi**arthrosis, **amphi**aster (in mitosis, the long spindle with asters at either end that forms during the prophase, or first stage), **amphi**bian, **amphi**biotic, **amphi**bious, **amphi**bole, **amphi**bolite, **amphi**bology (a double or doubtful meaning; ambiguity), **amphi**brach (see p. 22, top of page), **amphi**chroic, **amphi**coelous, **amphi**ctyony, **amphi**gory (a piece of nonsense writing, as in burlesque), **amphi**macer (see **Clavis**), **amphi**mixis, **amphi**pod, **amphi**prostyle, **amphi**stylar, **amphi**theater, **amphi**thecium, **amphi**tropous; **amphis**baena.

Explore *Peripatetic philosophers* (as a beginning, see **Clavis**).

NB: *Ambush, ambulia,* and *ambrosia* are not in this family.

> **Quote**: The quality of words, the company they keep, their strange and sometimes unaccountable fortunes as they journey down through the centuries are rewarding fields of exploration. J. Donald Adams

wordbuilders #2, 3

Greek *allos*, **other, mutually**, yields **all**onym (*allo-*[*] + *onym*, **name**); **allo**gamy, **allo**graph, **allo**metry (the study and measurement of the relative growth of a part of an organism in comparison with the whole), **allo**morph, **allo**pathy, **allo**patric (in *biology*, of or pertaining to species of organisms occurring in different but often adjacent areas; often used of populations of related organisms unable to crossbreed because of geographic separation), **allo**phane, **allo**phone, **allo**saurus, **allo**tropy (*tropos*, **way**); **parall**el. [*]If a prefix or leading root ends in *o*, that letter is usually dropped if the first letter of the following element begins with a vowel. Do not confuse the assimilated forms of **all**egation, **all**eviate, **all**iteration, and especially **all**ocate, **all**ocution, with the prefix *allo-*.

Greek *pachys*, **thick**, yields **pachy**cephalic (**thick-headed**), **pachy**dactylia, **pachy**derm (literally, **thick-skin**), **pachy**dermia, **pachy**hemia. There are three species of pachyderms: *elephant, rhinoceros, hippopotamus*.

wordextras

Table d'hôte, French for **table of the host**, a common table for hotel guests, is also a meal for which one pays a fixed price—*prix fixe* (pronounced pree FEEKS)—as opposed to *à la carte*, **by the menu**, with a separate price for each item on the menu. Pronounced in English TAHB ul DOTE, or TAB ul DOTE.

Nazi is a clipping of German *Nationalsozialist*, **National Socialist Workers' Party**.

Exit, literally, **He, She**, or **It goes out**, is from Latin *exire*, **to go out**. Both *exit* and the plural *exeunt* were originally stage directions. *Exit*, however, has become a noun, denoting one's going or passing out, or the way by which one **goes out**, as *a theater exit*, or that which **goes off**, as on an interstate highway. From *ire* is *ambition*, p. 6.

Fascia, from *fasciare*, **to swathe, wrap with bands**, designates in Britain an instrument panel, as of an automobile. See p. 57 for *fasciate*. *Fascia* is also used in anatomy, architecture, and biology, all referring to a band or strip.

Bikini, a very brief two-piece swimsuit for women, and named after Bikini Atoll, an atomic testing site in the Marshall Islands, suggests the explosive effect on the viewer. *Atoll* is a ring-shaped coral island nearly, or completely, surrounding a lagoon. Pronounced: A (as in *bat*) tole.

Common element base: ambulare   **Meaning**: to go about, to walk
IE base: *al-*, **to wander**, related to *amphi-* and *ambi-*, **around**; yields *ombudsman* (see p. 193) and *umlaut*.
German: *gehen*, **to go**, **pass**, **leave**, **run**

Clavis

ambulance: in French, *hôpital ambulant*, **moving** (itinerant) hospital. An *ambulatory* patient in a hospital is one who is able **to walk** or move about, that is, not confined to a bed, or not bedridden: lit., **riding a bed**.

ambulacrum: an alley, or a **covered walkway**; also called *ambulatory*; further, one of the radially disposed areas of echinoderms, e.g., sea urchins, starfishes; so called from the rows of locomotive suckers.

ambulatorial: in reference to a forest animal, describes its mobility by **walking**, rather than by running, leaping, or crawling. *Brachiation*, on the other hand, refers to the **use of the arms**, as the gibbon's, for moving from one branch to another. In *botany*, *brachiation* indicates those trees or plants with widely spread branches arranged in alternating pairs, like arms. The maple, for example, has *brachiated* branches. Compare with *decussate*, forming an X, p. 58. See *brachium*, p. 21.

amble: French; in reference to horses, **to move** by lifting two feet on one side together; the noun is *ambler*.

ambition: *itere*, **to go**, as in *exit* (see p. 5); **to go about**. Later, **a going about** (seeking votes); thus, a strong desire to succeed, especially for a particular goal. See p. 208, Item 113. for more words from *itere*.

preamble: *pre-*, **before**; **to go before**; an introduction to a document stating its purpose, for example, the *Preamble* to the *United States Constitution*. *Preambles* usually begin with a series of *Whereas* statements, followed by resolutions, beginning with *Therefore*.

somnambulist: *somnus*, **sleep**; **one who walks**, or is addicted to **walking**, in one's **sleep**. *Somnambulist* is synonymous with *noctambulist*, literally, **night walker**. Pronunciation: sahm NAM byoo list.

purlieu: *American Heritage* indicates that *purlieu* is probably from *ambulare*; *Webster's New World*, from *puraler*, **to go through**. Both references indicate it originally referred to an outlying area. Now, it can mean a place that one visits often or habitually; a haunt. Pronounced: PURL yoo.

exile: *ex-*, **out** + IE base *al-*, **to wander**; whence Greek *alaomai*, **I wander**; **I am banished**.

amphibrach: *brachys*, **short**; **short at both ends**, or short before and after; a trisyllabic metrical foot in Greek and Latin verse containing one long syllable between two short ones, or, in English, one accented syllable between two unaccented ones, e.g., ro-MAN-tic; ex-PLO-sion. See pp. 22, 39.

amphimacer: *macron*, **long**; **long at both ends**; a metrical foot in Greek and Latin verse consisting of one short syllable between two long ones, or in English, of one unaccented syllable between two accented ones, e.g., HES-i-TATE. (See *tribrach*, p. 22; see p. 169, for more poetry terms.) Pronunciation: am FIM uh ser.

Peripatetic: capitalized, pertaining to the philosophy of Aristotle, who conducted discussions while **walking** outside the Lyceum, a lecture hall, of ancient Athens. In lowercase, **moving from place to place**; **itinerant**, which can be used as both an adjective and a noun. See p. 208, Item 113 for *itere*.

wordextras

Democracy, from Greek *demos*, **people** + *kratein*, **to rule**, designates a government in which the people hold the ruling power, either directly or indirectly, or through elected representatives; rule by the ruled; majority rule. There is *Demopolis* (**People City**), AL, in Marengo County. See *republic*, p. 1, under **wordextras**. See *aristocracy*, p. 38.

Cheddar cheese was originally made in *Cheddar*, a village in Somerset, England.

Gouda cheese was originally made in *Gouda*, a city in the Netherlands. Pronunciation: GOW duh, or GOO duh.

Decoy, from Dutch *de-*, **the** + *kooi*, **cage**, originally designated a place into which wild ducks and geese were lured for capture. Now, an artificial bird or animal, or sometimes a trained live one, used to lure game to a place where it can be killed. More figuratively, a thing or person used to lure or tempt into danger or a trap, e.g., a police decoy.

Farad, the basic unit of electrical capacitance, is named for Michael Faraday (1791-1867), an English scientist.

Ohm, after G. S. Ohm (1789-1854), a German physicist, is the basic unit of electrical resistance. Reciprocal to the ohm is *mho* (pronounced moh, and the reverse spelling of *ohm*), the unit of electrical conductance.

```
                              Word Cluster No. 4

        annual              annals              anno           anniversary
        annuity          per annum          superannuated        annuary

     centennial            biennial           perennial         millennium
      triennial            viennial          decennium         quadrennium
     septennial           sextennial          octennial          centenary


  Common elements_____Inferred Meaning_____
```

Romance Cognates	French	Romanian	Italian	Portuguese	Spanish
	an, année	an	anno	ano	año

Word with disguised Latin root: solemn (see **Clavis**)

Latin phrases: *anno mundi (A.M.), anno Domini (A.D.), anno Hegirae (A.H.), anno Hebraico, annos vixit (a.v.), anno urbis conditae, anno humanae salutis (A.H.S.), annus magnus*

Placenames: Centenary (AL, IN, NY, OH, VA, SC); Centennial (AZ, CO, GA, IN, MI, OH, PA, WY)

Spanish: *el cumpleaños* (see **Clavis**) [see p. 133 for using *el* instead of *los*]

Greek: *horos,* from IE *yer-,* **time, season,** but has come to mean **hour,** as in *horoscope* (to observe the *hour* of one's birth); from this root is also *gherkin,* literally, **unripe,** or a cucumber before it has matured; *year* and German *Jahr* words, which follow, are cognates.

German: *Jahrestag* (**anniversary**); *Jahreswende* (**turn of the year;** New Year); *Jahrzehnt* (**decade**); *Wanderjahr* (**a year of travel**) by a journeyman to gain experience.

---
wordextras

Flak is the acronym for German *Fliegerabwehrkanone,* **antiaircraft guns,** literally, **cannons.**

Fiat is a one-word Latin sentence, **Let it be done.** As a *noun,* it is a form of an order from a source of final authority, and usually begins with *fiat;* as an *adjective,* it applies to what is based only on an authoritative order, as "fiat money," or money not backed by gold or silver. Other one-word sentences throughout the book include *affidavit* (see p. 80, **Clavis**), *caret, deficit, do* (**I give**), *exit* (see p. 5, **wordextras**), *placebo* (**I shall please**), *tenet, veto* (**I forbid**).

The plural of *criterion* is *criteria;* thus *The criterion is. . .; the criteria are. . .; one* of the criteria *is. . .* In the latter example, the singular verb *is* agrees with singular subject *one.*

The *Virgin Islands* were named *Las Virgenes,* **the virgins,** by Christopher Columbus in 1493, reputedly in honor of the legendary 11,000 virgin followers of St. Ursula, who were killed in 238 A.D., by the Huns.

Bureau, French for a **writing table** or **desk,** is from Old French *burel,* **coarse cloth** used as a table cover, and is ultimately from Latin *burra,* **wool, a shaggy garment.**

Fascinate, from *fascinare,* **to bewitch, charm,** originally meant to put under a spell. Now, to attract or hold motionless, as by a fixed look or by inspiring terror; more commonly, **to hold the attention of.**

Hebrew *shofar* is a ram's horn used in ancient times as a signaling trumpet, and still blown in synagogues on Rosh Hashana (**first of the year:** the Jewish New Year) and at the end of Yom Kippur (**Day of Atonement**).

Chaste, from Latin *castus,* **pure,** means "not engaging in unlawful sexual activity; virtuous"; the same base produces *castigate,* **to punish or rebuke severely,** as well as *chasten, chastise, chastity; caste, castrate, castrato; incest.*

---
wordbuilder #4
Latin *alter,* **other,** yields **alter** itself, **alter**able, **alter**ation, **alter**cation, **alter**ity; **alter**nate, **alter**native, **alter**nator; **altr**uism, **altr**uistic; **aliquot; alter** ego, **alter** idem, sub**altern;** et **alibi** (et al.), et **alii** (et al.),[*] as well as *adultery, alien, alias,* and *alibi* (contraction of *alius ibi,* **elsewhere**), an accused's best defense.

[*]*Et al.* stands for both *et alibi,* **and elsewhere,** and *et alii,* **and others.** (See p. 104, **wordextras.**)

A Writing Tip: Distinguish the difference between *lightning* and *lightening,* both of which are from *light,* **to illuminate.** *Lightning* often accompanies thunder; *lightening* is the process of becoming lighter, or brighter, as the *lightning* was *lightening* the starless sky. Another use of *lightening* from *light* that means **having little weight** is the process of relieving or making less burdensome, as in *lightening one's burdens.* (See **IE base,** p. 112.)

7

Common element base: annus **Meaning**: year
IE base: *atno-*, from *at-*, **to go**; thus, the meaning in German and Latin elements, "**to go** through the cycle of a **year**."

Clavis

annals:
record of events arranged in a **yearly** sequence without comment or interpretation. See also *annals* in a literary handbook, or on the Internet.

perennial:
per-, **through**; **through the years**; lasting or active through the year or through many years; lasting an indefinitely long time; **enduring**, as *perennial happiness, perennial poverty*. As a *noun*, refers to a *perennial* plant, as differentiated from an *annual*, which must be planted yearly.

superannuated:
from *superannuari*, **to be too old**; too old, feeble, or worn out for further work or service; discharged from service, especially with a pension, because of old age or infirmity. SYNONYMS: anachronistic, obsolete, old-fashioned, outdated. See *antediluvian*, p. 10.

anno Domini:
abbreviated A.D., **in the year of the Lord**; in the (given) year since the beginning of the Christian era; can also mean **old age**.

anno Hegirae:
abbreviated A.H., **in the year of the Hegira** (Arabic for **flight**); the flight of Mohammed from Mecca to Medina, and the first year of the Moslem era, A.D. 622.

anno lucis:
in the year of light, from Genesis 1:3, "Let there be light."

anno urbis. . .:
abbreviated A.U.C., **in the year of the founded city**; the ancient Roman way of reckoning dates from Rome's founding, circa 753 B.C.

annuit coeptis:
He (God) has smiled on our undertakings; from Virgil's *Aeneid* (IX, 625); motto that appears on the reverse side of the Great Seal of the United States. The translation is not literal.

annus magnus:
literally, **great year**; in *astronomy*, the cycle of 26,000 years in which a complete revolution of the celestial bodies occur; also known as *Platonic year*.

aere perennius:
more lasting than brass, or **bronze**. Horace (65-8 B.C.), Roman poet, known for his odes and satires.

solemn:
originally, *sollennis*, from *sollus*, **whole** + *annus*: **entire year**; from association with **yearly**, or **annual**, religious festivals. SYNONYMS: earnest, grave, sedate, serious, sober, staid.

el cumpleaños:
Spanish: literally, **the culmination of years**; thus, one's birthday.

Centenary College, Shreveport, Louisiana; founded 100 years *after* the Methodist Church was established in the United States; in lowercase, ***centenary*** means 100 **years**, and refers to **100 years later**.

wordextras

Latin ***ignoramus***, **We take no notice**, was originally a law term written on a bill when the evidence was not sufficient for proceeding with the action; now, applied to persons distinguished for their ignorance and stupidity. The word is probably a result of the name of a character that played the part of a lawyer in *Ignoramus*, 1615, a play by George Ruggle (1575-1622). The play is in Latin; an English translation can be found on the Internet.

Govern is from Greek *kybernan*, **to steer**, **pilot**, which evolved into *gubernare*, **to pilot a ship**. *Govern* now means to exercise authority over; to rule; to administer. The adjective is *gubernatorial*; the nominal, *governor*, as of a State.

A ***reputation*** (*re-*, **back** + *putare*, **to think, suppose, reckon**) is gauged by what other people think about a person, business, etc. From *putare* is ***putative***, generally considered or deemed such; reputed; as in *a putative ancestor*.

Pheasant, the chickenlike, nidifugous game bird, is named after the Phasis River, in the ancient country south of the Caucasus Mountains, on the Black Sea, in what is now Georgia. It has been said that the birds were numerous near the mouth of the Phasis. See p. 86 for *nidifugous*.

Anorak is Greenlandic Eskimo for a heavy jacket with a hood; a parka. ***Parka***, literally, **pelt**, is from Alaskan Russian. See p. 56, under **wordextras**, for more on *parka*.

Poncho, from Araucanian, was originally a woolen cloth used for a covering against the elements of the Andes. Araucanian is a native Indian language of Chile.

Word from a place: *bedlam*, dialectal pronunciation of *Bethlehem*; from Hospital of St. Mary of Bethlehem, an old insane asylum in London, known for its noise and confusion; now, any noisy, confused place or situation.

Word Cluster No. 5

ante	antebellum	antecessor	antecedent
antechamber	antedate	antediluvian	antefix
antejuramentum	antemortem	antemundane	antenatal
antependium	antepenult	anteroom	antescript
antenuptial	antemeridiem(a.m)	antemeridian	anteversion
antecede	antecedence	antechoir	anterior

Common element_____Inferred Meaning_____

Romance Cognates	French	Romanian	Italian	Portuguese	Spanish
	avant*	inainte	avanti	antes	ante

*Partridge says this element occurs only in such Gallicisms as *avant-garde*, from *ab ante*.

Words from disguised Latin roots: ancestor, ancient, antlers, antipasto (*anti* is a respelling of *ante*), antic, anticipate, antique, advance, advantage, avant-garde, dance, rampart, vamp; penny ante

Latin phrases: *Ante barbam doces sene*: **You teach old men before your beard has come.**
status quo ante, ante cibum: **before meals** (in prescription writing, abbreviated a.c.)

Latin law term: *ante litem notam*: **before litigation has commenced**

Spanish phrase: *Antes de que digan*: **Tell before they tell.** Be proactive rather than reactive.

Explore *antecedent* and *consequent* as musical terms; *antecedent* as a concept in grammar, logic, and mathematics.

Related Greek: *anti-*, **against**: enantiomorph; antagonist, Antarctic, anthelion, anthelix, anthelmintic, antonym; antibacterial, antibaryon, antibiosis, antibiotic, antibody, antichrist, anticlimax, anticline, anticlinorium, antidepressant, antidote, antidromic, antienergistic, antifreeze, antifriction, antihistamine, antimatter, antipathy, antiphone (see *anthem*), antistrophe. In addition to its use as a Greek drama term, *antistrophe* designates the repetition of words in reverse order; in addition, the repetition of a word or phrase at the end of successive clauses for rhetorical effect. *Anthem* is from **antiphone**. See p. 45 for more *anti-* words in the *contra-*, **against**, family.

Sanskrit: *Vedanta* (see **Clavis**)

wordextras

The modern word **booty** comes from Middle Low German *büte*, **a distribution**, or **a sharing**. When *büte* entered English, it began to take on its present meaning: something taken illegally and then shared in the fashion of the pirates and freebooters. See *sack* under **wordextras**, p. 55.

A **ledger**, in which credits and debits are posted, comes from Old English *leggen*, **to lie flat**. At first, a *ledger* lay flat in one place and was open for inspection. A *ledge* is a **shelf**, or shelflike projection, as in mountains and oceans.

The plural of **axis** is *axes*; **crisis**, *crises*; **genesis**, *geneses*; **hypothesis**, *hypotheses*; **oasis**, *oases* (see p. 10); **paralysis**, *paralyses*; **parenthesis**, *parentheses*; **stasis**, *stases*; **synthesis**, *syntheses*; **testis**, *testes*; **thesis**, *theses*.

The plural of **curriculum** is *curricula* (see **wordbuilder #1**, p. 1); **stadium**, *stadia* (see p. 51 for more on *stadium*); **podium**, either *podia* or *podiums*; **locus**, *loci*. The plural of *alumnus* (male) is *alumni*; *alumna* (female), *alumnae*.

A wind system that reverses its direction seasonally, or one that blows constantly between land and adjacent water, and produces both dry and wet seasons, is **monsoon**, from Middle Dutch *monssoen*. Prior to the Dutch version, the word was Portuguese *mação*, which itself is from Arabic *mausin*, **time**, **season**. The adjective is *monsoonal*.

Ashcan, or *ash can*, is Navy slang for a depth charge, or a bomb, dropped from a ship or airplane and explodes under water; it is used especially against submarines.

Baja California, a peninsula in Mexico, is Spanish for **lower California**, and is divided into two states: *Baja California Norte* (**north**) and *Baja California Sur* (**south**). See p. 143 for more on *peninsula*.

Embrocate, from Greek *em-*, **in** + *brechein*, **to wet**, means to moisten and rub a part of the body with oil or liniment.

A Writing Tip: *Correlative conjunctions* come in pairs: *either . . . or*; *neither . . . nor*; *not only . . . but also*; *whether . . . or*; *both . . . and*. The grammatical structure following the second half of the pair is the same as that following the first half, e.g., Dr. Rebecca Keller is *not only* a chemistry professor at the University of New Mexico, *but also* a home school consultant. Dr. Keller is *both* a chemistry professor *and* a home school consultant.

9

Common element base: ante-, a prefix   **Meaning**: before
IE base: *anti-*, **before**, **opposite**, **against**, and yields **English** *until* as well as **Sanskrit** *antah*, **end**, in *Vedanta*.

Clavis

antediluvian: with *diluvium*, **flood**, **before the flood**; specifically referring to the time before the biblical flood. SYNONYMS: anachronistic, old, old-fashioned, primitive. As a *noun*, an *antediluvian* person or thing. Compare with *superannuated,* p. 8. See p. 110 for more on *antediluvian*.

anteversion: with *vertere*, **to turn**, an abnormal, forward displacement of a bodily organ, especially, the uterus.

penny ante: a game of poker in which the *ante* is limited to **one cent**. *Ante* is the stake one must put into the pot **before** receiving cards. *Ante up* means **to pay**.

antlers: with *oculis*, **eye**; originally, *anteocularis*, **located before the eyes**, the deciduous horns of an animal of the deer family; in German, *Augensprossen*, **eye sprouts** (see p. 141). See *window*, p. 142.

ancestor: with *cedere*, **to go**, the same bases as *antecedent*, **that which goes before**, and *antecessor*, **one who goes before**. In *law*, the person from whom an estate has been inherited.

rampart: French *rempart*, from Provençal *amparer*; ultimately from Latin *re-*, **again** + *ante-* + *parare*, **prepare**; **to fortify a place**. Provençal is the language of Provence, a region in southern France, and was the first Roman province, thus the name. *Provençal* is pronounced PROH vahn SAHL.

anticipate: from *ante-* + *capere*, **to seize**; literally, **to seize beforehand**; to prevent by action in advance, as "to anticipate an opponent's blows." Many other applications. The *i* of *anti-*, Partridge says, is a confusion with *ante-*. It may also be a structural connective, making the word easier to pronounce.

antipasto: as in *anticipate*, above entry, *anti-*, **before** (*not* **against**) + Italian *pasto* (from Latin *pascere*, **to feed**); appetizers originally served with olive oil and vinegar before the main meal.

Vedanta: Sanskrit; the essence of the *Veda* (cognate of Latin *videre*, **to see**; see p. 213, Item 187); any one of the four ancient sacred books of Hinduism. *Veda*, **knowledge** + *antah*, **an end**, implies **complete knowledge**; the *Veda* teaches that one's goal is unity with Brahman, the Creator. See *Trimurti*, p. 195. Compare with *Rig-Veda, Yajur-Veda, Sama Veda*, and the *Atharvaveda*.

advance: from Vulgar Latin *abantiare*, which is from *ab ante*, **from before**. SYNONYMS: forward, further, progress, promote; the shared meaning of the synonyms: **to help or move ahead**.

anthem: from Greek *antiphona*, literally, **sounding against**; evolved into Old English *antefn* and later Middle English *antefne*. Originally, *anthems* were sung responsively, or *antiphonally*.

dance: *Webster's Third* indicates that *dance* is from *ab ante*, literally, **in front of** (see *advance*, above); there is also a tenuous association with *tendere*, **to stretch** (see p. 190); *dance* refers to ballet, interpretive dancing, and other dancing of an artistic nature.

wordextras

Lens is from Latin *lentil*, because of the similarity of the shapes of a *lens* and the eye of a *lentil*.

Imprimatur, **let it be printed**, was originally a Roman censor's permission to publish; it has come to mean **approval** or **sanction**, and is from Latin *imprimere*, **to print**, and from which are derived *impress* and *imprint*. *Imprimatur* is pronounced either IM pri MAHT ur, or, IM pri MATE ur.

Gourmet and *gourmand* may both be from Old French *gormet, gromet*, **a wine taster**, **servant**. As the words evolved, *gourmet* came to designate "one who is fond of fine food," whereas *gourmand* designates "a glutton, an epicure." Both words are related to Middle English *groom*, originally a man or boy who tended, fed, and curried horses.

The Scottish dialectal phrase ***in the gloaming*** can be read as "in the glowing twilight," or *dusk*. The first stanza of the song by the same name, by Meta Orred, reads "*In the gloaming*, oh, my darling!/When the lights are dim and low,/And the quiet shadows softly come and go./When the winds are sobbing faintly with a gentle, unknown woe,/ Will you think of me and love me,/ As you did once long ago?"

Covet and *cupidity* are from *Cupid*, **desire**, **passion**; *covet* means **to envy**; *cupidity,* **a strong desire**, especially for wealth. In Roman mythology, Cupid was the god of love, and associated with Greek Eros.

Oasis, pronounced oh AY sis, is Coptic (Egyptian) for "a fertile place in the desert." *Oasis*, CA, is on the Salton Sea.

Word Cluster No. 6

arms	armistice	disarm	alarm	gendarme
armament	armamentarium	disarmament	armure	armiger
armature	armadillo	rearmament	armilla	armoire
armigerous	armillary	armlet	armada	armor

Common element_____Inferred Meaning_____

Romance Cognates	French	Romanian	Italian	Portuguese	Spanish
	arme	arma	arma	arma	arma

Doublets: armada:army; ambry:armoire

Triplets: armor:armature:armament

Word with disguised Latin root: ambry

Placenames: Armada, Michigan; Armadillo, Mexico

French words and phrases: *maître d'armes; arme blanche* (see p. 1)*; armoire*

Latin phrases: *O fama ingens, ingentior armis!* **great by reputation, greater still by feats of arms**
nugis armatus: **armed with trifles**; *arma pacis fulcra; arma virunque cano* (see **Clavis**)*; arma accipere*

Motto of the State of Mississippi: *Virtute et armis*: **By valor and by arms**
Motto of the University of Wyoming: *Cedant arma togae* (See **Clavis** for translation.)

German: *Waffen*, **weapons**; *bewaffnen*, **to arm**; *Luftwaffe*, **air weapon**, German air force during World War II; *Wehrmacht*, **defense force**, the German armed forces during World War II. [All German nouns are capitalized.]

> **Quote**: Scarcely any of our intellectual operations could be carried on to any considerable extent without the agency of words. Peter Roger

---

wordextras

German *leitmotif, leitmotiv*, is **leading motive**, or **theme**. Developed by Richard Wagner, a *leitmotif* is a short, recurring musical theme to represent a given character, emotion, etc. Also, any dominant recurring theme.

Creole French *lagniappe*, or *lagnappe*, is **something extra**, as a small present given to a customer; broadly, something given or obtained by way of good measure, such as "a baker's dozen." Pronounced: lan YAP, or LAN YAP.

Bayonet is named after *Bayonne*, France, where the weapon was first made. The early French *baïonnettes* were short, flat daggers. As a *verb*, to stab, prod, or kill with a bayonet. There is *Bayonne*, New Jersey.

Refulgent, from Latin *re-*, **back**, **again** + *fulgere*, **to shine**, "to reflect light," means "brilliant, shining, radiant, glowing, resplendent." *Effulgent*, **to shine out**, is a synonym of *refulgent*.

Cloak, a loose outer garment, is from *clock*, from the garment being shaped like a clock, or bell. *Clock* itself comes from Middle Latin *clocca*, **bell**, from the shape of old clocks. In school buildings of the past, there were cloakrooms, where students placed their coats, caps, and umbrellas in inclement weather.

Mojo, probably of Creole origin, and related to Gullah *moco*, **witchcraft**, is a charm or amulet thought to have magic powers. In *slang*, **power**, **luck**, etc., as of magical or supernatural origin.

In Scottish history, *wappenschawing*, **weapons-showing**, was a review or mustering of men under arms, held at periodic intervals in each district. Also *wappenschaw*. Pronunciation: WAHP un SHOW ing.

Irredentist, from *(Italia) irredentista*, **unredeemed Italy**, designated regions inhabited by Italians but under foreign control. A section of Somalia was one such region before the United Nations demarcated boundary lines in 1960.

A loooonnnnng word: *pneumonoultramicroscopicsilicovolcanoniosis*. Robert W. L. Smith, in *Dictionary of English Word-Roots*, notes that there are no long words in the English language, only a succession of shorter pieces, each of which has a meaning of its own. Pneumono + ultra + micro + scopic + silico + volcano + connective ni + osis.

Common element base: armare   **Meaning**: to arm; thus, arms, shield, weapon
IE base: *ar-*, **joined together**, yields **Greek** *arthron*, **joint**. See p. 204, Item 63, for a list of *arthro-* words.

Clavis

armada: Spanish; an **armed** force; a fleet of warships. *Spanish Armada*—a Spanish fleet deployed against England in 1558, but destroyed by the British.

armadillo: Spanish; a small mammal living in the SW US and Mexico; it has very simple teeth, or no teeth at all (edentate), its shield or bony plates being its protection, or **armor**. See p. 64 for *Edentata*.

armament: Latin plural, *armamenta*; in English, often *armaments*; all the military forces, **weapons**, and equipment of a nation; the guns and other military equipment of a warship, warplane, tank, fortification, etc.; a large force for offense or defense; an arming or being armed for war.

armamentarium: originally, **an arsenal**; now the total store or aggregate of resources, apparatus, knowledge, etc., as that of a physician or an attorney.

armature: from Latin *armatura*, **arms**, **equipment**; any **shielded** or protective covering, and is applied equally to plants, animals, warships, warplanes, tanks; in the case of plants, applies to burs, spurs, thorns, etc.; of animals, to claws, scales, teeth, talons, etc.; also, the part that revolves in an electric motor or dynamo. *Armature* means the same as *armor* in certain senses.

armigerous: *gerere*, **to bear**; of, having, or entitled to have a coat of arms. An *armiger* was originally an armorbearer for a knight. *Gerere* also produces **ger**und, exag**ger**ate, belli**ger**ent, denti**ger**ous.

armistice: literally, **a standing still of arms**; thus, *Armistice Day*, November 11, 1918, marked the end of World War I. *Stice* is also in *interstice* and *solstice* (see *stare* family, **Word Cluster No. 90**, p. 179).

alarm: originally, in Old Italian, *all'arme*; **to the arms**, or **weapons**.

ambry: from *armarium*, **a chest for tools or arms**; later, though now archaic, a locker, cupboard, or pantry; also, a niche in a church for sacramental vessels, vestments, etc. A doublet of French *armoire*.

gendarme: from French *gens d'armes*, **men at arms**; a rural policeman in France. Pronounced approximately ZHÂN darm. See p. 133 for other words from *genere*, **to beget**, **produce**.

Cedant arma. . .:   motto of University of Wyoming: **let arms give place to the toga**, from Cicero, *De Officiis* and *In Pisonem*.

Arma virumque cano: **Arms and the man I sing**: opening words of the *Aeneid*, by Virgil.

wordextras

Brother in Russian—a cognate of English—is **brat** (pronounced brot). See *cognate*, p. 134.

Innuendo, from Latin *innuere*, **to nod to**, was once used in a Roman court in quoting a statement first made definite by a nod. *Innuendo* has come to mean **indirect reference**, usually implying something derogatory; **insinuation**. As a law term, *innuendo* is a plaintiff's interpretation of allegedly libelous or slanderous material; also, a parenthetical explanation or specification in a pleading.

School is from Greek *schole*, **leisure**, which privileged male children could spend their free time in doing. In Spanish, *escuela*; French, *école*; German, *Schule*; Yiddish *shul*, **synagogue**. See p. 3 for another *school*.

Latin **dexter**, **right**, means **on the right-hand side**; in *heraldry*, on the right-hand side of a shield (the left as seen by the viewer). Other words from *dexter*: **dexter**ity, **dexter**ous, **dextr**al, **destr**ose, **dextr**ous; **dextro**cardia, **dextro**gram, **dextro**rotation, **dextro**rse; **dexio**tropic; ambi**dextr**ous; and the archaic but interesting word *destrier*. *Destrier* designated a war horse, a charger, which was on the "right of the squire leading him." Pronounced: DES tree.

Word from an animal: *behemoth*, any animal or thing that is huge and very powerful; may originally have been the hippopotamus. It could also be the animal mentioned in Job 40:15-25. Pronounced: bih HE muht.

A Writing Tip: Distinguish between *stationary* (adjective) and *stationery* (noun) both of which come from Latin *stare*, **to stand**; both also pertain to **standing or staying in one place**. Example: It is not difficult to hit a *stationary* target. *Stationery* refers to writing materials. Example: We will need new *stationery* when the ZIP code is changed. The *er* in *letter* is a mnemonic for remembering the correct use and spelling of *stationery*. Originally, *stationers* stayed in one place rather than peddle their wares from door to door. See p. 180, under **Clavis**.

Word Cluster No. 7

audit(or)	auditorium	audition	audience	audile
inaudible	auditory	audient	audiencia	subaudition
audiology	audiovisual	audiogram	auditive	audiometer

Common elements_____Inferred Meaning_____

Romance Cognates	French	Romanian	Italian	Portuguese	Spanish
	ouïr	auzi	udire	ouvir	oir

Doublets: obeisance:obedience

Words with disguised Latin roots: obey, obedience, oyez, aural, auscultate (do not confuse with *osculate*, p. 146)

Latin phrases: *audi alteram partem; Exaudi; de auditu*

Romance phrases: Spanish: *de oídas*; French: *ouï-dire* (both mean **by hearsay**)

Spanish proverb: *Quien mal dice, peor oye*: **He who speaks evil, hears worse.** (See pp. 65, 123.)

NB: *Audacious* is not in this family. See **Clavis**; also see p. 45, under **Latin Phrases**.

Greek *acou-, acu-,* **hearing**: **acou**stic, **acou**esthesia; **acou**stogram; **acusis** (**normal hearing**); brady**acusia**, dipl**acusia**, hyp**acusia**, hyper**acusia**; an**acusis**, dipl**acusis**, dys**acusis**, hyp**acusis**, hyper**acusis**, noso**acusis**, odyn**acusis**, osteo-**acusis**, par**acusis**, presby**acusis** (*presbys-*, **old**; hearing associated with old people), pseud**acusis**; opto**acoustic**.

> **Quote**: Every workman in the exercise of his art should be provided with proper implements. . . . The writer as well as the speaker employs the instrumentality of words; it is in words that he clothes his thoughts; it is by means of words that he depicts his feelings. It is therefore essential that he be provided with a copious vocabulary. Peter Roget

wordextras

Cereal is from *Ceres*, Roman goddess of agriculture and grain. There is *Ceres*, Virginia, in the southwestern part of the state. Spanish *cerveza*, **beer**, is also from *Ceres*.

Nice originally meant **ignorant**, from the Old French form of Latin *nescius*, **not knowing**. On the way from Latin to English, it meant in Old French *lazy* as well as *dull*, and in Middle English, *simple*. *Nice* was later to take on more favorable meanings: *fastidious, delicate, exact; pleasing, agreeable, delightful*; in addition, *virtuous, respectable, decorous*. *Nice* is an example of *melioration*, a linguistics term, designating the process by which the meaning or connotation becomes more positive. See *egregious*, p. 88, for an example of *pejoration*, the opposite of *melioration*.

Originally, a *barber* was a *bearder*, one who removed *beards*, or whiskers. *Whiskers* on certain fish, like the catfish, are called *barbels*.

Robust is from Latin *robustus*, **oaken**, **hard**, **strong**, and further from *robur*, **hard variety of oak**; consequently, one who is *robust* is **strong and healthy**; in the same family is *corroborate*, **to further strengthen**; confirm, substantiate.

Quail, **to draw back in fear**, to lose heart or courage, to cower, probably comes from *coagulare*, **to clot**. The bird *quail* is not related, coming from Middle Latin *cuacula*, probably being echoic of the sound it makes.

wordbuilder #5

Latin *clamare*, **to cry out**, yields **clam**ant, **clam**atorial, **clam**or, **clam**orous; ac**clam**ation, de**clam**ation, ex**clam**ation, pro**clam**ation, re**clam**ation; ex**clam**atory; **claim**, **claim**ant; ac**claim**, counter**claim**, de**claim**, dis**claim**, ex**claim**, pro**claim**, quit**claim**, re**claim**; dis**claim**er; chamade; réclame. *Clamant* means **noisy**; also, **demanding attention, urgent**. An *exclamatory sentence* is followed by an exclamation point (!). *Clamatorial* describes those birds—over 8,000 species—known for their singing as well as for feeding on insects taken while the birds are in flight.

A Writing Tip: Use *fewer* to indicate a *smaller number* of *countable* items; use *less* to indicate a *smaller amount* of a *noncountable* entity. Example: There were *fewer cars* on the road this evening; there was *less traffic*. Interestingly, *more* is used for both *countable* and *noncountable* entities, e.g., *more cars, more traffic*, respectively.

Common element base: audire   **Meaning**: to hear, to listen
IE base: *au-*, **to perceive**, to place perception, to feel; yields **Greek** *aesthetics, anesthesia*, where the prefix *an-* is a negative; thus, an *anesthetic* causes a loss of feeling. **German** *hören*, **to hear**; *schwerhörig*, **hard of hearing**.

Clavis

auditorium: *-orium*, **place**; a place where "something" is **heard**; the space set apart for the *audience* in a public place; a building for public gatherings; a building or hall for speeches, concerts, plays, etc.

audient: in the early Christian Church, one permitted to attend, thus **hear**, the services in the narthex, or the vestibule, but dismissed after the sermon; as an *adjective*, **hearing, listening, giving attention**.

audiencia: Spanish; literally, **a hearing**; a tribunal in which the sovereign of Spain gave his personal attention to matters of justice; a tribunal of two chambers, one for civil and one for criminal jurisdiction.

audiology: *-logy*, **scientific study** (from Greek *logos*, **word**), **the science of hearing**; the evaluation of hearing defects and the rehabilitation of those who have such defects. See p. 120 for more *–logy* words.

audit: a formal examination and checking of accounts or financial records, as *an audit by the Internal Revenue Service*; as a *verb*, to attend a college class as a **listener** without receiving a credit.

auditor: originally, the Roman official who **heard** the bookkeeper's own interpretation of the financial accounts; a person authorized to audit accounts; also, one who audits, or attends a course of study without expecting or receiving a credit; the capacity of a judge in a case—he or she **hears** both sides.

auditory: of or related to **hearing**; attained, produced, or experienced through *hearing*, as *auditory images of great music*; having to do with *hearing* or the organs of *hearing*.

obey: *ob-*, **to**; originally, *obedire*, **to listen to**; to submit to the control of; to conform to or comply with, e.g., falling objects *obey* the laws of physics; to be guided by, as to *obey* one's conscience. See p. 140 under **Clavis**. "Children, *obey* your parents." Ephesian 6:1

obeisance: and *obedience* are doublets; the act of **hearing** in the sense of *listening to*, or *heeding*. *Obeisance* was formerly used in the sense of *obedience*; it came to be an act of respect, e.g., bowing, curtsying, kowtowing, saluting. *Obedience* is the act of *obeying*. See previous entry.

oyez: or *oyes*; an interjection; imperative of Anglo-French *oir*. **Hear ye**; spoken three times to open court in England; usually pronounced "O yes." As a *noun*, a cry of "oyez." Spanish: *oír*, **to hear**.

auscultation: *auris*, **ear** + IE *kel-*, **to incline**; the act of **listening** to the sounds of the heart and lungs through a stethoscope, an instrument for "looking at the chest (or breast)." Greek *skopein*, **to examine**.

acouesthesia: Greek *esthes*, **sense**; **the sense of hearing**.

osteoacusis: Greek *osteos*, **bone**, + *akousis*, **hearing**; **hearing by bone conduction** (for low frequencies), as opposed to nerve conduction (for high frequencies).

audacious: not in this family, but from *audere*, **to dare**; not restrained by a sense of shame or propriety; rudely bold; the nominal is *audacity*. SYNONYMS: bold, brave, courageous, intrepid, valiant. See p. 45.

Audi alteram partem: **Hear the other side**, interpreted as "No man should be condemned unheard." *Black's*

---
wordextras
Posse, short for Latin *posse comitatus*, **the power of the county**; hence, a force with legal authority. A *posse* includes all those whom a sheriff might summon into service, especially in searching for an escapee. See *possess*, p. 176.

Rasher, a thin slice of bacon for frying or broiling, may come from the same source as *raze*: *radere*, **to scrape**. While *raze* originally meant **to scrape** or **graze**, **to wound slightly**, it now means **to tear down completely**; level to the ground; demolish. *Raze* and *raise* are homonyms; although pronounced the same, they have quite opposite meanings.

---
wordbuilder #6
Greek *exo-*, **out, outside**, yields **exo**teric, **exo**tic (**foreign**; as a *noun*, a foreign or imported thing; also, a plant that is not native), **exo**tica; **exo**dontia (*odont*, **tooth**), **exo**dus (*hodus*, **way**), **Exo**dus (second book of Bible, detailing the exodus from Egypt), **exo**smosis (*osmos*, **impulse**); **exo**biology, **exo**carp, **exo**centric, **exo**crine, **exo**cytosis, **exo**dermis, **exo**gamy (see pp. 4, 44), **exo**genous, **exo**pathic, **exo**skeleton, **exo**sphere, **exo**spore, **exo**thermic, **exo**toxin, **exo**tropia.

Word Cluster No. 8

bat	battle	battlement	abate	abattoir
abator	battalion	batten	battery	abatement
bate	batter	battered	débat	rebate
batting	combat	combatant	battering ram	debate

Common elements_____**Inferred Meaning**_____

Romance Cognates	French	Romanian	Italian	Portuguese	Spanish
	battre	bate	battere	bater	abatir

Word with disguised Latin root: rabbet (in full: rabbet joint: a groove or recess cut in the edge of board or plank)

Romance words and phrases: *abat-voix, abat-vent, abat-sons, abat-jour; battue; hors de combat; abattis, bastón* (Spanish for "walking cane"), *battalia, batterie*

Placenames: Baton Rouge, LA (see p. 149); Bayou La Batre, AL; there is a *Battle Creek* in each of the following states and provinces: ID, IA, MI, MT, NE; Saskatchewan.

French phrase: *cheval de bataille*: **war horse**; charger; figuratively, **strong point**; forte; favorite subject; hobby

French expression: *battre l'eau avec un baton* (see **Clavis**)

Explore *débat* as a literary term, as in *The Owl and the Nightingale*, circa 12th century. See **Clavis**.

Explore *battaglia* (**music combat pieces**) in *Harvard's Music Dictionary*.

> **Quote**: Great leaders are great leaders because through their command of vocabulary power and culture, they are able to make others see and feel what they see and feel. Gain this power for yourself and you will have at your service the greatest force ever put into the hands of mankind.
> Joseph G. Brin

wordextras

Serendipity is from "The Three Princes of Serendip," a Persian fairy tale, where the princes make fortunate discoveries quite by accident. *Serendip* translates *Sri Lanka*, formerly Ceylon. *Serendipity* was coined by Horace Walpole (1717-97), English writer and 4th Earl of Oxford. He used the word and explained its derivation in a letter written January 28, 1754. His collected letters number more than 3,000, some of which are still extant. See p. 115.

Sabbath, from Hebrew *shabbath*, **He rested**, designates the seventh day of the week. In commemoration of Christ's resurrection [God's finished work], many Christians observe Sunday, the first day of the week, as the Sabbath.

Papier-mâché, French for "masticated," or "chewed paper," is paper pulp that can be molded into various objects. *Papier*, as well as English *paper* and Spanish *papel*, is ultimately from Greek *papyrus*, the name of the plant from which paper was originally made. *Masticate* is from Latin *masticare*, **to chew**; it can also mean to grind, cut, or knead rubber to a pulp. Pronunciation: PAY per muh SHAY.

The *Eiffel Tower*, after Alexandre Gustave Eiffel (1832-1923), the French engineer who designed it, is an iron framework in Paris, built as the centerpiece for the International Exposition of 1889. With a height of 984 feet, it is almost twice that of the Washington Monument's 555 feet. When built, it was the highest structure in the world.

wordbuilder #7

Latin *vestis*, **clothing**, **garment**, yields such disparate terms as **vest** (both an item of clothing and a legal term indicating unconditional right), **vest**ment; de**vest**, di**vest**, in**vest**, re**vest**; in**vest**ment, in**vest**iture, trans**vest**ite, tra**vest**y; re**vest**ment. *Revetment*—while usually regarded as a military term, denoting protection of a bunker—is any protection of an embankment, for instance, a retaining wall or a levee on the Mississippi. This root is not related to *investigate* or *vestige*, both of which refer to "track," or "footprint." See both *investigate* and *vestige*, p. 146.

A Writing Tip: Make certain that all necessary words are included in a sentence. Example: Women entering a military academy can expect haircuts *as short as the male cadets*. The italicized phrase should be *as short as those of the male cadets*. I wanted to drive all the way *to Alabama*, or at least *(to) Georgia*. [coming from Virginia]

Common element base: battuere   **Meaning**: to beat, to strike

Latin verb of unknown origin. **German**: *schlagen*, **to beat, to hit**, as in *ausschlagen*, **to strike out** (at someone)

Clavis

battery: in *law*, any illegal **beating** or touching of another person either directly or with an object. ***Assault and battery***: the carrying out of threatened physical harm or violence; an intentional and unlawful beating (see p. 182). More generally, *battery* designates a device for generating electrical current by chemical reaction; also, an artillery military unit, which *strikes* its opposing forces.

battalion: a large group of soldiers arrayed for *battle*; any large group joined together in some activity. In the US Army, a tactical unit made up of three or more companies, batteries, or analogous units; it is normally commanded by a lieutenant colonel and is the basic building unit of a division.

battle: from Old French *bataille*; further from Low Latin *batalia*, which originally referred to an exercise in fighting and fencing for gladiators and soldiers; now, any struggle, conflict, as *a battle with cancer*; *The Battle of the Bulge*, from December 16, 1944, to January 25, 1945; a decisive American victory in WWII. Classical *pugnare*, **to fight**, yields *pugilism, pugilist, pugnacious, expugn, expugnable, inexpugnable, impugn, impugnable, oppugn, oppugnant, repugn, repugnant*.

battue: French; **beating** the underbrush and woods to drive out game towards hunters; figuratively, wanton slaughter. Pronounced: ba TOO, or ba TYOO. [short *a* as in *bat*]

abate: from Old French *abattre*; *a-*, **down**; **to beat down**; in *medicine*, to lessen or decrease pain or other symptoms. The same elements are in *abattis*, next entry.

abattis: or *abatis*; from Old French *abattre*; a barricade of felled trees with branches facing the enemy; also, a barbed wire entanglement for defense. Pronounced: AB uh tis, or French AB uh TEE.

abattoir: from *abate*: literally, a place for "beating down" animals; a slaughterhouse.

rebate: *re-*, **back**; to give back part of an amount paid; to make a deduction from a bill; also used as a noun.

abatjour: French *jour*, **day**; that which **throws down light**; an aperture that deflects light. See p. 103.

abat-vent: French *vent*, **wind**; that which **throws down wind**; in a belfry, for example, a series of sloping boards that break the wind without obstructing the passage of air; wind deflector. See p. 199.

abat-voix: French *voix*, **voice**; **a voice deflector**, especially one behind a speaker's stand. See p. 213, Item 191.

débat: a type of literary composition in which two or more characters, usually allegorical, **discuss** or **debate** a subject; an extended discussion, debate, philosophical argument between two characters in a literary work. Compare *tenson*, **tension**, a lyric poem of dispute composed by Provençal troubadours in which two opponents speak alternate stanzas, lines, or groups of lines, usually identical in structure. Troubadours also engaged in *partimens*, lyrical poems with a more limited range of argument than the *tenson*. A prime example of *débat* is *The Owl and the Nightingale*.

hors de combat: French, **out of battle**, or **combat**; disabled. Compare with *hors d'oeuvre*, **outside the works**, or apart from the main dish; an appetizer, or an antipasto. See *forum, forest, foreclose, faubourg*, p. 50.

battre l'eau avec un bâton: **to beat the water with a stick**; to make vain efforts.

wordextras

Plaudit is from the imperative plural of Latin *plaudere*, **to clap** (the hands). At the close of a Roman play, an actor announced the end of the performance by calling out, *Plaudite!* **Applaud!** In English, the *e* of *plaudite* seems to have been regarded as a silent vowel, then dropped completely.

Enervate, **to deprive of strength, force, vigor**, is from Latin *ex-*, **out** + *nervus*, **nerve**. SYNONYMS: 1: unman, unnerve; 2: debilitate, deplete, drain, sap, undermine, weaken. See *sine nervis*, p. 178.

A French expression used in English: *Je ne sais quoi*, literally, **I don't know what**: an undefinable quality setting one, or something, apart; something elusive, or hard to describe or express. Pronunciation: zhun say KWAH.

A Writing Tip: Hyphenate two or more words used as a single modifier *before* a noun, e.g., "She is a *well-known* athlete," but "The athlete is *well known*." A hyphen is not used when the first word of such a modifier is an *-ly* adverb. For example: a *half-finished* task, but a *partly finished* task.

```
┌─────────────────────────────────────────────────────────────────────────────────┐
│                            Word Cluster No. 9                                      │
│                                                                                    │
│  benefit        benefaction     benefactor       benefic        beneficent        │
│  benefice       beneficial      beneficiary      beneficite     Benedictus        │
│  benediction    benison         benevolent       benign         benignant         │
│                                                                                    │
│    bonito       bonus           embonpoint       bonny          boniform          │
│  debonair                                                       bonification       │
│                                                                                    │
│  Common elements_____Inferred Meaning_____  │
└─────────────────────────────────────────────────────────────────────────────────┘
```

Romance Cognates	French	Romanian	Italian	Portuguese	Spanish
	bon, bien	bun, bine	buono, bene	bom, beme	bueno, bien

Doublets: benediction:benison

Words with disguised Latin roots: bounty, boon (companion)

Placenames: Benedicta, ME; Bon Agua, TN; Bon Air, AL; Bon Secour, AL (see p. 1); Bonita, MS; Bonsecours, Quebec; Benevolence, GA; Bountiful, WA; Terrebonne Bay, LA; Bonne Terre, MO; Terrrebonne, OR; Terrebonne, Quebec. There is a *Bonanza* in each of the following states: AK, AR, GA, ID, KY, MO, OR, TX, UT.

Latin phrases: *contra bonos mores*; *bene vale; bonafide; nota bene* (**NB**); *cui bono? cui malo?*

French words and phrases: *bon vivant, bon mot, bon voyage, à bon marché, bon appétit, bonjour, bon ami, à bon droit, bénéficiaire, bienvenue, bonne nuit, bonne chance*

French proverb: *à bon chat, bon rat* (see **Clavis**)

Italian phrases: *ben trovato* (**well found**)*; ben tornato* (**welcome home**)*; ben venuto; ben mercato; a bene placito*

Spanish words and phrases: *muy bien* (**very well**)*, buenas noches* (**Good night**)*, buenos días* (**Good day**)
Bien vengas, mal, si vienes solo: **Welcome, Misfortune, if thou comest alone.** Cervantes (1547-1616), Spanish writer

Motto of the State of Maryland: *Scuto bonae voluntatis tuae coronasti nos*: **With the shield of thy good will hast thou crowned us.**

Motto of the University of the South: *Ecce quam bonum*: **Behold, how good.** Psalms 133:1

NB: *Bonfire*, from *bone fire*, originally referred to the fire that burned the bodies following a plague or war.

Greek: *eu-*, **good, well**: **eu**calyptus (**well-covered**, from the covering of the buds), **Eu**charist, **eu**clase, **eu**demonia (see p. 62), **eu**diometer, **Eu**dora (**good gift**), **Eu**gene, **eu**genics, **eu**logy, **eu**onymus, **eu**pepsia, **eu**phemism, **eu**phonious, **eu**phonium, **eu**phoria, **eu**photic, **eu**phuism, **eu**plastic, **eu**ploid, **eu**pnea, **eu**thanasia; **ev**angel, **the gospel, good news**.

Sanskrit: *swastika*, literally, **a sign of good luck**; well-being. *Swastika* was an ancient cosmic or religious symbol, and adopted by Nazi Germany in 1935. Pronounced: SWAHS tih kuh.

wordextras

To cavil, from *calvari*, **to deceive**, is to object when there is little reason to do so; to resort to trivial faultfinding; to carp; quibble *at*, or quibble *about*. The parents *caviled at* the school board's ruling on revised boundaries.

To cater, ultimately from Vulgar Latin *acceptare* (*ad-*, **to, toward** + *capere*, **to take hold**), means "to provide food," "to serve as a caterer." In a figurative sense, to take special pains in seeking to gratify another's needs or desires: with *to*; as the new tax law *catered to the wealthy*, not to those who really needed it.

Vacuum, from *vacuus*, **empty**, has remained unchanged from its original spelling. As a *noun*, a space with nothing at all in it; completely empty space; as an *adjective*, of a vacuum; describing that which is empty; as a *verb*, to clean with a vacuum cleaner; in full, *to vacuum-clean*. The plural of *vacuum* is either *vacuums* or *vacuua*.

Convivial, from *con-*, **with** + *vivere*, **to live**, originally had to do with a feast or festive activity. It now means **sociable, jovial**; fond of eating, drinking, and good company. See p. 187 for *convivial* paired with *symbiotic*.

Graham crackers are named after Sylvester Graham (1794-1851), a US dietary reformer, and Presbyterian minister, who advocated the use of whole-wheat flour and a vegetarian diet. Often ridiculed, he was called "the poet of bran and pumpkins" by Ralph Waldo Emerson, with whom Graham associated. See *transcendentalism*, p. 193.

an aphorism: **Don't change horses in the middle of the stream.** Don't discount experience in a leader.

Common element bases: bene, bonus   **Meaning**: well, good

IE base: *due*, **to do**, **perform**, **show favor**, **revere**; yields **Greek** *dunasthai*, **to be able**, as in **dynam**ic, **dynam**ite, **dyn**asty, aero**dyn**e, geo**dyn**amics; **German**: *gut*, **good**; *guten Tag*, **good day**; *guten Morgen*, **good morning**

Clavis

bon ami:	French; **good friend** (BOH nah ME); in uppercase, the name of a cleaning compound, and pronounced bon AMI, as in *Miami*. The compound Bon Ami® first appeared over 100 years ago; since promotion was only by printed media, customers without knowledge of French pronounced the name of the product as they perceived it in English. The compound "hasn't scratched yet."
bonafide:	with *fidere*, **to have faith**, **trust**; **in good faith**, as *a bonafide contract*; without dishonesty, fraud, or deceit. See p. 80 for further information and the corresponding German word.
cui bono?	**to whose good?** Interpreted as **to whose benefit?** Who stands to gain from this? Sometimes translated: For what useful purpose? "*Cui bono* is ever of weight in all agreements. *Black's*. It was a Roman lawyer's maxim when at a loss to tell where the responsibility for a crime lay, the best choice was to inquire who reaped the benefit of it. Opposite to *cui malo?* **to whose harm?**
debonair:	from Old French *debonaire*, **of good breed**; pleasant and friendly in a cheerful way; genial; affable; can also mean an easy and carefree manner; jaunty; sprightly.
embonpoint:	French; **in good condition**; a well-fed appearance; plumpness; corpulence (see p. 49).
à bon chat…:	French proverb: **to a good cat, a good rat**; quid pro quo; tit for tat.
bonne chance:	French for **good luck**; an expression of good wishes. Pronounced: bon SHAWNS.
benediction:	and *benison*, doublets; with *dicere*, **to speak**, **to speak well**, to hallow, to bless; an invocation of divine blessings, especially at the end of a religious service; also, an assurance of divine blessing. *Benediction*, directly from Latin; *benison*, from Old French. [*-tion*: noun-forming suffix]
nota bene:	symbol *NB*, **note well**; directing attention to something important; used in this book to indicate words that appear by form to be related to root under consideration, but are *not* related.
euthanasia:	with Greek *thanatos*, **death**, **good** or **pleasant death**; as an act of mercy, painlessly putting to death one suffering from an incurable or distressing disease; there are both *passive* and *active* forms of euthanasia.
euphoria:	with Greek *pherein*, **to bear**, **well-borne**, **easy to bear**. An exaggerated feeling of **well-being**; high spirits, especially if such a feeling is without obvious cause.
eugenics:	Greek *eu-* + Latin *genus*, **birth**; **well-born**; the study of hereditary improvements, especially of human improvement by genetic control. *Eugenics* is plural in form but used with a singular verb. [Many words ending with *-ics* have the same grammatical construction as that of *eugenics*: *acoustics*, *aesthetics*, *analytics*, *ceramics*, *economics*, *ethics*, *genetics*, *harmonics*, *kinesics*, *kinetics*, *linguistics*, *logistics*, *mathematics*, *metrics*, *physics*, *poetics*, *politics*, *semantics*, *statistics*, *tactics*.]

wordextras

Sabotage is from French *sabot*, **wooden shoe**; the verb from which *sabotage* derives is *saboter*, **to work badly**. In retaliation for poor working conditions, disgruntled factory workers often threw their *sabots* into the machinery.

Espionage, from French *espionner*, **to spy**, and further from Italian *spione*, "the act of spying," is ultimately from Latin *specere*, **to see**, which also yields *aspect*, *expect*, *inspect*, *introspect*, *prospect*, *respect*, *retrospect*, *suspect*; *despise*. Another Latin verb meaning "to see" comes from *videre*: *video*, *evident*, *provide*, *envious*; *visible*, *vision*, *visionary*, *envision*, *provision*, *revision*, *television*, *improvise*; *visa*, *view*; *déja vu*. See p. 212, Item 171.

A Writing Tip: Use a comma between **coordinate adjectives** not joined by *and*. Do *not* use a comma between **cumulative adjectives**. **Coordinate**: First Lady Jacqueline Kennedy was an attractive[,] gracious lady. **Cumulative**: Jacqueline Kennedy wore a **dark blue tweed suit**. *Tweed* modifies *suit*; *blue* modifies *tweed suit*; *dark* modifies *blue tweed suit*. If "and" can be inserted between the adjectives without distorting the meaning of the sentence, the adjectives are coordinate, e.g. Jacqueline Kennedy was *a gracious* **and** *attractive lady,* or if the adjectives can be transposed, e.g. Jacqueline Kennedy was *a gracious, attractive lady* [the first sentence with transposed adjectives]. See **A Writing Tip**, p. 179, for more information on coordinate versus cumulative adjectives.

Word Cluster No. 10

bicycle	bicyclic	biracial	bilingual	binomial
bisect	bivalve	biceps	bidentate	biped
bifoliate	biennial	bifocal	bimestral	bicuspid
bicameral	bilateral	bimarine	bitheism	bigeminate
biconjugate	bicorn	biduous	bibasic	biligulate
bilabial	bifurcate	bigamy	bifid	bibeveled
binary	binaural	binocular	combination	binate
bissextile	bisaxillary	biscuit	combine	binovular
bisferious	bisiliac	biscotti	recombinant	
		bistort		

Common elements_____Inferred Meaning_____

Romance Cognates	French	Romanian	Italian	Portuguese	Spanish
	bis, deux	bi, dubbe	due	dois, duas	dos

Words with disguised Latin roots: balance (see *equipoise*, p. 76), barouche, dual, duel, deuce, duodenal, double, duet, dyad, dubiety, dubious, doublet, dozen, doubt, pinochle, redoubtable (not related to *redoubt*)

Placenames: Bivalve, CA, MD, NJ; Dos Cabezas (**Two Heads**), AZ; Dos Palos, CA; Dos Rios (**Two Rivers**), CA; Two Egg, FL; Twodot, MT; Two Medicine Creek, MT, Two Ocean Pass, WY. There are many others.

Latin phrases: *Bis peccare in bello non licet*: **It is not permitted to blunder twice in war.**
Bis vincit qui se vincit victoria: **Twice does he conquer who conquers himself in the victory.** Given among maxims of Publius Syrus, a writer of mimes (dramatic dialogues), in 1 B.C.

French phrases: *tête-bêche* (see **Clavis**), *à deux*, **of or for two**; **between two**; **intimately**

Italian music word: *duo*, **duet**, a composition for two voices or two instruments

Explore *bicinium* and *tricinium*; *binary* and *ternary* music forms; also, *combination tone. Harvard's*

Greek cognates: *di-*, **two**: **di**chondra, **di**chromate, **di**chroscope, **di**cotyledon, **di**crotic, **di**ploma, **di**lemma, **di**ptych
dich(o)-, **in two**, **asunder**: **dicha**sium, **dich**optic [*dicho-* + *optic*], **dicho**gamy, **dicho**geny, **dicho**tomous, **dicho**tomy

Greek *didumous*, **two, twin, testicles**: **didym**ium (a rare metal, formerly considered an element, but later found to be a mixture of *two* elements), **didym**ous; **didym**algia, **didym**itis, **didym**odynia; **didym**ospore; epi**didym**is.

German cognate: *zwei*, as in **Zwieback**, the linguistic equivalent of *biscuit*. (See **Clavis**.)

Related French term: *Double-entendre*, **double meaning**, is a term with two meanings, especially when one of them has a risqué or indecorous connotation; can also mean "ambiguity." Usual pronunciation: DOO blon TAHN dreh.

wordextras

Tawdry, describing that which is **cheap, flashy, gaudy, showy, sleazy**, is from a syllabic merging of *St. Audrey*, especially as in *St. Audrey's laces*; these laces were gaudy neckpieces sold at St. Audrey's fair in Norwich, England.

Munificent, from *munus*, **gift** + *facere*, **to make**, means **very generous in giving**; lavish; characterized by great generosity. Example: Many universities receive *munificent* bequests from wealthy individuals and large corporations. See p. 55 for *remuneration*. Pronounced: myoo NIF uh sunt.

An *adjective*, *spurious* originally meant **false, of illegitimate birth**, from the noun *spurius*, **bastard**. *Spurious* describes that which is outwardly similar or corresponding to something without having its genuine qualities; of deceitful nature or quality, as *a spurious signature*. In *botany*, like in appearance, but unlike in structure or function. SYNONYMS: artificial, counterfeit, ersatz, synthetic.

Rhinestone translates French *caillou du Rhin*: so called because it was originally made at Strasbourg (on the Rhine). *Rhinestone* is a bright, colorless gem made of hard glass, often cut to imitate a diamond.

an aphorism: *A bird in the hand is worth two in the bush.* **Certainty is better than uncertainty**; possession is better than prospect. A low-paying job is better than the mere possibility of a higher-paying one.

Common elements: bi-, bin-, bis-, bini-   **Meaning**: two; twice; two by two

IE base: *dwo-*, **two**; thus, *two, twelve, twain, tweed, twilight, twin, twine*. When counting with the fingers, Old English *twalif*, **twelve** is "two left over"; Old English *endleofan*, **eleven**, "one left over."

Clavis

bicameral: with *camera*, **room**; **two rooms** or **chambers**, as in most legislatures. The United States Congress and 49 of the 50 states have such bodies; only Nebraska has a *unicameral* legislature. As a medical term, having **two cavities** or **chambers**. See *unicameral*, p. 26.

biceps: with *capit*, **head**; **two heads**; any muscle having two heads or points of origin, but especially the large muscle at the front of the upper arm that flexes the elbow joint; also, the large muscle at the back of the thigh that flexes the knee joint; compare *triceps, quadriceps*. See p. 85 under **wordextras**.

bicuspid: with *cuspis*, **point**; a tooth with a **two-pointed** crown. The canine, a one-pointed tooth, is a cuspid. See *canine*, p. 27, under **Word Cluster No. 14.**

biduous: with *dies*, **day**; consisting of **two days**, as *a biduous fever*.

bifoliate: with *folium*, **leaf**; in *botany*, **having two leaves**. See p. 206, Item 90, for other words from *folium*.

bisect: with *secare*, **to cut**; **to cut in two**; in *geometry*, to cut into two *equal* parts. As an intransitive verb, **to divide**, **fork**; the noun is *bisection*.

balance: modification of *bi-* + *lanx*, **scalepan** (as in the zodiacal sign of Libra), from early devices using **two suspended pans** for weighing; *lance* is the plural of *lanx*. A sentence is *balanced* when grammatically equal structures are used to express contrasted, or similar, ideas. Explore *balance* as a rhetorical device.

binaural: with *auris*, **ear**; **having two ears**; of or involving the use of *two ears*; designating sound production or transmission in which at least *two sources of sound* are used to give a *stereophonic* (**solid sound**) effect. See p. 111 for other words from *stereo-*, **solid**. See *ocular*, p. 142.

biscuit: from Middle Latin *bis cocium*, **twice-baked**; clipped from Old French *pain bescuit*, **twice-baked bread**; in French, *bread* is *pain*; in Spanish, *pan*. Twice-baked is *Zwieback* in German. A *companion* is one who shares bread with another; *company* is from same roots as *companion*. See p. 26 under *comrade*.

bissextile: *bis*, **twice** + *sextus*, **sixth**; now referring to leap year. The background of this word is so tortuous, the reader is referred to a college-edition dictionary.

barouche: from German *Baratsche*; ultimately from Latin *birotus*, **a two-wheeled carriage**; however, the barouche is *four-wheeled*.

tête-bêche: French; **double-headed**; with heads touching; postage stamps that are printed upside down to each other.

doubt: from *dubious*, literally, **to be two**; ultimately from Latin *dubitare*, **to waver in opinion**. Compare *doubt* with *redoubtable*, **fearsome**, **formidable**. *Doubt* is not related to *redoubt*, which is from *reducerer* (see p. 25, **wordbuilder #15**). See *Webster's New World* for explanation of erroneously inserted *b* in *dou̲bt*.

dozen: from Middle English *dozeine*; Old French *dozaine*; ultimately from *duodecim*, **twelve**; from *duo* + *decem*, **ten**. See p. 58 for *duodenal*, as *a duodenal ulcer*.

wordextras

French *insouciant*, **blithely indifferent**, **carefree**, is from *in-*, **not** + *soucier*, **to trouble, to upset**, and ultimately from Latin *sollicitare*, **to agitate**. Pronunciation: in SOO see unt; also, in SOO shunt. See *sans-souci*, p. 178.

In Greek drama, *tragedy* meant **goat song**. Possibly, the reason is that a goat was offered as a sacrifice to the gods during the annual drama festival; another possible reason is that the actors in the *satyr* play—one section of the entire drama, or *tetralogy*—were dressed as goats rather than as horses. For more on *satyr* and *tetralogy*, see p. 162.

Ferret, from Italian *fioretti*, **floss silk**, and ultimately from Latin *flos*, **flower**, is a narrow ribbon of cotton, wool, silk.

Sauna is Finnish for "a very hot, dry bath," which originated in Finland, where the bath is followed by a light beating of the skin with birch boughs or by a brief plunge into cold water.

Duel, from Latin *bellum* (from Old Latin *devellum*), **war**, is a type of physical combat between two persons. Other words from *bellum* are *bellicose, belligerent, rebel* (rebeldom, rebellion, rebellious), *antebellum, postbellum, casus belli*, an event provoking war or used as a pretext for making war; also the variants *revel* and *revelry*.

Sectional Word Cluster Test

INSTRUCTIONS: For each set of words from Latin and Greek (and sometimes, French, Spanish, and German), write the common meaning in the blank.

Example: **hypo**tenuse, **hypo**thesis, **sub**ject   <u>under</u>

	Presection Answer	Postsection Answer
11. ab**brev**iate, **brev**ier, **brevi**ped, a**bridge**	_____	_____
12. **calor**ie, **cal**enture, non**chal**ant, **chowder**	_____	_____
13. bi**cameral**, uni**cameral**, in **camera**, **chamber**	_____	_____
14. **can**ine, **Can**is Minor, **cyn**ic, **cyn**odon	_____	_____
15. **cap**tion, **cap**size, for**ceps**, eman**cip**ate	_____	_____
16. per **cap**ita, de**cap**itate, bi**ceps**, ker**chief**	_____	_____
17. **carni**vorous, **carn**ation, pan**creas**, **sarco**phagus	_____	_____
18. **centri**fugal, geo**centric**, andro**center**, **centr**oid	_____	_____
19. de**cad**ent, cas**cad**e, de**cid**uous, re**cid**ivist	_____	_____
20. **circum**ference, **circa**dian, re**search**, **peri**meter	_____	_____

_____   _____
Presection Score   Postsection Score

Note: Enter scores for this test and the following ones after completing this section; then, enter them on p. xvii.

Sectional Wordbuilder Test

Throughout the book and as a supplement, there are wordbuilders; these wordbuilders are designed to help you build a family of words from a single root.

	Presection Answer	Postsection Answer
8. What is the meaning of *dactyl-* as in **dactylo**graphy, ptero**dactyl**?	_____	_____
9. What is the meaning of *ana-* as in **ana**chronism, **ana**biosis?	_____	_____
10. What is the meaning of *anima-* as in **anima**l, **anima**te?	_____	_____
11. What is the meaning of *chron-* as in **chron**icle, syn**chron**ize?	_____	_____
12. What is the meaning of *–tom-* as in appendec**tom**y, ana**tom**y?	_____	_____
13. What is the meaning of *anth-* as in **anth**ology, chrys**anth**emum?	_____	_____
14. What is the meaning of *dors-* as in **dors**al, en**dors**e?	_____	_____
15. What is the meaning of *duc-* as in **duc**tile, e**duc**ate?	_____	_____
16. What is the meaning of *-itis* as in appendic**itis**, bronch**itis**?	_____	_____
17. What is the meaning *-oma* as in fibr**oma**, sarc**oma**?	_____	_____
18. What is the meaning of *blast-* as in **blast**ema, odonto**blast**?	_____	_____

Presection Score   Postsection Score

After entering the scores here, enter them on pp. xviii.

Word Cluster No. 11

breve	breviger	abbreviate	breviped	brevicaudate
brevet	breviate	breviconductor	brevifoliate	breviloquence
breve rest	breviary	brevicipitid	brevimanu	brevipennate
brevier	brevity	breviductor	breviflexor	breviradiate
				brevirostrate

Common elements_____**Inferred Meaning**_____

Romance Cognates	French	Romanian	Italian	Portuguese	Spanish
	bref (m); brève (f)	bref, scurt	breve	breve	breve

Doublets: abbreviate:abridge

Latin phrases: *Ars longa, vita brevis* (see **Clavis**). *Ira furor brevis est*: **Anger is a brief madness.** Horace
Est brevitate opus, ut currat sententia: **Terseness is needed that the thought may run free.** Horace

Spanish proverb: *Oración breve sube al cielo*: **Short prayers mount to heaven.**

Related words (see **IE base**, p. 22): **brace**ro (Spanish: **farmhand**), **brace**let, garde-**bras**, **brace** and bit (a drill, **bit**, with a handle, **brace**); em**brace***, vam**brace**; **Brazos** River, a**brazo** (**an embrace**), **brass**iere; amphi**brach** (see pp. 6, 39); medical words beginning with *brach-*, **arm**, as in **brach**ial, **brach**iate, **brach**ium; **brach**ialgia; **brachio**gram, **brachio**pod, **brachio**tomy; **pretzel**. *There is another *embrace*, as *to embrace a jury* (to try illegally to influence the jury); this *embrace* is from French *braise*, **coals, to set fire to**; other forms: embracer, embracery.

German: *kurz* as in *kurz und gut*: **short and good**; in short; in summary.
Kurz is der Schmerz, und ewig ist die Freude: **Brief is the pain and eternal is the joy.** Friedrich von Schiller (1759-1805), German dramatist and poet.

wordbuilder #8
Greek *dactyl*, **finger**, yields *dactyl* itself—a *foot* of poetry (see p. 169), **dactylo**gram (**a fingerprint**), **dactylo**graphy (the science of *fingerprinting*), **dactyl**ology (the use of the *finger* alphabet, or sign language), **dactylo**scopy (the identification and classification of *fingerprints*), penta**dactyl**, ptero**dactyl**; pachy**dactyl**ia; and **date** (the fruit of the palm tree). Old Provençal changed *dactyl* to *datil*, from which *date* is derived; the fruit is shaped similar to the *fingers*.

wordextras
Amenable, describing one who is responsive, submissive, and open to suggestions, originally described "one who can be threatened or driven." Latin *minare*, from which *amenable* is derived, meant "to drive or herd animals."

Pen, the writing utensil, is from Latin *penna*, **feather**, from the early practice of writing with quills. From the root are *penna, pennant, pennate, pennon, pennatisect, penniform; bipennate, brevipennate* (see **Word Cluster**, above), *paripennate, tripennate; empennage; pinnacle, pinnate, bipinnate; digitipinnate*.

Pencil, penicil, penicillate, penicillin, and *penicillium* are diminutives of Latin *penis*, **tail**.

Interloper, one who **runs** (or, **leaps, lopes**) **between**, is from Latin *inter-*, **between** (see p. 97, **Word Cluster No. 49**) + Middle Dutch *lopen*, **to run**, and Old English *hleapan*, **to leap**. An *interloper* was originally one who encroached on the trading rights of others, and first designated independent traders, or those not affiliated with Muscovy Company or the East India Trading Company. Now, an intruder, a meddler. Compare *elope*, **to run away** (to marry).

Old English *mynster*, now **minster**, is a doublet of *monastery*, from Greek *monos*, **one, alone**. A *minster* usually designated the church belonging to a *monastery*, e.g., Westminster Abbey. *Minster*, Ohio. See *minister*, p. 128.

Middle English *virago*, from Latin *vir*, **man**, is a quarrelsome, shrewish, nagging woman; a scold. *Virago* is related to *werewolf*, **man-wolf**. See p. 22 under **wordextras**. See p. 102 for *virtual*.

Allegory, from Greek *allos*, **other** + *agoreuein*, **to speak in assembly**, describes one thing under the image of another. *Allegories* are often used for teaching or explaining ideas, moral principles, etc. A well-known allegory is John Bunyan's *Pilgrim's Progress* (1678), portrayed as a dream of setting out on a journey from this world to heaven.

Delphinium, the larkspur, is so named because of the resemblance of its nectary to a *dolphin*. The *delphinium* is a member of the buttercup family, bearing spikes of spurred, irregular flowers, usually blue, on tall stalks, several species of which are poisonous. [*Nectary*: the part of a flower that secretes nectar.]

Common element base: brevis   **Meaning**: short, brief

IE base: *mregh-u-*: **short**; **Latin**: *brachium*, **arm**, yields *brachy*-prefixed medical words, for example, **brachy**-cephalic (having a relatively **short** or broad head); also, amphi**brach** (see pp. 5, 39), tri**brach** (see **Clavis**, below); in addition, **shorter**; thus, the upper (or, *shorter*) arm of the body (the part of the arm that extends from the shoulder to the elbow); also yields *pretzel* (see **Clavis**).

Clavis

brevity: from *brevitas*, **shortness**, shortness of time or duration; briefness; the quality of expressing much in a few words; **conciseness**; **terseness**.

breviger: with *gerere*, **to carry**; a friar carrying a license (*breve*), an authorizing letter, for begging.

brevier: an 8-point print size, for typesetting *breviaries*—books containing the daily offices and prayers of the Roman Catholic Church, or of the Orthodox Eastern Church.

abridge: and *abbreviate*, doublets; *abridge*, **to shorten by condensing**; an *unabridged* dictionary is complete, not shortened; *abbreviate*, **to shorten by omitting**. *Abbreviate*, directly from Latin; *abridge*, through French.

bridge: through association with *abridge*, above entry, it might be inferred that *bridge* is a means of shortening distances, as over a river; instead, it comes from Anglo-Saxon *bricg*, **a wooden causeway**.

brief: a **condensed** statement of the main arguments or ideas in a speech or piece of writing; in *law*, a written document outlining the main facts of a case. As an *adjective*, of short duration or length, as *a brief visit*.

pretzel: from German *Brezel*; ultimately from *brachium*, **arm**; originally, a biscuit baked in the form of crossed *arms*, and given to children as a reward for saying their prayers.

brumal: from Latin *bruma*, **winter**; pertaining to the **shortest** day of the year, **the winter solstice**, around December 21; **wintry**; indicative of, or occurring in, the winter. *Bruma* is from *brevissima*, superlative of *brevis*.

merry: and *mirth* are from Old English *myrge*, but ultimately from the same IE base that yields the Latin words. The underlying meaning of these words is that *happiness* and *mirth* are of **short** duration.

tribrach: *tri-*, **three**; a metrical foot consisting of three **short** syllables, two belonging to the *thesis* (unstressed part), and one to the *arsis* (stressed part). See *amphimacer*, p. 6; see other poetry terms, p. 169.

Ars longa, vita brevis: **Art is long, life is short**; the 19th-century American poet Henry Wadsworth Longfellow translated it: **Art is long and time is fleeting.**

wordbuilders #9, 10, 11

Greek *ana-*, **again**, **over**; also **up**, **against**, **throughout**, yields **ana**basis, **ana**baena, **Ana**baptist, **ana**batic, **ana**biosis, **ana**chronism, **ana**clastic, **ana**coluthon, **ana**crusis, **ana**dem, **ana**dromous, **ana**glyph, **ana**lysis, **ana**mnesis, **ana**morphism, **ana**pest (see p. 169), **ana**phase, **ana**phora (the repetition of a word or phrase at the beginning of successive clauses, lines of poetry, etc. Example: Dr. King's "I Have a Dream"), **ana**plastic, **ana**thema, **ana**strophe, **ana**tomy, literally, **a cutting up**. The following are double-prefixed compounds: **ana**katadidymus, **anana**phylaxis.

Latin *anima*, **life**, **soul**, yields **anima** itself; **animal**, **anima**ted, **anim**osity, **animus**; **anim**advert; in**anima**te (**not animate**), un**anim**ous, equ**anim**ity, long**anim**ity, magn**anim**ous (see p. 122), pusill**anim**ous, trans**anim**ation.

Greek *chronos*, **time**, yields **chron**ic (existing over a period of time; opposite to *acute*), **chron**icle, **Chron**icles I, II (Old Testament books), **chrono**gram, **chrono**graph, **chrono**logy, **chrono**meter, **chrono**scope; iso**chron**e; dia**chron**ic, mono**chron**ic, poly**chron**ic, sub**chron**ic, syn**chron**ic; ana**chron**ism, para**chron**ism, pro**chron**ism, syn**chron**ism; geosyn**chron**ous (satellite); **crony**. Many newspapers have *Chronicle* as part of their name.

wordextras

In English folklore, *werewolf*, from IE *wiros*, **man** + Old English *wulf*, **wolf**, was a person changed into a wolf, or one capable of assuming the form of a wolf at will; **lycanthrope**. Also spelled *werwolf*. See *virago*, p. 21.

Bazaar and *bizarre*, though pronounced the same, come from different sources and have different meanings. Persian *bazaar*, **market**, designates a street of shops and stalls in Middle Eastern countries; also, any shop for selling various kinds of goods; a sale of various articles, usually to raise money for a club, church, etc. French *bizarre* is from Italian *bizzarro*, **angry**, **fierce**, **strange**; it is further from Spanish where it meant **bold**, **knightly**. Synonyms: fantastic, grotesque. Consider the *bizarre* tales of ratiocination by Edgar Allan Poe; see p. 157.

Word Cluster No. 12

calefaction	**cale**scent	**cale**nture	de**cale**scent
calefy	**cali**duct	**calor**ification	in**cale**scent
calor	**calor**ic	**calor**ie	re**cale**scence
calorescence	**calor**imeter	**calor**ific	trans**cale**nt

Common elements_____Inferred Meaning_____

Romance Cognates	French	Romanian	Italian	Portuguese	Spanish
	chaleur	cald	calore	calor	calor

Words with disguised Latin roots: caldera, chowder, chafe, nonchalant, scald, chauffeur, camouflage

Doublets: caldron:chaldron

Placenames: Caliente (CA, NV); Ojo Caliente (**Hot Eye**), NM; Rio Caliente, Mexico

French words and phrases: *chaud, chaud-froid, chaudière, chauffe-pieds, réchauffé*

Italian music term: *con calore* (see **Clavis**)

Spanish phrase: *hace calor* (see **Clavis**)

Greek *therm*, **heat**: **Therm**os™ (see **Clavis**) **therm**ometer, **therm**onuclear, steno**therm**, and **Therm**idor, the eleventh month in the French Revolutionary War calendar; also a style of preparing seafood in brandy.

Placename: Thermal, California (near Salton Sea)

German: *heiss*, **hot**; pronounced HICE.

wordextras

German *Lebensraum*, or **living room**, is the space, room or territory needed, or deemed necessary, to satisfy economic necessities. See p. 26 under IE base. [In German, all nouns, whether common or proper, are capitalized.]

Migraine, coming from Greek *hemi-*, **half** + *cranium*, **skull**, is a headache involving only one side of the head. The adjectival form is *migrainous*, as *a migrainous headache*.

With *extra-*, **beyond**, *extravagant*, **straying beyond**, especially beyond the usual limits, shares its root with *vagrant* and *vagabond*, both of which denote persons who *wander* or *stray* from place to place.

With *sidus*, Latin for **star**, when one *considers* an issue, "the *stars* are studied closely." A *sidereal day* measures 23 hours, 56 minutes, and 4.091 seconds of mean solar time. *Mean solar time* or *mean time* designates time based on the hypothetical mean of the sun: used as a basis for standard time because it has exactly equal divisions. Each time zone is equal to 15° of the 360°-circumference of the earth. *Mean sun* is a hypothetical concept: the sun is thought of as moving uniformly along the celestial equator at a speed equal to the actual sun's *average* speed along the ecliptic, because the sun does *not* travel along the ecliptic at a uniform rate. *Desire*, **to await from the stars**, is also from *sidus*.

wordbuilder #12

Greek *–tom-*, from *temnein*, **to cut**, yields **tome**; a**tom**, dia**tom**; arthro**tome**, epi**tome** (see *epitomize*, below) micro**tome**, myo**tome**, osteo**tome**; a**tom**ic, dia**tom**ic, tetra**tom**ic; ana**tomy**, appendec**tomy**, auto**tomy**, cranio**tomy**, dicho**tomy**, episio**tomy**, gastro**tomy**, hystero**tomy**, kerato**tomy**, litho**tomy**, necro**tomy**, nephro**tomy**, neuro**tomy**, osteo**tomy**, os**tomy**, phlebo**tomy**, pleuro**tomy**, polycho**tomy**, rhizo**tomy**, sclero**tomy**, stereo**tomy**, teno**tomy**, tracheo**tomy**, tricho**tomy**, vago**tomy**, varico**tomy**, vaso**tomy**, zoo**tomy**; ent**om**ology*; epi**tom**ize, lobo**tom**ize; **tm**esis (see p. 81, under **wordextras**). With *a-*, **negative**, *atom*, for instance, is that which **cannot be cut further**, at least, as thought so in ancient Greek times; with *ana-*, **again, completely**, *anatomy* is that which is **cut up completely**; and *tome* is a single, usually large, volume *cut from a larger work*, e.g., an *encyclopedia* is **cut** into several volumes, or *tomes*. *Entoma*, **insect**, is "that whose body is *cut into* segments"; *entomology* is the branch of zoology that studies insects scientifically. Do not confuse *entomology* with *etymology*, the study of word origins. The **Clavis**, as well as the **wordextras**, of this book gives *etymological* notes.

Motto of Brown University, Providence, Rhode Island: *In Deo speramus*: **In God we hope.**
Motto of Goucher College, Baltimore, Maryland: *Gratia et Veritas*: **Grace and Truth.**
Motto of University of Denver: *Pro scientia et religione*: **For science and religion.**

Common element base: calor **Meaning**: heat
IE base: *kel(e)-¹*: **warm**

Clavis

caldron:	and *chaldron* are doublets; from *caldarium*, **a pot for boiling**. Although both are from Old French, they came into English in different periods and from different dialects.
caldarium:	from *caldarius*, **pertaining to warming**; in ancient Rome, a room for taking **hot** baths.
caldera:	Spanish; from *caldarium*; see above; the basin, or crater, of a volcano formed by an explosion or the collapse of the cone; the diameter of the *caldera* is many times that of the volcanic vent.
calenture:	a fever caused by intense humid **heat** in the tropics that affects sailors' minds, often causing them to imagine the sea a green field, and into which they have often jumped.
calorie:	the amount of **heat** necessary to raise the temperature of one gram of water one degree, from 14.5° to 15.5° Celsius, when the water is at atmospheric pressure.
calorimeter:	an apparatus for measuring amounts of **heat**, as in a chemical combination, friction, etc.
incalescent:	*in-*, **intensive** + *-escent*, **increasing, becoming, in the process of**; thus, **becoming hotter**; now rare, for *calescent* itself means **to become increasingly warmer**. With *–escent* meaning "becoming," an *adolescent*, a noun, is one who *is becoming an adult*; *adolescence* is the period of life between puberty and maturity; and *obsolescent*, an adjective, describes that which is *becoming obsolete*.
recalescence:	*re-*, **again**; **growing hot again**; a sudden and temporary increase in glow and temperature of hot iron or steel when it reaches one or more particular temperatures in the cooling process.
chowder:	from French *chaudière*, **a hot pot**; further from *caldarium* (see second entry); a thick soup or stew.
chafe:	from Latin *calefacere*, **to make warm**; can mean either **to stimulate** or **to annoy**.
chafing dish:	a dish that keep foods **warm** while being served.
chauffeur:	**a stoker**, one who stokes the fire; originally, the operator of a steam-driven car.
hace calor:	Spanish; literally, **it makes heat**; it is warm (or, hot).
con calore:	Italian: in *music*, with **warmth**, passion.
Thermos™:	trade name for an insulated container, invented by Scottish physicist Sir James Dewer (1848-1923). A *Thermos bottle*, for instance, keeps hot drinks hot, and cold drinks cold.
lukewarm:	Middle English *luke warme*, where *luke* means **tepid**, and is from **IE base**, above. Literally, *lukewarm* means **tepid-warm**, or **warm-warm**.

wordextras

Bellwether originally designated a castrated male sheep (wether) with a bell tied around its neck; the other sheep in the flock followed him. It has come to designate one who takes the lead or initiative, but formerly the leader of a foolish, sheeplike crowd; also, anything suggesting the general tendency or direction of events, style, trends.

From Latin *insula*, **island**, ***insulin***, the protein hormone developed in the pancreas, and which regulates the metabolism of carbohydrates (sugar), is from "the islets of Langerhans"; the islets are named after Paul Langerhans (1847-1888), a German histologist. From *histo-*, **tissue**, *histology* is the study of microscopic tissues of the body.

Contrite, from *com-*, **together** + *terere*, **to rub**, means **repentant**. ***Contrition***: remorse for having done wrong; in *theology*, sorrow for having offended God. *Trite, attrition, detrital, detrition, detriment, termite* are also from *terere*.

Qualm, from Old English *cwealm*, **death**, **disaster**, now usually means "a twinge of conscience." All present uses of *qualm* meliorate, or make more positive, the original meanings. SYNONYMS: compunction, misgiving, scruple.

A Writing Tip: Avoid sweeping generalizations. Even when the facts are accurate, they may be numerically insufficient to support a generalization. Generalizations like the following may contain some elements of truth, but they claim far too much: *The very rich avoid paying income taxes. College professors have no real concern for their students. A businessman is not interested in the arts. Mediterranean people are hot-tempered. Sweeping generalizations* are also known as *stereotypes* (*stereos*, **solid**); thus, *solid impressions* before all the facts are known.

```
┌─────────────────────────────────────────────────────────────────────────────────┐
│                          Word Cluster No. 13                                      │
│                                                                                   │
│  camera            cameral             bicameral           camerata               │
│  cameralist        cameralistic        unicameral          camerate               │
│  camerlengo        camerina            camaraderie         Camorra                │
│                                                                                   │
│  Common elements_____Inferred Meaning_____     │
└─────────────────────────────────────────────────────────────────────────────────┘
```

Romance Cognates	French	Romanian	Italian	Portuguese	Spanish
	chambre	camera	camera	câmara	cámara

Words with disguised Latin roots: comrade, chum, chamber, chimney, chamberlain, chambered nautilus; cabaret

Latin phrases: *camera lucida; camera obscura; in camera* (see **Clavis**)

Romance words and phrases: *camarade; camerista; camarero; camarilla* (Spanish for a small meeting room; also, a group of secret or confidential advisers; cabal; see *cabal*, p. 47, **wordextras**)

French words and phrases: *bon camarade; chambré* (**chambered**; brought to room temperature, said of certain wines); *femme de chambre, chambre à coucher; chambre d'ami*

NB: See *chambray* (a fabric), p. 97.

German: *Kamerad*, plural *Kameraden*: used by German soldiers in World War I in appealing for quarter (mercy granted to surrendering foe).

---

wordbuilders #13, 14, 15

Greek *anthos*, **flower**, yields **anth**emion, **anth**er, **anth**esis (not related to *thesis*), **antho**dium; **antho**carpous, **antho**logy (originally, **a garland**; now a collection of literary works), **antho**phore; an**anth**ous (**lacking flowers**), poly**anth**us; ex**anth**ema, chrys**anth**emum. NB: *Anthem*, from *anti-*, **against**, is *not* related to this root (see pp. 10, 77).

Latin *dorsum*, **back**, yields **dors**ad, **dors**al, as *a dorsal fin*, **dors**um; **dors**iduct, **dors**iflexion, **dors**ispinal; en**dors**e; **dos**-à-**dos** [in English, *do-si-do*; a square-dance figure in which the dancers pass each other right shoulder to right shoulder and circle each other *back to back*]; **dos**sier; intra**dos** (in *architecture*, the inside curve or surface of an arch or vault); para**dos** (an embankment of earth along the back of a trench, as to protect against fire from the rear).

Latin *ducere*, **to lead**, yields **duc**at, **duce**, **duct**, **duct**ile; ab**duct**, ad**duct**, con**duct**, de**duct**, e**duct**, in**duct**, pro**duct**; aque**duct**, dorsi**duct**, via**duct**; pro**duce**, re**duce**, repro**duce**, tra**duce**; e**duc**ate (**to lead out**), e**duc**ator, tra**duc**ianism; en**due**, sub**due**; **duke**, **duch**ess, Il **Duce** (**the leader**), re**doubt** (**a stronghold**; unrelated to *doubt*, see p. 20).

---

wordextras

Kindergarten is German for **children's garden**. The first kindergarten in the United States was established at Watertown, Wisconsin, for children of German immigrants. See p. 134 under **IE base**.

Though meaning **rough, abrupt**, *brusque* is not from *abrupt*; rather, it is from Latin *ruscum*, **butcher's broom**. SYNONYMS: bluff, blunt, crusty, curt, gruff. His *brusque* manner cost him many friends.

Lord is from Anglo-Saxon *hlafweard*, **loaf-ward**, or **keeper of the bread**. See *lady*, p. 197; p. 165 for *lordly* and *lordling*; p. 172 for *steward* for its similarity to *hlafweard*.

Snoop, **to look about in a sneaking, prying way**, is from Dutch *snoepen*, **to eat snacks on the sly**. *Snoop* is also a noun, designating a person who snoops.

Dilapidated, from Latin *dis-*, **apart** + *lapidare*, **to throw stones at**, describes that which is in a state of disrepair; broken down; ruined; hence, **shabby and neglected**. Both *dilapidated* and *lapidary* come from *lapis*, **stone**. *Lapidary*, or *lapidarist*, designates one who cuts, polishes, and engraves precious stones. *Lapidary* is also used as an adjective.

Isinglass, from Dutch *huizenblas* (*huizen*, **sturgeon** + *blas*, **bladder**), is a form of gelatin prepared from the internal membranes of fish bladders, used as a clarifying agent and adhesive; also designates a form of **mica**, especially in the form of thin, transparent sheets of muscovite. **Muscovite**: a type of mica, used as an electrical insulator.

Consummate, from *con-*, **with** + *summa*, **sum**, means **perfect, complete, supremely skillful**, as *a consummate pianist*. As an *adjective*, pronounced kun SUM it; as a *verb*, **to bring to completion**, as *to consummate a marriage with sexual intercourse*. Pronounced: KAHN suh MATE. See *sum* under **Clavis**, p. 184.

Vichyssoise, a smooth, thick soup made with potatoes, leeks, and cream, originated in Vichy, a city in France.

Common element base: camera   **Meaning**: room, chamber

IE base: *kamer-*: **to bend, a vault**; yields **Greek** *kamara*, **vaulted chamber**; **Old English** *heofon*, **heaven**.

German: *Zimmer*: **room** (of a house); *Raum* (**space**; see *Lebensraum* under **wordextras**, p. 23).

Clavis

camera:	directly from Latin, but ultimately from Greek (see **IE base**); a **chamber**; specifically, the chamber of a judge. When the photographic camera device was invented, it was first called *camera obscura*, **dark chamber**, or dark room.
unicameral:	*uni-*, **one**; designating a legislative body of only **one chamber**, or **house**, such as that of the State of Nebraska. All other States of the United States as well as the Federal Government have *bicameral* legislatures, the House of Representatives and the Senate (see *bicameral*, p. 20).
comrade:	French *camarade*; from Spanish *camarada*: **chambermate**: does not contain prefix *com-*, as in *companion*, although the meanings are similar. See *companion*, under *biscuit* (**Clavis**), p. 20. *Camaraderie*, **comradeship**, is also from *camarada*.
chum:	shortened from *chambermate*; pronounced *chomber*, or *chumber* in 18th-century England.
camerlengo:	in the Roman Catholic Church, a cardinal in charge of the papal treasury.
chamberlain:	originally, an attendant of a lord or ruler; an attendant of the Pope.
camerata:	largest order of crinoids (echinoderms); *echinoderm*, **prickly skin**; marine animals with a water vascular system, and usually with a hard, spiny skeleton and radial body, and includes star-fishes and urchins.
chambered nautilus:	also called *pearly nautilus*, a cephalopod of the genus Nautilus, and having a spiral, **chambered** shell, with pearly white septa (plural of *septum*, **dividing wall**). Explore "The Chambered Nautilus," a poem by Oliver Wendell Holmes (1809-94), US writer and physician.
chamber business:	judicial business transacted by a judge in his or her **chambers** as distinguished from business that must be transacted by the court in session; also known as *in camera*, **in the chamber**.
chimney:	from Middle English *chimene*, **fireplace**; further from Latin *caminus*, **furnace, flue**; ultimately from Greek *kaminos*, **oven, fireplace**. From the same IE root that yields *camera*.

wordbuilder #16

Greek *–itis*, **inflammation**, yields appendic**itis**, arthr**itis** (**joints**), bronch**itis** (**bronchial tubes**), burs**itis**, encephal**itis** (**brain**), hepat**itis** (**liver**), laryng**itis**, mening**itis** (**membrane**), neur**itis** (**nerves**), nephr**itis** (**kidney**), orch**itis** (**testes**), oste**itis** (**bone**), phleb**itis** (**veins**), rhin**itis** (**nose**), tendon**itis**, tonsill**itis**, urethr**itis**, vagin**itis**. Many others; see onelook.

wordextras

Epaulet, an ornamental shoulder board used in the military to indicate a particular rank or honor, is a diminutive of French *épaule*, **shoulder**. *Épaule* itself is from Latin *spatula*, a diminutive of *spathe*, **flat blade**; indicating that which is **flat**, as is the kitchen utensil and a paint spreader; in *botany*, *spatulate* leaves are **spoon-shaped** in outline and attached at the narrow end; in *zoology*, spoon-shaped or spatula-shaped.

The *Ferris wheel* is named for its builder, George Ferris (1859-96). Constructed for the World's Fair in 1893, the wheel was Chicago's answer to the Eiffel Tower, built in 1889, for the Paris exhibition (see p. 15). The wheel had a diameter of 250 feet, a circumference of 825 feet, and a height of 264 feet. Each car could hold 60 people!

Town, from Middle English *to(u)n*, **an enclosed place**, originally designated a nightly encampment. In Anglo-Saxon times, farmers often did not live on the land they tilled, but gathered with their own family and other families in "tons" for security against wild beasts and marauders. Some of these encampments evolved into established communities, often with the emergent leader's name designating the community, a practice continued as *towns* were established in North America, e.g., Brock**ton**, MA, MT; Charles**ton**, SC; Clay**ton**, AL, Warren**ton**, VA.

A Writing Tip: Conjunctive adverbs bridge sentences or parts of sentences. When a conjunctive adverb appears between independent clauses in a compound sentence, it is preceded by a semicolon (;) and followed by a comma. Examples: Scott goes to school full-time[;] *moreover*[,] he works 40 hours a week. I helped the magician set up his props[;] *furthermore*[,] I let him saw me in half. The apple trees must be sprayed[;] *otherwise*[,] the spider mites will kill the blossoms. See p. 28 for more on *conjunctive adverbs* under **A Writing Tip**.

```
┌─────────────────────────────────────────────────────────────────────────────┐
│                          Word Cluster No. 14                                  │
│                                                                               │
│ canine (K-9)     caniniform      canicule      Canicula        canary         │
│ Canary Island    Canis Major     Canis Minor   canaille        canine tooth   │
│                                                                               │
│ Common elements_____Inferred Meaning_____ │
└─────────────────────────────────────────────────────────────────────────────┘
```

Romance Cognates	French chien	Romanian caîne	Italian cane	Portuguese cão	Spanish can

Words with disguised roots: chenille, chien, kennel, quinsy

Placenames: Point au Chien, LA; Prairie du Chien, WI; Bayou du Chien, TN; Dog Town, AL; Dog Walk, KY

Latin phrases: *cane pejus et angue*: **worse than a dog or a snake**
canis in praesepi: **dog in a manger**; *Cave canem*: **Beware of the dog**

French phrases: *entre chien et loup*: **between dog and wolf**, i.e., when it is impossible to distinguish one from the other; in the twilight; at dusk; *chien méchant*: **wicked dog**; beware of the dog.

Greek cognates: cynic, Cynics, Cynicism, cynologist, cynical, cynosure, cynodon(tia), cynorexia (see p. 209, Item 134), Procyon (see *Clavis*, under *Canis Minor*). The Cynics form the link between Socrates and the Stoics.

Explore *cynicism* of Antisthenes, Crates, Zeno, and Diogenes; also, Butler's *Way of All Flesh*, and Maugham's *Of Human Bondage*.

Germanic words: kennelhound, dachshund, keeshond, poodle (originally, *Pudelhund*, **puddle dog**)

Welsh: corgi (*corr*, **dwarf** + *ci*, **dog, or guard**); the full name of the breed is Welsh corgi, bred for herding cattle.

wordextras

Stalag abridges German *Stammlager*, originally, **base camp**; in World War II, *Stalag* came to mean Prisoner of War camp, thus the title of the movie *Stalag 17*, released in 1953, starring William Holden.

Latin *emeritus* (*ex-*, **out of** + *merere*, **to earn**; thus, **because of merit**) is an honorary position bestowed on the holder because of his or her distinguished service to an institution. The term is most often applied to retired pastors and college professors. Thomas H. Estes, Ph.D., is Professor Emeritus of Reading, University of Virginia.

Parboil modifies French-English *perbullire*, **to boil thoroughly**. By an early mistake, the first syllable was connected with the meaning of *part*, and the word has thus come to mean **to partially boil**.

Alligator is from Spanish *el legarto*, **the lizard**. In addition to a large reptile of the crocodile family, also designates a machine, tool, etc., with a strong, movable, often toothed saw. Because of its rough skin, *avocado* is often called "alligator pear." *Avocado* itself is from Nahuatl *a'wakah*, **testicle**, because of its shape. See *orchid*, p. 86.

Arraign, ultimately from Latin *ratio*, **reason**, is to call a defendant before a court to answer to an indictment (a formal charge). Other than its use as a law term, *arraign* means "to accuse of wrong, inadequacy, or imperfection."

Blithe, from German *blithia*, **light**, **bright** (said of the sun), means **gay**, **joyful**, **cheerful**; also, **jocund**, **jovial**, **jolly**.

Schooner, probably from Scottish *scun*, **to skip a flat stone across water**, is a sailing vessel with two or more masts; *schooner* is also short for *prairie schooner*, the sturdy covered wagons used by pioneers to cross the American prairies. Most prairie schooners were Conestoga wagons, made in Conestoga Valley, Lancaster County, PA.

Taj Mahal, Persian for **best of buildings**, is a famous mausoleum, a tomb, at Agra, India, built 1630-48, by Shah Jahan for his favorite wife, who had borne his 14 children, and who died in childbirth.

Coulee, originally French *coulée*, from *couler*, **to flow**, and ultimately from Latin *colare*, **to strain**, is a deep gulch or ravine in the Northwest. There is the Grand Coulee Dam on the Columbia River, in northeast Washington. The dam is 550 feet high, five feet short of the height of the Washington Monument, and is almost a mile wide. From *couler* are also *colander* (a sieve), *percolate; coulisse, couloir; portcullis; piña colada. Coulee* and *couloir* are doublets.

Spanish *guano*, from Quechua *huanu*, **dung**, is manure of sea birds, found especially on islands off Peru; any natural or artificial fertilizer resembling this, as *bat manure*. Quechua, language of the Incan empire, is still widely spoken.

Condone, from *con-*, **intensive** + *donare*, **to give**, is to **forgive**, **pardon**, or **overlook** (an offense); to look the other way as if the offense did not occur. The parents *condoned* their children's boisterous drinking party. See p. 73.

Common element base: canis   **Meaning**: dog
IE base: *kwon-*: **dog**; thus, the Greek cognates on previous page.

Clavis

canary:
when discovered, a group of unnamed islands were consequently called *Insula Canaria* (Canary Islands) supposedly because of the wild **dogs** already there. The explorers also found small, greenish-brown birds that they called *canaries* from the dubbed name of the islands, or from the similarity of their color to that of the dogs (it's anybody's guess). Through modification in the domesticated state, the color of the canary has changed to a light, clear yellow. *Canary* also designates a lively court dance of the 16th century, as well as a sweet wine from the Canary Islands, once popular in England.

canaille:
from French; further from Italian *canaglia*, **pack of dogs**; rabble-rousers; pejorative term for the masses of common people. (See *canaille* in **Quote**, p. 185.)

Canis Major:
the larger dog, a constellation in the Southern Hemisphere; contains Sirius, the brightest star in the sky, and 8.7 light years (or 52.2 billion miles) from Earth.

Canis Minor:
the smaller dog, a constellation in the equatorial region of the Southern Hemisphere, near Hydra and Monoceros; contains *Procyon*, a binary star that rises "before" the **Dog Star**.

cynophilist:
with *philos*, **love**, **dog lover**. *Philos* is one of three main Greek words for *love*; the two others are *eros*, **sexual love**, and *agape*, **Godly love**. *Philos* is also found in *Philadelphia*, *philanthropy*, *philharmonic*, *philodendron*, *philogyny*, *philosophy; heterophil, homophile, pedophile*. See *philology*, p. 199.

Cynics:
a philosophical sect, found in the 300's B.C. by Antisthenes of Athens, and a disciple of Socrates. The basic tenet of Antithenes was that virtue rather than pleasure is the chief end of life, and therefore, the only good; further, that self-control is the only means of achieving virtue.

Among the enthusiastic followers of Antisthenes was Diogenes, who carried the principles of Antithenes and the Cynics to an extreme. To illustrate, it is said that Diogenes refused the common comforts of life, sleeping, for instance, in a tub instead of in a bed. See more on Diogenes, p. 132.

Funk says the sect degenerated into one of self-righteousness, an attitude that gained for them the derisive sobriquet—*Cynics*—**like a dog**, or **snarlers**.

kennel:
Middle English, *kenel*; Old French *chenil*, from Late Latin *canile*; a **dog house**.

wordbuilder #17
Greek *-oma*, **swelling**, **tumor**, yields carcin**oma**, cyst**oma**, dacry**oma**, fibr**oma**, glauc**oma**, gli**oma**, granul**oma**, hemat**oma**, lymph**oma**, melan**oma**, my**oma**, myx**oma**, neur**oma**, sarc**oma**. Many others. See onelook.com.

wordextras
Quonset hut, a prefabricated metal structure once common on military installations, is so named because of its being designed and manufactured at Quonset Point, RI. *Quonsets huts* were modeled after the *Nissen huts* of Great Britain.

Moult, or *molt*, is from Latin *mutare*, **to change**, as in *mutation*. In the Middle Ages, an *l* was erroneously inserted in the manner of *fault*. *Molting* refers to the casting off of hair, outer skin, horns, or feathers at certain intervals, prior to replacement of the castoff parts by new growth: said of certain animals, as reptiles, birds, deer.

Flirt may be from Old French *fleureter*, **to move from flower to flower**; the base of *fleureter* is *fleur*, **flower**, as in *fleur-de-lis*, **flower of the lily** (in *heraldry*, an emblem resembling an iris or a lily).

Flour, from "flower" of the wheat, or the best wheat, is from French *fleur de farine*, **flower of the meal**.

German *Linzer torte* is a rich Austrian pastry with a bottom crust and a lattice top of spiced ground-almond dough and a raspberry jam filling. *Torte* is German for *cake*; from Italian *torta*, **twisted** (**bread**).

Sluice, from Latin *excludere*, **to shut out**, is an artificial channel or passage for water; as a *verb*, it can mean "to wash off with a rush of water" or, to draw off by, or as by means of, a sluice. See p. 205, Item 74, for *claudere*, **to close**.

A Writing Tip: **Conjunctive adverbs** can express *addition* (furthermore, also, moreover); *contrast* (even so, however, on the other hand); *exemplification* (for example, for instance); *result* (hence, therefore, thus); an *alternative* (instead, otherwise, on the other hand); *time relationship* (then, later, next, meanwhile); *emphasis* (indeed, in fact, certainly). See **A Writing Tip**, p. 26, for sample sentences using conjunctive adverbs. **Note**: If conjunctive adverbs consist of more than one word, they are often called "transitional expressions."

```
┌─────────────────────────────────────────────────────────────────────────────┐
│                          Word Cluster No. 15                                  │
│                                                                               │
│  caption        captious       capias            capstan        captive      │
│  captivate      captor         capture           capable        capsule      │
│  capacity       capacious      capillary         mercaptan       capacitor   │
│                                                                               │
│  forceps        inception      interception        accept        except      │
│  susceptible    deception      contraception       susceptible   concept     │
│  precept        conception          ceptor        intussusception            │
│                                                                               │
│  conceive          perceive          receive              deceive            │
│  conceit           receipt           deceit            apperceive            │
│                                                                               │
│  recipe         participle     recipient      emancipate       anticipate    │
│  incipient      municipal      principal      principle        participate   │
│                                                                               │
│ Common elements_____Inferred Meaning_____  │
└─────────────────────────────────────────────────────────────────────────────┘
```

Romance Cognates	French	Romanian	Italian	Portuguese	Spanish
	capture	capta	cattura	captura	captura

Words with disguised Latin root: cable, caitiff, catch, chassis, chess, prince, princess, chase, enchase, purchase

Doublets: recuperate:recover; catch:chase; caitiff:captive; casket:caisson; conceit:conception

Triplets: prince:principal:principle

Latin phrases: *Capiat qui capere posit*: **Let him take who can**; *facile princeps*: **easily chief** (or **first**) *ad captandum vulgus* (see **Clavis**)*; particeps criminis* (**a partner in crime; accomplice**)

Related words: comprehend, prehensile (see p. 211, Item 152 for *prehendere*), entrepreneur, enterprise

Explore *negative capability* as used by Keats in referring to Shakespeare.

Germanic words: haven; heave; Copenhagen (**protected harbor**), capital of Denmark

wordextras

To eat humble pie, that is, **to undergo humiliation**, especially that of admitting one's error and apologizing, is from a pie made of *hombuls*, the edible organs of a deer or hog. In Anglo-Saxon times, a *humble pie* was often served to the servants after a deer hunt.

Voyage, now mainly a trip by water, was originally a trip by land, and comes from Old French *veiage*, and further from Latin *via*, **way**. In Latin, *veiage* was *viaticum,* which, in ancient Rome, designated money or supplies provided a vicar or envoy as traveling expenses. In the Roman Catholic Church, *Viaticum* designates the *Eucharist*, the sacrament of *Holy Communion*, when given to a dying person or one considered to be in danger of death.

Montevideo (pronounced MAHNT uh vuh DAY oh), the capital of Uruguay, and situated on a mountain, may have been named from a Portuguese sailor's cry, "*Monte vide eu*," **I see a mountain**. With not a mountain in sight, *Montevideo*, Minnesota, is pronounced monte VID ee oh.

Both *irascible* and *irate* are from Latin *irasci*, **to be angry**. Both adjectives, *irascible* means **easily angered**, **quick-tempered**; *irate*, **angry**, **wrathful**, **incensed**.

Amicus curiae, **friend of the court**, designates a person who offers, or is called in, to advise a court on some point of law that directly affects the case in question. Pronunciation: uh MY kus KYOOR ee.

French *maraud*, **tomcat**, yields the English verb *to maraud*, "to rove in search of plunder; make raids."

Disgust, from *dis-*, **negative** + *gustus*, **a taste**, **relish**, is a sickening distaste or dislike; deep aversion; repugnance; as a *verb*, to cause to feel disgust; be sickening; be repulsive. See p. 105 under *ragout*, **wordextras**. Spanish: *No me gusta*: **I don't like it**. Other words from *gustus* include **gust**atory, **gust**o; de**gust**ation.

Appeal, from *ad-*, **to, toward** + *pellere*, **to drive**, is to make a request to a higher court for the rehearing or review of a case. From *pellere* is *repeal*, as well as *compel, dispel, expel, impel, propel, repel*; *pulsate, pulse; compulsion, compulsive*; *expulsion, expulsive*; *impulse, impulsion, impulsive*; *propulsion, propulsive*; *repulse, repulsion, repulsive*.

Complacent, from *com-*, **intensive** + *placere*, **to please**, means **satisfied**, especially **self-satisfied**, or **smug**. Other words from *placere* include *placable, placate, placet, placid, implacable; complaisant*; English: *please, pleasure*.

Common element base: capere **Meaning**: to seize, grasp, hold, take

IE base: *kap-*: **to grasp**, yielding Germanic *haft, have, haven, heave, heavy, heddle, behoove*. The synonymous IE root *ghabh-* means **to give** or **receive**, as in *habit*. See **Word Cluster No. 45**, p. 89. **German**: *halten*, **to hold** (see p. 188); *fassen*, **to seize**; *nehmen*, **to take, seize**.

Clavis

capias: in *law*, a writ issued by a court directing an officer to arrest, or **seize**, the person named: from *capias*, the first word of the writ.

conceit: *conceit* and *conception* are doublets; however, they entered English through different routes and at different times. *Conception*, from *conceptio*, **taking hold**; *conceit*, from the verb *conceive*, from Old French *conceivre*, refers to a fanciful idea; also, a fanciful idea about oneself. Explore *conceit*, from Italian *concetto*, as a metaphoric figure of speech.

recipe: Rx symbol on prescriptions; usually assumed to mean "**Take** this medication as prescribed," but more likely directed to the apothecary of old, "*Take* these instructions and follow closely in dispensing," the same as cookbook instructions, e.g., "*Take* two eggs. . . ." *Sig.* on a prescription is the abbreviation for *Signature*, the physician's instructions to the patient; *Disp.* abbreviates *Dispense*, **Weigh out**, or **Measure**, the set of instructions to the pharmacist. See p. 68 for *bis in die*, a prescription term.

purchase: from Old French *purchasier*, which is from either *per-*, or *pro-* + *chase*; consequently, **to pursue, to seek to obtain**. Its more general meaning is "to obtain for money or by paying a price." In *law*, the acquisition of land, buildings, etc. by means other than inheritance or descent.

prince: and principal:principle; from Latin *princeps*, **first, chief**; further from *primus*, **first** + *capere*; thus, **first-taker**. A *prince* is *first* in line to seize the throne; a *principal* takes *first* place as a teacher and *was* in earlier years, the **first**, or **head teacher**; a *principle* is a *first* rule and ends in *le*, as in *ru̲le̲*. While *princip̲a̲l* may function as a noun, e.g., the *principal* [leader, capital (sum)], or as an adjective, e.g., the *principal* role, *princip̲le̲* is used only as a noun; *principled*, as in *high-principled*, is an adjective.

forceps: from *formus capere*, **hot taker**; formerly, tongs used by smiths for removing objects from the furnace; now used especially by dentists, jewelers, midwives, obstetricians, surgeons.

recuperate: from Latin *recuperare*, base of both *recover* and *receive*; akin to *recipere*, **to bring back**. *Recuperate*, **to get back**, or recover (losses, health, reputation, etc.)

ad captandum vulgus: **to catch the crowd**; to please the common folk, a logical fallacy; essentially the same as *ad populum*, **to the people**, or saying what the people want to hear. Other logical fallacies can be found on the Internet.

---

wordextras

Promulgate, to make [a document, law, decree] known by "public" declaration, is probably from Latin *provulgare*, **before the people**. *Vulgar, vulgarity, Vulgar Latin, Vulgate, divulge* are from *vulgus*, **the common people**.

Tinsel, an aphesis of Old French *estincelle*, **spark, spangle**, is from Middle English *stansilen*, "to ornament with sparkling colors or pieces of metal," which yields *stencil*. *Stencil* is further from Latin *scintilla*, **spark, particle**, from which are *scintillate, scintillant*. *Scintilla* itself is often heard in the expression "not a scintilla of evidence"; *scintillate*, as in *a scintillating personality*. See p. 46 for *scintillate* used in **An exalted aphorism**.

Congress, from Latin *congresus*, **a meeting**, is from the past participle of *congredi*, **to come together**. The elements of *congress* are *com-*, **with, together** + *gradi*, **to walk**. *Congress* means variously **a meeting, sexual intercourse, social interaction, an association or society**. See **wordbuilder #54**, p. 145, for more words from *gradi*.

Bête noire, French for **black beast**, is a person or thing that is disliked or feared, and therefore avoided. Pronounced: bet NWAR, or in English bate NWAR. Plural is *bêtes noires*, but is pronounced the same as the singular.

French ***fait accompli***, **accomplished fact**, is something already done or in effect, making opposition or argument useless. Pronounced: FATE uh cohm PLEE. See other French expressions, p. 131. See *res judicata*, p. 106.

Abash, from Old French *esbahir*, **to astonish** (from *baer*, **to gape**), means **to make embarrassed** and ill at ease; to make self-conscious; disconcert. I was *abashed* that I forgot part of my memorized speech.

A Writing Tip: *All together* [two words] describes a group as **acting or existing collectively**; *altogether* [one word] means **wholly, entirely**. The family was **all together** for the reunion. The runners managed to start **all together**. Joan was **altogether** pleased with her new position. The parents weren't **altogether** elated with Susie's new boyfriend.

Word Cluster No. 16

cap	cape	capitalize	capitate	capitular
decapitate	capitulate	recapitulate	capillary	capitellum
capitol	capital	capitulum	capo	caput
caprice	caporal	escape	captain	capuche
biceps	triceps		precipitous	sinciput
quadriceps	precipice	amboceptor	precipitate	occiput

Common elements_____Inferred Meaning_____

Romance Cognates	French cap, chef	Romanian cap	Italian capo	Portuguese cabeça	Spanish cabeza

Doublets: captain:chieftain; chapter:capital; chef:chief; cattle:chattle

Words with disguised Latin roots: achieve, cabbage, cabotage, caddie, cadet, caudillo, cauliflower, chamfron, chape, chapeau, chapel, chaplain, cole, corporal, handkerchief, hatchment, kale, kerchief, mischief, muscovado (Spanish and Portuguese for "unrefined; of inferior quality"; denotes the dark raw sugar remaining after the molasses has been extracted from the juice of cane sugar; see p. 127)

Latin phrases: *per capita* (see **Clavis**), *crux capitata*

Romance phrases: *da capo (DC)*, *a capella*, *cap-a-pie*, *chef d'oeuvre*, *el dolor de cabeza* (Spanish: **pain of the head**: headache), *El Caudillo, chef d'orchestre, tête-bêche* (see **Clavis**, p. 20), *a capriccio*

Placenames: Capitol, MT; Cabeza, TX; Dos Cabezas (**Two Heads**), AZ; Cabeza de Tigre (**Tiger's Head**), Venezuela

Latin phrase: *Caput inter nubile condo*: **Amid the cloud I hide my head**. Virgil [*head* has been translated "fame"]

German words from Latin: *Das Kapital; Kapelle*; kohlrabi, **cabbage turnip**

Greek *cephalos*, **head**: **cephal**ad, **cephal**ic; en**cephal**itis, electroen**cephalo**gram (EEG); acro**cephalic**, brachio-**cephalic**, eury**cephalic**, hydro**cephalic**, macro**cephalic**, micro**cephalic**, pachy**cephalic**, pro**cephalic**.

German: *Kopf* (of a person); *Chef* (of a firm); *Haupt* (of a government).

---

wordextras

French ***foible*** (from *feeble*) originally designated the weaker section of the sword blade in fencing; ***forte***, the stronger part. One's own human weaknesses are called *foibles*, and one's strong points, *fortes* (pronounced fortz); the Italian music term *forte* (**loud**, as opposed to *piano*, **soft**; from Latin *planus*, **smooth**) is pronounced FORE tay.

Sack, a dry white wine from Spain popular in England during the 16th and 17th centuries, was originally *wyneseck*, from French *vin sec*; *sec* is from Latin *siccus*, **dry**. A *siccative* promotes drying. Spanish: *sed*, **thirst, thirsty**.

Target, from Middle French *targette*, is a diminutive of *targe*, **a shield**. Historically, *target* designated a small shield, especially a round one. It now designates a round, flat board, often marked with concentric circles, set up to be aimed at, as in archery or rifle practice. *Target* is also the name of a nationwide department store chain.

Aberration, from *ab-*, **from** + *errare*, **to wander**, is a departure from what is right, true, correct, normal. Snow in June is an *aberration*. Can also mean **mental derangement** or lapse. The adjective is *aberrant*.

Inveterate, from *vetus*, **old**, means "firmly entrenched over a long period; deep-seated," as *an inveterate gambler*, or *an inveterate liar*. *Vetus* also yields *veteran* as well as *veterinarian*, originally, one who treated "old" animals.

Saber, from Hungarian *szablya* and Polish *szabla*, is a heavy cavalry sword with a slightly curved blade. As a *verb*, to strike, wound, or kill with a saber. See *bayonet*, p. 11.

Spanish ***vanilla*** comes from Latin ***vagina***, **sheath, case, pod**. *Vanilla*, a type of orchid, has podlike capsules, the extract of which is used as a flavoring in cooking, baking. See *orchid*, p. 86.

Word pairs are those sets of words that have a one-on-one correspondence. There are a number of word pairs from Anglo-Saxon and Latin respectively, e.g., almighty:omnipotent; bitterness:acerbity; boyish:puerile; bravery:valor; buy:purchase; clothes:habiliments; dwelling:residence; foresee:provide; foretell:predict; friendly:amicable; gainsay:contradict; heal:cure; hearten:encourage; hearty:cordial; home:domicile. Note the ***word triads*** from Anglo-Saxon, Latin, and Greek respectively: earthly:terrestrial:geological.

Common element base: kaput **Meaning**: head; beginning; hood (from that which covers the head)
IE base: *kaput*: **head**; **Russian**: *ataman*, a Cossack chief; **Polish**: *hetman* (from German *hauptmann*, a Cossack leader). Another word for *head* is **French** *tête*, as in *tête-à-tête*, which comes from **Vulgar Latin** *testa*, **pot**. The phrase is literally *pot-to-pot* or *head-to-head*, an intimate conversation between two people.

Clavis

capital:	and *chapter* are doublets; *capital* is from *capitalis*, **of the head**; *chapter*, from *capitulum*, **small head**. *Capital* has various uses in both its noun and adjective functions. *Capitol* is a d<u>o</u>med building.
per capita:	Middle Latin; **by heads**, for each person, as in *income per capita*; original Latin: *in capita*; in *law*, **equally to each heir**.
cap-a-pie:	from Middle French; **head to foot**; in Provençal *de cap a pé*; pronounced CAP uh PEE. Latin, *a capite ad calcem*, **from head to heels**. See p. 152 for *Piedmont*, **foot of the mountains**.
biceps:	*bi-*, **two**; **two-headed**; a muscle having two heads, or points of origin; the large muscle at the front of the upper arm or the corresponding muscle at the back of the thigh. See *muscle*, p. 85.
occiput:	*oc-*, assimilation of *ob-*, **against**; **the back part of the skull** or **head**. The adjectival form is *occipital*. See **Word Cluster No. 70**, p. 139, for *ob-* family.
sinciput:	*sin-*, from *semi-*, **half**; **half the head**; the upper part of the skull or head; especially, **the forehead**. Pronounced: SIN sih PUT; the adjectival form is *sincipital*, pronounced sin SIP ut 'l.
amboceptor:	*ambo-*, **both** + *receptor*; in *bacteriology*, an antibody able to damage or destroy a microorganism or other cell by connecting the complement to it.
kerchief:	*ker* in *kerchief* and *cur-* in *curfew* are from French *couvrir*, **cover**; *kerchief*, **a covering for the head**; *curfew*, from Middle French *cuevre feu*, *covrefeu*, **cover the fire**, a signal to extinguish village fires and retire for the evening. *Handkerchief*, an English-French hybrid, is that which covers the *head* but small enough to be held in the *hand*. *Smackover*, Arkansas, in French, is *sumac couver*, popularly said to be **covered with sumac**; named by French explorers. See p. 54 for *couvade*.
mischief:	Anglo-Saxon *mis-*, **wrong**; that which comes to a bad or **wrong head** or end.
achieve:	through Middle French, from *venir a chief*; from Latin *venir ad caput*, **come to a head**; to reach one's potential. SYNONYMS: accomplish, discharge, effect (as a verb), execute, fulfill, perform.
chef:	and *chief* both occurred in Old French; short for *chef de cuisine*, **head of the kitchen**; therefore, *head chef* is redundant. A *king's* reign is his *kingdom*; a *chef's* reign is his or her *chefdom*.
escape:	in Vulgar Latin *excappare*, **to leave one's cape behind**. SYNONYMS: avoid, eschew, evade, shun.
cattle:	and *chattle* from *vivum capitale*, **livestock**, the principal or *head* means of wealth; therefore, property used in trading. *Fee* in Anglo-Saxon and Latin *pecus*, as in **peculate, peculiar, pecuniary** and *impecunious* (literally, having no cattle; having no money, penniless) also pertained to livestock.
cabbage:	Middle English *cabage, caboche*, from Old French *boce*, **swelling**, with prefix *ca-*, perhaps suggested by Latin *caput*. Consequently, *cabbage* may mean **a swelled head**, or that which resembles a swelled head. From *cabbage* is derived Dutch *koolsla*, **coleslaw**.
encephalitis:	Greek *encephal*, **brain** + *-itis*, **inflammation**; **inflammation of the brain**.

wordextras

Midriff, or *diaphragm*, is from Middle English *mydhrif*; *hrif*, **belly**, is ultimately from Old English. The *midriff* is approximately midway between the breasts and the waistline. See p. 50, under **IE base**.

Plutocracy, **rule by the wealthy**, is from Greek *ploutos*, **wealth** + *kratein*, **to rule**. *Plutocracy* is extended to mean "a group of wealthy people who control or influence the government." Other words with *–cracy* include aristo**cracy** (**the best**), auto**cracy** (**self**), demo**cracy** (**the people**), geronto**cracy** (**the elderly**), gyneco**cracy** (**women**), iso**cracy** (**equals**), kakisto**cracy** (**the bad**), merito**cracy** (**the elite**), mobo**cracy** (**the mob**), ochlo**cracy** (**the mob**), strato**cracy** (**the military**), techno**cracy** (**scientists and engineers**), theo**cracy** (**God; a god or gods**). *Pancratium* (pan-, **all** + *kratos*, **strength**), an ancient Greek athletic contest involving both boxing and wrestling, is also from *kratein*.

Word Cluster No. 17

carnal	**carn**ification	in**carn**adine	**carn**elian	**carn**assial
carnation	in**carn**ate	**carn**ival	rein**carn**ation	**carn**ivorous
carnifex	**carn**isauria	dis**carn**al	**carn**iferous	**carn**ify
carnose	**carn**age	de**carn**ate	**carn**iliter	dis**carn**ate

Common elements_____**Inferred Meaning**_____

Romance Cognates	French	Romanian	Italian	Portuguese	Spanish
	chair	carne	carne	carne	carne

Words with disguised Latin roots: carrion, caruncle, charnel, charqui (same as beef jerky), crone

French phrase: *rire entre cuir et chair*: **to laugh between skin and teeth**; to laugh in one's sleeve

Spanish phrases: *el carnero*, **mutton**; *la carne de vaca*, **meat of the cow**; beefsteak; *chili con carne*

Related words: currier, cuirass, excoriate, coriaceous (from Latin *corium*, **leather**)

IE base of related words, previous entry, and of Greek *kreas*, **flesh**, words, e.g., **creat**ine, **cre**odont, and pan**creas**, is *kreu(s)-¹*, **raw flesh**, and yields the following Latin-based words: crude, cruel, ecru (see **Placename**), and recrudesce.

Placename: Ecru, Mississippi; see p. 99 under **wordextras**.

> **Quote**: When words fail, wars begin. When wars finally end, we settle our disputes with words. Wilfred Funk

---

wordextras

French *croissant* translates—though not literally—German *Hörnchen*, **little horn**. In 1689, the Viennese celebrated their defeat of the Turks, who had attempted to overrun Vienna, by baking a rich pastry in the form of "the little horn" that appeared on the Turkish battle flag. Symbolically, the Viennese continued to celebrate their victory by devouring *Hörnchens* in great quantities. What appeared to the Viennese as *a little horn* struck the French pastry makers as a "crescent," translated *croissant*. A *crescent* is the waxing or the waning phase of the moon. New Orleans is known as the **Crescent City**, because its being situated on a *crescent*, or **sharp bend**, of the Mississippi.

Recant is from Latin *re-*, **back** + *cantare*, **to sing**; thus, **to sing back**; to withdraw or renounce beliefs or statements formerly held, especially in a formal or public manner.

Authorities differ on the origin of *dungeon*. All agree that Middle English *donjon* originally referred to an earth-covered cellar for storing fruits and vegetables; *donjon* later came to mean a dark underground cell, vault, or prison. One authority says the cellar was "covered with dung"; another says that *donjon* meant "keeper of the lord's castle," from Latin *dominus*. See *danger*, **wordextras**, p. 35; see *daunt*, p. 2.

Tantamount, **equivalent in value or effect**, is from Anglo-French *tant amunter*, **to amount to as much**, as in "His silence was *tantamount* to an admission of guilt."

BASIC English, a term coined by Charles Ogden (1889-1957), English educator and linguist, and consisting of 850 words, is an acronym for British, American, Scientific, International, Commercial.

BASIC, a subprogram of FORTRAN, acronym for *Formula Translation*, is itself an acronym of Basic All-Purpose Symbolic Instruction Code.

Grand Prix, **great prize**, is short for *Grand Prix de Paris*, was originally in 1863 an international horse race.

Canvass, probably from the use of a *canvas* for sifting, is to try to get votes, orders; **solicit**. As a *verb*, also, to examine or discuss in detail; look over carefully. *Canvas*, from Latin *cannabis*, **hemp**, is a closely woven, coarse cloth of hemp, cotton, or linen, often unbleached, and used for tents, sails, etc.; a sail or set of sails; a specially prepared piece of canvas on which an oil painting is made; **the canvas**: the canvas-covered floor of a boxing ring.

an aphorism: **It's a foolish fish that gets caught by the same bait twice**. It is folly not to benefit from a bitter or painful experience. Similar to the following: *Fool me once, shame on you; fool me twice, shame on me.*

Common element base: carnis

Meaning: flesh, meat

IE base: *sker-¹*: **to cut**, yielding *shear, harvest*; **German**: *Fleisch*: *flesh* or *meat*

Clavis

carnal:
pertaining to the body, its passions and its appetites; **fleshly**; **sensual**; **impure**; **sexual**.

carnation:
originally, a flower with a pinkish or **flesh** tint; by permutation and cross-fertilization, now in a variety of colors. *Carnations*: **flesh-colored** tints used in paintings.

carnival:
from French *carnaval* or from Italian *carnevale*, both of which appear to come from Middle Latin *carnem levare*, **to remove meat**. See p. 112 for a different interpretation.

carnification:
in some Christian denominations, especially in the Roman Catholic Church, the belief in *transubstantiation*, or that at a certain point in the worship service, the bread of the Eucharist, Holy Communion, or Lord's Supper is changed literally into the **flesh of Christ**, and the wine becomes the blood of Christ; from Jesus' statement, "This is my body, take and eat; this is my blood, take and drink." Some other denominations see this statement as symbolic or hyperbolic. See *hyperbole* under *hyperbola*, p. 184.

carnivorous:
vorare, **to devour**, **eat**; describing those animals, as lions and tigers, that are **meat-eaters**. There are also *carnivorous* plants that consume small frogs as well as insects; those plants that devour only insects are described as *insectivorous*, e.g., bladderwort, pitcher plant, Venus' flytrap.

carnassial:
describing teeth adapted for **tearing apart flesh**; said of carnivorous animals; analogous to *canines* (or, **dog teeth**) in humans. The *canine* is a sharp-pointed tooth between the incisors and the bicuspids.

incarnate:
in-, **in**; **in the flesh**; Christians believe that Jesus Christ is the embodiment of God; He is *God Incarnate*, or **God in the Flesh**. In Hinduism, *incarnation* is called *avatar*, **he crosses down**, or **he passes beyond**.

sarcophagus:
originally, in Greek, *(lithos) sarkophagos*, **flesh-eating** (**stone**); then, in Latin, *sarcophagus (lapsis)*. The ancient Greeks buried their dead in limestone vaults to hasten decomposition of the body. Now, a burial vault, especially an ornamental one, such as the *Tomb of the Unknown Soldier* (now, *Tomb of the Unknowns*), in Arlington National Cemetery, Arlington, VA; a *sepulcher*, pronounced SEP ul ker; a *mausoleum*; capitalized, the tomb of Mausolus (Persian satrap, ruler over Caria, c. 376-353 B.C.); the *Mausoleum* was one of the *Seven Wonders of the World*. Pronounced sar KAHF uh gus.

anasarca:
Greek *ana-*, **throughout** + *sarx*, **flesh**; **throughout the flesh**; generalized edema (an abnormal accumulation of fluid in the body), known formerly as *dropsy*, which itself is an alteration of Greek *hydrops*, **water**.

---

wordbuilder #18

Greek *blastos*, **shoot, sprout**, yields **blast**ic, **blast**ema; **blast**oma; **blast**ocarpous, **blast**ocele, **blast**ocyst, **blast**ocyte, **blast**oderm, **blast**ogenesis, **blast**omere, **blast**omycosis, **blast**ophore, **blast**osphere, **blast**ospore, **blast**otomy; amphi**blast**ula; angio**blast**, archi**blast** (egg protoplasm), ecto**blast**, ento**blast**, epi**blast** (the outer layer of cells in an embryo), erythro**blast**, hemato**blast**, hypo**blast**, idio**blast**, melano**blast**, meso**blast**, myelo**blast**, neuro**blast**, odonto**blast**, osteo**blast**, para**blast**, stato**blast**, tropho**blast** (*trophein*, **to nourish**); hetero**blast**ic, holo**blast**ic.

---

wordextras

The expression *Alas!* is from Old French *a las*, "**Ah, weary (that I am)**," with *las* from Latin *lassus*, **weary**. *A las* finally passed into English as one word. Compare with *lassitude*, p. 94, under **wordextras**.

Exhilarate and *hilarious* are from *hilaris*, **glad**. *Exhilarate*: **to make cheerful**, **merry**, **lively**; also, to invigorate or stimulate. *Hilarious*: **noisily merry**; boisterous; joyous; producing great merriment; very funny.

Spokane, Washington, is Salish for **the sun**. *Salish*, from *salst*, **people**, is a group of North American Indian people in the northwestern North America; also, their language.

Olympia, capital of Washington, is named for the *Olympic Mountains*, the highest peak of which is Mt. Olympus.

A Writing Tip: **Semicolons** (;) separate independent clauses when there's no *coordinating conjunction* in between. The city banned the homeless from downtown[;] they had no place to go. The sentence with a *coordinating conjunction*: The city banned the homeless from downtown, *so* they had no place to go.

Romance Cognates	French	Romanian	Italian	Portuguese	Spanish
	centre	centru	centro	centro	centro

NB: In Greek mythology, *Centaur* referred to a race of monsters with a man's head, trunk, and arms, and a horse's body and legs; also, the constellation *Centaurus*. *Centaury* is a small plant of the gentian family; the centaur Chiron was said to have discovered medicinal qualities in the plant.

Note: Do not confuse this root with *centum*, **100**, as in **cent**ury, **cent**urion, **cent**ennial (see p. 58, under **IE base**), or with *kentesis*, **puncture**, as in **cent**esis, arthro**cent**esis, entero**cent**esis, and pneumo**cent**esis (see p. 205, Item 71).

German: *Zentrum*.

> **Quote:** No knowledge of a science can be properly acquired until the terminology of that science is mastered, and this terminology is in the main of Greek and Latin origin. Spencer Trotter

wordextras

Accolade, from Latin *accolare* (*ad-*, **to** + *collum*, **neck**), **to embrace**, was formerly used in conferring knighthood; then, a tap on the shoulder with the flat of a sword. *Accolade* has come to mean **praise**, **approval**.

Both *typhoon* and *tycoon* contain the Chinese element *t'ai*, **big** or **great**. *Typhoon* was originally in Cantonese *t'ai fung*, **great wind**, and is related to *Typhon*, who, in Greek mythology, was the Father of Winds. *Tycoon* in Ancient Chinese was *t'ai kun*, or **great monarch** (from Cantonese *kuan*, **official**), and is now applied to any wealthy or powerful businessman or industrialist. See p. 43 under **wordextras**.

Old French *danger*, originally meaning "absolute power of an overlord," is from Latin *dominium*, **lordship**, and further from *dominus*, **master**. See *dungeon*, p. 33; *daunt*, p. 2; *damsel*, p. 125; *condominium*, p. 147.

Garrison, *garment*, and *garnish* are from Old French *garnir*, **to protect**. Thus, a military *garrison* is protected, or fortified, with troops, guns, etc.; a *garment* protects one's body; *garnish* can mean *to decorate, adorn, embellish, trim*, as *to garnish a steak with parsley*, or *garnish a cake with frosting or candles*. In law, *garnish* means to attach money or property to satisfy a debt owed by the defendant. The legal process is termed *garnishment*.

Ersatz, from German *ersetzen*, **to replace**, is *replacement*, but meaning *substitute*, especially something synthetic; that which is used to replace something natural or genuine; as an *adjective*, **artificial**. *Oleomargarine*, for example, is *ersatz butter*.

Italian *seraglio*, **enclosure**, **padlock**, is the part of a Muslim household where wives or concubines live; **harem**; also, the palace of a Turkish sultan.

Abstruse, from *abs-*, **away** + *trudere*, **to thrust**, describes that which is difficult to understand, as algebra, calculus, chemistry, and physics are for many people. See p. 213, Item 179, for more words from *trudere*.

Ad hoc, Latin for **to this**, indicates "for a special case only," as *an ad hoc committee* to study the feasibility of a particular project; opposed to "standing committee," one that is permanent, especially of a legislative body.

Unagi, Japanese for **grilled eel**, is popular not only for its flavor but also for its stamina-giving properties. It is rich in protein, calcium, vitamins A and E, and is traditionally eaten during the hottest months of the year.

Common element base: kentron   **Meaning**: center; also, sharp point
IE base: *kent-*: **to prick, jab**: also yields **Greek** *kestos*, hence *cestus*, a woman's belt or girdle. Other meanings.

Clavis

center:
originally, the stationary **point** of a compass; thus, when *center* is used as an intransitive verb, it is followed by *on, upon, in,* or *at*, not by *around* or *about*.

centriciput:
with *caput*, **head**; the central part of the upper surface of the skull between the *occiput,* **the back of the head**, and the *sinciput,* **the forehead**. See *occiput, sinciput*, p. 32.

centrifugal:
with *fugere*, **to flee**; **fleeing from the center**; coined by Sir Isaac Newton (1642-1727), to indicate moving or tending to move away from the center. In *botany*, describes flower clusters that develop from the center outward; in *physiology*, pertains to impulses transmitted away from a nerve center; tending or directed away from centralization, as of authority. *Centrifugal sugar* is that which is freed from liquid by a centrifugal machine, or a centrifuge. See p. 86 for more on *centrifugal*.

centripetal:
with *petere*, **to seek**; **seeking the center**; other words from *petere*: **petition, petulant, appetite,** *compete, competent, competition, competitor, impetigo, impetus, perpetual, repetition; repeat; propitiate;* also, *fathom* (see p. 187). See p. 86 for more on *centripetal* contrasted with *centrifugal*, **fleeing the center**.

centrum:
in *anatomy*, the **center** of a vertebra supporting the disks in a spinal column; in *botany*, the central air space in hollow-stemmed plants.

centromere:
with *meros*, **a part**; a very small body near the nucleus in most animal cells, usually near the **center** of the chromosome, to which the *meres* attach themselves in the process of mitosis. See **word-builder #48**, p. 115, for more words from *meros*; see p. 50 for *chromosome*.

centrosema:
with *sema*, **sign**, **symbol**; a genus of tropical American vines with sharp leaves. Other words from *sema*: *semantics,* **semaphore** (see p. 177), *seminology, sematic, aposematic, monosemy, polysemy*.

acrocentric:
Greek *akros*, **high**, **topmost**, **extreme**; having or relating to a subterminal centromere.

eccentric:
Greek *ek-*, **out**; **out of center**; deviating from customary character or practice. In *geometry*, **not concentric**, or not having the same center; in *astronomy*, describing an elliptical orbit; as a *noun, an eccentric person*; also, a device in mechanical engineering.

anthropocentric:
Greek *anthropos*, **man**; the philosophy that *man* is the **center** of the universe. See p. 93 for other words containing *anthropos*, such as **anthropology, anthropomorphic**; also, p. 204, Item 61.

heliocentric:
Greek *helios*, **sun**; having the *sun* as the **center**. Other words from *helios*: **helium, heliacal, helio**latry, **heliometer, heliosphere, heliostat, heliotaxis, aphelion, parhelion, perihelion, isohel**.

heterocentric:
Greek *heteros*, **other**; made up of rays that are neither parallel nor meeting in one point; said of a ray of light. See other *heteros* words, such as **heteronym, heterosexual**; p. 207, Item 104.

wordextras

Nova Scotia, or *New Scotland*, was the name applied to this peninsula of Canada, by King James I. The ancient poetic name for *Scotland* was *Caledonia*; the Caledonia Canal in northern Scotland extends northward from the Atlantic to Moray Firth, a length of 60 miles. See p. 143 for more on *peninsula*; see p. 9 for *Baja California*.

Adirondack, an American Indian tribe, is Algonquian for **bark eaters**. The tribe was known to eat tree bark when food was scarce. There are the Adirondack Mountains in northeast New York State.

Spanish ***piñata***, originally meaning **pot**, but ultimately from Latin *pinea*, **pine cone**, now designates a clay or papier-mâché container, hung from the ceiling on certain festivals, especially birthdays, and broken in a game by blindfolded children who take turns wielding a stick so as to release the piñata's contents of toys and candy.

Spanish ***posada***, from *posar*, **to lodge**, is further from Latin *pausare*, **to stop**. *La Posada* is a nine-day festival preceding Christmas in Latin American countries marked by a candlelight procession that reenacts Mary and Joseph's search for lodging. The festival is also held in many SW US communities, and in other parts of the country.

Adhere, from *ad-*, **to** + *haerere*, **to stick**, means "to stick fast; stay attached." ***Cohere*: to stick together**.

Jaguar, from Tupi *jaguara*, is the largest New World predatory cat, found from SW US to Argentina.

36

Word Cluster No. 19

regi**cide**	pesti**cide**	insecti**cide**	sui**cide**	sorori**cide**
uxori**cide**	matri**cide**	patri**cide**	fratri**cide**	parri**cide**
caduceus	**cad**ence	cas**cade**[*]	**cad**ucity	de**cad**ent
oc**cas**ion	**cas**e	cas**cad**e[*]	**cas**ualty	de**cad**ence
ac**cid**ent	ac**cid**ental	ac**cid**ence	oc**cid**ent	de**cid**e
de**cid**uous	re**cid**ivist	in**cid**ent	in**cid**ental	coin**cid**e
ex**cise**	s**ciss**ors		s**ciss**ion	circum**cis**ion
pre**cise**	pre**cis**ion		s**ciss**ile	pré**cis**
con**cise**	con**cis**ion	circum**ciss**ile		de**cis**ive
in**cise**	de**cis**ion			

[*]*Cascade* is listed twice because of the duplicated root.

Common elements _____ **Inferred Meaning** _____

Romance Cognates	French	Romanian	Italian	Portuguese	Spanish
	coup, coupe	cadere	cadere	cair	caer

Doublets: chance:cadence; cadence:cadenza   **NB**: Neither *exercise* nor *exorcise* is in this family.

Words with disguised Latin roots: Caesarian, caesura, capon (a castrated rooster; see *poulard*, p. 95), cement, coupon, chisel, chute, decay, decoupage, escheat, parachute, rescind, sheath

Latin phrases: *Ilex deciduas,* **deciduous holly** (possum haw); *casus belli,* **occasion for war**

Placenames: Accident (Arkansas, Maryland); Coupon, Pennsylvania; Coupon Bight (a bay), Florida

IE *skei-,* **to split**: **sci**ence, **sci**licet, **sci**olism; ne**sci**ence, con**sci**ence, con**sci**ous; omni**sci**ence; **sci**re facias; plebi**sci**te, pre**sci**ent, ad**sci**titious (added from an external source; supplemental; as *adscititious leaves, adscititious evidence, adscititious remarks*), **nice** (from *nescire*, originally, **not knowing, to be ignorant**; see **wordextras**, p. 13).

Greek: **schism**, **schism**atic; **schisto**carp, **schisto**some; **schiz**ogony, **schiz**oid, **schiz**ophrenia (see p. 80, **wordextras**).

Motto of the University of Michigan: *Artes, Scientia, Veritas*: **Arts, Science, Truth**

Related words and phrases from French: coup, coupé, coup de grâce, coup de main (see p. 199).

> **Quote**: Add 1800 words to your vocabulary and you can graduate from the ordinary to the superior. John H. Steadman

wordextras

French ***prestige***, from Latin *praestigiae,* from *pre-,* **before** + *stringere,* **to bind**, originally meant **illusion, trick**. The word characterized one who performed tricks of magic while *blindfolded,* thus an illusion brought on by magic; now, the power to impress or influence, as because of success, wealth, status. SYNONYMS: authority, influence, renown, weight. *Prestige* is not related etymologically to *prestidigitation,* from, *preste,* **quick** + *digitus,* **finger**.

French ***chignon***, a variation of *chaînon,* **link**, is from Latin *catena,* **chain**. *Chignon* is a knot or coil of hair worn at the back of the neck. *Catena* is also the base of *concatenation,* a writing principle of connecting sentences to form a unified paragraph; *concatenation* is also used as computer term to designate linking subsets of programs. See p. 204.

Accost, from *ad-,* **to** + *costa,* **side, rib**, is to approach and speak to; greet first without first being greeted. The following words are from *costa*: ***costal***, ***costrel***, ***infracostal***, ***intercostal***, and ***coast***; Spanish *chuleta,* **porkchop**.

Pettitoes is probably from Old French *petite oye,* **goose giblets,** *petite* being from *petty,* **small**. The word has come to mean "pigs feet as an article of food"; by association with *toes,* the feet or toes, especially a child's.

Word from a literary character: ***braggadocio***: **a braggart**; **vain, noisy boasting**. Coined by English poet Edmund Spenser (1552?-99); alteration of *Braggadocchio,* a character in *The Faerie Queen* (1599), who personifies vainglory. The word is formed from Middle English *brag* + Italian ending. There is *Braggadocio,* Missouri.

Common element base: caedere   **Meaning**: to kill, to cut, to fall
IE base: *caedere* from *(s)khai*, **to strike**; **Latin** *cadere* from *kad-*, **to fall**, **die**; **German**: *Schnitt*, **a cut of** (veal, mutton)

Clavis

case:
an **example**, **instance**, or **occurrence**, as *a case of measles*, or *a case of carelessness*; a person being helped as by a doctor or social worker, thus the term *case worker*. Many other applications.

decadent:
from Latin *decadere*, **to fall away**; characterized by a process, condition, or period of decline, as in morals, art, literature, etc.; capitalized, a group of 19th-century, chiefly French writers, characterized by a highly mannered style and an emphasis on the morbid and perverse. See *fin de siècle*, p. 82.

Occident:
from Latin *occidere*, **to fall**, or **to set**, as the sun; applied by Asian countries to the west of them; the Western Hemisphere. Compare *Orient*, from *orire*, **to rise**; see *Oriental*, p. 76, under *equator*.

excise:
ex-, **out**, **away**; **to cut away**, or **out**, as *to excise* a tumor; **not** related to *excise tax*, a fee paid for a license to carry on certain occupations, sports, etc.; the original was *accensare*, **to tax**.

précis:
French; from Latin *praecidere*, **cut short**, or **cut off in front**; a summary of essential points; an abstract; pronounced pray SEE, or PRAY see.

uxoricide:
Latin *uxor*, **wife**; **the killing of a wife by her husband**; also, **a man who murders his wife**; *filicide* (**one's own child**); *fratricide* (**brother**); *genocide* (**a race**); *matricide* (**mother**); *parricide* (**both parents**); *patricide* (**father**); *regicide* (**king**); *sororicide* (**sister**); *suicide* (**oneself**).

chance:
and *cadence* are doublets; *chance*, that which **befalls** one; in *speaking*, *cadence* is the **falling** of the voice; in *dancing* or *marching*, a measured movement (by the numbers); in *music*, *cadence* indicates a harmonic ending, e.g., V^7, or **dominant seventh**, to I, or **tonic**.

decoupage:
French; from *de-*, **away** + *couper*, **to cut**; a form of art in which **cut-up** pieces are pasted to form a collage. *Coupe de cheveux*: **a haircut**. French *collage*, from *colle*, **paste**, is from Greek *kolla*, **glue**, as in *protocol*, p. 159, and *papier collé*, a kind of collage in which the pasted objects form a pattern.

escheat:
French: **that which falls to one**, especially property that reverts to the manor, a form of precedence in feudal law. In US law, that which **falls to the state** in the absence of heirs.

cement:
from Latin *caedere*, **to cut**; originally, rough stone, marble chippings, used to make lime.

science:
from Latin *scire facias*: **that you may cause to know**, with the idea that a subject is *dividied into parts* that can be discerned; formerly, **knowledge**, **learning**.

scissors:
from *cisoria*, plural of Latin *cisorium*, **cutting tool**. The English spelling is altered after Latin *scissor*, **one who cuts**.

ptomaine:
from Greek *ptoma*, **a corpse**, or **dead body**; further from *piptein*, **to fall**; a class of alkaloid substances, some of which are poisonous, found in decaying animal or vegetable matter; hence, **ptomaine poisoning**, an early term for food poisoning. Pronounced TOE mane.

wordextras

Arcane, from Latin *arcanus*, **closed**, **secret**, describes that which is **esoteric, mysterious, hidden, recondite**, as contrasted with that which is **clear**, **lucid**, **direct**. *Arcanus* also yields *arcanum*, with basically the same meaning, but can also mean **a secret remedy**, **an elixir**. There is *Arcanum*, Ohio, near Dayton.

Tabasco, an extremely hot pepper grown in south Louisiana, originated in *Tabasco*, a province of Mexico.

Chihuahua, an ancient Mexican breed of very small dogs with large, pointed ears, comes from the name of the State in northern Mexico, on the US border.

Acerbic, **sour**, **severe**, is from Latin *acerbus*, **bitter**. The judge cast some *acerbic* remarks at the culprit.

Aristocracy, **rule by the best**, is from Greek *aristos*, **best** + *kratein*, **to rule**; thus, a government ruled by the best citizens; can also indicate those considered the best in some way, as "an aristocracy of researchers." *Aristocracy* is similar to *oligarchy*, **rule by the few**. See other *–cracy* words, p. 205, Item 76.

A Writing Tip: *Irregardless* is not a word. Never use it! *Regardless* of the situation, *regardless* is the word to use "irregardless" that some so-called educated people persist in using *irregardless*. Spread the word!

```
┌─────────────────────────────────────────────────────────────────────────────┐
│                          Word Cluster No. 20                                  │
│                                                                               │
│  circa         circle        circlet       circline      circuit   circuitous│
│  circulant     circular      circulate     circulatory   circadian circension│
│  circinate     circulus      circovarian(circum- + ovary)                     │
│                                                                               │
│  circumcise          circumference      circumlocution      circumnavigate    │
│  circumvent          circumstance       circumfluent        circumambulate    │
│  circumspection      circumscribe       circumscissile      circumdiction     │
│  circumvolve         circumflex         circumnutation      circumscription   │
│                                                                               │
│  Common elements_____Inferred Meaning_____ │
└─────────────────────────────────────────────────────────────────────────────┘
```

Romance Cognates	French	Romanian	Italian	Portuguese	Spanish
	cercle	cerc	circolo	circulo	círculo

Mathematical terms: circumference of ellipse, incircle of triangle, circle of Apollonius

Words with disguised Latin and Frankish roots: curb, curvature, curvet, cirque; search, research, recherché; also, ranch, range, arrange, derange, ribbon, rink, ringhals

Latin phrases: *Si monumentum requiris, circumspice*: **If you seek his monument, look around**.
circuitus verborum: **a circuit of words**; circumlocution
circulus in probando: **a circle in the proof**; reasoning in a circle; a vicious circle
duas tantum res anxius optat, panem et circenses

French phrases: *chercher la petite bête*: **to search for the little beast**: to be excessively finical
cherchez la femme: **look for the woman** (in the case)

Research *ricercare* and *ricercata* in a music dictionary.

Greek *peri-*, **around**: **peri**anth, **peri**apsis, **peri**apt, **peri**blem, **peri**cardium, **peri**carp, **peri**clinal, **peri**cope, **peri**cranium, **peri**cycle, **peri**derm, **peri**gee, **peri**gynous, **peri**lune, **peri**meter (see **Clavis**, under *circumference*), **peri**natal, **peri**neum, **peri**od (see p. 109), **peri**odical, **peri**odontics, **peri**pheral, **peri**phrasis, **peri**phrastic, **peri**scope.
from *amphi-*, **around, both**: **amphi**aster (*aster*, **star**; in *mitosis*, the long spindle with asters at either end that forms during the prophase, or first stage), **amphi**bian (*bios*, **life**; an animal that can live on both land and water), **amphi**biotic, **amphi**bole, **amphi**bology (double or doubtful meaning; ambiguity, especially from uncertain grammatical construction), **amphi**brach (see pp. 6, 22), **amphi**chroic, **amphi**mixis, **amphi**pod, **amphi**theater.

Chemical Symbols

Ag is from Latin *argentum*, **silver**. *Argentina* is from the same source, *silver* being the object of the early Spanish explorers' quest.

Au is from Latin *aurum*, **gold**, which also yields *aureate*: **golden, gilded** (see *oriole*, p. 175); splendid, ornate, often affectedly so.
NB: Do not confuse *aurum* with *aura*, or with *aural*, pertaining to *an aura* or *to the ear*; the latter is from *auris*, **ear**.

Cu is from Latin *cuprum*, **copper**. There is Copperhill, Tennessee.

Fe is from Latin *ferrum*, **iron**. There is Ferrum, Virginia.

Hg is from Latin *hydrargyrum*, but ultimately from Greek *hydrarguros*, **silver water**; thus, *mercury*.

K is from Latin *kalium*, **potassium**, which itself is from Dutch *potasch*, **potash**.

Na is from New Latin *natrium*, **sodium**.

Pb is from Latin *plumbum*, **lead**. A *plumber*, in Roman times, worked with **lead pipes**. See *aplomb*, as well as *plumb bob*, p. 105.

Sb is from Latin *stibium*; the symbol for *antimony*. Used in medicines, pigments, matches, and for fireproofing.

Sn is from Latin *stannum*, **tin**.

W is the symbol for *tungsten*, which in German is *Wolfram*, from Swedish for **heavy stone**.

Common element base: circus   **Meaning**: around, circle, ring

IE base: *sker-³*; also *ker-*: **to turn, bend**; **German** *Kreis*, **circle**; **Greek** *krikos*, **ring**, and yielding *cricoid*, the ring-shaped cartilage forming the lower part of the larynx.

Clavis

circadian:
with *dies*, **day**; literally, **around a day**; in *biology*, designating behavioral or physiological rhythms associated with the 24-hour cycles of the earth's rotation. See **Clavis** note, p. 68.

circa:
around, about: used before an approximate date, e.g., circa 1500 A.D.

circus:
originally, *amphitheatre circular*, which in ancient Roman times was used for exhibitions of horsemanship, athletic contests, chariot races, and gladiatorial spectacles.

circinate:
from *circinatus*, **to make round**; from *circinus*, **a pair of compasses**; **rounded**, **circular**, specifically, rolled into a coil on its axis with the apex in the center, or rolled up from the tip, as the new fronds of a fern, or the tongue of a butterfly.

circumcision:
with *caedere*, **to cut**; a circumcising, or being circumcised, either as a religious rite, as of Jews and Muslims, or as a hygienic measure; in the Bible, figuratively, **a cleansing of sin**.

circumference:
with *ferre*, **to bear**, or **to carry**; **the distance around a circle**. The Greeks used *perimeter* for the distance **around** any figure, including circles. The formula for finding the circumference of a circle, $C=\pi d$, uses the initials of Latin *circumference* (C) plus Greek *perimeter* (π, or pi) and *diameter* (d), the distance across a circle. The ratio of the *perimeter* to *diameter* is equal to the value of π (approximately 3.1416); that is, there is the equivalent of 3.14 diameters in the *circumference* (or, *perimeter*) of a circle. See p. 155 for *circumference* listed under *ferre*, **to bear**.

circumfluent:
with *fluere*, **to flow** (see **Word Cluster No. 42**, p. 83); **to flow around**; surrounding in the manner of a fluid; encompassing, e.g., the earth and its *circumfluent* air. Pronounced sir KUM floo unt.

circumlocution:
with *loqui*, **to speak**; **speaking in a roundabout manner**; prolixity; evasion in writing or speaking. Instead of directly answering the question, the senator resorted to *circumlocutions*.

circumstance:
with *stare*, **to stand**; **standing around**; basically, a fact or essential condition or determining factor, as in "circumstances alter cases." Explore *circumstantial evidence*, a law term. See p. 180.

search:
from Old French *cerchier*, **to go around in a circle**; as a *noun*, **a careful examination**, as *a title search*; as a *verb*, **to probe**, as *to search one's motives* or *one's conscience*; **to canvass**, as *to search for the lost child*. Synonyms: examine, explore, rummage. See *canvass*, p. 33, **wordextras**.

recherché:
French; from *research*; sought out with diligence and care; rare, choice, uncommon; endowed with social graces; can also mean **too refined**. Pronounced: ruh sher SHAY; ruh SHER SHAY.

Kreis:
German; an **encircled**, or enclosed combat area; also, a unit of government in Germany corresponding to a county in the United States.

Si monumentum requiris, circumspice: **If you seek his monument, look around**; epitaph of the architect Sir Christopher Wren (1632-1723), in St. Paul's Cathedral in London, the church itself being his own great work. Similar to the motto of the State of Michigan: **If you seek a pleasing peninsula, look around you**. Actually, the state of Michigan comprises two peninsulas: *the Upper* and *the Lower*, which are separated by Lake Huron and Lake Michigan.

Panem et circenses: **bread and circuses**; said to be that which satisfied the common folk of ancient Rome.

wordextras

Colossal, **huge, gigantic**, and *coliseum*, a *huge* building or stadium for sports events, exhibitions, etc., are both from *Colossus*, a giant statue of Apollo, honoring the sun god, Helios, set at the entrance to the harbor of Rhodes around 280 B.C., and was included among the *Seven Wonders of the World*. Approximately the height of the Statue of Liberty, Colossus took 12 years to complete; soon after *its* completion, the *statue* was destroyed by an earthquake. [*Statue* in the preceding sentence is an example of *a delayed antecedent*, with the pronoun *its* coming *before*, instead of *after*, the antecedent. *Antecedent* means **that which comes before**. Consequently, *antecedent* denotes the word, phrase, or clause to which a pronoun refers, for example, *man* is the antecedent of *who* in "the man who spoke." *Antecedent* has other applications in *mathematics* and *logic*.]

Sectional Word Cluster Test

INSTRUCTIONS: For each set of words from Latin and Greek (and sometimes, French, Spanish, and German), write the common meaning in the blank.

Example: **hypo**tenuse, **hypo**thesis, **sub**ject   <u>under</u>

	Presection Answer	Postsection Answer
21. **clar**inet, **clar**ify, de**clar**e, de**clar**ative sentence	_____	_____
22. **clav**icle, **clav**is, con**clav**e, en**clav**e, ex**clav**e	_____	_____
23. **contra**puntal, **contra**vene, **counter**point, **anti**dote	_____	_____
24. **cord**ial, con**cord**ance, **card**iac, peri**card**ium	_____	_____
25. **corp**ulent, **corp**oration, in**corp**orate, chromo**some**	_____	_____
26. **cruc**ify, ex**cruc**iating, Vera **Cruz**, **cruise**	_____	_____
27. **cub**icle, **cub**it, in**cub**us, in**cumb**ent, suc**cumb**	_____	_____
28. **culp**rit, **culp**able, ex**culp**ate, mea **culpa**	_____	_____
29. **deca**thlon, **deca**pod, **Deca**polis, **dean**, **dime**	_____	_____
30. **deist**, **theist**, **theo**cracy, **div**ine, a**dios**, a**dieu**	_____	_____

          _____   _____
          Presection Score   Postsection Score

Note: Enter scores for this test and the following ones after completing this section; then, enter them on p. xvii.

Sectional Wordbuilder Test

Throughout the book and as a supplement, there are wordbuilders; these wordbuilders are designed to help you build a family of words from a single root.

	Presection Answer	Postsection Answer
19. What is the meaning of *aug-, auct-* as in **aug**ment, **auct**ion?	_____	_____
20. What is the meaning of *auto-* as in **auto**crat, **auto**mobile?	_____	_____
21. What is the meaning of *endo-* as in **endo**blast, **endo**cardium?	_____	_____
22. What is the meaning of *erg-* as in en**erg**y, all**erg**y, syn**erg**ism?	_____	_____
23. What is the meaning of *gamy-* as in apo**gamy**, exo**gamy**?	_____	_____
24. What is the meaning of *bar-* as in **bar**ium, **baro**meter?	_____	_____
25. What is the meaning of *bio-* as in **bio**graphy, **bio**meter?	_____	_____
26. What is the meaning of *flect-, flex-* as in genu**flect**, re**flex**?	_____	_____

Presection Score   Postsection Score

After entering the scores here, enter them on pp. xviii.

```
┌─────────────────────────────────────────────────────────────────────────────┐
│                          Word Cluster No. 21                                  │
│                                                                               │
│   clarify            clarifier            clarin            clarina           │
│   clarion            clarinet             clarity           clarificant       │
│   clarification      clarified butter     clarion           clarain           │
│   claret             claro                declare           declaration       │
│ declarative                               clarabello        declaredly        │
│                                                                               │
│ Common elements_____Inferred Meaning_____│
└─────────────────────────────────────────────────────────────────────────────┘
```

Romance Cognates	French clair	Romanian clar	Italian chiaro	Portuguese claro	Spanish claro

Words and phrases with disguised Latin roots: chanticleer, chiaroscuro, clair de lune, clairvoyant, clerestory, éclair, éclaircissement, en clair; glair; English: clear; Spanish: claro

Placenames: Claire (New Brunswick; Saskatchewan); Clarina, Ontario; Clearwater (FL; Manitoba); Eau Claire (**Clear Water**), WI; Montclair, NJ; Mont Clare, PA; Montclare, SC; Claremont (MN, NH, NC, SD)

Explore *claret stain* and *clarificant* as terms used in medicine.

Greek *phainein*, **to appear**, **show**: **phant**asm, **phant**asmagoria; **phant**om; **phan**erogram; allo**phane**, cello**phane**; hiero**phant**, syco**phant**, tono**phant**; epi**phan**y, theo**phan**y; dia**phan**ous; **fant**asy; **pant**; tif**fany**; **phen**omenon; **phase**, ana**phase**, di**phase**, inter**phase**, meta**phase**, poly**phase**, pro**phase**, telo**phase**; multi**phasic**; em**phas**is.

The preceding words are from IE *bha-[1]*, **to shine**, which also yields the *phos* and *photo* subfamilies, which mean **light**, as in **phos**e, **phos**phorous, centra**phose**; **photon**, **photo**graph, **photo**synthesis; many others.

German: *klar*, **clear**: *Aufklärung*, **enlightenment**; **solution**; **answer**; *an sich klar*, **self-sufficient**; and *klarlegen (stellen)*, **to clear up**, explain.

wordextras

In the military services, the ranks are of Latin origin except the lowest and highest in the Navy—*seaman* and *admiral*. While *seaman* is Anglo-Saxon, *admiral* is Arabic. By way of Old French *amiral*, *admiral* was originally in *amîr a' ali*, **the high leader**. See *sergeant*, p. 135; *lieutenant*, pp. 118, 187; *corporal*, p. 50.

Though **colonel** is pronounced "kernel" in English, it originated from Latin *columna*, which evolved into Italian *colonello*, **a small column**, designating an officer in charge of a *column* of troops.

Shingles, an acute virus disease, is from Latin *cingulum*, **belt**, from *cingere*, **to gird**, which translates Greek *zone*, **a girdle**. *Shingles*: a nontechnical term for *herpes zoster*. *Herpes*: **creeping**; *zoster*, akin to *zone*.

Vietnam is a Chinese compound originally meaning "those strangers to the south" of China.

Crisscross, from Middle English *Christcros*, **Christ's cross**, designates a pattern of crossed lines; as a *verb*, to move to and fro across. Helicopters *crisscrossed* the area of the sea where the sailor fell overboard.

Fierce, from Latin *ferus*, **wild**, **savage**, describes anything of a cruel or savage nature, as *a fierce dog*, *a fierce storm*; it can also mean **intensely eager**, also, **intense**, as *a fierce appetite* or *a fierce embrace*. Compare *feral*, *ferocious*.

From Turkish *durb*, and further from Arabic *darb*, **drub** means "to beat with a stick or club"; to defeat soundly; also, to abuse with words; berate; as a *noun*, a **blow**, as with a club.

wordbuilders #19, 20

Latin *augere*, **to increase**, yields the roots *auct, aug, auth, aux*, the respective bases of **auct**ion, **auct**ioneer, **auct**orial; **aug**ment, **aug**mentation, **aug**ur, **aug**ury, **aug**ust; in**aug**urate; **auth**or, **auth**ority, **auth**orize; co**auth**or; **aux**esis, **aux**iliary (see p. 191), **aux**in; **aux**ochrome, **aux**ocyte, **aux**otrophic; onych**auxis** (**nail overgrowth**); auteur, octroi (a tax on certain goods entering a town; the place where this tax is collected; the official or officials collecting the tax).

Greek *autos*, **self**, yields **aut**ism, **aut**istic; **aut**archy, **auth**entic (*auto-* + *hentes*, from IE *sen-*, **to prepare**, **achieve**; **self-prepared**), **auto**ecious, **auto**psy (**a self-viewing**); **auto**biography, **auto**chthon, **auto**clave, **auto**cracy, **auto**crat, **auto**didact, **auto**erotism, **auto**gamy, **auto**genesis, **auto**genous, **auto**giro, **auto**graph, **auto**hypnosis, **auto**mation, **auto**mobile, **auto**nomy, **auto**phyte, **auto**telic, **auto**tomy, **auto**trophic. German: *Autobahn*: with *Bahn*, **road**, a super-highway in Germany. **NB**: *Auto-da-fé*, Portuguese for *act of faith*, is not from *autos*. See p. 80, under **Clavis**.

Common element base: *clarus*   **Meaning**: bright, clear, lustrous

IE base: *kel³*: **to call**, **to cry out**; thus, *claim, claimant, acclaim, reclaim; clamant, clamor* (see **wordbuilder #5**, p. 13).

Clavis

clarain:	one of the materials composing the **lustrous** layers in some coals.
claret:	short for *vin claret*, **clear**, or **clarified wine**; dry, red table wine of Bordeaux, France.
clarinet:	a musical instrument with a **clear** tone; a member of the woodwind family in a symphonic orchestra. The *clarinet* has a single reed attached to the mouthpiece; the *oboe* (or, *hautbois*, French for "high wood") has a double reed. See p. 4 for more on *oboe*; p. 95 for *English horn*, also a woodwind.
clerestory:	**clear story**; the upper part of a wall, specifically of a church, containing windows for **lighting** the nave, the central part of the church or cathedral. Pronounced: KLIR stor ee.
declare:	*de-*, **down**, **away**; **to clear down** or **away**; to make clear. Synonyms: announce, assert, aver, proclaim, promulgate, publish. See p. 30 for *promulgate*, under **wordextras**.
declarative:	describing that which **clarifies** or asserts, as *a declarative sentence*, the other functional types of sentences being *interrogative, imperative*, and *exclamatory. Declarative sentences* often **classify**, **compare and contrast**, **define**, **describe**, **exemplify**, **narrate**. *Declaration of Independence*: a formal statement, written mainly by Thomas Jefferson and adopted July 4, 1776, by the Second Continental Congress, **declared** the 13 American colonies free and independent of Great Britain. The document is permanently displayed at the National Archives on Constitution Avenue, Washington, DC.
clairvoyant:	*voyant*, present participle of French *voir*; from Latin *videre*, **to see**; **clearly viewing**; it is often used as a synonym for *extrasensory perception*, or ESP; having keen insight; as a *noun, a clairvoyant person*. The noun form is *clairvoyance*, the ability to perceive things not in sight. See p. 213, Item 187.
éclair:	French for **flash**, **lightning**; from *éclairer*, **to illuminate**; an oblong custard-filled French pastry with chocolate icing: so named because eaten in a flash, one authority indicates.
clara:	Spanish; in full: *clara de huevo*, **white of an egg**; bald spot; thin spot in a fabric; *a las claras*, **clearly**; **openly**; ¡*claro!* **Certainly!** In Spanish, exclamation points and question marks precede as well as follow exclamatory and interrogative sentences, respectively.
emphasis:	Greek *en-*, **in** + *phainein*, **to show**; **a showing in**; the force of expression, thought, feeling, action, etc., that impresses, or stresses. The verb form is *emphasize*, **to stress**.
phantom:	and *phantasm*, from *phainein*, **to show**; something apparently seen but having no physical reality. In Platonic philosophy, *phantasm* denotes objective reality as perceived and distorted by the five senses.
sycophant:	Greek *syco*, **fig** + *phainein*, **to show**; **one who shows the sign of the fig**, the fig being the symbol for denouncing a criminal; hence, an informer, a flatterer; a slavish self-seeker. See *janissary*, p. 3.
diaphanous:	Greek *dia-*, **through**, **across** (as in **dia**gnosis, **dia**gonal, **dia**meter, **dia**rrhea); **showing through**; allowing **light** to show through; hence, transparent or translucent; also, describing a delicate form; vague and indistinct; airy. Pronounced: die APH uh nus. See p. 193 for other *dia-* words.
hierophant:	Greek, *hieros*, **sacred**, **holy**; **a holy showing**; an interpreter of sacred mysteries, especially an expounder of Eleusian mysteries. Eleusis, the site of the mysteries, was a town in Greece and the birthplace of Aeschylus (525-456 B.C.), a Greek writer of ninety tragedies. See p. 170 for other *hiero-* words.
theophany:	Greek, *theos*, **God**; a manifestation of **God** or a **deity**. See pp. 59, 199 for other *theo-* words.
chanticleer:	from Old French *chantecler*, **one singing loud**, or **clear**; the name of a rooster in the medieval bestiary epic *Reynard the Fox*. There are many sites devoted to this epic on the Internet.

---

wordbuilder #21

Greek *endo-*, **within**: **end**odontics (*odous*, **tooth**; **within the tooth**; an *endodontist* is a dentist specializing in root canals), **endo**smosis, **endo**steum, **endo**stosis; **endo**biotic, **endo**blast, **endo**cardial, **endo**cardium, **endo**carp, **endo**centric, **endo**commensal, **endo**cranium, **endo**crine, **endo**cytosis, **endo**derm, **endo**gamy, **endo**gen, **endo**genous, **endo**lithic, **endo**lymph, **endo**mixis, **endo**morph, **endo**phyte, **endo**sperm, **endo**thermal, **endo**toxin. Many others.

```
┌─────────────────────────────────────────────────────────────────────────────┐
│                          Word Cluster No. 22                                  │
│                                                                               │
│  clave          conclave        clavichord       enclave                      │
│  clavel         autoclave       claviger         clavis                       │
│  clavicle       exclave         clavicula        clavier                      │
│                                                                               │
│  Common elements_____Inferred Meaning_____      │
└─────────────────────────────────────────────────────────────────────────────┘
```

Romance Cognates	French clé (clef)	Romanian cheie	Italian chiave	Portuguese chave	Spanish llave

Words and phrases with disguised Latin and Indo-European roots: cembala (harpsichord), clef sign, roman à clef (a type of novel), kevel (a nautical term); lot, lotto, lottery, allot

Words with related meanings: clause, claustrophobia, cloister, cloisonné, eclosion, conclude, preclude, seclude

Note: *Clavate* (**club-shaped**), *clavicorn* (a beetle family), and *clavus* (**a corn on the foot**) are related to this family.

Music term: *Chiave trasportata* was a late-16th-century system of writing vocal music with all the clefs moved up or down from their normal position, usually by a third, i.e., the third tone in the diatonic scale.

Explore *The Forty-Eight*, popular name of the 48 preludes and fugues in Bach's *Well-Tempered Clavier I and II*.

German music words: *Schluss*, **conclusion**, *Schlüssel*, **clef**, *Schluss-satz*, **closing phrase**. *Piano*, the instrument, is *Klavier*, from French *clavier*, originally, **a key holder**. [As an *adjective*, Italian *piano* means **soft** in music.]

wordextras

There are a number of Japanese words in English, including *hara-kiri*, **belly-cutting**, a form of ritual suicide; *hibachi*, **firebowl**; *bonsai*, **potted tree**; *kamikaze*, **divine wind**; *tycoon*, **great ruler** (see p. 35); *samurai*, **exalted warrior**; also, *kudzu*, a prostrate leguminous vine used widely for hay and forage and for erosion control, especially in the South.

Browse, a noun, from Old Saxon *brustian*, **leaves, twigs, and young shoots**, is that on which deer nibble; as a *verb*, **to nibble**, as to eat or read in a casual way; thus, a library's *browsing* area; also, to look casually over articles for sale.

Decant, to pour wine from a bottle without stirring up the sediments, is from Latin *de-*, **from** + *canthus*, **edge, rim, corner**. *Canthus* denotes either corner of the eye, where the eyelids meet; there is *epicanthus*, which refers to the *epicanthic fold*: a small normal fold of skin from the upper eyelid sometimes covering the inner corner of the eye, as in many Asian people; also occurs with certain abnormal conditions, as in Down syndrome.

Barter, of uncertain origin, may be from Old French *barater*, **to cheat**. In current usage, *barter* means "the exchange of goods and services without the exchange of money." *Barter* is also a verb, both transitive and intransitive.

Okefenokee Swamp in southeast Georgia, is an American Indian name for **trembling earth**. Encompassing 700 square miles, it extends into northeast Florida. There is also *Dismal Swamp*, in southeast Virginia; see p. 124.

Veranda, Hindi for **balcony**, designates an open porch or portico, usually roofed, along the side of a building. The word was borrowed from Portuguese *varanda*, where *vara* meant **pole** or **staff**, and further from Latin, meaning **a wooden trestle**, or **forked stick** for spreading out nets. The IE base also yields *vacillate* and *vary*.

Prism, Greek for **something sawed**, is a solid figure whose ends are parallel, polygonal, and equal in size and shape, and whose sides are parallelograms. In *optics*, a transparent body, as of glass, whose ends are equal and parallel triangles, and whose sides are parallelograms: used for refracting or dispersing light, as into the spectrum. The colors of the rainbow are thus visible by shining light through the prism.

Surreptitious, from *sub-*, **below** + *rapere*, **to seize**, means "done, gotten, made in a secret, stealthy way; acting in a secret, stealthy way. SYNONYMS: clandestine, covert, furtive, secret, underhanded. See *rapture*, p. 130, **wordextras**. Pronounced: SUR up TISH us.

wordbuilder #22

Greek *ergon*, **work**, yields **erg** (the measurement unit for work), **erg**ograph, **erg**ometer, **erg**onomics; en**erg**esis, en**erg**etic, en**erg**etics, en**erg**ize; en**erg**y, all**erg**y, syn**erg**y; Demi**urge*** (**worker of the people**); chem**urgy**, lit**urgy**, metall**urgy**; par**erg**on (*para-* + *ergon*), zym**urgy**; leth**argy**; s**urg**ery; **arg**on, georg**ic**. *In Platonism, the creator of the world; in Gnostic and certain other philosophic systems, a supernatural being, imagined as creating the world in subordination to the Supreme Being. Compare *ergon* with *opera*, **work**, as in *opera, operation, operator*.

Common element base: clavis, from *claudere*, **to close**   **Meaning**: key
IE base: *kleu-*: **hook, wooden plug**, and yields *lot*, **a hook**; **a forked branch**; **Greek** *cleistos*, **closed**, as in *cleistogamy, cleistogamous* (see **Clavis**). See **wordbuilder #23**, below.

Clavis

clavicle: the **collarbone**; from French *clavicule*, a diminutive of *clavis*; literally, **small key**, from the shape of the collarbone. See p. 187, **Scientific Medical Terms**?

Clavis: key; glossary. As used in this book, the explanatory notes are **keyed** to the common element's meaning. As such, the *Clavis* helps associatively bond the meaning of the element.

claviger: one who keeps the **key** or **keys**; a custodian; a warden; also, a club bearer.

clavichord: with *chord*, **string**, an instrument in which the strings are struck by *claves*, or **keys**; a successor to the *harpsichord* in which the strings were *plucked*, and the predecessor of the *piano(forte)*, literally, **soft-loud**, in which the dynamics are controlled by both the touch and the damper pedal.

conclave: *con-*, **with**; literally, **with a key**; a small room where a group may be *closed* in, especially where cardinals are sequestered to elect a pope; any private, or secret, meeting; *to be in conclave*, to be engaged in a secret meeting. See *cabal*, p. 47.

enclave: a political unit enclosed by foreign elements, as though a **key** projecting inward, e.g., the former West Berlin was an *enclave* of East Germany. *Exclave* is an area isolated in an alien territory, e.g., West Berlin was an *exclave* of West Germany. *East* and *West* were used prior to reunification.

roman à clef: **roman** (novel) with **a key**, in which characters are **keyed** to actual persons, and one in which the reader is expected to identify them under the guise of fiction. Examples: Peacock's *Nightmare Abbey*; Huxley's *Point Counterpoint*; and Hemingway's *The Sun Also Rises*. In German, *roman à clef* is *Schlüsselroman*. Pronounced: roh mahn a CLAY.

clause: from Medieval Latin *clausa*, **close** of a rhetorical period; conclusion of a legal argument, hence, a section of a law. Explore use as a grammar term, especially *dependent* and *independent clauses*.

cloister: originally, that portion of a monastery **closed** off to the laity; a place of religious seclusion: monastery or convent; an arched way or covered walk along an inside wall. See p. 205, Item 74.

cleistogamous: from Greek *kleistos*, **closed** + *gamous*, **pertaining to marriage**; in *botany*, characterized by self-fertilization in an unopened, budlike state. See **wordbuilder #23**, below.

---

wordbuilders #23, 24

Greek *gamos*, **marriage**, **sexual reproduction**: **gam**ete; **gamo**genesis, **gamo**phyllous, **gamo**sepalous; a**gam**ous; allo**gamy**, apo**gamy**, auto**gamy**, big**amy**, deutero**gamy**, dig**amy**, dicho**gamy**, endo**gamy**, exo**gamy**, hetero**gamy**, homo**gamy**, hyper**gamy**, iso**gamy**, miso**gamy** **(hatred of marriage)**, mono**gamy**, opsi**gamy** (see p. 165), poly**gamy**, syn**gamy**, xeno**gamy**; cleisto**gam**ous (see **Clavis** entry above), crypto**gam**, miso**gam**ist; *gameto*: **gameto**cyte, **gameto**genesis, **gameto**phore, **gameto**phyte. Try your luck on the *–gamy* quiz, p. 4, bottom of page.

Greek *baros*, *barys*, **heavy**: **bar**ite, **bar**ium (symbol: Ba); **bar**itone; **baro**gram, **baro**graph, **baro**meter, **baro**scope; **bary**sphere, **bary**tone (or, baritone); **bary**on; anti**bary**on; iso**bar**; centro**baric**, hyper**baric**, hypo**baric**.

---

wordextras

Italian *sonata*, **a sounding**, was originally an instrumental composition, as opposed to *cantata*, **something sung**; from Latin *sonus*, **sound** (see p. 212, Item 170). See p. 204, Item 67, for more words from *cantar*, **to sing**.

Sonnet, French, from Italian through Provençal, is ultimately from Latin *sonus*, **sound** (see p. 212, Item 170). The diminutive suffix indicates that *sonnet* is **a small sound**, or **a small song**.

Bantam, a former Dutch residency in Java, denotes a small, domestic fowl; it has been extended to **a small**, **but aggressive person**. As an *adjective*, *like a bantam*; **small and aggressive**. A *bantamweight* designates a boxer between a flyweight and a junior featherweight, with a maximum weight of 118 pounds.

Adulate, from *ad-*, **to** + *ulos*, **tail**, is literally **to wag the tail**, as a dog to its master; to fawn upon; to admire intensely or excessively. Other forms: *adulation* (noun); *adulator* (noun); *adulatory* (adjective).

Hormone, from Greek *hormon*, **to stimulate**, **excite**, is originally from *horme*, **impulse**.

Word Cluster No. 23

contrast	**contro**l	**contra**ry	**contra**riety
contraceptive	**contra**dict	**contra**fugue	**contra**band
contrafact	**contra**puntal	**contra**riwise	**contra**petal
contralateral	**contra**gredient	**contra**flexure	**contra**mundum
controversy	**contro**vert	**contro**versial	**contro**versial
contrecoup	**contre**danse	**contre**temps	**contre**-jour
counter	**counter**mand	**counter**weight	**counter**clockwise
counteract	**counter**feit	**counter**move	**counter**espionage
countermine	**counter**point	**counter**poise	**counter**balance
counterpart	**counter**pane	**counter**vail	en**counter**

Common elements_____**Inferred Meaning**_____

Romance Cognates	French	Romanian	Italian	Portuguese	Spanish
	countre	contra	contro	contra	contra

Word with disguised Latin root: country

Latin phrases: *contra bonos mores*: **contrary to good manners**; *contra mundum*: **against the world**
contra pacem: **against the peace**; *pro et contra*: **for and against**; *Ne cede malis, sed contra audentior*[*] *ito*. **Yield not to misfortunes, but go more boldly to meet them**. Virgil
[*]*Audentior* is not related to *audire*, **to hear** (see p. 13), but to *audere*, **to be bold**, as in *audacious* and *audacity* (see *audacious*, p. 14).

French phrases: *au contraire*: **on the contrary**; *à contrecoeur* (see **Clavis**)

Religious movements: Catholic Counter-Reformation (countering the *Protestant Reformation*)

Portuguese phrase: *remar contra a mare*: **to row against the tide**

Explore *counterpoint* and *contrafactum* as music terms. See **Clavis**.

Greek: *anti-*, **against**: **ant**agonist, **ant**alkali, **Ant**arctic, **anth**elion, **anth**elix, **anth**elmintic; **ant**onomasia, **ant**onym; **anti**bacterial, **anti**baryon, **anti**biosis, **anti**biotic, **anti**body, **Anti**christ (see 1 John 2:18), **anti**climax, **anti**clinal, **anti**clinorium, **anti**coagulant, **anti**cyclone, **anti**depressant, **anti**disestablishmentarianism, **anti**dote, **anti**lithic, **anti**nomian, **anti**pyretic, **anti**thesis, **anti**type; **anth**em (from *antiphon*). See more on *anthem*, p. 10, under **Clavis**.

wordextras

Mayday, an international distress call, is the English version of French *(venez) m'aider*, "(Come to) **my aid**." **Help me**! (See p. 199, under **French Phrases**.) *SOS* is a wireless distress signal in Morse code (. . .- - -. . .), and probably stands for "Suspend Other Services," rather than "Save Our Ship."

Laissez faire, French for "**Let** (the people) **do** (as they please)," is the policy or practice of noninterference; in *government*, the policy of letting leaders of industry and business fix their own rules of competition, the conditions of labor, etc., without governmental regulation or control. Pronunciation: LES ay FER.

The plural of Anglo-Saxon *goose* is *geese*, but the plural of Prakrit *mongoose* is *mongooses* (see p. 53). In Prakrit, *mongoose* was *manguso*, which evolved into Hindi *magus*. Prakrit is an Indic language.

Aegis, from Greek *aigis*, originally referred to the short goatskin cloak of Zeus. In Greek mythology, *aegis* was a shield borne by Zeus and later by his daughter Athena and occasionally by Apollo. *Aegis* has come to mean **protection**, **sponsorship**, **auspices**. See p. 198. Pronunciation: EE jis.

Banal, from Old French *ban*, **legal control**, designating objects such as ovens or mills that belonged to feudal serfs, has come to mean **common**, **ordinary**, **dull** or **stale** as because of overuse; **trite**; **hackneyed**; **insipid**.

Argyle, after a clan tartan of County Argyll in Scotland, describes a pattern of diamond-shaped figures in different colors. *Argyles*: argyle socks, patterned in the manner of the Argyll tartan.

Crew, from Middle English *creue*, **increase**, **growth**, is ultimately from Latin *crescere*, **to grow**. Other words from *crescere* include **create**, **creative**, **creature**; **recreate**; **crescendo**, **crescent**; **increase**, **decrease**; **procreant**; **increment**; **accrete**, **concrete**; **croissant**; **recruit**. See more on *croissant*; also, New Orleans, the Crescent City, p. 33.

Common element: *contra-*   **Meaning**: against, over against, opposite; also, facing, on the contrary
IE base: *kom-*, yields **Latin** *cum-, com-*, **with, together**; **Greek** *cenobite* (*koinos*, **common** + *bios*, **life**; a member of a religious order living in a monastery or convent), *epicene* (**common to both sexes**), *koinonia* (**fellowship of a church**).

Clavis

contralto:	formerly, *contra alto*, or the lowest of the three women's parts, sung **against** the highest men's part, *alto*. *Contralto* has been clipped to *alto*, which is now the *lower* of the two women's parts. Present-day four-part harmonic structures do not utilize the male alto part or mezzo-soprano. See *alto*, p. 4.
contraband:	short for *contrabannum*, **against decree**; forbidden, or verboten, merchandise. ***Verboten***, a German loanword, corresponds root by root with Anglo-Saxon *forbidden*. See p. 77 for other *ban-* words.
contradict:	with *dicere*, **to say**; **to say against**, the root-by-root equivalent of Anglo-Saxon *gainsay*, as in "I *gainsay* the weather forecaster that it will rain tomorrow." See more on *gainsay*, pp. 31, 132. See p. 65, for other words from *dicere*.
contrafact:	a 16th-century musical setting of the Mass, a chorale, or hymn, by replacing the text of a secular song with religious words. Martin Luther's "A Mighty Fortress Is Our God" is an example of *contrafact*; the hymn tune *Ein' Feste Burg*, to which the hymn is sung, was originally music for a German beer-drinking song. In addition, *The Star-Spangled Banner* is sung to the tune of an old English folksong.
contraflexure:	with *flectere*, **to bend, curve**; a **bending in opposite directions**, like the curve of an ogee; a point of contrary flexure or inflexion that in a fixed beam is a point of zero-bending moment. In *architecture*, an *ogee* is a double curve in the shape of an elongated *S*.
contrapuntal:	from *contra punctum*, **against the point**; yields the noun *counterpoint*; in *music*, **point to point**; extended to mean **melody against melody**. See *polyphony* as it pertains to *counterpoint*, p. 154. Huxley's *Point Counterpoint* is a superb example of *roman à clef* (see **Clavis**, p. 44).
countermand:	with *mandare*, **to command**; to cancel or revoke a command by a **countering order**. In *law*, a *countermand* may be expressed or implied.
countermine:	a military mine for **intercepting** or **destroying** an enemy mine; as a *verb*, *to counterplot*: to defeat a plot with another one.
country:	formerly, the area or region that was **over**, **against** another region or area; may have meant "spread out" as one left the city.
à contrecoeur:	French; **against the heart**; reluctantly; against the grain. There is *Contrecoeur*, Quebec. See listing of *Contrecoeur* in the *cord-*, **heart**, family, p. 47.
encounter:	*en-*, **in**; **to meet unexpectedly**; also, to meet in conflict or battle; as a *noun*, can mean "a hostile confrontation." SYNONYMS: action, battle, campaign, combat, skirmish.

wordextras

With *nasus*, **nose** + *torquere*, **to twist**, ***nasturtium***, **twisted nose**, is so called because of the flower's pungent odor; however, the American *nasturtium* does not have a pungent odor; the *marigold*—**Mary's gold**—is indeed pungent.

Azalea, from Greek *azaleos*, **dry**, was adopted to indicate "the dry plant," or one that thrived in dry, or well-drained soil. The *azalea* is a member of the genus *Rhododendron*. See p. 89, under **wordextras**.

Persian has given English some very colorful words: ***azure, caravan*** (see p. 166), ***check, checkmate, chess, divan, jasmine, khaki*** (see p. 68), ***lemon, lilac, mogul, orange, paradise, shawl, sherbet, taffeta, turban***. Not so poetic or colorful are ***baksheesh*** (**a tip**; more often, a bribe) and ***satrap*** (**a ruler**).

Agrarian, from *ager*, **a field**, and from which ***acre*** is derived, relates to land or to the ownership or division of land.

Debut, **to play first, to lead off**, is from French *jouer de but*, **to play for the mark**, and designates the first appearance before the public, as of an actor; more popularly, the formal introduction of a young woman into society. A *debutant* is a person—male or female—making a debut; a *debutant̲e* is a girl or woman making such a debut. Pronunciation of *debut*: day BYOO.

An exalted aphorism: *Scintillate, scintillate, asteroid miniscule*. **Twinkle, twinkle, little star**. Moral: Beware of using unfamiliar words that may *obfuscate* the meaning. See p. 140 for *obfuscate*; see *scintillate*, under *tinsel*, p. 30.

Word Cluster No. 24

cordate	**cord**iform	ac**cord**	ac**cord**ant
cordial	con**cord**	ac**cord**ian	ac**cord**ance
cordiale	con**cord**ance	dis**cord**	dis**cord**ant
disac**cord**	miseri**cord**	re**cord**	ob**cord**ate

Common element_____**Inferred Meaning**_____

Romance Cognates	French coeur	Romanian cord	Italian cuore	Portuguese coraçao	Spanish corazón

Words with disguised roots: courage, encourage, discourage; quarry (one meaning); core; chord (one meaning)

Placenames: Accord, NY; Coeur d'Alene, ID; Coeur d'Alene Mountains, MT; Creve Coeur (MO, IL); Contrecoeur, Quebec (see p. 46). *Creve Coeur* is French for "broken heart": **utter discouragement**.

Latin phrases: *corda serata fero* (see **Clavis**); *Concordia discors*: **discordant harmony**. Horace

French phrases: *à coeur joie*: **to one's heart's content**; *à coeur ouvert*: **with an open heart**; *entente cordiale*: **friendly understanding**; *Accordez vos flûtes*: **Tune your flutes**: Settle your differences. *cri de coeur, affaire de Coeur; Coeur de Lion; à contrecoeur*

Spanish phrase: *cuan lejos de los ojos, tan lejos del corazón*: **as distant from the heart as from the eye**; out of sight, out of mind [Vow of Simón Bolívar, the so-called *Jorge Washington of South America*: *Mi corazón nunca descansaré o mis manos nunca se cansarán hasta que las cadenas que unen nuestro país con España se rompan.* **My heart shall never rest nor my hands ever tire until the chains that bind my country to Spain are broken.**] See p. 4 for more on Simón Bolívar, under *altiplano*.

Greek cognates: *kardia*, **heart**: **card**iac, **card**ialgia (*algia*, **pain**), **card**iodynia (*odyne*, **pain**), **card**ioid; **card**iocele, **card**iocentesis, **card**iogram, **card**iologist, **card**iolysis, **card**iophony; a**card**ia, bathy**card**ia, brachy**card**ia (*brachys*, **short**; same as *bradycardia*), brady**card**ia (*bradys*, **slow**; slowness of the heartbeat), dextro**card**ia, exo**card**ia, lepto**card**ia, mega**card**ia, megalo**card**ia, tachy**card**ia (*tachys*, **swift**; excessive rapidity in the action of the heart); diplo**card**iac (*diplos*, **double**; having the heart completely divided or double, one side systemic, the other pulmonary), endo**card**ium, epi**card**ium, myo**card**ium, peri**card**ium; myo**card**itis; electro**card**iogram (EKG, or ECG).

wordextras

French *raison d'être*, **reason for being**, is the justification for the existence of some action or policy. Pronounced: RAY zone DET, or RAY zone DET ruh.

Intoxicate, from Latin *in-*, **in** + *toxicum*, **poison**, originally meant "to put poison into" by means of poisoned arrows. In Greek, *toxicon* referred to a poison used in bows meant to kill or maim.

Chicory, a plant whose root can be mixed with coffee or used as a coffee substitute, can be traced through Middle English *cocoree*, to Latin *cichorium*, and ultimately to Greek *kikhora*, meaning **chicory**, **endive**, **succory** (from *sycory*, an older form of *chicory*).

Coffee, originally in Arabic *quhwah*, became Turkish *kahve*, and Italian *caffè*. *Café*: French for **coffee house**, restaurant, or bar. *Caffeine* and *cafeteria* are also from the Arabic word. Other Arabic words in English include *adobe*, *alcove, amber, azimuth, cotton, mattress* (see p. 82), *saffron, sugar, syrup, zero*.

American Indian languages have contributed many words to English: *chipmunk* (*achitamo*, **squirrel**); *hickory* (**pohickery**); *menhaden*, **a small fish** (**fertilizer**; probably so used because the Indians taught the European colonists how to use the fish to enrich the soil); *moose* (*moos*, **eats off the bark**); *powwow* (**medicine man**, sorcerer); *raccoon* (*aracun*, **the scratcher**); *skunk* (*segogw*); *tepee* (**dwelling**); *tomahawk* (*tamahaac*, **axe**, used either as tool or weapon); *wapiti* (Shawnee, **one with a white rump**; elk). *Wapiti* is pronounced WAHP ut ee.

Glade, an open space in a wood or forest, is from Old English *glad,* from Germanic *glatt*, **smooth**.

Cabal, from Hebrew *kabala*, **received lore, tradition**, produces *cabala*, **occultism**, as well. *Cabal* has come to mean a secret association comprising a few designing persons. By a mere coincidence, the British cabinet under Charles II (1660-85) consisted of five persons, the initial letters of whose last names made up *cabal*: Clifford, Arlington, Buckingham, Ashley, and Lauderdale. SYNONYMS: conspiracy, intrigue, machination, plot. See *conclave*, p. 44.

Common element base: cord   **Meaning:** heart

IE base: *kerd¹*: **heart**, and yields **Greek** *kardia*, **heart** (see p. 47). The Greek word refers to the **physical heart**; the Latin is more *figurative*. IE base also yields **Old Irish** *machree*, as well as **Latin** *credere*, **to believe**, as in **cred**ence, **cred**enza (see p. 79), **cred**o, **cred**ible, **cred**ulous, in**cred**ible, mis**creant**, **grant** (see p. 205, Item 77).

Clavis

chord:
in *music*, **string**, as in *harpsichord* (see p. 44, under *clavichord*); here, however, it is an apheresis of *accord*, **to the heart**, thus, harmony; in *music*, three or more harmonic tones sounded together. [*Apheresis*, or *aphesis*, is the loss of one or more sounds at the beginning of a word, e.g., *squire* for *esquire*. There is a technical difference between *apheresis* and *aphesis*; *aphesis*, the dropping of a short unaccented vowel at the beginning of a word, is a form of *apheresis*.]

cordial:
that which warms the **heart**, whether a friendship or an aromatic liqueur. Also used as an adjective. ADJECTIVE SYNONYMS: amiable, affable, genial, good-natured, obliging.

concord:
con-, **together**; thus, of the same mind, or, **heart**; from *concord* are derived *concordant*, **harmonious, agreeing**; *concordat*, **a formal agreement**, a pact; and *concordance*, **a statement of agreement**. A *concordance* is also an alphabetical index of the main words in a text or corpus of texts, showing contextual occurrences of a word, for example, *a concordance of the Bible*, or *of Shakespeare*.

accord:
ac-, assimilation of *ad-*, **to, toward**; **to the heart**; **to make agree**; **reconcile**. SYNONYMS: agree, conform, correspond, harmonize, tally; as a *noun*, mutual agreement; harmony.

discord:
dis-, **negative**; **lack of concord**; thus, **disagreement**; in *music*, a lack of harmony in tones sounded together. *Concord*, on the other hand, is a combination of sounds pleasant to the ear, such as thirds, triads, sixths, and dominant seventh chords. *Concord* and *discord* are used as aesthetic rather than technical categories. SYNONYMS: contention, dissension, strife.

record:
re-, **again**; **again to the heart**; from Old French *recorder*, **to call to mind, to remember**; from Latin *recordari*. In *law*, the commitment to writing, as authentic evidence, of something having legal importance; anything written down, as for documentation. Also used as a verb.

obcordate:
ob-, **against**; in *botany*, describing a **heart-shaped** leaf joined at the stem of the apex, or tip.

misericord:
or, *misericorde*; **merciful heart**; originally, a relaxation of the strict observance of a rule or rules in a monastery or convent. Also, a dagger used in the Middle Ages for giving the death stroke (*coup de grâce*) to a mortally wounded knight. See *parlor* for an example of *misericord*, p. 101.

Coeur de Lion:
French; **heart of the lion**; Richard I, or *Richard Coeur de Lion*, or **Richard the Lion-Hearted**, King of England, 1189-1199. After becoming king, he joined Philip Augustus of France in a crusade to the Holy Land. He captured Acre (now, Akko, a city in Israel), but could not retake Jerusalem.

à contrecoeur:
French; **against the heart**; against the grain; grudgingly; against one's wishes. See pp. 45, 46.

cri de coeur:
French; **cry from the heart**, an outrage, or an impassioned appeal, protest, complaint; *outrage* is from *outré*; see p. 198. Approximate pronunciation of *cri de coeur*: krete KER.

corda serata. . .:
I carry a heart locked up; punning motto of the Lockhart family.

pericardium:
peri-, **around**; **around the heart**; the thin, closed membranous sac enclosing the heart and the origins of the great blood vessels. Compare with *myocardium*, **muscle-heart**, middle layer of the heart wall.

machree:
Irish; *mo*, **my** + Old Irish *cride*, **heart**; **My heart**; **my dear**; an Anglo-Irish term of endearment, as in *Mother Machree*.

---

wordextras

Anglo-Saxon *wordhoard* designated one's **hoard**, or **store of words**; thus, one's vocabulary.

Ridicule, from Latin *ridere*, **to laugh**, is to laugh at in a joking, jesting, or contemptuous manner; *ridere* also yields *ridiculous*, *deride*; *risibility, risible*; *derision, derisive*; *riant*. Spanish: *risa*, **laughter**.

Word Cluster No. 25

corpus	corporal	corporation	incorporate
corpulent	corpuscle	corporeal	corposant
corporeity	corparative	incorporeal	corps
intracorporeal	corporality	corpuscular	corpse

Common elements_____Inferred Meaning_____

Romance Cognates	French	Romanian	Italian	Portuguese	Spanish
	corps	corp	corpo	corpo	cuerpo

Words with disguised Latin root: corsage, corselet (a piece of armor), corset, corsetiere, corsetry

Short Latin phrases: *corpus albicans, corpus delicti, corpus juris*: **a body of law**; *habeas corpus, corpus luteum, corpus vile*: **worthless matter**; *corpus callosum, corpus cavernosum, corpus Juris Canonici, Corpus Juris Civilis*

Other Latin phrases: *corpus sine pectore*: **a body without a soul**. Horace
Corpora nostra lente augescunt, cito extinguuntur: **Bodies are slow in growth, rapid in decay**. Tacitus
mens sana in corpore sano (see **Clavis**)

French phrases: *à corps perdu* (**with lost body**; impetuously; headlong); *esprit de corps* (see **Clavis**)

Placenames: Corpus Christi (**Body of Christ**), Texas; Corps, France

Greek: *soma*, **body**: **soma**tic, **soma**tagenic, chromo**some**; see p. 212, Item 169, for other *soma* words.

German: *Körper*; thus, *Körperanlage*, **constitution**; *Körperbau*, **one's build**; *Körperchen*, **particle, corpuscle**; *Körperflege*, **care of the body**; *körperlich*, **bodily, physical**; *Körperreich*, **material world**.

Irish: leprechaun (see **Clavis**)

wordextras

Fortnight—**two weeks**—contracts *fourteen nights*. A newspaper issued once every two weeks is often called a *fortnightly*. In earlier times, many public libraries were known as *fortnightlies*, because of lending books for two weeks.

Longshore is an aphesis of the adverbial "along shore," describing that which exists, occurs, or works along the shore or a waterfront; the nominal is **longshoreman**. See *aphesis*, p. 48, under *chord*. See *stevedore*, p. 178.

Zenith, Arabic for **road**, and taken to mean **road over one's head**, is the point in the sky directly overhead; also, the highest point or state; culmination. The opposite of *zenith* is *nadir* (see p. 53 under **wordextras**).

The legal term *lien* originally meant **ligament** or **tie**. Coming from Latin *ligare*, **to bind**, and yielding *legato* (see p. 155 for *staccato*), *lien* (**a binding**) is a claim on the property of another as security for the payment of a just debt.

Heinous, originally from French *hair*, **to hate**, and akin to German *hassen*, **to hate**, has come to mean **outrageously evil or wicked**, as *a heinous crime*. Synonyms: atrocious, flagrant, monstrous. Pronounced: HAY nus.

Menial, from *manere*, **to remain**, is also the base of *manor, mansion, manse*. In Anglo-French (also called Middle English), the language spoken in England after the Norman Conquest in 1066 through the Middle Ages, *menial* was spelled *meiniee*, **a family retainer, servant**, coming to mean "of, or fit for servants," as in *menial labor*, thus **servile; low; mean**. As a *noun*, **a domestic servant**; also, a servile, low person.

Glebe, from Latin *gleba*, **clod, lump of earth**, designates a piece of church land forming part or all of a benefice. [A *benefice* was originally land held by a feudal tenant for services rendered to the owner; now, an endowed church office providing a living for a vicar, rector, pastor, etc.] There is *Glebe Road*, Arlington, Virginia.

Palatial, from Latin *palatium*, **palace**, means "of, suitable for, or like a palace"; **large and ornate; magnificent; stately**, as *the palatial homes of the antebellum South; the White House is a palatial edifice*.

Cermet coalesces ceramic metal, a bonded mixture of ceramic material and a metal. Tough and heat-resistant, *cermet* is used in gas turbines, nuclear reactor mechanisms, etc.

Motto of University of Georgia
Et discere et rerum exquirere causas
Both to learn and to investigate the causes of things

Common element base: corpus   **Meaning**: body

IE base: *kwrep-*: **body**; from this base is **Old English** *hrif*, **belly**, as in *midriff* (see p. 32).

Clavis

corsage: the **waist** or the **bodice** of a dress, as well as a floral arrangement worn as a fashion accessory upon the *bodice*, the upper part of a woman's dress. Pronounced: COR sahzh, or COR sahj.

corps: in the *military*, a separate branch or department of the armed forces having a specialized function; it is also a tactical unit of ground combat forces between a division and an army; commanded by a lieutenant general, a corps comprises two or more divisions and auxiliary service troops. Pronounced *core*, the word is singular; the plural is spelled the same, but pronounced *corz*.

corporal: a Communion cloth; in the *military*, a junior non-commissioned officer (NCO), who originally was head of a **body** of men. The military meaning may possibly have come from *caput*, **head**, or **chief**. Also, an *adjective*, as in *corporal punishment*. See p. 31, **Words with disguised Latin roots.**

corporation: a legal entity, or **body**, that exists independently of the person or persons who have been granted the charter creating it and that is invested with many of the rights given to individuals; for example, a *corporation* may enter into contracts, buy and sell property, experience profits and losses, the same as individuals.

corporeal: of, for, or having the nature of the **body**; physical; bodily; not spiritual, as *corporeal desires*. Two related nominal forms are *corporeality* and *corporeity*. Pronounced: kor POR ee ul.

corposant: from Portuguese *corpo-santo*, **holy body**, **St. Elmo's fire** (after St. Elmo, patron of sailors); *corposant* denotes a visible, electric discharge from charged objects, as the tip of masts, spires, trees, airplanes, and seen sometimes during electrical storms.

corpulent: **fat and fleshy**; **stout**; **obese**; **overweight**; the nominal form is *corpulence* or *corpulency*: fatness or stoutness of **body**.

intracorporeal: *intra-*, **within**; a medical term meaning "situated or occurring **within the body**."

corpus delicti: **body of the crime**: the material substance upon which a crime has been committed, for example, the stabbed corpse of a murdered person, or the charred remains of a house burned down; generally consists of two elements: the act itself, and the criminal agency of the act.

esprit de corps: **spirit of the body**; group spirit; unity. Although a **body** of people, such as a military unit, is *heterogeneous*, dedication to a common cause fosters *homogeneity*, or *esprit de corps*. See p. 212.

chromosome: *chroma*, **color** + *soma*, **body**: colored **body**; any of the microscopic bodies that carry the genes. *Chromosomes* **color**, or stain, deeply with basic dyes and are especially conspicuous during mitosis. See *centromere*, p. 36, for more on *chromosome*. See *soma* words, p. 212, Item 169.

psychosomatic: pertaining to phenomena that are both *psychological* and *physiological*; both *psychic*, pertaining to the **mind**, and *somatic*, pertaining to the **body**; having bodily symptoms of a psychic, emotional, or mental origin. For example, a headache may arise from mental stress.

leprechaun: Old Irish; **small body**; in Irish folklore, one of a race of elves, pygmies, sprites, or goblins, who were cobblers and who possessed hidden treasures. See more on *leprechaun*, p. 112.

mens sana in corpore sano: **a sound mind in a sound body**, the philosophy of the Romans in promoting athletics after the concept of the Greek *gymnasium* (see p. 207, Item 100, for *gymn-*, **nude**, family), **a place to exercise in the nude**. Consider *gymnosophists*, an ancient Hindu sect of ascetics who contemplated in the nude.

wordextras

The base of *foreign, forest, foreclose, forfeit, forum, faubourg*, and *hors d'oeuvres*, is Latin *foris*, **outside**; in Greek, *agora*; thus, *agoraphobia* is fear of open places, or fear of the marketplace. Spanish *fuera*, **outdoors**.

Middle English *vinegar*, from *vin*, **wine** + *aigre*, **sour**, is "sharp, or sour, wine." See *garlic*, p. 119.

Menhir, from Breton *men*, **stone** + *hir*, **long**, is a tall, usually rough, upright megalith, probably erected as a Neolithic monument either alone or as part of a row or circle. See *cromlech, dolmen*, p. 123; *Stonehenge*, p. 125.

Word Cluster No. 26

crucial	cruciate	crucify	crucifix	crucifixion
crucifer	excruciate	cruciform	cruciferae	excruciating

Common element_____Inferred Meaning_____

Romance Cognates	French	Romanian	Italian	Portuguese	Spanish
	croix	cruce	croce	cruz	cruz

Words with disguised Latin roots: croisé, cruise, crusade, Crusades, lacrosse (see p. 177) **English**: cross

Latin words and phrases: *Crucifixus; Via Crucis; a cruce salus; In Hac (Cruce) Salus*
Christi crux est mea lux: **The cross of Christ is my light.**

French words and phrases: *croisement, croisez, crosez, Croix de guerre, Croix de feu* (see **Clavis** for all terms)

Placenames: Las Cruces, NM; Marine on St. Croix, MN; Veracruz, CA; Vera Cruz, Mexico; Holy Cross, KY; Holy Cross College, Worcester, MA; Delacroix (**of the cross**) Island, LA

Types of crosses: *crux ansata*: **cross with a handle**; the ankh, an ancient Egyptian symbol representing life
crux capitata, crux commissa: the tau cross: shaped like a capital tau, the 19th letter, T, of the Greek alphabet
crux decussata: X-shaped cross, the cross of Saint Andrew; see *saltire*, p. 182.
crux gammata, crux immissa, crux stellata

By folk etymology: crucible (see **Clavis**)

German words and phrases: *Kreuz, Kreuzer*, and the familiar *das Rote Kreuz*, **the Red Cross**. *ans Kreuz schlagen*, **fix or nail to the cross**; *das Kreuz machen*, **to make the sign of the cross**; **to cross oneself**; *zu Kreuze kriechen*, **to humble oneself**; **to repent**.

wordbuilder #25

Greek *bios*, **life**, yields **bi**otic; **bi**ome, **bio**chemistry (the science that deals with the chemistry of **life** processes in plants and animals), **bio**cide, **bio**genesis (the principle that **living** organisms originate only from other closely similar **living** organisms), **bio**gnosis, **bio**graphy, **bio**herm, **bio**logy, **bio**meter, **bio**phagous, **bio**sphere; aero**be**, micro**be**; aero**bic**, anaero**bic**; rhizo**bium**; sym**bi**ont; ana**biosis**, sym**biosis**; photo**biotic**, sym**biotic**; entero**bi**asis, as well as the motto of the fraternity Phi Beta Kappa, the initials for *philosophia biou kuberenetes*, **Philosophy, the guide of life.**

wordextras

Mile is from Latin *milia passum*, **1,000 paces**; it was the practice in the Roman Empire to mark off such distances with a stone (thus the term *milestone*); instead of *1,000 paces*, a mile now measures 5,280 feet.

During ancient Greek times, *stadium*, now designating **a sports arena**, was not only an arena, but also a measurement of distance, based upon the length of a particular foot race, equal to 607 feet. In *biology*, designates a period or stage in the life history of an animal or plant. The plural of *stadium* is either *stadiums* or *stadia*. See p. 9, **wordextras**.

Emolument, from *mola*, **millstone**, shares the same base as *molar*, **grinder** (tooth), and is compensation for services rendered; *emolument* appears to be that which has been "ground out," or worked for tediously.

Svelte, also spelled *svelt*, and pronounced as such, is from Latin *evellere*, **to pull out, to stretch out**. Meaning **slender, thin, lithe**, *svelte* appears to convey that a person so described has been "stretched thin."

Patio, from Spanish, is an aphesis (see p. 48 for aphesis, under *chord*) of Latin *spatium*, **space**. *Patio* is a courtyard or inner area open to the sky, as in Spanish and Spanish-American architecture; a paved area, as one adjacent to a house, for outdoor cooking and dining.

Vicar is a person who acts in place of another. Capitalized (in full: **Vicar of Christ**), the pope, regarded as the earthly representative of Christ. See p. 213, Item 186. A *vicarious* experience is one that is substitutionary, e.g., *vicarious authority, vicarious menstruation, vicarious punishment, vicarious sacrifice, vicarious thrill.*

Dolabriform, from Latin *dolabra*, **pickax**, means **shaped like an ax**, as are certain leaves.

Motto of the University of Vermont: *Studiis et rebus honestis*: **For studies and noble achievements.**
Motto of the State of Iowa: **Our liberties we prize, and our rights we will maintain.**

Word from Greek mythology: *stygian*, **dark, gloomy, hellish**, from the *River Styx*, which encircled Hades, or Hell.

51

Common element base: crux   **Meaning**: cross
IE base: *sker-³*: **to turn, bend**; yields **Latin** *curvus*, **curve**; **Spanish**: *curva*, **curve**

Clavis

The Cross: in Christianity, the symbol of atoning redemption, signifying Christ's death on the **Cross** for one's sins.

Crux: capitalized, the **Southern Cross**, a heavenly constellation; in lowercase, *a cross* as an instrument of torture; hence, a difficult problem, a turning point, as *the crux of the problem*; also, the determinative point of an issue.

crucial: **cross-shaped**; **of supreme importance**; critical; decisive, as *a crucial election*; severe; difficult; trying, as *a crucial decision*; in *medicine*, having the form of a *cross*, as *a crucial incision*.

cruciate: **cross-shaped**; in *medicine*, the **cross-shaped** ligaments of the knee; in *botany*, having leaves or petals arranged in the form of a **cross**; in *zoology*, **crossing**: said of wings; in *entomology*, wings **crossing** diagonally when at rest: said of certain insects.

excruciate: *ex-*, **from, out of**; **from**, or **out of**, **the cross**; to inflict with intense pain, anguish, torture, torment, as though made to suffer upon *a cross*; the adjective *excruciating* means **intensely painful**; **extreme**, as *excruciating care*; **very careful**, as *excruciating attention to detail*.

cruzado: an old gold coin of Portugal having a *cross* on the reverse side. A coin's face is its *obverse* side.

Vera Cruz: **True Cross**; Cortez originally named the city in Mexico *Villa Rica de la Cruz*, **Rich City of the Cross**. Vera Cruz is also a state of Mexico, the capital of which is Jalapa (in full: Jalapa Enriquez).

cruise: from Dutch *kruise(n)*; originally, **to cross** (the ocean by ship); now, to sail (or ride) to and from place to place, as for pleasure or in search of something; in *forestry*, to go over a wooded area to estimate its lumber yield; as a *noun*, the action of cruising. See *journey*, p. 104.

croisez: and *croisement*: indications **to cross** the hands in piano playing.

crucible: from *cruse*, **earthen pot**; a container made of a substance that can resist great heat; by *folk etymology* (see **Note**), associated with *crux* (genitive of *cruces*), as if a lamp burning upon a cross. Explore *The Crucible*, a play by Arthur Miller (1915-), concerning the witchcraft trials of Salem, MA, and the burning of the so-called witches. **Note**: *Folk etymology* refers to unscientific etymology; popular but incorrect notion of the origin and derivation of a word; e.g., *hangnail* is actually from *agnail*, **pain nail**.

Croix de guerre: **war cross**; a French decoration for bravery in battle.
Croix de feu: **fire cross**; a French decoration awarded during World War I.

---

wordextras

Agree, from Old French *agreer*, **to receive kindly**, is originally from Latin *gratus*, **pleasing**, which also generates *gratuity, gratitude, gratify, gratuitous, congratulate, ingratiate, ingratitude*; *ex gratia* (**as a favor**, with no legal obligation); *grace, gracile, gracious*. *Gratis*: **free**, **without charge**. Spanish *gracias* (**thank you**).

Horde is from Turkish *ordu*, **camp**, **army**. Centuries ago, the army of the Turkish Mongols swept across Asia, moving into countries in great numbers to defeat the local inhabitants. *Horde* has come to mean "a large number of people on the move." SYNONYMS: crowd, mob, multitude, swarm. See related *Urdu*, p. 167.

In medieval times, *falsehood* referred to an uneducated or lay person wearing the hood of the medical profession; has come to mean an untruth, a lie. *No falsehood can endure the Touch of celestial temper*. John Milton.

Lacuna, **ditch**, **hole**, **pool**, designates a space where something has been omitted or has come out; **gap**; **hiatus**; especially a missing portion in a manuscript, text, etc. In *anatomy* and *biology*, a space, cavity, or depression; specifically, any of the small osseous (bony) cavities that are filled with bone cells. *Lacunar*, an architectural term, designates a ceiling made up of sunken panels. *Lagoon*, a shallow lake or pond, comes from the same source.

Tora, Japanese for **tiger**, was the war cry of the Japanese attackers of Pearl Harbor. The 1970 movie *Tora! Tora! Tora!* dramatized the Japanese attack on Pearl Harbor and the series of American blunders that allowed it to happen.

Word from a literary character: *gargantuan*, **gigantic**, **enormous**; from *Gargantua*, a giant king, noted for his size and prodigious feats and appetite; the main character of *Gargantua*, a *satire* by François Rabelais (1552). See more on *satire*, p. 172, and under *tetralogy*, p. 162. Compare *Brobdingnagian*, p. 144.

Word Cluster No. 27

cube	cubic	cubicular	cubiculum	cubicle	cubism
cubit	cubital	cubitiere	cubitus	incubate	incubus
succubus	cuboid	concubine	cubomancy	cubiform	cuboctohedron

accumbent   decumbent   incumbent   procumbent   recumbent   succumb

Common elements_____**Inferred Meaning**_____

Romance Cognates	French	Romanian	Italian	Portuguese	Spanish
	cube	cuib (nest)	cubo	cubo	cubo

Words with disguised Latin roots: couvade (see **Clavis**), covey, hive (of bees)

Latin term: *cubiculum hospitale*: **guest room**

Prescription term: *hora decubitus*, abbreviated *hor. decub.*: **at bedtime**

Spanish proverb: *Quien te cubre te descubre*: **Whoever covers you discovers you.**

NB: Neither *cucumber* nor *encumber* is in this family. There is also a tropical American shrub, *cube*, pronounced kyoo BAY, which is probably *not* related to this root.

German *liegen*, **to lie down**: *Es liegt an Ihnen*: **It depends on you**; *so viel es an mir liegt*: **as far as I am concerned.**

wordextras

In Spanish, *Wednesday* is *miércoles*, from *Mercury*, the messenger of the gods in Roman mythology. *Monday*, in Spanish, is *lunes*, from *luna*, **moon**, the base of *lunatic*; *moon* is also the base of English *Monday* or *Moonday*, from Anglo-Saxon *monandaeg*, **moon day**. The second day was sacred to Luna, Roman goddess of the moon. In German, Monday is *Montag*; in Dutch, *maandag*, both **moon day**. See p. 113 for English *Wednesday*, **Woden's Day.**

Arabic *nadir*, **opposite the zenith** (see p. 49), is that point in the celestial sphere directly opposite the zenith and directly below the observer. Also, **one's low point**; time of one's greatest depression.

Proxy, **one who acts for another**, from Latin *procurator*, **one who takes care of**, is one who is employed to manage the affairs of another. Also, a person authorized to act for another; agent or substitute.

Ambush, from Old French *embuschier*, **in the bushes**, originally indicated lying in the bushes waiting to attack. As a *verb*, **to hide in ambush**; to attack from ambush. In Latin, *ambush* was *imboscare*. Spanish: *bosque*, wood of a forest.

Hindi has contributed a number of words to the English languages, including the following: *bandanna* (see p. 85), *bangle*, *bungalow* (from *bangla*, **a thatched house**; in the manner of the "Bengalese"), *cashmere, cheetah, chintz, chit, chutney, coolie, copra, cot, cummerbund, curry, dinghy, dungaree* (see p. 97), *guru, juggernaut* (see p. 149), *jungle, khaki, kismet, loot, mogul, mongoose* (see p. 45), *nabob, nirvana, pajamas* (see p. 151), *pariah, pundit, sahib, sari, seersucker* (*sirsakar*, **milk and sugar**), *shampoo* (see p. 184), *toddy, swami, yoga.*

Cincinnati, Ohio, is named in honor of *Cincinnatus*, who left his plow to become dictator of Rome. An American organization of former officers of the Revolutionary War took for themselves the plural of this name; it is from this organization's name that the city was named.

Nullity, from Latin *nullus*, **none**, is the condition of being null; futility; nothingness; a mere nothing.

Little Rock, capital of Arkansas, is so named after a rocky promontory in the Arkansas River. At 1450 miles, it is the fourth longest river in the United States, flowing through Colorado, Kansas, Oklahoma, and Arkansas.

Italian *pesto*, a sauce of ground fresh basil and garlic mixed with olive oil, and used especially over pasta, is from Latin *pinsere*, **to pound**. *Pestle*, as in *pestle and mortar*, is from *pinsere* as well.

An exalted aphorism: *Members of an avian species of identical plumage congregate*. **Birds of a feather flock together.** An interpretation: Those of like interests often form their own circles, cliques, or coteries.

A Writing Tip: The subordinating conjunction *while* is sometimes carelessly used in the sense of *and* or *but* [two of the seven *coordinating* conjunctions: for, nor, or, so, yet], thus creating false subordination. **Faulty**: My brother wants to study law *while* I want to study biology. **Corrected**: My brother wants to study law, *and* I want to study biology. [or] My brother wants to study law, *but* I want to study biology.

Common element base: cubare

Meaning: to lie down

IE base: *ker-²*: **to bend**, **curve**, yielding such diverse words as *kyphosis, vertebra, howitzer* (see p. 101), *height*.

German: *liegen*, **to lie down**, **rest**, **repose**, **be recumbent**, **lodge**

Clavis

cubism:	an artistic movement in France beginning in 1907 that featured **cubes** and surfaces of geometrical planes; abstract art. So called from a remark by Henri Matisse (1869-1954), who referred to the predominant "small cubes" in a painting by Georges Braque (1882-1963).
cubit:	during Roman times, the elbow (on which one **lies**) when reclining; an ancient unit of linear measure, originally equal to the length of the arm from the tip of the middle finger to the elbow—usually from 17 to 22 inches. See more on *elbow*; also, *akimbo*, p. 71.
accumbent:	*ac-*, assimilation of *ad-*, **to**, **toward**; **lying to**; lying down; in *botany*, **lying against some other part**: said especially of certain cotyledons (first leaves of a plant).
decumbent:	*de-*, **down**; **lying down**; lying on the ground, as if too weak to stand; in *botany*, **trailing on the ground**, and rising at the tip, as some stems.
incumbent:	*in-*, **on**; **lying**, **leaning**, or **resting upon** something else; imposed as an obligation or duty; required; obligatory; as a *noun*, one holding a specified office or ecclesiastical benefice.
procumbent:	*pro-*, **forward**; **lying face down**; prone; in *botany*, trailing along the ground without rooting: said of a stem, or a vine.
recumbent:	*re-*, **back**, **down**; **lying down**; resting; idle; in *biology*, designating a part that leans or lies upon some other part or surface.
concubine:	*con-*, **with, together**; **to lie down with**; a mistress. In *law*, *concubine* has a specialized meaning.
incubus:	*in-*, **in**, **upon**; **to lie down upon**; in medieval times, a demon thought to lie upon sleeping persons, especially women, with whom the demon sought sexual intercourse; now any **oppresssively heavy burden**, as "the incubus of his defect." Also, a *nightmare* (see p. 132, **IE base**).
cuboctohedron:	one of the thirteen Archimedean solids having as faces six equal squares and eight equal regular triangles; the solid is formed by cutting off the corners of the **cube**. *Oct-*, as in *octagon*, *octamerous*, *octopus*, and *October*, **eight**; *October* was the eighth month in the Roman calendar (see p. 165).
cubomancy:	*–mancy*, **divination**; **divination using dice**. Other words with *–mancy*: *chartomancy*, *chiromancy*, **palm reading**; *geomancy*, *necromancy*, *oneiromancy*, *pyromancy*, *rhabdomancy*.
couvade:	**a hatching**; from French *couver*, **to hatch**; **to sit upon eggs**; a practice among certain primitive people in which the husband of the woman in delivery takes to his bed as if he himself were bearing the child, submitting himself to fasting, purification, and certain taboos. *Couvrir*, **to cover**, from *cubare*, also yields *curfew* and *kerchief* (see both on p. 32 under *kerchief*).
kyphosis:	from *kuphos*, **bent** + *osis*, **condition**; abnormal bending or curving of the spine, with rearward convexity; **hunchbacked**, or Pott's curvature.

wordextras

In the song "Begin the Beguine," *beguine* is a rhythmic dance of Martinique, whose music has been popularized in the U.S. Capitalized, *Beguine*, meaning **beggar**, is a sisterhood that began in the Low Countries (Belgium, the Netherlands, Luxembourg) in the 12th century. See Benelux, p. 81.

Banshee, from Old Irish *bean*, **woman** + *sidhe*, **fairy**, meant **woman of the fairies**. In Irish and Scottish folklore, a *banshee* was a spirit in the form of a woman whose appearance and mournful wailing under the windows of a house was a sign that a loved one in that house would soon die; thus, the phrase "screaming like a banshee."

Escalator®, a trademark, is probably from French *escalade*, **climbing** + *elevator* (see p. 112). *Escalate*, a back-formation of *escalator* is "to increase, enlarge, or intensify," especially a war.

Celsius, the temperature scale whose boiling point is 100° and whose freezing point is 0°, is named after its inventor, Anders Celsius (1701-1744), a Swedish astronomer. See *Fahrenheit*, p. 56.

Latin law phrases: culpa levis; culpa levis in concreto; culpa levis in abstracto; culpa levissima; culpa lata; mea culpa; ad vitam aut culpam

Other Latin phrases: *Culpam poena premit comes*, **Punishment presses hard upon the heels of crime**. Horace
Felix culpa! **O fault most fortunate!** St. Augustine, in alluding to the fall of Adam and Eve, and the consequent coming of Jesus, the Redeemer.

Similar root: *menda*, **defect, error, flaw**: **mend**, **mend**acious (**not truthful; lying or false**), **mend**acity (**a lie; falsehood**), **mend**icant (**asking for alms; begging**); a**mend**, a**mend**ment, a**mend**s, e**mend**, e**mend**ate.

NB: *Inculcate* is not in this family (see **Clavis** note). Neither is *culpeo*, a South American animal resembling a dog.

German equivalents: *Schuld*, **guilt**, and *Tadel*, **fault**.
Phrases with *Schuld*: *eine Schuld abtragen*: **to pay off a debt**; *einem die Schuld geben*: **to lay the blame on someone**; *schuldvoll*: **full of guilt**; guilty.
Phrases with *Tadel*: *an einem keinen Tadel finden*: **to be unable to find fault with a person**; *ohne Tadel*: **blameless**

wordextras

Vandal is from *the Vandals*, a Germanic tribe that overran Gaul, Spain, and North Africa and sacked Rome in A.D. 455. Note *sack*, below. *Vandalism* is the malicious or ignorant destruction of public or private property, especially of that which is beautiful or artistic; *to vandalize* is to destroy or damage public property maliciously.

Sack, as in *sacking the quarterback* and in *sacking a captured city*, is from Italian *sacco*, **to plunder**, from *sack* or *bag*. In ancient times, vandals and plunderers physically "sacked" their loot; figuratively, the linebacker attempts *to sack his booty*, the quarterback. See *booty*, p. 9.

Halibut, originally *halybutte* in Middle English, means **holy flatfish**, from its being eaten on holy days.

Cockroach is the English spelling and pronunciation of Spanish *cucaracha*.

Middle English *scaffold* is from French *catafalque*, from *cata-*, **down** + *fala*, **wooden siege tower**. *Catafalque* is a raised structure on which the body of a deceased person lies in state; *scaffold* can mean either a temporary structure for holding workmen and materials during construction, or an elevated platform on which a criminal is hanged.

Latin *remuneration*, from *re-*, **back, again**, + *munus*, **gift**, is the "act of giving back," in the sense of "compensating, paying, recompensing, rewarding." *Munificent* is from the same root; see p. 19.

To rake over the coals means "to criticize sharply; censure; scold."

Scion, from Old English *kith*, **sprig**, is a shoot or bud of a plant, especially one for planting or grafting; also, a descendant; offspring. Pronounced SIGH un.

Agnostic, from *a-*, **negative** + *gnosis*, **knowledge**, is one who believes that the human mind cannot know whether there is a God or an ultimate cause, or anything beyond material phenomena. An *atheist*, from *a-*, **negative** + *theos*, **God**, denies the existence of God.

Disparage, from Old French *desparagier*, originally meant "to marry one of inferior rank," or "below one's par." It has come to mean "to lower in esteem; discredit; also, to speak slightingly of; show disrespect for; belittle," as *to disparage another's achievements*.

Motto of the State of Alabama: *Audemus jura nostra defendere*: **We dare to defend our rights**.

Word from a person's name: *bowdlerize*, **to expurgate**; after Thomas Bowdler (1754-1825), English editor who, in 1818, published an *expurgated* Shakespeare. *Expurgate* means to purge or remove passages considered obscene or otherwise objectionable from a book. Thomas Jefferson *expurgated* the New Testament of the miracles of Jesus.

Common element base: culpa
IE base: *mend-*: **a flaw**, **a shortcoming**; **physical defect**

Meaning: guilt, fault, blame; also, misbehavior

Clavis

culpable:
deserving **blame**; blameworthy. *If he acts according to the best reason he hath, he is not* **culpable**, *though he be mistaken in his measures.* William Sharp, pseudonym of Fiona Macleod (1855-1905).

culpatory:
from *culpatus*, past participle of *culpare*, **to blame**. Synonyms: accusing, censorious.

culprit:
contraction of <u>culpable</u>, <u>prit</u> *a averer nostre bille*, **Guilty**, **ready to prove our case**: opening words spoken by the prosecutor in a Roman court; in present usage, the person accused of a crime or offense, as in court; an offender.

exculpate:
ex-, **out**; **to free from blame**; declare or prove guiltless; *inculpate*: **to impute blame**; charge, or incriminate; *inculpatory*: describing the facts that tend to establish **guilt**, as in *inculpatory evidence*.

culpa levis:
levis, **light**; **light** (as of weight) or **ordinary negligence**; excusable neglect as opposed to *culpa lata*, **gross negligence**. *Levis* is also found in *levitate, levitation, elevate, elevator*.

mea culpa:
I am guilty. It is my fault, as "He pleaded *mea culpa* to the charge." Pronounced: MAY ah KOOL pah.

amend:
and *emend* are from Old French *amender*; ultimately from Latin *emendare*, **to correct**. *Amend* means "to change or revise, as a legislative bill, law, constitution," whereas *emend* means "to correct," as a scholarly text.

emend:
ex-, **out**; **to take flaws out**; to make scholarly corrections or improvements in a text. *Emendate*: same as *emend*; *emendation*: the act of emending. Note difference in *amend* and *emend*.

mendacious:
lying, untruthful; from *mendacis*, genitive of *mendax*; describing that which has a **flaw**, whence *emend*, **to correct a fault** (see previous entry). *Mendicant*, **a beggar**, **one who has a flaw**, from the same root as *amend*. *Mendacity* is the quality or state of being *mendacious*; a falsehood (see *falsehood*, p. 52).

inculcate:
not in this family, but included because of its orthographic similarity to *inculpate*; *in-* + *calx*, **heel of foot**; **to trample in, to impress upon**, as *the inculcation of honesty*. *Calx* is also the base of <u>recalcitrant</u>, **kicking back** (as of a mule); hard to handle or deal with; refusing to obey. (In different dictionaries, check the origin of *causeway* for relationship to *calx*.)

ad vitam aut culpam: **for life or until misbehavior**; during good behavior; equivalent to *quamdiu bene se gesserit*: **so long as he conducts himself well**.

---

wordextras

Chinese *ke-tsiap* is transliterated **ketchup** (also, *catsup*), originally, **spiced fish sauce**.

With Latin *pre-*, **before**, *precocious*, from a verb that means **to cook beforehand**, came to mean "ripening prematurely"; in *botany*, blossoming before the leaves sprout. See *apricot* and *cuisine*, p. 127; see *fugacious*. p. 86.

Arrant, from Latin *errare*, **to wander**, or **to go stray**, means "notorious, egregious, unmitigated," as *the arrant luxury of a cruise ship*; *an arrant fool*; *an arrant liar*. We are *arrant* knaves, all; believe none of us. Shakespeare

Russian has contributed many words to the English language, including *borsch* (**beet soup**, but originally from *parsnip*, or *turnip*, the original ingredient); *borzoi* (**swift**, and designating a particular breed of swift dog); *mammoth*; *parka* (originally, **animal skin**; see p. 8); *samovar* (**self-boiler**; see p. 123).

Fahrenheit, the temperature scale with a boiling point of 212° and a freezing point of 32°, was developed by Gabriel Daniel Fahrenheit (1686-1736), a German physicist resident in Holland. See *Celsius*, p. 54.

Altruism, **selflessness**, **devotion to the cause of others**, is from Latin *alter*, **another**; in *biology*, behavior by an animal that is not beneficial, or may be harmful, to itself but that benefits others of its species. Opposed to *egoism*.

Mai tai, Tahitian for **good**, is a cocktail made with rum and fruit juices, often garnished with pineapple or other fruit or with a tiny orchid. Pronounced: MY TY (equal stress).

Whisk, from Old Norse *visk*, originally referred to a **wisp**, and came to mean **brush**, **broom**.

Word from a person's name: *chauvinism*, blind enthusiasm for military glory; from Nicolas Chauvin, a legendary French soldier extremely devoted to Napoleon I, and notorious for his attachment to the lost imperial cause.

Word Cluster No. 29

decane	decurion	decanal	decigram	deciliter
decuple	decistere	decade	decimate	decibel
Decembrist	decare	decile	deciare	decimeter
December	decennium	duodecimo	decimal	decurion
decemvir	decennary	decussate		
decapod	decastere	Decameron	decagram	decagon
Decalogue	Decapolis	decathlon	decaliter	decahedron
decanormal	decastyle	decasyllabic	decacanth	decadrachm

Common elements_____**Inferred Meaning**_____

Romance Cognates	French	Romanian	Italian	Portuguese	Spanish
	dix	zece*	dieci	dez	diez

*The *z* is an influence of the Dacian language. Dacia, an ancient kingdom, and later a Roman province, approximates the area of modern Romania. See p. 103.

Words with disguised Latin roots: dean, denarius, denary, dicker, dime, doyen, dozen, duodenal

German: *zehn*, **ten**: *Zehnender*: **a stag of ten points**; *Zehner*: wine of the year **1910**; **soldier of the Tenth Regiment**; *in den Zehnern stehen*: **to be in one's teens.**

Russian: *dessiatine*, originally, **a tithe**; a unit of land measure equal to about 2.7 acres

> **Quote**: It is my experience that the short path to the simple and precise English needed by a man of science lies through the tongues of Homer, Horace, and Virgil. Henry Crew

wordbuilder #26

Latin roots *flect-, flex-*, from *flectere*, **to bend, curve**, yields respectively **flect**ion; circum**flect**, de**flect**, in**flect**, re**flect**; re**flect**ance; in**flect**ion, re**flect**ion; re**flect**or; genu**flect***; **flex**, **flex**ible, **flex**ile, **flex**ion (in *anatomy*, the bending of a joint or limb by contraction of *flexor* muscles), **flex**uous (winding or wavering), **flex**ure (a bending, curving, or flexing, as of a heavy object under its own weight); circum**flex**, re**flex**; dorsi**flexion**, in**flexion**; re**flex**ive. *Genuflect*, **to bend the knee**, as in reverence or worship, can also mean to act in a submissive or servile way.

wordextras

Retreat, from *retract*, **to pull back**, is used as both a noun and a verb. As a *noun*, a withdrawal to a safe place or from a dangerous situation, as from the forward line of battle; also, an organized group withdrawal from regular activities, as for religious contemplation. In the military, *retreat* is both a bugle call and a ceremony to mark the lowering of the National flag at sunset; as a *verb*, **to move back**. *Retreat* and *retract* are from *re-*, **back** + *trahere*, **to draw**, **pull**. NOUN SYNONYMS: cover, refuge, sanctuary, shelter; VERB SYNONYMS: ebb, recede, retract, retrograde.

Saturday—in Latin, *Saturni dies*, or **Saturn's Day**—translates Greek *hemera Khronu*, **Cronus' Day.**

Elite, the choicest, finest, best, most distinguished, or most powerful of anything considered collectively, is from the same Latin base as *elect*, that is, *electus*, past participle of *eligere*, **to pick out**, or **to select**. Only *elite* soldiers are granted the honor of guarding the Tomb of the Unknowns. *Elite* also designates a size of type for typewriters.

Bath Mitzvah, pronounced bat MITZ vuh, is Hebrew for "daughter of the (divine) law." In the Jewish faith, *Bath Mitzvah* is a ceremony for a 12-year-old girl, marking her acceptance of religious duties and responsibilities. See p. 165 for *Bar Mitzvah*, a similar ceremony for a 13-year-old boy.

Altricial, from *alere*, **to feed**, describes birds whose newly hatched young are helpless and are not mature enough to fly or search for their own food. Baby birds are also described as *nidicolous* (*nidus*, **nest** + *colere*, **to dwell**). See p. 86.

A *milliner*, originally, **inhabitant of Milan**, Italy, is one who designs, makes, trims, or sells women's hats.

Fasciate, from Latin *fascia*, **a band**, **sash**, means "bound with a band or filet." In *botany*, abnormally enlarged and flattened, as some plant stems. In *zoology*, marked by broad colored bands, as of certain insects. See *fascia*, p. 5.

Common element base: decem   **Meaning**: ten (*deci-*, tenth)
IE base: *dekm*: yields **Greek** *deka* and **Latin** *decem*, as well as *centum* (**100**), as in **cent**ennial, **centi**pede*, **cent**ury, **cent**urion; **centi-**, **100**th: **centi**me, **centi**grade (see *Celsius*, p. 54), **centi**gram, **centi**liter, **centi**meter, **centi**poise, **centi**stoke. *Centi- can also mean **100**, as in *centipede*, the only known word with this particular construction.

Clavis

December: the **tenth** month in the Roman calendar. The months of September (**seventh**), October (**eighth**), and November (**ninth**) are also known by their numerical prefixes; July and August were also similarly known before they were renamed for the caesars Julius and Augustus. See p. 165 under **wordextras**.

decemvir: **ten men**; one of a body of ten Roman magistrates; especially, a member of one of the two such bodies appointed in 451 and 450 B.C. to draw up a code of laws. Pronunciation: dee SEM vir.

decimate: from *decimus*, **tenth**; originally, to kill a **tenth** of the people; now usually the obliteration of almost everyone; semantic shift from specific to general.

decibel: abbreviated **db**; *bel*, from Alexander Graham Bell (1847-1922), inventor of the telephone; a unit that expresses the relative difference in power between two different acoustic or electric signal levels; usually equal to **ten** times the common logarithm of the ratio of the two levels; it is sometimes necessary to use 20 times the common logarithm.

decussate: to cross or cut so as to form an **X**, the Roman numeral for **ten**; **intersect**. See p. 6, under *ambulatorial*.

dean: from *decanus*, a person who was head of a group of **ten** men—probably first, soldiers; then, monks; and later, college students. The adjective describing the office of a dean is *decanal*. Explore the relationship between *dean* and *tithingman*, the chief of a *frankpledge*, consisting of ten families.

dime: from Latin *decima pars*, **tenth part**; then Middle English *disma* for Old English *tithe*; both *tenth* and *tithe* are from earlier Anglo-Saxon *teoth*; in addition to a *tithe* being the first **tenth** of one's income given to the church, it also referred to a unit of civil administration, originally consisting of a frankpledge, or ten families. See *frankpledge* and *tithingman*, previous entry.

dicker: from *decuria*, **a set of ten**, especially of animal hides for trading; now, to bargain or barter, especially over trifles. In *politics*, to make a deal by bargaining.

duodenum: *duo*, **two** + *den*, **ten** = **twelve**; a section of the small intestine the ancient Roman physicians estimated to be the length of the breadth of *twelve* fingers. The adjective is *duodenal*. See *dozen*, p. 20.

decathlon: Greek *athlon*, **award**, **prize**, as in *athlete*; from *athlein*, **to contest for a prize**; a **ten-event** athletic contest consisting of various distances of runs; hurdles; javelin and discus throws; shot put; pole vault; and jumps. *Athlon* is similar to *agon*, **struggle**, **contest**, as in **agon**, **agon**y, antagonist, and protagonist.

Decameron: Greek *hemera*, **day**; **ten days**; a collection of a hundred tales (published 1353) by Giovanni Boccaccio (1313-1375), presented as stories told by a group of Florentines to while away **ten** days during a plague.

Decalogue: Greek *logos*, **word**; **Ten Words**, or the *Ten Commandments*, recorded first in Exodus 20, and later in Deuteronomy. *Deuteronomy*, literally, **second law**, gives a second iteration of the original laws.

Decapolis: Greek *polis*, **city**; an ancient region in northeast Palestine, mostly east of the Jordan, occupied by a confederation of **ten cities**.

decastyle: Greek *style*, **column**; an architectural term for **ten columns** across the front of a building. Other types of architecture with *–style* are as follows: amphipro**style** (having columns at the front and back, but none along the sides), epi**style** (the same as *architrave*), hypo**style**, peri**style**, and pro**style**.

wordextras
Fido, formerly a common name for a dog, is from Latin *fidere*, **to trust, to have faith in**. See **Word Cluster No. 40**.

Askance, pronounced uh SKANS, is perhaps from Vulgar Latin *quam si*, **how if**; its meaning is influenced by Dutch *schuin*, **sidewise**. The word, an adverb, can mean "with a sidewise glance," or "with a look of suspicion or disapproval," as in "The professor looked at me *askance* when I asked her to raise my grade."

Mirabile dictu means **wonderful to tell**; the verb *mirari*, **to wonder at**, yields *miracle, miraculous, mirador* (from Spanish: a balcony, turret, etc. that affords a fine view), *mirage, mirror, admire; marvel*. Spanish: *mirar*, **to view**.

```
┌──────────────────────────────────────────────────────────────────────────────┐
│                         Word Cluster No. 30                                    │
│                                                                                │
│  deity        deify         deist          deistic        deific              │
│  deodar       deicide       deipotent      deodand        deification         │
│                                                                                │
│  Common elements_____Inferred Meaning_____│
│                                                                                │
└──────────────────────────────────────────────────────────────────────────────┘
```

Romance Cognates	French	Romanian	Italian	Portuguese	Spanish
	dieu	dumnezeu	dio	deus	dios

Words with disguised Latin roots: day, deuce (one meaning), divinity, drat, gossip, joss

Latin phrases: *Agnus Dei; Deus vobiscum; Dei gratia; Dei judicium; Deo volente; Deus ex machina*
Vox populi, vox Dei; Adjuvante Deo labor proficit; Lux est umbra Dei; Deus nobis fiducia
ad majorem Dei gloriam: **to the greater glory of God**. Motto of the Jesuits

Italian phrase: *Dio mio*, **dear me**!   **French words and phrases**: *prie-dieu; maison-dieu; adieu*

Spanish phrase: *Vaya con Dios*, **Go with God**, a parting prayer; also, a popular song of the 1950s

Motto of El Salvador: *Dios, Unión, Libertad*: **God, Union, Liberty**
Motto of the State of Arizona: *Ditat Deus*: **God enriches**.

Placename: Deovolente (**God willing**), Mississippi

Greek: *theos*, **god, God**: **theo**bromine, **theo**centric, **theo**cracy, **theo**cracy, **theo**dicy, **theo**gony, **theo**logy, **theo**phany, a**theo**ism, apo**theo**sis, pan**theo**ist, pan**theo**on, en**theo**usiasm (**having God within**). See pp. 42, 199 for other *theo-* words.

Proper Names (from *theos*): Timothy (**honoring God**); Dorothy, **Theo**dore (latter two names: **gift of God**)

German: *Gott*, as in *Gott befohlen!* **God be with you!** *Gott sei Dank!* **Thank God!**

---

wordextras

Free-lance, **a free agent**, especially a nonstaff writer who accepts commissions for special assignments, originally was a knight not in service to a feudal lord and who offered his services—and his lance—as a mercenary. *Free-lance* can also designate a person who contends in a cause without personal allegiance.

Berceuse, from French *bercer*, **to rock, lull to sleep**, is a lullaby, a cradlesong. It is also a piece of instrumental music with a rocking or lulling effect. *Berceuse* is from *berceau*, **cradle**, and ultimately from Vulgar Latin *bertium*, **woven basket**. Pronunciation: ber SOOZ.

Amp, the basic unit of electric intensity, is from André A<u>mp</u>ère (1775-1836), French mathematician and physicist.

Volt, the basic unit of electromotive force, is named after Conte Alessandro <u>Volt</u>a (1745-1827), Italian physicist, and a pioneer in the study of electricity.

Trade winds, denoting those winds that blow toward the equator from the northeast on the north side of the equator, and from the southeast on the south side, are so called from their "treading" or "tracking" in a path. Both *trade* and *tread* are from the IE base, *dra-*, **to run, to step**.

Jipijapa, from a place in Ecuador, is a plant of Central and South America, whose leaves yield a flexible, durable straw used for hats; **Panama hat**. Pronounced HEE pee HAH puh.

Ha-ha has an uncertain background; it means a **fence, wall**, etc., set in a ditch around a garden or park so as not to hide the view from within. *Ha-ha* is also written without the hyphen—**haha**.

Amenity, from Latin *amare*, **to love**, means a pleasant quality; attractiveness; anything that adds to a person's comfort. *Amenities*: the courteous acts and pleasant manners of polite social behavior.

Exquisite, **carefully sought out**, is from Latin *ex-*, **out** + *quaerere*, **to ask**. *Exquisite* means "carefully done or elaborately made," as *an exquisite wedding gown*; highly sensitive; keenly discriminating, as *an exquisite taste for French wines*, or *an exquisite ear for classical music*. SYNONYMS: choice, dainty, delicate, elegant, rare.

Motto of University of Indiana and of Yale University: *Lux et Veritas*: **Light and Truth**
Motto of the University of South Carolina: *Emollit mores nec sinit esse feros*: **Learning humanizes character and does not permit it to be unrefined** (or, **cruel**). Ovid, *Epistles to Pontus*, 2, 9, 48.
Motto of the State of New York: *Excelsior*: **Higher**.

Common element base: deus   **Meaning**: god, God
IE base: *deiw-*: the same base as *day*, and originally meant **to shine**, is found in *sky, heaven, god.*

Clavis

deification: with *ficare*, **to make**, the philosophy that when one dies, the soul is absorbed into **God**; also, the act of making (something) **a god**; *deify*, **to make into a god**, as *to deify money.*

deism: a natural religion based on human reason and morality, and on rejection of supernatural intervention in the conduct and affairs of mortal beings. *Deism* affected the writings of Thomas Jefferson, Benjamin Franklin, and Thomas Paine, writer of *Common Sense*. Jefferson, in fact, expurgated the New Testament of the miracles performed by Jesus. See *bowdlerism*, p. 55.

adeus: *adieu* and *adiós*, Portuguese, French, and Spanish, respectively, meaning **to God**: equivalent of *goodbye*, or God be with ye. See Italian *ciao*, **your slave**, p. 181.

deus ex machina: a transliteration of Greek *theos ek mekhanes*, **God from a machine**; in Greek and Roman drama, a god mechanically lowered onto the stage to resolve the conflict; the *denouement*, **untying the knot**. As a dramatist, Euripides employed this technique; Abrams notes that novelists have used this technique as well, for example, Charles Dickens in *Oliver Twist*, and Thomas Hardy in *Tess of the d'Urbervilles*. Pronounced: DAY uh eks MAH kee nuh.

eudiometer: Greek *eu*, **good** + *dios*, from *Zeus*, **god of the sky**; originally, an instrument for measuring the amount of oxygen in the air; now, an instrument for measuring and analyzing gases.

theobromine: Greek *broma*, **food**; **food for the gods**. A genus of trees of the chocolate family; its leaves and seeds are used both as a diuretic and as a stimulant. See *nectar and ambrosia*, **food of the gods**, p. 194.

enthusiasm: **in God**; possession by a god; inspiration. The adjectival form is *enthusiastic*. See p. 199.

pantheism: *pan-*, **all**; the doctrine that *God* is not a personality, but that all laws, forces, manifestations, etc. of the universe *are* God; the belief that God and the universe are one and the same.

apotheosis: *apo-*, **from**, **away**; the act of raising a person to the status of a **god**; attributing divinity to a human being; deification; the glorification of a person or thing; a glorified ideal, as *the apotheosis of a fair trade policy*. Pronounced: uh PAHTH ee OH sis; or, AP uh THEE uh sis.

wordextras

Magazine, from Arabic *makhzan*, **storehouse**, can designate a storage depot, a supply chamber for rounds in a rifle, space in a camera for holding film, as well as a periodical with a storehouse of information. There is *Magazine*, as well as *Magazine Mountain*, in Arkansas. Greek *thesaurus*, **a treasure, collection**, is a treasury or a storehouse, as of words, synonyms, stories. For more on *thesaurus*, see p. 77.

The computer term *bit* coalesces <u>bi</u>nary + dig<u>it</u>; a bit is equivalent to 0 (zero) or 1 (one).

Baud, from J. M. E. <u>Baud</u>ot (1845-1903), French telegrapher and inventor, who improved the speed of telegraphic transmission, is a variable unit of computer data transmission speed, equal to one bit per second. See *bit*, above.

Halitosis, from Latin *halitus*, **breath** + *osis*, **bad condition**, means "bad breath." *Exhale, inhale* are also from *halitus*.

Pidgin, a simplified form of speech, usually a mixture of two or more languages, probably represents the Chinese pronunciation of *business*.

Embarrass, from Italian *imbarrare*, **to bar**, **impede**, means to cause to feel self-conscious, confused, or ill at ease. SYNONYMS: abash, discomfit, disconcert, faze, rattle. [There are two r's and two s's in *emba<u>rrass</u>*.]

The *Bernoulli* removable computer cartridge, manufactured by Omega, and based on the principles of fluid dynamics, is named after Swiss scientist Daniel Bernoulli (1700-1782). Much of Bernoulli's work in fluid dynamics has been codified in "the Bernoulli effect," the phenomenon of internal pressure reduction with increased steam velocity in a fluid. *This work as well as a number of related files was originally stored on a single 20-megabyte Bernoulli cartridge*. It now stores easily on a smaller-size 250-megabyte Iomega® Zip disk.

Fibonacci, a 13th-century Italian mathematician, developed what is now called the *Fibonacci series*, a sequence of integers in which each integer after the second is the sum of the two preceding ones, e.g., 1, 1, 2, 3, 5, 8, 13, 21, 34, 55, etc. This pattern of numbers has been observed in such diverse entities as beehives, sea shells, pine cones, leaf arrangements, and branching plants. There are many sites on the Internet devoted to Fibonacci numbers.

Sectional Word Cluster Test

INSTRUCTIONS: For each set of words from Latin and Greek (and sometimes, French, Spanish, and German), write the common meaning in the blank.

Example: **hypo**tenuse, **hypo**thesis, **sub**ject   <u>under</u>

	Presection Answer	Postsection Answer
31. eu**demon**, **demono**logic, pan**demon**ium	_____	_____
32. **denti**loquy, mast**odont**, orth**odont**ist, **dan**delion	_____	_____
33. **dict**ionary, e**dict**, pre**dict**, ver**dict**, bene**dict**ion	_____	_____
34. **dia**ry, sine **die**, circa**dian**, carpe **diem**	_____	_____
35. **dis**ease, **dis**criminate, **des**sert, **di**mension	_____	_____
36. con**dole**ment, in**dol**ent, **dolori**fuge, an**alge**sic	_____	_____
37. **don**ation, par**don**, con**done**, e**diti**on, ren**diti**on	_____	_____
38. **equi**lateral, **equi**nox, **egal**itarian, **Ecua**dor	_____	_____
39. **fab**le, in**fant**, in**fant**ry, pro**phet**, dys**phas**ia	_____	_____
40. af**fid**avit, con**fide**, con**fid**ant, con**fid**ent	_____	_____

                                                    _____   _____
                                                    Presection Score   Postsection Score

Note: Enter scores for this test and the following ones after completing this section; then, enter them on p. xvii.

Sectional Wordbuilder Test

Throughout the book and as a supplement, there are wordbuilders; these wordbuilders are designed to help you build a family of words from a single root.

	Presection Answer	Postsection Answer
27. What is the meaning of *fac-*, *fic-* as in **fac**tory, dif**fic**ult?	_____	_____
28. What is the meaning of *fig-*, *fic-* as in **fig**ment, **fic**tion?	_____	_____

_____   _____
Presection Score   Postsection Score

After entering the scores here, enter them on pp. xviii.

```
┌─────────────────────────────────────────────────────────────────────────────┐
│                        Word Cluster No. 31                                    │
│                                                                               │
│   demon            demoniac          demonology         pandemonium           │
│   demonolatry      demonomania       demonize           demonologic           │
│   eudemon         eudemonia          demonian           demonophobia          │
│                                                                               │
│  Common element_____Inferred Meaning_____   │
└─────────────────────────────────────────────────────────────────────────────┘
```

Romance Cognates	French démon	Romanian diavol-drac	Italian demone	Portuguese demônio	Spanish demonio

Latin phrases: *diaboli advocatus; diabolus in musica*

Italian phrases: *Fra diavolo* (**Brother Devil**, 1760-1806, born Peter Pezza); *aver un diavolo per capello*

French words and phrases: *diable*, flavored with hot spices, as *sauce diable*
C'est là le diable: **There is the devil**. There's the rub. *C'est un pauvre diable*: **He's a poor devil**.
diable à quatre: **the devil to pay**; uproar; rumpus
avoir le diable au corps; *la beauté du diable* (see **Clavis**)

NB: *Diabolo*, a toy, is not in this family, though it is often associated with Italian *diavolo*.

German: *Teufel*, as in *Den Teufel an die Wand malen*. (See **Clavis**.)

wordbuilder #27

Latin *facere*, **to do, make**, yields **faç**ade, **fac**et, **fac**ile, **fac**ilitate, **fac**ulty; **fac**simile; **fact**, **fact**icity, **fact**ion, **fact**itious, **fact**itive, **fact**ual, **fact**ure; **fact**otum (*fact* + *totum*, **all**); bene**factor**, male**factor**; cale**factory**, ol**factory**; manu**fact**ure; af**fect**, con**fect**, de**fect**, ef**fect**, in**fect**, per**fect**, pre**fect**; con**fect**ion, re**fect**ion; re**fect**ory; bene**fic**iary, dif**fic**ult, arti**fic**ial; bene**fit**, pro**fit**; **feas**ible; **fet**ish; counter**feit**, sur**feit**; **feat**, **feat**ure; de**feat**; par**fait**; confetti (originally, **sweetmeat**); doublets: fashion:faction; aficionado (see p. 163, under **wordextras**); *deficit*: **There is lacking**. There are many other words from *facere*, e.g., -**fact**ion, satis**fact**ion; -**fic**ation, grati**fic**ation; -**fic**ient, ef**fic**ient, suf**fic**ient.

wordextras

French ***reveille***, from Latin *re-*, **again** + *vigilare*, **to watch**, is a trumpet call to awaken soldiers and sailors; also, the first formation of the day in the military. *Vigil, vigilant, vigilante, invigilate, surveillance* are also from *vigilare*.

Celtic ***crag*** is a steep, rugged rock that rises above others or projects from a rock mass; note the cognates in Welsh *craig*, Irish *carraig*, Gaelic *creag*. The IE base is *kar-*, **hard**.

Doctor, from Latin *docere*, **to teach**, was originally "a teacher," and was applied to any learned man, evidenced by **Doctor of Laws, Doctor of Letters, Doctor of Philosophy**. It was not until the Middle Ages that *doctor* designated more particularly a *medical* doctor, **a physician**.

Caboose, from Middle Dutch *kabuys* or *kambuis*, originally meant **cabin house**; a ship's gallery.

Cookie, from Dutch *koekje*, a diminutive of *koek*, is akin to Norse *kaka*, English *cake*; also related to German *Kuchen*, **cake, pastry**; *Küche*, **kitchen**. *Kitchen* in Spanish is *la cocina*.

Parasite, from *para-*, **alongside** + *sitos*, **grain, food**, originally designated "one who eats at the table of another," and in ancient Greece, one who flattered and amused his host in return for free meals. See *plurivorous*, p. 154.

Beijing, the capital of China, is a combination of *bei* and *kin*, **northern capital**.

Chimney, from Latin *camera* and Greek *kaminos*, originally designated **a chamber for burning**. See p. 26.

German ***panzer***, **armor**, is ultimately from Latin *pantex*, **belly**, and designated a German armored vehicle, especially a particular tank used in World War II. From the Latin word is also *paunch*, a large, protruding belly; a potbelly.

Misandry (*misos*, **hatred** + *andros*, **man**) means **hatred of men**. ***Misogyny*** means **hatred of women**.

Polo, from a Tibetan dialectal variation of *pulu*, properly the name of the ball used in the game, is played on horseback by two teams of four players each. It is the favorite sport of Charles, Prince of Wales.

Acute, from Latin *acuere*, **to sharpen**, has various meanings: having a sharp point; keen or quick of mind, or wit; sensitive to impressions, as *acute hearing*; severe and sharp, as pain, jealousy; severe but of short duration, as *acute appendicitis*; also, less than 90°, as *acute* angles. *Acumen* and *ague* are also from *acuere*. See *ague*, p. 124.

Common element base: demon (daemon)　　　　　　　　　　　　　　　　　**Meaning**: evil spirit

In Greek, *daemon* meant **divine power**, thus *eudemonia*, under **Clavis**.

IE base: *da-*: **to divide**; yields *geodesy, eventide*, and **Greek** *demos*, **division of society**, and has come to mean **the people**, as in **demo***graphy,* **demo***cracy,* **en***demic,* **epi***demic,* **pan***demic* (see p. 205, Item 83). Though *demon* is now semantically related to *devil, devil* itself is from **Greek** *diaballein*, **to throw across**, and shares its root with *parable* (see p. 102), *emblem, parabola*, and *metabolism*, e.g., a *parable* is a story *thrown alongside* to illustrate a general truth. One of the most notable of Jesus' parables is that of *The Prodigal Son* (Luke 15:11-32). Nathan's parable of David's taking the one ewe lamb rebukes him for his illicit affair with Bathsheba (II Samuel 12:1-23).

Clavis

demoniac:　　as a *noun*, one who is possessed by a **demon**, such as the Gadarene demoniac, recorded in the *Synoptic Gospels*; as an *adjective*, arising or seeming to arise from possession by a demon; befitting or suggesting of a demon. **ADJECTIVAL SYNONYMS**: fiendish, frenzied. See more on the *Synoptics*, p. 142, under *synopsis*.

demonolatry:　　Greek *latrein*, **to worship; the worship of demons**. Other *–latry* words include *astrolatry* (**stars**), *bibliolatry* (**books**), *heliolatry* (**sun**), *iconolatry* (**icons**), *idolatry* (**idols**), *monolatry* (**self**), *necrolatry* (**the dead**), *ophiolatry* (**snakes**; see *ophicleide*, p. 1), *zoolatry* (**animals**).

demonomania:　　Greek *mania*, **madness**; delusion of being possessed by a **demon**. Other *–mania* words include *bibliomania* (**books**), *dipsomania* (**alcoholic drink**), *kleptomania* (**stealing**).

demonize:　　*–ize*, a verb-forming suffix; **to make into a demon**; to characterize or conceive of as evil, cruel, inhumane, as *to demonize one's enemies*; to bring under the influence of demons.

eudemonia:　　Greek *eu-*, **well, pleasant**; happiness resulting from an active, rational life. Here, *demon* means **spirit**. *Eudaemonism*: a theory that the highest ethical goal is happiness and personal well-being. See *eudemonia* in the *eu-*, **good, well, pleasant** family, p. 17.

pandemonium:　　Greek *pan-*, **all; the abode of all devils**; in Milton's *Paradise Lost*, the capital of Hell; in lower-case, a place or scene of wild disorder, uproar, or confusion. **SYNONYMS**: babel, bedlam (see p. 8), clamor, din, hubbub, hullabaloo, noise, racket.

diaboli advocatus:　　also, the reverse, *advocatus diaboli*, **devil's advocate**; in Roman Catholic Church theology, originally, an official selected to examine critically the facts and to raise objections in the case of a deceased person nominated for beatification or canonization. Also, one who pleads the unpopular side in an argument.

la beauté du diable: **the beauty of the devil**; the bloom and freshness of youth in a face not otherwise beautiful.

avoir le diable au corps: **to have the devil in one's body**: to be deliberately annoying.

Den Teufel an die Wand malen: **Speak of the devil and there he is.**

> **Quote**: Human destiny hinges upon the accuracy of thought transmission.
> Joseph G. Brin

wordextras

Starboard, literally, **steer board**, originally referring to the large oars on the **right side** of a medieval ship, has come to mean the right side of a ship or an airplane as one faces forward, toward the bow.

Invidious, from Latin *envy* (*invidere*, **to look askance at**), has only pejorative meanings: jealous, hateful, defamatory, obnoxious. *Webster's New World* says also "giving offense by discriminating unfairly," e.g., *invidious comparisons*.

Obsequious, from *ob-*, **toward** + *sequi*, **to follow**, originally meant **complying with**; **prompt, obedient, dutiful**. Through pejoration, it has come to mean **showing fawning attentiveness, sycophantic, servile, subservient**.

With Greek *okto*, **eight** + *pous*, **foot**, *octopus* is literally **eight feet**, but more like **arms**, or **legs**. There are three optional plural forms for *octopus*: octopuses, octopi, octopodes.

Biloxi, MS, was originally French *Bilocchy*, and was the name of an Indian people living in lower Mississippi.

Word Cluster No. 32

Latin

dental	**dent**ilation	**dent**inator	**dent**ion	**dent**ilingual
dentiloquy	**dent**iphone	**dent**ist	**dent**oid	**dent**iculate
dentifrice	**dent**igerous	**dent**ation	**dent**el	**dent**icle
dentelle	**dent**ures	**dent** corn	**dent**il	**dent**ilitis
dentellate	bi**dent**ate	**dent**ine	**dent**algia	**dent**ate
e**dent**ate	tri**dent**	in**dent**	in**dent**ured	

Greek

mega**dont**	ortho**dont**ics	**odont**osis	peri**odont**ist
mes**odont**	macr**odont**	**odont**oid	**odont**ophobia
mon**odont**	micr**odont**	**odont**itis	ex**odont**ia
cre**odont**	mast**odon**	**odont**oclast	end**odont**ics

Common elements_____**Inferred Meaning**_____

Romance Cognates	French	Romanian	Italian	Portuguese	Spanish
	dent	dinte	dente	dente	diente

Words with disguised roots: dandelion (see **Clavis**), redan (a double notching or jagging, as in the teeth of a saw)

Italian term: *al dente* (see **Clavis**)

French phrases: *prendre la lune avec les dents*: **to seize the moon with the teeth**: to aim at possibilities
prendre le mors aux dents: **to take the bit in the teeth**: to fly into a passion; apply oneself unrestrainedly; buckle down

German: *Zahn,* as in *Löwenzahn,* a calque, or literal translation, of French *dandelion*. See **Clavis**.

wordextras

With **re-**, **back**, **again** + *bursa*, **bag**, *reimburse* means **back into the purse**, or **pocket**. *Bursa* also yields **bursar (a college treasurer)**, **burs**ectomy, **burs**itis **(the inflammation of the bursae**, pouchlike cavities, especially those containing a fluid that reduces friction, between a tendon and the bone), **burs**iform, **burs**opathy, dis**burse**; purse.

The ***question mark*** (?) originated from *quaestio*, Latin for a *querying*, or *asking*, sentence. The first letter of *quaestio* was placed upside down and superimposed upon the last letter *o*; this mark was placed, as it is today, after a sentence asking a question. Over the years, the *q* lost part of its curve and the *o* became smaller, finally becoming a mere dot. In Spanish, an inverted question mark also *precedes* an interrogatory sentence.

Rhapsody is from Greek *rhapsoidos*, **one who strings songs together**; also, **a reciter of poetry**. In ancient Greece, also designated a part of an epic poem suitable for a single uninterrupted recitation; in *music*, an instrumental composition of free, irregular form, suggesting improvisation. See **wordbuilder #42**, p. 109.

Halloween coalesces *Hallowed evening*, the night before All Saints' Day on November 1. Prior to the Christianization of England, however, the Druids celebrated *All Witches' Day* on that date, the pagan New Year, when ghosts supposedly walked at midnight and witches rode to their covens on broomsticks. Although Christianity attempted to eradicate the witch festival by giving it a religious significance, little goblins, often dressed as witches and ghosts, still go from house to house on Halloween, looking for treats on the last night of October.

Shilly-shally, acting in a vacillating manner, is a reduplication of "Shall I or shall I not?"

Mediterranean is Latin for **middle of the land**. The *Mediterranean Sea* is squeezed in between Europe and Africa.

Croupier, **one who rides on the croup**, that is, the top of a horse's rump, originally was an inferior assistant. In charge of the gambling table, a *croupier* rakes in and pays out the money.

The Lord's Prayer uses mostly Anglo-Saxon words; *debt, trespass, temptation*, and *deliver* are from Latin. In Latin, "Our Father," the first words in the prayer, is *Paternoster*; in Latin itself, usually written *Pater Noster*.

Amorphous, from *a-*, **without** + *morphe*, **form**, means **shapeless**. In *biology*, without definite or specialized structure, as some lower forms of life; in *chemistry* and *mineralogy*, not crystalline. See p. 209, Item 124, for other words from *morphe*, e.g., **morpheme, morphosis, morphology**, allo**morph**, ecto**morph**, meso**morph**; ana**morph**ism.

Common element base: dens (genitive: dentis)   **Meaning**: tooth
IE base: *dent-*: **tooth**

Clavis

dentoid:
—*oid* (*eidos*, **shape, form**; thus, **similar to**), **tooth-shaped**. Other words with –*oid*: *anthropoid*, **man**; *asteroid*, **star**; *blastoid*, **bud, shoot**; *helicoid*, **helix: spiral**; *hominoid*, **man**; *hyaloid*, **glass**; *ichthyoid*, **fish**; *lipoid*, **fat**; *odontoid*, **tooth**; *ornithoid*, **bird**; *paranoid* (*nous*, **mind**); *phylloid*, **leaf**; *rhizoid*, **root**; *spheroid*, **sphere, globe** (see p. 111) *steroid*, **solid**; *toxoid*, **poison**; *trapezoid*, **table**.

indent:
in-, **in**; to make a **toothlike** incision into; an indented paragraph appears as though it were bitten into. *Paragraph*, **written alongside**, was the medieval scribe's indication (¶) in the margin, that is, **alongside the text**, that a new subject had been introduced. [*para-*, **beside** + *graphein*, **to write**]

indenture:
same basis as *indent*; the contract for an *indentured servant* was made in duplicate and then torn in half; the corresponding notched, or **toothed**, edges allowed for positive identification; the original of one half and the duplicate of the other were given each to the master and to the servant. Also, a format certificate, e.g., voucher, prepared for purposes of control.

dandelion:
and German *Löwenzahn*, **tooth of the lion**, from the fancied resemblance of the leaf's shape to a lion's tooth. It is not certain if the French and Germans arrived at the name independently, or if one is a calque, or literal translation, of the other.

Edentata:
e-, elision of *ex-*, **without**; **without teeth**; an order of mammals having only molars, or no teeth at all, for example, the armadillos, aardvarks, sloths. See p. 12 for more on *armadillo*.

dent corn:
Zea mays indentata, a variety of corn with kernels that are **indented** at the top.

al dente:
Italian; literally, **to the tooth**; firm to the bite; chewy: said especially of pasta.

odontochirugical:
pertaining to **dental surgery**; *chirugia*, Greek for **surgery**, is **to work by hand**. *Cheir*, **hand**, also yields *chiropractor*; both surgeons and chiropractors use their hands. Other words with *chiro-*: *chirography, chiromancy, chiropody, enchiridion*, **a handbook**. Latin *manus*, **hand**, yields *manual, manufacture, manuscript*. Spanish: *mano*, **hand**. See **wordbuilder #22**, for *erg-*, p. 43.

orthodontics:
Greek *orthos*, **straight**; the dental practice of straightening or correcting abnormally aligned or positioned teeth. Other words with *ortho-*: **orthicon, orthoptic, orthotics**; *orthodox, orthograde* (see **wordbuilder #54**, p. 145, for more *grad-* words), *orthography, orthopedics*; more on p. 163.

periodontal:
Greek *peri-*, **around**; **around the teeth**; thus, pertaining to the tissue and structures surrounding the teeth. A dentist specializing in this field is a *periodontist*.

mastodont:
Greek *mastos*, **breast**; **breast tooth**; an extinct mammal resembling the elephant; from the **nipple-shaped** protuberances on the teeth.

microdont:
Greek *mikros*, **small**; **having very small teeth**; also, *microdontous*.

Word from a person's name: *gerrymander*, an arbitrary arrangement of political boundaries; from Elbridge *Gerry* + (*sala*)*mander*, from the shape of an election district formed in 1812 in Massachusetts when Gerry was governor.

wordextras

Contumacious, from *com-*, **intensive** + *tumere*, **to swell**, means **haughty, stubborn, disobedient**, "swollen" with one's own importance. The noun is *contumacy* (KAHN tyoo muh see, or KAHN tuh muh see), the stubborn refusal to submit to authority, especially of a court of law; insubordination; disobedience. Other forms of the word are *contumely* (a noun, even though it ends in *-ly*, which indicates mainly adverbs), and *contumelious*, an adjective.

With *urbs*, **city**, **conurbation** refers to an extremely large, densely populated metropolitan area, usually a complex of suburbs and smaller towns with a large city at their center. Compare *megalopolis*, **great city**, p. 122. See also **Greek cognates**, p. 65. Other words with *urb-* include **urban, urbane, urbanize, exurban, suburban, urbi et orbu**.

Bond paper, paper with rag content, was originally used for printing government bonds, bank notes, etc.; now, any strong, superior grade of paper used for documents, letterheads, certificates, etc.

Eugenics, from *eu-*, **well, good** + *genus*, **birth, race, species, kind**, is the science of human improvement. Other words ending in *-genic* include anthropo**genic**, cryo**genic**, crypto**genic**, dacryo**genic**, hallucino**genic**, lacto**genic**.

Word Cluster No. 33

diction	**dict**ator	juris**dict**ion	inter**dict**ion
dictionary	**dict**ature	vale**dict**ion	e**dict**
dictate	ad**dict**	contra**dict**ion	ver**dict**
dictum	in**dict**	bene**dict**ion	pre**dict**
vin**dic**ate	ab**dic**ate	pre**dic**ate	pre**dic**ant
in**dic**ate	in**dic**ative	pre**dic**ament	de**dic**ate

Common elements_____**Inferred Meaning**_____

Romance Cognates	French	Romanian	Italian	Portuguese	Spanish
	dire	zice[*]	dire	dizer	decir

[*]The z is an influence of the Dacian, an ancient language of the Thracian people; see p. 103.

Doublets: benediction:benison; malediction:malison

Words with disguised Latin roots: condition, dight, bedight, diseur (masculine), diseuse (feminine), digit, ditto, ditty, disk (unusual relationship to Greek), index, indite, judex, judge, preach, prejudice (see p. 106), teach, vendetta (see p. 153), vengeance, avenge, revenge, veridical

Latin phrases: *nemine contradicente* (abbreviated nem. con.); *dictum sapienti sat est*, **a word to the wise is sufficient** (Plautus, 254?-184 B.C., a Roman writer of comedies)*; obiter dictum* (see **Clavis**); *mirabile dictu*, **wonderful to tell**; see p. 58; *horribile dictu*, **horrible to relate**; *ipse dixit*, **he himself has said it**; compare with *ex cathedra*, pp. 175, 207.

Old French phrase: *voir dire*: **to say the truth**; an oath given by a witness that he, or she, will tell the truth in regard to questions concerning his, or her, competency

Spanish proverb: *Quien mal dice, peor oye* (see pp. 13, 123)

Placenames: Benedicta, ME; Lac Indicateur, Quebec. There is an *Index* in the following states: KY, NY, NC.

Explore *poetic diction* in a literary handbook, such as *Abrams'*, or the Internet.

Greek cognates: deic_tic, apo**dic**tic, para**digm**, policy [from *apodeixis* (contract)], **dic**ast, syn**dic**, syn**dic**ate, theo**dic**y, Eury**dic**e. Another *policy* comes from Greek *polis*, **city**, as in **poli**ce, cosmo**poli**tan, megalo**polis**, necro**polis** (a cemetery, especially in an ancient city); Deca**polis** (an ancient region of Palestine, occupied by a federation of ten Greek cities); the American cities: Anna**polis**, MD; Cosmo**polis**, WA; Demo**polis**,[*] Indiana**polis**, IN; Kanna**polis**, NC; Minnea**polis**, MN, as well as many others. [*]Demo**polis**, AL, is **people city**. Compare with *republic*, p. 1.

German words and phrases: *Wörterbuch*, **wordbook**: dictionary
Wortwörtlich: **word for word**, or verbatim
Aus seinen Worten spricht Begeisterung: **His words express enthusiasm.**
frei aus dem Kopf sprechen: **to speak extemporaneously**
aufs Wort gehorchen: **to obey implicitly**

A Writing Tip: It is often difficult to catch one's own writing mistakes, especially the small ones, such as omitting a word, such as *an, in, the*, and *on*; substituting one word for another, such as *in* for *on*; or inserting an unnecessary word. One of the best ways to proofread your work is to read it aloud. By doing so, you are able to hear a harsh word or to hear if you've used the same word too close together. It's better to take the extra time than to be embarrassed by your reader finding the mistake. The authors of this book are as guilty as anyone else; students are often in a delirium of joy to find a professor's having made an error in a handout.

> **Quote**: It is fatal to the highest success to have command of a noble language and to have nothing to say in it; it is equally fatal to have noble thoughts and to lack the power of giving them expression.
> Hamilton Wright Mabie

Common element base: dicere

Meaning: to point out in words, to speak

IE base: *deik-*: **to point out, pronounce solemnly**, from which is **Old English** *taecan*, **to show, instruct**, thus **to teach**; **German**: *sprechen*, **to speak**; *unterrichten*, **to teach**

Clavis

diction:
as a general term, signifies the selection of **words** in a work of literature, whether they are *abstract* or *concrete*, *Latinate* or *Anglo-Saxon*, *colloquial* or *formal*, *technical* or *common*, *literal* or *figurative*. Also, manner of speaking or singing; choice of words; wording; enunciation. See *verbiage*, p. 130.

addict:
ad-, **to**; originally, **to assign to**, as by a court of law; has come to mean **bound to**; given over to another as a slave; thus, one may be addicted, or made a slave, to alcohol, drugs, or work; also, an ardent supporter, as *an addict to one's political party*; devotee, as a *baseball or television addict*.

valedictorian:
vale, **farewell**; **one who speaks farewell**; the highest-ranking student of a graduating class; the *salutatorian*, the second-ranking student, *salutes* or greets the assembly. *Salute*: **to wish health to**. See *salutatorian*, p. 168. *Assembly* is from *simul*, **together**, which also yields *simultaneous*, *same*.

verdict:
vere, **truly**; **a thing truly said**, as *the verdict of the jury*; a jury is sworn to pronounce the truth, or *verdict*; any decision or judgment; the finding of a judge on a matter.

obiter dictum:
obiter (*ob-*, **over**, **against** + *ire*, **to go**; thus, **to fall**); a **statement** made in passing; an incidental remark, especially one made by a judge, that has no bearing on the case. *Obiter* shares its constituents with *obit*, *obituary*; the verb *ire* is also found in *itinerary, adit, exit, coitus, introit* (see p. 100); see p. 208, Item 113, for more words from *ire*.

predicate:
pre-, **before**; as a *verb*, **to speak before**, or **to address**; also, to establish a base, as to *predicate* an argument upon certain facts; in *grammar*, the verb and its complements, or that which is said about a subject. In addition, that which completes the meaning of a copula, or linking verb, as a *predicate noun*, e.g., Dr. Smith is *president* of the college; or as a *predicate adjective*, e.g., Dr. Smith is *amicable*. In Latin, the inflected verb precedes, or "predicates," the subject.

abdicate:
ab-, **off**; **to deny**, **renounce**; to give up formally (a high office, throne, authority, etc.); to surrender or repudiate (a right, responsibility, etc.). King Edward VIII *abdicated* the British throne in 1936.

vindicate:
vim, **force**; **to clear from criticism, blame, guilt, suspicion**. Alexander Pope (1688-1744) in his *Essay on Man* wrote "Eye Nature's walk, shoot folly as it flies/And catch the manners living as they rise: Laugh where we must, be candid when we can/But *vindicate* the ways of God to man."

preach:
from Old French *prechier*; further from Latin *praedicare*, **to say or proclaim before**; the paired Old English synonym is *foretell*. *Paired synonyms* indicate a root-by-root correspondence; see other word pairs on p. 31. See p. 160 for more on *preach*.

paradigm:
para-, **alongside** + *deigma*, **example**, from IE base *deik-*, **to point out**; thus, a pattern or model. In *grammar*, an example of declension of nouns or conjugation of verbs. See p. 210, Item 140.

Word from a person's title: *sandwich*; from John Montagu, 4th Earl of Sandwich (1718-92), for whom slices of roast beef between bread were made so that he could stay at the gambling table without interruption for meals.

wordextras

Algebra, from Arabic *al*, **the** + *jabara*, **to reunite**, means "the reunion of broken parts." Arabic *al-* is found in a number of other words in English: *albacore, albatross, alchemy, alcohol, alcove, alfalfa* (see p. 142), *algarroba* (**the carob** tree or its pods), *alidade, alkali, alkanet*; *Alhambra*, CA. *Alhambra*, **the red house**, refers to the *citadel* of the Moorish kings near Granada, Spain, built during the 13ᵗʰ and 14ᵗʰ centuries. Washington Irving (1783-1859), regarded as the first serious American novelist, popularized the citadel in *The Alhambra*. Many Spanish words show the influence of the Moors' occupation of Spain, e.g., *alfombra* (**carpet**), *almohada* (**pillow**), *almuerzo* (**lunch**).

Mien, aphetic of *demeanor*, but altered after French *mine*, **look**, **air**, denotes **one's appearance; a way of looking; manner; bearing; carriage; deportment**. My father had the *mien* of a college professor.

From Old French *estraier*, **estray**, in *law*, denotes a stray and unclaimed domestic animal.

Retaliate, from *re-*, **back** + *talio*, **punishment in kind**, and akin to Welsh *tal*, **compensation**, is **to return like for like**, especially to return evil for evil; pay back injury for injury. Synonyms: avenge, revenge. *Revenge* is also a noun.

```
┌─────────────────────────────────────────────────────────────────────────────┐
│                         Word Cluster No. 34                                   │
│                                                                               │
│     circadian              meridian              quotidian                    │
│ post meridiem (p.m.)    triduum (or, triduo)      pridian                     │
│   postmeridian           antemeridian        antemeridiem (a.m.)              │
│        dial                  diary               eudiometer                   │
│                                                                               │
│   French days of the week: lundi (Monday), mardi, mercredi, jeudi, vendredi,  │
│   samedi, dimanche                                                            │
│                                                                               │
│ Common elements_____Inferred Meaning_____  │
└─────────────────────────────────────────────────────────────────────────────┘
```

Romance Cognates	French jour*	Romanian zi	Italian giorno*	Portuguese dia	Spanish dia

*French and Italian cognates are from Latin *diurnalis*, from which the word cluster is also derived. Related words listed under *jour(n)* family, **Word Cluster No. 52**, p. 103: *journal, sojourn; diurnal, terdiurnal, tridiurnal.*

Words with disguised Latin roots: Midi, dismal, diet (one meaning), dietary; clandestine (possibly)

Latin terms: *Dies Irae, sine die, dies non, bis in die, diem perdidi, carpe diem, per diem, post diem*

Latin phrase: *Nulla dies sine linea*: Pliny, *Natural History*, 35, 356 (10), 22: **No day without a line.** It was the custom of Apelles never to let a day be so busy that he should not by drawing a line practice his art; from this came the cited Latin saying, meaning "Never let a day go by without doing something to increase your skills."

Diaries: Samuel Pepys, John Evelyn, Bulstrode Whitelocke, George Fox, Jonathan Swift, John Wesley, Fanny Burney, Samuel Sewell, Sarah K. Knight, William Byrd.

Old English: *daeg* yields *daisy* (**day's eye**), *dawn*, and is a cognate of German *Tag* as in *Guten Tag* (**Good day**).

wordextras

Geyser, Icelandic for **gusher**, and the name of a certain hot spring in Iceland, is ultimately from Old Norse *göysa*, **to gush**. The most famous geyser in the United States is *Old Faithful*, in Yellowstone National Park, Wyoming. *Spa*, a mineral spring, is a celebrated watering spot in Belgium. There is *Spa*, Kentucky.

Mesa, Spanish for **table**, from Latin *mensa*,* is a flat-topped natural elevation, more extensive than a butte, and less extensive than a plateau. There is a *Mesa* in each of the following states: AZ, CO, ID, MS, WA. *The ***Mensa Society***, a group of individuals with high IQs, is from the same Latin word. The society invites candidates to the *table*, without regard to race, religion, academic degrees, or social status.

Italian *fioritura*, **blossoming**, from Latin *flora*, **flower**, is a trill, an appoggiatura, or any other ornamentation added to a melody, as in virtuoso singing. Pronunciations: fioritura: fyoh ree TOO rah; appoggiatura: uh PAHJ uh TOOR uh.

Italian *subito*, **suddenly**, is from Latin *subire*, **to approach, to spring up**, and in music indicates **quickly, abruptly**: a direction to the performer; pronounced SOO bih TOE. *Sudden* is from the Latin verb.

Suave, from Latin *suavis*, **sweet**, describes one who is smoothly gracious or polite; polished. It can almost mean "blandly ingratiating." SYNONYMS: bland, diplomatic, politic, urbane. Spanish: *suave*: **sweet, smooth.**

Niggle, from Norwegian *nigla*, is "to spend excessive time on inconsequential details"; it can also mean "to criticize constantly in a petty manner." The participial form *niggling* means "petty, inconsequential"; it can also mean "demanding excessive care, attention, etc."; fussy.

Duffel, the material from which military utility bags (called **duffel bags**) are made, was originally from *Duffel*, Belgium. *Duffel* has been extended to include the essential clothing and equipment carried by a woodsman, hunter, or yachtsman; also a camper's kit or equipment.

Gelding, from Old Norse *gelda*, **to castrate**, is a castrated male animal, especially a horse.

In *botany*, *acinaciform* means "shaped like a scimitar." Pronunciation: ASS uh NASS uh form.

Faux pas, French for **false step**, denotes an embarrassing social blunder; an error in etiquette; a tactless act or remark, as to tell a hostess that her party was boring. Pronounced foh PAH. The plural is spelled the same, but pronounced foh PAHZ.

Pith, from Old English *pitha*, has come to mean **the essential part**; substance, gist. *Pithy*: **concise**.

Common element base: dies   **Meaning**: day

IE base: *deiw*: **to shine**; therefore, **divine, of the sky, luminous**. **Latin** *deus*, **god**, as in **French** *adieu* and **Spanish** *adiós* (both, **to God**) comes from this root. The luminous sky was often confused with the gods, especially Apollo. The Greek root that corresponds to Latin *dies* is *hemera*, yielding *ephemeral*, *ephemeris*, *hemeralopia* (opposite to *nyctalopia*; see p. 142), *Decameron*, see p. 58, and *hexaemeron*, the six days of the Hebrew account of creation.

Clavis

diary:
: from Latin *diarium*, originally, **daily allowance for food or pay**; a daily written record, especially of one's own experiences, thoughts, etc.; a book for keeping such a record.

circadian:
: *circa-*, **about, around**; **lasting for a day**; in *biology*, pertaining to certain physiological rhythms associated with the 24-hour cycle of the earth's rotation. *Jet lag* is an example of the disruption of one's *circadian* rhythms. See **Clavis** note, p. 40.

meridian:
: from *meridies*, **noon, south**, and further from *medius* (*mid-* + *dies*); originally meant "the hour of noon"; the representation of the great circle of the earth by longitudes; also, a high point.

pridian:
: from *prior*, **before**; **on the day before**; of or relating to a previous day or to yesterday; also, former, as *a pridian monarchy*, or *the pridian days of one's youth*.

quotidian:
: *quot*, **as many as**; daily; recurring every day; everyday; usual or ordinary; anything, especially a fever, that recurs daily, or every day. Note *everyday* as an adjective, as *an everyday occurrence*.

Dies Irae:
: **Day of Wrath**; a medieval hymn concerning Judgment Day, which began with *Dies Irae*.

bis in die:
: **twice a day**, abbreviated *b.i.d.* in prescription writing; part of *Sig.*, abbreviation of *Signature*, **instructions to patient**. See *recipe*, p. 30, for other prescription terms; see p. 72 for *Dolobid*®.

sine die:
: **without a day**; when Congress adjourns *sine die*, for example, no date is set to reconvene; *adjourn*, **to the day**, sets a specific day to reconvene. See *adjourn*, p. 104, for the practical meaning.

carpe diem:
: **seize the day**, a philosophy expressed in Herrick's "To the virgins," which begins with "Gather ye rosebuds while ye may," echoing Pierre de Ronsard, of France. The phrase was used earlier by Horace to express the idea of "Let us drink and eat, for tomorrow we may die." The longer phrase from his *Odes*, 1, 11, 8, is translated "Enjoy the day, trusting the morrow as little as possible." *Carpe diem* was the underlying theme of the movie *Dead Poets Society*. See *tempus fugit*, **time is flying**, p. 86.

dismal:
: Old French *dis mal*; from Latin *dies mali*; originally, **evil days** in the medieval calendar; causing gloom and depression; thus, dark and gloomy; depressed; miserable. See p. 69, under **NB**.

Midi:
: French; **midday**; from *mi*, **half**; further from *medius* + *di*; actually means **south**; specifically **southern France**.

---

wordextras

Flummery, from Welsh *llymru*, **soured oatmeal**, means any soft, easily eaten food; it can also mean **meaningless flattery** or **silly talk**.

Essay, from Anglo-French *assay*, is probably from *exigere*, **to weigh out**. A short literary composition on a particular theme, usually in prose and generally analytic, speculative, or interpretive, an *essay* "weighs out" the facts.

Boneset, a plant of eastern North America, is so called because it supposedly helped knit broken bones. The plant is also called *thoroughwort, agueweed, feverwort*.

Khaki, from Hindi, with identical spelling, meant **dusty, dust-colored**. *Khaki* was originally Persian *khak*, **dust, earth**. Meaning **dull yellowish brown**, *khaki* also denotes a strong, twilled cloth of this color, used especially for military summer uniforms. In the plural, *khakis*, a khaki uniform or pair of trousers. See p. 46, for other Persian words.

Almanac, possibly of Coptic* origin, is a yearly calendar of days, weeks, and months with astronomical data and weather forecasts; also, a book published annually, containing information, usually statistical, on many subjects, such as the population of world cities and the measurement of geographical areas. *Copt refers to an Egyptian who is a descendant of Egypt's ancient inhabitants, or who is a member of the Coptic Church. See p. 163 for more on Coptic under *adobe*.

Antipathy (*anti-*, **against** + *pathos*, **feeling**) is a firm dislike of a person or thing. Pronounced: an TIP uh thee.

Word Cluster No. 35

disability	**dis**afforest	**dis**agree	**dis**arm	**dis**arm
disaster	**dis**card	**dis**cern	**dis**charge	**dis**close
discriminate	**dis**course	**dis**cover	**dis**course	**dis**courage
disdain	**dis**ease	**dis**embogue	**dis**enchant	**dis**engage
disgrace	**dis**guise	**dis**gust	**dis**may	**dis**nature
disinterested	**dis**parage	**dis**sonance	**dis**tend	**dis**tinguish
distend	**dis**tract	**dis**turb	**dis**calced	**dis**carnate
differ	**di**gest	**dif**ficult	**dif**fidence	**dif**fuse
dilate	**di**luent	**di**lute	**di**luvian	**di**mension
divest	**di**rect	**di**eresis	**di**vest	**di**latory

Common elements_____**Inferred Meaning**_____

Romance Cognates: In the Romance languages, the Latin root remains unchanged, or with assimilations and truncations, e.g., *dif-* before roots beginning with *f*; *di-* before roots beginning with *g, l, m, r, v*.

Words with disguised Latin roots: dirge, dirigible, directrix, diriment, dessert, dinner, descant

NB: The following words are not in this family: dismal (see p. 68), dismay, distaff, distich, distill.

Note: This element is *not* related to the Greek prefix *dys-*, **bad**, **wrong**, as in **dys**crasia, **dys**entery, **dys**function, **dys**genic, **dys**graphia, **dys**kinesia, **dys**lexia, **dys**logistic, **dys**menorrhea (painful or difficult menstruation), **dys**pareunia (sexual intercourse that is physically painful or difficult), **dys**pepsia (impaired indigestion), **dys**peptic (of, causing, or from dyspepsia; morose; grouchy; as a *noun*, a person suffering from dyspepsia), **dys**phagia (difficulty in swallowing), **dys**phasia, **dys**phonia, **dys**phoria, **dys**plasia, **dys**pnea, **dys**rhythmia, **dys**tonia, **dys**topia, **dys**trophic (of or caused by *dystrophy*; of a lake or pond derived from a bog and characterized by brown, humic matter, high acidity, and poorly developed fauna and flora), **dys**trophy, as in *muscular dystrophy*; and **dys**uria (painful urination). (See **Word Cluster No. 62**, p. 123 for a partial list of these words paralleled with the Latin counterpart *mal-*.)

A proverb: A word fitly spoken is like apples of gold in a setting of silver.
Proverbs 25:11

---

wordbuilder #28

The elements *fic-, fig-*, from Latin *fingere*, **to form**, **mold**, **shape**, **devise**, yield **fic**tile, **fic**tion, **fic**tionalize, **fic**tional, **fic**titious, **fic**tive, meta**fic**tion; traf**fic**; **fig**ment, **fig**ural, **fig**urant, **fig**urative, **fig**ure, **fig**urine; con**figure**, dis**figure**, pre**figure**, trans**figure**; con**figur**ation, pre**figur**ation, trans**figur**ation; ef**fig**y; fainéant (adjective: **lazy**, **idle**; as a *noun*, **a lazy**, **idle person**; pronounced FAY nee unt), faint, feign, feigned, feint. From the IE base—*dheigh*—that yields the Latin elements are also Greek *paradise* and Anglo-Saxon *lady* (see p. 197).

wordextras

"Mushing" dog is a corruption by English dog sled, or sledge, drivers in pronouncing French *Marchons!* **Let's march on!** See *Iditarod*, an annual dog sled race in Alaska, from Anchorage to Nome, p. 147.

Verdure, from Latin *vivere*, **to be green**, indicates the fresh green color of growing plants. That which is **verdant**, an adjective, is covered with green vegetation, as in *the verdant meadow*; can also mean "inexperienced, immature."

Stalwart, **firm**, is short for Old English *statholwyrthe*: *stathol*, **foundation** + *writhe*, **worth**; hence, having a firm foundation; strong and well-built. SYNONYMS: brave, firm, resolute, robust, strong, sturdy, unyielding, valiant.

Mustang and *mestizo* are from Latin *miscere*, **to mix**, as in *miscellaneous, miscegenation, promiscuous*. See more words from *miscere*, p. 208, Item 120.

Ipse dixit, Latin for **he himself has said** (**it**), is an arbitrary or dogmatic statement; an unsupported assertion, usually by a person of standing. Similar in meaning to *ex cathedra*; see pp. 175; 207, Item 102.

Astonish and *astound* are from *ex-*, **intensive** + *tonare*, **to thunder**. *Astonish* is **to surprise** with something that seems unbelievable; *astound* suggests causing **a shocking astonishment** that leaves one helpless to think or act. From *tonare* are also **detonate** and **tornado**. As far as can be determined, these are the only English words from *tonare*.

Common element base: dis-　　　　　**Meaning**: general negative: not, away, apart, opposite of, reversal

Clavis

disaster:　　Greek *aster*, **star**; **falling apart of the stars**; that which is **ill-starred**. Synonyms: calamity, catastrophe. *Aster* also forms the base of *asterisk*, **little star**, and *astronaut*, **star traveler**; the Latin counterpart is *stella*, as in *stellar*, *constellation* (**a group of stars**), and *Estelle*. See p. 212, Item 173.

discalced:　　*calceatus*, **sandal**, **shoe**; **barefoot**, as members of certain religious orders. Other words from *calceatus*: *calceolate* (**shaped like a slipper**, the middle petal of an orchid), *calceiform*, and *chaussure*.

discard:　　originally, in certain card games, **to throw away a card** that had been dealt; **abandon**; **to get rid of**, especially as useless, unimportant, or of no value.

discourage:　　*courage* from *cor*, **heart**; **to deprive of courage**, **heart**, **hope**, or **confidence**; **dishearten**.

discover:　　**to uncover**; to find, or to find out something that already existed, as Ponce de Leon *discovered* Florida. Do not confuse with *invent*, **to come in**, to make something that did not exist before, as Thomas A. Edison (1847-1913) *invented* the light bulb and the phonograph. See *invent*, p. 200.

discriminate:　　from *discern*, the verb of which is *cernere*, **to separate**; thus, **to constitute a difference between**; differentiate; to recognize the difference between; distinguish; also, to show partiality *for* or *against*.

disdain:　　*dain* from French *deign*; from Latin *dignus*, **worthy**; when treated with *disdain*, or "beneath one's dignity," a person's **dignity**, or **worth**, **is taken away**. Verb Synonyms: contemn, despise, scorn, scout.

disease:　　**not at ease**; an abnormal or pernicious condition. Synonyms: ailment, malady; also, affection, a disorder of a specific organ, as *an affection of the liver*; *affection* also means a fond or tender feeling.

disembogue:　　*em-*, a variant of *in-*, **into** + *bogue*, from *bucca*, **cheek**; to pour out its waters at the mouth, as the Mississippi *disembogues* into the Gulf of Mexico. *Buccinator*, a cheek muscle, is also from *bucca*.

disinterested:　　not influenced by personal interests or selfish motives; **impartial**, as of a judge, an umpire, referee, or arbiter; not to be used for *uninterested*, **having or showing no interest**, concern, or feelings, as a student *uninterested* in a professor's lecture.

disparage:　　*par*, **equal**; originally, to marry one below one's own *par*, or below one's own status; to belittle another's accomplishments or achievements; to discredit.

descant:　　*cantus*, **song**; **apart from the song**; a subordinate melody that embellishes the fixed melody or air; a *descant*, pitched higher than the fixed melody, can be played or sung.

dessert:　　from Old French *desservir*, **to serve away**; originally, to clear the table and prepare for the final course.

dilate:　　*di-*, truncation of *dis-* + *latus*, **side**, **wide**; thus, to make wider or larger; cause to expand or swell; stretch; also, to write or speak in detail about a subject. From the same root are **latitude**, **lateral**, **bilateral**, **collateral**, **equilateral**, **multilateral**, **trilateral**, **unilateral**. See other *-late* words, p. 155.

diffuse:　　from *fundere*, **to pour**; **to pour away**, or **to pour in different directions**; in *writing*, using more words than are necessary; **prolix**, **wordy**. [*dif-* assimilates *dis-*, thus, making words whose roots begin with *f* easier to pronounce: *differ*, *difference*, *differential*, *difficile*, *difficult*, *diffident*, *diffract*.]

dinner:　　both *dinner* and *dine* are probably from Vulgar Latin *disjejunare*, **to break one's fast**; *disjejunare* itself comprises *dis-* + *jejunus*, **fasting**, **hungry**, **empty**. *Jejunum*, the middle part of the small intestine, between the duodenum and the ileum, was thought by the ancient Romans to be *empty*.

Word from a person's name: *Machiavellian*, characterized by craft, cunning, and deceit; from Niccolò Machiavelli (1469-1529), an Italian statesman and political theorist; author of *The Prince* (1513), which established him as the father of the modern science of politics. In Elizabethan literature, hundreds of references connect him with the Devil or the Evil One.

A Writing Tip: You can often increase the emphasis on a single-word adverb or a brief adverbial phrase by moving it to the beginning of the sentence. *Gerald searched frantically for his car keys.* Change to: ***Frantically**, Gerald searched for his car keys.* Tom *excitedly* told his friends he had won the lottery. ***Excitedly**, Tom told his friends he had won the lottery.*

Word Cluster No. 36

dolor	**dolor**ic	**dolor**ific	**dolor**ous
dolorifuge	**dolor**imeter	**dolor**ogenic	con**dol**e
con**dol**ence	con**dol**ement	in**dol**ent	**Dol**obid®

Common elements_____Inferred Meaning_____

Romance Cognates	French	Romanian	Italian	Portuguese	Spanish
	douleur	doliu*	dolor	dor	dolor

*Romanian *doliu* means "in mourning."

Placenames: Doloroso, Mississippi; Dolores, Colorado

Related word: hangnail (see **Clavis**)

Latin phrases: *via dolorosa, Mater dolorosa* (see **Clavis**)
Nocet empta dolore voluptas: **Pleasures brought by pain are injurious**. Horace
Infandum, regina, jubes renovare dolorem. Virgil. **Unspeakable, O queen, is the grief thou biddst me renew**.
(reply of Aeneas, when relating the history of Troy's destruction)

Italian phrases: *Nessun maggior dolore che ricordarsi del tempo felice nella miseria*: **There is no greater grief than to remember times of happiness in the midst of wretchedness**.
"A sorrow's crown of *sorrow* is remembering happier things." Dante
I gran dolori sono muti: **Great griefs are silent**.

NB: *Dolce, dulce, dulcimer*, and *doldrums* are not in this family.

Greek: *algos*, **pain**: **alge**sia; **alge**simeter; **algo**lagnia; **algo**meter; an**alge**sic; cox**algia** (**hip pain**), metr**algia** (**pain in the uterus**), my**algia** (**muscle pain**), nephr**algia**, (**kidney pain**), neur**algia** (**nerve pain**), nost**algia** (**a longing for home**), oophor**algia** (**pain of the ovaries**). An identically spelled root means **cold**, as in **alg**id, **alge**facient, **algo**facient, **algo**scopy. *Algogenic* can mean either **causing pain** or **causing cold**; in the latter meaning, lowering the body temperature below normal. [*Algology* is the scientific study of algae; also called *phycology*.]

Greek *odyne*, **pain**: **odyn**acusis; **odyn**ometer, **odyn**ophagia, **odyn**ophobia; an**odyne**; aden**odynia**, all**odynia**, arthr**odynia** (**joints**), cephal**odynia** (**head**), dermat**odynia** (**skin**), dors**odynia** (**back**), gastr**odynia**, gnath**odynia**, hepat**odynia**, my**odynia**, neur**odynia**, odont**odynia**, orchi**odynia**, oste**odynia**, ot**odynia**, phall**odynia**, pod**odynia**.

wordextras

Akimbo, as in *arms akimbo*, is Old Norse for "arms in a keen bow," as in showing defiance or frustration. *Elbow*, "bow of the ell," is from Latin *ulna*, **arm** + **bow**. *Ell*, a former English unit of length (as of cloth), equaled 45 inches. See *cubit*, p. 54.

Celerity, from Latin *celer*, **speed**, means "swiftness in acting or moving." *Accelerate*, **to speed up**, and *decelerate*, **to decrease speed**, are also from *celer*. [Unrelated *celery* and *celeriac* are vegetables.] See *alacrity*, **wordextras**, p. 3.

Quintessence, **fifth essence**, is the essence of a substance in its purest, most distinctive and concentrated form. With the four elements of the universe construed as being *earth*, *air*, *fire*, and *water*, the ancients believed that the *fifth essence*, **ether**, filled celestial or heavenly spaces.

Anomaly, from Greek *an-*, **negative** + *homalos*, **even** (from *homo-*, **same**; see p. 94, under **NB**), indicates that which is **not even**, thus "irregularity." In *astronomy*, the angular deviation of a planet from its perihelion. *Perihelion*: the point nearest the sun in the orbit of a planet, comet, or man-made satellite; opposite of *aphelion*.

Italian *paparazzo*, the plural of which is *paparazzi*, was originally **a scribbler**; also, a rummager in old newspapers. The plural now designates mainly **freelance photographers**, who take candid shots, often in an intrusive manner, of celebrities for newspapers or magazines.

Transmogrify, a pseudo-Latin formation, means **to change completely**, especially in a grotesque or strange manner.

Axel, a jump in figure skating in which the skater takes off from one skate, does one and a half turns in the air, and lands on the other skate, facing in the opposite direction but moving in the same direction. Requiring coordination and timing, this difficult jump is named after Norwegian figure skater *Axel* Paulsen (1865-1938).

Common element base: dolere   **Meaning**: to feel pain, to suffer
IE base: *del-³*: **to split, carve, cut**; **German**: *Schmerz*, **pain**; *Kummer*, **grief**; *Depression*, **depression**

Clavis

Dolobid®:   a Merck Sharp & Dohme trade name for an analgesic, given **twice daily for pain**. (b.i.d.: *bis in die*, prescription writing for "twice a day"; see p. 68); see p. 30, under *recipe* for other prescription terms.

dolorifuge: *fugere*, **to flee**; that which makes **pain, grief, sorrow flee**; an analgesic; a painkiller, as in "The doctor prescribed a *dolorifuge* to relieve the patient's arthritic pains."

condole: *con-*, **with, together**; **to express pain**; mourn with another in sympathy; commiserate.

condolement: from *condole*; the sharing of another's grief or sorrow. Latin *condolement* is paired with Greek *sympathy*; they share a root-by-root correspondence in meaning. See other word pairs, p. 31.

indolent: *in-*, **not**; **no pain**; lazy; idle. Work apparently *grieves* or *pains* the would-be worker, so that in idleness, he (or she) is *not pained*. In *medicine*, causing little, or no pain, as *an indolent tumor*. Compare Greek *analgesia*, below; note relationship of *algia* to a coined medical word, *nostalgia*, a longing, or, pining, to return home. *Nostalgia* translates German *Heimweh*, **homesickness**. Explore the story of *Nestor*, who in Greek mythology, was a wise old counselor on the side of the Greeks at Troy, and one of the few warriors to return safely to Greece.

dolorous: **very sorrowful**, sad, mournful; painful; as the *dolorous expressions* of "those who lead lives of quiet desperation." Henry David Thoreau (1817-62), American essayist, and author of *Walden*.

Dolores: shortened version of Spanish *Maria de los Dolores*, **Mary of the Sorrows**.

Via Dolorosa: **the Way of Sorrow**, the traditional path that Christ trod to Golgotha, the place of His crucifixion. There are many musical renditions concerning *Via Dolorosa*.

Mater dolorosa: **The Sorrowing Mother**, a song representing Mary in sorrow for the sufferings of her son; also a painting by Titian (c. 1490-1576). See p. 179 under **Latin Phrases**.

hangnail: by folk etymology, associated with *hang*, but was originally *agnail*; in Old English, *angnaegl*, **pain nail**. The root *ang* also yields *anger, anguish, angina, angst, anxious*; in addition, *quinsy* (see p. 27, under **Words with Disguised Roots**).

neuraglia: Greek *neuron*, **nerve**; severe sharp **pain** along the course of a nerve.

analgesia: Greek *an-*, **not, without**; a state of not feeling painful stimuli although fully conscious. The adjectival form is *analgesic*. Compare *anesthesia*, **loss of feeling**, from *an-*, **not** + *esthesia*, **feeling**.

wordextras

Both *rancid* and *rancor* are from Latin *rancere*, **to be rank**; *rancid*, an adjective, describes that having the bad smell or taste of stale fats or oils; **spoiled**; **repugnant**. *Rancor*, a noun, is a continuing and bitter hate or ill will; deep spite or malice. Synonyms of *rancor*: antagonism, animosity, animus, antipathy, enmity, hostility.

Neufchâtel, a soft white cheese similar to cream cheese, and made from skimmed milk, was first made in Neufchâtel, Switzerland. Pronunciation: NOO shah TEL.

Antithesis, from *anti-*, **against** + *thesis*, **a standing**, means **exact opposite of**, as *hate is the antithesis of love*. See other words from *thesis*, p. 117; with *anti-*, p. 9, 45. See *antipathy*, p. 68. Pronunciation: an TITH uh sis.

Vitiate, from Latin *vitium*, **vice**, **fault**, is to make imperfect, faulty, or impure; to spoil, corrupt; to weaken morally, debase, pervert; also, to invalidate, as a contract. (See use of word in **An exalted aphorism**, below.)

An exalted aphorism: A plethora of individuals with expertise in culinary techniques *vitiate* the potable concoction produced by steeping certain comestibles. Simplified: **Too many cooks spoil the broth**. Variations: **Two many nurses kill the baby. Too many captains run the ship onto the reef**. Following the advice of many can often be more harmful than following no one's advice. See *vitiate* in **wordextras**, above.

Word from Greek mythology: *tantalize*, to tease by arousing expectations that are repeatedly disappointed; from *Tantalus*, a king, son of Zeus, doomed in the lower world to stand in water that always receded when he tried to drink it, and under branches of luscious fruit he could never reach.

Word Cluster No. 37

donate	**don**ee	con**don**e	par**don**
donation	**don**or	con**don**ation	par**don**er
date	**dat**um	**dat**a	**dat**ive
edi**tor**	edi**tion**	ren**dit**ion	extra**dit**ion
edi**tor**ial	per**dit**ion	tra**dit**ion	ven**dit**ion

Common elements_____**Inferred Meaning**_____

Romance Cognates	French donner	Romanian da ceva	Italian dare, donare	Portuguese dar	Spanish dar

Words with disguised Latin roots: add, addendum, betray, dado, deodand, die (plural, dice), dot (see **Clavis**), dowager, dower, dowry, endow, perdu, perdue, rent, render, rendezvous, surrender, traitor, treason, vend

French phrase: enfants perdus (see p. 78).

Latin phrases: *Timeo Danaos et dona ferentes*: **I fear the Greeks even when they are bringing gifts**. Virgil
The enemy are not to be trusted even when they seem friendly.
honorarium donum; *Dono dedit* (**given as a gift**; abbreviated d.d.); *editio princeps*

Italian phrase: *dà tempo al tempo*, **give time to time**: give things time to mature

Spanish proverbs: *Al hombre mayor, darle honor*: **To the great man give honor**. See pp. 93, 121.
Dádivas quebrantan peñas: **Gifts break rocks**.

A prayer: *Dona nobis pacem*: **Give us peace**. Often set to music, as a canon, or round.

Greek cognates: dose, apodosis, antidote, anecdotal, anecdote (see **Clavis**), epidote

wordextras

Cashier, both the noun and the verb, while pronounced the same, are from different sources. The noun—an officer in a bank or business in charge of paying and receiving money—is from Middle French *casse*, **money box**. The verb—to dismiss from a position of command or responsibility, especially in dishonor—is from Latin *quassare*, **to shake**, as though "shaken loose" from one's position.

Eleemosynary, from Greek *eleos*, **mercy**, **pity**, **charity**, describes that which is "charitable," as *an eleemosynary institution*, such as a children's home. Pronunciation: EL ih MAHS uh NAIR ih. *Alms* is also from *eleos*.

Madeira Islands, north of the Canaries, is Portuguese for Latin *materia*, **timber**, from the dense forests covering the islands when they were discovered by the Portuguese in 1418; *madeira* is also an amber-colored fortified wine from the islands. There is *Madeira School for Girls*, Greenway, Virginia, near Washington, DC.

Apocalypse, from *apo-*, **from** + *kalyptein*, **to cover**, means **to disclose**, and refers to certain Jewish and Christian writings (c. 200 B.C.-A.D. 300), depicting symbolically the ultimate destruction of evil and the triumph of good. Revelation, the last book of the New Testament, is an example of *apocalypse*.

Words describing animals also describe certain humans, e.g., *anserine*, like a *goose*: **silly**, **foolish**; *aquiline*, ~ *eagle*; *asinine*, ~ *ass*; **foolish**; *bovine*, ~ *cow*: **stolid**, **dull**; *canine*, ~ *dog*; *caprine*, ~ *goat*; *corvine*, ~ *crow* or *raven*; *equine*, ~ *horse*; *feline*, ~ *cat*: **sly**, **stealthy**; *hircine*, ~ *goat*; *ovine*, ~ *sheep*; *pavonine*, ~ *peacock*; *taurine*, ~ *bull*; *ursine*, ~ *bear*; *vulpine*, ~ *fox*: **stealthy**, **sly**.

Coming from *vorare*, **to eat**, words ending in –*vorous* describe what a person, animal, or other living thing eats. For example, an animal or bird that feeds on spiders is *arachnivorous*; *carnivorous* refers to **meat-eaters**, such as lions and tigers; certain dogs are *ossivorous*, **bone-eating**; *herbivorous*, feeding on grass and other plants.

Ecclesia, **church**, is Greek for **called-out ones**, and in secular Greece, referred to elected city officials. Pronunciation: eh KLEE zee uh, or, eh KLAY zee uh.

A Writing Tip: *Infer* and *imply* are NOT used interchangeably. *To infer* means to draw a conclusion from observations; *to imply*, to indicate indirectly or by allusion. Examples: I *inferred* that the student had passed the test because of his beaming smile. The student *implied* that he would receive an A in the course because he had always maintained a 4.0 grade-point average and had graduated *summa cum laude* from a community college. [an actual case of a student of one of the authors]

Common element bases: donare, dare   **Meaning**: to give
IE base: *do-*: **to give**; **German**: *geben*; *zurückgeben*, **to give back**; *achtgeben*, **to give heed**; **to pay attention**
Russian: *dacha*, **a country house**, a summer house, or villa in Russia, used as a vacation retreat

Clavis

date:
> first word in Roman letters, **giving** the place and time of writing, as *data Romae*, **given at Rome**. In media parlance, a datelined story retains the original meaning; in English, note proclamations that begin, "**Given** under my hand. . ." Compare *datum* and its plural, *data*, **that which are given**.

dative:
> in *grammar*, a **giving** case; in many Indo-European languages, designating the case that marks the indirect object as well as the object of certain other verbs and prepositions.

pardon:
> *per-*, **through, completely, quite; to forgive thoroughly and completely**. Compare *pardon* with *amnesty*, a general pardon, or forgiveness, for offenders by a government, especially for political offenses. *Amnesty* and *amnesia,* are from Greek *a-*, **negative** + *mne-*, **memory**. See p. 208, Item 121, for other words from *mnasthai*, **to remember**, e.g., *mnemonic(s)*.

dot:
> **a woman's marriage dowry**; pronounced dawt; from *Do*, a one-word Latin sentence, meaning "I give." The adjectival form is *dotal*. Not related etymologically to *dot*, **a speck**.

dowry:
> a variant of *dower*; "that which has been **given**"; money or property brought by a bride to her husband at marriage; specifically, a *dowry* is the part of the interest of a deceased man's real estate allotted by law to his widow for her lifetime.

endow:
> Middle English *endouen*, from Latin *dotare*, **to provide with a dowry**; to provide with some talent, quality, as *endowed* with courage, honesty, fortitude, perseverance; also, to give money or property so as to provide an income for the support of an institution, such as a college, hospital.

editor:
> *e-*, elision of *ex-*, **out; to give out**, one who publishes, brings forth; *edition* shares the same elements. An *editorial* gives the opinion on a particular issue by the editor, publisher, or owner of a newspaper or magazine; the *adjectival* form, characteristic of an editor or an editorial, as *editorial comments*.

honorarium:
> from *honorarium (donum)*, once a **gift** made upon one's appointment to a *post of honor*; now, a fee for services rendered, especially for those services on which custom or propriety forbids a price to be set.

render:
> from Latin *reddere*, **to restore**; *red-*, **back, to give back**; can also mean **to give in return**, as **to render good for evil**; relinquish. SYNONYMS: deliver, restore, translate, yield.

rendezvous:
> unaltered from Old French *rendez vous*, **present yourselves**; from *render*, previous entry. A prearranged meeting place; in the military, to bring troops and equipment together at a specified time and place; also, a place of popular resort; a haunt.

add:
> from *addere*, **to give to**, or to put to; to append. Adjective: either *add\u0251ble* or *add\u0268ble*. See *sum*, p. 184.

perdition:
> *per-*, **intensive; to give completely**, but actually meaning "to lose completely." In *theology*, the loss of the soul; damnation; Hell.

traitor:
> and *tradition*, from *tradere*, **to give over**; one who commits treason. See more on *traitor* under *treason*, p. 194. Our doubts are *traitors*/And make us lose the good we oft might win/By fearing to attempt. Shakespeare

anecdote:
> Greek *an-*, **not** + *ek-*, **out; not given out**; originally, little-known, interesting facts of history or biography; now, a short, unelaborated account of an interesting or humorous incident. Explore further under *Short Story*, in *Abrams'*, or the Internet, using Google or Yahoo.

dose:
> Greek; **that which is given**; a specified amount; also, an ingredient added to wine to strengthen it.

---

wordextras

Aggravate, from *ad-*, **to** + *gravis*, **heavy**, is **to make worse**; make more burdensome, troublesome, etc. The obese man *aggravated* his health by continuing to smoke even after the doctor advised him of the dire consequences. *Aggravate* should not be used as a synonym for *annoy*. A situation is *aggravated*; a person is *annoyed*.

With *e-*, **out** + *bullire*, **to boil**, *ebullient* means "bubbling; boiling over; effervescent; overflowing with enthusiasm." Carl's *ebullient* nature gained him many friends. Pronunciation: ih BOOL yunt.

```
┌─────────────────────────────────────────────────────────────────────────────┐
│                          Word Cluster No. 38                                  │
│                                                                               │
│  equivalent         inequity          equitable          equiaxed            │
│  equivocal          equivocation      equinox            equifinal           │
│  equilibrist        equilibrant       equilibrium        equipluve           │
│  equidistant        equipoise         equiform           equative            │
│  equable            equator           equate             adequate            │
│  equanimity         inadequate        equalitarian       equal               │
│                                                                               │
│  Common elements_____Inferred Meaning_____ │
└─────────────────────────────────────────────────────────────────────────────┘
```

Romance Cognates	French	Romanian	Italian	Portuguese	Spanish
	égal	egal	eguale	igual	igual

Doublets: equivoque:equivoke   **French word**: egalitarian

Placenames: Equality, AL, IL, IN, MN, MO, ND; Equinunc, PA. (*Equinunc* is probably of Indian origin.)

A country: Ecuador, in South America (see **Clavis**)

Mathematical terms: biquadratic *equation*; *equal* sign (=)

Latin phrases: *in equilibrio*; *Omnia mors aequat*: **Death levels all things** (or, **makes all things equal**). Claudian

French phrase: *C'est égal*: **It is equal**: it's all the same.

Motto of the State of Nebraska: *Equal* before the law

Explore the difference in *equivoque* and *equivocation* as literary devices.

Other Latin words: from *par-*, **equal**: **par**, **par**ity, **par**lay; com**par**e, com**par**ison; **peer**, **pair**, herb **Par**is (originally *herba paris*, **herb of a pair**, in allusion to an even number of flower parts), non**par**eil (**not equal**; thus, unequaled; unrivaled; peerless; also refers to the painted bunting, a brightly colored bird), **par**imutuel (as in horseracing). These words are also listed p. 149, as belonging to **Word Cluster No. 75**, the *part/port* family.

Greek *iso-*, **same**, **equal**: **iso**bar, **iso**bath, **iso**cheim, **iso**chore, **iso**chromatic, **iso**chrone, **iso**clinal, **iso**cracy, **iso**cyclic, **iso**diametric, **iso**dimorphism, **iso**dose, **iso**dynamic, **iso**gamete, **iso**gamy, **iso**genous, **iso**geotherm, **iso**gloss, **iso**gonic, **iso**gony, **iso**gram, **iso**hel, **iso**hyet, **iso**logous, **iso**mer, **iso**metrics, **iso**metropia, **iso**metry, **iso**morph, **iso**nomy, **iso**piestic, **iso**pleth, **iso**pod, **iso**sceles (see **Clavis**), **iso**seismal, **iso**stasy, **iso**there, **iso**tonic, **iso**tope, **iso**tropic.

NB: *Equine, equitant, equitation, equerry, equestrian*, all pertain to horses, from *equus*, **horse**.

Motto of the State of North Carolina: *Esse quam videri*: **To be rather than to seem.**

Word from Greek mythology: *protean*, **assuming many forms**; from *Proteus*, a sea god that could change his own appearance at will; in lowercase, *proteus* is one who changes his or her appearance or principles easily; one who is wishy-washy. Pronunciation of *protean*: PROTE ee uhn. This word is not related to *proto-*, **first**; see p. 159.

Common element base: aequalis   **Meaning**: equal

From Latin *aequus*, **plain**, **even**, **flat**; root cannot be traced beyond Latin. **German**: *gleich*, as in *Gleichheit*, **equality**

Clavis

equanimity: *animus*, **mind**; **of even mind**; the quality or characteristic of being calm and even-tempered, especially under stress. SYNONYMS: composure, nonchalance, serenity. Pronounced: EK wah NIM uh tee.

equator: divides the earth into two **equal** parts, the northern and southern hemispheres. The Prime Meridian 0° through Greenwich, England, and called Greenwich Mean Time, and the International Date Line at 180° in the Pacific Ocean, divide the earth into eastern and western hemispheres, or Oriental and Occidental, respectively. See *International Date Line*, p. 98; *Orient*, p. 38; *sphere*, p. 111.

equilibrium: *libra*, **a balance**; that which is **equally balanced**; equal balance between any powers, influences, etc.; equality of effect; in *chemistry*, for example, the condition when reaction and its reverse reaction proceed at equal rates.

equinox: *nox*, **night**; **equal night**, designating the time when the sun crosses the equator, making night and day of **equal** length in all parts of the Earth. The *vernal equinox* occurs around March 21, and the *autumnal equinox,* around September 21. Compare *summer* and *winter solstices*, respectively, around June 21 and December 21, literally, when *the sun stands still*. See more on *solstice*, p. 180.

equipoise: *poise* from *pendere*, **to weigh**; **equal distribution of weight**; state of balance, or equilibrium; weight or force that balances another; counterbalance. See *balance*, p. 20; see p. 210, Item 141 for *pendere*.

equivocal: *vox*, **voice**; having two or more meanings; that can have more than one interpretation; purposely vague, misleading, or ambiguous, such as *an equivocal reply*. See *Magnavox®*, p. 121.

egalitarian: from French; describes the **equality** for all citizens with respect to social, political, and economic rights; rallying philosophy of the French Revolution, the motto of which see on p. 113.

Ecuador: so named because the *equator* passes directly over that country, as well as Colombia and Brazil in South America. The capital of Ecuador is *Quito*, pronounced KEE toe.

iniquity: *in-*, **not**; **not equal**; lack of righteousness or justice; therefore, **sin**. Compare King David's prayer in Psalm 51:2: "*Wash* me thoroughly from my *iniquity*, and *cleanse* me from my *sin*." Many of the psalms are written in parallel structure, with the second phrase repeating the thought of the first, often synonymically. For example, *cleanse* and *sin* are synonyms of *wash* and *iniquity*, respectively. The entire 51st Psalm is a paradigm of Hebrew parallelism.

isosceles: Greek *isos-*, **equal** + *skelos*, **leg**; a triangle with two legs *equal*. There are also *isosceles trapezoids*.

isocracy: Greek *isos-*, **equal** + *kratein*, **to rule**; a system of government in which all persons have equal political power. See p. 205, Item 76 for other –*cracy* words, e.g. *auto**cracy**, demo**cracy**, pluto**cracy***.

isogloss: Greek *isos-*, **equal** + *glossa*, **tongue**, **speech**; an imaginary line of demarcation between regions differing in a particular feature of language, as on a point of pronunciation, syntax, etc.

wordextras

Gingham, from French *guingan*, is originally from Malay *genggang*, **striped**; *gingham* is a yarn-dyed, plain-weave cotton fabric, usually in stripes, checks, or plaids.

Budget, from Middle English *bougette*, **small bag**, and further from Latin *bulga*, **leather bag**, was originally portions of one's income set aside in "small leather bags," for recurring expenses. One can also *budget* one's time. Also, a limited stock or supply of something, as "His *budget* of patience was running out." See *bursa*, p. 63.

Regret, from Gothic *gretan*, **to weep**, is to feel sorry about or mourn for a person or thing gone, lost, etc. NOUN SYNONYMS: compunction, contrition, remorse. As far as can be determined, there are no other words from *gretan*.

Arbiter, originally, **one who goes to a place**, a witness, a judge, is a person selected to judge a dispute; an umpire.

Tarnish, from French *ternir*, means **to make dim**, as in *to tarnish one's reputation*; *to tarnish a memory*.

Word from Greek mythology: *Sisyphean*, **an unending, arduous task**; from *Sisyphus*, an avaricious king of Corinth condemned in Hades to roll uphill a huge stone that constantly rolled to the bottom as he neared the top.

```
┌─────────────────────────────────────────────────────────────────────────────┐
│                          Word Cluster No. 39                                  │
│                                                                               │
│  infant              fable           preface*          fame                   │
│  infantile           affable         prefacer*         famous                 │
│  infantry            ineffable       prefacial*        defamatory             │
│  infante             fabulist        prefatory         infamy                 │
│  infanticide         fabulous                          infamous               │
│                                                                               │
│    fate              confess         profess           profession             │
│    fatal(ity)        professor       professorial      professional           │
│                                                                               │
│      *The fac in these words is not related to facere, to make, to do, as in  │
│      face, façade (wordextras, p. 131), or to manufacture (Clavis, p. 126).   │
│                                                                               │
│  Common elements_____Inferred Meaning_____  │
└─────────────────────────────────────────────────────────────────────────────┘
```

Romance Cognates	French	Romanian	Italian	Portuguese	Spanish
	fabuler	fabula	fama	falar	fama

Words with disguised Latin roots: fay (one meaning), fairy**

Romance words and phrases: *femme fatale, damnum fatale, enfant terrible, enfants perdus, fantoccini, fabliau(x), enfant de famille, affabile*

Latin phrases: *data fata sectus*: **following what is decreed by fate**. Virgil
Confiteor: **I confess**. A prayer of public confession. Roman Catholic Church
Odi profanum vulgus et arceo: **I hate the unhallowed rabble and keep them far from me**. Horace

**Explore* *fairy tale* collections. See *Thrall's*. Both Yahoo and Google search engines have extensive listings.

Related words from IE *bha-²*, **command**: **ban**, **banns**, **ban**al, **ban**dit, **ban**ish, aban**don**, contra**band**. See p. 46 for more on *contraband*, under **Clavis**.

Related Greek *phanai*, **to speak**: a**phasia**, brady**phasia**, cata**phasia**, dys**phas**ia, endo**phasia**; pro**phe**sy, pro**phe**t from *phone*, **sound**: **phone**, **phon**eme, **phon**emics, **phon**ics, **phon**ogram, **phon**ograph, **phon**ology, **phon**ometer, **phono**scope, allo**phone**, dia**phone**, homo**phone**, hypo**phone**, micro**phone**, poly**phone**, geo**phone**, hydro**phone**, stereo**phon**ic, tele**phone**, xylo**phone**, anti**phon**e (anthem), sym**phon**y; eu**phem**ism; eu**phon**ious; **blame**, **blaspheme**.

wordextras

Greek ***thesaurus***, **treasure**, **collection**, has come to mean a treasury, or storehouse, of words; also a list of subject headings or descriptors, usually with a cross-reference system for use in the organization of a collection of documents for reference and retrieval; also a function of most word-processors. See *magazine*, p. 60.

Assassin, from Arabic *hashshash*, **hashish addict**, is from the plant *hashish*, **hemp**. Originally, *Assassins* were members of a secret order of Moslem fanatics who terrorized and killed Christian Crusaders, between the 11th and 12th centuries.

Whiskey, from Irish and Scottish *usquebaugh*, means "water of life." *Akvavit*, also a distilled spirit, is the Scandinavian cognate of Latin *aqua vitae*, **water of life**. Russian ***vodka*** is a diminutive of *voda*,* **water**; originally, a fermentation of wheat, but now usually made from potatoes. *There is *Voda*, Kansas, between WaKeeney and Quinter on Interstate 70.

Synecdoche, from Greek *synekdoche*, **a receiving together**, is a figure of speech in which a *part* is used for a *whole*, as *bread* for *food*; or conversely, in which a *whole* is substituted for a *part*, as *army* for *soldier*, or *The White House* for the *President*. The meaning of *synecdoche* is similar to that of *metonymy*, p. 135. See other *sym-*, *syn-* words, p. 161. Pronunciation: sih NEK duh kee.

A pizza restaurant is properly a ***pizzeria***, not *pizzaria*.

Magnet, from *Magnetis lithos*, **stone of Magnesia**, is a material, such as iron, that has the power to attract like material.

Disoblige is to refuse to oblige or do a favor for; **to slight**; **offend**; to inconvenience; incommode.

Arbitrary, from the same source of *arbiter* (see p. 76), means **random**, **capricious**; not fixed by rules. SYNONYMS: dictatorial, doctrinaire, dogmatic.

Common element base: fari   **Meaning**: to speak, to talk

IE base: *bha-²*: **to speak**; **Greek** *pheme*, as in *blaspheme*, **to speak evil of**; **English**: blame
German: *sprechen*, as in *Sprechen Sie langsam, bitte*: **Please speak slowly**.

Clavis

fable:
a moral tale from folklore in which animals **speak**; may also be so named because tales were originally **oral**. The most famous fables are those of Aesop, a Greek slave who lived about 600 B.C.; other noted fabulists include Gay (England), La Fontaine (France), Lessing (Germany), Krylov (Russia), Thurber (United States); *fable* may also refer to any fictitious narrative.

fabliau:
a medieval genre of literature *recounting* a short comic or satiric tale in verse and dealing with middle- or lower-class characters (and originally **told** by trouvères); *fabliaux* were often obscene and earthy. Explore "The Pardoner's Tale" and "The Miller's Tale" in Chaucer's *Canterbury Tales*. Compare *fabliau* with *conte* (pronounced as one syllable), a short fictitious story, especially a tale of venture. *Trouvère*, or *trouvere*: a class of lyric and narrative poets and poet-musicians.

preface:
from *praefatio*, **to speak before**; an introductory statement to an article, book, or speech, telling its subject, purpose, plan, etc.; something preliminary or introductory; prelude; the adjectival form is *prefatory*, as in *prefatory remarks*. Pronunciations: *preface*: PREF ice; *prefatory*: PREF uh TOR ee.

infant:
in-, **negative**; **one who cannot speak**; *infantry*: often thought to be those **not allowed** to speak; however, *infants*, or younger persons, who usually did not own a horse, were conscripted for the *infantry*; during the Middle Ages, only the older upper-class men who usually owned horses were allowed to join the cavalry. In Spanish and Portuguese, infantrymen, or *peóns*, **foot soldiers**.

enfants perdus:
French for **lost children**; military troops in a hopeless battle; related in meaning to Dutch *verloren hoop*, **forsaken troops**, and by variant folk etymology, *forlorn hope*, or **a faint hope**. General as well as military usage. See p. 73, under *French phrase*.

infamous:
in-, **not**; **not well-spoken of**; famous or well-known in a derogatory sense; having a bad reputation; notorious. In *law*, the loss of certain rights, when persons are convicted of particular crimes. *Infamous crimes* are those punishable by imprisonment in a penitentiary rather than in a jail.

profess:
pro-, **before**; **to speak before**; thus, a college or university professor (who **speaks before** a class); to declare or admit openly, as *to profess one's beliefs*.

dysphasia:
Greek *dys-*, **wrong, abnormal**; a clinical term expressing the impairment of **speech** resulting from a brain lesion (wound).

apophysis:
Greek *apo-*, **away**; any natural outgrowth or process, especially on a vertebra or other bone.

flowerwords

Flowers are often named after the botanist, or other person, who discovered them; sometimes, they are named simply in honor of someone. Examples: *begonia, bougainvillea, camellia, claytonia, dahlia, forsythia, fuchsia, gardenia, magnolia, poinsettia, wisteria, zinnia*.

begonia: Michel Bégon (1638-1710), French governor of Santo Domingo; a patron of science.
bougainvillea: Louis Antoine de Bougainville (1729-1811), French navigator and explorer.
camellia: G. J. Camelli (1661-1706), Moravian Jesuit missionary who brought specimens from Japan to London in 1738. The state flower of Alabama, where it blooms in January and February.
claytonia: J. Clayton (1685-1773), American botanist.
dahlia: A. Dahl, 18th-century Swedish botanist. The flower is a native of Mexico, and is its state flower.
forsythia: William Forsyth (1737-1804), English botanist. Discovered in China.
fuchsia: Leonhard Fuchs (1501-66), German botanist. See *digitalis*, p. 110.
gardenia: Alexander Garden (1730-91), American botanist.
magnolia: Pierre Magnol (1638-1715), French botanist. State flower of Mississippi. [Of the 17 varieties, there are eight in the Eastern United States alone.]
poinsettia: Joel R. Poinsett (d. 1851), U.S. ambassador to Mexico, where he found the plant growing wild.
wisteria: Caspar Wistar (1761-1818), American anatomist.
zinnia: J. G. Zinn (d. 1759), German botanist.

Word Cluster No. 40

fidate	af**fid**avit	per**fid**y	con**fid**e	con**fid**ential
con**fid**ent	dif**fid**ent	**fid**elity	**fid**uciary	in**fid**el
con**fid**ant	**fid**ucial	**fid**eism	**fid**ucity	sol**fid**ian

Common elements_____Inferred Meaning_____

Romance Cognates	French foi	Romanian fidel	Italian fede	Portuguese fé	Spanish fe

Words with disguised Latin roots: fay, foy, affiance, fiancé, fiancée, davy, defiance, defy

Placenames: Santa Fe (NM, TN); Confidence, IA; Fidelity (IL, MO); Defiance, IA; Fort Defiance (AZ, NM)

Latin phrases: *Bona fide polliceor*: **I promise in good faith**. Cicero
Confido et conquiesco: **I trust and am at rest.**
semper fidelis; adeste fidelis; bona fide; bona fides; Deus nobis fiducia; Fidei Defensor (see **Clavis**)
Nulla fides fronti: **No trust in the countenance**; also, *Ne fronti crede*: **Do not trust the face.**
Compare the last two phrases with *Macbeth*, I, 4, 11, "There is no art to find the mind's construction in the face."

Portuguese phrase: *auto-da-fé* (see **Clavis**)

French phrases: *de bonne foi*, **in good faith**; *ma foi*, **my faith!** upon my word! indeed!

Motto of George Washington University: *Deus nobis fiducia*, **God our trust**

Related derivatives: **fed**eration, **fed**eral, con**fed**erate, con**fed**eration, Con**fed**erate States of America

Latin *credere*, **to trust, believe**: **cred**ence, **cred**enda, **cred**ential, **cred**entialism, **cred**enza (from Italian *fare de credenza*, **to make confidence; to taste**; a type of buffet or sideboard; also, a piece of dining room furniture for holding linen, silver, china), **cred**ible, **cred**it, **cred**itable, **cred**itor, **cred**o, **cred**ulity, **cred**ulous (tending to believe too readily, especially with little or no proof, e.g., describing the child who believes the moon is actually made of green cheese); in**cred**ulity; ac**cred**it, dis**cred**it, disac**cred**it, micro**cred**it; dis**cred**itable; in**cred**ible; mis**cre**ant, re**cre**ant (**cowardly, craven**); **cre**ed. Spanish: *creer*, **to believe**; *no lo puedo creer*, **I can't believe it.** See pp. 48, 205.

Explore *confidant* (*confidante*, feminine) as a literary term. In a drama or novel, a *confidant* plays only a minor role in the action, but serves the protagonist as a trusted friend to whom he can confess his intimate thoughts. A famous *confidant* is Dr. Watson in A. Conan Doyle's detective stories about Sherlock Holmes.

wordextras

Piccolo, Italian for **small**, is a musical instrument considerably smaller than a flute. Not only is it smaller, it is also pitched an octave higher; as an *adjective*, **smaller than usual**, as *a piccolo banjo*.

Tympani, the plural of *tympano*, **kettle drum**, is further from *tympanum*, **ear drum**.

Atascadero, California, is Spanish for **mudhole**, certainly not a complimentary name for such a beautiful city. However, residents attest that after a rain, the name is appropriate, at least in times past.

Bessemer, Alabama, known for its former steel mills, is named after a process of producing steel, invented by English engineer Sir Henry Bessemer (1813-1898). The Bessemer process removes impurities by forcing a blast of air through the molten iron. Bessemer is a suburb of Birmingham, the Pittsburgh of the South.

Expiate, from *ex-*, **out** + *piare*, **to appease**, means to make amends or reparation for wrongdoing or guilt; atone for, as *to expiate one's sins by acts of penance*; to pay the penalty of; suffer for wrongdoing or guilt. The nominal form is *expiation;* the adjectival, *expiatory*. Other words and forms from *piare*: **pi**acular; **Pi**età, **pi**etism, **pi**ety; **pi**osity, **pi**ous; ex**pi**able, inex**pi**able; im**pi**ety; im**pi**ous; **pi**ty.

Maelstrom, from Dutch *malen*, **to grind, whirl around** + *stroom*, **stream**, is any large or violent whirlpool, and was first applied to a famous strong, swirling tidal current off the west coast of Norway. In lowercase, a violently confused or dangerously agitated state of mind, emotion, affairs, etc. A famous story by Edgar Allan Poe is titled "A Descent into the Maelstrom." See p. 157 for *ratiocination*, a process of rational thinking used in many of Poe's tales.

Archaic, from Greek *archein*, **to begin**, means belonging to an earlier period; ancient; anachronistic. My bank uses *archaic* methods of bookkeeping; it still issues a handwritten receipt for deposits.

Common element base: fidere   **Meaning**: to trust, to have faith in

IE base: *bheidh-*: **to persuade, compel, confide**; **German**: *Glauben*, **faith in a religion**; *Treue*, **faithfulness**.

German *Treue* is akin to **English** *true*, the basis of which is **Old English** (Germanic) *treow*, **faith**.

Clavis

fidate:	to exempt in chess from capture (as in problems).
fideism:	the view that everything that can be known with certainty about God or divine things can be known by **faith** and never by reason alone. Pronunciation: FEE day IZ um; also, FIE dee IZ um.
fiducial:	based on firm **faith**; used as a standard of reference for measurement or calculation, as *a fiducial point*; relating to or characteristic of a legal trust or fiduciary; see next entry.
fiduciary:	from *fiducia*, **trust, a thing held in trust**; designating, or of a person, who holds something in **trust** for another; of a trustee or trusteeship, as *a fiduciary guardian* for a minor child.
affidavit:	a one-word Latin sentence: **He has stated it on faith**; a written, voluntarily sworn declaration; *ex parte*, **from one side only**, with no cross-examination. Compare *deposition*, a sworn statement made out of court and used when the case for which it was made comes to trial.
affiance:	*af-*, assimilation of *ad-*, **to, toward**; **a pledging of oneself**, especially to another, as in a wedding ceremony; though now archaic, **trust, confidence**. Other words with *af-*: **af**fable, **af**ferent, **af**finity.
diffident:	*dif-*, assimilation of *dis-*, **not**; originally, **not trusting**; lacking self-confidence. Milton refers to the *diffidence of God*, or **not trusting God**. *Diffidence* has acquired an internalized focus, however; it now means lack of confidence in oneself. ADJECTIVE SYNONYMS: bashful, coy, modest, shy, timid.
infidel:	*in-*, **negative**; a person who does not believe in a particular religion, especially the prevailing one; among Christians, a non-Christian; among Muslims, a non-Muslim.
perfidy:	from *per fidem decipi*; *per-*, **an intensive**; **a deception of faith**; the deliberate breaking of faith; betrayal of trust; treachery. Adjectival form: *perfidious*. See *warlock*, pp. 108, 167.
defy:	*de-*, **down, away**; **away** (or, **down**) **with faith**; hence, to reject, renounce, or repudiate. Also, to resist or oppose boldly or openly; to resist in a baffling way, as *the puzzle defied solution*.
bona fide:	**in good faith**, as *a bona fide contract*; genuine; *bona fides*: lack of fraud or deceit; in German, *in gutem Glauben*. See *bona fide*, p. 18.
auto-da-fé:	Portuguese; **act of faith**; a ceremony prior to the burning of a heretic. Do not confuse with Greek *auto-*, **self**, as in **auto**cratic, **auto**gamy, **auto**graph, **auto**mobile, **auto**nomy, **auto**nomous, **auto**psy (see **wordbuilder #20**, p. 41).
Fidei Defensor:	**Defender of the Faith**, one of the many titles of the monarchs of England; abbreviated *Fid. Def.*, or *F.D.*, on British coins.
semper fidelis:	*semper*, **always**; **Always Faithful**; motto of the United States Marine Corps; shortened to *semper fi*.

wordextras

Galore, from Irish *go leor*, **enough**, means "more than enough, abundant, plentiful." *Galore* is used postpositively, that is, after the noun, e.g., at the company picnic, there were salads and fried chicken *galore*. In English, adjectives usually precede nouns except when following linking verbs. See *beaucoup*, p. 103.

Dollar is from Low German and Modern Dutch *daler*, **dale**, **valley**, from German *thaler*. *Dollar* itself is a clipping of *Joachimsthaler*, a coin originally made in 1519 from silver mined at St. Joachimstal (**Joachim's Valley**), Bohemia (modern Czechoslovakia); the mine now produces uranium.

Schizophrenia, from Greek *schizein*, **to split** + *phren*, **mind** + *-ia*, **condition**, is "the condition of a split mind." *Schizophrenia* is a mental disorder characterized by indifference, withdrawal, hallucinations, and delusions of persecution and omnipotence, often with impaired intelligence. See p. 37.

Latin *quidnunc*, Latin for "**What now?**" is an inquisitive, gossipy person; a busybody; a yenta, or yente (Yiddish).

Word from Greek mythology: *Procrustean*: **drastic, ruthless**; enforced conformity; from *Procrustes*, an innkeeper who seized travelers, tied them to a bedstead, and either stretched them or cut off their legs to make them fit the bed.

Sectional Word Cluster Test

INSTRUCTIONS: For each set of words from Latin and Greek (and sometimes, French, Spanish, and German), write the common meaning in the blank.

Example: **hypo**tenuse, **hypo**thesis, **sub**ject   <u>under</u>

	Presection Answer	Postsection Answer
41. **fin**ish, **fin**ite, **fin**itude, de**fine**, in**fin**ite	_____	_____
42. **flu**id, in**flu**enza, con**flu**ence, in**flux**	_____	_____
43. **fug**itive, centri**fug**al, re**fug**ee, vermi**fuge**	_____	_____
44. **greg**arious, con**greg**ation, e**greg**ious, **agora**phobia	_____	_____
45. **hab**eas corpus, **hab**it, reha**bil**itate, pro**hib**it	_____	_____
46. **hered**ity, **heir**, **heir**loom, in**herit**, **herit**age	_____	_____
47. **Homo** sapiens, **homi**cide, Ecce **homo**, ad **hom**inem	_____	_____
48. **in** absentia, **in** esse, **in** loco parentis	_____	_____
49. **inter**action, **inter**cede, **inter**state, **inter**vene	_____	_____
50. **intra**coastal, **instra**state, **intra**venous, **intra**uterine	_____	_____

_____	_____
Presection Score	Postsection Score

Note: Enter scores for this test and the following ones after completing this section; then, enter them on p. xvii.

Sectional Wordbuilder Test

Throughout the book and as a supplement, there are wordbuilders; these wordbuilders are designed to help you build a family of words from a single root.

	Presection Answer	Postsection Answer
29. What is the meaning of *eco-, ecu-* as in **eco**nomy, **ecu**menical?	_____	_____
30. What is the meaning of *firm-* as in **firm**ament, in**firm**ary?	_____	_____
31. What is the meaning of *galact-* as in **galact**ic, dys**galact**ia?	_____	_____
32. What is the meaning of *lact-* as in **lact**ate, **lact**eal?	_____	_____
33. What is the meaning of *cine-, kine-* as in **cine**ma, **kine**tics?	_____	_____
34. What is the meaning of *dorm-* as in **dorm**itory, **dorm**ant?	_____	_____
35. What is the meaning of *frater-* as in **frater**nity, **frater**nal?	_____	_____
36. What is the meaning of *gran-* as in **gran**ary, pome**gran**ate?	_____	_____
37. What is the meaning of *fract-* as in **fract**ure, re**fract**?	_____	_____
38. What is the meaning of *carp-* as in **carp**ology, poly**carp**ous?	_____	_____
39. What is the meaning of *brady-* as in **brady**cardia, **brady**kinetic?	_____	_____

Presection Score   Postsection Score

After entering the scores here, enter them on pp. xviii.

Word Cluster No. 41

fine	finish	final	refine	definition
finite	finance	finesse	confine	finial
finitude	financier	infinity	define	finical
finicky	infinitive	affinity	infinitesimal	paraffin

Common element_____Inferred Meaning_____

Romance Cognates	French	Romanian	Italian	Portuguese	Spanish
	fin	sfirsir	fine	fin	fin

Words with disguised Latin root: trepan:trephine (*tres*, **three** + *fines*, **ends**); doublets (in this book, joined by colons)

French phrase: *fin de siècle* (see **Clavis**)

Latin phrases: *ad finitum*; *mali principii malus finis*: **the bad end of a bad beginning**
Certum voto pete finem: **Set a definite limit to your desires.** Horace
Nervi belli pecunia infinita: **Plenty of money is the sinews of war.** Cicero
Finis coronat: **The end crowns the work.** *finem respice*: **consider the end,** or the **consequences**.

Italian phrase: *La commedia è finita*: **The comedy is ended.** Closing words of the opera *I Pagliacci*, by Leoncavallo. Compare French *tirez le rideau, la farce est jouée*: **Bring down the curtain, the farce is over.** Rabelais (1494-1553; French satirist and humorist: said to be his last words

Literature phrase: moment of *final* suspense (see **Clavis**)

Greek: from *teleo*, with same basic meaning as *finis*: **tele**stich, **teleo**logy; talisman.

NB: Unrelated to Greek *tele-*, **afar**: **tele**genic, **tele**gony, **tele**graph, **tele**phone, **tele**vision (see p. 212, Item 177).

wordbuilder #29
Greek *eco-*, *(o)ec-*, from *oikein*, **to dwell, inhabit**, yields **eco**nomy, **eco**logy, **eco**species, **eco**system, **eco**tone, **eco**type; **ecu**menical; andr**oecium**, gyn**oecium**; aut**oecious**, di**oeceious**, heter**ecious**, homo**ecious**, mon**ecious**, syn**oecious**, tri**oecious**; parish, parochial (from *para-* + *oikos*), diocese (*dia-*, **through**; *dioikein*, **to keep house**).

wordextras
Furlough, from Dutch *verlof* and German *verlaub*, **to permit**, is a leave of absence, especially, a leave granted to enlisted military personnel for a specified period; as a *verb*, **to lay off employees**, especially temporarily.

Smorgasbord, from three Swedish words, **smear** (from *smör*, **butter**), **goose**, and **board**, is a buffet of a great variety of dishes, both hot and cold. *Smorgasbord* can also mean a heterogeneous mixture; a mélange; hodgepodge.

The plural of **radius** is either *radii* or *radiuses*; *locus, loci*; *isthmus, isthmi*. The plural of *focus* may be either *focuses* or *foci*, pronounced FOH sigh. As a *verb*, the third-person singular is *focuses*. See more on *focus*, p. 111.

The feminine form of Hindi *rajah* (in India, a prince or chief) is *rani*, or *ranee*. See p. 163, **Word Cluster No. 82**, under **Disguised Roots**. [*Hindu* designates "a people of India"; *Hindi*, their language.]

Benelux is the acronym for Belgium, Netherlands, and Luxembourg considered together; also designates the tripartite customs union formed by these countries in 1947. See more on *Benelux*, p. 54, under *beguine*, **wordextras**.

Greek *tmesis*, from *temnein*, **to cut**, means "a cutting." In *grammar* and *rhetoric*, the separation of a compound word, now generally for humorous effect; for example, "what place soever," instead of "whatsoever place," or "abso-bloody-lutely." See other words from *temnein*, p. 23. Pronounced: TMEE sis.

Infirm, **not firm or strong physically**; weak, unstable; also **not secure or valid**, as *an infirm title to property*. An *infirmary* is a place for the care of the sick, injured, or infirm, especially in the military. See **wordbuilder #30**, p. 83.

Indulge, from Latin *indulgere*, **to be kind to, to yield to**, cannot be further traced with certainty. Variously, the word means **to yield to, to satisfy a desire**; to give oneself up to, as *to indulge one's craving for chocolate*; to be very lenient with; to humor. SYNONYMS: baby, pamper, spoil. Related forms: *indulgence* (noun), *indulgent* (adjective).

Ardent, from *ardere*, **to burn**, means warm or intense in feeling; passionate; as *an ardent follower* of a particular religion, or *an ardent fan* of one's athletic team.

Common element base: finere   **Meaning**: to end; hence, limit, boundary
IE base: *dhigw-*: **to stick in**; the source of *dike, ditch, fix,* and **Latin** *figere*, **to fasten**, **attach**: **fix**, **fix**ate, **fix**ation, **fix**ative, **fix**ture, af**fix**, ante**fix**, in**fix**, pre**fix**, suf**fix**, trans**fix**; traf**fic**; sof**fit**; idée fixe; prix fixe (see *table d'hôte*, p. 5).

Clavis

finite: having measurable or definable **limits**; *infinite*: lacking limits or bounds; *the Infinite Being*, **God**.

finale: Italian; in *music*, the **last** piece, division, or movement of a composition; the concluding part of any performance, course of proceedings, etc.; the end. Pronounced: fuh NAL ee; fuh NAH lay, or lee.

finicky: from, and the same as, *finical*; excessively particular or exacting; overly dainty or fastidious; difficult to please; fussy; colloquially, persnickety (Scottish dialect).

finance: originally, **to end** an obligation; now, more likely, to begin one.

financier: one who provides the **finances** for an enterprise or undertaking. One pronunciation: FIN un SIR.

fin de siècle: French; **end of the century**; specifically, the **end** of the 19th century (especially, the last ten years), and designates a period free from social and moral traditions; formerly used to refer to progressive ideas and customs, but now generally used to indicate **decadence**. See *decadent*, p. 38.

affine: *af-*, assimilation of *ad-*, **to**, **toward**, and in this word, meaning **related**; in *mathematics*, of or pertaining to a transformation that maps parallel lines to parallel lines and finite points to finite points.

define: *de-*, **down**; **to set a limit to**, **to bound**; to describe exactly; to give the distinguishing features of; to state the meaning or meanings of a word; there are both *dictionary* and *extended* definitions. Related forms: *definite, definitive* (adjectives); *definition, definitude* (nouns).

infinitive: *in-*, **negative**; **without end**; the simple, uninflected form of a verb without reference to person, number, or tense, and in English, most often preceded by *to*, as in *to run*, *to educate*. Infinitives can function as nouns, as in Romeo's "*To be* or not *to be*," and "How much easier it is *to be* critical than *to be* correct," Benjamin Disraeli, Earl of Beaconsville. Infinitives are also used in verbal phrases, as in "He wished *to become an actor*."

ad infinitum: **to infinity**; forever; endlessly; without limit; figuratively, what appears like infinity, e.g., "The speaker droned on *ad infinitum*." Pronunciation: ad IN fuh NITE um.

talisman: French and Spanish for Arabic *tilsam*, but originally from Greek; that which is **completed**. A consecrated object believed by some to hold magical charms.

moment of final suspense: designating the ray of hope just before the catastrophe of a tragedy. Explore phrase further; listed under "dramatic structure" in most handbooks of literary terms. Search Yahoo or Google.

wordextras

Mattress, ultimately from Arabic *matrah*, was originally something **thrown** or **laid**, as to lie on; **a cushion**; passed into Italian as *materasso*; eventually, into Middle English (a combination of Anglo-Saxon and Old French) as *materas*.

Ascetic, from Greek *askein*, **to exercise**, **train for athletic competition**, is a person who lives a life of contemplation and rigorous self-denial for religious purposes; anyone who lives with strict self-discipline and without the usual pleasures and comforts; also, a monk, or hermit. As an *adjective*, describes such a person or way of life.

Villain, from Vulgar Latin *villanus*, **a farm servant**, is further from Latin *villa*, **country house**, **farm**. A *villain* is a person guilty of, or likely to commit, great crimes; also, a wicked or unprincipled character in a novel, play, etc., who opposes the protagonist. A related word is *villein*, any of a class of feudal serfs who by the 13th century had become freemen in their legal relations to all except their lord, to whom they remained subject as slaves.

Measly properly denotes "infected with measles." Informally, *measly* means "meager, contemptibly slight, worthless, or skimpy." Example: The rich, old man left the waiter only *a measly tip*.

Poultice, a hot, soft, moist mass, as of flour, herbs, mustard, etc., often spread on cloth, and applied to sore or inflamed parts of the body, is from Latin *pulvis*, **powder**, and is the base of *pulverize*, **to crush or grind to dust**.

Word from a person's name: *Byronic*; from George Noel Gordon, 6th Lord Baron Byron, an English poet. SYNONYMS: cynical, equivocal, ironic, passionate, romantic. Lord Byron (1788-1824) contributed to the creation of the Byronic hero with deeds as much as words. The remarkable story of his life can found on the Internet.

Word Cluster No. 42

fluent	fluid	affluent	superfluity	transfluent
defluent	profluent	effluent	fluence	influence
confluence	mellifluous	refluent	influenza	diffluent
		circumfluent		
flux	afflux	efflux	influx	reflux
fluvial	subfluvial	effluvium	fluviomarine	interfluve

Common elements_____Inferred Meaning_____

Romance Cognates	French	Romanian	Italian	Portuguese	Spanish
	fluide	fluid	fluido	fluido	fluido

Words with disguised roots: fluctuant, fluctuate, flume, flow, flood   **Doublets**: influence:influenza

French term: *roman fleuve* (**river novel**): a long novel, often in a number of volumes, dealing with a cross section of society, several generations of a family, etc.

Greek: *rrhe*, from *rhein*, **to flow**, yields the following words: **rheo**base, **rheo**logy, **rheo**meter, **rheo**phile, **rheo**stat, **rheo**taxis, **rheo**tropism; cata**rrh**; blenno**rrhea**, broncho**rrhea**, dia**rrhea**, dysmeno**rrhea**, gono**rrhea**; leuko**rrhea**, logo**rrhea**, meno**rrhea**, pyo**rrhea**, rhino**rrhe**a (**runny nose**), sebo**rrhea**; hemo**rrh**age, hemo**rrh**oid.

German phrase: *Flut von Worten*: **a torrent of words**

Quote: Although the study of Greek has been for centuries an essential part of the higher education of Englishmen, the language would not have contributed greatly to the English vocabulary if it had not happened to be particularly fitted to supply the need for the precise technical terms of science.
Henry Bradley

wordextras

Japan is a transliteration of a Chinese compound, *Jipenkuo*, **land of the origin of the sun**; this phrase was later modified to Japan's sobriquet: Land of the Rising Sun. The early settlers of Japan gave the islands the collective name *Nihon*, now *Nippon*, a compound of *Nicchi*, **sun** + *Hon*, **origin**, thus showing their acceptance of the older Chinese label. See *Levant*, p. 112.

Raconteur, from French *raconter*, **to recount**, is a person skilled in telling stories or anecdotes. *Raconter* is from *re-*, **again** + *a(d)-*, **to** + *co(u)nter*, **to count, to tell**. Pronounced RACK ahn TOOR, or RACK un TOOR.

Mein Kampf, by Adolph Hitler, is German for **My Struggle**, his autobiography.

Thrall is Anglo-Saxon for **slave, serf**; originally, *to enthrall* meant "to make a slave of; enslave." It has come to mean "to hold as if in a spell; captivate; fascinate."

Bandit, from Italian *bandito*, and further from *bandire*, **to outlaw**, denotes a **robber**, especially one who preys on travelers on the road; brigand; highwayman; anyone who steals, cheats, exploits, etc. See other *ban-* words, p. 77.

Astute, from Latin *astus*, **craft, cunning**, describes one having a clever or shrewd mind; also, crafty, sly, wily.

Tatter, from Old Norse *töturr*, **rags, tatters**, means a torn and hanging shred or piece; seen also in *tatterdemalion*.

Pillow, from Latin *pulvinus*, originally meant **cushion**. In German, *pillow* is *Pfühl*; in Spanish, *almohada*.

wordbuilder #30

Latin *firmare*, **to make strong**, yields **firm**, **firm**ament, af**firm** (SYNONYMS: assert, avouch, declare, warrant), con**firm**, disaf**firm** (to deny or contradict a former statement; in *law*, to refuse to abide by a contract, agreement; repudiate), discon**firm**, in**firm** (see p. 81 under **wordextras**); con**firm**ation, con**firm**atory, con**firm**ed (as *a confirmed bachelor*), in**firm**ary, in**firm**ity; cantus **firm**us (**fixed song**, an existing melody used as the basis for a new polyphonic composition); terra **firm**a (**solid ground**); **farm**; and the music term *fermata*, **pause**, which comes from Italian *fermare*, **to stop**. Spanish *firma* is one's signature, that which *affirms*, or *confirms*, that which is signed.

Common element base: fluere   **Meaning**: to flow
IE base: *bhleu-*: **to swell**, **well up**, yielding **Greek** *phluzein*, **to boil over**; thus, *phlyctena*, *a blister*; and *phloos*, **phloem**, **tree bark** (swelling with growth). IE base also yields *rhyme, rhythm, stream*.

Clavis

confluence: *con-*, **together**; **a flowing together**, especially of two or more streams or rivers, as Cobb Island, Maryland, is located at the *confluence* of the Potomac and Wicomico; also, **a coming together of people**; crowd; throng. [In his autobiography, a student of the Virginia author of this book wrote that he lives on Cobb Island, which is at the *intersection* of the Potomac and the Wicomico. He was led to see that rivers don't *cross*, as at an intersection, but *flow together*. He remarked that he would be the only person on Cobb Island who knew the meaning of the word.]

affluent: *af-*, assimilation of *ad-*, **to**, **toward**; **flowing in**. As an *adjective*, **flowing freely**, as *an affluent imagination*; can also describe one who is wealthy, as though riches "flow to" that person, e.g., *an affluent congressman*; a tributary; for example, Pea River, in Alabama, is an *affluent* of the Choctawhatchee, which itself is an *affluent* of, or disembogues into, the Gulf of Mexico. The nominal form is *affluence*, **a flowing toward**; great plenty; wealth, opulence. Pronounced: AF loo unt.

effluent: *ef-*, assimilation of *ex-*, **out**; **flowing out**; something that flows out or forth, especially a stream flowing out of a lake or other body of water; also, an outflow of a sewer, storage tank, irrigation canal, or other channel. Other words with *ef-*: **ef**face, **ef**fect, **ef**feminate, **ef**fervesce, **ef**ficient, **ef**fete, **ef**figy, **ef**fort.

influence: *in-*, **in**; that which **flows in**; originally thought to be an ethereal fluid which flowed from the stars and which affected people's actions and character. As a *verb*, **to affect**.

influenza: Italian; often shortened to *flu*; from *influence*, previous entry; ancient astrologers believed that the infection was influenced by, or **flowed in from**, the stars. *Influence*, as a noun, and *influenza* are doublets.

refluent: *re-*, **back**; **flowing back**, ebbing, as the tide to the sea. The nominal form is *refluence*. In the same sense, *fluctuate* means to move back and forth or up and down; rise and fall. Pronounced: REF loo unt.

mellifluous: *mel*, **honey**; **flowing like honey**, as *a mellifluous voice*. Other words from *mel*: *melliferous* (**producing honey**), *caramel, oenomel, molasses; mildew, mousse*. Pronounced: muh LIF loo us.

ossifluence: *os*, **bone** (genitive: *ossis*); a dissolution, or softening, of bone. Pronounced: ah SIF loo unce.

superfluous: *super-*, **above**, **over**; **flowing over**; more than is needed, wanted, or useful; surplus; excessive; not needed, as *superfluous words*; irrelevant, as *a superfluous remark*. Pronounced: soo PUR floo us.

interfluve: *inter-*, **between**; the land between two streams or river valleys; another source says, the region of higher land between two rivers that are in the same drainage system.

flume: an artificial water channel for producing power or conveying logs, fish, etc.; also, a ravine or gorge with a stream **flowing** through it. *The Flume* is a major tourist attraction in the White Mountains of New Hampshire.

catarrh: Greek *kata-*, **down** + *rhein*, **to flow**; that which **flows down**; formerly applied to inflammation of the mucous membranes of the nose, head, and throat, and which caused an increased flow of mucus; *mucus*, noun; *muc<u>ou</u>s*, adjective. *Catarrh* is rarely used now.

rheostat: Greek *stat*, **stable**; a device that **sets the flow** of an electrical current. Engineers' definition: a device that varies the resistance of an electrical circuit without interrupting the circuit; thus, **a light dimmer**. See p. 180 for more on *rheostat*.

wordextras

Livid, from Latin *lividus*, and akin to *livere*, **to be black and blue**, describes that which is discolored by a bruise; has come to mean grayish-blue; lead-colored, as in *livid with rage*. See *lavender*, p. 110.

Ossa and *Pelion* are mountains in Thessaly, northeastern Greece, 6,490 ft. and 5,252 ft., respectively. To be faced with overbearing obstacles and burdens is sometimes referred to as "to pile Ossa on Pelion."

Word from a person's name: *maudlin*, **tearful**, **emotional**, **foolishly sentimental**; from the sorrowful and repentant Mary Magdalene, who washed the feet of Jesus with her tears. Luke 7:37.

```
┌─────────────────────────────────────────────────────────────────────────────┐
│                          Word Cluster No. 43                                  │
│ fugue            subterfuge         febrifuge          centrifugal            │
│ fugacity             fugie          calcifuge          counterfuge            │
│ fugitate           refuge           vermifuge          heliofugal             │
│ fugitive          refugee           dolorifuge         tenifuge               │
│ fugal            fugacious          nidifugous         refugium               │
│                                                                               │
│ Common elements_____Inferred Meaning_____       │
└─────────────────────────────────────────────────────────────────────────────┘
```

Romance Cognates	French	Romanian	Italian	Portuguese	Spanish
	fuir	fugi	fuggire	fugir	fugar

Words with disguised roots: fuidhir (in ancient Ireland, a stranger-refugee), feverfew

Early American style of music: fuging tune (see **Clavis**)

Placenames: Refugio, Texas (in Refugio County) has a colorful history (check Google); Refugio Azules, Chile

Latin phrases: *in meditatione fugae; fugit irreparabile tempus; fugit hora; tempus fugit*
Fugaces labuntur anni: **The years glide swiftly on.**
Quid sit futurum cras, fuge quaerere: **Avoid asking what tomorrow will bring forth.** Horace
Dum loquimur fugerit invida aetas: **Even as we speak, grim Time speeds swiftly away.** Horace
Faenum habet in cornu, longe fuge: **He has hay on his horn** (the mark of a dangerous bull); **flee from him**. Horace

Explore *The Art of the Fugue*, *St. Anne's Fugue*, and *The Cat's Fugue* in a music dictionary.

wordextras

When the early Romans flexed their biceps, there appeared to be a small mouse racing up and down their upper arm. Consequently, the biceps was called *muscle*, or **little mouse**. Depending on how used, *biceps* can be either singular or plural; an alternate spelling for the plural is *bicepses*. See **Clavis**, pp. 20, 32, for more on *biceps*. See *mussel*, p. 113.

Miasma, from Greek *mianinein*, **to pollute**, referred to a poisonous atmosphere thought to arise from swamps and to cause disease. *Miasma* now most often refers to any noxious, or befogging, atmosphere or influence.

Myopia, from Greek *myein*, **to shut** + *ops*, **eye**, "to shut, or blink, the eye," has come to mean **near-sightedness**, and in *ophthalmology*, a condition of the eye in which parallel rays are focused in front of the retina.

Bandanna, or *bandana*, from Hindi, originally "a method of dyeing," came from Sanskrit *bandhana*, **tying** (so called because the cloth is tied in a way to prevent certain parts from receiving the dye). *Bandana* designates a large colored handkerchief, usually with a figure or pattern. See p. 53, under *Indian words*.

Canorous, from Latin *canere*, **to sing**, means richly melodious; pleasant-sounding; musical, as *the canorous sounds* of nightingales, finches, linnets, canaries, and larks. Pronounced: kuh NOR us.

Inebriate, from *in-*, **intensive** + *ebriare*, **to make drunk**, is "to intoxicate"; figuratively, to excite, exhilarate.

Sutler, from 16th-century Dutch *soeteler*, **to do dirty work**, denotes a person following an army to sell food, liquor, etc., to its soldiers. In modern use, a civilian provisioner to an army post often with a shop on the post.

Austere, from Greek *auein*, **to dry**, is an adjective meaning "having a severe or stern look, manner, etc."; very plain.

Affable, from *ad-*, **to** + *fari*, **to speak**, means "pleasant and easy to approach or talk to." SYNONYMS: amiable, cordial.

wordbuilders #31, 32

Both Greek *galactos* and Latin *lactos* mean **milk**; *galactos* is extended to mean **stars**, from a mass of stars appearing *milky*, as *the Milky Way*; **galact**ic (pertaining to both *milk* and *stars*), **galact**oma (same as *galactocele*, a tumor of the milk gland), **galact**agogue, **galact**ose, **galact**osis; **galacto**blast, **galacto**cele, **galacto**gen, **galacto**graphy, **galacto**-pexy, **galacto**phagous (**feeding on milk**), **galacto**phore, **galacto**poietic, **galacto**rrhea; dys**galact**ia, extra**galact**ic, inter**galact**ic, intra**galact**ic; neo**gala**; **galaxy**, meta**galaxy**, proto**galaxy**.

Latin: **lact**am, **lact**arene, **lact**ary, **lact**ate, **lact**ation, **lact**eal, **lact**escent, **lact**ic, **lact**one, **lact**ose; **lacti**ferous, **lacti**fugal, **lacti**fy, **lacti**genous, **lacti**gerous, **lacti**vorous; **lacto**bacillus, **lacto**genic, **lacto**meter; **lact**yl; ab**lact**ation, de**lact**ation, mis**lact**ation, super**lact**ation; pro**lact**in; **lettuce** (because of its *milky* juice); Spanish *café con leche* (**coffee with milk**); French *café au lait* (**coffee with milk**; also, **pale brown**).

Common element base: fugere   **Meaning**: to flee
IE base: *bheug-¹*: **to flee**; **German**: noun, *Flucht*; verb, *flüchten*

Clavis

fugacious: adjective; passing away quickly; **fleeting**; ephemeral, evanescent; in *botany*, withering; falling soon
               after blooming, as some flowers; the nominal form is *fugacity*. See *precocious* as a botany term, p. 56.

fugitive: as a *noun*, **one who flees**, especially from justice or from the law; as an *adjective*, **fleeting**, as *fugitive
               thoughts*, or of passing interest, as *a fugitive essay*.

nidifugous: *nidus*, **nest**; **fleeing from the nest** (shortly after hatching), as a chicken, turkey, grouse, pheasant. Those
               remaining in the nest until mature enough to fly, such as robins, wrens, sparrows, are described as
               nidicolous, where the contrasting verb is from *colere*, **to dwell**. See *altricial*, p. 57.

fugue: in *music*, a canon or contrapuntal composition in which melodic themes are imitated by the successive
               voices, as though one theme is chasing (or, conversely, **fleeing from**) the other. In *medicine*, a dis-
               turbed state of consciousness.

fuging tune: early 19th-century Protestant hymn type characterized by *polyphony* and *imitations*. *Polyphony* is the
               juxtaposition of a number of individual but harmonizing melodies; *imitation* is the repetition of a
               theme in different parts of a composition with or without changes in rhythm, key, voice, or intervals.

centrifugal: **center-fleeing**; in a whirlpool, for example, the force of water that goes, or **flees**, to the outside.
               Compare with *centripetal*, which *seeks* **the center**. Other words from *petire*, **to seek**: *appetite* (to **seek**
               after, as for food or knowledge), *petition, petulant, perpetual, compete, impetigo, impetuous, impetus,
               repetition, competent, propitiate* (to cause to become favorably inclined, as sacrifices made to *pro-
               pitiate* the gods; see p. 139); *repeat*. See p. 36, for more on *centrifugal*.

refuge: *re-*, **back**, **away**; a place **to flee away to**; a place providing protection, asylum, shelter; a haven, sanc-
               tuary. A person seeking *refuge* is a *refugee*.

subterfuge: from *subterfugere*, **to escape secretly**, or **under**; a plan to evade or escape an unpleasant or difficult
               situation. SYNONYMS: artifice, feint, guile, ruse, trick.

tempus fugit: **time is flying**. Compare *carpe diem*, **seize the day**, p. 68.

Die Kunst der Fuge: **The Art of the Fugue**: the last work of J. S. Bach, published posthumously.

wordbuilder #33

Greek *kinein*, **to move**, yields **cine**ma; **kin**ase, **kin**en; **kine**sics, **kine**sis, **kine**tic; **kine**tics; **kine**matics; **kin**esthesia;
kinescope; **kine**sodic; **kine**siology; **kine**toblast; dys**kine**sia; cyto**kine**sis, dia**kine**sis, hyper**kine**sis, hypo**kine**sis,
photo**kine**sis, psycho**kine**sis, tele**kine**sis; entero**kin**ase, strepto**kin**ase, uro**kin**ase; pharmoco**kine**tics.

wordextras

Raze, though a homonym of *raise*, is quite its opposite. From Latin *radere*, **to scrape**, *raze* originally meant "to
scrape, or to erase completely." It now means to tear down completely, to level to the ground. Other words from the
verb include *abrade, corrade; erase, abrasion, abrasive, erasion;* as well as *rascal* and *tabula **rasa*** (see next entry).

Tabula rasa, **erased tablet**, or **board**, is Latin for "clean slate," a philosophy that describes the mind before impressions are recorded upon it by experience; also, something existing in its original, pristine state.

Orchid, from Greek *orchis*, **testicle**, is so named because its roots are shaped like testicles. *Orchitis* is the inflammation of the testicles; two other words with *orchid* meaning "testicle" are as follows: ***orchid**ectomy* (surgical
excision of the testicles), *crypt**orchid**ism* (*kryptos*, **hidden**; a congenital condition in which one or both testicles fail
to descend into the scrotum). *Orchidology* is the branch of horticulture dealing with orchids.

Virulent, from *virus*, means **extremely poisonous** or injurious; spiteful; full of hate and enmity, as *a virulent remark*.

Trepidation, from Latin *trepidare*, **to hurry with alarm**, **to tremble**, originally meant "an involuntary shaking; quak-
ing; quivering." It has come to mean "a state of dread or alarm; nervous agitation; apprehension; fright." The word is
often heard in the phrase "fear and trepidation," which is redundant, but is used for emphasis. *Intrepid*, with prefix
in-, **not**, means **not afraid**; thus, **bold**. SYNONYMS of *intrepid*: audacious, bold, brave, courageous, plucky, valiant. See
p. 149 for more on *intrepid*.

Mascot, from Provençal *masco*, **sorcerer**, is any person, animal, or thing, supposed to bring good luck.

86

<table>
<tr><td colspan="4" align="center">Word Cluster No. 44</td></tr>
<tr>
<td>gregarian
gregarine
gregaria</td>
<td>gregal
segregate
egregious</td>
<td>gregarious
congregate
congregation</td>
<td>aggregate
desegregation
disaggregation</td>
</tr>
<tr><td colspan="4">Common element_____Inferred Meaning_____</td></tr>
</table>

Romance Cognates	French grégaire	Romanian gregar	Italian gregge	Portuguese gregário	Spanish gregario

Roman Catholic Church committee: *Congregatio de Propaganda Fide*, a committee of cardinals established in 1622 by Pope Gregory XV for supervising foreign missions of the Church.

Latin phrases: *spec gregis*: **the hope of the flock**. Virgil
dux gregis: **the leader of the flock**; *qualis rex, talis grex*: **like king, like people**
Epicuri de grege porcus: **a hog from the drove of Epicurus**; a glutton. Horace

Italian phrase: *Egregio Signore*: **Distinguished Sir**, a polite form of address

Explore *Congregationalism* as the impetus for establishing early American universities, especially Harvard.

Greek: **agora**philia, **agora**phobia, all**egor**y, cat**egor**y, par**egor**ic, pan**egyr**ic (**encomium, eulogy, tribute**)

wordextras

Sub rosa, Latin for "under the rose," means **secrecy**. The rose has been a symbol of secrecy since Roman times.

Greek *dioecious* (*di-*, **two** + *oikos*, **house, surroundings**), means having male reproductive organs in one individual and female organs in the other; having separate sexes. See **wordbuilder #29**, p. 81. Pronunciation: die EE shus.

Yacht, from Old Dutch *jaghtschip*, or **chasing ship** (against pirates), is known for its speed and agility.

Catamaran, from Tamil, a language of southern India and Sri Lanka, means **tied together**. Originally, two logs lashed together, catamarans were—and still are—propelled by paddles or sails. Pronounced: KAT uh muh RAN.

Modem, a coined computer term, coalesces *modulator* + *demodulator*.

Pennsylvania, with Latin *sylva*, **forest**, is "Penn's Woods," named in honor of William Penn, the early American Quaker who founded the colony in 1682. From *sylva* are also *sylvan, silva, silvical, silvicide, silvicolous, silviculture*.

Charisma is Greek for **divine gift, favor, talent**, bestowed for a special purpose. This meaning has been extended to include a special quality of leadership that captures the people's imagination. The adjective form is *charismatic*.

Dainty, coming from *dignus*, **worth**, means a choice food; delicacy; as an *adjective*, **delicious and choice**, as *a dainty morsel*; delicately pretty or lovely. SYNONYMS: fastidious, nice, particular, squeamish. Other words from *dignus*: **digni**tary, **digni**ty, **digni**fied, con**dign**, in**dign**ant, in**dign**ity, **deign**, dis**dain**; *infra* **dig** (**beneath one's dignity**).

Eerie, from a Northern England dialect and from Scottish, and further from Middle English *eri*, **filled with dread**, originally meant **timid and frightened**; uneasy because of superstitious fear; has come to mean **mysterious, uncanny**, or **weird**, in such a way to frighten or disturb.

wordbuilders #34, 35

Latin *dormire*, **to sleep**, yields **dorm**itory (dorm), **dorm**ant, **dorm**itive, **dorm**er windows, and **dorm**ouse. *Dormouse*, an Old World rodent, is named probably from its being nocturnal and a hibernator; it is often found to appear sleeping. *Dormer windows* are often installed in attics, transforming them into "sleeping rooms."

Latin *frater*, **brother**, yields **frater** (the eating room, or refectory, of a monastery), **frater**nal, **frater**nity, **frater**nize, con**frater**nity; **fratr**icide; **friar**. The words for English *brother* are similar in Danish, Dutch, French, German, Gypsy (Romany), Italian, and Russian (see *brot*, p. 12), as well as other languages of the Indo-European family.

Though University of Virginia, founded by Thomas Jefferson, does not have an official motto, the following sentence from an 1820 letter from Mr. Jefferson to Mr. Roscoe, and inscribed at the east entrance to Cabell Hall, serves as one of the guiding principles of the university:

Here we are not afraid to follow truth wherever it may lead,
nor tolerate any error so long as reason is left to combat it.

Common element base: grex (genitive: gregis)   **Meaning**: flock, group, herd, multitude
IE root: *ger-¹*: **to gather**; yields **Old English** *crammian*, **to stuff**, thus, **to cram**; **Greek** *ageirein*, the base of *agora*, **assembly**, **marketplace**; thus, *agoraphobia*, fear of the marketplace, or fear of being in a crowd (see p. 50).

Clavis

gregal:
belonging to or characteristic of a **company** or **multitude**; although now an obsolete term, it may be encountered in researching older references.

gregarine:
a **group** of parasitic sporozoan protozoans in the digestive tract of insects, crustaceans, earthworms, etc. Used here as a noun, it can also serve as an adjective: of, or pertaining to, these protozoans; as an adjective, also *gregarinian*.

gregarious:
inclined to **flock**, or to associate with others of one's own kind; can describe either people or plants, such as irises, that grow in clusters, or in a colony; also describes a constant series of waves caused by the regular movement of the sea at all times; thus, *gregarious waves*.

congregation:
con-, **with**, **together**; **flocked together**, or a group that assembles for a special purpose, usually for religious services. A minister, priest, or rabbi, is often called the ***pastor*** (see p. 129), which has the same root as *pasture*, where the flocks feed. Thus, a pastor "feeds" the assembled flock, or congregation. Greek ***synagogue***, **a coming together**, is also a congregation, or an assembly. Note relationship of *synagogue* to *agoraphobia* (under **IE** above), as well as *panegyric*, below. The elements *agogue* and *agora* pertain to "an assembly." See *assembly*, p. 66.

egregious:
e-, elision of *ex-*, **out of**; **separated from the flock**; originally, **to stand out favorably**; now, **standing out for undesirable qualities**, e.g., *an egregious liar*, or *an egregious error*. Example of semantic degeneration, or *pejoration*; compare *melioration*. See *nice*, under **wordextras**, p. 13, for an example of melioration. Other words with *e-*: **e**bullient, **e**closion, **e**cru, **e**dentate, **e**ditor, **e**ducate, **e**ject.

segregate:
se-, **apart**; **apart from the flock**; to set apart from the others or from the main mass or group; isolate; in *biology*, to separate in accordance with Mendel's laws, a set of four principles dealing with genetics. As an *adjective—segregated—***separated**, **isolated**; thus, conforming to a system that segregates racial groups, such as slavery in the Old South and apartheid in South Africa.

aggregate:
ag-, assimilation of *ad-*, **to**, **toward**, **addition to**; **to gather into**, or to consider as, a whole. In *biology*, gathered into clusters; in *geology*, as a noun, a node of similar materials in a rock; also used as verb.

disaggregate:
dis-, **apart**; **to break down**, **or separate into constituent parts**, as to classify or analyze, as *to disaggregate census data* according to household size, age, nationality, marital status, sex, etc.

panegyric:
Greek *pan-*, **all**; **a bringing together**; hence, a public meeting; formerly, *logos panegurikos*, a speech for a public festival. Now a formal speech or writing, praising a person or an event.

paregoric:
Greek *para-*, **alongside**; **beside the assembly**; a medication that relieves pain. Original meaning appears to be the calming influence of "talking over in the marketplace."

wordextras

Alfresco, from Italian *al fresco*, **in the cool**, means **outdoors**, **open air**, as *to dine alfresco*, or *an alfresco café*.

Hypochondriac, from Greek *hypo-*, **under** + *chondros*, **cartilage**, originally referred to one suffering from melancholia (**dark bile**), which was believed to arise from "under the cartilage" of the breastbone. It has been said that hypochondriacs don't feel good unless they feel bad. See p. 99 for *endochondrial*.

Robot and ***orphan*** are closely related, both pertaining to **work**. In Old Slavic, *rabota* meant **work** or **labor**, and originally *compulsory labor*, or drudgery. ***Orphan***, though now meaning a child deprived of one or both parents, meant a child, with or without parents, who had **to work** to support himself or herself.

Debauch, from Old French *des-*, **away from** + *bauch*, **tree trunk**, originally meant to separate branches from the trunk. The word has come to mean "to lead away morally; to corrupt; to deprave." The nominal form is *debauchery*.

Catacomb, from Greek *kata-*, **down**, **by** + *tumbas*, **graves**, is "at, or by, the graves." Usually in the plural, *catacombs* are underground burial places. As an actual place, *Catacombs* is a region between the second and third milestones of the Appian Way, a highway out of Rome, and begun by Appius Claudius Caecus, in 312 B.C.

Avarice, from Latin *avarus*, **greedy**, and further from *avere*, **to desire**, means **too great a desire to have wealth**.

88

Word Cluster No. 45

habit	habitation	habitual	habitat
inhabit	habitable	habitué	cohabit
habitude	habile	habilitate	habiliments
inhibit	adhibit	prohibit	exhibit

Common elements_____Inferred Meaning_____

Romance Cognates	French	Romanian	Italian	Portuguese	Spanish
	avoir	avea	avere	haver	haber

Doublets: debt:debit

Words with disguised Latin roots: able, ability, binnacle, debenture, debt, dishabille, due, duty, endeavor, gavel, malady, prebend, provender

Latin phrases: *Habeas corpus ad faciendum et recipiendum*: **You should have the body for doing and receiving**, meaning basically the same as the following three law terms:
Habeas corpus sum causa: **You should have the body of the cause.**
Habeas corpus ad prosequendum: **You should have the body for prosecuting.**
Habeas corpus ad subjicendum: **You should have the body for submitting.**

Spanish words: *la habitación* (**one's home**); *el habitante* (**inhabitant**); *habilidoso* (**capable**)

wordbuilder #36

Latin *granum*, **grain**, yields **gran**ary, **gran**ge, **gran**ite, **gran**ular, **gran**ulate, **gran**ule; pome**gran**ate; **gren**ade; **gar**ner, **grav**y; en**grain**, in**grain**; fili**gree**. *Einkorn* (originally German) shares a common meaning with the Latin element, and means "one-seeded wheat." With *pome*, **fruit**, *pomegranate* is "seeded, or granulated, fruit."

wordextras

Nainsook, a soft, light fabric, often with a woven stripe, is from Hindi *nainsukh*, **pleasing to the eye**.

Pun, from Italian *puntiglio*, **fine point**, from Latin *pungere*, **to prick**, is the humorous use of a word, or words, that are formed or sounded alike but have different meanings, in such a way as to play on two or more of the possible applications. Other words from *pungere*: ***punc**tate, **punc**tilio, **punc**tilious, **punc**tual, **punc**tuate, **punc**tuation, **punc**tulate, **punc**ture; com**punc**tion, ex**punc**tion; contra**punc**tal; **pung**ent, ex**pung**e; **poign**ant; **point**, counter**point**; counter**pane***. See more words on p. 205, Item 71; p. 211, Item 155. See *punctilious*, p. 146.

Sauerkraut is German for **sour cabbage**; *sauerbraten*, **sour roast**, is a dish made of beef marinated in vinegar with onion, spices, etc., before cooking.

Ludicrous, from Latin *ludere*, **to play**, originally described "a show," "public games." From laughing at that which was a show came to mean "causing laughter because of absurdity." Other words from *ludere*: ***ludic***; al**lude**, col**lude**, de**lude**, e**lude**, inter**lude**, pre**lude**, post**lude**; e**lud**ible, ine**lud**ible; al**lusion**, col**lusion**, de**lusion**, disil**lusion**, e**lusion**, il**lusion**; al**lusive**, col**lusive**, de**lusive**, e**lusive**, il**lusive**.

The *rhod* of *Rhode Island* and *rhododendron* means **rose**, **rose-red**. See *azalea*, p. 46.

Procrastinate, from Latin *pro-*, **forward** + *crastinus*, **of tomorrow**, means "to put forward until tomorrow." It can mean putting off doing something until a future time; more often, to postpone or delay needlessly.

Awry, from Middle English, means **with a twist to the side**; not straight; askew; wrong; amiss. Even before the rain, our carefully laid picnic plans had gone *awry*. Pronounced: uh RYE.

Shirt and *skirt* were originally the same word, coming from Old Norse *skyrta*, **short**. During the 800's, Scandinavians from Denmark and Norway invaded England, bringing with them a host of words used in English today, including the pronouns *they, them*, and *their*. In addition, most words in English beginning with *sk-* are Norse, e.g., *skep, skerry, skewer, ski, skid, skill, skin, skip, skit, skitter, skittish, skoal, skull, sky*. There are many others that do not begin with *sk-*, e.g., *birth, both, call, die, dirt, eat, egg, fellow, flat, get, guess, happy, ill, knife, leg, lift, loan, loose, low, odd, rid, rotten, same, scare, sister, slaughter, though, thrift, tight, till, trust, ugly, want, weak, window*. *Window*, **wind eye**, comprises *vindr*, **wind** + *auga*, **eye**. See *Augensprossen*, p. 10, under *antlers*.

Common element base: habere   **Meaning**: to have, to hold
IE base: *ghabh-*; also *ghebh-*: **to give**, **receive**; related to IE *kap-*, see **Word Cluster No. 15**, p. 29. **German**: *haben*

Clavis

habit:
: that which one **holds** onto; by extension, the clothing of a particular person, especially one in a religious order. As a *verb*, **to dress**, **clothe**; hence, *rehabilitate*, **to reclothe**; **to render fit again**.

habitué:
: French; a *habitual* frequenter of a particular place. Pronounced: huh BICH oo AY.

habeas corpus:
: **you shall have the body**, from the first words of the writ. In *law*, one of a variety of writs that may be issued to bring a party before a court or judge, having as its functions the release of a seizing party from unlawful restraint; various meanings, but underlying them all are safeguards for individual freedoms. Interestingly, *individual* originally meant "not divisible; not separable."

cohabit:
: *co-*, truncation of *com-*, **with**, **together**; **to dwell**, or **abide**, **together**; to live together in a sexual relationship, especially when not legally married.

dishabille:
: French; *dis-*, **apart**, **away**; the state of being **partially unclothed**, or in night clothes.

prohibit:
: *pro-*, **before**; **to have before**; to refuse to permit; forbid by law or by an order; to prevent. SYNONYMS: ban, enjoin, forbid, hinder, interdict.

debt:
: and *debit* are doublets; from *debere*, **to owe**; in *theology*, that which requires forgiveness or reparation; therefore, a **sin** or a **trespass**. For example, in the Lord's Prayer, note the phrase "Forgive us our *debts*," sometimes couched as "Forgive us our *trespasses*." See p. 63 for more on the prayer.

debenture:
: receipts used in Roman times began with *debentur mihi*, **there are owing to me**; now, a bond backed by the general credit of the issuer rather than a specific lien on particular assets.

prebend:
: *pre-*, **before**; **to have before**; originally, the state support of a private person, and later the revenues of a church that go for the pastor's salary, or that which is paid before other obligations or debts. Related forms: *prebendal* (of a prebend), *prebendary* (a person receiving a prebend).

provender:
: from the same base as *prebend*, previous entry, but means "dry food for livestock," such as hay, corn, and oats; fodder. *Fodder*, from German *Futter*, is a cognate of English *food*.

endeavor:
: from Old French *deveir* (now *devoir* in French as well as in English), **duty**; from *se mettre en deveir*, **to try to do**; as "He *endeavored* to do his best"; *to express one's devoirs*: acts or expressions of due respect or courtesy, such as thanking the host before leaving the function one has been invited to. *Endeavor* is also a noun, as in "He made an *endeavor* to save the child."

ability:
: from *habilis*, **easily handled**, **having the power to do**, as *the ability to sing*.

malady:
: from *male habitus*, **badly kept**, out of condition; a disease; illness; sickness; often used figuratively, as in *the malady of discontent*, or *the malady of boredom*. See p. 124 for more on *malady*.

Word from a literary character: *quixotic* [often capitalized]; visionary, impractical; of or like *Don Quixote*, the hero in Saavedra Cervantes' satirical romance by the same name (1615). In a chivalrous but unrealistic way, Don Quixote tries to rescue the oppressed and to fight evil, yielding the term "tilting at windmills." In this use, *tilt* means "to poise or thrust one's lance, or to charge at one's opponent." See p. 104, under *picaresque*.

wordextras

Vignette, diminutive of French *vigne*, **vine**, originally was an ornamental design of vine leaves, tendrils, and grapes, and used as an illustration on a page of a book, magazine, etc., as at the beginning or end of a chapter or section; now, a short, delicate literary sketch.

Rhodesia, now *Zimbabwe*, a country north of South Africa, was named after Cecil John Rhodes (1853-1902), a British financier and administrator. Rhodes desired to promote the expansion of the British Empire in South Africa. The Rhodes scholarship was established by his will. Rhodes scholars, who come from Britain and the United States, spend two or three years at Oxford University, Oxford, England.

New Hampshire, one of the 13 original colonies, is named after *Hampshire*, a county on the south coast of England.

Tallahassee, capital of Florida, is from Creek *talwa*, **town** + *hasi*, **old**; thus, **old town**.

heredity	hereditary	hereditament
hereditarian	hereditarianism	hereditable
hereditas	inherit	inheritance
heritable	disinherit	heritage
heres	heritor	heir
heirloom	heirship	heirdom
heir apparent	heir presumptive	heir at law

Common elements_____Inferred Meaning_____

Romance Cognates	French	Romanian	Italian	Portuguese	Spanish
	héritier	ereditar	erede	herdeir	hereder

Latin phrases: *Absens haeres non erit*: **The absent shall not be the heir.**

hereditas jacens: **lying**, i.e., **inactive inheritance**, a vacant succession (see more in **Clavis**)

damnosa hereditas (or, *haereditas*): **a damaging inheritance**, i.e., one that entails loss. For example, the taxes due on inherited property are more than the property itself is worth.

Quote: To be a power one must know how to use language; and how can you place words together unless you know their derivation and their real meaning?
Henry Kraeman

wordextras

After the Norman French conquered England—but mind you, not the English people, nor the English language!—it has been recorded that the French lords sent the Anglo-Saxon serfs into the forests to fetch *mousserons*. By the serfs' mispronouncing the French word, we now have **mushrooms**; the Anglo-Saxon cognate is *moss*. Consequently, there is no meaning of *mush* or *room* in *mushroom*. See p. 204, Item 66, for Greek root for *moss*.

Butler, from Old French *bouteillier*, **bottle bearer**, was originally in charge of the wine cellar; this position evolved into one in charge of the plates, tables, and liquors.

Sinister is from Middle English *sinistre*, **left, on the left**, hence, **injurious, baleful, ominous.** The early Romans believed that unfavorable omens appeared to one's left; in augury—the practice of divination from omens—the left side was regarded as inauspicious.

Addis Ababa, the capital of Ethiopia, is Amharic—the native language—for **new flower**.

From Latin *timere*, **to fear**, are *timid, timorous, intimidate,* the only known English words from the verb *timere*.

Forbear, from Old English, is "to refrain from; avoid or cease doing, saying, etc." Dialectally, *forbear* has come to mean **to endure, tolerate.** SYNONYMS: abstain, refrain. Do not confuse with *forebear*, **an ancestor.**

Bemuse, **to muddle or stupefy**; to plunge into thought; and *amuse*, **to keep pleasantly enjoyably occupied or interested**, are both from Middle English *musen*, **to ponder, loiter**, and means **to think deeply and at length.**

Middle English *surfeit* is from Latin *super-*, **beyond** + *facere*, **to do**; thus, **that which is overdone**; also, too great an amount or supply; excess of, as *a surfeit of compliments*; overindulgence; satiety. Pronounced SUR fit.

wordbuilders #37, 38

Latin *frangere*, **to break**, yields **fract**ion, **fract**ious, **fract**ure; diff**ract**ion, inf**ract**ion, ref**ract**ion; **frag**ile, **frag**ment, ossi**frag**e (or, osprey; **bone-breaker**), saxi**frag**e, suf**frag**e, in**fring**e, **frail:frag**ile; fracas, defray.

Greek *karpos*, **fruit**, originally that which can be **plucked** or **harvested**, yields **carp**el, **carp**ology, **carp**ophagous (**fruit-eating**), **carp**ogonium, endo**carp**, mono**carp**ous (**bearing only one fruit**), oligo**carp**ous (**bearing little fruit or few fruits**), poly**carp**ous (**bearing many fruits**, or **much fruit**), and schizo**carp**; **harvest**. *Carpet*, that which has been *plucked*, is related etymologically to this element. Do not confuse this element with an identically spelled root, meaning **wrist**, as in **carp**al, **carp**us and meta**carp**al, as well as **varve**, an annual layer of sedimentary material.

Common element base: heres   **Meaning**: heir

There is no English translation; however, the IE base is *ghe-*: **to be empty**; **leave behind**; **let go**; **release**. The IE base yields **Greek** *choros*, **place**, **region**, from which are **chor**ography and *anachroism*, not to be confused with *anachronism*, p. 22, **wordbuilders #9** and **#11**. Do not confuse *chorography*, the technique of mapping a region, with *choreography*, p. 171, under *orchestra*. **German**: *Erbe*: **heir**, **heritage**, **inheritance**; *erben*, **to inherit**.

Clavis

heritage:

property that is or can be **inherited**; something other than property passed down from preceding generations; **legacy**; **tradition**; the status or lot acquired by a person through birth; **birthright**, as *a heritage of affluence and position, a heritage of aristocracy, a heritage of poverty.*

heritor:

from *hereditary*; an inheritor, or **heir**.

heir apparent:

the **heir** whose rights to a particular property or title cannot be denied if he outlives his ancestor and the ancestor dies *intestate*, that is, **without a will**.

heir presumptive:

an **heir** whose rights to a particular property or title will be lost if someone more closely related to the ancestor is born before the ancestor dies.

hereditarianism:

a doctrine that individual differences may be accounted for on the basis of *heredity*, or genetics.

heirloom:

loom, from Old English *geloma*, **utensil**, **tool**; a valued possession passed down in a family through succeeding generations; in *law*, an article of personal property included in an inherited estate. The *loom* of *heirloom* is the same as the one that designates a machine or device used for weaving.

hereditas jacens:

in *civil law*, a prostrate or vacant **inheritance**; the state of an inheritance not being accepted, or denied.

inherit:

originally, to transfer property to an **heir**; now, to receive property from an ancestor at the ancestor's death.

Black's Law Dictionary gives many additional terms usually omitted in even unabridged dictionaries, e.g., heirs and assigns; heirship; heir special; heirs per stirpes, heir unconditional, hereditary right to the crown.

The following phrase is from *Black's*: *Heirs at law shall not be disinherited by conjecture, but only by express words or necessary implication*, a maxim that the ancestor must clearly cut off an heir and that such disinheritance is not lightly inferred.

wordextras

Hysteria is from Greek *hystera*, which in Latin is **uterus**, and in Anglo-Saxon, **womb**. The ancient Greeks believed that *hysteria* was caused from an upsetting of the uterus. Two other common words with *hystera* are **hyster**ectomy and **hystero**tomy. Medical dictionaries, as well as the search engine *onelook*, list many others.

Halcyon, a legendary bird, and identified with the kingfisher, was believed to have a peaceful, calming influence on the sea at the time of the winter solstice, floating its nest on the sea and magically calming the waves during high tide. *Halcyon* has come to mean **happy**, **idyllic**, **peaceful**, especially in the phrase *halcyon days*, usually with nostalgic reference to earlier times. See p. 180 for more on *solstice*; p. 106 for *siesta*.

Halo, from Greek *halos*, **threshing floor**, came to designate the **ring of light** around the sun or moon; also, the radiant light surrounding the head of a divine or sacred personage, or of an ancient or medieval monarch. See p. 171 for *orchestra* for original meaning similar to *halo*. See p. 165 for *halos*, **salt**, **sea**.

Q.V. stands for *quod vide*, **which see**, and in research materials instructs the reader to look up the cited reference for fuller or further details.

The *Smithsonian Institution*, in Washington, DC, is named after James Smithson (d. 1829), a British scientist. Born in France, he was educated at Oxford University, England. Known for his research in both chemistry and mineralogy, he donated $500,000 to the United States for the establishment of a scientific institution. *Smithsonite*, a zinc carbonate, is named for him as well. See p. 2, **A Writing Tip**.

Arizona, **little springs**, is Papago, the language of the Indian people living in what is now the state of Arizona.

Bequeath, verb, and *bequest*, noun, are from Old English *cwethan*, **to say**, which also yields **quoth**. *Bequeath* is to leave (property) to another by last will and testament; also, to hand down, pass on, as *to bequeath his talent to his son*.

Word Cluster No. 47

homicidal	homicidious	homiculture	hominine
homicide	hominid	hominal	hominism
hominian	hominoid	hominivorous	hominiform

Common elements_____**Inferred Meaning**_____

Romance Cognates	French	Romanian	Italian	Portuguese	Spanish
	homme	om	uomo	homem	hombre

Words and phrases with disguised Latin roots: homage, homager, hombre, homunculus, human, humane, humanities; exhume, transhumance, humble, humiliate, humility; ombre (also, omber)

Placenames: Humansville, MO; Humble, TX; Humble City, NM; Hombre River, Honduras; Humble, Denmark; Salar de Hombre Muerto, Argentina (extensive salt mines in the Andes); listed also on p. 131.

Latin phrases: *legalis homo*: **a legal man**; a man of full legal rights
Homo sum, humani nihil a me alienum puto. Terrence. **I am a man; I consider nothing that is human alien to me.**
Ecce homo; homo homini aut deus aut lupus; Homo sapiens; homo vulgaris; novus homo; Quot homines,
tot sententiae; Te hominem esse memento; Principia, non homines; Iesus Hominum Salvator; Lux hominum vita

French phrases: *homme d'esprit; l'homme propose et Dieu dispose*
le style est l'homme même (often misquoted as *Le style, c'est l'homme*)

Spanish proverb: *Al hombre mayor, darle honor*: **To the greater man give honor.** See pp. 73, 121.

Greek: *anthropos*, **man**: **anthrop**oid (*-oid*, from *eidos*, **form**; **resembling a human**; **apelike**, as *a brutish man with anthropoid features*); **anthropo**centric (see **Word Cluster No. 18, p. 35**), **anthropo**genesis, **anthropo**graphy, **anthropology**, **anthropo**metry, **anthropo**morphic, **anthropo**morphism, **anthropo**phagi (literally, people-eaters; **cannibals**), **anthropo**pathy, **anthropo**sophy, lyc**anthrop**y, mis**anthrop**ist, phil**anthrop**ist. See p. 204, Item 61.

German: *Mann* (specific); *Mensch* (general).

wordextras

Montreal is the French spelling of *Mount Royal*, **King's Mountain**, around which the city is built. A city and seaport in southwest Quebec, Canada, *Montreal* is located on an island in the St. Lawrence River.

Venezuela, Spanish for **Little Venice**, was so called by the Venetian explorers, from the natives' houses being built on stilts, as in Venice, the Italian name of which is *Venezia*. The city of Venice is built on more than 100 small islands in the Lagoon of Venice. Instead of hailing a taxi, one would hail a gondola to traverse the canals of Venice.

Hurricane, from Spanish *huracán*, has no constituent meaning; it is simply the West Indian (Taino) word for a violent tropical *cyclone* with winds of 73 or more miles per hour, often accompanied by torrential rain, and originating mainly in the West Indies. A *cyclone* is any windstorm with a violent, whirling movement, such as a tornado. *Tornado* appears to be from *tornar*, **to turn**; more likely, it is from *tonare*, **to thunder**.

Gibraltar is named for Arab general Tarik ibn Zaid, who captured the rock in A.D. 711. Its original name in Arabic was *Jebel-al-Tarik*, or "Mountain of Tarik." Known as the *Rock of Gibraltar*, the word has come to indicate any strong fortification, or unassailable fortress. The "rock" is a symbol of Prudential Insurance Company.

Scapula, originally meaning **spade**, from the use of the bone as a spade, is either of two flat, triangular bones in the back of the shoulders of humans; thus, **the shoulder blade**. The plural is either *scapulae*, or *scapulas*.

Himalayas, the world's highest mountain range, is from Sanskrit, meaning **House of Snows**, or **The Snowy Range**. Actually, the Himalayas consist of several parallel ranges. Its highest peak is Mount Everest. See *continent*, p. 188.

The *negative* forms of many adjectives are in much greater use than their *positives*, e.g., ill-fated, ill-founded, ill-judged, ill-mannered, ill-starred, ill-suited, ill-tempered, ill-timed, ill-treat; illicit, immutable, impassible (unable to suffer or feel pain), impervious, inadvertent, inclement, incongruous, incontrovertible, ineffable, inexplicable, innocuous, inscrutable, insuperable; nonchalant, nonentity, nonexistent; unassuming, unblinking, unbounded, unbridled, uncalled-for, unceremonious, uncompromising, unconscionable, uncouth, unequivocal, unhinged, unkempt, unraveled, unwitting; disheveled, disordered, dispeople.

Common element base: homo   **Meaning**: man

IE base: *dhghem-*: **earth**; yields **English** *guma*, base of *groom*, thus *bridegroom*; **Greek** *khthon*, as in *chthonic*, *autochthon*; **Greek** *khamai*, **on the ground**, as in *chameleon*, *chamomile*, and *germander*; **Russian**, *zemstvo* (a local administrative body in czarist Russia; and **Persian-Hindi**, in India, *zamindar*, **a tax collector**; also, **a landholder**.

NB: Do not confuse the Latin root with **Greek** *homo-*, **like**, **equal**, **same**, as in *homogamy*, *homogeneity*, *homogenize*, *homogeneous*, *homophone* (any of two or more letters representing the same speech sound; also, **homonym**), *homosexual*, *homopterous*, *homosphere*, *homosporous*, *homotaxis*, *homozygous*. See p. 207, Item 105.

Clavis

hominine: resembling or characteristic of **man**.

homage: originally, a vassal's service; now, respect, tribute, honor, especially as in "paying *homage* to the dead."

hominid: also, *hominoid*, **a man-like creature**; any of a family of two-legged primates, including all forms of **humans**, both extinct and living; corresponds to Greek *anthropoid*, also, **a manlike creature**, but can also mean **a man that resembles an ape**, either in size, gait, appearance, or intelligence.

homunculus: diminutive of *homo*; **a little man**; a diminutive human; dwarf; manikin; pygmy.

ad hominem: **to the man**, a logical fallacy of attacking one's opponent personally rather than his or her views. For example, "What did President Jimmy Carter know about running the country? He was only a Georgia peanut farmer." This fallacy fails to mention that he was an honor graduate of the United States Naval Academy, with a degree in nuclear physics. Other logical fallacies of reasoning include *ad populum, arguing in a circle, argument from ignorance, bandwagon appeal, begging the question, complex question, confusing the issue, either-or, hasty generalization, hypothesis contrary to fact, name-calling, non sequitur, red herring, shifting ground, slanting, slippery slope, unrepresentative example.* There are many others, which can be found in most college composition texts, or on the Internet; search for "logical fallacies." See *ad captandum vulgus*, p. 30.

Ecce homo: "Behold the man," said Pilate, the Roman governor of Judea, when he presented the accused Jesus to his own people for trial after he had found no fault in Him. John 19:15

novus homo: **new man**; one who rises to distinction through his own efforts rather than by the prestige of his family.

homicide: with *caedere*, **to kill**; any killing of a human being by another; murder, manslaughter.

Homo sapiens: **wise**, or **knowledgeable man**; scientific classification of modern man.

abominate: by folk etymology, **away from the man**, but etymologically, **away from the omen**; to regard as an ill omen; to have feelings of hatred and disgust for; **loathe**; abhor. The noun is *abomination*.

exhume: *ex-*, **out of**; **to remove from the earth**; to remove a corpse from the grave, usually for forensic examination; also, to disinter; *terr*, **earth**, as in *terrace*, *terrain*, *terrestrial*, *terricolous*, *territory*, *extraterrestrial*, *Mediterranean* (see p. 63, **wordextras**), *inter*. See p. 192 for more on *inter*.

anthropophagi: plural of *anthropophagus*; *phagus*, as in *sarcophagus*, **flesh-eating**, is the Greek designation for **man-eaters**, or cannibals. See more words from *phagein*, **to eat**, p. 128, **wordbuilder #51**.

wordextras

Lassitude, **weariness**, from Latin *lassus*, **faint**, **weary**, is the state of being tired and listless; languor; weariness of body and mind from mental strain, oppressive climate, disruption of one's circadian rhythms (jet lag), etc.; also a condition of indolent indifference; debility. See *Alas*, p. 34, under **wordextras**. See *circadian*, p. 40, **wordextras**.

Surtax, from *super-*, **beyond** + *tax*, is a tax on something already taxed; as a *verb*, to levy a surtax on.

wordbuilder #39

Greek *bradys*, **slow**, yields **brady**acusia (**dullness of hearing**), **brady**cardia (**slow heartbeat**), **brady**glossia (**slowness in speaking**), **brady**kinetic (**slowness of bodily movement**), **brady**lalia (**slowness of speech**), **brady**lexia (**slowness of reading** not attributable to lack of intelligence), **brady**logia, **brady**phagia (**slowness of eating**), **brady**phrasia, **brady**pnea (**slowness of breathing**), **brady**rhythmia, **brady**stalsis, **brady**uria (**slowness in urination**, often due to an enlarged prostate in men). Do not confuse this root with *brachi*, **arm** (p. 21), or with *brachy*, **short** (p. 22).

94

Word Cluster No. 48

inborn	incentive	incarnate	inoculate	inchoate
inundate	intuition	incipient	inbreed	indebted
impulse	immediate	impact	impregnate	impress
imbroglio	imbrue	immanent	imminent	immigrate
immix	imply	implicate	import	importance
illuminate	illustrate	irrigate	irritate	irrupt

NB: The prefix of the foregoing words is not a part of *image, imbricate, imperial,* and *imitate.*

Common elements_____Inferred Meaning_____

imbalance	imbecile	immaculate	immature	immortal
imperfect	impossible	impropriety	impudent	impuissance
inactive	inapposite	inapt	incest	injury
illegal	illegible	illicit	illimitable	irrevocable

The prefix in these words means *not.*

injury	impel	impetus	impinge	impugn

The prefix in these words means *against.*

incandesce	indurate	impair	implore	incentive

The prefix in these words *intensifies* the root.

Latin phrases: *in absentia, in extremis, in fine, in loco parentis, in meditatione fugae, in media res, in memoriam, in re, in flagrante delicto, in ovo, in pari causa, in parvo, in patrimonio, in pectore, in perpetuum, in persona, in propria persona, in statu nascendi, in statu quo, in petto*

> **Quote**: The terms used in the scientific world are largely, and in some sciences, almost exclusively, derived from the classics. Bernard Walker

wordextras

Polecat is often used for Algonquian *skunk*; *pole* is an English respelling of Old French *poule*, **chicken**, which yields *poultry* as well. Literally *chicken cat*, a *polecat* is notorious for raiding the chicken coop. Other words from *poule* are **pullet**, a young hen; **poulard**, a young hen spayed for fattening; any fat young hen; **poulterer**, a dealer in poultry and game. The Spanish cognate is *pollo*, as in *arroz con pollo*, or "rice with chicken." See *capon*, p. 37.

Cunning, the present participle of Middle English *cunnen*, **to know**, has a number of meanings, both meliorative and pejorative. The meliorative meanings include "made or done with skill or ingenuity; attractive; pretty; cute." The pejorative meanings include "skillful in deception; sly." See p. 13 for *melioration* and *pejoration*, under *nice.*

With German *Glock*, originally **clock**, then **bell**, *glockenspiel*, "to play with bells," designates the musical instrument with small bells that are struck with wooden mallets. **Note**: Nouns in German are capitalized, whether proper or common. If used as English words, they are **not** capitalized, e.g., *kindergarten*, **children's garden**.

The ***English horn*** is not a horn as are tubas, trumpets and trombones, but is a member of the woodwind family, as are the *flute, piccolo* (see p. 79), *oboe* (see p. 4) and *clarinet* (see p. 42). Woodwinds are so called because they were originally made of wood; *woodwinds* is often shortened to *winds*, as in *the winds section.*

Hooky (also, *hookey*), as *to play hooky from school*, is probably from Dutch *hoekje*, **hide-and-seek**, from *hoek*, **corner**; hence, to hide around the corner (from school).

Stubborn, akin to Dutch *stok*, **a stick**, can be used to describe not only persons who are obstinate and hard to deal with, but also situations, such as *a stubborn campaign* (**doggedly persistent**), *a stubborn cold*, *a stubborn headache* (**hard to handle**). The word can be applied to animals as well, such as *a stubborn mule.*

Surrey, a light pleasure carriage, was first built in *Surrey*, a county in southeast England.

As a *verb*, ***muster***, from Latin *monstrare*, **to show**, means "to assemble or summon troops," as for inspection. See p. 171 for *monument* and other words from *monstrare*. As a *noun*, any assemblage, especially of military troops.

Common element base: Indo-European en-   **Meaning**: in, on, into, against

The IE base yields **Latin** *inter-*, between; *intra-*, within (see **Word Clusters Nos. 49, 50** respectively); **Greek** *endos*, *entos*, within. Another meaning of *in-* corresponds to **Anglo-Saxon** *un-*, **not**, as in *unable, unnecessary*. Another meaning of *in-*, **negative** is from IE *ne-*, as in *necessary, nefarious, neuter* (originally, **not either**), as well as words beginning with *neg-*, as in *neglect and negligee*. *In-* can also mean **to, toward**, and is often used as an **intensifier**.

Clavis

in absentia: **in absence**, as of an accused person, e.g., *condemned* **in absentia**, or as of a person earning a degree, but not present to receive it in person; thus, *to graduate* **in absentia**.

in esse: **in essence**; in being; in existence; opposed to *in posse*, **in possibility**.

in extremis: **in extremity**; at the point of death.

in media res: **in the middle of things**; in the middle of the action, rather than at the beginning.

in memoriam: **in memory of**; used especially in epitaphs, inscriptions on tombstones.

in re: **in reference to**; regarding; often used in the title of a law case.

imbibe: *im-*, **in**; *bibere*, **to drink**; **to drink in**, or to absorb as if by drinking; to take in with the senses of mind, as *to imbibe the poetry of Robert Frost and Emily Dickinson*.

imbecile: *im-*, **negative**; *bec* from *baculus*, **rod** (the same root as is in *bacterium*, **a rod**-shaped microorganism); **without a rod**, or without support; formerly a term to denote **one with mental retardation**, it now denotes **a very foolish or stupid person**. See p. 2 for *bacterium*.

impropriety: *im-*, **not**; with *propriety*, **the quality of being improper** (from *proprius*, **one's own**). Other words from *proprius* include **proper, property, proprietary, proprietor,** *appropriate, inappropriate, expropriate, impropriate*. The Spanish word for "own" or for "one's own" is *propio*. See *idio-*, p. 214, Item 201.

impudent: *im-*, **negative**; *pudere*, **to be ashamed**; **to *not* be ashamed**; impertinent, saucy, rude; disrespectful.

impugn: *im-*, **against**; *pugnare*, **to fight**; **to fight against**; to criticize; to find fault, as *to impugn the values of one's parents*. SYNONYMS: contradict, deny, gainsay. See other *pug-* words, p. 211, Item 154.

illustrate: *il-*, assimilation of *in-*, **in** + *lustrare*, **to illuminate**; to make clear; explain; to make easily understood by giving examples, comparisons; to exemplify. See other *lustr-* words, p. 208, Item 116.

imminent: *im-*, assimilation of *in-*, **in** + *minere*, **to project**; **likely to happen without delay**, as *an imminent storm*, or *an imminent judgment in a case*. Not to be confused with *eminent*, although both come from the same verb. ***Eminent***: with *ex-*, **out**, literally, **projecting out**; celebrated, distinguished, famous.

inchoate: *cohum*, **the strap from plow beam to yoke**; originally, **to harness, to hitch up**; thus, in the initial or early stage; just the beginning; incipient. Pronounced: in KO it, or in KO ATE.

inundate: *unda*, **wave**; **to cover with waves**; thus, to cover with, or as if with a flood; deluge; as *to be inundated with requests*. See more *unda-* words, p. 213, Item 181.

annoy: from *esse alicui in odio*, **to be in hatred of someone** or **something**; Compare *odious* and *odium*. SYNONYMS: bother, irk, plague, tease, vex.

in flagrante delicto: **during the blazing of the crime**; the act itself; red-handed; flagrant.

wordanalysis

See relationship between **_enemy_** and **_inimical_**. Begin by seeing that *en-* and *in-* are from Latin *in-*, **not**; note that *em-* of *enemy* and *im* of *inimical* are variants of Latin *amicus*, **friend**; further from *amare*, **to love**. *Enemy* means "not a friend," and *inimical*, "not friendly," hostile. Finally, see that *inimical* is the adjectival form of *enemy*. *Amity*, from the same root, means "friendship." There is an *Amity* in each of the following states: IN, MO, OH, OR, NY.

Word from a person's name: *sadist*, one who enjoys cruelty or infliction of pain; *from* Marquis de Sade (full name: Donatien Alphonse François de Sade) (1740-1814), who incurred infamy by torturing the women he loved. Thus, a *sadist* is one who receives neurotic sexual pleasure from torturing his or her lovers. *Sadist* has been extended to include anyone who derives pleasure from inflicting pain. *Marquis* is a title; in French, pronounced mar KEY.

intercede	interdict	interciliary	intercostal
intercourse	interfere	interfoliate	interject
interlude	interpose	interstate	internecine
interpolate	intervene	interrupt	interdigitate
interbreed	interregnum	interlocutor	intercept
interrogate	interpellate	interpret	internal
interior	interim	interaction	interosseus
interest	intersex	interstice	interureteral
entrecôte	entremets	entresol	entrepreneur
entrepôt	entredeux	entrefer	entre nous

NB: *Entrechat*, a particular leap in ballet, is not in this family. The prefix is *en-*.

Common elements_____**Inferred Meaning**_____

Romance Cognates	French	Romanian	Italian	Portuguese	Spanish
	entre	între	entro	entre	entre

Words with disguised Latin roots: enterprise, entertain, intestine, entrails, denizen, intellect, intimate

Latin phrases: *ad interim* (abbreviated *ad init.*; **in the meantime**; temporarily; temporary), *primus inter pares*

French phrases: *entre nous, entr'acte, rire entre cuir et chair*: **to laugh between skin and teeth**; laugh in one's sleeve

Placenames: Enterprise, AL (site of the monument to the boll weevil, that which caused the area to diversify its agricultural base from simply cotton to cotton, peanuts, and corn, as well as tree farms, cattle-raising, and catfish ponds); there is also an *Enterprise* in each of the following states: IL, IN, KS, MS, OR, UT. Intercourse: AL, PA.

Explore *interlude* as a historical dramatic term.

Explore the following in a music dictionary: *calculation of interval, intermezzo, entrée, entrata.*

What is the common meaning of the following sayings or aphorisms?
Seven captains run the ship on the reef.
Too many cooks spoil the broth.
Seven nurses kill the baby.
As with any proverb, aphorism, or old saying, begin the interpretation by deriving its actual meaning; then, determine the moral, or its general application. See p. 72 for interpretation.

---

wordextras

Damask, a durable, lustrous, reversible fabric as of silk or linen, in figured weave, and used for table linen and upholstery, is from *Damascus*, the present capital of Syria, where it was first made.

Dungaree, a coarse denim fabric, is from Hindi *dungri*. See Hindi words, **wordextras**, p. 53.

Denim was originally *serge de Nîmes*, Nimes being the city in France where the fabric was first made.

Chambray is a smooth fabric of cotton, originally made in Cambrai, a city in northern France. See **NB**, p. 25.

Muslin, the name of a strong, often sheer, fabric of plain weave, especially a heavy variety used for sheets, pillow-cases, etc., was first made in Mosul, a city in Iraq.

Gauze is a very thin, light, transparent, loosely woven material, as of cotton or silk; also, any similar but stiff material, as of thin wire; in addition, a thin mist. Originally Persian *kaz*, then Arabic *kazz*, **raw silk**; later, Spanish *gasa*; then French *gaze*; finally English *gauze*.

Mouton, pronounced MOO tahn, is French for *sheep*, but means in English "sheepskin processed to resemble seal or beaver."

Patent leather is a leather with a hard, glossy, usually black finish; made by a process that was formerly *patented*.

Common element base: inter-, a prefix

Meaning: between, among

This prefix is related to *intra-* and *intro-* (see p. 99, **Word Cluster No. 50**).

Clavis

internal:
: from *internus*, **inward**, which yields *intern*, also spelled *interne*; **inner**; **interior**; opposed to *external*; having to do with or belong to the **inner** nature of a thing; intrinsic, as *internal evidence*; *internal investigation* (as of a police department), *internal criticism*, as of the Bible, Shakespeare.

interpose:
: *ponere*, **to put**, **place**; **to place or put between**; insert; to put forward as an intervention, as "The chairperson *interposed objections* to the committee's recommendation."

interval:
: *vallum*, originally, **between the ramparts**, or space between the outer breastworks and the soldiers' tents; now, any space between two points, either in time or space; in *music*, the pitch between two tones, represented by notes on a staff. *Contravallation* also comes from *vallum*.

Int'l Date Line:
: an imaginary line drawn north and south through the Pacific, largely along the 180° meridian. At this line, by international agreement, each calendar day begins at midnight, so that when it is Sunday, for example, just west of the line, it is Saturday just east of it. The International Date Line divides the earth into the western and eastern hemispheres; the 0° meridian passes through Greenwich, England. The equator divides the earth in southern and northern hemispheres. See *equator*, p. 76.

inter vivos:
: **between living persons**; from one living person to another, as *a transaction inter vivos*. Compare *donatio* and *mortis causa*; search on Google.

primus inter pares:
: **first among equals**; said of the Chief Justice of the U.S. Supreme Court. His dual roles are Chief Justice of the United States and the head of all Federal courts. See more on p. 160.

intimate:
: from *intimus*, superlative of *intus*, and describes the **inmost** character of a thing; fundamental; essential; also marked by a close, warm relationship. As a *verb*, originally, to make known formally; now, to hint at or to imply. As a *verb*, the last syllable rimes with *mate*; as an adjective, the accent is on the first syllable. As a *noun*, *a close companion*. In law, *intimation* is a formal announcement or declaration. See *intrinsic*, p. 100.

denizen:
: *de-*, **from** + *intus*, **within**; **from within**; an inhabitant of, e.g., deer are *denizens of the forest*; whales, *denizens of the deep*. Also, a frequenter of a particular place; habitué (see p. 90).

entertain:
: *tain* from *tenere*, **to hold**; **to hold the attention of**; thus, to amuse; to have as a guest; to consider, as *to entertain an idea*. See more on *ten* root, **Word Cluster No. 94**, p. 187.

entrepreneur:
: French; from *entreprendre*, which is also the base of *enterprise*, **to seize between**; one who *seizes*, or assumes, the risks of venture for the sake of potential profits. See p. 211, Item 152.

entre nous:
: French; **between us**; between ourselves; in confidence. Pronounced: AHN treh NOO.

entrepôt:
: French; **a holding place**; an immediate collection point for shipment of goods. Same roots as *interpose*, **to place between**, as *to interpose no objections*.

entredeux:
: French; *deux*, **two**; **between two**; something placed **between two things**; insertion.

wordextras

Chagrin, directly from French, and originally meaning **sadness**, now means "anxiety, grief, vexation." Example: I was *chagrined* for receiving a low grade on a test for which I had studied diligently. Pronounced: shu GRIN.

French *frisson*, originally from Latin *frigere*, **to be cold**, means "a shudder, chill, quiver, tingle," as *a frisson of delight*, or *a frisson of fear*. Approximate pronunciation: free SOHn.

Pilgrim, from Latin *peregrinus*, **foreigner**, is further from *per-*, **through** + *ager*, **field**. A *pilgrim* is one who travels about, as though *through the fields*; a wanderer. The band of Puritans who established Plymouth Colony in 1620 were Pilgrims, having sought religious freedom in Holland before *peregrinating* to the New World. Over 100 communities, cemeteries, and other entities bear the name *Pilgrim*, or *Pilgrims Rest*. Search USGS on the Internet.

Fee, Middle English for **estate**, **fief**, **payment**, can be traced to Old English *feoh*, **cattle**, **property**. It originally meant heritable land held from a feudal lord in return for service; then, the right to hold such land. Explore *fee simple*.

Romance Cognates: All the Romance languages have retained the Latin form.

Words with disguised Latin roots: intrinsic, dedans, dentro (Spanish contraction of *de entro*), introrse

Latin phrase: *intra vires*, **within the powers**; within the legal power or authority of an individual or corporation; opposed to *ultra vires*, **beyond the powers**

Related Greek: *entos*, **within**: **enter**ic, **enter**itis (inflammation of the intestines), **enter**on (**the alimentary canal**), **entero**cele, **entero**centesis, **entero**stomy, **entero**virus; dys**enter**y, mes**enter**y, ex**enter**ate, par**enter**al; gastro-**enter**itis, coel**enter**on; **ento**blast, **ento**cele, **ento**cyte, **ento**phyte, **ento**proct, **ento**zoon; entrails; esoteric.
endon, **within**: **end**odontics (*odontos*, **tooth**: the field of dentistry dealing with root canals), **end**osmosis, **end**osteum, **end**ostosis; **endo**biotic, **endo**blast, **endo**cardial, **endo**cardium, **endo**carp, **endo**centric, **endo**chondral (see relationship to *hypochondria*; p. 88), **endo**commensal, **endo**cranium, **endo**crine, **endo**cytosis, **endo**derm, **endo**gamy (the custom of marrying only within one's own group; in *botany*, self-pollination among flowers), **endo**genous, **endo**lymph, **endo**mixis, **endo**morph, **endo**parasite, **endo**phyte (a plant living within another plant), **endo**plasm, **endo**scope, **endo**skeleton, **endo**sperm, **endo**spore, **endo**thecium, **endo**thermal, **endo**toxin, **endo**tracheal.

> **Quote**: It is obvious that we cannot begin to be citizens in a democracy if we are only partly capable of understanding our own language, if we cannot distinguish critically between truth and falsehood, between sense and nonsense; if we do not realize that language and the word are still more powerful than the atom bomb, that like a weapon it can be used for or against us. Victor Grove

wordextras

Placebo, a one-word Latin sentence, means **I shall please**; in Roman times, referred to an inactive substance to satisfy a patient's demand for medication; in medical research, a *placebo* is used for the control group; in the Roman Catholic Church, a vespers service for the dead. Other one-word Latin sentences are listed throughout the book.

The Scandinavians enriched our language with *utlager*, **beyond the law**, or **outlawed**, therefore, *outlaw*, originally a person deprived of legal rights and protection; the killing of such a person was not a legal offense. Also used as a verb.

Story is the shortening of *history*; the *story* of a house or building comes from the practice in earlier times of painting murals on successive floors of public buildings to depict sequential episodes of a historical period.

Nitwit, a person regarded as stupid or silly, is probably from German *niht*, **nothing** + Middle English *wit*, **intelligence**; therefore, **one who knows nothing**.

Ecru, **light tan**, **beige**, is from Old French *escru* (from Latin *ex-*, **intensive** + *crudus*, **raw**), in reference to the color of unbleached, or *raw*, linen. *Crude*, *crudités* (raw vegetables cut up and served as hors d'oeuvres, usually with a dip or sauces), and *erudite* are also from *crudus*. See word pair erudite:learned, p. 185. There is *Ecru*, MS; see p. 33.

Gaucho is a cowboy of mixed Indian and Spanish ancestry, living on the South American pampas; see p. 100.

Scrimmage, from *skirmish* (see p. 100), is a rough-and-tumble fight; tussle; confused struggle. In *football*, short for *line of scrimmage*; for sports in general, a practice session or game between two different teams or two units of the same team.

Motto of the University of Denver: *Pro scientia et religione*: **For science and religion**
Motto of Duke University: *Eruditio et Religio*: **Learning and Religion**
Motto of the State of New Mexico: *Crescit eundo*: **It increases by growing**

Common element base: intro-, intra-   **Meaning**: within, in, on the inside, inwardly, on
IE base: *en-*, **in**, and found in **Italian** *mountebank*; **German**: *drinnen*, **inside**, **within**
Both *inter-* and *intra-* are from a common base; however, in present-day usage, *inter-* means **between**, **among**, whereas *intro-* and *intra-* usually mean **within**. For example, *interstate commerce* involves trade between States of the United States, while *intrastate commerce* involves trade within a single State. Furthermore, *interstate highway*, e.g., I-95, from Maine to Florida, versus *intrastate highway*, e.g., *within California*, or within any particular state. The older US-designated routes are also *interstate highways*, such as US1, again from Maine to Florida, but are not designated as such.

Clavis

intramural: *murus*, **wall**; **within the walls**, and thus describes sports played **within** the confines of the school rather than between schools. *Varsity*, the highest level of a sports program between schools, is from a British dialectal pronunciation of *university*. As a medical term, **within the walls of an organ**.

intravenous: *venous*, **pertaining to veins**; **in**, or **directly into**, **a vein or veins**, as *an intravenous injection*.

intrauterine: **within the uterus**; an *intrauterine contraceptive device* (IUD) is any of various devices, as a coil or loop of plastic, inserted into the uterus as a contraceptive.

intrinsic: *intra-* + *sequi*, **to follow**; **to follow within**, private, secret; now, generally, describing the essential nature of a thing. See **Clavis** note on *intimate*, p. 98.

introduce: *ducere*, **to lead**; **to lead in**; to lead or bring into a given place or position: SYNONYMS: insert, interject, interpolate, interpose. SYNONYMS for *introduction*: foreword, preamble, preface, prologue. An overture (from *aperture*, **opening**) *introduces* the different motifs in an opera. See p. 25, **wordbuilder #15**.

introit: with *ire*, **to go**, as in *itinerary, adit, exit, obit, obituary*; a psalm or hymn sung or played at the opening of a Christian service, and as the choir enters the sanctuary. See other *it-* words, pp. 66, 194, 208.

introvert: *vertere*, **to turn**; **to turn inward**; to direct one's interest, mind, or attention, upon oneself; also, a noun.

intestine: from *intus*, **within**; originally referred to the *internal* affairs of a country or community, e.g., *an intestine dispute* was an internal, or domestic quarrel or misunderstanding; more often, a noun, referring to the lower part of the *alimentary* canal. *Alimentary,* along with **alimony** and **alma mater,** shares the same root, meaning **to nourish**. See p. 4 under **IE base**. *Alma mater* literally means **nourishing mother**.

entrée: in France, refers to the first course of a meal, usually appetizers or hors d'oeuvres. In the United States, *entrée* designates the main dish.

dysentery: *dys-*, **bad**; **bad intestines** (bowels); intestinal inflammation with intense abdominal pain and diarrhea. *Diarrhea*—**to flow through**. See other *dia-* words, p. 193.

endocrine: Greek *krinein*, **to separate**, **to secrete within**, as *endocrine glands*. See **wordbuilder #21**, p. 42.

Intracoastal Waterway: a mostly inland water route, extending 1550 miles along the Atlantic coast from Boston to Florida Bay and 1116 miles along the Gulf Coast from Carrabelle, Florida, to Brownsville, Texas. See *dismal*, p. 124.

wordextras

Ubiquitous, **every place at the same time**, or, at least, appears to be so, is from Latin *ubi*, **where** + *que*, **any**. In the summertime, Minnesota is notorious for its *ubiquitous* mosquitoes.

From the Dutch, we have ***coleslaw***, which combines *kool*, **cabbage** and *sla*, **salad**.

Skirmish, originally from Old High German *skirmjan*, **to protect**, is a brief fight or encounter between small groups, usually an incident of a battle; any slight, unimportant conflict; brush; as *a skirmish with the law*. See p. 99 for *scrimmage*.

Felony is a major crime, as murder, arson, or rape, for which statutes usually require a greater punishment than for a misdemeanor. Those convicted of a *felony* are usually incarcerated in a penitentiary rather than in the local jail.

Pampas are the extensive, treeless plains of Argentina and some other parts of South America. See *gaucho*, p. 99.

Fiend, from Old English *feond*, **the one hating**, was originally an evil spirit; devil; now, **an inhumanly cruel person**.

Word from the name of a place: *billingsgate*, foul language; after the fish market in London, notorious for the foul language used there. See p. 120 under *obloquy*.

Sectional Word Cluster Test

INSTRUCTIONS: For each set of words from Latin and Greek (and sometimes, French, Spanish, and German), write the common meaning in the blank.

Example: **hypo**tenuse, **hypo**thesis, **sub**ject   <u>under</u>

	Presection Answer	Postsection Answer
51. pro**ject**ile, e**ject**, pro**ject**or, **jetty**, para**ble**	_____	_____
52. **jour**nal, ad**journ**, bon**jour**, so**journ**	_____	_____
53. **jud**icial, **judg**ment, **jus**tice, hoosegow	_____	_____
54. con**jug**ate, con**junct**ion, **junta**, sy**zygy**	_____	_____
55. **lava**, **lava**tory, ab**lut**ion, antedi**luv**ian	_____	_____
56. **lev**ee, **lev**er, e**lev**ator, al**lev**iate, re**lev**ant	_____	_____
57. **liber**ate, **Liber**ia, **liber**al, il**liber**al, **liber**tarian	_____	_____
58. **liter**al, **liter**ate, il**liter**acy, trans**liter**ate	_____	_____
59. **loc**ation, al**loc**ate, **lieu**tenant, **thesis**, hypo**thesis**	_____	_____
60. **loqu**acious, ventri**loqu**ist, sol**iloqu**y, e**loc**ution	_____	_____

_____   _____
Presection Score   Postsection Score

Note: Enter scores for this test and the following ones after completing this section; then, enter them on p. xvii.

Sectional Wordbuilder Test

Throughout the book and as a supplement, there are wordbuilders; these wordbuilders are designed to help you build a family of words from a single root.

	Presection Answer	Postsection Answer
40. What is the meaning of *gastr-* as in **gastr**ic, **gastr**itis?	_____	_____
41. What is the meaning of *hydr-* as in **hydr**ant, **hydr**angea?	_____	_____
42. What is the meaning of *-od-* as in ex**od**us, **od**ometer?	_____	_____
43. What is the meaning of *sphere-* as in **sphere**, hemi**sphere**?	_____	_____
44. What is the meaning of *ster-* as in chole**ster**ol, **ster**eotype?	_____	_____
45. What is the meaning of *glyp-* as in **glyp**todont, hiero**glyph**ics?	_____	_____
46. What is the meaning of *myel-* as in **myel**algia, polio**myel**itis?	_____	_____
47. What is the meaning of *mut-* as in **mut**ation, com**mute**?	_____	_____
48. What is the meaning of *mere* as in ecto**mere**, poly**mere**?	_____	_____
49. What is the meaning of *derm-* as in epi**derm**is, **derm**atology?	_____	_____

_____	_____
Presection Score	Postsection Score

After entering the scores here, enter them on pp. xviii.

```
                          Word Cluster No. 51

   eject                adjective          project           objective
   abject              interject          projector         introjection
   inject               subject           projectile         reject
   deject             conjecture           object             jet
     jactation          adjacent          disject            jetty
     jactitation      superjacent           ejaculate        jetsam

   Common elements_____Inferred Meaning_____
```

Romance Cognates	French	Romanian	Italian	Portuguese	Spanish
	jeter	ejecta	gettare	jogar	echar

Words with disguised Latin root: agio, ballet, disease, ease:adjacent, ghetto, gist, joist, jut, malaise

Latin phrases: *hic jacet* (**here lies**: a tombstone inscription; an epitaph); *alea jacta est, disjecta membra* (see **Clavis**)

French terms and phrases: *jet d'eau*, **a jet of water**; an ornamental jet of water; fountain
jeter de la poudre aux yeux: **to throw dust in the eyes**; to mislead
jeter le manche après la cognée: **to throw the handle after the hatchet**; give up a thing in despair
objet d'art (see p. 140, under **Clavis**); *jeté* (in *ballet*, a leap from one foot to the other)

Greek cognates: di**esis** (double dagger: a symbol (‡) used as a reference mark), par**esis**, syn**esis** (see **Clavis**), en**ema**

Greek *ballein*, **to throw**: **ball**ad, **ball**ade, **ball**et, **ball**ista, **ball**istics; amphi**bole**, hyper**bole**; cata**bol**ism, disco**bol**us, ec**bol**ic, epi**bol**y, meta**bol**ism, hyper**bol**a, para**bol**a, sym**bol**; devil (dia**bol**ic), em**blem**, pro**blem**; para**ble** (see p. 62); palaver, parley, parliament (see p. 144), parlor (see **wordextras** below), by parol (**oral testimony**), parole. **NB**: balloon.

German: *werfen*, as in *die Augen auf eine Sache werfen*, **to cast a glance at a thing**.

wordextras

In earlier times, ***parlor***, from French *parler*, **to speak**, designated the living room, or where guests were entertained. In medieval monasteries, such rooms were called *parlatoriums*, designating special chambers where monks were allowed to break their silence and speak with visitors, and sometimes with each other. See p. 144 for *parliament*.

Fiasco, **flask**, meaning "a ridiculous failure," is from Italian *(far) fiasco*, (**to make**) **a bottle**. Possibly, the *failure* was due to one's nipping the bottle excessively.

Howitzer, from German *Haubitze*, and ultimately from Old Czech *haufnice*, originally meant **a sling**, as in *slingshot*. A modern *howitzer*—a mainstay of the artillery—is a short cannon with a low muzzle velocity, firing shells in a relatively high trajectory. See p. 54, top of page.

Tequila, from Nahuatl *Tuiquila*, and originally the name of an Aztec tribe, was probably the first distilled liquor in America, inasmuch as the Aztecs were known to have drunk it before Cortez arrived. It is made from a variety of the agave plant, grown mostly in volcanic soil near Jalisco, the tequila capital of the world; *Jalisco* is also the capital of the State of Guadalajara. *Nahuatl* is the language of the ancient Aztecs and is still spoken in parts of Mexico.

Chopsticks is Pidgin English for Chinese *k'wai-tsze*, **the quick ones**.

The ***Missouris***, from Illinois (Indian tribe) *ouemessourit*, meant **person who has a canoe**. From this tribal meaning was derived the name of the state of Missouri.

Gadget may have come from French *gâchette*, **catch of a lock**, and a diminutive of *gâche*, **a bolt**, **catch**. It probably came into English when Britain's merchant marine, impressed with the small mechanical parts of new-style rifles in France, stumbled across the word, and then continued to use it for any small mechanism that is more costly than helpful. *Gadget* usually denotes any interesting but relatively useless or unnecessary object.

Abundance and ***abound*** are from *ab-*, **away** + *undare*, **to rise in waves**. See p. 213, for more words from *unda*.

Motto of Columbia University: *In lumine tuo videbimus lumen*: **In thy light shall we see light**. Psalm 36:9.
Motto of the State of Montana: *Ora y Plata*, Spanish for **Gold and Silver**
Motto of the University of Delaware: *Scientia sol mentis est*: **Knowledge is the sun of the mind**.
Motto of the State of Idaho: *Esto Perpetua*: **Let her be eternal**.

Common element base: jactare   **Meaning**: to throw, hurl, cast
IE base: *ye-*: yields **Latin**: *jacere*; **Greek**: *hienai*: **to send**, **throw**; **English**: mount; **Welsh**: *meneth*, **mountain**

Clavis

abject:	*ab-*, **from**; **thrown from**; of the lowest degree; miserable; wretched, as *abject poverty*. Also, lacking self-respect, degraded, as *an abject coward*.
adjective:	*ad-*, **to**; **thrown to**, but more like "that which is added to," as to nouns to qualify or modify them. *Adjective* is also used as *an adjective*; in *law*, for example, **dependent** or **procedural**, as *an adjective issue*; and **mordant, caustic**, as *adjective dyes*. See p. 150, under *parse*.
conjecture:	*con-*, **with, together**; **to throw together**, to guess; as a *noun*, an inferring, theorizing, or predicting from incomplete or uncertain evidence; **guesswork**.
interject:	*inter-*, **between**; **to throw between**, or **among** (other things), which accounts for *interjection* as a part of speech, or an exclamation *thrown in* without grammatical connection, e.g., ah! ouch! well! See p. 150, under *parse*, for the derivation of the other parts of speech.
projectile:	*pro-*, **forward**; that which is **thrown forward**, an object that can be *hurled* or *shot forward*, as a cannon shell, bullet, javelin, or rocket. As an *adjective*, designed to be thrown or hurled forward, as *projectile forces*; in *zoology*, that can be thrust out, as *a projectile tentacle*.
jactitation:	in *medicine*, **excessive restlessness**; in *law*, a false boast or claim that causes harm to another.
adjacent:	*ad-*, as in *adjective*, above; **thrown to**; now, **lying close to**; adjoining; as "the home *adjacent* to ours is a bungalow." An unusual doublet is *ease*. *Adjacent* comes directly from Latin; *ease*, through Old French *aise*, a contraction—and corruption—of Latin *adjacens*.
ejaculate:	*e-*, elision of *ex-*, **out**; **to eject or discharge abruptly**; also, to utter suddenly; exclaim, as to utter a paroxysm (an outburst). [In *medicine*, *paroxysm* is a sudden attack, or intensification, of symptoms.] *Ejaculate* also means to eject or emit semen. (In *paroxysm*, *par-* is an elision of Greek *para-*, **beyond** + *oxys*, **sharp**, as in *oxymoron*, a figure of speech, meaning "acutely silly," "absurd.")
synesis:	*syn-*, **together**; **a throwing together**; or, closer to the actual meaning, **a sending together**; a grammatical construction that conforms to the meaning rather than to the strict syntactical agreement, e.g., "Has *everyone* (singular antecedent) washed *their* (plural pronoun) hands?" or "If *anyone* [singular] arrives, tell *them* [plural] to wait." "If the *group* (collective singular noun) becomes too large, we can split *them* in two." The rule: *Pronoun<u>s</u>* are to agree with *their* antecedents.
parable:	*para-*, **alongside**; **thrown alongside of**; a short, simple story, usually of an occurrence of a familiar kind, from which a moral or religious lesson may be drawn. See p. 62, under **IE base**.
hyperbole:	*hyper-*, **over, beyond**; **a throwing beyond**; an excess; a figure of speech expressing an exaggerated or extravagant statement not meant to deceive, e.g., *I could sleep for a week. This suitcase weighs a ton.* See *literally* as used hyperbolically, p. 116. Jesus often taught by hyperbole, e.g., I am the true vine.
alea jacta est:	**the die is cast** (an exclamation attributed to Julius Caesar upon crossing the Rubicon). See p. 174 for additional information on the origin of "crossing the Rubicon."

Word from the name of a place: *buncombe*, or *bunkum*, often shortened to *bunk*; **humbug, insincere talk**; originally, insincere speechmaking by a politician intended merely to please local constituents; from "a speech for Buncombe (North Carolina)," by Congressman Felix Walker in 1820 before the U.S. House of Representatives.

---

wordextras

Virtual, from *virtue*, **manliness, strength, worth**, has come to mean "being such practically or in effect" although not in actual fact or name, e.g., *a virtual impossibility*, or *the virtual memory* (of a computer). *Vir*, a Latin word for **man**, yields the adjective *virile*, **manly, forceful, sexually potent, capable of copulation**. See p. 213, Item 189.

Ordeal, from Germanic *uzdailjan*, **to deal out, allot, judge**, originally was an ancient method of trial in which the accused was exposed to physical dangers, from which he or she was supposed to be divinely protected if innocent; now, any difficult, painful, or trying experience; severe trial. See p. 106 under **IE base**.

Idée fixe, French for **fixed idea**, is an obsession. *Idée reçue*, **received idea**, is a generally accepted idea; convention.

```
┌─────────────────────────────────────────────────────────────────────────┐
│                         Word Cluster No. 52                               │
│                                                                           │
│  journal          journalist        journalese        journalism          │
│  journey          adjourn           journeyman        sojourn             │
│                                                                           │
│  Common element_____Inferred Meaning_____   │
└─────────────────────────────────────────────────────────────────────────┘
```

Romance Cognates	French	Romanian	Italian	Portuguese	Spanish
	jour*	zi**	giorno	dia	dia

*The common element, which is French, from Latin *diurnalis*, is also the base of the Italian, Portuguese, and Spanish elements.

**The *z* of the Romanian element is influenced by Dacian, the language of Dacia, an ancient kingdom and later a Roman province between the Carpathian Mountains and the Danube. Renamed *Romania* as a tribute to the purest Latin spoken outside of Rome, Romanian is now distantly removed from Latin, being supplanted by Dacian and the Slavic languages of neighboring countries. See pp. 57, 65.

French words and phrases: *bonjour, abatjour, au jour, jour de fête, jour des morts, jour maigre, permis de séjour, l'ordre du jour, d'aujourd'hui en huit, d'aujourd'hui en quinze, le jour viendra, au jour le jour, le potage du jour, bonheur du jour, en plein jour, soupe du jour*

Popular French phrase: *Le jour de gloire est arrivé!* from *La Marseillaise*, the national anthem of France; *Marseillaise*, **of Marseille**; first sung by Marseille volunteers in 1792 during the French Revolution

A couplet: *Vienne la nuit sonne l'heure/Les jours s'en vont je demeure.* Apollinaire (1880-1918), French poet

Journals: John Woolman (1720-72), an Early American Quaker, known for his opposition to slavery (his *Journal* was published posthumously); William Byrd (1674-1744), a Colonial Virginia planter.

wordextras

Is **grammar** glorious or magical? In England during the Middle Ages, there was quite a mixture of languages: Anglo-Saxon (Old English), Norman French, Church Latin, Court Latin, Danish, Norse, as well as Celtic, a native language. To speak well, or to know one's *grammar* was to possess *glamour* [a Scottish variant of *grammarye*], or magic. *Grammar* comes from Greek *graphein*, **to write**, which yields **graph, graphite; autograph, mimeograph, paragraph, polygraph, telegraph; agraphia, dysgraphia; biography, calligraphy, orography, orthography; graft.**

A French word common in the South is **beaucoup**, pronounced properly as boh KOO, but usually BOO KOO, and means "an abundance of," as in "We caught *beaucoup* fish"; similar in meaning to Irish *galore*, used postpositively, as in "We caught fish *galore*." See *galore*, p. 80.

Squirrel, from Greek *skiouros*, is **shadow tail** (*skia*, **shadow** + *oura*, **tail**). In Latin, *skiouros* was changed to *sciurus*, and in Old French evolved into *escuriuel*. By the time of Chaucer, it had evolved into *squirel*. Since about a third of a squirrel is its bushy, fancy tail, *squirrel* is quite appropriate for the tree rodent.

Japanese **Shinto** is formed from two earlier Chinese words: *shin*, **god** or **spirit**, and *tao*, **way of life**. **Shinto** is a primitive religion that emphasized ancestor worship, and prior to the defeat of Japan in 1945, was the state religion of the country. It is still the prevailing religion in postwar Japan.

Boise, Idaho, from French *boisé*, **wooded**, **covered with trees**, was so named by early French explorers. **Boiserie**, pronounced BWAH zuh REE, denotes wood paneling on the walls of a room.

Oklahoma, **red people**, is from Choctaw *okla*, **people** + *homma*, **red**; compare with *Pensacola* (p. 111).

The **fallopian tubes** are named after Gabriele *Fallopio*, a 16th-century Italian anatomist. *Fallopian* is also in caps.

Poll, probably from Middle Dutch, originally referred to the **top of the head**, or to the *head* itself. It came to mean an individual person, especially one among several; then, a counting, listing, or register of persons, especially of voters. In the US, the 24th Amendment in 1964 abolished the *poll tax* as a prerequisite for voting.

Geisha, from Sino-Japanese *gei*, **art** (of dancing, singing) + *sha*, **person**, denotes a Japanese woman trained in singing, dancing, the art of conversation, etc., to serve as a hired companion to men.

Blatant, coined by Edmund Spenser (1552-99), and from Latin *blaterare*, **to babble**, or from English dialect *blate*, **to bellow**, means disagreeably loud or boisterous; glaringly conspicuous or obtrusive, as in *blatant ignorance*.

Common element base: jour
IE base: *dieu-*; see p. 68, under **IE base**.

Meaning: day

Clavis

journal:
and *diurnal*; both are from Latin *diurnalis*, **daily**, but entered English through different routes, and took on various meanings and spellings. In German, *journal* is *das Tagebuch*, **the day book**.

Although *diurnal* means **daily**, it is used in the sense of being opposite to *nocturnal*, **pertaining to the night**; thus, *diurnal* is an adjective (except when it denotes a service book containing prayers for daytime use), whereas *journal* is a noun.

In *botany*, *diurnal* describes those flowers that open in the daytime, but close at night; in *zoology*, describes those animals that are active only in the daytime, such as the coatimundis, prevalent from Texas to Central America.

As a record of daily occurrences, *journal* is a part of the title of many newspapers, as an account of the **daily** news events. In Middle English, *journal* referred to a book containing forms of worship for the day hours (see *diurnal*, above). *Journal* also designates the part of a rotating axle, shaft, or spindle that turns in a bearing, probably from the earth's turning, or rotating as on a "daily" basis.

journalese:
a style of writing and diction characteristic of many newspapers, magazines, and tabloids; facile or sensational style, often with many clichés. Explore *yellow journalism*.

journey:
originally, a **day's** trip by horseback, since the land trip could be broken into **daily** units interrupted by overnight periods of rest; now refers to an extended land trip as distinct from a sea voyage. In German, *die Tagereise*, **a day's ride**, or trip. See *cruise*, p. 52.

journeyman:
originally, in French, *à la journée*, **by the day**; then the noun, *journalier*, one who worked **by the day**; in German, *Tagelöhner*—**day earner**. Now, *journeyman* refers to a trained, competent worker.

adjourn:
ad-, **to**, **toward**; **to the day**; originally, to suspend (a session) until a specified day, has come to include "to suspend indefinitely." *Adjourn* can also mean "to move from one place to another," as in "After dinner, we *adjourned* to the living room." See *adjourn*, p. 68, under *sine die*.

sojourn:
sub-, **under**; **under a day**; as a *verb*, to live someplace temporarily, as on a visit; as a *noun*, a temporary stay; a visit. The extent of one's life is often referred to as a *sojourn*.

le potage du jour: French; or *soupe du jour*: **soup of the day**; in France, usually a thick soup of vegetables or beans, and most often the first course of the meal.

---

wordextras

Forecastle was originally the foremost of two castlelike structures on medieval ships. From this vantage point, the lookout had a panoramic view. Pronounced FOKE sil, or FORE KAS ul.

Et al. is the abbreviation for Latin *et alii*, **and others**. The term is usually seen in the case of multiple authors, where one author's name is listed, followed by *et al.*; it is also used where there are multiple parties in a court case. Note that there is no period (.) after *et*, since *et* is a complete word. See **wordbuilder #4**, p. 7.

Opaque, from Latin *opacus*, **shady**, can mean **hard to understand**. SYNONYMS: dark, dim, dusky, murky, obscure. As a *verb*, to make *opaque*. The noun form is *opacity*, as a spot on the cornea or lens of the eye.

Spinster is **one who spins**. *Spinning* was an accepted activity for unmarried, older women in times past to fill their time in doing. A *spinster* was also called **old maid**, a mild term of contempt.

Picaresque, from Spanish *picaro*, **rogue**, pertaining to sharp-witted rogues or vagabonds, also describes a type of fiction that deals with the adventures of a hero who is, or who resembles, a vagabond. Examples: Cervantes' *Don Quixote* (see p. 90); Twain's *Huckleberry Finn*; Dickens's *Martin Chuzzlewit*; Fielding's *History of Tom Jones*.

Blight may be from Middle English *bliknen*, **to lose color**, which itself is from Old Norse *blikja*, **turn pale**. *Blight* is any atmospheric or soil condition, parasite, or insect that kills, withers, or stunts the growth of plants.

Pedant, from Greek *pais*, **child**, is one who puts unnecessary emphasis on minor or trivial points of learning; a narrow-minded teacher who insists on exact adherence to a set of arbitrary rules. See *page*, p. 105.

Word Cluster No. 53

judicial	judiciary	prejudice	judicable
judicious	judicature	injudicious	adjudicate
just	judicatory	justiciary	adjust
justice	justiciable	justifiable	adjudge
judge	judgment	judgmental	injury
jury	abjure	adjure	injure
jurisdiction	jurisprudence	perjury	perjure(d)
		objurgate	conjure

Common elements_____Inferred Meaning_____

Romance Cognates	French	Romanian	Italian	Portuguese	Spanish
	juge	judeca	giudice	juiz	juez

Word with disguised Latin root: hoosegow (see **Clavis**)   **Doublets**: adjudge:adjudicate

Latin words and phrases: *jus, jus conubi, jus accrescendi, jus abutendi, jus ad rem, jus civile, sub judice, jus gentium, res judicate, justitia omnibus, ad judicium, corpus juris, de jure* (opposite of *de facto*)

Translated Latin phrases: *Summum jus, summa injuria* (See **Clavis**.)
jus et norma loquendi: **the law and rule of speech.** Horace
jurare in verba magistri: **to swear to the words of the master.** Horace

French phrase: *juste milieu*: **the just** (or, **golden**) **mean**; specifically, a method of government that holds a middle course between extremists.

Placenames: Justice (KY, IL, NC, OK); Justiceburg, Texas

Motto of Paraguay: *Paz y justicia*: **Peace and Justice**
Motto of the District of Columbia: *Justitia omnibus*: **Justice for all.**
Motto of the State of Georgia: **Wisdom,** *Justice*, **and Moderation**

wordbuilder #40

Greek *gaster*, **stomach**, yields **gastr**ea, **gastr**ic, **gastr**ula, **gastr**ulation; **gastr**ectomy, **gastr**itis; **gastr**oenteritis, **gastr**olith, **gastr**onomy, **gastr**opod, **gastr**oscope, **gastr**otomy, **gastr**otrich, **gastr**ovascular; micro**gastr**ia; di**gastr**ic, entero**gastr**ic, hemo**gastr**ic, hepato**gastr**ic, pneumo**gastr**ic; epi**gastr**ium, hypo**gastr**ium, meso**gastr**ium.

wordextras

Ragout, pronounced ra GOO, and from French *ragoûter*, **to restore the appetite**, is a highly seasoned stew of meat and vegetables. *Ragout* is ultimately from Latin *re-*, **again** + *ad-*, **to** + *gustus*, **taste.** *Gustation*, **gustatory**, **gusto**, and *disgust* are from the same root. See *disgust*, p. 29. Spanish: *No me gusta*: **I don't like it.**

French ***bouillabaisse***, a fish stew, and a specialty of Marseille, is from the imperative of Provençal *bouia*, **to boil** + *abaissa*, **to lower**, "[that which] **boils and settles.**" Pronunciation: BOO yah BESS, or BASE; also, BOOL yah BESS.

Nexus, from Latin *nectere*, **to bind**, refers to a **connection, tie, link** between individuals of a group, members of a series, etc.; a means of connection between things. Other words from *nectere*: ad**nexa**, an**nex**, con**nect**.

Imperious, from the same Latin base as *empire* and *imperative*, describes one who is "overbearing, arrogant, domineering, dictatorial." A situation that is *urgent* or *imperative* can also be described as *imperious*.

Aplomb, from French *à*, **to** + *plomb*, **plumb**, and further from Latin *plumbum*, **lead**, describes that which is perpendicular in the manner of a plumb bob. SYNONYMS: assurance, poise, self-confidence, self-possession. See p. 39 for chemical symbol for *lead*.

The noun ***broach***, a **brooch** or **ornamental pin**, and the verb, **to start a discussion of, bring up, introduce**, are from Middle English *broche*, **a pin, peg, spit.** To *broach* a subject is to have something to *pin* it on.

Page, as *a senate page*, from Greek *paidion*, **boy**, originally referred to a boy training for knighthood, and who attended a knight; later, it referred to a boy attendant or servant, especially one serving a person of high rank. See p. 148 for *page* of a book. See *pedant*, p. 104.

Motto of the State of Kansas: *Ad astra per aspera*: **To the stars with difficulty.**

Common element base: jurare   **Meaning**: to take an oath; swear

Base of *jurare* is *jus*, **right**, **law**; **IE base**: *yewes-*: **law**; together with *deik*, **to judge**; see IE base, p. 66.
German: *schwören*, **to swear**; *richten*, **to set right**; *urteilen*, **to judge**, from which is *ordeal*. See p. 102.

Clavis

judicial:
: of **judges**, **law courts**, or their functions; allowed, enforced, or set by order of a judge or law court.

Judgment Day:
: in *theology*, the time of **God's final judgment** of all people; end of the world; doomsday. *Dies Irae*.

judgmental:
: having to do with the exercise of **judgment**; making or tending to make judgments as to value and importance; often specifically, making judgments or evaluations lacking in compassion, tolerance, objectivity, especially those that are moral or personal.

judicious:
: having, applying, or showing sound **judgment**; wise and careful. SYNONYMS: prudent, sage, sapient, wise. Showing poor judgment is to be *injudicious*.

adjudicate:
: a doublet of *adjudge*; *ad-*, **to**, **toward**; **to judge**, **decide**; in *law*, to hear and settle a case by judicial procedure; also, to serve as a judge in, or on, a dispute or problem. In *law*, the noun *adjudication* is "a judge's decision," or "a court ruling." Pronounced ad JOO dih KATE.

prejudice:
: *pre-*, **before**; **a judging beforehand**, or before knowing all the facts. Associating *prejudice* (often misspelled *predjudice*) with *prejudge* aids in correct spelling, i.e., no *d* before the *j*.

res judicata:
: Latin; **a matter judged**; a case already decided; therefore, pointless to discuss the matter further; similar to French *fait accompli*, **accomplished fact** (see p. 30); also, similar to French *chose jugée*.

jury:
: Old French *jurée*, from *jurer*, **to swear**; theoretically, a group of one's peers *sworn* to extract and distill the truth of witnesses' statements.

injury:
: *in-*, **not** + *jus*, **right**, **justice**. SYNONYMS: grievance, injustice, wrong.

perjury:
: *per-*, **through**; the willful telling of a lie while under lawful oath or affirmation to tell the truth in a matter material to the point of inquiry. Related forms: perjure, perjured, as *perjured testimony*.

adjust:
: *ad-*, **to** + *juxta-*, **near**; to arrange; to change so as to fit; often confused with *just*, and came to mean "to make right." Another word with *juxta* is *juxtapose*, **to place side by side**. See p. 107.

unjust:
: English-Latin hybrid. English *un-*, **not**, for *in-*, **opposite**, **not** + *just*; not just or right; unfair; contrary to justice. *Unjust* is the adjectival form of the noun *injustice*.

hoosegow:
: American slang for **jail**, from Spanish *juzgado*, **courtroom**; further from Latin *judicare*, **to judge**. Americans who were tried in Mexican courts pronounced and spelled *juzgado* approximately the way they heard it, since *j* in Spanish is pronounced as *h*. The place where one was judged became the place where one was jailed after being sentenced.

---

summa jus, summa injuria: **the highest law, the highest injustice.** The rigor of the law may be the height of injustice.

wordextras

Spanish *siesta* is from Latin *sexta hora*—**sixth hour** after sunrise—the hottest part of the day. It is a time for merchants to close their shops and relax in the coolness of the shade. Analogous to Greek *calm*, from *kaumas*, **heat of the sun**. Greek merchants also closed their shops in the *calm* of the day. *Calm* has come to mean *peaceful, restful, tranquil, halcyon, serene, still*. See more on *halcyon*, p. 92; *tranquil*, p. 194; *siesta*, p. 212, Item 164.

Rathskeller, a German-type restaurant, usually below street level, is from German *rath*, now *rat*, **council**, **town hall** + *keller*, **cellar**, because of its often being located in the cellar of the town hall.

Col, from Latin *collum*, **neck**, is a gap between peaks in a mountain range, used as a pass. *Col* is also a term used in meteorology: the point of *lowest* pressure between two *anticyclones* or the point of *highest* pressure between two *cyclones*. Other words from *collum*: **coll**ar, **coll**et, dé**coll**etage (the noun form of *décolleté*) dé**coll**eté (cut low as to bare the neck and shoulders: said of some dresses); **col**porteur; ac**col**ade (see p. 35), machi**col**ate, machi**col**ation, de**coll**ate (**behead**), torti**coll**is (**twisted neck**: a medical term).

Instigate (*in-*, **intensive** + *stigare*, **to prick**) means **to urge on, incite to some action**, especially to some wrongdoing, as *to instigate a riot*. The synonym *incite* means **to urge**, either favorably or unfavorably. See *stigma*, p. 114.

106

Word Cluster No. 54

jugal	jugulum	jugum	conjugate	bijugate
jugular	jugulate	jugate	conjugal	conjugant
junction	conjunct	juncture	subjugate	injunction
conjunction	subjunctive	junctive	adjunct	conjunctiva
join	conjoin	conjunctive	disjunct	rejoinder
disjoin	subjoin	enjoin	rejoin	subjoinder

Common elements_____**Inferred Meaning**_____

Romance Cognates	French	Romanian	Italian	Portuguese	Spanish
	joug	jug	giogo	jugo	yugo

Related words: join, joint, conjoint, disjoint, joust, jostle, jument, junta, junto, juxtapose, juxtaposition, yoke

Placenames: Junction (ID, IL, NY, OH, TX, UT); Junction City (AR, CA, GA, KS, KY, MT, NC, OH, OR, WI)

Motto of the University of Cincinnati: *Juncta juvant. Alta petit.* See p. 3 for translation.

Latin phrase: *Juncta juvant*: **Things united aid each other.** Union is strength.

Greek cognates: from *zygon,* **yoke**: zygoma, zygosis (pl. zygoses), zygote, zygodactyl, zygomorphous, zygophyte, zygapophysis, zygoptera, zygospore; heterozygous, homozygous, azygous; syzygy, zeugma (grammar terms): compare *zeugma* with *syllepsis*; epizeuxis. Explore *syzygy* as used by both Sidney Lanier and Edgar Allan Poe.

Sanskrit cognates: yoga, Yogi, Yuga

wordextras

A *palindrome* is a word or phrase that reads the same backward as forward; for example, "A man, a plan, a canal, Panama," referring to President Theodore Roosevelt, and his plan to build the Panama Canal. Also, Madam, I'm Adam. *Palin* is Greek for **again**, but usually means **backwards**, as in *palimpsest*; and *dramein* is **to run**, as in **drome**dary; aero**drome**, hippo**drome**, and syn**drome** (a set of symptoms that usually **run together**), ana**dromous** (going from salt water to fresh water or up rivers to spawn: said of salmon, shad, etc.), cata**dromous**, dia**dromous**. *Palindromic arthritis* clears up in reverse order of its onset. See p. 206, Item 86, for other *drome* words.

A *felluca* is a long, narrow sailing vessel propelled by oars or lateen sails, used mainly along the Mediterranean coast. Coming from Italian *felucca*, it is further from Arabic *fulk,* **ship**. Pronounced: fu LUCK uh.

Pirogue, pronounced pih ROGUE, a canoe used on the Louisiana bayous, comes from Spanish *piragua*, which is further from Carib, an Indian language of northern South America. The *pirogue* was originally a hollowed-out tree trunk.

Kayak is Eskimo for **a canoe made of skins**, especially sealskins, stretched over a frame of wood to cover it completely except for an opening in the middle for the paddler. As far as can be determined, *kayak* has no constituent meaning. *Eskimo*, however, probably means "snowshoe net makers."

Alliteration, often called **initial rhyme**, is the repetition of an initial sound, usually of a consonant or a consonant cluster, in two or more words of a phrase or a line of poetry. Example: *Princess of primitive promise, awake! Gladness and glory shall glow in thy cheeks!* Alliteration is quite alive today in such expressions as "busy bee," "busy as a beaver," "cool as a cucumber," "labor of love," "friend or foe." See p. 116 for more on *alliteration*.

Burgeon, generally, **to grow or expand**, is from Old French *burjon*, **a bud**. Specifically, *burgeon* means to put forth buds, shoots; to sprout; to grow or develop rapidly; proliferate, flourish. The *burgeoning* suburbs have decreased the natural habitat of many birds and wild animals.

Hangar, from French, and sometimes said to be from a place where gliders were *hung* from the ceiling, is more likely from Middle Dutch *hamgaerd*, **home guard**, and designates a shelter used to house, repair, etc., an airplane. In French, *hangar* designates simply "a shed."

An aphorism: Every man thinks his own geese swans. Every parent thinks his or her own children are the best. Witness the many bumper stickers extolling one's progeny, such as "My child is an honor student at Lake Ridge Middle School, Woodbridge, Virginia."

Common element base: jugere **Meaning**: to join, to yoke
IE root: *yeug-*: **to join**. German, *binden*, **to join**; *Joch*, **yoke**, a cognate of *join*.

Clavis

jugal:
: **connected** or **united as by a yoke**; designating or pertaining to a bone of the upper cheek; also known as *zygomatic arch*, a bony arch on either side of the face just below the eye in many vertebrates, consisting of a *zygomatic bone* that fuses with the *zygomatic process* of the temporal bone. See p. 107 for more words from *zygo-*.

conjugal:
: *con-*, **with**, **together**; **yoked together** in marriage; thus, *conjugal bliss*; matrimonial; connubial.

conjugate:
: *con-*, **with**, **together**; as a verb, **to yoke together**; in *grammar*, to give the various inflected forms of a verb. In *botany*, describes a type of sexual reproduction in protists (one-celled organisms, such as algae, yeasts, protozoans) in which the transfer of the gametes is passed through connecting tubes; also, growing in pairs, as leaflets on the axis of some leaves. In *chemistry*, NH4, as an example, is a conjugate of NH3; *conjugation* also designates a class of organic molecules with alternating single and double carbon-carbon bonds. In *linguistics*, that which has the same derivation and usually some likeness in meaning; otherwise known as *cognate*.

conjugant:
: *con-*, **with**, **together**; either of a pair of organisms, cells, or gametes undergoing **conjugation**.

subjugate:
: *sub-*, **under**; **under the yoke**; therefore, **submission**. When the Romans conquered a country or an area, they set up a yoke, and with spears, forced the victims of the country or area to pass *sub jug(um)* as a symbol of submission, or subjugation.

adjunct:
: *ad-*, **to**, **toward**; **joined to**; a nonessential addition; something added to a thing or body, but not an integral part of it, e.g., *an adjunct professor*, one who teaches part-time, but is not a member of the regular faculty. Also, "The new bride became his wife, but remained an *adjunct* to his family." Depending on its place in the sentence, *adjunct* can be either an adjective or a noun.

conjunction:
: *con-*, **with**, **together**; **a joining together**; denotes words, such as the coordinates *and, but*, and *or*, which join other words, phrases, and clauses. There are also *subordinate* conjunctions, such as *if, when, as, because, though*; these conjunctions introduce phrases and clauses that are subordinate to the principal clause. In *astronomy*, denotes the condition of being in the same orbital longitude, e.g., *planets in conjunction*. Also used generally, e.g., "The FBI, in *conjunction* with local police, apprehended the suspect." See *conjunction*, under *parse*, p. 150.

subjoin:
: *sub-*, **under**; to add something at the end of what has been stated; **append**; literally, **to hang to**.

yoga:
: Sanskrit; **a yoking**; **union**; a mystic and ascetic discipline that seeks liberation of self, and union with the supreme spirit or universal soul through intense concentration, deep meditation, and controlled breathing, as well as through assuming certain postures.

syzygy:
: *sy-*, truncation of *sym-*, **together**; **a yoking together**; a pair of things, especially a pair of opposites. In Greek and Latin prosody, a group of two feet, as a *dipody*. Dipody: from Greek *di-*, **two** + *pod*, **foot**. In *astronomy*, *syzygy* denotes the nearly straight-line configuration of three celestial bodies, e.g., the sun, moon, and earth, during a solar or lunar eclipse. Pronounced: SIZ uh jee.

zygospore:
: in *botany*, a thick-walled, resting *spore* (a small reproductive body), formed by **conjugation** of two isogametes, as in certain phycomycetous fungi and in certain green algae.

---

wordextras

Ink, from Greek *en-*, **in** + *kaiein*, **to burn**, **to burn in**, came to mean "purple ink," and was shortened to *enc*, which Middle French changed to *enque*. In Middle English, the age of Chaucer, it was spelled both *inke* and *enke*.

Anglo-Saxon *waerloga*, from *waer*, **faith** + *leogan*, **to lie**, came into Modern English as ***warlock***, **a breaker of the faith**, or **oath breaker**. *Warlock* now designates a man who is thought to have magic powers, as in practicing black magic; a male witch. See more on *warlock*, p. 167; see *perfidy*, p. 80.

Afrikaans ***gemsbok***, from German *gemse*, **chamois** + *bok*, **buck**, is a large antelope of South Africa.

Narrate, from Latin *narrare*, **to tell**, is "to tell a story in writing or speech; to give an account of something."

```
┌─────────────────────────────────────────────────────────────────────────────────┐
│                          Word Cluster No. 55                                      │
│                                                                                   │
│  lava         lavabo        lavendula     lavation      lavage       lavatory     │
│  lavish       lavender      lave          lavatic       laver        lavement     │
│                                                                                   │
│       ablution         abluent           dilute              elute               │
│       diluent          dilutee           dilutant            elutriate           │
│                                                                                   │
│    antediluvian        diluvion          alluvion          colluvial             │
│       alluvium         colluvium         eluvium           colluvies             │
│                                                                                   │
│  Common elements_____Inferred Meaning_____│
└─────────────────────────────────────────────────────────────────────────────────┘
```

Romance Cognates	French	Romanian	Italian	Portuguese	Spanish
	laver	spala	lavare	lavar	lavar

Words with disguised Latin roots: lather, latrine, launder, loment, lotic, lotion, lye, deluge

Romance words and phrases: *el lavabo, la lavandera, diluendo, lavasse* (diluted, or weak, coffee)

Placename: Alluvial City, Louisiana (because of the alluvial deposits of the Mississippi). In Saint Bernard Parish, Alluvial City is at the terminus of Route 46. (In Louisiana, *counties* are known as *parishes*.)

French phrases: *après moi le deluge; laver la tête* (see **Clavis**). *Passons au déluge*: **Let us pass on to the Deluge**. Let us come to the point. Racine (1639-99), French poet and dramatist

NB: *Pollution* is probably not in this family; neither is *laveer*, a Dutch word that means "the side of ship toward the wind"; thus, to beat against the wind in sailing. The word is now archaic, but may be encountered in old texts.

```
┌─────────────────────────────────────────────────────────────────────┐
│   Quote: No writer or speaker who ignores the roots of Latin and Greek│
│          derivatives is secure from egregious error. Stuart Sherman   │
└─────────────────────────────────────────────────────────────────────┘
```

wordextras

Parfait, French for (**something**) **perfect**, is a dessert made of layers of different flavors of ice cream and usually garnished and served in a tall glass. Pronounced: pahr FAY.

Exacerbate, **to aggravate, to make worse, to embitter**, is from Latin *ex-*, **completely** + *acerbus*, **bitter, harsh**. One can *exacerbate* a pain or an illness, or a situation. **Acerb**ate, **acerb**ic, **acerb**ity, and **acrid** are also from *acerbus*.

Delirium, **a raving in madness**, from Latin *de-*, **away** + *lira*, **line, furrow**, is "to turn the furrow awry" (while plowing). *Delirium*, noun; *delirious*, adjective. Both the noun and the adjective can be used figuratively, e.g., a *delirium* of joy, and *delirious* with joy, respectively. See *delirium* used in **A Writing Tip**, p. 65.

Vermont, from French *Verd Mont*, is **green mountain**. The Green Mountains dominate much of the state's landscape. Vermont's neighboring state New Hampshire is known for its White Mountains.

Callow, from Latin *calvus*, **bald**, originally meant "still lacking the feathers needed for flying"; unfledged; young and inexperienced; immature; lacking adult sophistication. *Calvus* also renders *Calvary*, **the place of the skull**.

Alabama was the name of a tribe of the Creek Confederacy originally inhabiting what is now southern Alabama.

Georgia was named for George II (1683-1760), king of Great Britain and Ireland (1727-60); born in Germany.

wordbuilder #41, 42

Greek *hydor*, **water**, yields **hydr**ant, **hydr**ate; **hydr**angea (see *angos*, p. 204, Item 62), **hydr**aulic; **hydro**cele, **hydro**cephalic, **hydro**gen, **hydro**geology, **hydro**graphy, **hydro**logy, **hydro**lysis, **hydro**pathy, **hydro**philic, **hydro**phobia, **hydro**phone, **hydro**phyte. Explore *Hydra*, a many-headed serpent or monster in Greek mythology.

Greek *(h)odos*, **way**, yields **od**ograph, **od**ometer; an**ode**, epis**ode**, ex**od**us, Ex**od**us, meth**od**, peri**od**, syn**od**; palin**ode**; stom**od**eum (the oral cavity in the digestive track of an embryo, that develops into the mouth).

Another *od*, from Greek *aeidein*, **to sing**, yields **ode** (an exalted poem), as well as com**edy**, ep**ode**, hymn**ody**, mel**ody**, mon**ody**, par**ody**, psalm**ody**, rhaps**ody** (see p. 63, under **wordextras**), and trag**edy** (see p. 20, under **wordextras**).

Common element base: lavere, lavare   **Meaning**: to wash, to flood

IE base: *leu(e)*: **to wash. German**: *Wasser*, **water**; *waschen*, **to wash**; see *Vaseline*®, p. 188.

Clavis

Lavabo:	**I shall wash**; in the Roman Catholic Church, a short ritual after the Offertory, in which the celebrant washes his fingers; also designates the basin used in the ritual.
lavage:	in *medicine*, the therapeutic **washing** out of a cavity or an organ, as the stomach, intestinal tract, or sinuses; also called *irrigation*.
lavish:	as a verb, **to wash** (with praise). William Caxton, who published the first book printed in English (c. 1474), wrote: "Ther was no *laves* in their speech." As an adjective, **profuse, prodigal, unstinted**, as *a lavish banquet*; as a *verb*, to give or spend on generously, as *to lavish praise* on someone.
lavender:	originally thought to come from its use as a **bath** perfume; more likely, it is from *livid*, its pale-purple color. See more on *livid*, p. 84, **wordextras**.
alluvion:	*al-*, assimilation of *ad-*, **to, toward**; the **wash** or **flow** of water against, or toward, a shore; an accession to land by the gradual addition of matter that then belongs to the owner of the land to which it was added (see *alluvium*, next entry). Synonyms: flood, inundation.
alluvium:	clay, silt, sand, gravel, or similar detrital (see p. 24) material deposited by **running** or **flowing** water, as along a river bed or the shore of a lake; *alluvion* and *alluvium* are often used interchangeably.
antediluvian:	*ante-*, **before**; **before the** (biblical) **flood**; figuratively, **outdated, anachronistic**. See p. 10.
ablution:	*ab-*, **away**; the act of **washing away**; usually in plural, *ablutions*: a symbolic religious rite of cleansing. In Psalm 51, King David pleads that God "wash away" his sins of adultery and murder.
dilute:	*di-*, truncation of *dis-*, **away**; **to wash away**; to thin down or weaken by mixing with water or other liquid; as an *adjective*, same as *diluted*, as in *the dilute speech of the candidate elicited little applause*.
deluge:	*de-* from *dis-*, **apart**; from *diluere*, **to wash away**; as a *noun*, **inundation, flood**; as a verb, **to inundate**, as to *deluge* one with requests.
lava:	first applied to the rushing (or, **flowing**) of rain through the streets after a flood; in Naples, Italy, the stream of molten matter issuing from Mount Vesuvius; now, such matter, either melted or solidified after cooling.
laundry:	properly, *laund̲ery*, from Middle English *lavandrie*, from Middle French *lavanderie*; probably formed after Old French *lavandière*, **a person who washes**.
ablutomania:	Greek *mania*, **madness, frenzy**; a psychological compulsion **to wash** one's hands.
elutriate:	*e-*, truncation of *ex-*, **out**; from *eluere*, **to wash out**; to purify, separate, or remove (ore, for example) by washing and settling.
laver la tête:	French; **to wash the head**; Synonyms: admonish, berate, rebuke, reprimand, reproach.

après moi le deluge: French; **after me, the deluge**; saying attributed to Louis XV.

Word from Roman mythology: *martial*, **warlike**; after Mars, the Roman god of war; identified with Greek Ares.

wordextras

Lachrymose, from Latin *lacrima*, **teardrop**, and akin to Greek *dakrys*, means **tearful, mournful**. Other words from this root are as follows: **lachrym**al, **lachrym**ator; **lacrim**al, **lacrim**ation, **lacrim**ator (or, lachrymator).

Digitalis means **belonging to the finger**. Named by L. Fuchs (1501-66), known for *fuchsia* (see p. 78), *digitalis*, or foxglove, has thimblelike flowers, after the German name *Fingerhut*, **finger house**; or *thymel*, Anglo-Saxon for *thimble*, or "thumb covering." See *Dudelsack, Handschuh*, p. 112.

Paddy, from Malay *padi*, means **rice in the husk**. In addition, *paddy* can mean rice in general, or a rice field; thus, the phrase *rice paddy*.

Word Cluster No. 56

lever	levator	cantilever	elevate
levy	levity	levee	leverman
levant	levanter	relevant	levitate
leverage	elevator	alleviate	levade

Common element_____**Inferred Meaning**_____

Romance Cognates	French	Romanian	Italian	Portuguese	Spanish
	lever	levier	levare	levanter	levantar

Words with disguised Latin roots: leaven, legerdemain, relief, relieve, bas-relief, mezzo-relievo, levy in masse

Latin phrases: *Sit tibi terra levis. Leve fit quod bene fertur onus.* See **Clavis**.
Curae leves loquuntur, ingentes stupent: **Light griefs find utterance, great ones are dumb.** Seneca (4 B.C.-A.D. 85), Roman philosopher, dramatist, and statesman

NB: *Leviathan*, *levigate*, and *levirate* are not in this family.

Germanic: lung, lights, light (in weight)   **Old Irish**: leprechaun

---

Quote: Reading is to the mind what exercise is to the body. Addison

---

wordextras

In Latin, *focus* meant **hearth**, or **fireplace**, the center of the home. In 1604, Johannes Kepler (1571-1630), German astronomer and mathematician, adopted *focus* to indicate the center, or the burning point, of a lens. See plural of *focus*, under **wordextras**, p. 81.

Cajole, **to coax with flattery, to wheedle**, is probably from French *cajoler*, "to chatter like a caged jay." Pronounced: kuh JOLE.

Pensacola, Florida, **hair people**, is from Choctaw *pansha*, **hair** + *okla*, **people**; compare with *Oklahoma*, p. 103.

Savannah, Georgia, may be from Spanish *sabana*. A *sabana,* or savanna, is a treeless plain, or relatively flat, open region, as the steppes of southeastern Europe and Asia, especially Russia. *Steppe* is a Russian word; see p. 189.

Florida was so named by Ponce de Leon (1460-1521); when he discovered the peninsula, it abounded with *flowers*.

Trencherman, from Old French *trenchier*, **to cut**, and further from Latin *truncare*, **to cut** (which yields *truncate*) is a **hearty eater**, one who eats much and heartily; originally designated a person who frequented a patron's table; **parasite, hanger-on**. Originally, *trencher* meant a wooden board or platter on which to carve or serve meat.

wordbuilders #43, 44, 45, 46

Greek *sphere*, **ball, globe,** yields **sphere**; **spher**oid; atmo**sphere**, bio**sphere**, exo**sphere**, hemi**sphere**, hetero**sphere**, homo**sphere**, meso**sphere**, strato**sphere**; possibly, **pearl,** from *spherule*, "a small globe." While Earth is usually thought of as a sphere, it is in fact a *spheroid*, flattened at the poles and bulging slightly below the equator. With *eidos*, **form,** *spheroid* means "similar to a sphere." Because the bulge is near the equator, the earth's circumference is greater around the equator than around the poles. At the equator, the circumference is 24,901.55 miles, whereas at the poles, it is 24,859.82, a difference of 41.73 miles. See *equator*, p. 76. See other *–oid* words, p. 64.

Greek *stereos*, **hard, solid,** yields **stere** (a cubic meter—being cubic, it is solid), **ster**agnosis, **ster**oid; **stere**obate, **stere**ometry, **stere**ophonic (**solid sound**), **stere**oscope, **stere**otropism, **stere**otype; andro**ster**one, chole**ster**ol (**solid gall**; first isolated in the gallbladder; some gallstones are almost pure cholesterol), testo**ster**one.

Greek *glyphein*, **to carve,** yields **glypt**ic (having to do with *carving* or *engraving*, especially on gems), **glypt**odont (*odous*, **tooth**); **glypt**ograph, **glypt**ology, **glypt**ostrobus; ana**glyph** (see p. 22), di**glyph**, geo**glyph**, hemi**glyph**, inter-**glyph**, litho**glyph**, petro**glyph**, photo**glyph**, soleno**glyph**, tri**glyph**; hiero**glyph**ics (**sacred carvings**; see p. 170).

Greek *myelos*, **marrow, spinal cord,** yields **myel**ic; **myel**algia, **myel**asthenia, **myel**analosis, **myel**itis; osteo**myel**itis (*osteo*, **bone** + *itis*, **inflammation**, the inflammation of bone marrow), polio**myel**itis (*polios*, **grey** + *itis*, **inflammation**, inflammation of the grey matter, or marrow, of the spinal cord).

Common element base: levare   **Meaning**: to raise, to rise; to make light; relieve
IE base: *legwh-*: **light**, having little weight (see **A Writing Tip**, p. 7); **German**: *erhoben*: **raised**

Clavis

leaven: an agent, such as yeast, that causes batter or dough to **rise**, especially by fermentation; as a *verb*, to add a leavening agent to; figuratively, to pervade with a lightening, enlivening, or modifying influence.

Levant: French, *levant*; Italian, *levante*: like *Orient*, **a rising up**, the place of the rising sun; thus, the countries of the eastern Mediterranean, as seen from Rome. Likewise, *Japan*, in Chinese, was *Jephenkuo*, a transliteration of the compound characters meaning "land of the day (or, sun)," as seen from China. See *Japan* under **wordextras**, p. 83; *Orient*, p. 38; *Oriental*, p. 76.

levee: a morning reception held by a nobleman **upon rising**; also, a **raised** embankment, as on the Mississippi, to prevent flooding; a levee also helps prevent flooding from irrigation; a river landing place: a pier.

leverage: the act of using a *lever*, a bar used as a pry; the increased force resulting from using a lever; increased means of accomplishing some purpose. Explore the business term *leveraged buyout*.

levy: **to raise** (taxes); in *law*, to seize property in order to satisfy a judgment; as a *noun*, the enlistment or conscription of young men for military service.

elevator: *e-*, elision of *ex-*, **out of**; that which lifts or raises up, e.g., an aircraft device that controls **up and down motion**; also, a device that hoists grains, etc. to a warehouse. See *Escalator*®, p. 54.

relieve: from *relevare*; *re-*, **again**; **to lift up again**; to free from a burden; to ease, reduce pain or anxiety. SYNONYMS: allay, alleviate, assuage, extenuate, lighten (see **A Writing Tip**, p. 7), mitigate.

carnival: originally from Latin *carne*, **meat** + *levare*; from Old Italian *carnelevare*, **taking meat away**; from Italian *carneval(e)*. *Carnival* is <u>not</u> just the day before Ash Wednesday, but the entire season preceding Lent, with Mardi Gras (**fat Tuesday**) being the last and best-known event of the season. By folk etymology, often associated with Italian *carne, vale*! **Flesh, farewell**! See p. 34.

leprechaun: from Old Irish, which shares many of its roots with Latin and is also part of the IE language family. *Lu*, **small** + *chorpan*; thus, **small**, or **light body**. See p. 50 under **Clavis**.

lung: from Middle English *lunge*; **light** in weight and movement; *lungs*: so called because of their lightness.

leve fit quod bene fertur onus: **Lightly lies the load that is cheerfully borne**. Ovid.
Sit tibi terra levis: **May the earth lie lightly upon thee**. (an old epitaph)

wordextras

Asthma, Greek for **panting**, designates a chronic disorder characterized by wheezing, coughing, difficulty breathing, and a suffocating feeling. Pronounced: AZ muh.

German *Dudelsack*, "doodle sack," means **bagpipe**; *Handschuh*, "hand shoe," **glove**; and *Fingerhut*, "finger hat," **thimble**. Anglo-Saxon *thimble*, "thumb covering," was a bell-shaped leather case to protect the thumb while sewing.

Celibate, from Latin *caelebs*, **unmarried**, refers to an unmarried person, especially one under vow to remain single; also, one who abstains from sexual intercourse; also used as an adjective. Nominal form: *celibacy*.

Ward, as in *a political ward, hospital ward*, or *ward of the state*, as well as **warden** and **warder**, comes from Old English *weardian*, **to protect**, **guard**. A *warder* is a person who guards; a watchman; in Britain, same as *warden*.

Bail, *bailiff*, and *bailiwick* all pertain to **power**, **control**, **custody**, and come from Middle English and Old French *baillier*, **to keep in custody**. With Old English *wik*, **village**, a *bailiwick* is the district of a *bailiff*, who, in England, was an administrative official of a district with power to collect taxes, serve as magistrate, etc. *Bailiwick* can also refer to one's particular area of activity, authority, interests, etc.; for example, *etymology*, the study of words, is the *bailiwick* of the authors of this book.

Word from Roman mythology: *mercurial*, **sprightly**, **volatile**; from *Mercury*, either the Roman god or the planet. *Mercurial* can also mean "eloquent, clever, shrewd, thievish."

an aphorism—See *aphorism*, p. 132, under **wordextras**.
Great cry but little wool. Those who do the most talking do the least work.
German version: *Viel Geschrei und wenig Wolle*: **Much cry and little wool**.

```
+----------------------------------------------------------------------+
|                      Word Cluster No. 57                              |
|                                                                      |
|  liberate         libertinage      liberalism      libertarian       |
|  liberator        liberal          libertine       liberty           |
|  liberticide      illiberal        libertinism     liberatory        |
|                                                                      |
|  Common elements_____Inferred Meaning_____ |
+----------------------------------------------------------------------+
```

Romance Cognates	French	Romanian	Italian	Portuguese	Spanish
	libre	liber	libero	livre	libre

Words with disguised Latin roots: livery, deliver, deliverance

Latin words and phrases: *libera, ad libitum, liberum veto* (see **Clavis**)*, liberum maritagium, pro libertate patriae; patria cara, carior libertas; libertas sub rege pio, Veritas liberabit vos, Semper liberi*

French phrase: *vers libre*: **free verse**   **Spanish phrase**: *cuba libre*: a drink of rum and Coca-Cola®

Name of country: Liberia (on the east coast of Africa; see **Clavis**)

American landmarks: Statue of **Liberty**, on **Liberty** Island, New York City; **Liberty** Bell, Philadelphia, PA

Motto of the University of Tennessee: *Veritatem cognoscetis et veritas vos liberabit*: **You shall know the truth and the truth will set you free**. John 8:32

Motto of the State of West Virginia: *Montani semper liberi*: **Mountaineers always free**.
Motto of the State of Massachusetts: *Ense petit placidam sub libertate quietem*: **By the sword she seeks calm repose under liberty**.

Motto of the State of New Hampshire: Live *Free* or Die

Motto of Colombia: *Libertad y orden*: **Liberty and Order**

Motto of the French Revolution: *Liberté, égalité, fraternité*: **Liberty, equality, brotherhood**. See p. 75.

Motto of Johns Hopkins University: *Veritas vos liberabit*: **The truth shall set you free**. John 8:32

Greek: eleutheromania; **Middle Dutch**: filibuster **(freebooter)**; **Anglo-Saxon**: friend

wordextras

Friday, named after Frigg, the Old Norse goddess of love and the wife of the god Odin, is identified with the Anglo-Saxon god Woden, and who is remembered by *Woden's Day*, or *Wednesday*. See p. 53 for more on *Wednesday*.

Monday, **Moon's Day**, is similarly known in French and Spanish, *lundi* and *lunes*, respectively. Both *lundi* and *lunes* are from Latin *luna*, **moon**. See p. 53 for additional information. See p. 67 for French days of the week.

Barrister, the term for a British attorney, is so called because the attorney being admitted to plead the defendant's case is at the *bar*, or the railing separating the defendant from the judge.

Demurrer is a plea in court proceedings to dismiss a lawsuit on the grounds that, although the opposition's statements may be true, they are insufficient to sustain the claim. *Demurrer* is from French *demur*, which itself is from *de-*, **intensive** + *morari*, **to delay**, as in *moratorium*, a legal delay. See *sine mora*, p. 178.

Meager, from Greek *makros*, **long**, means **thin**, **lean**, **emaciated**; of poor quality or small amount; not full or rich; inadequate, as *a meager allowance*, or *a meager performance*. In compounds, *macro-* means **large**, **enlarged**, or **elongated** (in a specific part), e.g., **macro**cephaly, **macro**cosm, **macro**gamete, **macro**molecule, **macro**nutrient, **macro**phage, **macro**phallic. See p. 208, Item 117 for more *macro-* words.

Chasm, from Greek *chasma*, **yawning**, **hollow**, **gulf**, is a deep rack in the earth's surface; an abyss, a bottomless pit.

Mussel, as well as *muscle* (see p. 85), is from Latin *mus*, **mouse**, because of its appearance.

wordbuilder #47

Latin *mutare*, **to change**, yields **mut**able, **mut**ate, **mut**ation, **mut**ative, **mut**ual, **mut**ualism; **muta**gen, **muta**genesis; com**mute**, per**mute**, trans**mute**; com**mut**ation, per**mut**ation, trans**mut**ation; im**mut**able, incom**mut**able; *mutatis mutandis*, "the necessary changes having been made." Other words from *mutare* include *miss* (one meaning), *molt*, *parimutuel* (see p. 75), *remuda* (in the Southwest, a group of extra saddle horses kept as a supply of remounts).

Common element base: liber   **Meaning**: free; not in bondage

IE base: *leudh-²-*: **to mount up**, **to grow**; the semantic evolvement to the Latin meaning is obscure.

Clavis

Libera:
: in the litany of the Roman Catholic Church, a funeral responsory sung after the Mass and prior to the final prayers for the deceased; from the first word of the responsory in Latin. *Responsory*: responsive verses, especially from the Psalms.

liberal:
: as an adjective, **free**, **noble**, or **generous**; as a noun, **one who is open**-minded, or not strict, in observance of orthodox, traditional, or established forms, ways, or mores.

libertine:
: in ancient Rome, a person who had been **freed** from slavery; now, usually refers to a man who leads an unrestrained immoral life; **a rake**; **roué**. See use of *libertine* under *primrose*, p. 160.

illiberal:
: *il-*, assimilation of *in-*, **not**; **not liberal**. Originally, lacking a liberal education; without culture; now, intolerant, bigoted, narrow-minded.

Liberia:
: originally, an African colony founded in 1820 for and by **freed** slaves of the United States. James Monroe (1758-1831), President of the United States during the colony's establishment, is the eponym of *Monrovia*, Liberia's capital. *Liberia* was established as an independent republic in 1847.

liberal arts:
: originally, **arts becoming a freeman**, as opposed to *artes serviles*, **arts of the servants**, the manual arts or vocational trades, such as crafts, masonry, carpentry. *Liberal arts* evolved to include language, music, philosophy, history, literature, and abstract science. S e e *trivium* (p. 196) and *quadrivium* (p. 162), required curricula in the medieval university.

liberum veto:
: the veto (or, **the liberty**) exercised by a single member, as of a legislative body under rules requiring unanimous consent. *Veto*, a one-word Latin sentence: **I forbid**; thus, an instrument of the check and balance system of Federal and State governments of the United States.

friend:
: Middle English *frend*; from Anglo-Saxon *freond*, **friend**, **lover**; from the same IE base as *free*. The connotation suggests that a *friend* is one with whom another can be free and open.

wordextras

Latin *jocus*, **joke**, spawns a number of witty words: *jocose, jocosity, jocular, jocund*. Note the use of *jocund* in a line from Wordsworth's "The Daffodils": A poet could not but be gay in such a *jocund* company (referring to *the company of daffodils*). *Jocose*: playful, humorous; *jocund*: cheerful, genial; *jocular*: joking, humorous, full of fun.

Adamant, **unyielding**, from Greek *adamas*, **hard metal**, **steel**, **diamond**, possibly meant "unbreakable." SYNONYMS: inflexible, implacable, obdurate. *Diamond* itself is from *adamas* (see p. 194).

German *Wunderkind*, **wonder child**, is a child prodigy. Pronounced: VOON der KINT.

Stigma, **tattoo mark**, from Greek *stizein*, **to prick**, **tattoo**, originally meant a mark burned into the skin of a criminal or slave; has come to mean "mark of disgrace." The verb yields the noun *astigmatism*, a medical term meaning "that which is without focus"; also, a distorted view or judgment, as because of bias. See p. 106 for Latin *instigate*.

Disseminate, **to scatter seed**, from Latin *dis-*, **apart** + *semen*, **seed**, has come to mean "to scatter far and wide," "spread abroad," "promulgate widely." See *seminary*, from the same root, p. 143.

Rugby is so called from its having first been played at *Rugby School*, Rugby, Warwickshire, England.

Soccer is a shortening and an alteration of *as(soc)iation* **football**, so called from the Football Association established in England in 1863 to set up rules for the game.

Clemency, from Latin *clemens*, **mild**, means **forbearance**, **leniency**, or **mercy**, as toward an offender or an enemy. *Clement, inclemency*, and *inclement* are the only other known forms of *clemens*.

Uxorious, from Latin *uxor*, **wife**, describes a man who overly dotes on his wife, or is irrationally fond of, or submissive to, her; *uxoricide*: the murder of a wife by her husband; also, a man who murders his wife.

Agenda, plural of *agendum*, and from *agere*, **to do**, **act**, is a list of things to be done, especially at a meeting.

Word from Greek mythology: *narcissism*, **extreme self-love or self-admiration**; sexual pleasure derived from observing one's own naked body; from *Narcissus*, a beautiful youth whom Echo loved. Narcissus failed to respond to Echo's love and, after her death, was condemned by the gods to pine away for the love of his own reflection.

```
┌─────────────────────────────────────────────────────────────────────────────┐
│                          Word Cluster No. 58                                  │
│                                                                               │
│  literacy          literal            illiteracy         literate             │
│  literary          literature         alliteration       obliteration         │
│  literalism        transliterate      preliterate        biliteral            │
│  literality        literalize         literally          triliteral           │
│  aliterate         antiliterate       heteroliteral      literim              │
│                                                                               │
│  Common element_____Inferred Meaning_____   │
│                                                                               │
└─────────────────────────────────────────────────────────────────────────────┘
```

Romance Cognates	French	Romanian	Italian	Portuguese	Spanish
	lettre	litera	lettera	letra	letra

Romance words and phrases: literature of the absurd; didactic literature; literature of sensibility; literatus; literati; literary property; literal contract; belles-lettres

Latin phrases: *litterae sine moribus vanae; Litteris dedicata et omnibus artibus; unicales litterae*
Vox audita perit, littera scripta manet: **The spoken words die, the written words remain.**

Compare *literal* versus *figurative* language in a literary handbook.

Explore the *letters* of Lord Byron, Lord Chesterfield, Charles Dickens, and Horace Walpole, as well as those exchanged between John Adams and Thomas Jefferson, some of the notable collections still extant.

┌───┐
│ **Quote**: The custom of forming compounds from Latin and Greek elements   │
│ prevails in all civilized countries in Europe and America, and if a useful   │
│ term of this kind is introduced in any one country, it is adopted with great │
│ promptitude into the language of all the rest. Henry Bradley   │
│   │
│ Henry Bradley (1843-1923), an English lexicographer, was editor of *Oxford   │
│ English Dictionary*. This may explain why he wrote "civilized countries" in │
│ the quote.   │
└───┘

wordextras

Spinach, from Arabic *isfanakh*, was brought to England by seagoing merchants; at first, the plant was considered a delicacy, which only the wealthy could afford. Spanish: *espinaca*. Other Arabic words are listed throughout the book, e.g., *admiral, albacore, albatross, algebra, magazine, mattress, nadir, safari, Sahara, zenith*.

Tomato is from Nahuatl, an Aztec language; *chocolate* is also from Nahuatl *xocolatl*, where *xococ* meant **bitter** and *atl*, **water**. With an advanced civilization, the Aztecs were an Amerindian people in what is now Mexico.

Pumpkin, from Greek *pessein*, **to cook**, **ripen** (by the sun), originally designated any gourd or melon not to be eaten until sun-ripened. See *apricot, precocious*, pp. 56, 127.

Anglo-Saxon *nog* in *eggnog* means **a strong ale** or **beer**. *Noggin*, 1/4 of a pint, was a measure for ale or liquor.

Disabuse means **to rid of false ideas**; undeceive; to free from error, fallacy, or misconception. The psychoanalyst completely *disabused* Tom of his feelings of superiority and grandeur.

Glut means **a surplus**, **an overabundance**. We had a *glut* of contributions but a *dearth* of volunteers, making it seem that people had rather give their money than their time. *Glut* and *glutton* are from Latin *gluttire*, **to devour**.

Karate, Japanese for **open hand** (*kara*, **empty** + *te*, **hand**), is an art of self-defense characterized chiefly by sharp, quick blows and kicks delivered to pressure-sensitive points on the body of an opponent.

wordbuilder #48

Greek *meros*, **part**, yields **mer**istic, a**mer**istic (*a-*, **negative**); **mero**blastic, **mero**crine, **mero**genesis, **mero**morphic, **mero**plankton, **mero**zoite; **meri**carp, **meri**stem; iso**mer**, meta**mer**, mono**mer**, poly**mer**, stereoiso**mer**; anti**mere**, ecto**mere**, arthro**mere**, centro**mere**, chromo**mere**, crypto**mere**, epi**mere**, micro**mere**, sarco**mere**, telo**mere**; allo**mer**ism, tauto**mer**ism; poly**mer**ic, poro**mer**ic; di**mer**ous, hepta**mer**ous, hetero**mer**ous, mono**mer**ous, octa**mer**ous, penta**mer**ous, tetra**mer**ous, tri**mer**ous; a**mer**istic. *Polymer*: *poly-*, **many**; any of numerous natural and synthetic compounds of usually high molecular weight consisting of up to millions of repeated linked units, each a relatively light and simple molecule, or monomere. See *polymerism*, under *onion* (under **wordextras**), p. 119.

Common element base: littera   **Meaning**: letter, literature
IE base: *deph-*: **to stamp**, yielding **Greek** *diphthera*, **prepared hide**, **leather**. See *diphtheria* in **Clavis** entry.
German: *Buchstabe*, **letter** (alphabetic character); *Brief*, **letter** (correspondence)

Clavis

literally:	in a **literal** or strict way; **virtually**. The author would *literally* turn the world upside down to gain recognition. When *literally* is used to mean *virtually*, its use is pure hyperbole intended for emphasis. See pp. 102, 184, for more on *hyperbole*.
literate:	as an *adjective*, able to read and write (**letters**); **well-educated**; having or showing extensive knowledge, learning, or culture. As a *noun*, one who possesses the adjectival qualities; a learned person. ***Literati***: persons interested in literature or the arts; scholarly or learned people.
literatim:	**letter for letter**; verbatim; in exactly the same words, as *a verbatim account* of the trial.
alliteration:	*al-*, assimilation of *ad-*, **to**, **toward**; repetition of consonant (**letter**) sounds in a sequence of adjacent words, e.g., from "Piers Plowman," 'In a s̲omer s̲eason, whan s̲oft was the s̲onne. . . ." See p. 107.
biliteral:	*bi-*, **two**; consisting of or employing **two letters** or types of letters; also, written in two different alphabets; a word, syllable, or root, consisting of two letters.
triliteral:	*tri-*, **three**; consisting of **three letters**; specifically, consisting of three consonants, e.g., most Semitic languages are *triliteral*.
obliterate:	*ob-*, **intensive** (see pp. 139, 140 for other meanings of *ob-*); **to erase the letters [completely]**; to leave no traces. SYNONYMS: delete, destroy, efface, expunge. The noun is *obliteration*.
preliterate:	*pre-*, **before**; of or belonging to a society not having a writing system for its language; as a *noun*, a person belonging to such a culture. SYNONYMS: illiterate, nonliterate, uncivilized.
transliterate:	*trans-*, **across**; to write or spell words in the corresponding **letters** of another language, the letters of which represent approximately the same sounds as those in the original language, e.g., Spanish transliterates *football* as *fútbol*; *beefsteak* as *biftek*; and *sweater* as *suéter*.
belles-lettres:	French; **beautiful letters**; a body of writing that includes poetry, fiction, criticism, and essays, the inherent imaginative and artistic value of which overrides its scientific and intellectual qualities. Compare the works of Lewis Carroll, e.g., *Alice in Wonderland*, *Through the Looking Glass*, with his esoteric works in mathematics, written under his real name, Charles Lutwidge Dodgson. See *portmanteau*, p. 156.
unicales litterae:	**letters an inch long**; handwriting used especially in Greek and Latin manuscripts of the 4th to 8th centuries, A.D. *Uncial* corresponds to *ounce*, a twelfth part of a *libra* in Roman times.
diphtheria:	Greek; **tanned hides**, originally used to write **letters**, characters, upon; an acute infectious disease characterized by leathery false membranes in the throat.

Litterae sine moribus vanae: **Literature without character is vain**: Motto of the University of Pennsylvania
Litteris dedicata et omnibus artibus: **Dedicated to literature and all the arts**. Motto of the University of Nebraska

wordextras

Both *squalid* (adjective) and *squalor* (noun) are from Latin *squalere*, **to be foul or filthy**.

Aspirin is from Greek *a-*, **negative** + *spirea*, **a genus of shrubs**. So named in 1899 by H. Dresser, German physicist, *aspirin* is compounded *without* the use of *spirea*, in which the natural acid is found.

Prosodic pertains to *prosody*, not to *prose*. *Prosody* is the science or art of versification, including the study of metrical structure, stanza forms, etc.; also refers to a particular system or style of versification and metrical structure, e.g., Dryden's or Whitman's *prosody*. Pronunciation: *prosody*, PRAHS uh dee; *prosodic*: pro SAHD ik.

Word from Greek mythology: *nemesis*, **an agent of destruction**; from *Nemesis*, the goddess of retributive justice, or vengeance; just punishment, retribution; anyone or anything by which, it seems, one must inevitably be defeated or frustrated. Plural: *nemes̲es̲*.

A Writing Tip: *A lot* is two words, whether "*a lot* on the corner for sale," or "*a lot* of houses for sale." ***All right*** is two words, just as ***all wrong*** is. ***Everyday*** is one word when used as an adjective, as in "everyday chores."

116

```
┌─────────────────────────────────────────────────────────────────────────────────────┐
│                              Word Cluster No. 59                                        │
│                                                                                         │
│      locate              locular           allocate          dislocate                 │
│      locomotion          locomotive        allocation        collocate                 │
│      localism            localize          relocate          locus                     │
│      localizer           bilocular           localization    local                     │
│ uxorilocal               matrilocal        patrilocal        locale                    │
│      locality            trilocular          unilocular      locative                   │
│      localite            location          interlocal      translocate                 │
│                                                                                         │
│ Common elements_____Inferred Meaning_____      │
└─────────────────────────────────────────────────────────────────────────────────────┘
```

Romance Cognates	French	Romanian	Italian	Portuguese	Spanish
	lieu	loc	luogo	lugar	lugar

Words and phrases with disguised Latin roots: lieu, in lieu of, lieutenant, milieu (*purlieu* is probably not in this family; see p. 6); lodge, loge, loggia, logistics, louver; couch, accouchement, accoucher

Placenames: Local, Missouri; Location, West Virginia; Harts Location, New Hampshire

Latin words and phrases: *in loco, loco citato, in loco parentis, locus standi, locus sigilli, locus poenitentiae, genius loci, ad hunc locum, ad locum, sub loco, locum tenens, lex loci, locus classicus, locus communis, locus criminis, da locum melioribus*; *dulce est desipere in loco*: **It is pleasant to act foolishly in the right place.** Horace

Literary term: local color (see **Clavis**)

Related German: *Gestalt*; in Gestalt psychology, developed in Germany, any of the integrated structures or patterns that make up all experience and have specific properties that can neither be derived from the elements of the whole nor be considered simply as the sum of these elements.
Stollen: **post**, in reference to its shape; a German bread containing fruits and nuts.

Germanic words: **stall, stall**ion, fore**stall**, in**stall**ment; stale, stolid, stultify, stilt, stout. Related to Greek *stel-*, from IE *stel-*. See p. 129.

Greek words from IE *dhe-*, **to place**: **theca, theca**te, apo**thec**ary, hypo**thec**ate; amphi**thecium**, apo**thecium**, endo-**thecium**; biblio**theca**; **thesis**, anti**thesis** (see p. 72), dia**thesis**, epen**thesis**, hypo**thesis** (see p. 190 under *hypotenuse*), meta**thesis**, parasyn**thesis**, paren**thesis**, pro**thesis**, pros**thesis**, syn**thesis**; nucleosyn**thesis**, photosyn**thesis**; **theme**, ana**thema**; anti**thet**, epi**thet**.

Words from Greek roots: *bodega* (Spanish), *boutique* (French); both mean "small store," and are from *apothecary*, a place to store (things), originally, a pharmacist or druggist; now, a pharmacy or drug store.

wordbuilder #49
Greek *derma(to)*, **skin**, yields **derm**ad, **derm**al, **derm**is; **derm**atalgia, **derm**atitis, **derm**atodynia (*odynia*, **pain**); **derm**atocele, **derm**atology, **derm**atophyte; blasto**derm**, ecto**derm**, endo**derm**, pachy**derm**; xero**derma** (**dry skin**); intra**derm**al; hypo**derm**ic, trans**derm**ic; epi**derm**is; lepto**derm**ous. The Latin counterpart is *cutis*, as in **cut**aneous, **cut**icle, **cut**in, **cut**inization, **cut**is; intra**cut**aneous, per**cut**aneous, sub**cut**aneous, trans**cut**aneous.

Word named from a person: *spoonerism*, from the Reverend Doctor W. A. Spooner (1844-1930); reversal of the initial sounds of two or more words, usually accidentally, but can be done purposely for a humorous effect; e.g., Let me "sew you to a new sheet," for "show you to a new seat"; you have "tasted two worms" for "wasted two terms"; a "blushing crow" for a "crushing blow," all of which are attributed to Dr. Spooner. Check "Spooner" websites for more examples. *Goldy Bear and the Three Locks* is a spoonerism of *Goldilocks and the Three Bears*.

six aphorisms
Never ride a free horse to death: **Do not abuse privileges that have been granted as favors.**
Difficult it is to sail across the sea in an eggshell. **It is foolish to attempt great tasks with meager means.**
In a calm sea, every man is a pilot. **It is the difficulties of life that test one's mettle.**
Don't count your chickens before they hatch. **Don't assume certainty for something that hasn't come to fruition.**
All that glitters is not gold. **That which appears promising may simply be more of the present situation.**
You can lead a horse to water, but you can't make him drink. **A person can be provided with incentives to pursue a goal, but it is up to that person to take advantage of them.**

Common element base: locus   **Meaning**: place; in *biology*, cavity, cell, chamber

American Heritage does not trace the root further; *Webster's New World* relates base to IE *stlokos*, from *stel-*, **to set up**, **stand**, **locate**, whence **stalk**, **stall**, **still**; **Greek** *stellein*, **to place**. **German nouns**: *Platz* (masculine); *Stelle* (feminine)

Clavis

locative:
: of, relating to, or being a grammatical case in certain inflected languages, such as Latin, Greek, Sanskrit, that indicates **place in**, **on which,** or **time at which**, as in Latin *dom*i̱, **at home**.

allocate:
: *al-*, assimilation of *ad-*, **to, toward**; **to place to**; to set apart for a specific purpose.

collocate:
: *col-*, assimilation of *com-*, **with, together**; to arrange or place together, especially side by side. While some authorities prefer this term exclusively instead of *co-locate*, the latter is justified when referring to two or more military units located on the same base or post, e.g., the DC Air National Guard and the Air Force One unit are co-located at Andrews AFB, Maryland.

couch:
: from *collocate*, previous entry; to lay something (down); as a *noun*, **a place to lie down**: an article of furniture on which one may sit or lie down. As a *verb*, can mean "to lower or bring down, especially, to lower a spear, lance, etc., to an attacking position"; also, "to put in specific or particular words"; to phrase; to express, as *to couch a demand in the form of a request*.

matrilocal:
: *matri-*, **mother**; relating to a housing pattern or custom in which a married couple lives with or near the wife's parents; *patrilocal* ~ with the husband's parents.

bilocular:
: *bi-*, **two**; in *biology*, having, or divided into, **two cells** or **chambers**.

in loco parentis:
: **in the position**, or **place**, **of parents**, or, of a parent's authority; gives designated adults temporary custody of children not their own. By statutory authority, most public schoolteachers are *in loco parentis* while the students they teach are under their care.

loco citato:
: abbreviated *loc. cit.*, **in the place cited**, or quoted; in *research*, a footnote denoting such.

lieutenant:
: French *lieu* (for *locus*) + *tenere*, **to hold**; **one who holds the place of another**. For example, a first lieutenant is "first in line" to hold the place of the captain, the next higher military grade in the Army and Air Force, a second lieutenant being "second." In civilian life, **an aide, deputy**. Compare *locum tenens*, **temporary substitute**, as for a doctor or clergyman. See more on p. 188.

locus standi:
: **a place to stand**; a right to be heard in court. Compare Greek *pou sto*, **where I may stand**. The complete phrase "Give me a place to stand, a lever long enough, and a fulcrum high enough, and I will move the earth" is attributed to Archimedes (287?-212 B.C.), a Greek mathematician and inventor, inventing, for example, the Archimedean screw, an ancient water-raising device.

locus sigilli:
: on legal documents, abbreviated *L.S.*, **place of the seal**; *L.S.* is often assumed to stand for **legal signature**, which in effect, it is. Both *seal* and *sign* are from *sigillum*, **a seal, mark**, and is the base of *signum*, **sign**. See more on p. 173.

locus classicus:
: **a classical passage**, important for the elucidation of a difficult word or subject.

milieu:
: French; **middle place**; from Latin *medius* + *lieu*; thus, **environment, surroundings**.

anathema:
: Greek *ana-*, **up** + *theme*, **a placing**; that which is set up, or dedicated to evil. Any strong curse; a person so cursed, or banned; as an adjective, **greatly detested**; viewed as accursed, damned.

Word from Greek mythology: *odyssey*, **a long voyage**, or a long series of wanderings, especially when filled with notable experiences, hardships, and tribulations. From the *Odyssey*, the second epic of Homer, recounting the wanderings and adventures of Odysseus during the ten years after the fall of Troy and his eventual return home. Identified with Latin *Ulysses*. Homer is also credited with writing *Iliad*, Latin for *Troy*.

A Writing Tip: Use *sic*, **thus it is**; **thus**; **so**, in [brackets] to indicate that a mistake or peculiarity in the spelling or the grammar of a foregoing word appears in the original work. Example: It is time for Frank and *I* [sic] *to make* vacation plans for the summer. *I* should be *me* since the *objective case* of pronouns is the subject of infinitives, in this case, *to make*. It is time for *him* (objective case) *to make* (infinitive) a decision.

An aphorism: *Wise men learn more from fools than fools from wise men.* **It is wise to learn from the actions of all people**.

118

```
                        Word Cluster No. 60

    loquent          loquacious        colloquy          soliloquy
    loquitor         loquacity         colloquium        obloquy
    eloquent         grandiloquence    colloquialism     breviloquence
    magniloquent     multiloquent                        ventriloquist

    locution         allocution        circumlocution    locution
    collocutor       interlocution     prolocutor        elocution

Common elements_____Inferred Meaning_____
```

Romance Cognates	French	Romanian	Italian	Portuguese	Spanish
	loquace	locvace	loquace	loquaz	locuaz

Latin phrases: *usus loquendi; loquitur (loq.); romanice loqui; jus et norma loquendi*: **the law and rule of speech**; ordinary usage. Horace

Greek *logos*, **word**, **reckoning**, **thought**, is similar to the Latin meaning: **log**ic, **logo**, **Logos**; **log**arithm; **logo**griph, **logo**machy; horo**loge**; ana**log**ous, homo**log**ous; apo**logue**, dia**logue**, Deca**logue**, ec**logue**, epi**logue**, mono**logue**, pro**logue**; ana**logy**, apo**logy**, eu**logy**; para**logism**, syl**logism**. See more words from *logos*, under IE base, next page.

Explore *dramatic* and *interior monologues* in a literary handbook, or search on Google or Yahoo.

Explore Edmund Spenser's *eclogue* (a pastoral or idyllic poem, often in *dialogue* form between two shepherds) in *The Shepheardes Calendar,* circa 1579, the entirety of which can be found on the Internet.

Explore the differences in *eulogy, encomium*, and *panegyric*, all pertaining to words of praise.

```
┌─────────────────────────────────────────────────────────────────────┐
│ Quote: It is the Word that opens the door of the treasure cave, the Word │
│ which builds the universe and commands its power. G. H. Bonner          │
└─────────────────────────────────────────────────────────────────────┘
```

wordextras

Onion, from Latin *uni-*, **one**, is translated **oneness**, or **union**. The *onion* consists of a number of united concentric layers as opposed to the *polymerism* of garlic, for example. See *polymer*, p. 115.

Garlic is from two Old English words—*gar*, **spear** and *leac*, **leek**; the plant is so called because of its spearlike leaves. *Garlic* and *vinegar* are not related etymologically. See p. 50 for *vinegar*.

Shamrock, from Old Gaelic *seamrog*, is a diminutive of *seamar*, **clover**.

R.S.V.P., the polite request for a response to an invitation, and the initial letters of *répondez s'il vous plaît*, is French for "Reply, if you please." Please respond, indicating your accepting or declining the invitation.

PASCAL, an elegant but simple multiuse computer program, is named after Blaise Pascal (1623-1662), the French philosopher and mathematician who built the first desk calculator-type adding machine.

Russian *pirogi*, from *pirog*, **pie**, is a small pastry turnover with a filling, as of cheese, meat, mashed potatoes.

Comprise and *compose* are not used interchangeably! The United States *comprises* fifty States and Territories; fifty States and Territories *compose*, or **make up**, the United States. The basis of *comprise* is *prehendere*, **to catch hold of**, **seize**, and is seen in *prehensile* and *comprehend*. *Compose* is from *ponere*, **to place**, **to put**; thus, to put together.

Bishop, from Greek *episkopos* (**epi-**, **over** + *skopein*, **to see**), is an **overseer**. In many Christian churches, a member of the clergy having authority over other clergy and usually supervising a diocese or a church district. The roots of *bishop* are those of *episcopal*, a particular type of church organization; in uppercase, a denomination.

Word from Greek mythology: *olympian*, **grand**, **imposing**; from the gods who supposedly lived on the slopes of Mount Olympus. *Olympian* can also mean **majestic**, **aloof**, **disdainful**.

an aphorism: *You can't have your cake and eat it too*. **One can't save money for the future and spend it at the same time**. A lesson in delayed gratification.

Common element base: loqui   **Meaning**: to speak, to talk

IE base: *tolkw-*: **to speak**, and by metathesis—the transposition or interchange of letters—*loqui*. The Greek family—*logo*—is the most productive of all classical word elements; from it are the *–logy* words, such as *anthropology*, *archeology*, *astrology*, *biology*, *cryptology*, *cytology*, *dactylology*, *dermatology*, *embryology*, *ethnology*, *gerontology*, *odontology*, *oenology*, *psychology*, *radiology*, *sociology*, *somatology*, *thanatology*. Many others.

Clavis

loquacious:
: very **talkative**; fond of talking; garrulous; the noun *loquacity* means **talkativeness**, especially when excessive or unnecessary.

obloquy:
: *ob-*, **against**; **a speaking against**; a strongly worded defamatory statement; abusive language; calumny (pronounced: CAL um nih); loss or damage to one's reputation. SYNONYMS: abuse, billingsgate (see p. 100), censure, invective, scurrility, vituperation. Pronounced: OB luh kwee.

soliloquy:
: *solus*, **alone**; **speaking alone or to oneself**; in *drama*, lines in which a character reveals his or her thoughts to the audience, but not to the other characters, as if speaking to himself/herself. In *Hamlet*, Polonius advises his son Laertes "neither a borrower nor a lender be," as well as "unto thine ownself be true, and it shall follow as night the day, thou canst not be false to any man."

allocution:
: *ad-*, **to, toward**; a formal address, especially one warning or advising with authority.

grandiloquent:
: *grandis*, **full-grown, great**; using high-flown pompous, bombastic words and expressions. SYNONYMS: euphuistic, flowery, prolix, turgid, verbose. Pronunciation: gran DIL uh kwent.

eloquent:
: *e-*, elision of *ex-*, **out**; **to speak out**; vividly forceful and expressive, as *an eloquent speaker*; vividly or movingly expressive or revealing, as *an eloquent monument*.

ventriloquist:
: *venter*, **belly**; literally, **one who speaks from the belly**; the early Romans believed that it was from inside the body that the sounds by a ventriloquist were made.

romanice loqui:
: **to speak in the Roman fashion**, or, the common way; refers to languages descended from Latin, the tongue of the Romans; the term *romance* was then applied to a fictitious story written in a Romance dialect, and still later, to a story of adventure or love in any language.

circumlocution:
: *circum-*, **around**; a roundabout, indirect, or lengthy way of expressing something either in speaking or in writing; **prolixity**; **periphrasis**. *Periphrasis* and *circumlocution* are word-pairs. See other word-pairs on p. 31. See more on *circumlocution*, p. 40.

apology:
: *apo-*, **from**; **a formal defense, justification**, as in *Apology* by English poet John Milton (1608-74); also, a statement expressing regret; also, **a poor example**, as "It was an *apology* for a meal."

syllogism:
: *syl-*, assimilation of *sym-*, **with, together**; **a reasoning**, or **a reckoning, together**; in *logic*, a form of deductive reasoning consisting of a major premise, a minor premise, and a conclusion. A *major premise* is a general statement—a truth that cannot be denied, as in the classic premise—*All men are mortal*. The *minor premise* is a specific instance of the generality, e.g., *Socrates was a man*. Notice that the last word of the minor premise is a form of the second word in the first premise—in this example, *man* and *men*, respectively. The conclusion is a natural deduction, or conclusion, of the two premises: Therefore (or, *Ergo*), *Socrates is mortal*.

---

wordextras

In the Roman Catholic Church, *novenas* are prayers recited for a **nine**-day period. *Novena* is from Latin *novenus*, **nine each**; the root, *nov-*, also yields *November*, the **ninth** month in the early Roman calendar. Do not confuse this root with *novus*, **new**, which yields *novel, novelty, novice, innovate, renovate*. Spanish *nueve*, **nine**; *nuevo*, **new**.

Reconnaissance, from French, is from the same Latin base as *recognize*, **to know again**. *Reconnaissance* is an exploratory survey or examination, as in seeking out information on enemy positions, installations, etc., or as in making a preliminary geological or engineering survey.

Contrive, from *con-*, **with, together** + a variant of *trope*, **a turn**, is to think up, devise, scheme, as *to contrive a plan to hear from his family*. *Contrived*, an adjective, means **artificial, labored**, as "contrived humor." A *contrivance* is something devised, as a mechanical device, or an ingenious plan. My hearing aids are simply a *contrivance* to get people to speak louder and clearer, or "up and out." [the experience of the Virginia author of this book]

120

Sectional Word Cluster Test

INSTRUCTIONS: For each set of words from Latin and Greek (and sometimes, French, Spanish, and German), write the common meaning in the blank.

Example: **hypo**tenuse, **hypo**thesis, **sub**ject   <u>under</u>

	Presection Answer	Postsection Answer
61. **magn**um, **magn**animous, **magni**ficent	_____	_____
62. **mal**ady, **mal**icious, dis**mal**, **dys**functional	_____	_____
63. **manu**script, **manu**facture, **chiro**practor, **chiro**pter	_____	_____
64. **min**or, **min**us, **min**uend, **min**uet, di**min**ish	_____	_____
65. **miss**ionary, ad**miss**ion, trans**mit**, com**mit**tee	_____	_____
66. **mort**ality, im**mort**al, "**Thanat**opsis," eu**than**asia	_____	_____
67. **nat**al, **nat**ional, **nat**ivity, neo**nate**, con**gen**ital	_____	_____
68. **nomen**clature, **nomin**ate, a**nonym**ous, syn**onym**	_____	_____
69. **nolo** contendere, persona **non** grata, **um**pire	_____	_____
70. **ob**sequious, **ob**literate, **oc**clude, **of**fer, **o**mit	_____	_____

_____   _____
Presection Score   Postsection Score

Note: Enter scores for this test and the following ones after completing this section; then, enter them on p. xvii.

Sectional Wordbuilder Test

Throughout the book and as a supplement, there are wordbuilders; these wordbuilders are designed to help you build a family of words from a single root.

	Presection Answer	Postsection Answer
50. What is the meaning of *leg-, lig-* as in sacri**lege**, e**lig**ible?	_____	_____
51. What is the meaning of *phag-* as in eso**phag**us, **phago**cyte?	_____	_____
52. What is the meaning of *rhino-* as in **rhino**ceros, **rhino**plasty?	_____	_____
53. What is the meaning of *lith-* as in **litho**graphy, mono**lith**ic?	_____	_____

_____   _____
Presection Score   Postsection Score

After entering the scores here, enter them on pp. xviii.

```
┌─────────────────────────────────────────────────────────────────────────────────────┐
│                              Word Cluster No. 61                                        │
│                                                                                         │
│ magnate            magnify            magniloquent        magnanimous                   │
│ magnitude          magnum             magnific            magnificence                  │
│                                                                                         │
│ magistrate         magistrand         magistery           magistral                     │
│                                                                                         │
│ major              majority           majesty             majestic                      │
│                                                                                         │
│ maxim              maximum            maximize            maximal                       │
│                                                                                         │
│ Common elements_____Inferred Meaning_____      │
└─────────────────────────────────────────────────────────────────────────────────────┘
```

Romance Cognates	French	Romanian	Italian	Portuguese	Spanish
	maître	major	magno	magno	magno

Words with disguised Latin roots: Bolshevik, Magus (plural, Magi), May, mayor, master, mister, mistral

Latin and Romance words and phrases: *maître d'hôtel, maître d'armes, force majeure; Magnificat; major-domo; ars magna; magna cum laude; Magna est veritas; Magna Christi Americana; magnum opus; nil sine magno labore, Magna Charta* (also, *Magna Carta*); *c'est magnifique!* See **Clavis**.

Latin phrases defined: *Stat magni nominis umbra*: **He stands, the shadow of a mighty name.**
Amor magnus doctor est: **Love is a great teacher.** St. Augustine
a maximis ad minima: **from the greatest to the least**
A bove majori discit arare minor: **From the older ox, the younger learns to plow.**
Adde parvum parvo magnus, acervus erit: **Add little to little and there will be a great heap.** Ovid
ad majorem Dei gloriam. See **Clavis**.

Spanish proverb: *Al hombre mayor, darle honor*. See pp. 73, 93.

Motto of the Benedictines: *Deo, Optimo, Maximo* (abbreviated D.O.M.): **To God, the Best, the Greatest**

Trade name: Magnavox™ (see **Clavis**)

Greek cognates: *mega*, **great**: **mega**cephaly, **mega**cycle, **mega**gamete (same as Latin **macro**gamete), **mega**hertz, **mega**lith (**a huge stone**, especially one used in Neolithic monuments or in the construction work of ancient peoples; see *cromlech*, p. 123), **mega**phone, **mega**pod, **mega**pode, **mega**scopic, **mega**spore; *megalo*: **megalo**dont, **megalo**ps, **megalo**nyx; **megalo**blast, **megalo**cardia, **megalo**cephalic, **megalo**cyte, **megalo**dactyly, **megalo**glossia, **megalo**graphy, **megalo**mania, **megalo**penis, **megalo**polis, **megalo**saur; acro**megaly**, adreno**megaly**; **omega** (see p. 127);

---

wordextras

Extricate, from Latin *extricare* (*ex-*, **out** + *tricae*, **vexations**), is "to set free or disentangle," as from a net, difficulty, embarrassment, etc.; also, to liberate gas from combination, as in a chemical process.

The *ville* of place names, e.g., *Louisville*, is from the same suffix as Old English *wich, wick*, all of which mean "village, hamlet." Examples: *Ipswich*, *Warwick*, MA; *Sandwich*, MA, NH; *Greenwich*, England.

Stymie, also *stymy*, the origin of which is unknown, is a golfing situation in which an opponent's ball obstructs the line of play of one's own ball; figuratively, an impasse; a quandary.

The phrase *hue and cry*, "public clamor or outcry," as *a hue and cry against the war*, is from Old French *hu*, **a warning interjection**, originally indicating a loud shout or cry by those pursuing a felon: all who heard were obliged to join in the pursuit; *hue and cry* also designates the pursuit itself.

Remnant, from *manere*, **to remain, stay**, is **that which is left behind**, or that which is left over; **remainder**; **residue**, as in *a remnant of his former self*, or *a remnant of his former pride*. Doublet of *remainder*.

Paltry, from Low German *palte*, **a rag**, means **practically worthless**; trifling; insignificant; contemptible, petty. The lawyer's efforts on my behalf were *paltry*; they didn't amount to much of anything except a large fee.

Evanesce, from *ex-*, **out** + *vanescere*, **to vanish**, means **to pass away**, **to disappear gradually**, **to fade away**. The adjectival form is *evanescent*.

Texas was originally an ethnic name, from Caddo *taysa*, **friends, allies**; also, the name given to officers' quarters on Mississippi steamboats because they were the largest cabins. Once a republic, Texas is known as **The Lone Star State**.

Common element base: magnus   **Meaning**: great

Mag-, **great**; *maj-*, **greater**; *max-*, **greatest**; **IE base**: *meg-*, yields Sanskrit *maha,* as in *Mahatma* Gandhi; English *much*; Greek *mega-*, as in ***megalith***; also, **one million**; compare **German**: *grosse*, **great**; *grosse Kinder*, **grown-up children**.

Clavis

magna cum laude: Latin; **with great honor**, or **praise**; an award conferred upon a college graduate; higher than *cum laude*, **with praise**, and lower than *summa cum laude*, **with highest praise**.

magnanimous: *animus*, **mind**; **great mind**; noble in mind; high-souled; especially, generous in forgiving or overlooking injury or insult; rising above pettiness or meanness; gracious; unselfish. Pronounced: mag NAN uh muhs; the nominal is *magnanimity*, pronounced: MAG nuh NIM uh tee.

magnate: from *magnas*, **great man**; a very important or influential person of rank, power, or distinction in any field of activity, especially in business or industry; formerly, in Hungary and Poland, a member of the upper branch of the Diet, the national legislative assembly.

Magnavox®: a trade name with the literal meaning of **Great Voice**, implying fidelity of sound.

magniloquent: *loqui*, **to speak**; lofty, pompous, or **grandiose** in speech or style of expression; also, boastful or bombastic. Pronunciation: mag NIL uh quent. See **Word Cluster No. 60**, p. 119, for *loqui* words.

magnum opus: *opus*, **work**; **great work**, especially the greatest achievement of an artist, musician, or writer. *Messiah*, an oratorio, is considered Handel's *magnum opus*; *Mona Lisa*, da Vinci's *greatest* portrait; *The Blue Boy*, Gainsborough's *greatest* painting; term may now suggest **irony** or **sarcasm**. In German, *Meisterstück*, literally, **master stroke**, but meaning **masterpiece**, translates *magnum opus*. *Meisterstück*, also, a very clever or well-timed action. See p. 146 under *oratorio*.

majesty: the dignity or power of a sovereign; sovereign power, as *the majesty of the law*; capitalized, a title used in speaking *to* or *of* a sovereign, preceded by *Your* or by *His* or *Her*, as appropriate.

majority: the **greater part** or **larger number**; more than half of the total; also, the number by which the votes cast for a candidate, bill, etc., receiving more than half the votes, exceed the number of remaining votes, e.g., if candidate A receives 100 votes; candidate B, 50; and candidate C, 30; candidate A has a majority of 20 (100 – 50 – 30 = 20). See *plurality*, p. 154.

maître d'hôtel: French; **master of the house**, and is often abbreviated *maître d'*; **headwaiter**. *Maître d'* also designates a sauce of melted butter, parsley, and lemon juice. Pronounced: mehtr doh TEL.

maxim: a concisely expressed principle or rule of conduct; a statement of general truth. SYNONYMS: adage, aphorism, epigram, proverb, saw, saying. (See *aphorism*, under **wordextras**, p. 132.)

Bolshevik: from Russian *bol'she*, **the larger**, **majority**; designates a member of the majority faction, *Bolsheviki*, of the Social Democratic Workers' Party, that formed the Communist Party after seizing power in the 1917 Russian Revolution, with the overthrow of Tsar Nicholas (1894-1918).

megalopolis: Greek *polis*, **city**; **great city**; an extensive, heavily populated, continuously urban area, including any number of smaller cities. Compare *conurbation*, p. 64.

acromegaly: Greek *akros*, usually meaning **high**, but in *medicine*, **extremities**; thus, the enlargement of the bones in the hands, feet, and face, resulting from chronic overactivity of the pituitary gland.

ad majorem Dei gloriam: abbreviated AMDG, **to the greater glory of God**. The motto of the Jesuits.
Nil sine magno labore: **Nothing without great effort**: motto of Brooklyn College.

wordextras

Kremlin, French for Russian *kreml'*, **citadel**, is the citadel, or stronghold, fortress, of any Russian city; ***the Kremlin***, the citadel of Moscow, houses the government offices of the former Soviet Union, and now of Russia.

Boca Raton, Florida, is Spanish for **rat's mouth**, after nearby Lake Boca Raton, from hidden rock that frayed, or "gnawed" ships' cables. Boca Raton is on the Atlantic coast.

Expression from Greek mythology: *Pandora's box*; from *Pandora*, the first mortal woman, who in curiosity opened a box, letting out all the human ills into the world. A later version recounts that Pandora let all human blessings escape and be lost, leaving only hope.

```
┌─────────────────────────────────────────────────────────────────────────┐
│                        Word Cluster No. 62                                │
│                                                                           │
│   malefactor      malfeasance      dismal          malicious             │
│   malaria         maliferous          malediction  malaise               │
│   malevolent      maloplasty          malapropism  malinger              │
│   malocclusion    maladroit           malnutrition malady                │
│   malpractice     malism              malign       malignant             │
│   malice          malversation        malodorous   malison               │
│                                                                           │
│   Common elements_____Inferred Meaning_____  │
└─────────────────────────────────────────────────────────────────────────┘
```

Romance Cognates	French mal	Romanian mal*	Italian male	Portuguese mal	Spanish malo

*In Romanian, only as a prefix does this element have the meaning of the common element; as a separate word, *mal* means "bank of a river."

Romance phrases: *mauvais sujet; de mal en pis; grand mal; petit mal; malgré lui; mal de mer*

Latin phrases: *De duobus malis, minus est semper eligendum.* **Of two evils, the lesser is always to be chosen.** Thomas à Kempis (1380-1471), German monk and scholar.
Ne cede malis, sed contra audentior ito. **Yield not to misfortunes, but go more boldly to meet them.** Virgil

Motto of the Order of the Garter, England's highest order of knighthood: *Honi* soit qui mal y pense*; often abbreviated *honi soit!* **Shame to him who thinks evil of it!** *The modern French spelling is *honni*.

Spanish phrases: *Quien mal dice, peor oye*: **He who speaks evil, hears worse.** (See pp. 13, 65.)
Cosa mala nunca muere: **A bad thing never dies.**
Quien canta sus males espanta: **He who sings chases away his troubles.**

Greek *dys-*, **abnormal, difficulty, impaired**: **dys**calculia, **dys**crasia (an abnormal imbalance in some part of the body, especially in the blood), **dys**entery (*entera*, **bowels**), **dys**emia (*–emia*, **blood condition**; any abnormal condition or disease of the blood), **dys**ergasia, **dys**function, **dys**genic (causing deterioration of hereditary qualities of a stock; opposite to *eugenic*), **dys**graphia, **dys**kinesia, **dys**lexia, **dys**logistic, **dys**menorrhea, **dys**pareunia (sexual intercourse that is physically painful or difficult), **dys**pepsia, **dys**peptic, **dys**phagia (*phagein*, **to eat**; difficulty in swallowing), **dys**phasia, **dys**phonia (*phone*, **sound**; impairment of the ability to produce speech sounds, as because of hoarseness), **dys**phoria, **dys**plasia, **dys**pnea, **dys**prosium, **dys**rhythmia (a lack of rhythm, as of the brain waves or in speech patterns), **dys**tonia (lack of muscle tone due to disease or infection of the nervous system), **dys**topia, **dys**trophic, **dys**trophy, **dys**uria (painful urination). See other *dys-* words, p. 69, under **Note**.

wordextras

Samovar, Russian for **self-boiler**, is a metal urn with a spigot, and is used to boil water for tea. See p. 56.

Cromlech, from Welsh *crom*, **bent, crooked** + *llech*, **flat stone**, is a Neolithic monument of megaliths, arranged in a circle and surrounding a mound or *dolmen* (Breton for **table stone**). See *Stonehenge*, p. 125; *megalith*, p. 121.

In Russian, the expression of praise for "Good job!" can be only phonetically spelled in English; it sounds like *horror show*, accented on the first syllable, and with a heavily rolled double *r*.

California is the Spanish name of a fabled island, i.e., an island existing only as an imaginary place.

The *ham* of placenames is Germanic for **home**, and later a **group of homes**, thus a village; *hamlet*, a small group of homes. Examples of *ham* in placenames: *Chatham, Chesham, Durham, Nottingham, Windham*, NH; also, Chatham, VA; Birmingham, AL, MI; Fultonham, NY, OH; Dedham, IA, MA. In German, *ham* is *Heim*, as in *Anaheim*, CA, *Arnheim*, OH, *Bergheim*, TX, *Manheim*, PA. There is also Mannheim, Germany.

wordbuilder #50

Latin *lect-, leg-, lig-* (from *legere*, **to pick, choose**), yield col**lect**, dia**lect**, ec**lect**ic*, e**lect**, idio**lect**, intel**lect**, neg**lect** pre**lect**, recol**lect**, se**lect**; **leg**ion, sacri**leg**e; di**lig**ence, e**lig**ible, neg**lig**ence, neg**lig**ee. *Negligee* implies that one has "neglected" to get fully dressed. *There is *Eclectic*, Alabama, north of Montgomery, near Wetumpka.

an aphorism: *Better a small fish than an empty dish.* **Better to be satisfied with a little than to have nothing.** It is better to receive a small pay increase than none at all. It is better to have a low-paying job than no job at all.

Common element base: mal(e)   **Meaning**: bad, ill, wrong
IE base: *mel-⁵*: **bad**. **German**: *schlecht*, as in *schlecht und recht*, **somehow**, but literally, **wrong and right**

Clavis

malady:
from Vulgar Latin *male habitus*, **badly kept**, **out of condition**. SYNONYMS: ailment, disease. See p. 90.

malaise:
French; **bad ease**; an indefinite feeling of discomfort, illness, or depression; also, a vague awareness of social decline, or of mental or moral well-being. Pronounced: mah LAZE, or mu LAZE.

malapropism:
after *Mrs. Malaprop*, in Sheridan's play *The Rivals*; from French *mal à propos*, **badly to the purpose**. Mrs. Malaprop humorously confused words of similar pronunciation, e.g., making *parsing reverence* (**passing reference**) to *allegories* (**alligators**) sunning themselves on the banks of the Nile.

malaria:
Italian; contraction of *mala aria*, **bad air** (of swamps), from the former notion that such air caused the illness, characterized by chills and fever, or the ague. *Ague* is from *febris acuta*, **acute fever**.

malice:
in *law*, **evil intent**; state of mind shown by intention to do something unlawful, as in *malice afore-thought*. SYNONYMS: grudge, ill will, malevolence, spite, spleen.

malign:
from Old French *malignier*, **to plot**, **deceive**, **to speak evil of**; further from Latin *malignus*; from *male* + base of *genus*, **born**. As an adjective, "showing ill will; malicious," as *a malign influence*. VERB SYNONYMS: asperse, calumniate, defame, libel, revile, slander, traduce, vilify, vituperate. ADJECTIVE SYNONYMS: baleful, dire, evil, injurious, sinister.

malinger:
from French *malingre*, **sickly**, **infirm**; further from Old French *heingre*, **lean**, **haggard**, to pretend to be ill or otherwise incapacitated in order to escape duty or work; **to shirk**. The noun is *malingerer*.

mal de mer:
French; *mer*, **sea**; **seasickness**; *mer* is also in *mermaid*; variant forms are in *marine*, *meerschaum*, and *cormorant*; the *Maritime* Provinces of Canada: Nova Scotia, New Brunswick, and Prince Edward Island. German *meerschaum*, **sea foam**, is used for tobacco pipes.

dismal:
from Old French *dis mal*; further from Middle Latin *dies mali*, **evil days** (of the medieval calendar); causing gloom or misery; depressing; dark and gloomy; bleak; dreary; depressed; miserable. *Dismal Swamp*, a 30-mile-long marshy, forested region between Norfolk, VA, and Albermarle Sound, NC; traversed by a canal that is part of the Intracoastal Waterway. See more on the waterway, p. 100.

dyscrasia:
Greek *krasia*, **a mixing**; **a disproportionate mixture**, an *abnormal imbalance* in some part of the body, especially of the blood; root also found in *idiosyncrasy*. Interestingly, *crater*, literally, **mixing bowl**, of a volcano is also from *krasia*. There is the Punchbowl National Park, a centuries-old crater, and site of a national military cemetery, in Honolulu, Hawaii.

dysmenorrhea:
Greek *meno*, **month** + *rhein*, **to flow**; **painful** or **difficult menstruation**. The root *rrh-* is also found in *blennorrhea, diarrhea, gonorrhea, rheostat, rheotaxis, rhythm*; and the *Rhein* (English: Rhine): a river in Switzerland, Germany, and the Netherlands. *Menstruate*, from Latin *mensis*, **month**.

dyspnea:
Greek *pnoe*, **breathing**; **labored** or **difficult breathing**, or respiration; normal when due to vigorous work or athletic activity. Pronunciation: dis NEE uh.

dysplasia:
Greek *plasis*, **a molding**; a disordered growth or faulty development of various tissues or body parts.

wordextras

Modicum, from Latin *modicus*, **moderate**, **due measure**, is a small amount or portion; a limited quantity; a **bit**, as *a modicum of interest*. Students have come to expect a *modicum* of eccentricity in tenured professors. Because his new book received poor reviews, the author enjoyed only a *modicum* of satisfaction from its publication.

Omaha, NE, is from a Siouan tribal name, meaning probably "upstream people." Omaha is on the Missouri River.

Specious, from Latin *speciosus*, originally meant **showy**, **beautiful**, **plausible**, and is further from *specere*, **to see**. *Specious* has come to mean "seeming to be good, sound, correct, logical, without really being so"; plausible but not genuine, as *a specious argument*. See p. 212, Item 171, for more words from *specere*.

A Writing Tip: Place semicolons (;) and colons (:) *outside* "quotation marks"; place commas (,) and periods (.) *inside* "quotation marks." Example: According to Shakespeare, the poet writes in a "fine frenzy"; by "fine frenzy," he meant a combination of energy, enthusiasm, imagination, and "a certain madness."

Word Cluster No. 63

mandate	manner(ism)	manipulate	manubrium
manicure	mandatory	manual	manufacture
maniple	manage	demand	manipulate
manifest	remand	countermand	commandment
management	manumission	mansuetude	remand
amanuensis	manuscript	manumit	manacle
commend	recommend	mancipate	emancipate

Common elements_____Inferred Meaning_____

Romance Cognates	French	Romanian	Italian	Portuguese	Spanish
	main	mina	mano	mao	mano

Doublets: manure:maneuver

Words and phrases with disguised Latin roots: maintain, maintenance, mortmain, legerdemain, mastiff, Maundy Thursday, mano, *mano destra*, manqué; writ of mandamus; manecilla (Spanish for "hand of a clock")

Latin phrases: *Manus haec inimical tyrannis*: **This hand is an enemy to tyrants**. *manu forti;* **with a strong hand**; by main force; *ad manum*: **at hand**; in readiness

French phrase: *mains froides, coeur chaud*: **cold hands, warm heart**

Romance words and phrases: *manicotti; La Manche; manège; coup de main, main droite*

Documents: *Manifest Destiny; Emancipation Proclamation; Communist Manifesto*

NB: *Manifold* (**many-fold**) is not in this family.

Greek: *cheir*, **hand**: **chir**al; **chir**urgeon; **chiro**graphy, **chiro**mancy, **chiro**pody, **chiro**practor (see **Clavis**), **chiro**pter, en**chir**idion (**a handbook**); **surgeon**, one who uses his or her hands . See other *chiro-* words, p. 64.

Afrikaans: commandeer, commando (through Portuguese)

Arabic: Although Arabic is not of the Indo-European family, the following Arabic words have meanings similar to that of the common element's, and especially to *command: ameer, emeer, emir, emirate*.

wordextras

A *suitor*, from Latin *sequi*, **to follow**, "followed" the damsel (see next entry) and dogged her footsteps (see other *sequi* words, **Word Cluster No. 87**, p. 173). Take care! Kingdoms are destroyed by bandits, houses by rats, and widows by *suitors*. Ihara Saikaku (1646-1693), a Japanese writer known for taking great risks in his works.

Damsel, from *dame*, is ultimately from a diminutive of Latin *domina*, which itself is from the masculine *dominus*, **master**. See *daunt*, p. 2; *dungeon*, p. 33; *condominium*, p. 147.

Amarillo, Texas, Spanish for **yellow**, is named probably after nearby Amarillo Creek, whose subsoil is yellow.

Schenectady, New York, is the Dutch form of Mohawk *skahnehati*, **on the other side of the pines**.

El Sobrante, California, is Spanish for *leftover*. When ranchos on the East Bay were divided, this area was "left over."

Los Angeles, California, founded in 1781 on a Spanish grant, was originally named *Nuestra Señora Reina de los Angeles*, **Our Queen Lady of the Angels**.

To *lollygag*, an informal usage, is to waste time in trifling or aimless activity; **to fool around**.

Cree *muskeg*, **swamp**, is a kind of bog or marsh containing thick layers of decaying vegetable matter, mosses, etc., found especially in Canada and Alaska and often overgrown with moss.

Stonehenge, from Middle English *ston*, **stone** + *henge*, **(something) hanging**, is a circular arrangement of prehistoric megaliths on Salisbury Plain, England, set up probably in the Neolithic period. See *dolmen, cromlech*, p. 123.

Vitriol, from *vitrum*, **glass**, denotes sharpness or bitterness of feeling, as in speech or writing. The adjective is *vitriolic*. Other words from *vitrum* include **vitrain**, **vitreous** (vitreous humor, or body), **vitric**, **vitrics**, **vitrine** (a glass-paneled cabinet or display case for art objects, curios, small trophies, etc.), **vitriform**, **vitrify**.

Common element base: manus   **Meaning**: hand

IE base: *man-²*; with compound *mandere* (*manus* + *dare*, **to give**), **to give into another's hands**, e.g., **mand**atory, **mand**ate; hence *Maundy Thursday* (see **Clavis**); com**mand**, counter**mand**, de**mand**, re**mand**.
German: *Hand*, as in *die Hand im Spiel haben*: **to have a finger in the pie**; *Handschrift*: **manuscript**; **handwriting**.
Spanish: *mano*; in *anatomy*, **hand**; in *zoology*, **foot**, **forefoot**, **paw**.

Clavis

mandate:	see IE base above; an authoritative order or **command**, especially a written one. In Roman law, a commission by which a person undertakes to do something for another, without compensation, but with indemnity against loss. *Mandate* is also a verb; the adjectival form is *mandatory*.
manubrium:	originally, a **handle**, **hilt**, **haft**; a handlelike structure, process, or part, especially, the portion of a jellyfish or other coelenterate that bears the mouth at its tip. Also, an anatomical process or part shaped like a handle, as the projection of the *malleus*, **hammer**, in the ear; in addition, the cranial portion of the sternum, or breastbone. *Sternum*: from IE base *ster-*, **to spread out**: a flat structure of bone and cartilage to which most of the ribs are attached.
manufacture:	French; from Middle Latin *manufactura*; *facere*, **to make**, originally, **to make by hand**; now, the making of goods and articles, mostly by computerized machinery, often on a large scale and with division of labor. See note under **Word Cluster No. 39**, p. 77.
manumission:	from Latin *manumissio*; further from *manumittere*, **to let go from the hand**; a freeing or being freed from slavery; **liberation**; **emancipation**. See words from *miss-*, *mitt-*, **to send**, p. 129.
maniple:	from *manipulus*, **handful**; from the *maniple* having been originally held in the **hand**, a long narrow strip of silk worn by the priest at Mass over the left arm near the wrist.
remand:	*re-*, **back**; literally, **to hand back**; **to send back**; to order to go back; in *law*, to send a prisoner or accused person back into custody; as a *noun*, a remanding or being remanded.
La Manche:	**The Sleeve**; the French name of the English Channel; in lowercase, **sleeve**; *le manche*, **handle**.
maneuver:	and *manure* are doublets; from *manu operare*; the original meaning of both, **to work by hand**.
mansuetude:	*suescere*, **to accustom**; therefore, **tameness**, **gentleness**. Related etymologically to *ethic*, **character**.
amanuensis:	from *servus a manu*, **a slave at hand**(writing); one who writes for another, especially one who is incapacitated. Pronunciation: uh MAN yoo EN sis.
coup de main:	French; **stroke of hand**; a sudden or surprise attack in force, as in war. Pronounced: kood MAn.
mortmain:	*mort* from *mori*, **to die**; **dead hand**; perpetual ownership; no other **hands** shall touch or own property deeded to a corporate body, such as a school or church. See more on *mortmain*, p. 132.
Maundy Thursday:	*Maundy*, from *mandatum*, first word in Latin in Jesus' prayer as he washed his disciples' feet at the Lord's Supper before his arrest; he **mandated** that his disciples love and serve one another, as he had loved and served them, and exemplified by his servant role. John 13.
chiropractor:	Greek; one who **practices** (health care) with the **hands** (by manipulating the muscles and bones). *Surgeon* also comes from the root *chiro*, **hand**; *surgery* in Greek was *cheirourgos*, **working with the hands**. Note the *urg* element, as in *en<u>erg</u>y* (see **wordbuilder #22**, p. 43).
chiropter:	Greek *pteron*, **wing**; literally, **hand-wing**; a flying mammal family which includes the bats; *pter* is also in *helicopter*, **helical wing**, or **spiral wing**, and *pterodactyl*, **wing-finger**. See p. 211.
emirate:	Arabic; the jurisdiction of an *emir*, **commander**, **ruler**; thus, the United Arab Emirates, formerly The Trucial States; *trucial* refers to a truce among the states not to trade with other countries.

Latin expressions: *persona grata*: **one who is welcome or acceptable**, especially a foreign diplomat acceptable to the government to which he or she is assigned; *persona non grata*: **an unwelcome person**.

An exalted aphorism: **Missiles of ligneous or petrous consistency have the potential of fracturing my osseous structure, but appellations will eternally remain innocuous.** *Sticks and stones may break my bones, but words will never hurt me.* A truer, modern version: Sticks and stones may break my bones, and words can sting like anything.

Word Cluster No. 64

minim	diminution	minute	minus
minimize	diminutive	comminute	minuscule
minimum	diminish	minutiae	minimal
minnow	diminuendo	minestrone	mince
minor	minister	minuet	minuend
minority	administer	miniature	ministration

Common element_____Inferred Meaning_____

Romance Cognates	French	Romanian	Italian	Portuguese	Spanish
	menu	mic, minim	minuto	miúdo	minuto

Words with disguised Latin roots: menu, minstrel, minaudière (a woman's small handbag), miniver, muscovado

Latin phrases: *Qui invidet minor est*: **He who envies is the inferior**; *a minori ad majus*: **from the less to the greater**

Italian proverb: *Pensa molto, parla poco, e scrivi meno*: **Think much, speak little, and write less.**

Spanish proverb: *De los enemigos los menos*: **The fewer the enemies, the better.**

Motto of Wellesley College: *Non ministrari sed ministrare*: **Not to be ministered unto but to minister.** Matthew 20:28

Explore *diminution* and its opposite, *augmentation*, in a music dictionary.

Eric Partridge notes that some uses of the Anglo-Saxon prefix *mis-*, as in *mischief*, were derived from the **IE base** that yields the *Common Element*.

Greek *micros*, **small**: **micro**n; **micro**dont (*odont*, **tooth**); **micro**bacterium, **micro**be (*bios*, **life**), **micro**biology, **micro**cephaly, **micro**cline, **micro**coccus, **micro**computer, **micro**cosm, **micro**cyte, **micro**encapsulation, **micro**fauna, **micro**fiber, **micro**fiche, **micro**flora, **micro**form, **micro**fossil, **micro**gamete, **micro**graph, **micro**gravity, **micro**habitat, **micro**lith, **micro**mere, **micro**meter, **Micro**nesia, **micro**phone, **micro**phyte, **micro**pyle, **micro**pyrometer, **micro**scope, **micro**seism, **micro**some, **micro**sphere, **micro**sporangium, **micro**spore, **micro**stomatous, **micro**stome, **micro**structure, **micro**surgery, **micro**tome, **micro**tomy, **micro**tubule, **micro**villus; photo**micro**graph; the Greek letter *omicron*, **small o**, as opposed to *omega*, **large o**; see p. 121.

NB: *Minnesinger* is not in this family. From German, *minnesinger* designates certain lyric poets and singers of the 12th to the 14th centuries. The basic meaning is "loving recollection."

wordextras

Apricot, related to both *precocious* and *cuisine*, in that they all are bound to Latin *coquere*, **to cook**, is extended to mean **to ripen**. *Apricot* transliterates Arabic *al-birquq*, "the early-ripened fruit." See *precocious*, p. 56.

Hiatus, from Latin *hiare*, **to gape**, **open**, means **an opening**. Thus, *hiatus* indicates a break or interruption in the continuity of a work, series, action, etc.; a missing part, gap, lacuna. In *phonetics*, a slight pause in pronunciation between two successive vowels in adjacent words or syllables, as between the sounds represented by the two adjacent e's in *see easily*, so that the words are not coalesced into "seezily," as well as in *he entered* and *reenter*.

Atrophy, from *a-*, **negative** + *trophein*, **to nourish**, **feed**, means **a wasting away**, especially of body tissue or an organ, or the failure of an organ to grow or develop, as because of insufficient nutrition. Other words from *trophein*: **tropho**logy; auto**trophy**, dys**trophy**, hyper**trophy**; hetero**trophic**, meso**trophic**, oligo**trophic**, poly**trophic**.

Cantilever, a bracket or block projecting from a wall to support a balcony, cornice, etc., has an obscure background. Some have associated *canti-* with Greek *kanthos*, **corner of the eye**; others associate it with *canis*, **dog**. Neither association is obvious. *Lever* is included in **Word Cluster No. 56**, p. 111. Pronounced: KANT 'l ee ver.

Charity is ultimately from Latin *carus*, **dear**; in Christianity, translates Greek *agape*, God's unconditional love for man. The meaning of both *charity* and *agape* is extended to include "love and good will for one's fellow man."

Mississippi is French for Illinois (Indian tribe) *missisipioui*, **big river**; with a length of 2,348 miles, the Mississippi is the chief river of the United States. It disembogues into the Gulf of Mexico. *Disembogue*: **to come out of the mouth of a river**, from *dis-*, **apart** + *bucca*, **cheek**. (A related Spanish word is *boca*, **mouth**; see *Boca Raton*, p. 122.)

Common element base: minuere　　　　　　　　　　　　　　　　　　　**Meaning**: to make small
IE root: *mei-²*: **small**: yields **Greek** *meion*, **less**, **lesser**, as in **mei**osis, **Mio**cene, **Mio**lithic.
Russian: *Menshevik,* **minority** group of the Russian Social Democratic Party; opposed the *Bolsheviks*, the **majority**.

Clavis

miniature:　　from Latin *minium*, **red lead**; later, **red head letters** of medieval manuscripts; by association with *minute*, has come to mean **small**, as *a miniature poodle*, or *a miniature dollhouse*.

mince:　　from Middle English *mincen*; further from *minuere*, **to cut or make small**, e.g., *to mince potatoes, to mince words*; *mincing*, affectedly elegant or dainty: said of a person or a person's speech, manner, etc.; characterized by affected daintiness, as *a mincing walk*.

minister:　　originally, one who was of **smaller**, or of **lesser** rank, and who acted upon higher authority, either governmentally or ecclesiastically, e.g., Prime Minister of England, the minister of a church, respectively. As a verb, **to serve**, as *to minister* to the needs of the elderly. Do not confuse *minister* with *minster*, which comes from *mono-*, **one**, **alone**; see **wordextras**, p. 21.

minor:　　as an *adjective*, **lesser** in size, amount, number, or extent; under full legal age; as a *noun*, a field of study in which students specialize, but less so than in their major. Other uses as a noun and as a verb.

menu:　　French; **small**, **detailed**; thus, a detailed list describing the bill of selections of a restaurant generally, but now also of a computer or a word processor, e.g., pull-down menu: a list of options available.

minuend:　　from *minuendum*, **to be diminished**; in *arithmetic*, the number or quantity from which another (the subtrahend) is to be subtracted. In 9-4=5, the *minuend* is 9. [*Subtrahend*: **to draw under**. The result of subtracting 4 from 9 is called "remainder," or that which *remains*, or is left over. See p. 213, Item 178.]

minuet:　　a slow, graceful dance for groups of couples, characterized by short, or **small**, steps; introduced in France in the 17th century; the music for this, in 3/4 time. Bach's *minuets* were written for the dance.

minute:　　Ptolemy's designation for the 60th part of a circle, and was originally *pars minuta prima*, **first small part**. The next division of the hour or the circle was *pars minuta seconda*, **second small part**. As an adjective, pronounced mih NOOT, or NYOOT. Sʏɴᴏɴʏᴍꜱ: diminutive, little, miniature, small.

minstrel:　　in the Middle Ages, a wandering lyric poet or singer; a **servant**, an **underling**, of entertainment.

micrometer:　　Greek *metiri*, **to measure**; an instrument for measuring very small distances, angles, diameters, etc.; used on a telescope or microscope; pronounced my KROM uh ter; also, a unit of length equal to one thousandth of a millimeter; pronounced MY krow ᴍᴇᴇ ter.

microcosm:　　Greek *kosmos*, **world**; **small world**; a diminutive, representative world, e.g., Many university classes are *microcosms* of the United Nations. Compare **cosmo**logy, the scientific study of the origins of the universe; **cosmo**naut, a Soviet or Russian astronaut; and **cosmo**politan, pertaining to or representative of all or many parts of the world, such as Los Angeles, New York City, Paris, London, Rome.

wordbuilder #51
Greek *phagein*, **to eat** (in some cases, **destroy**, **consume**), yields **phago**cyte; a**phag**ia, dys**phag**ia (**difficulty in swallowing**), macro**phage**; eso**phag**us; eury**phagous**, mono**phagous**; anthropo**phagous** (pertaining to cannibalism), carpo**phagous** (**fruit-eating**), entomo**phagous** (**insect-eating**); cyto**phag**y, geo**phag**y; necro**phag**ia, omo**phag**ia; sarco**phag**us. Originally, the IE root *bhag-¹* meant "a share of food," thus yielding Sanskrit *Bhagavad-Gita*, **Song of the Blessed One**, a sacred Hindu text. It is a philosophical dialogue found in the *Mahabharata*, one of the ancient Sanskrit epics. The entire *Bhagavad-Gita* may be accessed online through either *Google* or *Yahoo*.

wordextras
Lucrative, **profitable**, from Latin *lucrari*, **to gain**, is further from *lucrum*, **gain**, **riches**; thus, *a lucrative business, a lucrative investment*, or *a lucrative marketing strategy*. The only other word from *lucrari* is *lucre* (1 Timothy 3:3).

Piquant, adjective, and *pique*, noun (also used as verb, as *to pique one's curiosity*), are from Old French *piquer*, **to sting**, **to prick**; both words may be from Latin *picus*, **woodpecker**. Sʏɴᴏɴʏᴍꜱ of *piquant*: pungent, racy, spicy. Nᴏᴜɴ sʏɴᴏɴʏᴍꜱ of *pique*: displeasure, resentment, umbrage. Vᴇʀʙ sʏɴᴏɴʏᴍꜱ: excite, provoke, stimulate.

Tort, from Latin *torquere*, **to twist**, is a **wrongful act**, **injury**, or **damage** (not involving a breach of contract) for which a civil action can be brought. *Tortfeasor*, **tort doer**, is one who commits or is guilty of a tort. See *travel*, p. 196.

Word Cluster No. 65

admit	commit	demit	emit	intromit
omit	permit	remit	submit	transmit

missile	mission	missionary	missive
admissible	admission	commissary	commission
dismiss	dismissal	emissary	emission
intermission	omission	remiss	emissive
transmission	compromise	premise	remission
promissory (note)	promise	surmise	permission
manumission	remise	demise	submission

Common elements_____Inferred Meaning_____

Romance Cognates	French	Romanian	Italian	Portuguese	Spanish
	mettre	trimite	mettere	miter*	mitir*

*These elements appear only in compound verbs, e.g., Spanish *remitir*.

Words with disguised Latin roots: Mass, Christmas, mess (of food), mess hall, message

Latin words and phrases: *mittimus; Nunc Dimittus*: **Now thou lettest depart**; first words in the Latin version of the song of Simeon, in blessing the Infant Jesus, Luke 2:29-32, used as a canticle in various liturgies.
Et semel emissum volat irrevocabile verbum. **And a word once uttered flies onward, never to be recalled.** Horace

French phrase: *mise en scène*: the staging of a play; the direction of a film

Greek: from *stellein*, as in dia**stole** and sy**stole**; apo**stle**; epi**stle**; peri**stal**sis, sy**stal**tic.

German: *senden*, as in *Sendenbote*, **a messenger**; *Sender*, **a transmitter**.

wordextras

Overture is the English spelling of Latin *aperture*, **opening**, as the aperture of a camera or telescope. An *overture* of an opera, oratorio, or symphony (four related sonatas) is the opening composition, and often introduces the recurring motifs. In general, any introductory proposal or offer; indication of willingness to negotiate, as *the enemy made overtures for a ceasefire*. **Symphony**: *syn-*, **with** + *phone*, **sound**: harmony of sounds, especially of instruments.

Abet, **to help**—especially in wrongdoing—is from the age-old occupation of hunting with dogs. The Germanic languages had a verb closely related to English *bite*; this verb *beita* meant "to cause to bite," but came to mean "to bait," as in the sense of "to sic a dog on." This Germanic word entered English through Old French *beter*, with the same meaning. The prefix *a-*, from Latin *ad-*, **to, toward**, was added to form *abeter*, **to egg on** or **incite**. By dropping the inflected verb ending *–er*, *abeter* passed into English as *abet*.

Pastor, now usually thought of as a minister, priest, or rabbi, basically means a **shepherd**. The base of *pastor* is *pascere*, **to feed**, as to feed the flock, or the congregation. The adjective *pastoral* basically describes the life of a shepherd; it can also describe rural life, especially that characterized by shepherds, dairymaids, etc. In addition, *pastoral* can describe a certain type of literature, or of music; there are also the *pastoral letters* of Paul in the New Testament. (For more on *pastoral*, see *congregation*, p. 88.) In Handel's *Messiah*, there is an instrumental interlude titled "Pastorale."

Berm, from Dutch *baerm*, is a ledge or space between the ditch and parapet in a fortification; also spelled *berme*. Colloquially, *berm* refers to a road shoulder.

Oyster, from Greek *ostreon*, is a type of mollusk, and is akin to *osteon*, **a bone**, from its bony, hard shell.

Peremptory, with Latin *per-*, **intensive** + *emere*, **to buy, take**, describes that which bars further action, debate, delay, question, etc., as *a peremptory challenge* (of a juror) in a court of law. Other words from *emere*: *exemplary, exempt, preempt, redeem*; *premium* (*pre-* **before** + *emere*); see p. 206, Item 89.

A Writing Tip: Distinguish between *flaunt* and *flout*. To *flaunt* is to make a gaudy, ostentatious, conspicuous, impudent, or defiant display, as *to flaunt one's new title*; *to flout* (originally, **to play the flute**) is to mock or scoff at; show scorn or contempt; to openly disregard, as *to flout the custom* of dressing smartly for an interview.

Common element base: mittere   **Meaning**: to send, to let go

IE base: *(s)meit(e)*: **to throw**, from which none other than *mittere*, the common element base, is derived.

Clavis

demise: from the same elements as *demit*; **to send down**; as a *noun*, **ceasing to exist**; **death**. In *law*, a transfer of an estate by lease, especially for a fixed period. As a *verb*, to transfer sovereignty by death or by abdication; pronounced dih MIZE.

premise: *pre-*, **before**; **that which is sent before**; used in deeds to avoid repeating the full description of the property; therefore, **an assumption**. In *logic*, one of the propositions, i.e., major and minor, of a syllogism. See *syllogism*, p. 120.

remise: from Middle French *remettre*, **to send back**; in *law*, to give up a claim to; to release by deed.

surmise: *sur-*, from *supra-*, **over**, **beyond**, **upon**; **to put** (or, **send**) **upon**; as a *noun*, an idea or opinion formed from evidence that is neither positive nor conclusive; conjecture; guess. See p. 184.

committee: from *commit*, **to send together**; thus, a group **sent** to consider, investigate, take action on, or report on some matter. There are both *ad hoc* and *standing* committees (see p. 35, under *ad hoc*).

remit: *re-*, **back**; **to send back**, as *to remit a payment online*; the nominal form is *remission*: release from the penalty of (sin, for example); temporary abatement of disease symptoms.

admissible: from the same elements of *admit*: *ad-*, **to**, **toward**; thus, **capable of being accepted**, as *admissible evidence*; allowable; worthy of being permitted to enter.

emissary: *e(x)-*, **out**; **one who is sent out** as a representative or an agent; a spy; can also be used as an adjective, for example, serving as an emissary; also, *emissary veins*. In *medicine*, providing an outlet, or a drain, referring especially to the venous outlets from the dural sinuses through the skull.

dimissory: *di-* from with *dis-*, **apart**, **away**; **sending away**; dismissing or granting leave to depart; describes a bishop's letter permitting a priest to move from one parish to another.

mise en scène: French; the action of putting onto a stage; the setting of a story, play, poem, etc.; **milieu**. For more on *milieu*, see p. 118, under **Clavis**. Pronounced: mee zahn SEN.

mittimus: Latin; **we send**; an authorizing legal document; specifically, a warrant for imprisoning a convicted person; also, a dismissal from office. Pronunciation: MIT ih mus.

apostle: Greek *apo-*, **away** + *stellein*, **to send**; one who is **sent** (**away**) on a special mission. Capitalized, *Apostles* were the twelve disciples (learners) *sent out* by Jesus to preach the gospel. See p. 157.

epistle: Greek *epi-*, **to** + *stellein*; **that which is sent to**, as a formal letter or missive. The epistles of the New Testament refer to the letters written by the Apostles, e.g., those of Paul, Peter, and John. Some biblical commentators believe that these epistles are more *personal* than formal.

wordextras

Rapture, from Latin *rapere*, **to snatch**, **seize**, is the state of being "seized" or carried away with joy, love, etc. *Rapere* also yields *rapacious, rapacity, rape, rapt, raptorial, surreptitious*. *Raptorial*, for example, describes that which is predatory, specifically, a group of birds of prey, such as the eagle, owl, vulture, with sharp talons and notched beak.

Shindig, a dance, party, entertainment, or other gathering, especially of an informal kind, is probably from a "kick in the shin," which could likely happen at a square dance with amateur dancers.

Misadventure, with *mis-*, **bad**, **wrong**, denotes an unlucky accident; a mishap; an instance of bad luck.

Mischief, from *mis-*, **bad**, **wrong** + *chever*, **end**, **head**, **come to a head**, means harm, damage, or injury, or annoyance.

Verbiage, from Old French *verbier*, **to speak**, **chatter**, and ultimately from Latin *verbum*, **word**, is an excess of words beyond those needed to express concisely what is meant; **wordiness**, **prolixity**; also, style of expression; **diction**, or manner of speaking. See *diction*, p. 66, under **Clavis**.

Votary, from *vovere*, **to vow**, is one who is devoted, given, or addicted to some particular pursuit, subject, study, or way of life; a devoted admirer; a devout adherent of a religion or cult; a dedicated believer or advocate.

A Latin term: *rara avis*, **rare** (or, **strange**) **bird**; an unusual person or thing. The plural is *rarae aves*.

mort	mortal	mortalism	mortality	mortgage
mortician	mortify	mortuary	amortize	antemortem
mortmain	immortelle	immortalize	immortal	postmortem

Common element_____Inferred Meaning_____

Romance Cognates	French	Romanian	Italian	Portuguese	Spanish
	mort	moarte	morte	morte	muerte

Words with disguised Latin roots: murder, murrain, morbid, moribund

Placenames: Buttes des Mortes, WI; Muertos Cay, Bahamas; Salar de Hombre Muerto, Argentina (also on p. 93)

Latin phrases: *rigor mortis, in articulo mortis; ante mortem; mortis causa; post mortem*
Dulce et decorum est pro patria mori: **Sweet and fitting it is to die for one's country.** Horace, *Odes*, 3, 2, 13.
Genus est mortis male vivere: **To live evilly** (or, **an evil life**) **is a kind of death.** Ovid

French phrase: *à la mort*: **to the death**; hence, very ill, melancholy.

Spanish sayings: *Cosa mala nunca muere*: **A bad thing never dies.** *Come se vive, se muere*: **As one lives, one dies.**

Greek *nekros*, **dead body**: **necr**osis, **necr**opsy; **necr**obiosis, **necr**olatry (**worship of the dead**; see p. 62 for other *–latry* words), **necr**ology, **necr**omancy, **necr**ophagia, **necr**ophilia, **necr**ophobia, **necr**opolis, **necr**otomy; inter**nec**ine (see **Clavis**) and per**nic**ious (**fatal, deadly**), the latter two being from Latin *necare*, **to kill**.

Greek: *nectar*, **drink of the gods**, and *ambrosia*, **food of the gods**, both assured the gods' immortality; also *thanatos*, **death**, as in **Thanatos** (*death* personified as a god; identified with Latin *Mors* (see **Word Cluster**, above), eu**than**asia, and William Cullen Bryant's poem "**Thanat**opsis," **a view of death**. See more on *nectar*, p. 194.

NB: *Morgue,* a place where the bodies of unknown dead persons are examined and identified, initially was the identification room of a prison. By association with the dead, *morgue* has come to apply to a collection of "dead news," e.g., back issues, photographs, clippings of newspapers, magazines, etc.

wordextras

Façade is from Italian *faccia*, **face**. Basically the "face" or front of anything, *façade* connotes a false or superficial appearance, as "He gave a *façade* of warmth, but inside he was a caldron of hate." Pronounced: fuh SAHD.

Dearth, from Old English *deore*, **high-priced**, originally meant costly, precious, or *dear*, which itself is from the same base. Consequently, *dearth* has come to mean "an inadequate supply of something"; also scarcity of food; famine; any scarcity or lack, as *a dearth of knowledge*, or *a dearth of joy*. Pronounced: durth. See *glut*, p. 115.

Hindi *mahout* is from Sanskrit *mahamatra*, **great in measure**, hence, **high officer**; in India and the East Indies, a *mahout* is an elephant driver or keeper. *Mahout* shares its root with *mahatma*, as in Mahatma Gandhi (1869-1948); assassinated; see p. 148. Pronounced: muh HOUT.

Copious, **abundant, plentiful**, is from *co-*, **together** + *ops*, **riches**. *Copy* and *cornucopia* are from the same elements.

Mormon, as explained by Joseph Smith, the founder of the Latter Day Saints, is *more mon*, **more good**. The headquarters of the Mormons is in Salt Lake City, Utah.

Hosanna, from Hebrew *hoshrah nna*, **save, we pray**, is an exclamation used to give praise to God.

Platitude, from Greek *platys-*, **flat**, and formed in the manner of *latitude* and *rectitude*, means a flat, dull, or commonplace quality, as in speech or writing; a commonplace or trite remark; a bromide; cliché; truism.

Some French Expressions

au courant: **with the current**; **up to date**, well-informed [pronounced: oh koo RAHN].
cause célèbre: **celebrated** (or, **famous**) **case**, either a case in law arousing considerable attention; or an incident or situation attracting much attention. Pronounced: kawz say LEH br.
noblesse oblige: **nobility obliges**; the principle that persons of high rank or social position are obliged to act nobly, as for kings and nobles to fight at the head of their troops. Many landlords often lack *noblesse oblige* in maintaining apartments for lease in depressed parts of the city. Pronounced: noh BLES oh BLEZH.

Common element base: mortis   **Meaning**: death

IE base: *mer-²*: **to rub away, harm**; yields **Old English** *mare*, thus *nightmare* (see p. 54, under *incubus*)

German: *Tod*, **death**, as in *Todesstrafe*, **capital punishment**; *sterben*, **to die**

Clavis

mortal:
: as an adjective, that must eventually **die**, as *all mortal beings*; of this world; of **death**; causing death, as *mortal wounds*; not to be pacified, as *a mortal enemy*; very intense; grievous, as *mortal terror*.

mortal sin:
: in Roman Catholic theology, sin that causes **death** of the soul, as opposed to *venial sins*, or those that can be forgiven, overlooked, excusable. *Mortal sins* can also be forgiven in the rite of confession, whereby the soul is restored to life. *Venia*: **grace, favor, forgiveness**.

mortalism:
: the doctrine that the soul is earthly, **dying** with the **mortal** body; the body and soul would then be resurrected together.

mortmain:
: literally, **dead hand**; directly from Middle English *morte-maine*; earlier, Old French *mortemain*; from Latin *mori*, **to die** + *manus*, **hand**. A transfer of real estate to a corporate body, such as a school, church, or charitable organization, for perpetual ownership; also, such property. See more on p. 126.

mortgage:
: Middle English *gage*, **pledge**; **dead pledge**; in *law*, a conditional assignment of property to a creditor as security for a loan. *Gage*, as in *engage*, shares its IE root, *wadh-¹*, with *wed, wage, wager*, and French *dégagé*: free and easy or unconstrained in manner or attitude; also, uncommitted, uninvolved, detached. Pronunciation of *dégagé*: DAY gah ZHAY.

immortelle:
: French: feminine form of *immortel*, **immortal, everlasting**; also designates any of various plants, whose blossoms keep their color and shape when dried, such as the strawflower, bittersweet, pussy toes; these plants are also called *everlastings*.

moribund:
: from Latin *moribundus*, **dying**; coming to an end; having little or no vital force left, as *a moribund cause*; *moribund customs*; *a moribund way of life*. Pronunciation: MÔR ih BUND; ô, as in *torn*.

thanatopsis:
: from Greek *thanatos*, **death** + *opsis*, **view of**; a term coined by William Cullen Bryant (1794-1878) for the title of his long poem that reflects his view on death. Written when the poet was only 17 years old, the poem remained largely unchanged until a few years before his death, when he added the final stanza, which begins with the well-known line: "So live, that when thy summons comes. . . ." Another poem that reflects his view of nature and death is "Ode to a Waterfowl."

internecine:
: *inter-*, **between**; **mutually destructive or harmful**, as *internecine warfare*; also, of or involving conflict within a group, although "within" is usually designated by *intra-*, as *an <u>intra</u>state highway* as opposed to *an <u>inter</u>state highway*. See p. 100, comments on *inter-* and *intra-*, top of page.

De mortuis nil nisi bonum: **About the dead, nothing except good**. The Greek form of this saying is probably from Diogenes (of Sinope), the Greek philosopher noted for founding the Cynical school of philosophy. See *Cynics*, p. 28.

Ave Caesar, morituri te salutant: **Hail Caesar, those who are about to die, salute thee**; spoken by the gladiators. *Gladius*, **sword**, is also in the name of a flower, *gladiolus*, with **sword**-shaped leaves; as a medical term, *gladiolus* names the central part of the sternum, or breastbone, which is also **sword**-shaped. The plural of *gladiolus* is either *gladioluses* or *gladioli*. See p. 3 for *ensiform* and *xiphoid*, both of which mean **sword**-shaped.

wordextras

Planet, from Greek *planen*, **to lead astray, wander**, meant originally those heavenly bodies with apparent motion, as distinguished from the fixed stars. A related word is *aplanatic*, **not wandering**, and describes optical systems that correct for spherical aberration of oblique rays of light passing through a lens. A *planetarium* is a complex revolving projector used to simulate the sun, moon, planets, and stars on the inside of a large dome.

Anglo-Saxon ***gainsay***, **to say against**, is to **contradict, deny, oppose, forbid**. See more on pp. 31, 46.

Aphorism, from Greek *apo-*, **away** + *horizein*, **to divide, to mark off**, is a concise statement of principle; or a short, pointed sentence expressing a wise or clever observation or a general truth. SYNONYMS: adage, epigram, proverb, saw, saying. *Aphorism* and *horizon* are related etymologically. [*Aphorisms* are listed throughout this book.]

Caret is the third-person singular of *carere*, **to lack**; therefore, **it is lacking**. A *caret* is indicated by the sign (^), and is used in writing or in correcting proof, to show where something should be inserted. See p. 133 for *car<u>a</u>t*.

nation(al)	natal	antenatal	innate
natural	postnatal	nature	agnate
naturalize	prenatal	native	enate
naturalism	neonatal	nativity	cognate

Common elements_____**Inferred Meaning**_____

Romance Cognates	French	Romanian	Italian	Portuguese	Spanish
	naissance	naste	nascita	nascimento	nacimiento

Words with disguised Latin roots: naïve, naïveté, nascent, renascent, née, puny:puisne; eigne, naïf (also, naïve); Noel; naissance, Renaissance, pregnant (one meaning), impregnate

Spanish phrases: *la navidad*, **birthdate**, as in *Feliz Navidad*, **Happy**, or **Merry Christmas**; compare *la navidad* with *el cumpleaños*, **accumulated years**; **one's birthday** [*el* is used instead of *los* when referring to *a* birthday]

Placenames: Natural Bridge, Virginia; Natural Steps, Arkansas; Natal, South Africa; Isla de Natividad, Mexico

Latin phrases: *Poeta nascitur, non fit*: **A poet is born, not made.**
Deficit omne quod nascitur: **Everything which is born passes away.** Quintilian
Naturam expellas furca, tamen usque recurret. **You may drive out Nature with a pitchfork, but she always comes back.** Horace

Spanish phrases: *Ninguno nace maestro*: **No one is born an expert.**
El hijo del tigre nace rayado: **The son of the tiger is born with stripes.**
(Similar to English expression: *Apples don't fall far from the tree*, e.g., Sons are very much like their fathers.)

Explore *naturalism* of William Wordsworth (1770-1850) and other Romantic writers; also research *nature* as a literary term. Explore the concept of *nature* in Thoreau's *Walden*.

Words from IE base: *gen-*, **birth**: **gen**der, **gen**e; **gen**eral, **gen**erate, **gen**eration, **gen**eric, **gen**erous; **gen**esis, **gen**etic(s), **gen**ital(s), **gen**ius; **gen**re, **gen**teel, **gen**uine; acro**gen**, anti**gen**, nitro**gen**, oxy**gen**; con**gen**ial; con**gen**ital; en**gen**der, trans**gen**der; allo**gen**eic, auto**gen**eic, iso**gen**eic; allo**gen**ic; eu**gen**ics; misce**gen**ation; andro**gen**y, bio**gen**y, cyto**gen**y, embryo**gen**y, pro**gen**y; hetero**gen**eous, homo**gen**eous; in**gen**ious; in**gen**uous; andro**gen**ous, ero**gen**ous, igni**gen**ous, terri**gen**ous; eu**gen**ism, mono**gen**ism, poly**gen**ism; deutero**gen**esis, syn**gen**esis. See *gentrify*, p. 159.

German phrase: *Auch ich war in Arkadia geboren*. Schiller. **I too was born in Arcadia**, i.e., I too have aspirations to the ideal.

---

wordextras

Era (plural), originally, **counters for calculating**, or **items of account**, has come to mean a basis for calculating or reckoning time by numbering the years from some important occurrence or given point of time, such as *the Christian era*, *the Napoleonic era*, the *Colonial era of American history*, *the Reconstruction Era*.

In ancient Rome, ***proscribe***, from *proscribere*, **to write before**, was the action of publishing the name of a person condemned to death or banishment, with the property of the condemned forfeited to the state. In present-day usage, to denounce or forbid the practice, use, etc., of; to interdict; to deprive of the protection of the law; to outlaw.

French ***ennui*** expresses weariness and dissatisfaction from inactivity or lack of interest; boredom. *Ennui* comes from the same base as *annoy*; note the similarity of spelling of *ennui* with the Middle French spelling of *annoy*: *enuier*. See more on *annoy*, p. 96, under **Clavis**. Pronounced: AWN wee.

Gauche, from Middle French *gauchir*, **to become crooked**, **warped**, means **awkward**, **tactless**, **lacking grace**, especially social grace; as in "I was offended by Tom's *gauche* remarks." Pronounced: gohsh. The noun is *gaucherie*.

Carat, from Greek *keration*, **little horn**, **carob seed**, is a unit of weight for precious stones and pearls. See p. 132 for *car̲e̲t*. See **wordbuilder #59**, p. 189.

Plantain, from Latin *planta*, **sole of the foot**, is a genus of plants; so called from the shape of the leaves. Another *plantain*, **plane tree**, is a banana plant yielding a coarse *fruit* eaten as a cooked *vegetable*; the latter *plantain* also refers to the fruit itself. In Spanish *plantain* is *plátano* and is probably misused for Carib *balatana*.

Common element base: natus   **Meaning**: birth, to be born

IE base: *gen-²*-: **birth**; yields **Old English** *kin*, *king*, *kind*, *kindergarten* (see p. 25); Greek *gonos*, as in **gon**ad, **gono**phore, arche**gonium**, carpe**gonium**, epi**gon**e, hetero**gony**, iso**gony**, cosmo**gony**, theo**gony**.

Clavis

Natal:
: province in South Africa; discovered by Vasco da Gama, Portuguese explorer, on Christmas Day, 1497; consequently named *Terra Natalis*, **Birth** (of Christ) **Land**.

nativism:
: favoritism toward **natives** rather than *immigrants*; favoring revival of an indigenous culture as opposed to that of acculturation; in *philosophy*, the doctrine of *innate* ideas.

nativity:
: capitalized, **the birth of Christ**; usually represented by a tableau (plural, tableaux) and occasionally by a *tableau vivant*, or a tableau with living creatures, both people and animals.

cognate:
: *co-*, **with** + *gnatus*, an older form of *nasci*, **to be born**; having the same ancestor(s); in *linguistics*, derived from a common original form, e.g., Russian *brat*, German *Brüder*, Latin *frater*, and English *brother* are cognates. English, German, Greek, Irish, Latin, Russian, Sanskrit, and Swedish are examples of cognate languages; they, as well as many others, belong to the preliterate Indo-European family. See *brat*, p. 12. *Sanskrit* is distinguished from *Prakrit*, the spoken language.

neonate:
: Greek *neos*, **new**; **a newly born individual**, especially an infant during the first month of life. A physician who specializes in the care of neonates is a *neonatologist*, NEE oh nah TAWL uh jist.

prenatal:
: *pre-*, **before**; **before birth**, or during pregnancy, as *prenatal health care*.

pregnant:
: *pre-*, **before** + Old Latin *gnesci*, **heavy with young**; can also mean **creative**, **inventive**, **replete**, as *pregnant*, or *nascent*, ideas.

naïve:
: French; also *naïf*; simple and credulous as though a child just **born**, e.g., *a naïve remark*, or *action*. SYNONYMS: artless, ingenuous, natural, unsophisticated. *Naïve* is the French cognate of Latin *native*. The noun form is *naïveté*, pronounced nah eve TAY; state of being naïve; unspoiled freshness.

née:
: French; from *naître*, **to be born**; pronounced originally NAY; now, often NEE; **name at birth**; mainly on legal documents and in marriage announcements; e.g., Mrs. Robert Jones, née Mary Smith.

Renaissance:
: also *Renascence*; from Middle French *renaistre*, **to be born again**; the intellectual and artistic movement beginning in 14ᵗʰ-century Florence (Italy) and extending throughout Europe by the 17ᵗʰ century; often regarded as a bridge or transition between medieval and modern times.

puny:
: of inferior size, strength, or importance; spelled *puisny* in Shakespeare's *As You Like It*; from Old French *puisné*, for *post natus*, **born after**, i.e., **younger**; therefore, **weaker**; often describes a runt.

gender:
: from Latin *genus*; then Middle French *gendre*, *genre*; the category at **birth**, or creation, that is, masculine, feminine, neuter (**not either**); consequently, **sort**, **kind**. *Genre*, a category of art or literature, is distinguished by a definite style, form, or content. Pronounced: ZHAHN ruh.

genesis:
: the **beginning**, **creation**, or **origin** of anything. Consider *Genesis*, the first book of the Pentateuch, literally, **five books** [the first five books of the Bible], in which the Hebrew account of the creation of the universe as well as the birth of Israel, the Hebrew nation, is set forth.

wordextras

Talisman, from Arabic *tilasm*, **magic figure**, **horoscope**, and ultimately from Greek *telos*, **an end**, is an **amulet**, something thought to bring good luck, keep away evil; anything thought to have magic power; a charm.

Tarmac, short for *tarmacadam*, is a "tarred" airport runway or apron; in Britain, **a paved road**; *macadam* is from the Scottish engineer John L. McAdam (1756-1836), who developed the modern process of paving roads.

Indefatigable (from *in-*, **not** + *defatigare*, **to tire out**) means **that cannot be tired out**; not yielding to fatigue; untiring. The base word is *fatigue*, **to be weary**, and further from *fames*, **hunger**; thus, **famished**.

Fecund is from Latin *fecundus*, **fertile**, which itself is from the IE base that yields *fetus*, **fruitful**; **productive**; **prolific**. Related words are *fecundate*, **to make fertile**; *fecundity*; *infecund*, **not fecund**, **not fertile**; **barren**; and *superfecundation* (see p. 184). Pronunciation of *fecund*: either FEE cund or FECK und; *fecundity*: fee KUN dih ty.

Word Cluster No. 68

nomial	nominal(ism)	nominate	nominee
denomination	denominator	ignominious	innominate
agnomen	cognomen	pronominal	surnomial
nomenclature	nominative	nomen	pronomial
nomenclater	nuncupative	praenomen	misnomer

Common elements_____Inferred Meaning_____

Romance Cognates	French	Romanian	Italian	Portuguese	Spanish
	nom	nume	nome	nome	nombre

Words and phrases with disguised Latin and Germanic roots: noun, pronoun, renown, nickname, namesake, surname; nom de guerre (**war name**; a pseudonym); nom de plume (**pen name**; pseudonym)

Placenames: Nome, Alaska (see **Clavis**; see *Tangent*, p. 186); Nombre de Dios (**Name of God**; **God's Name**), Mexico

Latin phrases: *in nominee Dei; in nomine Patris et Filii, et Spiritus Sancti*
Quid rides? Mutato nomine, de te fibula narratur. **Why do you laugh? Change the name, and the story is told of you.** Horace
Stat magni nominis umbra: **Here stands the shadow of a mighty man.**
Nomina stultorum parietibus haerent: **The names of fools stick to the walls**; similar to "Fools' names and fools' faces are always found in public places."

Explore *innomine* in a music dictionary; *onomatopoeia* in a literary dictionary.

Greek: *onyma*, **name**: acr**onym**, all**onym**, an**onym** (an anonymous person; a pseudonym), an**onym**ity, an**onym**ous, ant**onym**, ep**onym** (a real or mythical person from whose name, the name of a nation, institution, city, etc., is derived, e.g., President Monroe is the *eponym* of *Monrovia*, the capital of Liberia; see p. 114), heter**onym**, hom**onym**, matr**onym**, met**onym**, met**onym**y (see *synecdoche*, p. 77), par**onym**, prot**onym**, pseud**onym**, syn**onym**, taut**onym**; as well as *onom(ato)* as in **onomato**poeia (see **Clavis**), **onoma**stic, par**onom**asia, and ant**onom**asia.

NB: *Binomial* and *monomial* are not in this family; they belong in the same family as Deutero**nom**y, anti**nom**ian, neo**nom**ian, and taxo**nom**y, from *nomos*, **law**. See p. 209, Item 130.

wordextras

Sergeant and *servant* are doublets, both coming from Latin *servus*, originally, **slave**. A *sergeant* "served" his master in battle. Other words from *servus* include *service, servile, servitude, deserve, desert* (one meaning), *dessert*.

Potpourri, any collection of unrelated items, as well as a scented mixture of dried flowers and spices, is from French, where it meant **rotten pot**. Pronounced: POH poo REE.

The Algonquian Indians enriched the English vocabulary with *chinquapin* (a type of chestnut), *pecan* (from Illinois *pakani*, **a hard-shelled nut**), and *persimmon* (**dried fruit**). See pp. 47, 181, for others.

Lugubrious, from *lugere*, **to mourn**, is to be exceedingly mournful, especially in a way that seems exaggerated or ridiculous. Pronunciation: luh GOO bree us, or luh GYOO bree us.

Culminate, **to climax**, **to reach the full limit**, is from *culmen*, **peak**, **summit**; *culminate* is a contraction of *columen*, which yields *column*, a slender, upright structure, and is usually a supporting or ornamental member of a building.

Ewer, from Old French *evier*, **water pitcher**, is ultimately from Latin *aquarium*, originally, **watering place for cattle**. An accessory to a wash basin in former years, a *ewer* is a large water pitcher with a wide mouth.

wordbuilder #52

Greek *rhinos*, **nose**, yields **rhin**itis, **rhin**odynia (*odyne*, **pain**); **rhino**byon (a nasal tampon), **rhino**cele, **rhino**ceros (**nose-horned**), **rhino**laryngology, **rhino**logist (a medical doctor specializing in problems of the nose), **rhino**meter (an instrument for measuring the nose or its cavities), **rhino**pathy, **rhino**pharyngitis, **rhino**plasty, **rhino**rrhea (*rhein*, **to run**; **a runny nose**), **rhino**scope, **rhino**stenosis, **rhino**tomy, **rhino**virus, and otorhino**laryngology.

Motto of the University of Oregon: *Mens agitat molem*: **Mind over the mass.**
Motto of Harvard University: *Veritas Christo et Ecclesiae*: **Truth for Christ and the Church.**

Common element base: nomen   **Meaning**: name
IE base: *nomen-*: **name**: **German**: *Name*, as in *Vorname*, **first name**.

Clavis

nomenclature:	from *nomenclator*; *clator*, **caller**, one who **called names**; originally, a slave who accompanied his master to tell him the names of people he met. Partridge says "a slave whose office it is, in a court of law, to call the names of the clients." Now, **a system of names**; systematic naming in any art or science, or for the parts of a mechanism.
Nome, Alaska:	westernmost city of the United States, farther west than Honolulu; some accounts of the origin of the name indicate that a cartographer wrote *Name?*, which was mistakenly changed to *Nome*. Others say a post office clerk wrote *No Name* (yet attached to the place), later contracted to *Nome*. *Nome* is the terminus of the Iditarod sled dog race (see p. 147), which begins in Anchorage.
misnomer:	Anglo-French *mis-*, **wrong**; **that which misnames**, as in the sentence: *When six-foot Shorty entered the room, we immediately knew that his nickname was a misnomer.*
pronoun:	*pro-*, **for**; **for a noun**; **in place of a noun**. There are several classes of pronouns: demonstrative (**this, that, these, those**), indefinite (**any, anyone**), intensive (**himself**), interrogative (**who**?), personal (**I, he, she, we**), reciprocal (**each other**), reflexive (**himself**), relative (**which, who, that**: introduces a phrase or clause with *related* antecedent in the main, or independent, clause).
surnomial:	*sur-* from *super-*, **over**; **pertaining to one's surname**, that is, the **family name**, or **last name**, as distinguished from a given name; *surname* can also apply to a name or epithet added to a person's given name, e.g., Ivan *the Terrible*, William *the Conqueror*; also, America *the Beautiful*.
nuncupative:	*nun* from *nomen*, **name**, and *cup* from *capere*, **to take**; **to take names**; delivered orally to witnesses rather than written, as *a nuncupative will*. Pronounced: NUN kyoo PATE iv. Compare *by parol*.
nom de guerre:	French: **war name**; a name taken by a French soldier upon entering military service; now, a fictitious name, for example, a cover name for those engaged in clandestine activity.
nom de plume:	French: **feather name**, or **pen name**, from an early practice of writing with quills. Authors often adopt a *nom de plume* for themselves, e.g., *Boz*, Charles Dickens; *Mark Twain*, Samuel Langhorne Clemens; *Elia*, Charles Lamb; *Lewis Carroll*, Charles Lutwidge Dodgson; *O. Henry*, William Sydney Porter; *George Eliot*, Mary Ann Evans; *George Orwell*, Eric Arthur Blair.
nomen novum:	in *biology*, a **new** taxonomic, or classification **name**. *Taxonomy* is *not* related to the common element; rather, the **law** (or, **order**) of arrangement, where *tax-* is also the leading element in *taxidermy*, **the arrangement of skin** (of a dead trophy animal, such as a bear or deer). See more *nom-*, **law**, words, p. 209, Item 130.
nomen nudum:	in *biology*, **naked name**; an invalid taxonomic name. To be valid, scientific classifications must consist of two names, the first, **General**, in uppercase; the second, **specific**, in lowercase, e.g., *Juglans regia*, taxonomically, **Walnut royal**, but grammatically, *royal walnut*; the soft-shelled, or California, walnut. See p. 164 for more on *Juglans regia*.
sine nomine:	**without a name**; Ralph Vaughn-Williams (1872-1958) composed a hymntune for which he could think of no appropriate name; hence, he called it *Sine Nomine*. There is also a **Nameless Creek** in the following states: AK, IN, NY, VA, WY; also, the towns *Nameless*: GA, TN, TX.
onomatopoeia:	*poiein*, **to make**; **to make names**; the formation of words that imitate natural sounds, e.g., *boom, buzz, crack, tinkle; bobwhite, chickadee, cuckoo, killdeer*; in *rhetoric*, the use of imitative and naturally suggestive words for their dramatic effect. Pronounced: ah no MAT o PEE ah.

wordextras

Perpendicular, **hanging straight**, from Latin *per-*, **intensive** + *pendere*, **to hang**, describes those lines at right angles to a given plane or line; apart from mathematics, *perpendicular* means **upright**, **vertical**, **very steep**. See *propensity*, p. 151; also, see p. 210, Item 141, for other words from *pendere*.

Hypotenuse, the longest side of a right triangle, was originally *pleura hypotenusa*, **side stretched under** (the right angle). With the triangle turned so that the *hypotenuse* lies on a plane, it would indeed be true to its literal meaning.

136

Word Cluster No. 69

nonage	**non**appearance	**non**chalant	**non**combatant
noncommissioned	**non**compliance	**non**conformist	**non**descript
nondurable	**non**entity	**non**essential	**non**feasance
nonpareil	**non**plus(ed)	**non**profit	**non**restrictive
nonsectarian	**non**standard	**non**suit	**non**violence

Common element_____Inferred Meaning_____

Romance Cognates: The form of *non-* has remained unchanged in each of the Romance languages.

Word from disguised Latin root: umpire (see **Clavis**)

Short Latin phrases: *non compos mentis; non detinet; non est; non est factum; non est inventus; non liquet; non obstante; non obstante veredicto; non placet; non possumus; non prosequitur; non sequitur; persona non grata; nolens volens; noli me tangere; nolle prosequi; nolo contendere*

Latin phrases translated: *Davus sum, non Oedipus*: **I am Davus, not Oedipus**: I am a plain man and no genius. Terence
Qui timide rogat docet negare: **He who asks timidly courts denial**. Seneca
principiis, non homines: **principles, not men**
nil nisi Cruce: **nothing but by the Cross**; no reward without suffering

Italian music term: *non troppo*: **not too much**, as in *adagio ma non troppo*, **slowly but not too much so**

NB: Do not confuse prefix with root *nonus*, **ninth** (from *novem*, **nine**), which yields ***noon***, from *nona hora*, **ninth hour**. A Roman Catholic office was once held at *nona hora* from sunrise (3 p.m.); the office was later moved to the middle of the day; thus, the middle of day took its designation from the name of the office. See *siesta*, pp. 106, 212.

> **Quote**: Particularly in science and in engineering is it true that the best word must be found. Mere approximation is not only inadmissible, but often worse than useless. It is not sufficient that an engineer's report be so written that it can be understood; it should be so written that it cannot be <u>mis</u>understood. And unquestionably, it is a fact that an inadequate and inaccurate statement is one of the most common and serious handicaps of the average graduate of a technological school. Lewis Buckley Stillwell

wordextras

Clique, probably an imitative word from the sound of clicking or of applause, and from Old French *cliquer*, **to make a noise**, now refers to a small, exclusive group that suggests snobbery. SYNONYMS: circle, coterie, set.

The ***dreadnought***, or ***dreadnaught***, from the *Dreadnaught*, the first of such a class of British battleships built in 1906, later designated any large, heavily armored battleship with many powerful guns. With its firepower, it "dreaded naught." *Dreadnought* also designates a coat made of a thick woolen cloth, as well as the cloth itself.

Vituperate is from Latin *vitium*, **fault** + *parare*, **to prepare**. To *vituperate* is "to find fault with"; to speak abusively to, or about. SYNONYMS: berate, revile, scold, upbraid. **Vituperation**: abusive language; the adjective is *vituperative*.

Quisling, **a traitor**, is from Vidkun Quisling (1887-1945), a Norwegian politician who betrayed his country to the Nazis during World War II and became their puppet head of state. After the war, Norway's Benedict Arnold was tried and executed by a firing squad. Norwegians say they are not proud for having given this word to the world.

Creosote, from Greek *kreas*, **flesh** + *soter*, **to save, preserve**, is obtained by the distillation of wood tar.

Pixilated, **led away by pixies**, means to be mentally confused; daft; whimsical; eccentric; puckish. *Pixilated* was altered from *pixie-led* and originally meant "lost." A *pixie*, or *pixy*, was a fairy, or other tiny supernatural being.

Ewe (pronounced yoo), **a female sheep**, is ultimately from Latin *ovis*, **sheep**; thus, *ovine* pertains to sheep.

A Writing Tip: Be careful to differentiate words with similar sound or spelling but with different forms or meanings: He is a good student; he has a *questionable* mind, but rather a *questioning* mind. Some other words to be careful of include *alley, ally; allusion, elusion, illusion; anecdote, antidote; anesthetic, antiseptic; angel, angle.*

an aphorism: *A crooked stick casts a crooked shadow*. One interpretation: **An evil person does evil things.**

Common element base: non-   **Meaning:** general negative—not

IE base: *ne-*: yields **Old English** *not, naughty, neither* (**not either**), *nothing, hobnob* (from **Middle English** *habben* + *nabben*, **to have and not to have**, originally in reference to "on and off in drinking")

Latin: *ne-, neg-*, as in ***nefarious, negate, neglect, negligent, negotiate; nice*** (see **wordextras**, p. 13), *nisi*.

Greek: *nepenthe* (a drug supposed by the ancient Greeks that induced forgetfulness of sorrow)

Old English prefix *un-*, as in ***uncomfortable, undaunted***; **Latin** *in-*, negative, as in ***inability, inactive, inadequate, inappropriate, incessant, indecent, insolvent***); **Greek:** *a-, an-*, as in ***apolitical, atrophy, anesthesia***.

Clavis

nonplused: **no more**; at a loss for words, as in "I was *nonplused* by his gratuitous remark."

nolle prosequi: abbreviated *nol. pros.*, **to be unwilling to prosecute**: said by the prosecutor in a criminal case; similar notice by the plaintiff in a civil suit. Pronunciation: NAWL ee PRAHS ih KWIE. See p. 173.

nolo contendere: no abbreviation; **I do not wish to contend**; said by the defendant, in which he will not make a defense, but will not admit guilt. Pronunciation: NOH loh kuhn TEN duh ree.

non liquet: **It is not clear**, abbreviated *N.L.*, a designation by one of the judges in a Roman court to indicate his opinion for not pronouncing a verdict.

noli me tangere: **Touch me not**; a warning against touching or interference; so called from Christ's warning to Mary Magdalene, from John 20:17 in the Vulgate Bible; in modern versions, "Touch me not, for I am not yet ascended to my Father. . . ."; also, the *touch-me-not*, a plant whose seed pods burst with the slightest touch. More information on *noli me tangere* in the *tang-* family; see p. 186.

non sequitur: abbreviated *non seq.*, **it does not follow**; in *logic*, a conclusion that does not follow from the basic premises; any irrelevant remark. See p. 174 under **Clavis**. Pronunciation: nahn SEK wih toor.

ne plus ultra: **no more beyond**, probably from "(Sail) no more beyond (this point)," allegedly inscribed on the Pillar of Hercules as a warning to seamen; now, **the highest point of perfection**. See p. 198.

umpire: in Middle English, *oumpere*; altered by faulty separation of *a noumpire*; in Middle French, *nomper*, **uneven**; **not on par** (with either side or team); hence, **an uneven number**; third person to render a decision in a dispute; a judge; an arbiter. As a *verb*, to serve as an umpire.

Non compos mentis: **not in a composed mind**; not having mastery of one's mind; insane. *Black's Law Dictionary* says this is a general term, embracing all varieties of mental derangements. *Insanity* is a legal, not a medical, term; the medical equivalent is *mental illness* or *psychosis*. *Black's* defines many of the other Latin phrases listed on the previous page.

wordextras

Suspicion in French is *soupçon* (pronounced soop SOHn, or SOOP sohn): **conjecture, hint, touch, trace**. Both words, as well as *suspect*, are from Latin *suspicere*, **to look from below**. See p. 212, Item 171, for *specere*, **to see**.

Imbroglio, Italian for *embroil*, is most often used to indicate a confused understanding or disagreement, especially, one of a bitter nature; also, a confused heap. Pronounced: im BROHL yoh.

Rococo, from French *rocaille*, **rock work**, is a style of art developed from the Baroque period that originated in France about 1720 and soon spread throughout Europe. As an adjective, in *architecture*, characterized by elaborate, profuse designs intended to produce a delicate effect; also describes that which is profuse, overdone, florid, and tasteless. The term is applied to music and literature as well. Pronounced: ruh KOE koe; occasionally, roh kuh KOE.

Parsimonious, from the noun *parsimony*, is based on Latin *parcere*, **to spare**. SYNONYMS: close, miserly, penurious, stingy. The ending *–ous* is an adjective-forming suffix, e.g., *atrocious* is the adjectival form of the noun *atrocity*.

Querulous, from Latin *queri*, **to complain**, means "inclined to find fault; complaining; full of complaint; peevish." From the same verb is *quarrel*, the nominal synonyms of which are *altercation, spat, squabble, wrangle*.

Quorum, genitive plural of *qui*, **who**, denotes the minimum number of members required at an assembly or meeting before business can be validly transacted.

Massif, French for "solid, massive" is a geological term for a mountainous mass broken up into separate peaks and forming the backbone of a mountain range. It also refers to a large block of the earth's crust that is isolated by boundary faults and has shifted as a unit. Pronounced: mah SEFE; MAH SEFE; MASS if. Take your pick!

138

Word Cluster No. 70

obbligato	obcordate	obdurate	obese	obey
obfuscate	obit	obituary	object	objective
objurgate	oblate	oblige	oblique	obliterate
oblivion	oblong	obloquy	obnoxious	obrogate
obscene	obscure	obsequious	observe	obsolescent
obsolete	obstacle	obsess	obstetrics	obstinate
obstipation	obstreperous	obstruct	obtrude	obtund
obverse	obviate	obvious	obconic	obligate

occident	occiput	occlude	occult	occupant	occupy
occur	occurrence	offend	offense	offensive	offer
offertory	office	official	officious	opportune	oppose
opposite	oppression	opprobrium	oppugn	opponent	oppress

Common elements_____**Inferred Meaning**_____

Romance Cognates: There have been some assimilations and other modifications in the Romance languages, e.g., in Italian, *object* is *oggetto*, *obstruct* is *ostruire*, and *obscene* is *osceno*.

Romance words and phrases: *objet d'art; objet trouvé; noblesse oblige* (see p. 131)

Placenames: Oblong, Illinois (the village advertises itself as "Only Oblong"); Obstrucción, Chile

Latin phrases: *obiter dictum; obit sine prole* (see **Clavis**)

Greek *epi-*, **upon, over:** ep**ode** (see p. 109), ep**onym**, ep**oxy**; epi**benthos**, epi**blast**, epi**boly**, epi**calyx**, epi**canthus**, epi**cardium**, epi**cedium**, epi**cene**, epi**center**, epi**cotyl**, epi**cranium**, epi**critic**, epi**cycle**, epi**deictic**, epi**demic**, epi**dendrum**, epi**dermis**, epi**didymis**, epi**dote**, epi**dural**, epi**fauna**, epi**focal**, epi**gastric**, epi**geal**, epi**gene**, epi**genesis**, epi**glottis**, epi**gone**, epi**gram**, epi**graph**, epi**gynous**, epi**lepsy**, epi**limnion**, epi**logue**, epi**mere**, epi**mysium**, Epi**phany**, epi**physis**, epi**phyte**, epi**scia**, epi**stasis**, epi**stle**, epi**taxis**, epi**taph**, epi**taxy**, epi**thet**, epi**tome**, epi**zoic**.

NB: *Obelisk, oboe,* and *obolus* are not in this family. See p. 4 for *oboe*.

Quote: Life and language are alike sacred. Homicide and verbicide — that is, violent treatment of a word with fatal results to its legitimate meaning — are alike forbidden. Oliver Wendell Holmes

wordextras

Reticent, **tending to be silent**, is from Latin *re-*, **again** + *tacere*, **to be silent**. SYNONYMS: reserved, secretive, silent. Other words from *tacere*: *tacet*; *tacit* and *taciturn* are synonyms of *reticent*. Pronunciation: RET uh sunt.

Propitiate (verb) and ***propitious*** (adjective) are from Latin *pro-*, **before, forward** + *petere*, **to seek**. *Propitiate*: to cause to become favorably inclined or disposed, as "to propitiate the gods." In *Christian theology*, Jesus became the *propitiation* for man's sin. SYNONYMS of *propitious*: auspicious, favorable. See pp. 36, 86, for more *pet-* words.

Cicatrix, also *cicatrice*, **a scar**, designates the contracted fibrous tissue at the place where a wound has healed; in *botany*, the scar left on a stem where a branch, leaf, etc. was once attached. Plural: cicatrices, or cicatrixes.

Bismarck, capital of North Dakota, is named after *Prince Otto von Bismarck*, Prussian chancellor of the German Empire (1871-1890), in recognition of financial aid to the local railroad by German investors.

wordbuilder #53

Greek *lithos*, **stone**, yields **lith**ic, **lith**ium (symbol: Li); **lith**agogue, **lith**arge (symbol: PbO); **litho**graphy, **litho**logy (the scientific study of rocks, usually with the unaided eye or with little magnification; loosely, the structure and composition of a rock formation); acro**lith**; mono**lith**ic, Neo**lith**ic. Compare with Latin *calx* as in **calc**ine, **calc**ium, **calc**ulus, **calc**ulate; **calc**ify (*-fy* from *facere*, **to make**). In addition, see p. 210, Item 143, for *petra* and *lapis*.

Words are as beautiful as horses, and sometimes as difficult to corral.
Used by permission of Ted Berkman, biographer and screenwriter.

Common element base: ob-　　　　　　　　**Meaning**: over, upon, against; down, toward; also, intensifier
In modern scientific and technical words, **inversely**, as in *obovate*, **inversely ovate**, as some leaf shapes.
IE base: *epi-*: **upon**, as in words listed on previous page.
Ob- assimilates to *oc-*, *of-*, and *op-* to correspond to the first letter of the root, e.g., <u>oc</u>cur, <u>of</u>fer, <u>op</u>pose; is truncated before *m*, as in <u>o</u>mission and <u>o</u>mit, the only words so formed.

Clavis

obey:　　　　from *audire*, **to hear**; to listen to; to heed. See p. 14, under **Clavis**, for more on *obey*.

obit:　　　　*it-* from *ire*, **to go**; **to die**, **expire**; a death notice, usually with a short biography of the deceased. Same as *obituary*.

obit sine prole:　a law term; **He died without issue**, or without fathering, or begetting, any children.

obfuscate:　　*fuscare*, **to obscure**; **to darken**; to cloud over; make dark or unclear; to muddle; confuse; bewilder. See p. 46 for an example of using *obfuscate*, under **An exalted aphorism**.

objurgate:　　*jurgare*, **to chide**, **chastise**; originally, **to sue at law**; to chide vehemently; upbraid sharply; rebuke; berate. The judge *objurgated* the accused before sentencing him to life in prison.

obstetrics:　　*stare*, **to stand**; **to stand over** (in delivery). Compare ***midwife***: Anglo-Saxon *mid*, **with + woman**. The practice of a midwife is called *midwifery*. Pronunciation: mid WIF ery, not mid WIFE ery.

obstinate:　　from *obstinare*, **to stand against**; **standing against**; thus, stubborn, mulish; difficult to manage, e.g., *an obstinate child; an obstinate headache; an obstinate fever*.

obbligato:　　*ligare*, **to bind**; **to bind to**; in *music*, originally, an added essential melody; now a part that can be omitted, e.g., a piano solo with *an oboe or violin obbligato* is complete without the added part. The root can also be found in *ligament, lien, legato*. See *legato*, p. 155.

objet d'art:　French; **art object**; a small object of artistic value; **bibelot, curio, trinket**. See p. 101.

obverse:　　*vertere*, **to turn**; **to turn toward**; as an adjective, facing or turned toward the observer; thus the face side of a coin; in *botany*, narrower at the base than at the top, as *an obverse leaf*. Also, a noun.

obtrude:　　*trudere*, **to thrust**; **to thrust forward**; push out; eject; to offer or force oneself or one's opinions upon others unasked or unwanted. See p. 213, Item 179, for other words from *trudere*, e.g., *extrude*.

obviate:　　*via-*, **way**; the same elements as *obvious*: literally, **in the way**; thus, easy to understand; plain, evident; as a *verb*, to do away with or prevent by effective measures; make unnecessary: "The need for a jury trial was *obviated* by the defendant's guilty plea."

opprobrium:　　*probrum*, **infamy**; **a reproach against**; disgrace inherent in or arising from shameful conduct; a cause of shame or disgrace. Synonyms: degradation, discredit, dishonor, disrepute, ignominy, infamy, obloquy, odium, scandal. Pronounced: uh PROH bree um. The adjective is *opprobrious*.

epicardium:　　Greek *epi-*, **over**, **above**; **over the heart**; the inner serous (watery) layer of the pericardium; the membranous sac enclosing, and lying directly upon, the heart. See p. 47.

epididymis:　　Greek *didymoi*, **double**, **two**, but means **testicles**. The *epididymis*, literally, **upon the testicles**, is a long, oval-shaped structure attached to the rear upper surface of each testicle; it begins the *vas deferens* (literally, the vessel that "brings down"), the highly convoluted duct that conveys sperm from the testicles to the ejaculatory duct (the urethra) of the penis.

epibenthos:　　Greek *benthos*, **depth of the sea**; the animals and plants living at a depth of 100 fathoms, or 600 feet.

Epiphany:　　Greek *epi-*, **upon**; literally, **a showing upon**; a Christian festival on January 6 in celebration of the manifestation of the divine nature of Christ to the Gentiles. *Epiphany* completes the twelve days of Christmas; often called "twelfth day." Other meanings.

wordextra
French *cul-de-sac*, **bottom of the bag**, has come to mean a **dead end** or a **blind alley**; also, a situation from which there is no escape. **Placenames**: Culdesac, ID; Cul de Sac, St. Martin; Plaine du Cul-de-Sac, Haiti. Note variations of spellings. When used as an adjective, e.g., *dead-end street*, **dead end** is hyphenated.

Sectional Word Cluster Test

INSTRUCTIONS: For each set of words from Latin and Greek (and sometimes, French, Spanish, and German), write the common meaning in the blank.

Example: **hypo**tenuse, **hypo**thesis, **sub**ject   <u>under</u>

	Presection Answer	Postsection Answer

71. bin**ocul**ars, in**ocul**ate, syn**opsis**, "Thanat**opsis**"   _____   _____

72. **omni**vorous, **omni**potent, **pan**creas, **pan**acea   _____   _____

73. **ora**tory, per**ora**tion, ad**ore**, inex**orab**le   _____   _____

74. **paci**fic, **paci**fist, **Paci**fic Ocean   _____   _____

75. **part**ner, **part**ition, **part**iciple, **pars**e   _____   _____

76. **ped**estal, im**ped**ance, deca**pod**, octo**pus**   _____   _____

77. **plur**al, ne **plus** ultra, **plu**perfect, non**plus**ed   _____   _____

78. **port**able, trans**port**, rap**port**, circum**fer**ence   _____   _____

79. **post**erior, **post**lude, **post**script (P.S.)   _____   _____

80. **prim**eval, **prin**ciple, **prin**cipal, **primo**geniture   _____   _____

_____   _____
Presection Score   Postsection Score

Note: Enter scores for this test and the following ones after completing this section; then, enter them on p. xvii.

Sectional Wordbuilder Test

Throughout the book and as a supplement, there are wordbuilders; these wordbuilders are designed to help you build a family of words from a single root.

	Presection Answer	Postsection Answer
54. What is the meaning of *grad-, gress-* as in **grad**uate, pro**gress**?	_____	_____
55. What is the meaning of *caco-* as in **caco**phony, **caco**genics?	_____	_____

	_____	_____
	Presection Score	Postsection Score

After entering the scores here, enter them on pp. xviii.

```
┌─────────────────────────────────────────────────────────────────────────┐
│                         Word Cluster No. 71                                │
│                                                                            │
│  ocular           ocularium         oculate          ocellus              │
│  oculus           binoculars        inoculate        ocellate             │
│  oculomotor*      monocle           oculist          oculogyric*          │
│              *There are many other medical words beginning with oculo-.   │
│                                                                            │
│  Common elements_____Inferred Meaning_____  │
└─────────────────────────────────────────────────────────────────────────┘
```

Romance Cognates	French	Romanian	Italian	Portuguese	Spanish
	oeil	ochi	occhio	ôlho	ojo

Words with disguised Latin root: antlers (see p. 10), atrocious, inveigle, pinochle, ullage (an interesting word!)

French words: oeillade (an amorous or flirting glance; ogle), oeil-de-boeuf (**eye of an ox**; a round or oval window)

Placenames: Ojo Amarillo (**Yellow Eye**); Ojo Caliente (**Hot Eye**); Ojo Feliz (**Happy Eye**) [all in New Mexico]; Ojos Azules (**Blue Eyes**); Ojo Agua (**Water Eye**) [both in Mexico]

Greek cognates: *ops*: Cycl**ops**, Pel**ops**; my**opia**, nyctal**opia**, scot**opia**; aut**opsy**, rhod**opsin**, syn**opsis**; met**ope**
opto: **opt**ic, **opt**ical, **opt**ician; **opto**metry; pan**optic**, syn**optic**, Syn**optic** Gospels; di**opt**er, di**opto**meter
ophthalmos: **ophthalm**ia, **ophthalm**ic, **ophthalm**ology, **ophthalmo**scope; ex**ophthalmos**; xer**ophthalm**ia
ommato: **ommat**eum (a compound eye, as of insects and crustaceans), **ommat**idium, **ommato**phobia, **ommato**phore

German: *Auge* as in *Augensprossen*, **eye sprouts**; see *antlers*, p. 10; *augenblicklich*, **in a wink**; immediately; *aus den Augen, aus dem Sinn*: **out of sight, out of mind**.

Germanic: daisy, **day's eye**; window (see **Clavis**); ogle, **to keep looking at**; **to make eyes at** (see *oeillade*, above)

wordextras

American Spanish *vamoose*, **to leave quickly**, is from Spanish *vamos*, **let us go**.

Iceberg, from Dutch *ijsberg*, is **ice mountain**. Only about a tenth of an iceberg, however, is above water.

Belfry, from Frankish *bergfrid*, **movable war tower**, originally had nothing to do with bells or bats. Its original meaning was **peace protector**, and was a tower used much like the legendary Trojan Horse.

In Greek drama, a *hypocrite* was an *actor*, or "one who played a part," but has come to mean one who pretends to be what he or she is not, especially one who pretends to be better than one really is. The element *hypo-* means "under"; *crite* is from *krinein*, **to separate, to discern**. Thus, *hypocrites* interpreted the parts they played, being benefited by masks to aid the viewers in identifying the actors' roles. In Greek drama, as today, actors often played multiple roles. *I dare swear he is no hypocrite, but prays from his heart.* Shakespeare

Sushi, Japanese for **raw seafood**, is rolls of seaweed-wrapped rice containing plain strips of raw seafood, raw fish, especially eels, as well as pickled vegetables, eggs, and the like.

Bane, from Old English *bana*, **murderer**, means **cause of death**, **ruin**, or **harm**, as in "Poachers are the *bane* of the rhinoceros." Also, a source of persistent annoyance or exasperation, as bumper-to-bumper traffic is the *bane* of metropolitan commuters. [The plural of *rhinoceros* can be either the same as the singular, or *rhinoceroses*.]

Profiterole is a small cream puff. While the base is French *profit*, there seems to be no rationale for the connection, other than *to profit* from selling it. Pronounced pruh FIT uh ROLE.

Handsome has not always been used only to describe a man who is good-looking. In Middle English, *handsom* meant "easily handled, handy, convenient." In addition to describing attractiveness that is *dignified* and *impressive* as opposed to *delicate* and *graceful*, as *a handsome man* or *woman*, it can also mean "large, impressive, considerable," as *a handsome house, a handsome raise, to win by a handsome margin*; "appropriate, fitting, seemly, proper, gracious," as *a handsome compliment*." Expresses more than *pretty*; less than *beautiful*.

Valiant, from *valere*, **to be strong**, describes one who is full of, or characterized by, valor; brave; resolute, determined. Other words from *valere* include *valence, valetudinarian, valid, validate, validity, valor, valorous, valuable, valuate, value, valued, valuta, ambivalent, invalid, convalesce, avail, countervail, ad valorem (tax)*.

Pindar (c. 522-438 B.C.), a Greek lyric poet, is particularly remembered for his odes, which have two metric forms: one for the *strophe* and *antistrophe* and another for the *epode*. *Pindaric* describes such odes.

IE base: *okw-*: **to see**, which yields **German** *Auge*, thus **English** *ogle*; **Greek** *ops*. See *window*, **Clavis**.

Clavis

ocular:	**pertaining to the eye**; of, for, or like the **eye**; **by eyesight**, as *an ocular demonstration*; as a *noun*, the lens or lenses constituting the eyepiece of an optical instrument. Many other native English nouns have no corresponding adjective, making it necessary to supply that lack from Latin, e.g., *aural*, ear; *capital*, **head**; *caudal*, **tail**; *filial*, **son**; *fraternal*, **brother**; *guttural*, **throat**; *labial*, **lip**; *manual*, **hand**; *maternal*, **mother**; *oral*, **mouth**; *paternal*, **father**; *pedal*, **foot**; *renal*, **kidney**; *uxorial*, **wife**; *vulnerable*, **wound**.
oculist:	a general term for an ***ophthalmologist***, a medical doctor specializing in diseases of the **eye**; or for an ***optometrist***, a specialist who examines (**measures**) the eyes and prescribes glasses.
binocular:	*bini-*, **double**; **double eyes**. As an adjective, using, or for the use of, **both eyes** at the same time. As a plural noun—*binoculars*—a binocular instrument, such as field glasses or opera glasses.
pinochle:	from French *binocle*; further, from New Latin *binoculus*, **two eyes**; possibly because the game is played with a double deck.
inoculate:	*in-*, **in**; to plant an **eye** (**bud**, **shoot**) **into**; to inject serum into a living body with a hypodermic needle.
inveigle:	from Middle French *aveugler*, **to blind the eye**; further from Latin *aboculus*, **away from the eye**. To lead away by deception; to lure; to entice or trick into doing or giving something; not related to *inveigh*, **to carry in**, or sail into; thus, **to censure**. See p. 156 for more on *inveigh*.
window:	from Old Norse *vindauga*, **eye of the wind**. *Auga* is also part of *Augensprossen*, **eye sprouts**. See p. 10, under *antlers*.
synopsis:	Greek *syn-*, **together** + *opsis*, **a seeing**; a visual image; hence, **a general view**. The adjectival form is *synoptic*. The *Synoptic Gospels* designate the first three books of the New Testament—*Matthew, Mark*, and *Luke*—which correspond closely in detailing the life and resurrection of Jesus. The *Gospel of John*, often referred to as *The Fourth Gospel*, is more theological and reflective than the Synoptics. See more on *Synoptics* under *demoniac*, p. 62.
autopsy:	Greek *autos*, **self**; **a self**-**viewing**; a postmortem examination and possible dissection of a corpse; seeing with one's own eyes, or seeing for oneself the cause of a death not obviously due to natural causes, and usually performed by a coroner; pronounced AW top see, not aw TOP see.
rhodopsin:	Greek *rhodos*, **rose**, **rose**-**red**; a purplish protein pigment, contained in the rods of the retina, necessary for vision in dim light. *Rhodos* is also found in *rhododendron*, **rose tree**, although the flowers may also be white or purple; also called *mountain laurel* (see pp. 46, 89).
nyctalopia:	Greek *nyx*, **night** + *alaos*, **blind**; **night blindness**; vision that is normal in daylight but abnormally weak when the light is dim. Compare *hemeralopia*, **day blindness**. See p. 68, top of page.

wordextras

Baroque, a style of art and architecture characterized by much ornamentation and by curved rather than straight lines, is from Portuguese *barroco*, **imperfect pearl**. In *music*, *baroque* characterizes highly embellished melodies and fugal or contrapuntal forms. See *fugal*, p. 85; *contrapuntal*, p. 46; see also *rococo*, p. 138.

Decamp is **to break or leave camp**; also, to go away suddenly, usually without telling anyone; **run away**; **abscond**. He *decamped* from the reception without expressing his devoirs to the host.

Alfalfa, a Spanish modification of Arabic *al-fasfasah*, means **the best fodder**. Arabic-speaking Moors from North Africa occupied Spain for 700 years, influencing and enriching the Spanish language, as well as the country's customs, architecture, cuisine, and art. See **wordextras**, p. 66, for more on *alfalfa*, under *algebra*.

A Writing Tip: Distinguish between *continual* and *continuous*; *continual* means **repeated regularly and frequently**. *During the monsoon season in the Philippines, it rains continually from September through April. Continuous* means **extended or prolonged without interruption**. *During the monsoon season in the Philippines, it often rains continuously for 24 hours*. In addition, the Amazon, the Black Warrior, the James, the Mississippi, the Nile, the Occoquan, the Potomac, the Rappahannock, the Susquehanna, and the Tombigbee flow *continuously*.

Word Cluster No. 72

omneity	omnibus	omnicorporeal	omnifarious
omnific	omnidirectional	omnificent	omnipotent
omnipresence	omnirange	omniscience	omnivorous

Common element_____Inferred Meaning_____

Romance Cognates: The element remains unchanged in each of the Romance languages.

Latin phrases: *Omnia mutantur nos et mutamur in illis; Non omnis moriar; Ab uno ad omnes omne bonum desuper; omnia vanitas; omnia vincit amor*
Omnium reum principia parva sunt: **The beginnings of all things are small.** Cicero
Omnibus invideas, livide, nemo tibi: **You may envy everybody, envious one, but nobody envies you.**

Motto of the Kappa Delta Rho Fraternity: *Honor Super Omnia*: **Honor above all else.**
Motto of the University of Nebraska: *Litteris dedicata et omnibus artibus*: **Dedicated to letters and all the arts.**
Motto of the states of Oklahoma and Illinois: *Labor omnia vincet*: **Labor conquers all things.**
Motto of the State of Nevada: **All for our Country.**

Greek *pan-*, **all**: **pan**acea, **pan**creas, **pan**demonium, **pan**egyric, **pan**genesis, **pan**gram, **pan**orama (see **Note**), **pan**sophy, **pan**theon, **pan**theist, **Pan**dora, as in *Pandora's box* (see p. 122), and dia**pas**on. Related *pen-* means **almost all**, as in **pen**ultimate and **pen**insula, e.g., *peninsula*, **almost an island**. *Peninsula*, OH, so named because of the topography created by the Cuyahoga River. French *presqu'île* yields *Presque Isle* [also, **almost an island**], a city in Maine. *Presque Isle* is surrounded by water on three sides by Presque Isle Stream and the Aroostook River. Do not confuse the prefix *pan-* with the Romance *pan*, **bread**, as in **pan**try and com**pan**ion (see p. 20 under *biscuit*), or with Anglo-Saxon *pan*, as in *frying pan, saucepan, dishpan*. **Note**: *Panorama* is shortened to *pan* in film and television.

wordextras

Impeccable, **not sinning**, from Latin *im-*, **not** + *pecca*, **sin**, has come to mean **flawless, without blemish or defect**; **faultless**, as one with *impeccable character*. See **Word Cluster No. 48**, p. 95, for other *im*-prefixed words.

Semester, from Latin *cursis semestris*, originally meant a period that "ran" for six months; compare *trimester*, a period of **three months**. See p. 1, **wordbuilder #1** for more words from *currere*, **to run**.

Seminary, from Latin *semen*, **seed**, was once thought of as a place where the **seed of truth** is planted. Although *seminary* is still used to indicate a preparatory school, more often it designates a graduate school where ministers, rabbis, and priests receive professional training in theology and pastoral duties. See *disseminate*, p. 114.

Abeyance, from Anglo-French *abeiance*, **expectation**, is further from Latin *ad-*, **to** + Vulgar Latin *batare*, **to gape, yawn**. *Abeyance* now means **temporary inactivity, state of suspended action**, as in "The judge's decision was held in *abeyance*, pending a report of the psychiatrist." Pronunciation: uh BAY unce.

Assonance, from Latin *ad-*, **to** + *sonare*, **to sound**, means **likeness of sound**. *Assonance* is a partial rhyme in which the stressed vowel sounds are *alike*, but with *unlike* consonant sounds, as in *late* and *make, moaning* and *groaning; meat* and *seat; plead* and *need*. See other words from *sonare*, p. 212, Item 170.

French *demitasse*, **small cup**, comprises *demi-* + *tasse*, **cup**. *Demi-* can mean either **half**, as in *demivolt*, or it can mean **less than usual** in size, power, volume, etc.; thus, *demitasse*. Do not confuse *demi-* in *demitasse* with *demi-* in *demigod* (Greek *demos*, **people**)—a mythological semidivine being—or with French *demijohn*, originally, *dame-jeanne*, **Dame Jeanne**, originally a fanciful name for the shapely bottle of glass or earthenware, with a narrow neck and a wicker casing.

French *moue*, pronounced moo, denotes a **small, pouting grimace** to show distaste or playful impudence, as in *My daughter made a moue when I suggested how to entertain a bat that paid her nocturnal visits. I told her she needed to get a 'bat' attitude.* [actual case of the Virginia author of this book]

Ad lib., an adverb, standing for *ad libitum*, **at liberty**, is a musical direction meaning **at one's pleasure**. Coming from the same source, *ad-lib* (hyphenated), a verb, means **to improvise; extemporize**. *Having lost his notes, the speaker had to ad-lib his comments.* [Using *his* before *speaker* is an example of "a delayed antecedent."]

Lumbricalis, from Latin *lumbricus*, **intestinal worm, earthworm**, designates any of the four small muscles in the palm of the hand and the sole of the foot; so called from the shape of the muscles. Plural: lumbricales.

Common element base: omni-   **Meaning**: all

IE base: *op-¹*: **to work, produce in abundance**; thus, from **Old English** are derived *oft, often*; **Latin** *opus*, **a work**, as in *opus* itself, *opera* (a plural of *opus*; also, *opus̲e̲s̲*), *operate*, *maneuver*, *manure*; *maneuver* and *manure* are doublets; original meaning: **to work by hand**; see p. 126. Also, **Latin** *copia*, **plenty**, as in *cornucopia, copious, copy*.

Clavis

omniety: that which is **all-pervading** or **all-comprehensive**; hence, the Deity. The term is rarely used now.

omnifarious: *fas*, **divine law; lawful, possible**; of all kinds, varieties, forms, as *omnifarious knowledge*; compare *bifarious*, in *botany*, arranged in two rows. Pronunciation: AHM nih FER ee us.

omnific: *facere*, **to make**; creating all things; *omnificent*: unlimited in creative power. See p. 61 for *facere*.

omniscient: *scire*, **to know**; having infinite knowledge; knowing all things. Nominal form: omniscience.

omnivorous: *vorare*, **to eat**; eating any sort of food, especially both animal and vegetable food; taking in *all* things indiscriminately, e.g., *an omnivorous reader*; *vorare* is also found in *vo̲racious*; *carniv̲orous,* **eating meat**, as certain animals, such as lions and tigers; and *herbiv̲orous*. See p. 214, Item 193.

diapason: Greek *dia-*, **across, through** + *pas-*, from *pan-*, **all**; short for *hediapason khordon sumphonia*, **concord through all the notes**; one of the two principal organ stops — *open diapason* and *closed diapason*; both engage the entire range of the organ.

panorama: Greek *horan*, **to see, to look**; an unobstructed, wide view of an extended area; a comprehensive, **all-inclusive** survey, as of a subject; a picture unrolled before the spectator in such a way as to give the impression of a continuous view. The word was coined by Robert Barker (1739-1806), a Scottish artist.

pantheon: Greek *theos*, **god; all the gods**. Capitalized, a circular temple in Rome; completed in 27 B.C., and dedicated to all the gods. Its height and diameter are exactly the same.

pandemic: Greek *demos*, **people**; pertaining to **all the people**; widespread, universal; in *medicine*, an epidemic (occurring in a particular region) over a wide geographic area.

pancreas: Greek *kreas*, **flesh; all flesh**; a large, elongated gland situated behind the stomach that secretes a digestive juice. The reasoning for the names of certain bodily parts is not always readily apparent.

omniscient; omnipotent; omnipresent: respectively, **all-knowing; all-powerful; present everywhere at all times**; the three terms are considered attributes of God.

Omnia mutantur, nos et mutamur in illis: **All things change, and we change with them.**
Non omnis moriar: **Not all of me shall die.** Horace, *Odes*, 3, 30, 6.
Omnia vincit amor: **Love conquers all things.** Virgil, *Eclogues*, 10, 69.

wordextras

Literally **a talking place**, ***parliament***, from French, demonstrates the influence of Norman French on the government of England. In 1066, the Norman French conquered England in the Battle of Hastings. See *parlor*, p. 101.

Supercilious, from Latin *super-*, **above** + *cilium*, **lower eyelid**, pertains to the **upper eyelid**, and describes one who is characterized by haughty scorn, as "by raising the eyebrows." Synonyms: arrogant, disdainful, haughty, proud, scornful. See more *super-* words, p. 183, **Word Cluster No. 92.**

From *Brobdingnag*, a fictional country of giants in Jonathan Swift's *Gulliver's Travels*, ***Brobdingnagian*** (pronounced BROB ding NAG ee uhn), means **of extraordinary size; gigantic; enormous**. Compare *gargantuan*, p. 52.

Also from *Gulliver's Travels*, above entry, *Lilliput* was a fictional land inhabited by tiny people about six inches tall. ***Lilliputian*** originally meant **of Lilliput or its people**, but has come to mean **very small, tiny**. Figuratively, *Lilliputian* designates **a narrow-minded person**, or describes such a person's output, as *a person with Lilliputian ideas*.

Amok is from Malay *amuk*, **attacking furiously**, in a frenzy; in a violent rage; berserk; losing control of oneself and behaving outrageously or violently; becoming wild or undisciplined. ***Berserk*** is from the Old Norse verb *berzerkr*, **clothed in bearskin** (*bera*, **bear** + *serkr*, **coat**). *Amok* is pronounced either uh MUCK, or uh MOCK.

Deprecate, from *de-*, **from** + *precari*, **to pray**, originally meant **to pray against**, as an evil; to seek to avert by prayer. It has come to mean **to disapprove of strongly; to belittle; to depreciate**. *Precarious* is also from *precari* (see p. 145).

Word Cluster No. 73

oracular	oracle	orad	oral	orant
orate	orator	oratori	oratory	oratrix
orotund	exorable	peroration	oratorio	orifice
orinasal	inexorable	peroral	adore	orison

Common elements_____Inferred Meaning_____

Romance Cognates	French *	Romanian vorbi**	Italian orare	Portuguese orar	Spanish orar

*French does not have a verb corresponding to these elements, but it does have such words as *orateur* and *oraison*.
**In Romanian, *ora* means *hour*.

Words with disguised Latin roots: Auriga, usher, orle   **Doublets**: oration:orison

Words with related meanings: oscillate (see p. 13, under *auscultate*); oscitancy, oscular, osculate, osculum; ostiary, ostiole, ostium (see **NB**, below.)

Latin phrases: *Laborare est orare; orando pro rege et regno* (see **Clavis**)
Ora pro anima: **pray for the soul (of)**; *Ore rotundo*: **with a round mouth**, i.e., with well-turned speech
Ora pro nobis: **Pray for us**; in the Roman Catholic Church liturgy, a plea to the saints

Spanish saying: *Oración breve sube al cielo*: **Short prayers mount up to heaven**.

Oracles of Delphi: Delphi: an ancient city on the slopes of Mount Parnassus where the oracles of Apollo were said to be received.

Latin *precari*, **to pray**: **prec**arious; im**prec**ate, de**prec**ate (see p 144, under **wordextras**), and English **prayer**. It is not related to *pretium*, **price**, which yields **prec**iosity, **prec**ious; ap**prec**iable, ap**prec**iate, de**prec**iate; ap**prais**al, and English **praise**, **price**; **prize** (one meaning), dis**prize** (archaic form of *dispraise*: **to speak of with disapproval; censure**).

Greek *stoma-*, **mouth, stomach**: **stoma**, **stoma**ch, **stoma**cher; **stom**odeum; **stoma**titis; **stoma**tology, **stoma**topod; cyclo**stome**, di**stome**, mela**stome**, mono**stome**, peri**stome**; ana**stom**osis. **Note**: *Stomacher* is an interesting word!

NB: Do not confuse the *os* words with another identically spelled Latin root, meaning **bone**, which yields **oss**ein (the organic basis of bone), **oss**eous, **oss**icle; **oss**iferous, **oss**ifluence (see p. 84), **oss**ifrage (osprey), **oss**ify, **oss**uary; oyster.

wordbuilder #54

Latin *gradus*, **a step**, from *gradi*, **to step, walk**, yields **grad**ate, **grad**ation, **grade**, **grad**ient, **grad**ine; **grad**ual, **grad**uate, **grad**us; ag**grade**, centi**grade**, de**grade**, digiti**grade** (walking on the *toes* with the heels not touching the ground, as cats, dogs, horses), inter**grade**, ortho**grade** (walking with the body upright), palmi**grade**, planti**grade** (walking on the whole sole, as a human or bear), prono**grade** (walking with the body parallel to the ground), retro**grade**, salti**grade** (see p. 182, **Clavis**), sub**grade**, tardi**grade**; de**grad**ation; **gress**orial (adapted for walking, as the feet of certain birds); con**gress**, e**gress**, in**gress**, pro**gress**, retro**gress**; ag**gress**ion, de**gress**ion, di**gress**ion, re**gress**ion, trans**gress**ion; de**gree**; grallatorial (describing those birds that walk on stilts, such as herons and cranes).

wordextras

Ostracize, from Greek *ostrakon*, **a shell, potsherd**, and akin to *os*, **bone**, originally meant to exile by votes written on tiles or potsherds. In ancient Greece, *ostracism* was the temporary banishment of a citizen by popular vote.

Elicit, **to draw forth**, as *to elicit a reply*, *to elicit the truth*, or *to elicit applause*, is from Latin *ex-*, **out** + *lacere*, **to entice**. Do not confuse with *illicit*, **unlawful, improper**, from *licere*, **to be permitted**, which yields *license* as well.

French *ingénue* is from Latin *ingenuus*, **native, inborn**. Also spelled without the accent, *ingenue* is the role of an *ingenuous* (**artless, innocent, naïve**) girl, especially as represented on stage. Quite the opposite of *ingenuous* is *ingenious*, **bright, resourceful, able, adroit**. Pronunciation: AN zhu NOO, or AWN zhu NOO.

Austin, capital of Texas, is named for Stephen F. Austin (1793-1836), US pioneer; known as the Father of Texas.

Lurid, from *luridus*, **pale, yellow, ghastly**, originally meant "deathly pale; wan"; glowing through a haze, as flames enveloped by smoke; then, vivid in a harsh or shocking way; startling; sensational; also, characterized by violent passion or crime; of any of several light or medium grayish colors ranging in hue from yellow to orange.

Common element base: orare   **Meaning**: to speak, argue, plead a case, pray; mouth
IE base: *or-*: **to speak**, **plead**, **pray**; *os-*: **mouth**, with which one *prays* or *speaks*. Johnson notes that if the pleading was with a deity, *orare* meant **to pray**.
German: *sprechen*, **to speak**, as in "*Sprechen Sie Deutsch?*" "**Do you speak German?**"

Clavis

orant: in early Christian art, representation of a female figure with outstretched arms and palms upward in a gesture of **prayer**.

oratorio: originally, **a small chapel**, where one **prays**; then, religious, musical compositions performed in the Oratory of St. Philip Neri of Rome. In addition to Handel's *Messiah*, other well-known oratorios include Bach's *Passion According to St. Matthew*, Brahm's *Requiem*, and Mendelssohn's *Elijah*.

orifice: *facere*, **to make**; **to make a mouth**; **a mouth**: an opening, vent, or aperture of a tube, cavity, etc., through which something passes. See **wordbuilder #27**, p. 61, for other words from *facere*.

orison: and *oration* are doublets; *orison*: **a spoken prayer**; Hamlet entreats Ophelia, "Nymph, in thy *orisons*, be all my sins remembered." *Oration*: an elaborate discourse delivered in a formal and dignified manner. See p. 185, bottom of page, for examples of other English-Latin doublets, or pairs.

peroration: *per-*, **through**; **a speaking at length**; also, the summary of a speech with emphatic recapitulation; a highly rhetorical speech; a high-flown or bombastic speech.

osculate: **to kiss**; **to touch**; in *biology*, to have characteristics in common; in *mathematics*, the point where two branches of a curve have a common tangent is said to be *osculant*, as though the branches are **kissing**. See English-Latin word pairs, p. 199, for kiss:osculate. See *tangent*, p. 186.

usher: from *os*, **mouth**; **door**, **entrance**; *ostiary*, **doorkeeper**; a porter.

orate fratres: **Brothers**, **pray**; in Roman Catholic liturgy, addressed by the celebrant to the congregation just before the Secret, a prayer after the Offertory and before the Preface.

Orando pro rege et regno: an ancient writ requiring that prayers be offered for peace and good government of the realm.

wordextras

Vestige, from Latin *vestigium*, means **footprint**; thus, an *investigator* "tracks" or "follows the footprints." Do not confuse *vestige* and *investigate* with *vest-* words; see **wordbuilder #7**, p. 15.

Punctilious, from Spanish *puntillo* or Italian *puntiglio*, and further from Latin *punctum*, **point**, describes one who is extremely careful about even the smallest details, or *points*. See *contrapuntal*, p. 46. See *punct-* words, pp. 89, 211.

Scrutiny, from Latin *scrutari*, **to examine carefully**, **rummage through odds and ends**, originally referred to picking carefully through the refuse to find that which was salvageable, and has come to indicate a close, careful, and continuous watch; the verb form, *scrutinize*, means to search carefully, as *to scrutinize a contract*. SYNONYMS of *scrutinize*: examine, inspect, scan; of *scrutiny*: examination, surveillance.

Gist, from Latin *jacet*, **it lies**, means the **essential part**, **main idea**, the main point of a matter, or substance of a longer statement. In *law*, the grounds for action in a lawsuit. SYNONYMS: essence, pith; colloquially, nub.

Lhasa apso, from *Lhasa*, **capital of Tibet** + *apso*, **sentinel**, designates a small dog with dense straight hair that hangs over the eyes and a tail that curls over the back.

Miami, Florida, is from Chippewa *omaugeg*, **peninsula people**; also from Chippewa is *Michigan*, **big lake**.

El Paso, Texas, was originally *El Paso del Norte*, **the north pass** (ford) **of the river** (the Rio Grande, **Big River**).

Buffalo, New York, may be from French *beau fleuve*, **beautiful river**, referring to the Niagara River.

The *Tombigbee* River in Alabama is Choctaw for **coffin maker** (*itombi*, **box**, **coffin** + *ikbi*, **maker**); it is so called from the burial boxes used by the Choctaws. The Tombigbee joins the Alabama, to form the Mobile River.

A Writing Tip: Avoid confusing the following words with similar spelling and sound, but with different meanings: amicable, amiable; arguable, argued; block, bloc; borne, born; cannon, canon; canvas, canvass; climactic, climatic; elicit, illicit; godly, godlike; epic, epoch; genteel, gentle, gentile; hated, hateful; historic, historical; human, humane; ingenious, ingenuous; intelligible, intelligent; marital, martial; peaceful, peaceable; practical, practicable; receipt, recipe; single, singular; waive, wave; waiver, waver.

Word Cluster No. 74

`pacific`	`pacifier`	`pacifism`	`pacifist`	`pacify`
`pact`	`paction`	`pactum`	com`pact`	im`pact`(ion)

Common elements_____Inferred Meaning_____

Romance Cognates	French	Romanian	Italian	Portuguese	Spanish
	paix	pace	pace	paz	paz

Words with disguised Latin roots: pageant, appease, pale (of stake), palette, impale, pagan, page (of book), peace, palisade, pay, peasant, propaganda, propagate, travail, travel

Doublets: travel:travail (These words are listed under the *tri-* family as well; see p. 195, **Word Cluster No. 98**.)

Latin words and phrases: *pace; pax, pax Regis, Pax Romana, pax vobiscum, Pax Dei, Pax Americana Pax Britannica, Pax Ecclesiae*

Placenames: La Paz, Bolivia; Isles-de-la Paix, Quebec; Paz de Río, Colombia

Latin phrases: *pactum illicitum; nudum pactum; pactum vestitum; pacta conventa*
Mars gravior sub pace latet: **A severer war lies hidden under peace.**
Qui desiderat pacem praeparet bellum: **Who wishes for peace, let him make ready for war.**
quo pax et gloria ducunt: **where peace and glory lead**
infecta pace: **without effecting peace.** Terence

Religious canon: *Dona nobis pacem*: **Give us peace.** In this instance, *canon* is a polyphonic music composition.

Germanic: fang, vang. A *vang* is a rope running from the end of a gaff to the deck, used to steady the gaff, thus keeping the sailboat from moving erratically.

wordextras

Safari is from Arabic *safariy*, **journey**, and further, from *safara*, **to travel, to set out.** *Safaris* are most frequently made in East Africa, especially in Kenya and in the Serengeti of northern Tanzania. The *Serengeti* is a large plain, part of which is set aside as a national wildlife sanctuary. *Serengeti* comes from Maasai, meaning "extended place."

Condominium, from the law term *dominium*, **ownership**, designates **joint sovereignty**, or **joint ownership**. Originally, *condominium* referred to the territory governed jointly by two or more states, but now refers to joint ownership in a multiunit structure, such as an apartment complex. The prefix *con-* means **with, together**. See *dungeon*, p. 147.

Des Moines, capital of Iowa, is from French *la rivière des Moines*, **the river of the Monks.** The Des Moines flows through the city.

Modesto, California, is so named because its founder, William Ralston, a prominent San Francisco banker, was too *modest* to allow the city to be named after him. In Spanish, *modest* is *modesto*.

Sahara is Arabic for *desert*; thus, *Sahara Desert* is redundant. Other major deserts include the *Mojave* (California), *Gobi* (East Asia; mainly Mongolia), *Negev* (Israel), *Arabian* (Egypt), *Painted* (Arizona).

Boomerang, a native Australian word, is a flat, curved stick that can be thrown so that it will return to a point near the thrower; it was used as a weapon by the Aborigines; also, something that goes contrary to one's expectations.

Iditarod, an abandoned town in Alaska, lends its name to the annual mushing dog sled race from Anchorage to Nome, a course of almost 1,000 miles. The race dates from 1925, when Nome was hit by an epidemic of diphtheria. A serum was transported from Anchorage to Nenana by train, and mushers then relayed it to Nome to save the residents of the town. See *Nome*, p. 136; see p. 69 for the origin of *mushing dog*.

French *chaussure*, from *chausser*, **to shoe**, and ultimately from Latin *calx*, **heel**, is an article of footwear: shoe, boot, slipper, etc. From the same source, *chausses* was a knight's medieval garment of mail for the legs and feet.

Word from a person's name: *boycott*; from *Captain Charles Boycott*, an English estate manager in County Mayo, Ireland, who was ostracized by his tenants because he refused to adjust their rent during the potato famine.

An exalted aphorism: Where there are visible vapors in ignited carbonaceous materials, there is conflagration. **Where there's smoke, there's fire.** Where there is evidence of an act, there is likely to be the act itself.

Common element base: pac, pax   **Meaning**: peace

IE root: *pag-*; also, *pak-*: **to fasten**, yielding **Latin** *pangere*, **to strike**, as by ramming into ground; thus, *pale* (the stake); also yields *peasant* and *pagan*; **German**: *Frieden*, **peace**.

Clavis

Pacific Ocean: so called by Magellan because of its **peaceful**, tranquil appearance; however, it is the most turbulent of oceans. The others are Atlantic, Antarctic, Arctic, Indian.

pacifism: the practice of using **peaceful** methods for settling disputes. Though Jesus, Mahatma Gandhi, and Dr. Martin Luther King, Jr. are often regarded as *pacifists*, they are properly regarded as proponents of nonviolence. Incidentally, *Mahatma* is Gandhi's title, from Sanskrit *mahatma atman*, **Great Soul**. *Mahatma* shares it base with Latin *magnus* and Greek *mega*, **great**. See *mahout*, p. 131.

pace: **peace**; **with all due respect to**; by leave of; with the consent of; contrary to the opinion of; used in expressing polite disagreement. Pronounced: PAY see, or PAH che.

pact: an **agreement** between persons, groups, or nations; compact; covenant. See **A Writing Tip**, p. 155.

appease: from Old French *apaisier*, **to make peaceful**, **to pacify**; to calm; to satisfy, as the limitation of nuclear arms escalation by political *appeasement*. SYNONYMS: conciliate, mollify, pacify, placate, propitiate.

pax regis: **peace of the king**; the peace assured to the people as their right by the king; one of the principal bases of the Constitution of the United States.

pax Romana: **Roman peace**; the peace dictated by the Roman conquerors; now, peace dictated to a subjugated people by their conquerors.

impact: both *impact* and *impinge* are from *in-*, **against** + *pangere*, **to strike**, **fasten**, **to drive in**; as a *noun*, **collision**; as a *verb*, **to force tightly together**.

impacted: wedged together at the broken ends, said of a fractured bone; pressed tightly together; also driven or placed in the alveolus (cavity of gums) in a manner prohibiting eruption into a normal position: said of a tooth.

page: *page* of a book is related to *peace*, both of which are from IE *pak-*, above. *Peace* **fastened**, or confirmed an agreement; sheets of paper became *pages* when bound or *fastened* in a book. Another *page*, as *a Congressional page*, is from Greek *paidos*, **child**, and was originally a boy attendant (see p. 105). *Paidos* also yields *pedagogical*, *pedagogy*, *pediatrician*, *pederasty*, *pedophilia*, *orthopedics*, and *encyclopedia*. See p. 151, under **wordextras**.

impinge: *im-*, **in** + *pangere*, **to strike**; **to strike in**, but more **to strike against**; to encroach, as to *impinge* on one's property or one's rights; to touch on or upon; have an effect on, as *increasing one's professional vocabulary impinges on one's success*. *Fang*, the tearing teeth of carnivorous animals, as well as the hollow teeth of venomous snakes, is also from *pangere*; however, *pang* (of pain) is not related. The last four entries are from the IE roots *pag-*, *pak-*, **to fasten**.

wordextras

Enigma, noun, and *enigmatic*, adjective, are ultimately from Greek *ainissesthai*, **to speak in riddles**. *Enigma* usually refers to a perplexing, baffling, or seemingly inexplicable person, matter, writing, situation, speech.

Chinese *moo goo gai pan*, **mushroom chicken slice**, is a dish consisting of chicken slices sautéed with black mushrooms and assorted vegetables. In pronunciation, each word is equally stressed.

Amontillado, after *Montilla*, a town in Spain, is a pale, relatively dry sherry. One of Edgar Allan Poe's most famous tales of ratiocination is "A Cask of Amontillado." Pronounced: ah MAHN tuh LAH doh. See p. 157 for more on *ratiocination*—pronounced RASH uh AHS uh NAY shun.

Cravat, a dialectal form of Croatian *Hrvat*, is a **neckerchief**, **scarf**, or **necktie**; used by the French in reference to scarves worn by Croatian soldiers. Pronounced: cruh VAT.

Evitable, from *e-*, **from** + *vitare*, **to avoid**, is that which is avoidable. *Inevitable* is that which *cannot* be avoided, as *the inevitable consequences of greed*. See p. 93 for negative forms of positive adjectives.

Motto of American University, Washington, DC: *Pro Deo et Patria*: **For God and Native Land**

```
┌─────────────────────────────────────────────────────────────────────────────┐
│                         Word Cluster No. 75                                   │
│                                                                               │
│   partake          partial          partible          participant           │
│   participate      participle       partison          partition             │
│   partner          partnership      party             apartment             │
│ impart             impartial        repartition       repartee              │
│   portion          apportion        proportion        disproportionate      │
│                                                                               │
│ Common elements_____Inferred Meaning_____   │
│                                                                               │
└─────────────────────────────────────────────────────────────────────────────┘
```

Romance Cognates	French partie	Romanian parte	Italian parte	Portuguese parte	Spanish parte

Words with disguised Latin roots: pair, par, parcel, parlay, parse, peer (one meaning), jeopardy

Doublets: particle:parcel

Latin phrases: *pro virili parte*: **for a man's part**; to the utmost of one's ability, as well as one is able
pars pro toto: **part for the whole** (see *synecdoche*, p. 77); *pro rata; particeps criminis*, **partner in crime**

French phrases: *esprit de parti*: **party spirit**; *parti pris*: **preconceived opinion**

Explore *chorale partita* in a music dictionary; also on Yahoo or Google.

Some authorities place the following words in this, the IE *per-* family; others place them in the related IE *par-* family: **par**, **par**ity, dis**par**ity, di**s**par**age, com**par**e, non**par**eil, im**pair**, **peer**, **peer**less, com**peer**, um**pire** (see p. 138), **par**lay*, herb **Paris**, au **pair**, **as an equal**; designating an arrangement in which services are exchanged on an even basis; also used as a noun, as *an au pair who helps with the housework in return for room and board*.

*Unrelated to *parley*, the base of *parlor* and *parliament*, all of which share their base with Greek *parable*, or "that which is thrown alongside." Note that *parable* (see p. 62) is in the same family with *paragraph, parabola*, and *paradigm*; see p. 210, Item 140, for *para-*, **alongside**. *Paradise*, however, is related to Greek *peri-*, **around**.

Afrikaans: apartheid (see **Clavis**)

wordextras

The symbol *lb.* is the abbreviation of Latin *libra*, **pound**; *oz.*, of Italian *onza*, **ounce**.

Juggernaut, from Sanskrit *Jaganath*, **lord of the world**, is the name of the leading Hindu god. Because frantic devotees allowed themselves to be crushed by the gigantic idol as it was being moved in procession, *juggernaut* has come to mean an irresistible, ruthless force that destroys everything in its path. *Juggernaut* is *not* related to *astronaut* and *cosmonaut*, where *naut* means **traveler**, **navigator**, thus, *star traveler* and *universe traveler*, respectively.

Intrepid, **not afraid**, **bold**, **fearless**, **dauntless**, is from Latin *in-*, **not** + *trepidare*, **to tremble**, **to be alarmed**. From *trepidare* is *trepidation*, **fear**, **alarm**, **dread**, as well as *tremulous*, or trembling movement; tremor. The tautological expression "fear and trepidation" is often heard, but is used for emphasis. See p. 86 for *trepidation*, **wordextras**.

Emulate, from Latin *aemulus*, means **to try to equal** or **to excel**. In computer technology, an *emulator* is software or hardware that allows one computer to perform the functions of, or execute programs for, another type of computer.

Baton Rouge, capital of Louisiana, is French for **red stick**, translating Choctaw *itu-uma*, **red pole**, a boundary mark; probably between the hunting grounds of two tribes.

Chef Menteur, French for **big**, or **chief**, **liar**, is a major thoroughfare in New Orleans. The French infinitive *mentir* is translated **to lie**. See *chef*, p. 32. The feminine form of *menteur* is *menteuse*, correlating with *masseur:masseuse*.

Aghast, "feeling great horror or dismay; terrified; horrified," is from Middle English *a-*, **intensive** + *gaestan*, **to terrify**, which also yields *ghost*. Consequently, if one is *aghast*, it is as though having seen a *ghost*.

The *Pullman* sleeping car, developed by George M. Pullman (1831-1897), was first used to bear President Lincoln's body from Washington, DC, to Springfield, IL, for burial.

Avuncular, originally "of a maternal uncle," can mean "of an uncle," or "having traits characteristic of an uncle," as in "Uncle Henry is known for his *avuncular* indulgence of his nieces and nephews." Pronounced: uh VUNG kyoo ler.

Erie, Pennsylvania, is Huron for **place of the long-tailed wildcat**.

Common element base: pars   **Meaning**: to divide from; to part from

IE base: *per-*: **to sell**, **hand over in a sale**, **make equal**; **German**: *Teil*, **part**, **portion**, **component**, **element**; *Stück*, **piece**; *Glied*, limb as "part" of the body.

Clavis

parse: from *pars orationis*, **part of speech**; describes the function of a word in a sentence, e.g., *sentence* in the preceding phrase is a *noun*, the object of the preposition *in*. A *preposition*, that which shows relationship, is *prepositioned* to its object. Each other part of speech is etymologically true to its function in the sentence, e.g., *noun*, from *nomen*, **name** (gives the name of a person, place, thing, concept, or a quality); *pronoun*, **for the noun** (or, in place of the noun); *adjective*, **thrown to** (the noun, or pronoun it modifies); *interjection*, **to throw between**, e.g., *Ouch! Help!*; *conjunction*, **a joining together**, e.g., *and, or, yet, so, but, for, nor*; *adverb*, **to the verb**; and *verb*, **word**, which in a Latin sentence was the **main word**, it being inflected to show person, tense, mood, and gender. In *software terminology*, *to parse* is to determine the syntactical structure of a computer language by decomposing the units into subunits and establishing a *concatenation* between them. See more on *concatenation*, p. 204, Item 68. See *conjunction*, p. 108.

partake: a hybrid of Latin *part* and Anglo-Saxon *take*; partial translation of *particeps* (*part + capere*, **to take**, **grasp**, **seize**), **to take part in**, as *to partake in the Thanksgiving dinner with friends and family*.

particle: from *particula* (a double diminutive of *pars*: *-cu*, *-le*); thus, **a very small part**. In sentence structure, a short uninflected and invariable part of speech, as an article (*a, an, the*); certain prepositions (*in, on, up*); conjunctions (*or, and, but*), and interjections (*Ah! Oh!*), used to show syntactical relationships. For example, *a, an*, and *the* are "noun markers," meaning that a noun invariably follows. In *physics*, *particle* is matter so small that its magnitude is insignificant though it has inertia and the force of attraction.

participle: a verbal which **participates** as an adjective. *Speaking*, a present participle, comes from the infinitive *to speak*. Notice the participle's use as an adjective in the following phrase: *his speaking voice*, and in the sentence: *Speaking softly*, the police officer calmed the frightened child. When used as a noun, *speaking* is called a *gerund*, e.g., *Speaking* before a large audience can be frightening; and from Shakespeare: the silence of pure innocence/Persuades when *speaking* fails. *Gerund* is from *gerere*, **to do**, **carry out**.

partition: a **parting** or **being parted**; division into **parts**; apportionment. Something that **separates** or **divides**, as an interior wall, dividing one room from another. In *law*, the process of dividing property; in *logic*, the separation of a class into its elements or parts. As a *verb*, to divide into parts or shares; apportion.

repartee: from French *repartir*, **to return quickly**; a quick, witty reply. SYNONYMS: humor, irony, satire, wit.

jeopardy: **divided joke**, or **game**, from Old French *jeu parti*, a game with even chances; ultimately from Latin *jocus parti*. In *law*, exposure to conviction and punishment; situation of an accused person on trial for a crime. In general usage, *jeopardy* means "peril, great danger." Explore the law term *double jeopardy*.

apartheid: Afrikaans; **aparthood**; **apartness**, or "the state of being apart"; the policy of strict racial segregation and discrimination in South Africa against the native Negroes and other dark-skinned peoples. Pronounced: uh PAR tate; uh PAR tite; uh PAR tide.

German has many words that are similar to English, for example, *Fuss*, **foot**; *Glas*, **glass**; *Lippe*, **lip**; *Mann*, **man**; *Milch*, **milk**; *Mutter*, **mother**; *Nacht*, **night**; *Onkel*, **uncle**; *Schwester*, **sister**; *Schulter*, **shoulder**; *Sohn*, **son**; *Sonne*, **sun**; *Tochter*, **daughter**; *Vater*, **father**; *Wasser*, **water**. All nouns in German are capitalized, whether proper or common.

wordextras

Gaudeamus igitur, **Let's rejoice**, are the opening words of a medieval German student song; a *gaudeamus* is now a time of merrymaking, especially of college students. The song "Gaudeamus igitur" is often regarded as one of the best in *The Student Prince*, a Sigmund Romberg Broadway musical, which was later made into a movie in 1954.

Purloin, from Old French *porloigner* (*por-*, **for** + *loin*, **far**), **to steal**, **filch**, is seen in the title in Edgar Allan Poe's short story "The Purloined Letter." See pp. 148, 157, for more on Poe's stories of ratiocination.

Word named from a place: *donnybrook*, **a rough**, **rowdy fight**; from *Donnybrook Fair* held annually at Donnybrook, near Dublin, Ireland, where there was much brawling and rowdiness. The word can also indicate a heated quarrel or dispute, as in "The school board ended in a *donnybrook* over censored library books."

Word Cluster No. 76

pedal	centipede	pedestrian	pedigree	pedometer
peduncle	biped	pediment	expedite	expedient
expedition	impedance	impede	impediment	impedimenta
pedestal	palmipede	quadriped	velocipede	sesquipedalian

Common elements_____Inferred Meaning_____

Romance Cognates	French pied	Romanian picor*	Italian piede	Portuguese pé	Spanish pie

*Includes entire leg—from foot to hip.

Words with disguised Latin roots: caliber, passepied, cap-a-pie, dispatch, fetlock, impeach, pawn, peon, petiole, pew, pied noir, pied-à-terre, Piedmont, pejorative, pessimism, pioneer, repudiate, talipes, trapeze, trapezium, trivet, vamp (part of shoe over the instep)

Latin phrases: *nec caput nec pedes*: **neither head nor tail**; total confusion
Ex pede Herculem (see **Clavis**); *aequo pulsat pede*: **(Pale Death) knocks with equal foot**. Horace

NB: *Pedant, pedantry, pediatrics, pedagogue, pedology, pedobaptism, pedodontics* (the professional care of children's teeth), *pedophilia, pederasty* (*eros*, **love**), *encyclopedia* (see **wordextras** below), and *orthopedics*—from Greek *paidos*, **child**—are not related to these Latin roots. See p. 148, under *page*.

French phrase: *à la mort*: **to the death**; hence, very ill, melancholy.

Greek: *pod*, **foot**: **pod**ium; **pod**agra, **pod**iatrist, **pod**iatry; **podo**carpus; a**pod**al, amphi**pod**, anti**pod**es, arthro**pod**, bi**pod**, cope**pod**, deca**pod**, gastro**pod**, hexa**pod**, iso**pod**, mega**pod**, octo**pod**, pleo**pod**, ptero**pod**, rhizo**pod**, sauro-**pod**, sym**pod**ium, tetra**pod**, tri**pod**; chiro**pod**ist; A**pus**, octo**pus**, platy**pus**, poly**p**; Italian: ap**pog**giatura.

Persian: *pajamas* (**foot garment**; see p. 53); *teapoy* (see p. 196 under **Clavis**); **Hindi**: *charpoy* (**a four-footed bed**)

wordextras

Sooth, from Old English *soth*, **truth**, is found in the phrase *in sooth*, **truly**, **in fact**; also in *forsooth*, **to be sure**, and in *soothsayer*, **one who speaks the truth**. *Soothsayer* is still used today to refer to a person who makes "true" predictions; probably the best-known soothsayer in literature is the one warning Caesar "to beware the Ides of March."

The Norse (mainly Scandinavians) have contributed a number of words to the English language, including *ransack*. Originally, "to search and plunder a place," *ransack* comes from *rannsaka*, which meant "to make a legal search of a house for stolen goods." The elements are *rann*, **house** + *saka*, **to seek**. *Ramshackle* is from the same elements.

Propensity, **an inclination forward**, is from Latin *pro-*, **forward** + *pendere*, **to hang**, as in *pendant, pendulous, pendulum, depend*. *Propensity* has come to mean a natural inclination or bent, as in "having a *propensity* for chocolates." See *perpendicular*, **wordextra**, p. 136; see other *pend-* words, p. 210, Item 141.

Front Royal, Virginia, is named after the **royal oak** that in the 1860s stood in the center of the town. During the Civil War, a sergeant, weary from trying to assemble the newly mustered troops, ordered them **to front the royal oak**. On the Shenandoah River, and in the Shenandoah Valley, Front Royal is situated at the northern terminus of the Skyline Drive, which makes its ascent into the Blue Ridge Mountains from the quaint, picturesque town.

Rebus, from French *rébus*, and further from the ablative plural of Latin *res*, **thing**, is "meaning indicated by *things*." A *rebus* is a kind of puzzle consisting of pictures or drawings of objects, signs, letters, etc., the combination of whose names suggests words or phrases. For example, *a picture of an eye* followed by an *L* succeeded by an *ampersand* (&) is a rebus for *island*. See *res* in *republic*, p. 1.

Abilene, Texas, has only one known source: Luke 3:1, in reference to Lysanias as the tetrarch of Abilene.

Originally, *encyclopedia* was the circle of education in the arts and sciences, in order to give a *child* a well-rounded education. *Encyclopedic*, **like an encyclopedia**, describes a person with knowledge of many subjects. See **NB**, above.

French *butte*, **mound**, is a steep hill standing alone in a plain, especially in the western US; a small *mesa*, Spanish for **table**. *Butte*, Montana, is named for the many buttes in the area. Pronounced: byoot. See *mesa, Mensa Society*, p. 67.

Atlanta, capital of Georgia, is named after Western and Atlantic Railroad, of which Atlanta was the eastern terminus.

Common element base: pes, pedis   **Meaning**: foot

IE base: *ped-*: **foot**; yields **Old English** *foot, fetter*; **Middle English** *fetlock, fetch*; **Russian** *podzol*; from **Greek**: *pilot, diapedesis, cypripedium; polyp* (see **Clavis**)

German: *Fuss*: **foot, base, bottom**, as in *Fussball*; *zu Fuss*, **on foot**

Clavis

pedestal:
: from Italian *piedestallo*; German *Stall*, **foot of a stall**; subsequently entered English through Spanish; the foot or bottom support of a column, statue, lamp, etc.

pedigree:
: from French *pied de grue*, **foot of the crane**, from the lines drawn on a genealogical chart resembling a crane's foot; **a line of ancestors**; record of ancestors; descent; lineage; ancestry.

Piedmont:
: from Italian *Piemonte*, and French *piémont*, **foot of the mountains**, a region of Italy in the upper valley of the Po River and at the base of the Alps. There are many *piedmont* regions in the United States. For example, in Virginia, the *Piedmont* ranges northwest from Fredericksburg to Front Royal, the northern terminus of the Blue Ridge Mountains. See more on *Front Royal*, p. 151.

expedite:
: *ex-*, **out**; **to extricate one's foot**; now, **to speed up, hasten**. Semantic change from *specific* to *general*. Compare *impede*, **to entangle the feet**; thus yielding *impediment*, as *a speech impediment*, such as lisping, stuttering. See *impeach*, p. 162, **wordextras**.

peon:
: from the same base as **pawn**, *pedonis*; originally, **one who has flat, wide feet**; **foot soldier**, one who cleared the way; in Spanish, *peón*, **a laborer**.

peonage:
: *–age*, **condition of**; the condition of a peon (see above entry); the system by which debtors or legal prisoners were held in servitude to work off a debt.

pioneer:
: originally, **a foot soldier**, one who cleared the way for the ensuing invaders; a person who goes before, preparing the way for others, as an early settler or a scientist doing exploratory work.

pteropod:
: Greek *pteron*, **wing**; **wing-foot**, designates small, thin-shelled, or shell-less *gastropods*, **ventral-feet**, or **stomach-feet**, such as snails and slugs, that swim by means of winglike lobes on their feet.

platypus:
: Greek *platys*, **flat**; **flat-footed**; certain aquatic animals native to Australia and Tasmania. Tasmania is named for the Dutch navigator, Abel Tasman, who discovered the island state of Australia, as well as New Zealand.

polyp:
: Greek *poly-*, **many**; **many-footed**; any of various coelenterates (a phylum of invertebrates), colonial or individual, having a mouth fringed with many small, slender tentacles bearing stinging cells at the top of a tubelike body, as the sea anemone or hydra. In *medicine*, designates a smooth projecting growth of hypertrophied (overgrown) mucous membrane in the nasal passages, bladder, rectum, etc. [The final letter of *polyp* is a shortening of *pod*, retaining only the first letter.]

ex pede Herculem: **from Hercules' foot**; by comparing the length of the stadium of Hercules at Olympus with the ordinary stadium of 607 feet, Pythagoras calculated the length of Hercules' foot, and from that, his height; thus, "From the sample, you may judge the whole."

---

wordextras

To be *exonerated* is have one's *onus*, or **burden**, removed, usually in a court of law; *onerous* means **burdensome**. SYNONYMS of *exonerate*: absolve, acquit, forgive, pardon.

Extenuate, **to make thin**, is usually heard in the phrase "extenuating circumstances," where the circumstances lessen or seem to lessen the seriousness of an offense or crime.

Coined by Lewis Carroll in *Through the Looking Glass*, **chortle**, a portmanteau word, combines probably *chuckle* and *snort*, meaning "to chuckle gleefully." A *portmanteau word* combines two other words in form and meaning, e.g., *smog* is from *smoke* and *fog*. See p. 156 for more on *portmanteau*. See p. 116 for more on *Lewis Carroll*.

Easel, a sturdy tripod to hold an artist's canvas, is from Dutch *ezel*, **ass**, interpreted, "little donkey."

Detroit, Michigan, from French *détroit*, **strait**, was first applied to the Detroit River, originally "Strait of Narrows."

Launch, from Old French *lanchier*, originally meant "to wield a lance." See another *launch*, p. 153.

```
┌─────────────────────────────────────────────────────────────────────────────┐
│                          Word Cluster No. 77                                  │
│                                                                               │
│  plural          pluralism        plurality         pluriel                   │
│  pluriaxial      pluries          pluriavial        pluricellular             │
│  plurilingual    plurisignation   plurivocal        plurivorous               │
│                                                                               │
│  Common elements_____Inferred Meaning_____     │
└─────────────────────────────────────────────────────────────────────────────┘
```

Romance Cognates	French	Romanian	Italian	Portuguese	Spanish
	plus, pluriel	plural	più, plurale	plural	plural

Words with disguised Latin roots: plus, nonplus, pluperfect, plus fours, surplus

Latin phrases: *E pluribus unum* (see **Clavis**)*; pluris petitio; ne plus ultra* (see *sans-pareil*, p. 178)

French phrase: *plus on est de fous, plus on rit*: **the more merrymakers, the more fun**; the more the merrier

Motto of Louis XIV of France: *ne pluribus impar*: **not unequal to many**; a match for the whole world

Explore *plurisignation* under *ambiguity* in most literary handbooks; also, explore *pluralistic idealism* versus *monastic idealism*. The terms can also be found on Google.

Greek: *poly-*, **many**: **poly**adelphous, **poly**andry (the state or practice of having more than one husband at the same time; in *botany*, the presence of numerous stamens in one flower; in *zoology*, the mating of one female with more than one male), **poly**anthus, **poly**basic, **poly**centrism, **poly**chromatic, **poly**clinic, **poly**cotyledon, **poly**cyclic, **poly**cystic, **poly**dactyl, **poly**ester, **poly**gala, **poly**gamy, **poly**glot, **poly**gon, **poly**graph, **poly**gyny (the state or practice of having two or more wives at the same time; in *botany*, having many styles or pistils; in *zoology*, the mating of a male animal with more than one female), **Poly**nesia, **poly**nomial, **poly**p,* **poly**phony, **poly**saccharide, **poly**syndeton, **poly**technic, **poly**theist, **poly**valent; hoi **polloi**; iso**pleth**, **pleth**ora (see p. 171), **pleo**nasm, **Plio**cene.
Polyp is from *poly-* + *pous*, **foot** (see **IE base**, p. 152, for additional information).

---
wordextras

Vendetta, Italian for Latin *vindicta*, the base of *vengeance* and *vindictive*, has come to mean a **prolonged feud**, marked by bitter hostility, as the decades-long *vendetta* between the Hatfields and the McCoys. See p. 65.

From Dutch *knapzak* comes **knapsack**, which originally meant "an eating bag."

The *shrapnel* shell was named after British General Henry Shrapnel (1761-1842), who invented it. This type of shell is filled with an explosive charge with many small metal balls that explode in the air over the objective.

Flaccid, **lacking in firmness**, is from Latin *flaccus*, **flabby**; **lacking force**; **weak**; **feeble**. Example phrases: *flaccid economy, flaccid leadership, flaccid muscles*. Pronounced: FLAK sid, or FLAS sid.

Jodhpurs, **riding breeches**, are named after *Jodhpur*, a city in India, where they were made and first became popular.

Rh factor, a group of antigens, is so called from having been discovered first in the blood of *rhesus* monkeys. The rhesus is a brownish-yellow *macaque* of India, often kept in zoos and used extensively in biological and medical research. *Macaque* is from Portuguese *macaco*, **monkey**. Pronunciation of *macaque*: muh KOCK.

Lincoln, capital of Nebraska, was named in honor of President Abraham Lincoln, 16th president of the United States.

Snorkel, from German *schnorchel*, **inlet**, **breathing tube**, is related to *schnarchen*, **to snore**.

Ravish, from *rapere*, **to seize**, originally meant to seize and carry away forcibly; to transport with joy or delight.

Launch, from Spanish or Portuguese *lancha*, and probably originally from Malay *lancharan*, **swift**, is the largest boat carried by a warship; an open, or partly enclosed, motorboat. See another *launch*, p. 152.

A Writing Tip: Distinguish between *compliment* and *complement*. Both come from Latin *plere*, **to fill**. A *compliment* fills one with praise, and *complement* fills or completes; for example, a salad *complements* a meal.

Word from a person's name: *galvanize*; from Luigi Galvani (1737-1798), an Italian physiologist and physicist. In addition to its scientific meaning, *galvanize* means "to stimulate, excite, startle," as the Japanese attack on Pearl Harbor in 1941 *galvanized* Americans' patriotic fervor.

Motto of the University of North Dakota: *Lux et Lex*: **Light and Law**
Motto of Emory University, Atlanta, Georgia: *Lex, Lux*: **Law, Light**

Common element base: pluralis   **Meaning:** more, many, several
IE base: *pek(e)-¹:* **to fill**, with derivatives meaning **abundance, multitude, plenty.**
German: *mehr,* **more,** as in *Mehrbetrag,* **a surplus;** *desto mehr,* **all the more;** *nie mehr,* **never again;** *immer mehr,* **more and more;** *mehr als,* **more than**
Sanskrit: poori, "that which fills or satisfies"; a deep-fried wheat bread of India

Clavis

plurality: in a contest with more than two candidates, the situation of a candidate receiving **more** votes than any other candidate, but not more than half; for example, of three candidates, *A* receives 36 percent (a plurality), *B*, 35 percent; and *C*, 29 percent. Had *A* received 51 percent, the outcome would have been a *majority.* See more on *majority*, p. 122.

pluralistic: **more** than one individual or classification; pertains to a complex social structure in which diverse groups maintain their own traditional characteristics within a common civilization. America is often thought of as a melting pot, and in some ways, it is; but it is also **pluralistic** or, **a salad bowl**; thus, a mixture, with different ethnic groups maintaining their own customs.

pluriaxial: in *botany,* **having several axes**; specifically, having flowers on secondary shoots. Compare *monaxial,* also, *uniaxial,* developing flowers on the primary axis or along a single axis.

plurilingual: *lingua,* **tongue**; **speaking many languages**; the Greek counterpart is *polyglot,* as *a polyglot city; polyglot* is also a noun: one who speaks **many** languages.

plurivorous: *vorare,* **to eat**; living upon **several** hosts, as *plurivorous fungi* or *plurivorous parasites.* See p. 61 for more on *parasite,* under **wordextras.** Pronounced: ploo RIV er us.

pluperfect: from *plus quam perfectum,* **more than perfect**; a tense in certain languages that corresponds to English *past perfect,* or that action that was completed *before* a *later* event; designated by *had,* as in "The accident *had* (~~before~~) happened an hour before it *was* (~~later~~) discovered."

plethora: Greek; **superabundance; excess**; more than enough; in *medicine,* overfullness of blood vessels or of the total quantity of any fluid in the body. Pronounced: PLETH er uh.

polysyndeton: Greek *syn-,* **with** + *dein,* **to bind**; the binding together with many structural connectives and conjunctions; the repetition of connectives or conjunctions in close proximity for rhetorical effect, e.g., here *and* there *and* everywhere; or "He has everything: a good salary, good looks, and a good wife." Opposed to *asyndeton,* e.g., Smile, shake hands, part. See *veni, vidi, vici,* p. 200.

polyphony: Greek *phone,* **sound**; the simultaneous combination of **two or more** independent melodic parts, especially when in close harmonic relationship. See *contrapuntal,* p. 46; see more on *polyphony,* p. 86. In *phonetics,* the representation of two or more sounds by the same letter, as *th* in *thin* and *then.*

Polynesia: Greek *nesos,* **island; many islands.** *Polynesia* includes the following major groups of islands: Hawaii, Samoa, Tonga, Society, Marquesas; compare *Micronesia* (small groups of atolls, north of the equator and east of the Philippines; includes the states of Chuuk, Kosrae, Pohnpei, Yap); *Melanesia* (**black islands,** possibly because of the darkness of the natives); includes Fiji, New Caledonia, New Guinea, and the Solomon Islands. There is also *Indonesia,* or **Indian islands,** an archipelago of more than 13,600 islands, extending farther than the distance from Maine to California.

più: Italian; from Latin *plus;* **more**; a direction in music, as in *più allegro,* **more quickly.**

E pluribus unum: one of the mottoes of the United States, and on its coins: **Out of many, one**; from many states is formed a union; also, possibly the forming of one nation from many nationalities.

wordextras
Porpoise, **swine fish,** is from Latin *porcus,* **pig** + *piscis,* **fish.** The porpoise is a small, usually gregarious toothed whale found in most seas. It has a torpedo-shaped body and a blunt snout. Related in appearance to *dolphins.*

Smithereens, from Irish *smidirini,* **fragments, little bits,** as *the demolition imploded the old factory to smithereens.*

French *jalousie,* from *jealousy,* is a **window louver**; probably so called from permitting one to see without being seen.

Louver, from Middle Dutch *love,* **gallery** (in a theater), originally designated an open turret on the roof of a building.

```
┌─────────────────────────────────────────────────────────────────────────────┐
│                           Word Cluster No. 78                                  │
│                                                                               │
│     portable            portage          portative          portato          │
│     porter              portfolio         portly            portamento        │
│   support              portmanteau       comport           deport            │
│   disport              export            import            important         │
│   purport              rapport           report           transport          │
│                                                                               │
│   Common element_____Inferred Meaning_____  │
└─────────────────────────────────────────────────────────────────────────────┘
```

Romance Cognates	**French**	**Romanian**	**Italian**	**Portuguese**	**Spanish**
	porter	purta	portare	portar	portar

Placenames: Export, PA. There is a *Portage* in each of the following states: AK, IN, ME, MI, PA, UT, WI. *Portage des Sioux*, MO. *Portage*: the carrying of boats or goods overland from one river or lake to another, or around rapids.

Words and phrases from French: *porte-monnaie; port de bras; en rapport; portmanteau*

Words with related meaning: opportune, importune, harbor

Other roots with similar meaning: *ger-*: belli**ger**ent (see p. 163), denti**ger**ous, exag**ger**ate; *gest-*: **gest** (or **geste**), **gest**ate, **gest**iculate, **gest**ure; con**gest**, con**gest**ion, di**gest**, di**gest**ion, e**gest**, in**gest**, sug**gest**, sug**gest**ion; *gis-*: re**gis**ter, re**gis**trar; *fer-*: **fer**tile, circum**fer**ence, con**fer**ence, dif**fer**, of**fer**, pre**fer**, suf**fer**, trans**fer**; **fur**tive; *-late* (from *ferre*): ab**late**, col**late**, ob**late**, p**r**o**late**, trans**late**, legis**late**or; *pher-*: **pher**omone, para**pher**nalia, Christo**pher** (**bearing Christ**); *phor-*: am**phor**a, ana**phor**a, dys**phor**ia, eu**phor**ia, meta**phor**, sema**phor**e, phos**phor**ous; ampul, ampulla; *vect-*: **vect**or, ad**vect**ion, con**vect**ion, e**vect**ion, in**vect**ive; con**vex**; *veh-*: **veh**ement, **veh**icle; in**veigh** (see **Clavis**).

Note: See p. 213, Item178, for *portrait*. See p. 149, **Word Cluster No. 75**, for *port-* with a different meaning.

German: *Führer*, or *Füehrer*, from *führen*, **to lead, to bear**. Title assumed by dictator Adolph Hitler (1889-1945), as head of Nazi Germany (1934-45). [See *Nazi*, p. 5, **wordextras**.]

wordextras

Arpeggio, from *arpeggiare*, **to play on a harp**, indicates the notes of a chord to be played in quick succession, as on a harp, instead of being played simultaneously. Pronunciation: ahr PEJ oh; or, ahr PEJ ee oh.

Staccato, aphesis* of past participle of *distaccare*, **to detach**, indicates distinct breaks between successive tones, usually indicated by a dot over or under the note to be so produced. *Staccato* is opposite to *legato*, **connected**, coming from *ligare*, **to bind**, the same as in *ligament*, and from which *lien*, a claim on one's property, is derived. See *lien, ligament*, and *ligature*, p. 49, under **wordextras**. [*Aphesis*: the loss of an initial, short unaccented syllable.]

Phylactery, from Greek *phylax*, **watchman**, is used for Hebrew *tefillah*, **prayer**, or that which *guards* one from evil. From *phylax* are *prophylactic*, **preventive, protective**, as *prophylactic medicine*; as a noun, **a condom**; also, *prophylaxis*, a term for "professional teeth cleaning," or that which *guards against* (literally, **before**) tooth decay.

Glean, **to gather, learn, find out**, is from Old Irish *digleinn*, **he gathers**. Originally, *glean* was used mainly as "to collect grain left by reapers"; now, **to find out facts**, so as to collect certain information, as *to glean the truth*.

Harvest, from Old English *haerfest*, means basically "a time for cutting." The word has a tortuous background.

Joust, a combat with lances between two knights on horseback, is from *juxta-*, **near, beside**. See *juxtapose*, p. 107.

Word from a person's name: *leotard*, from Jacques *Léotard*, 19th-century French aerial performer; a one-piece, tight-fitting, garment that covers the torso, and worn by dancers, acrobats, etc. *Léotard* advised the men of his day to wear clothing that accentuated their natural features. From *leotard* is *unitard*, a leotard that also covers the legs and, sometimes, the feet.

A Writing Tip: Distinguish between *among* and *between*. Ordinarily, use *among* with three or more entities, *between* with two. The prize was divided *among* several contestants. You have a choice *between* going to law school or going to medical school. NOTE: *Between* is sometimes used when more than two are involved, if the relationship is thought of as each individually with each of the others, as in "a treaty *between* four powers," or "a stake between three trees," meaning the stake is equidistant from each of the trees. A stake could also be *among the trees* if no specified relationship exists between them. *American Heritage Dictionary* has a usage note that is quite helpful.

Common element base: portare   **Meaning**: to carry
IE base: *per-*[2]: **to lead, pass over**; yielding **Old Norse**: *firth, fiord*, or *fjord*; **Germanic**: *fare, farewell, wayfaring*.
Greek: *poros*, yielding *emporium*; **Avestan**: *Euphrates*, with **Greek** *eu-*, **well, good**, "good, or easy, to cross over."
German: *Führer*, from *fuhren*, **to lead** (see previous page); *Träger*, **porter**

Clavis

port arms:	in the military manual of arms, with the rifle across the chest, so as **to carry** it.
portfolio:	*folium*, **leaf**; a sheaf of papers one can **carry**; also, the office of a cabinet member or minister of state, as well as an investor's itemized list of securities. See p. 206, Item 90, in *folio* family.
portmanteau:	French; *manteau*, **mantle, cloak**; **a traveling case**; *a portmanteau word* is formed by merging the *sounds* and *meanings* of two words, e.g., *slithy* from *slime* and *lithe*; *chortle* from *chuckle* and *snort*, made famous by Lewis Carroll in *Alice in Wonderland*. See p. 116 for the real name of Lewis Carroll; also, see p. 152 for more on *chortle*.
portamento:	Italian; **the act of carrying**; a continuous glide effected by the voice, trombone, or bowed stringed instrument in passing from one tone to another. Most music terms are Italian.
import:	*in-*, **in**; **to carry in**; to bring in from the outside; to bring goods from another country, especially for purposes of sale; as a *noun*, **signification**; **importance**.
port de bras:	French; **carriage of the arm**; an arm movement in ballet.
rapport:	French; *re-*, **back** + *ad-*, **to**; a close or sympathetic relationship; *en rapport*, **in harmony**; **in sympathy**; **in accord**. The detective was able to establish *rapport* with the suspect.
asportation:	*as-*, truncation of *abs-*, **away**; **the act of carrying away**, especially, in *law*, the felonious removal of goods or merchandise from the place where they were deposited.
opportune:	Some philologists place this word in this, the *portare* family; others, in *fare*, while still others place both *port* and *fare* in the larger IE *per-* family, meaning **to lead**, or **to pass over**. *American Heritage* indicates that *opportune* means **towards port**, thus, *favorable* or *propitious*. The opposite is *inopportune*, as in "The day before payday is an *inopportune* time to ask me for a loan."
purport:	*pur-* from *pro-*, **forth**; **to bear forth**; to profess or claim as its meaning; to give the appearance, often falsely, of being, intending, etc., as in "selfish behavior that *purports* to be altruistic." As a *noun*, drift, meaning, sense, tenor; also, intention, object.
transport:	*trans-*, **across**; **to carry across**; to carry from one place to another, especially over long distances; to carry away with emotion; enrapture, as being *transported* by an operatic aria; also, **to banish**, as *to transport one to a penal colony*.
report:	*re-*, **back**; **to carry back**; in *law*, a formal account or record of a court case, decision, etc.; plural, report<u>s</u>: the official record, published periodically, of court cases, decisions, etc.
inveigh:	from *invehere*, **to bring in**; a violent verbal attack; to talk or write bitterly about. The root is also the base of *vehement*, *vehicle*. Do not confuse with *inveigle*; see p. 142.

wordbuilder #55
Greek *kakos*, **bad, evil, poor, harsh**, yields **cac**onym; **caco**demon (**an evil spirit or devil**), **cac**oepy, **caco**ethes (**bad habit**; a hankering to do something; mania), **caco**genesis, **caco**genics, **caco**graphy (**bad handwriting**), **caco**phemism, **caco**phony (**harsh-sounding**), and **caco**plasty; **kakisto**cracy (government by the least qualified or most unprincipled citizens). **NB**: *Cacomistle*, Nahuatl for "half cougar," a slender, long-tailed, raccoonlike carnivore of southwest United States and Mexico, is not in this family. *Nahuatl* is the native Aztec language of Mexico; still widely spoken.

Medical terms: **caco**demonomania (a condition marked by delusions of being possessed by evil spirits); **cac**odyl (*cako-*, **bad** + *ozein*, **to smell** + *hyle*, **matter**; a foul-smelling compound of arsenic and methyl), **caco**ethic, **caco**geusia, **caco**melia, **cac**osmia (*caco-* + *osmia*, **smell**), **caco**plasty, **caco**rhythmic, **caco**thenics, **caco**trophy.

wordextra
Japanese *kimono*, **a thing for wearing**, is from *ki*, **wearing** + *mono*, **a person**, or **thing**, depending on how *mono* is used. A loose-fitting robe, the *kimono* is worn by both men and women.

```
┌─────────────────────────────────────────────────────────────────────────────┐
│                           Word Cluster No. 79                                  │
│                                                                                │
│  postbellum         posterior         posterity          postern              │
│  postexilic         postface          postgeniture       postgraduate         │
│  posthumous         posthypnotic      postiche           postlude             │
│  postmarital        postmortal        postmortem         postnasal            │
│  postnatal          postorbital       postpone           postposition         │
│  postprandial       postscript        postil             preposterous         │
│                                                                                │
│  Common element_____Inferred Meaning_____ │
└─────────────────────────────────────────────────────────────────────────────┘
```

Romance Cognates: The form of *post* has remained unchanged in each of the Romance languages.

Latin phrases: *Post cineres gloria sera venit*: **After one is reduced to ashes, fame comes too late.** Martial
Post hoc, ergo propter hoc; **after this**; **therefore, because of this** (a logical fallacy; see **Clavis**)
a posteriori vs. *a priori*; *ex post facto*; *post meridiem* (p.m.); *postmeridian*: **pertaining to the afternoon**

Related Latin *pone* (from *ponere*, **to place**): com**pon**ent, de**pon**ent, ex**pon**ent, op**pon**ent, pro**pon**ent; post**pone**
pose: ap**pose**, com**pose**, decom**pose**, dis**pose**, ex**pose**, ex**posé**, im**pose**, inter**pose**, juxta**pose**, op**pose**, pro**pose**,
pur**pose**, re**pose**, sup**pose**, trans**pose**; apro**pos** (from French *à propos*, **to the purpose**), malapropism (see p. 124).
posit: **posit**ion, **posit**ive; de**posit**, re**posit**; ap**position**, com**position**, contra**position**, dis**position**, juxta**position**,
pre**position**, pro**position**; ap**positive**, dia**positive**, dis**positive**, post**positive**, pre**positive**; see *post*, p. 195.

Variant forms: from *ponere*: **post**ure, pro**vost**; com**pound**, ex**pound**; puisny, puny (see p. 134).

Greek *apo-*, **away**: **ap**helion, **ap**heresis, **ap**horism (see p. 132); **apo**apsis, **apo**calypse, **apo**carpous, **apo**chromatic,
apocope, **apo**crine, **apo**crypha, **apo**dictic, **apo**dosis, **apo**gamy, **apo**gee (see p. 192), **apo**logy (see p. 120), **apo**logue,
apomixis, **apo**phyge, **apo**physis, **apo**sematic, **apo**siopesis (see **Clavis**), **apo**pletic, **apo**stasy, **apo**stle (see p. 130),
apostrophe (see pp. 158, 212), **apo**thecary (see pp. 117, 157), **apo**them, **apo**theosis, **apo**thegm, **apo**dosis vs. protasis.

┌──┐
│ **Quotes**: If you want your child to achieve success with his studies in │
│ college, look to his vocabulary. W. D. Templeton   │
│   │
│ The ill and unfitting choice of words wonderfully obstructs the under- │
│ standing. Francis Bacon   │
└──┘

wordextras

Grisly, from Old English *a grisan*, **to shudder with fear**, means **ghastly**, **repugnant**, **horrifying**, **gruesome**, **macabre**, as "the grisly murder scene." Though not etymologically connected to the *grizzly*, or grey, bear, the two words are pronounced the same. Surely, a *grizzly* bear can indeed be *grisly*! As a noun, *grizzly* can mean the bear itself, or as an adjective, to describe such a bear. In other words, the animal is a *grizzly*, or a *grizzly bear*.

From Latin *peccare*, **to sin**, Spanish *peccadillo* is **a small sin** or **fault**, and is often heard in the phrase "an innocent peccadillo"; coming from the same root are *peccable*, *peccavi*, *impeccable*, and *impeccant*.

Ratiocination, from Latin *ratiocinari*, **to reckon**, is the process of reasoning, especially reasoning by using formal logic; the process of exact thinking; a reasoned train of thought. The mysteries of Edgar Allan Poe are exemplars of ratiocination. See p. 148 for "A Cask of Amontillado," one of his mystery, or ratiocination, tales.

Labyrinth, from Greek *labyrinthos*, is a structure containing an intricate network of winding passages hard to follow without losing one's way; a maze. Although noted as from Greek, it is of pre-Hellenic origin.

Brownsville, the southernmost city in Texas, and on the Mexican border, is named after Fort Brown, which itself was named for Major J. Brown, who was killed defending the fort in 1846.

Latin titles of books
John Gower's *Confessio Amantis*, **The Confessions of a Lover**; Oscar Wilde's *E Tenebris*, **Out of Darkness**
Cotton Mather's *Magnalia Christi Americana*, **Great Works of Christ in America**
John Dryden's *Annus Mirabilis*, **The Wonderful Year**, a poem giving the three remarkable events of the year 1666 (England's war with the Dutch, the Plague, and the Great Fire of London)
Henryk Sienkiewicz's *Quo Vadis?* **Whither Goest Thou**?

Common element base: post-   **Meaning**: behind, back, afterwards
IE base: *apo-*: **off**, **away**, **back**; **German** *nach*, as in *Nachmittag*, **afternoon**, **after midday**

Clavis

posterior:
: comparative of *posterus*, **following**; later, **following after**; **succeeding**; **at or toward the rear**; **behind**, specifically, *dorsal*, as opposed to *anterior*; in *botany*, on the side next to the main stem. In *anatomy*, of or pertaining to the dorsal side of the body. Colloquially, *posterior*, sometimes in the plural, refers to the derrière, or the buttocks. Pronunciation of *derrière*: DER YER, or DER ee ER.

postgraduate:
: as an *adjective*, of, taking, or describing a course of study **after graduation**, as *a postgraduate degree*, or *a postgraduate student*; as a *noun*, a student taking such a course or courses.

posthumous:
: from *postumous*, **last**, superlative of *posterus*, **following**; in Late Latin, altered to mean *bury*, as if meaning "born after the father is buried." In incorrectly pronouncing the word as post HUME us, and by associating the accented syllable with *humus*, **earth**, or **ground**, it was generally assumed that *posthumous* meant "after one is buried in the ground." Correct pronunciation: PAHS chu mus. *Posthumous* can also mean "published after the author's death; or "arising or continuing after one's death," as *the posthumous effects of Dr. Martin Luther King's speech "I Have a Dream."*

ex post facto:
: **from (the thing) done afterward**; done or made afterward, especially when having retroactive effect, as an *ex post facto law*.

a posteriori:
: in *logic*, denoting reasoning from facts or particular instances to general principles, or from effects to causes; **inductive**; **empirical**. In other words, the conclusions come **after** the facts are presented. This book's **word clusters** are written on the principles of *a posteriori*—one examines examples of words using a common root, and then concludes or infers the root's general meaning. Compare *a priori* (p. 160), the opposite of *a posteriori*. The **wordbuilders** are developed on the principles of *a priori*.

postil:
: contraction of *post illa verba*, **after these words**; **an annotation**; marginal notes; also, a short homily or commentary on a passage of Scripture; also spelled *apostil*, *apostille*.

preposterous:
: *pre-*, **before**; **before the following**, or, **before that which follows**; originally, with the first last and the last first; inverted; now, so contrary to nature, reason, or common sense as to be absurd, foolish, laughable, ludicrous (see p. 89), ridiculous (see p. 48), silly.

postiche:
: French; from Italian *posticcio*, **artificial**; from Latin *appositus*, **apposite**—placed next to. As an *adjective*, **counterfeit**; also, superfluously decorative; as a *noun*, **a substitute**, pretense; also, **a hairpiece**.

aposiopesis:
: Greek *siopan*, **to be silent**; a rhetorical device: a sudden and dramatic breaking off of a thought in the middle of a sentence, as if the speaker was unwilling or unable to continue. For example, "The horror of the murder scene—no! I must erase it from my mind." Pronounced AP oh SIGH oh PEE sis.

apostrophe:
: Greek *strophein*, **to turn**; **to turn away**; in *rhetoric*, the addressing of a usually absent person or a personified thing, as in "*O Liberty*, what things are done in thy name!" In *grammar*, designates the mark (') that shows possession, e.g., *the boy's bicycle*; it also shows the omissions of a letter or letters in contractions, e.g., *doesn't* for *does not*. In addition, the apostrophe is used in nonsyntactic plurals, such as "There are four *a*'s in Alabama, four *e*'s in Tennessee, and four *s*'s in Mississippi." "Remember to cross your *t*'s and dot your *i*'s." In Greek drama, an *aside*, as used by Shakespeare.

Post hoc, ergo propter hoc: **After this, therefore because of this**; an example of fallacious reasoning where one argues that a prior event was the cause of a later event. For example, there is the story of the rooster who believed that his crowing caused the sun to rise, until one day he forgot to crow, and the sun rose of its own accord.

---

wordextra
Keen, from Irish *caoninim*, **I wail**, is a custom of wailing for the dead; as a verb, to make a wailing, shrill, or mournful sound suggestive of a keen. Another *keen* comes from Old English *cene*, basically meaning **wise**, **learned**, also means **having a sharp edge**, as *a keen knife*; **piercing**, as *a keen appetite*; **strong**, as *a keen desire*.

Word from a place: *canter*, the pace at which the pilgrims rode their horses on the journey to the Canterbury Cathedral; from Chaucer's *Canterbury Tales*. An English poet and author of the 14th century, Geoffrey Chaucer (c. 1340-1400) wrote in Middle English, a combination of Anglo-Saxon and Norman French.

```
┌─────────────────────────────────────────────────────────────────────────────────┐
│                            Word Cluster No. 80                                    │
│                                                                                   │
│  prim           primacy        primage        primary        primate             │
│  prime          primer         primeval       primitive      primo               │
│  primogeniture  primordial     primrose       primulaceous   imprimis            │
│                                                                                   │
│  Common elements_____Inferred Meaning_____ │
└─────────────────────────────────────────────────────────────────────────────────┘
```

Romance Cognates	French premier	Romanian prim	Italian primo	Portuguese primeiro	Spanish primero

Words with disguised Latin roots: preach, preacher, premier, priest, prince, principal (used as both adjective and noun), principle (used only as a noun), prior, priory, priority, pristine, prone; approach, rapprochment

Triplets: principle:principal:prince (see **Word Cluster No. 15**, p. 29)

Latin words and phrases: *principium; princeps; primum mobile; prima facie; primus inter pares; primipara; primus; a priori; Potior est qui prior est*: **He is preferred who is earlier**. First come, first served. Terence *Decipit frons prima multos*: **The first appearance deceives many**; *a priori* vs. *posteriori* (See **Clavis**.)

Italian: *la primavera; la prima donna*   **Spanish**: *primero*

Explore *priesthood of the believer* not only as a theological term, but also as a social and political term.

Explore *primitivism* as a principle in art.

Greek cognates: **proton**; **proto**col (*kola*, **glue**; originally first leaf glued to a manuscript; the code of ceremonial forms and courtesies, of procedure, etc.), **proto**history, **proto**lithic, **proto**nema, **proto**pathic (in *physiology*, designating or of certain sensory nerves having limited sensibility, that respond to heat and pain from a general area), **proto**plasm, **proto**plast, **proto**stele, **proto**trophic, **proto**type, **proto**xylem, **proto**zoan, **proto**zoophage.

Word from Greek mythology: *chimera*, **a foolish fantasy**, or an absurd creation of the imagination; from *Chimera*, a fire-breathing monster, usually represented as having a lion's head, a goat's body, and serpent's tail; in *biology*, a living structure or organism in which the tissues are of varied genetic origin, sometimes as the result of grafting. Pronunciation: kie MIR uh. The adjective form is *chimerical*: imaginary, fantastic, absurd, impossible, visionary.

Word from a Greek legend: *Augean*, **difficult and unpleasant**; from *Augeas*, king of Elis, who had a stable that held 3,000 oxen and that had remained uncleaned for 30 years until Hercules cleaned it in *one* day by diverting a river (or, two rivers) through it. Pronounced oh JEE un.

---

wordextras

Legend, from *legere*, **to read**, originally a collection of saints' lives, is from Middle Latin *legenda*, "lesson to be read," so called because appointed to be read on respective saints' days. It has come to mean a story handed down for generations among a people and popularly believed to have a historical basis, although not verifiable. It also refers to a person whose deeds or exploits are much talked about in his or her own time.

The suffix *–phobia* indicates an irrational fear of; for example, *agoraphobia*, **fear of the marketplace**, **open spaces**; *autophobia, isolophobia*, or *monophobia*, ~ **being alone**; *arachnephobia*, ~ **spiders**; *astrophobia*, ~ **stars**; *claustrophobia*, ~ **closed spaces**; *cryophobia*, ~ **freezing**; *rhabdophobia*, ~ **being beaten**; *necrophobia*, ~ **a cadaver**; *ailurophobia, felinophobia, gatophobia*, ~ **cats**. *A Thesaurus of Medical Word Roots*, by the authors Danner and Noël, lists over 300 phobias, both by phobia and by the thing feared; many others can be found on the Internet.

The *burg* of placenames is an earlier version of *borough*, and originally meant **fortified**, or **walled**, **town**. In Virginia alone, there are over a dozen city and town names ending in *–burg*: Blacksburg, Christiansburg, Edinburg, Fredericksburg, Harrisonburg, Leesburg, Lynchburg, Middleburg, Pearisburg, Petersburg, Rustburg, Scottsburg, Strasburg, Williamsburg, as well as two counties: Lunenburg, Mecklenburg.

Albuquerque, New Mexico, is named after the Duke of Alburquerque, viceroy (1702-11) of New Spain. At its greatest extent, New Spain included Mexico, Central America north of Panama, the West Indies, and the Philippines.

Gentrify, from *gentry*, **noble or high birth** + *facere*, **to make**, means to convert a deteriorated or aging area of a city into a more affluent middle-class neighborhood, as by remodeling dwellings, often displacing the poor.

Chasuble, a sleeveless outer vestment worn over the alb by priests at Mass, is a diminutive of *casa*, **hut**, **cottage**.

Common element base: primus   **Meaning**: first, before, chief
IE base: *per-¹*: **beyond**, whence **English** *far*, *first*.

Clavis

prim: stiffly formal, precise, moral, etc; proper; demure; *primming*: assuming a prim expression.

primate: Middle English *primat*; from Latin genitive *primatis*, **of the first**; an archbishop, or the highest-ranking bishop in a province; any of an order of mammals, including man, the apes, monkeys, lemurs, characterized by flexible hands and feet, both with five digits.

primer: pronounced PRIM er, **a basic handbook** in any subject, especially in *reading*, e.g., *McGuffey's Readers*; pronounced PRY mer, can mean any of the following: a small explosive charge; someone who primes; an undercoat of paint; that which stimulates or catalyzes action.

primitive: can describe a self-taught artist whose work is characterized by a naïve or simple quality, e.g., that of Grandma Moses (1860-1961). In *grammar*, the form from which a certain word is derived. In *algebra* and *geometry*, a form from which another is derived; the term is also used in biology.

primrose: probably from Middle French *primerole*, then altered to *prima rosa*, **first rose**; a spring flower; as an adjective, **pleasant**, as *a primrose path*, an allusion to Shakespeare's having Ophelia declare to Hamlet: *Do not, as some ungracious pastors do/Show me the steep and thorny way to heaven/While he like a libertine treads **the primrose path** of dalliance*. **Dalliance**: dallying, flirting, toying, trifling.

prima donna: literally, **first lady**; originally, the leading female soloist in an opera company; now, as well, a temperamental and conceited performer; informally, *prima donna* can refer to anyone of either sex who is imperious, overbearing, vain, or arrogant.

imprimis: **in the first place**—used to introduce a list of items or considerations; the name of many business entities and publications in the United States.

prima facie: **at first sight**; or on the *face* of it; self-evident; on first view, before further examination; describing evidence sufficient to establish a fact unless disproved. Pronounced: PRY muh FAY shee ee.

primordial: *ordiri*, **to begin**; **the first in time**; existing at or from the beginning; not derivative; fundamental; original; in *biology*, the earliest formed in the development of an organism, organ, structure, etc.

preach: *pre-*, **before** + *dicere*, **to speak**; **to proclaim to**; especially to a religious congregation. See p. 66 for more on *preach*.

primeval: *aevum*, **age**; of the earliest times or ages; primal; primordial, as *primeval forests*, *primeval innocence*.

a priori: *a-*, **from** + **prior**, ablative of *prior*, **first**; a type of reasoning from cause to effect or from generalization to particular instances; deductive; opposite to *posteriori*. See p. 158 for more on *a posteriori*.

prototrophic: Greek *trophein*, **to nourish**; able to synthesize its required growth factors: said of original organisms from which auxotrophic mutants are derived; having the nutritional requirements of the normal or wild type. [*Auxotrophic*: designating an organism requiring additional nutritional substances.]

primus inter pares: **first among equals**, as the Chief Justice of the Supreme Court; he is also the Chief Justice of the United States. See more on p. 98.

primum mobile: **first moving** (thing); **prime mover**. A rendering of Arabic *al-muharrik alawwal*; in *medieval astronomy*, the outermost concentric sphere conceived as carrying the spheres of the fixed stars and the planets in their daily revolution.

Word from Egyptian mythology: *phoenix*, **a symbol of immortality**. The *phoenix* was a beautiful, lone bird that lived in the Arabian desert for 500 or 600 years and then consumed itself in a fire, rising renewed from the ashes to start another long life. It has come to refer to a person or thing of unsurpassed beauty; a paragon. Figuratively, a *phoenix* is a person or institution that rises from the ashes of its own destruction vigorous enough to start anew. *Phoenix*, the capital of Arizona, is said to be named after the legendary bird.

Word from Greek mythology: *atlas*, **a book of maps**; from the representations of the Titan *Atlas* upholding the heavens on his shoulders, common in the 16ᵗʰ-century books of maps. In mythology, Atlas was compelled by the gods to support the world on his shoulders forever; by extension, *atlas* is any person who bears a heavy burden.

Sectional Word Cluster Test

INSTRUCTIONS: For each set of words from Latin and Greek (and sometimes, French, Italian, Spanish, and German), write the common meaning in the blank.

Example: **hypo**tenuse, **hypo**thesis, **sub**ject   <u>under</u>

	Presection Answer	Postsection Answer
81. **quadr**ate, **quadri**vium, **quatr**ain, **quart**et	_____	_____
82. **regi**men, cor**rect**, di**rect**ion, **orth**odontics	_____	_____
83. **sal**ary, **sal**ami, **sauce**, **saus**age, **halo**gen	_____	_____
84. **salu**te, **salu**tation, **salu**brious, Gesund**heit**	_____	_____
85. **sanct**uary, **sacr**ed, conse**cr**ate, exe**cr**ate	_____	_____
86. **sat**ire, **sati**sfy, **sat**urate, **pleth**ora	_____	_____
87. **sec**ond, **seq**uence, sub**sequ**ent, pur**sue**, **suite**	_____	_____
88. **sess**ion, super**sede**, sub**sid**ize, cat**hedr**al	_____	_____
89. **sine**cure, **sans**-souci, **sin** duda	_____	_____
90. **stat**ionery, tran**sist**or, armi**stice**, **thesis**	_____	_____

_____   _____

Presection Score   Postsection Score

Note: Enter scores for this test and the following ones after completing this section; then, enter them on p. xvii.

Sectional Wordbuilder Test

Throughout the book and as a supplement, there are wordbuilders; these wordbuilders are designed to help you build a family of words from a single root.

	Presection Answer	Postsection Answer
56. What is the meaning of *sym-, syn-* as in **sym**phony, **syn**tax?	_____	_____
57. What is the meaning of *calli-* as in **calli**graphy, **calli**opsis?	_____	_____
58. What is the meaning of *cata-* as in **cata**pult, **cata**comb?	_____	_____

_____	_____
Presection Score	Postsection Score

After entering the scores here, enter them on pp. xviii.

Word Cluster No. 81

quatrain	quart	quarter	quartile
quatran	quatrefoil	quartet	quarto
quaternary	quaternion	quatern	quarter horse
quadrate	quadratic	quadrant	quadruple
quadrangle	quadriceps	quadrennial	quadruped
quadrivial	quadrivium	quadripartite	quadrat

Common elements_____Inferred Meaning_____

Romance Cognates	French	Romanian	Italian	Portuguese	Spanish
	quatre	patru*	quattro	quarto	cuatro

*There are no q's in Romanian.

Words with disguised Latin roots: cadre, cahier, carillon (see **Clavis**), catercornered (also, catercorner), quarantine (see **Clavis**), quarrel (one meaning), quarry (one meaning), quire (of paper), squad, squadron, square, trocar

Prescription term: *quater in die* (q.i.d.); see **Clavis**

French term: *Louis Quatorze*: designated the style of architecture, furniture, art, etc., that prevailed during the reign of Louis XIV.

Greek *tetra-*, **four**: **tetr**acid, **tetr**ad, **tetr**arch, **tetr**archy, **tetr**atomic, **tetr**ode, **tetr**oxide; **tetra**basic, **tetra**branchiate, **tetra**chloride, **tetra**chord, **tetra**cycline, **tetra**gon, **Tetra**grammaton, **tetra**hedron, **tetra**logy (see **Clavis**), **tetra**merous, **tetra**meter (see p. 169), **tetra**petalous, **tetra**ploid, **tetra**pod, **tetra**sporangium, **tetra**stich, **tetra**syllable, **tetra**valent; **tess**alate, **tess**era, dia**tess**aron; **tra**pezium, **tra**pezoid (see p. 64, under *dentoid*). **NB**: Tetrazzini.

Trademarks: Teflon®, from poly**tetra**fluoroethylene + **on** (*-on*, an arbitrary suffix for synthetic products, e.g., Dacron®, nylon, rayon)

Anglo-Saxon: *farthing* (a former small British coin, equal to **one-fourth** of a penny); **Dutch**: *firkin* (a small, wooden tub for butter, lard, etc.; a unit of capacity equal to **one-fourth** barrel; *-kin* is a diminutive: *bumpkin, catkin, napkin*).

wordbuilder #56

The Greek prefixes *sym-*, *syn-*, **with**, **together**, yield dozens of words, e.g., **sym**biont, **sym**biosis, **sym**bol, **sym**metry, **sym**pathy, **sym**petalous, **sym**phony, **sym**podium, **sym**posium (see p. 199, **wordextras**), **sym**ptom; **syn**agogue, **syn**apsis, **syn**carpous, **syn**chronous (geo**syn**chronous), **syn**copate, **syn**dactyl, **syn**dicate, **syn**drome (see p. 107 under *palindrome*), **syn**ecdoche (see p. 77, under **wordextras**), **syn**eresis, **syn**ergism, **syn**ezesis, **syn**od, **syn**onym, **syn**opsis, **syn**optic, **syn**tax, **syn**thesis, **syn**thetic. In the specialized fields, there are many others; for example, in *medicine*, there are **sym**blepharon, **sym**pathectomy; **syn**cytial, **syn**ovia. Assimilated forms are as follows: *syl-*: **syl**lable, **syl**lepsis, **syl**logism (see p. 120 under **Clavis**); *sys-*, **sys**taltic (**sys**tole), **sys**sarcosis (the connection of bones by muscle); as well as poly**syn**deton (see p. 154, under **Clavis**). Truncated to *sy-*: **sy**stem, **sy**zygy (see p. 108).

NB: *Syllabus*: originally, **list**; altered from Latin *sillybus*, and further from Greek *sillybos*, a parchment strip used as a label. In *academics*, a summary or outline containing the main points of a course; in *law*, brief notes preceding and explaining the decision of law in the written report of an adjudged case.

wordextras

Laser is the acronym for *light amplification by stimulated emission of radiation*; ***maser***, *microwave amplification by stimulated emission of radiation*.

Glom, from Gaelic *glaum*, **to snatch**, means **to seize**, **grab**; **to steal**; **to look over**, **view**, **see**, **stare at**. Sports enthusiasts often stay *glommed* to the television to watch their favorite teams.

Minacious, from Latin *minari*, **to threaten**, means **menacing**, **threatening**; other words from this verb are **men**ace, a**men**able, pro**men**ade, **min**atory, e**min**ent, im**min**ent, pro**min**ent, pro**mon**tory; de**mean** (one meaning), de**mean**or.

Memphis, Tennessee, on the Mississippi, is named after the capital of ancient Egypt, on the Nile, just south of modern-day Cairo. Memphis is the home of the blues and the birthplace of rock 'n roll.

Montana, from Latin *montana*, **mountainous regions**, is sometimes called "Mountain State of the Northwest."

Common element base: quadrus   **Meaning**: four, square
IE base: *kwetwer-*: yields **Old English** *feower*; **German** *vier*; **Greek** *tetra*, all pertaining to **four**.

Clavis

quadratic: in *algebra*, involving a quantity or quantities **squared** but none raised to a higher power; a *quadratic equation* is one in which the second power, or **square**, is the highest to which the unknown quantity is raised.

quadriceps: *caput*, **head**; the **four**-headed, large extensor muscle of the front of the thigh.

quadrivium: in the medieval university, the **four** *mathematical* subjects leading to the Master of Arts degree: arithmetic, astronomy, geometry, music. In this curriculum, *music* was considered *not* as an art in the modern sense of the word, but as a science, bordering on mathematics and physics (acoustics). See *trivium*, p. 196; *liberal arts*, p. 114.

quarter horse: so called because of its high speed up to **one**-**fourth** mile.

quatran fever: a fever that occurs every **fourth** day, by inclusive counting, i.e., with two days between attacks.

quarter note: a music note equal to **one**-**fourth** of a measure's time; receives one beat in 4/4 time; one-half, in 2/2 time. A *quarter note* has a stem and filled-in, or solid, head; a half note has a stem and a clear head.

quatrain: a stanza or poem of **four** lines, usually with the rhyme scheme abab, abba, or abcb. In the Shakespearean, or Elizabethan, sonnet, there are three quatrains plus a rhymed couplet, for a total of 14 lines. A typical rhyme scheme in a Shakespearean sonnet is abab cdcd efef gg. See *stanza*, p. 180.

quater in die: abbreviated *q.i.d.*; in prescription writing, **four times a day**. Compare *b.i.d.*, **twice a day**, p. 68.

quarantine: from Italian *quarantina giorni*, **forty days**; originally, the period that a ship carrying persons with a contagious disease was detained in the port of entry under strict isolation to prevent the disease from infecting the area's people. Related in principle to French *cordon sanitaire*, **sanitary line**, a line of checkpoints around a quarantined area.

cadre: French; **the frame of a picture**; from Latin *quadrum*, **a square**; basic framework; key personnel, mainly of a military training unit. In Spanish, a *picture*, as of art, is *cuadro*.

carillon: French; from Latin *quaternio*; originally, **a set of four bells**; also, an imitative organ pipe. One of the most famous carillons in the United States is at the Netherlands Memorial, on the grounds of the Iwo Jima Memorial, adjacent to Arlington National Cemetery and Fort Myer, Arlington, Virginia.

quarry: originally, **a place for squaring stones**; can also mean diamond-shaped tile or glass. Another *quarry*, **prey**, **game**, is from Latin *cord*, **heart**, or from *cuir*, **hide**; authorities differ on the origin.

tetralogy: **four** related works—especially operas or novels—by a single composer or author; also, a set of dramas, consisting of *three tragedies* and *a satyr play*, which probably was a *satire*, presented in sequence at the festival of Dionysius in Athens. See **Clavis** note on *satyr*, p. 20; for additional information on *satire*, see p. 172.

wordextras

Impeach has a tortuous derivation, but is ultimately from *impede*, **to entangle the feet**. The basic elements are Latin *in-*, **in** + *pedica*, **fetter**, from *pes*, **foot**. In Late Latin (A.D. c. 200-c. 600), these elements coalesced into *impedicare*, **to fetter**, **to entangle**, which yields *impediment*. In Old French (A.D. c. 800-c. 1550), the word evolved into *empechier*, **to hinder**; in Middle English (a combination of Old French and Anglo-Saxon, and the language of Chaucer), *empechier* evolved into *empechen*. *To impeach* is to challenge or discredit a person's honor, reputation, etc. In particular, *impeach* means "to bring a public official before the proper committee on a charge of wrongdoing."

Belie, from Old English *beleogan*, **to deceive by lying**, is "to give a false idea of, contradict, misrepresent," as in "The newspaper reporter *belied* the facts of the article"; "His ashen face and trembling hands *belied* his calm attitude."

Houston, Texas, is named after Samuel Houston (1793-1863), US general and statesman, and president of the Republic of Texas (1836-1838). An Army post (*Fort Sam* Houston) in San Antonio, TX, is also named after him.

Ocean was originally thought of as "the outer sea," in contrast to the inland Mediterranean Sea. See *Pacific Ocean*, p. 148, for the names of the five oceans.

Word Cluster No. 82

regal	**reg**alia	**reg**ality	**reg**ency
regent	**reg**icide	**reg**ime	**reg**imen
regiment	**reg**imentation	**reg**ion	**reg**ius
regnal	**reg**ular	**reg**ulatory	**reg**ulate
regulation	**reg**uline	**reg**ulus	inter**reg**num
rectangle	**rect**ify	**rect**itude	**rect**o
rector	**rect**um	ar**rect**	cor**rect**
di**rect**	di**rect**ion	di**rect**ory	e**rect**(ion)
e**rect**or	insur**rect**ion	resur**rect**ion	**rect**ocele

Common elements_____**Inferred Meaning**_____

Romance Cognates	French	Romanian	Italian	Portuguese	Spanish
	règle	drept	regola	regra	regla

Words and phrases with disguised roots: address, adroit, alert, dirge, dirigible, dress, droit, droit du seigneur (**right of the lord**); ergo, maladroit, rajah, rani (see p. 81); real, realm, reckon, redress, regal, reign, resource, resurge; Rex, rial, rich, right, rigible, Risorgimento (lit., resurrection); royal, rule, ruler, rye, source, vive le Roi!

Doublets: resurge:resurrection

Latin phrases: *oratio recta; Juglans regia; Pithecanthropus erectus*   **French term**: *ancien régime*

Motto of the State of Arkansas: *Regnat populus*: **The people rule.**
Motto of the State of Maine: *Dirigio*: **I direct.**

Contemporary Quote: *Esse non recte intelligi est*: **To be is to be misunderstood.**
Used in speech by William J. Bennett, Ph.D., former U. S. Secretary of Education

NB: *Register* is not in this family, but rather from *gerere*, **to carry, make**, and yields *gerund* (see p. 150), *belligerent* (see p. 155); *gestate, gesticulate, gesture*. Neither *regale* nor *regatta*, originally, a gondola race, is in this family.

Greek: *orthos*, **straight**: **orth**icon, **orth**odontics (see p. 64), **orth**optic, **orth**otics; **ortho**biosis, **ortho**center, **ortho**cephalic, **ortho**chorea, **ortho**chromatic, **ortho**clase, **ortho**clastic, **ortho**dox, **ortho**doxy, **ortho**ëpy, **ortho**genesis, **ortho**gnathous (**having straight jaws**), **ortho**gonal, **ortho**grade (see p. 145, **wordbuilder #54**), **ortho**graphy (*graphien*, **to write**, correct spelling; method of spelling), **ortho**keratology, **ortho**kinetics, **ortho**logy, **ortho**melic, **ortho**metry, **ortho**molecular, **ortho**pedics (originally, the practice of straightening *children's* bones), **ortho**pteran, **ortho**rhombic, **ortho**scope, **ortho**static, **ortho**stichy, **ortho**tropous (*tropein*, **to turn**; in **botany**, **growing straight**); an**ortho**site.

Spanish Words and Placenames in English

Conquistador, **conqueror**, is from Latin *quaerere*, **to seek, demand, acquire**, hence, to get what one seeks.

Aficionado, a devoted follower of some sport, art, activity, etc., is from Latin *afficere*, **to influence**, from which are *affect, affection*, the base of which is *facere*, **to make, do, act** (see p. 61, **wordbuilder #27**).

Renegade, from Latin *renegare* (**re-**, **again** + *negare*, **to deny**), repeatedly denies his or her former beliefs; one who abandons his or her party, principles, customs, etc.; an apostate. *Renege*, to back out of a deal, is from *renegade*.

Pueblo, an Indian communal village mainly in Arizona and New Mexico and built of adobe or stone, is from Latin *populus*, **people**. (See **Placenames** below.)

Adobe, usually associated with American Indians, is originally from Arabic *at-tuba* (**al-**, **the** + Coptic *tobe*, **brick**). *Adobe* designates an unburnt, sun-dried brick; also, a building made of adobe, especially in the Southwest. Words such as *adobe* demonstrate the influence of the Arabic-speaking Moors who conquered and inhabited Spain for almost a thousand years. See p. 68 for more on *Coptic*, under *almanac*. See *adobe*, p. 47, under *coffee*.

Arroyo, originally from Latin *arrugia*, **shaft** or **pit** (in a gold mine), means either a dry gully, or a rivulet or stream.

Placenames: Pueblo, CO; Pueblo Bonito (**Beautiful Town**), NM. Pueblo Bonito, located in the Chaco Culture Historic Park, is the largest of the prehistoric ruins. Pueblo de Luna (**Moon Town**), NM; Pueblo Grande (**Big Town**), AZ; Santa Fe (**Holy Faith**), NM. Also, Puebla, both a state and a city in Mexico.

Common element base: regere   **Meaning**: to rule, thus straight, right, ruler (thus, king)
IE base: *reg-¹*: **to move in a straight line**; **German**: *regieren*, **to rule**; noun, *Reich*; thus, Hitler's *Third Reich*

Clavis

recto: in *printing*, the **right**-**hand** page of a book; the front side of a leaf; opposed to *verso*.

rectocele: Greek *kele*, **hernia**, **rupture**; a hernial protrusion of the rectum into the vagina.

arrect: *ar-*, assimilation of *ad-*, **to**, **toward**; **rigidly erect**; lifted up; raised, as the *arrect* ears of a rabbit, mule, burro, or donkey.

regal: **of a king**; royal; characteristic of, like, or fit for a king.

regalia: rights or privileges belonging to a **king**; prerogatives of sovereignty; extended to mean **splendid clothes**; **finery**.

interregnum: *inter-*, **between**; **between kings**, or between reigns; the interval between the death of a king and the choosing of his successor. The designation for an **acting ruler** is *interrex*.

Juglans regia: taxonomically, **Walnut king**; scientific classification for the soft-shelled, or California, walnut; translated from Latin, **the King's walnut**, or **the royal walnut**. See p. 136, under *nomen nudum*.

rectify: *-fy* from *facere*, **to make**; **to make straight**; to put or set right; **correct**; **emend**; in *chemistry*, to refine or purify a liquid by distillation, especially by fractional or repeated distillations.

dress: from Old French *drecier*, **to set up**, **arrange**; from *directus*, **to lay straight**.

dirigible: from same base as *direct* (*di-*, **apart**); that which is able to be **directed**, as a lighter-than-air craft.

reign: the government or power of a **king**. SYNONYMS: English, *kingdom*; French, *règne*; Latin, *regnum*; German, *Reich*. The French, Latin, and German words are cognates of *reign*.

surge: *sub-*, **from under** + *regere*; as a *noun*, a sudden, strong increase, as a wave billow, or swell of the ocean; also, an electrical power surge. As a *verb*, to increase suddenly or abnormally. Not to be confused with its homonym *serge*, a fabric, from Latin *serica*, **silken garments**.

resurrection: *re-*, **again**; **to surge** or **rise up again**, a basic tenet of the Christian faith; resurge.

Rex: Latin; **ruler**, **king**, the official title of a reigning king; *rex non potest peccare*, **the king can do no wrong**.

adroit: from French *à droit*, **rightly**; therefore, **skillful**, **dexterous**; opposite to *maladroit*, from French *mal*, **wrong** + *adroit*. SYNONYMS of *maladroit*: awkward, clumsy, gauche (see p. 133), inept.

alert: from French *alerte*; further from Italian *all'erta*; from Latin *ad illam erectam*, **on the height**, on the lookout. "On the alert" is tautological, i.e., using unnecessary words, for *l'* of *all'* means "the."

porrect: *por-*, from *pro-*, **forward**; **to direct forward**; in *zoology*, stretched out or forth; extended, especially forward, as *porrect mandibles*, or jaws.

Pithecanthropus erectus: from Greek *pithekos*, **ape**; from an earlier IE root *bhidh*, **dreadful**, which evolved into Latin *foedus*, **ugly**; combined with Greek *anthropos*, **man**, and Latin *erectus*, denotes "an ugly man who holds himself erect," i.e., not walking on all fours like an animal.

Orando pro rege et regno: an ancient writ requiring that prayers be offered for good government of the realm.

NB: *Regale*, from French *régaler*, is further from Old French *gale*, **joy**, **pleasure**. As a *verb*, *regale* means "to entertain by providing a splendid feast"; further, to delight with something pleasing or amusing, as "to regale the class with amusing anecdotes"; as a *noun*, **a feast**, **choice food**, **delicacy**, though its use as a noun is now archaic.

wordextras

Jai alai is from Basque *jai*, **festival** + *alai*, **merry**, thus "merry festival." Also called *pelota*, Spanish for "ball," *jai alai* is an extremely fast court game popular in Spain, Latin America, and the Philippines. *Jai alai* is somewhat like handball, played usually by two or four players, with a long curved wicker basket strapped to the wrist. [The language of the Basques appears to be unrelated to any other language.] Pronounced: HI LIE, or HI uh LIE.

In radio, *AM* stands for *amplitude modulation*; *FM*, for *frequency modulation*.

Word Cluster No. 83

salad	**sal**ada	**sal**ami	**sal**ariat	**sal**ary
salé	**sal**eratus	**sal**iferous	**sal**ify	**sal**imeter
saline	**sal**magundi	**Sal**ol	**sal**tern	**sal**ting

Common elements_____Inferred Meaning_____

Romance Cognates	French	Romanian	Italian	Portuguese	Spanish
	sel	sare	sale	sal	sal

English bound compounds: saltbox (a type of colonial New England house), saltbush, saltcellar, saltpan, saltpeter, saltshaker, saltwater, saltworks, saltwort; **unbound compounds**: salt grass, salt lick, salt marsh, salt pork

Words with disguised Latin roots: sass, sassy, sauce, saucer, saucy, sausage, coleslaw (**cabbage salad**)

Placenames: Salina, KS; Salinas, CA; Saline, MO; Salton Sea, CA; Salt Lake City, UT; Salt River, AZ

Latin phrases: *cum grano salis* (See **Clavis**); *Sal sapit omnia*: **Salt seasons everything.**

French phrase: *un propos salé*, **a salty remark**; **a coarse remark**; biting; pungent; indelicate

Note: Do not confuse this root with the *sal* in *salute* (see **Word Cluster No. 84**, p. 167), or with another family that includes *saltire, assault, somersault, desultory*, and *insult* (see **Word Cluster No. 91**, p. 181).

Greek: *halos*, **salt**: **hal**oid (see p. 64 for other words with the suffix *–oid*), **halo**biont, **halo**gen, **halo**phile, **halo**phyte, **halo**steresis, **halo**thane. Do not confuse this root with *halo* in the medical term **halometer**, a device for measuring the halo around the optic disk. For more on *halo* as a single word, see p. 92, under **wordextras**.

German: *Er liegt tüchtig im Salz*: **He is in a pretty pickle.** *Du hast es noch im Salz (liegen)*: **You have it coming to you.**

Word named after a place: *mecca*, **an ultimate goal**; a place one yearns to go to; a place visited by many people; from *Mecca*, the birthplace of Mohammed and thus a holy city of Islam, which Moslems are required to visit once in their lifetime if they are physically able. The city of Mecca is located in Saudi Arabia, near the Red Sea.

wordextras

Insinuate, from Latin *sinus*, **bend**, **curved surface**, **hanging fold of a toga**, is **to wind one's way into**, thus provoking gradual doubt or suspicion. See *sincere* on p. 177 under **NB**. *Sine* and *cosine* are also from *sinus* as well.

In the Roman calendar, *July* and *August* were known by their numerical designations—*Quintilis, Sextilis*—as are *September* through *December*. Later, *Quintilis* and *Sextilis* were renamed *July, August*, to honor the caesars Julius and Augustus, respectively. The Roman calendar had only ten months. See **Clavis** note, under *December*, p. 58.

Polonaise, the French feminine form of *polonais*, **Polish**, is a stately Polish dance in triple time, almost processional in character. *Polka*, which is Czech, is also a Polish dance; *Polka* itself means "Polish woman," *Polak* being "Polish man." The base of these words is Slavic *polje*, **field**.

Bar Mitzvah, Hebrew for **son of duty**, or **son of the commandment**, designates a 13-year-old Jewish boy, who has arrived at the age of responsibility; also, the ceremony celebrating his coming of age. See *Bath Mitzvah*, p. 57.

Brogue, **a heavy work shoe**, from Irish *brog*, **a shoe**, is originally from Old Norse *broc*, **leg covering**. *Brogan*, coming from the same source, is also a heavy work shoe, fitting high on the ankle. *Brogue*, referring to the pronunciation peculiar to a dialect, is from Irish *barrig*, **hold on the tongue**.

Lordly, from Old English *hlafordic*, means "of, like, characteristic of, or suitable to a lord"; specifically, **noble**; **grand**; also, **haughty**; **overbearing**. *Lordling* designates an unimportant or minor lord: usually contemptuous. See p. 25 for more on *lord*.

Scuba is the acronym for *Self-Contained Underwater Breathing Apparatus*.

With *opsi-*, **late** + *gamos*, **marriage**, *opsigamy* is the instance of **marrying late in life**. See other words from *gamos*, e.g., allo**gamy**, bi**gamy**, cleisto**gamy**, exo**gamy**, poly**gamy**, pp. 4, 44.

Vellum, from Middle French *velin*, **prepared calfskin**, is a fine kind of parchment prepared from calfskin, lambskin, or kidskin, used as writing parchment or for binding books. *Veal*, **the meat of calves**, is from the same source. See *parchment*, p. 166.

Common element base: sal   **Meaning**: salt
IE base: *sal-¹*; **German**: *Salz*; **Greek**: *halos*; **Sanskrit**: *salila*, **salty**; a salt marsh

Clavis

salina: Spanish: a **salt** marsh, pond, or lake not connected with the sea; *Salina*, California (near Monterey), is so named from the salt deposits formed at its mouth.

salada: Mexican Spanish for **salt-covered plain** in the Southwest where an ancient salt lake has evaporated.

salary: Roman soldiers were at one time paid in cakes of **salt**; consequently, the expression, "He is not worth his *salt*." SYNONYMS: emolument, fee, stipend, wage.

salariat: **salaried workers** as opposed to *wage earners*. Labor laws define salaried workers, e.g., managers and executives, as exempt from the wage-hour laws, whereas nonexempt employees, or wage earners, are accountable by the hour.

salinity: noun form of *saline*; the average *salinity* of Great Salt Lake in Utah is almost six times that of the ocean. No fish can live in this environment; neither can a person sink in it. The noun-forming suffix *–ity* changes adjectives into nouns, e.g., able, *ability*; ambiguous, *ambiguity*; chaste, *chastity*; infinite, *infinity*; possible, *possibility*; profound, *profundity*; responsible, *responsibility*; sane, *sanity*.

saltern: from Old English *sealtaern*; *aern*, **house**, **saltworks**, but literally, **salt house**; a place where **salt** is made, as by evaporation of natural brines. *Barn* is also from *aern*, originally denoting a *barley house*.

saleratus: from New Latin *sal aeratus*, **aerated salt**; sodium bicarbonate; baking soda.

saliferous: *ferre*, **to bear**; producing or containing salt. Pronunciation: suh LIF er us.

sal volatile: Modern Latin; **volatile salt**; a mixture of ammonium bicarbonate and ammonium carbonate, especially in aromatic solutions for use as smelling salts.

halobiont: Greek *bios*, **life**; an organism living in a **saline** environment, as the sea.

halophile: Greek *philos*, **love**; an organism that flourishes in a **saline** environment.

halophyte: Greek *phyton*, **plant**; a plant that thrives in soils having a high content of various **salts**. Many halophytes resemble true *xerophytes*, or plants that thrive in a climate with limited water supply. Greek *xero* means **dry**, as in *Xerox*®, manufacturer of **dry copiers**. See p. 214, Item 196.

cum grano salis: **with a grain of salt**; with allowances or reservations; with due skepticism.

wordextras

Shogun is Japanese, but originated in China; originally, *chiang chun*, **military leader**.

Caravan, from Persian *karwan*, comes into English through Italian *caravana*; as far as can be determined, *caravan* has no constituent meaning. In Persian, Italian, and English, the inherent meaning has remained intact: a company of travelers, especially of merchants or pilgrims traveling together for safety, as through a desert. It can also mean "a number of vehicles traveling together." See p. 46 under **Persian words**.

Tarantella, a vivacious folk dance of the 16th and 17th centuries, is related to *Taranto*, a seaport in southeast Italy, and to the *tarantula spider*, itself named after *Taranto*. It has been said that *tarantism*, a disease thought to be caused by the spider bite, could be cured by dancing the *tarantella*. It is suggested, however, that you consult a doctor.

Dernier cri is French for **the latest cry**; **the latest fashion**; also, **the last word**. Pronunciation: der nyay KREE.

Dour, from Gaelic *dur*, **rough and rocky land**, means **sullen, gloomy**. This word is ultimately from Latin *durare*, **to last, harden**, which also yields ***durable, dural, duration, endure, epidural, indurate, obdurate, perdure, Duron***®.

Quell, from Old English *cwellan*, **to kill**, has come to mean "to crush; subdue; put an end to, as *to quell a riot*"; also, **to quiet, allay**, as in *to quell one's fears about terrorism*.

Quench, from Old English *cwencan*, **to extinguish**, has not changed its basic meaning; in addition to *extinguish*, *quench* means **to put out**, as *to quench fire with water*; **to satisfy**, as *to quench one's thirst*.

Parchment, from Latin *charta Pergamena*, **paper of Pergamum**, where used as a substitute for papyrus, is the skin of an animal, usually a sheep or goat, prepared as a surface on which to write or paint. See p. 165 for *vellum*.

```
                    Word Cluster No. 84

salubrious       salubrity        salutary         salutation
salutatorian     salutatory       salute           salutiferous
salvable         salvage          salvation        salvatory
salve            salvific         salvo            salver
                                  salvor

Common elements_____Inferred Meaning_____
```

Romance Cognates	French	Romanian	Italian	Portuguese	Spanish
	salut	salut	salute	saúde	salud

Words with disguised Latin roots: safe, safety, sage, save, saving, savior, Savior, sir-reverence

Latin phrases: *In Hac Cruce Salus*: **in this Cross, salvation**; *Salve Regina; Salus*; *Iesus Hominum Salvator (IHS)*, **Jesus, Savior of Men**; *salva fide*, **with safety to one's honor**; keeping one's word

Country: *El Salvador*, the capital of which is San Salvador (see **Clavis**)

Latin hymn title: *O Salutaris Hostia*: **O Saving Victim**, in the Roman Catholic Church, the first words of the hymn used at the beginning of the Benediction of the Blessed Sacrament.

Motto of the State of Missouri: *Salus populi suprema lex esto*: **The welfare of the people shall be the supreme law.**
Motto of the State of Florida: *Civium in moribus rei publicae salus*: **In the character of its citizens lies the welfare of the state.**

Greek *holo-*, **whole, well-preserved**: **hol**istic, **hol**y, **hol**iday, **hol**iness; **holo**blastic, **holo**caust, **Holo**cene, **holo**cephalic, **holo**crine, **holo**gamous, **holo**gram, **holo**graph, **holo**hedral, **holo**metabolism, **holo**morphic, **holo**phrastic, **holo**phytic (obtaining nutrition by photosynthesis, as do green plants and some bacteria), **holo**plankton, **holo**type; cat**hol**ic.

wordextras

Plaintiff and *complain* are from Latin *plangere*, **to lament**, or **cry out**, originally shown by striking or beating the chest. Thus, a *plaintiff* **cries out**, or *complains* against the defendant; from the same root is *plaintive*, **mournful, sad**, as though *crying out*. *Plaint* and *plangent*, as in *plangent waves* beating upon the shore, are also from *plangere*.

Atone, from Middle English *at onen*, means **at one**; thus, **to become reconciled**. The nominal is *atonement*, "satisfaction given for wrongdoing, injury, etc."; in the Christian faith, the effect of the sufferings and death of Jesus Christ in redeeming mankind through one's faith, and bringing about the reconciliation of God and man.

Tabernacle, from Latin *tabernaculum*, **tent**, or **temporary shelter**, is a diminutive of *taberna*, **hut, shed, tavern**. Capitalized, *Tabernacle* designates the portable sanctuary carried by the Jews in their wanderings from Egypt to the Promised Land; later, the Jewish temple (Exodus 25-27). *Tavern* comes shares the same background as *tabernacle*.

Ramadan, Arabic for **the hot month**, the ninth month of the Islamic calendar, also designates the daily fast that is rigidly followed from dawn until sunset during each day of the month. Compare *Ramadan* with Jewish *Passover* and Christian *Lent*, even though the linguistic meaning of *Lent* is simply *a lengthening of days*.

Urdu, spoken mostly by Pakistanis, and from Hindi *zaban-i-urdu*, **language of the camp**, can be traced further to Turkish *ordu*, which is also the base of *horde*; thus, a great number of soldiers in a camp. See p. 52 for *horde*, under **wordextras**.

In the 4th and 5th centuries, A.D., *Britain*, as England was then called, was invaded by a number of Germanic tribes, but mainly the Angles, the Saxons, and the Jutes. The most predominant of these tribes were the Angles; consequently, Britain came to be called *Angleland*. Still later, *Angleland* became known as *Engleland*, and finally *England*. The language of these tribes was called Anglo-Saxon, or Old English, consisting mainly of one-syllable, or monosyllabic, words. There were many words, however, of two syllables, such as **brother** (*brothor*); **furlong** (*furlang*, **length of a furrow**); **lady** (*hlæfdige*, **bread kneader**; see p. 197); **lord** (*hlafwœrd*, **loaf warden**); **midwife** (*mitwif*, **with woman**; see p. 196); **neighbor** (*neahgebur*, **nearby farmer**; see p. 185); **steward** (*stiweard*: **a keeper of pigs**); **warlock** (*wœrleogan*, **truth-breaker**; see p. 108). See p. 91 for more on *England*. See *lord* and *steward*, p. 172, under *steward* (**wordextras**).

In ancient Greece, *chiliarch* (*chilioi*, **a thousand** + *archos*, **leader**), was the military commander of a thousand men. *Chiliasm*: the belief in the coming of the millennium. Pronunciation: *chiliarch*: KIL ee ark; *chiliasm*: KIL ee AZ um.

Common element base: salutare   **Meaning**: to salute; to wish health to
IE root: *sol:* **whole**, **complete**, **health**, **safe**, **well**; **German**: *sicher*; **well**, *gut*; **health**; *Gesundheit*, **health**

Clavis

salute:
to wish health to; hence, **to greet**; in the *military*, a form of respect by raising the right hand to the forehead; other forms of saluting are dipping, or lowering, the flag or firing a cannon. *The United States flag, however, is **never** dipped, or lowered, in salute to anyone or to any other country.*

salutatorian:
ranking immediately below the valedictorian in academic standing, the one who **greets** or **wishes health** to the guests. See p. 66, under *valedictorian*.

salvage:
from *salvare*, **to save**, and closely related to *salus*, **health**, **sound condition**; as a *noun*, basically the rescue, or saving, of a ship and cargo at sea from peril, such as fire, shipwreck, capture; there are many extended meanings; as a *verb*, to save or rescue from shipwreck, fire, flood, etc.

salvation:
directly from Old French; with same base as *salvage*, previous entry. As a theological term, **spiritual rescue** from the consequences of sin; **redemption**; **a buying back**. See *emp-* words, p. 206, Item 89.

salvo:
from *salute*, above; a discharge of weapons, either by artillery or by small arms, as a form of **greeting** for a visiting dignitary. There is another *salvo*, from the same root, and is short for *salvo jure*, a legal phrase meaning **right reserved**, thus a **saving** clause; a reservation. *Salvo* also means **a hostile broadside**, but one in which it is intended **to secure** (or **make safe**) one's own position.

San Salvador:
capital city of *El Salvador*, **The Savior**. The conquering Spaniards, or conquistadors, named this city in honor of Christ, the Savior—*San(to) Salvador*, **Holy Savior**.

holocaust:
Greek *kaustos*, **burnt**; **burnt whole**; originally, an offering, the whole of which was burned; now, great or total destruction of life, especially by fire. There is the *Holocaust Memorial Museum* (on 14th Street, three blocks south of the National Mall) in Washington, DC.

holohedral:
Greek *hedra*, **base**, **side**, **seat**; as a suffix, *-hedral* pertains to a geometric figure or crystal with a specified number of surfaces; thus, *holohedral*: having the full—**whole**—number of planes, or facets, required for complete symmetry: said of a crystal.

holomorphic:
Greek *morphe*, **form**; having the two ends symmetrical: said of a crystal. It is sometimes necessary to massage the meaning of the elements into the total meaning of a word. In this instance, *holo-* means **symmetrical**, whereas it usually means **whole**, **complete**.

holophrastic:
Greek *phrazein*, **to speak**; expressing an entire sentence or phrase in one word, e.g., *affidavit*, **He has stated it on faith**; *caret*, **There is lacking**; *deficit*, **It is lacking**; *placebo*, **I shall please**; *veto*, **I forbid**.

catholic:
Greek *kata-*, usually meaning **down**, but in this case, **completely**; **of general scope or value**; **all-inclusive**; **universal**; often capitalized when referring to the Christian church as a whole.

An idiom: **to lie fallow**: **to be idle**, **uncultivated**, as *the field lay fallow*; *a fallow mind*; *a fallow gold market*; also, **not pregnant**, as *a fallow mare*. There are a number of reasons farmers let their fields *lie fallow*, but mainly to kill weeds and to make the soil richer. There is another *fallow*, which means **pale-yellow**, **brownish yellow**.

wordextras

Stipend, an allowance or a fixed payment for services rendered, is from Latin *stipendium*, a compound of *stips*, **a contribution of a small coin** + *pendere*, **to hang**, **weigh out**; thus, the weighing out of a small coin. SYNONYMS: emolument, fee, pay, salary, wage. See *perpendicular*, p. 136; see other *pend-* words, p. 210, Item 141.

The ***marathon***, a foot race of 26 miles, 385 yards, and run over an open course, is from the legend of the Greek runner who ran the same distance from Marathon, an ancient Greek village in East Attica, to Athens to tell of victory over the Persians (490 B.C.). Some legends say that the runner collapsed and died upon relating the news.

Chalcography, from *chalkos*, **copper** + *graphein*, **to write**, is the art of engraving in copper or brass.

Lent—the 40 days from Ash Wednesday to Easter—in Old English was *lengten*, meaning simply *lengthening* of daylight hours. Dutch cognate: *lente*; German, *Lenz*, which itself means "springtime." See more on *Lent*, p. 167.

Word named for a place: *meander*, **to wander aimlessly**, from the Menderes River in Asia Minor, known for its winding, or *meandering*, course. The ancient name of the Menderes was *Meander*. As a noun, *meander* designates an ornamental design of winding and crisscrossing lines. The adjective form is *meandrous*, as *a meandrous river*.

168

```
                        Word Cluster No. 85

        sanctify      sanction        sanctified       sanctimony
        sanctity      sanctuary       sanctum          Sanctus
    sacrosanct        sacrament       sacred           sacrifice
        sacrist       sacristan       sacrilege        sacrum
        sacroiliac    sacristy        obsecrate        consecrate
        sacrosanct    sacral          execrate         desecrate

    Common elements_____Inferred Meaning_____
```

Romance Cognates	French	Romanian	Italian	Portuguese	Spanish
	saint	psfînt	santo	santo/sao	santo

Words with disguised Latin roots: corposant, sacerdotal, sainfoin, saint, sexton

Doublets: sexton:sacristan

Placenames: Sacramento, CA, KY; Sacré-Coeur, Quebec; Sao Paulo, Brazil (a state of Brazil; also the capital of the state; Brazil's largest city). *Sao*: **saint**. Brazil is the only country in South America whose language is Portuguese.

Latin phrases: *Sacrum Romanum Imperium* (**Holy Roman Empire**; empire of west-central Europe comprising the German-speaking peoples and northern Italy; begun in A.D. 800 with the papal crowning of Charlemagne as emperor or, in an alternate view, with the crowning of Otto I in A.D. 962)*; Sanctum Sanctorum* (**holy of holies**; colloquially, **a private room or retreat**; **den**), *os sacrum*: **sacred bone**.

German: *Weihnachten*, **consecrated**, or **Holy Night**; Christmas Night

Poetry Terms

Iamb, the origin of which is obscure, is a metrical foot of *two* syllables, the first *unaccented*, the other *accented*, or the first short and the second long, e.g., To **strive**/to **seek**/to **find**/and **not**/to **yield**.

Dactyl, Greek for **finger**, is a metrical foot of *three* syllables, corresponding to the three joints of the index finger, the first long followed by two short ones, e.g., **Take** her up/**Ten**derly. See p. 21 for more on *dactyl* as a root of other words.

Anapest, from Greek *ana-*, **back** + *paiein*, **to strike**, is a metrical foot of *three* syllables, so called from reversing the *dactyl*, previous entry. An *anapest* has two short syllables followed by a long one, e.g., And the **sheen**/of their **spears**/was like **stars**/of the **sea**. Probably the most familiar poem in this meter is "Twas the **night**/ before **Christ**mas."

Trochaic, from Greek *trochaios*, **running**, is a metrical foot of *two* syllables, the first, stressed followed by an unstressed one, e.g., **There** they/**are**, my/**fifty**/**men** and/**wom**en.

Spondaic, from *spondee*, Greek for **libation**, is a metrical foot of *two* long or stressed syllables, e.g., as in the first two feet of the following line: **Good strong/thick stu**/pefy/ing in/cense smoke. Browning

Pyrrhic both describes and is a foot of *two* successive syllables with equal light stresses, as in the second and fourth feet in the following line: My way/is to/begin/with the/beginning. Lord Byron, *Don Juan*.

A *foot* of poetry is a rhythmic unit of two or more syllables; the combination of a strong stress and the associated weak stress or stresses that make up the recurrent metric unit of a line.

Meter is either the **number of feet** in a line of verse, e.g., *pentameter* (**five feet**), or the **combination of the number and the kind of feet**, e.g., *iambic pentameter* is a line with **five feet of iambs**. *Dimeter* is a line of two feet; *trimeter*, a line of three feet; *tetrameter*, a line of four feet.

A Writing Tip: The possessive, not the objective, case of a pronoun modifies *gerunds*, those verbals that end in *–ing* serving as nouns. "Would you mind *my* helping you set the table?" not "Would you mind *me* helping you set the table?" This type of modifier is called *gerundial possessive*. [The ending *–ing* also indicates a *participle*, which "participates" as an adjective. Example of *–ing* gerund: *Running* can be good for you. Example of *–ing* participle: *Running* to the bus stop, Gerald fell and sprained his ankle. *Running* modifies *Gerald*, or who was running. See *participle*, p. 150.] **Note**: Transformational grammarians do not totally subscribe to the gerundial possessive rule.

Common element base: sacer   **Meaning**: holy, sacred
IE base: *sak-*: **to sanctify**; **German**: *heil*, **safe**; *heilig*, **holy**; **Greek** *hiero-* is not a cognate; however, this root yields **hier**archy, **hiero**cracy (government by priests or other clergy), **hiero**dule (see **Clavis**), **hiero**glyph (**holy carving**; for other *glyph* words, see p. 111, **wordbuilder #45**), **hiero**logy (the religious lore of a people), **hiero**phant.

Clavis

sacrament:	can mean a sum deposited by the two parties in a suit, in the sense of **dedicating** themselves to a resolution; in some Christian churches, any of certain rites regarded either as a means of grace or as a manifestation of grace. *Baptism* and *Communion* are usually regarded as the two basic sacraments.
sacrifice:	*facere*, **to make**; **to make holy or sacred**. Christians inherited the ancient Hebrew concept of *sacrifice*, the offering of a cherished possession, such as an unblemished lamb; as a *noun*, the act of offering the life of a person, animal, or some object, in propitiation of or homage to a deity. Christians regard Jesus Christ as the sacrificial Lamb. Also used as a baseball term.
sacristan:	a person in charge of a *sacristy*, a room in a church where the *sacred* vessels, vestments, etc. are kept. A doublet of *sacristan* is *sexton*; however, a sexton usually maintains the church property.
sacrum:	short for *os sacrum*, lowest bone of the spine; translates Greek *hieron osteron*, **sacred bone**, because in sacrifices, it is said this bone was not consumed in the fire; posterior section of the pelvis.
sacroiliac:	in *anatomy*, the juncture of the *sacrum* (see *sacrum*, above) and the *iliac*. *Iliac* is from *ilium* (plural, *ilia*), the uppermost and widest of the bones composing one of the lateral halves of the pelvis.
sacrosanct:	**sacred holy**, or **sacred sacred**; very sacred, holy, or inviolable. The noun is *sacrosanctity*.
sacrilege:	*legere*, **to gather up**, **take away**; the taking away of something sacred; originally referred to temple robbers. The roots *lect-*, *leg-* also means **to read**, as in *lectern*, *lecture*, *legible*, *lesson*; also, **to choose**, as in *collect*, *dialect*, *eclectic*, *elect*, *intellect*, *neglect*, *prelect*, *recollect*, *select*; *elegant*.
sanctimony:	affected **piety** or righteousness; religious hypocrisy; *sanctimonious*: pretending to be very holy or pious; hypocritical.
sanctuary:	**a holy place**, as a building set aside for worship of the divinity or of one or more deities; any church or temple, particularly a holy place within a church or temple; also, a place of refuge or protection; immunity from punishment or the law. SYNONYMS: asylum, haven, refuge, retreat, shelter.
sanctum:	short for *sanctum sanctorum*, **holy of holies**; **a sacred or holy place**; a private room or study where one is not disturbed. The plural is either *sanctums* or *sancta*.
desecrate:	*de-*, **away**; **to take away the sacredness of**; to treat as not sacred; **profane**.
consecrate:	*con-*, **together**; **to sanctify or make holy**. President Lincoln declared at Gettysburg, "But, in a larger sense, we cannot *dedicate*—we cannot **consecrate**—we cannot *hallow*—this ground." Excellent example of *parallel repetition* as a rhetorical device; the main verbs are synonyms.
execrate:	*ex-*, **out** + *sacrare*, **to consecrate**; originally, **to call down evil upon**; to curse; to speak abusively or contemptuously of; to denounce scathingly; to loathe; detest; abhor. The root is truncated because of the *s*-ending sound of the prefix *ex-* (eks).
obsecrate:	*ob-* (see **Word Cluster No. 70**, p. 139); **to beseech** (on religious matters); though now rarely used, the word means "to beg (for something) or supplicate (someone)"; **entreat**.
hierodule:	Greek *doulos*, **slave**; in early Greece, **a temple slave**, dedicated to the service of a god.
hieroglyphic:	Greek *glyphein*, **to carve**; **holy carvings**; *hieroglyphics*, a method of writing in ancient Egypt, using pictures instead of alphabetic letters; has come to mean **hard to understand**, **illegible**.

Word from a plant: *sardonic*, **bitterly ironic**, **sarcastic**; from *Sardinian herb*, that when chewed supposedly distorted the chewer's face. There is no etymological connection between *sardonic* and *sarcastic*.

A word from Greek history: *solon*, a lawmaker or legislator, especially a wise one; from *Solon*, an Athenian statesman and lawgiver, who lived circa 638-558 B.C. *Solon* framed the democratic laws of Athens.

<table>
<tr><td colspan="5" align="center">**Word Cluster No. 86**</td></tr>
</table>

sate	**sat**iate	**sat**ient	**sat**iety	**sat**ire
satisfaction	**satis**fy	in**sat**iable	in**sat**iate	**sat**urate
polyun**sat**urated	dis**satis**fy	**sat**iable	**sat**irize	**sat**urable

Common elements_____Inferred Meaning_____

Romance Cognates	French	Romanian	Italian	Portuguese	Spanish
	saturer	satul	saturare	saturar	saturar

Word with disguised Latin root: asset   **Old English**: sad

Latin phrases: *Dictum sapienti sat est*: **A word to the wise is sufficient.** Plautus, Roman writer of comic dramas
satis eloquentiae sapientiae parum: **enough eloquence but too little wisdom**
sat cito, si sat bene: **soon enough, if but well enough.** Cato
Satis quod sufficit: **What suffices is enough.** Enough is as good as a feast.
Sat pulchra, si sat bona: **Beautiful enough if (she is) good enough.** Handsome is as handsome does.
Satis verborum: **enough of words**; enough said.

Explore *Satire in Music* in *Harvard's Dictionary of Music*.

NB: Do not confuse this root with the linguistic term ***satem***, from Avestan (Old Persian).

Latin *plenus*, **full**: **plen**ary, **plen**ish (now used only in Scottish), **plen**itude, **plen**teous, **plen**ty, **plen**um; com**plete**, incom**plete**, de**plete**, re**plete**; ex**ple**tive; im**ple**tion, su**ppletion**; com**ple**ment, im**ple**ment, su**pple**ment; comple-mentary (or, comple**ment**al), com**pli**ment, compli**ment**ary; accom**plish**, mani**ple**; com**ply**, sup**ply**; re**plen**ish, also, Greek **pleth**ora (see p. 154), **pleth**oric, iso**pleth** (*iso-*, **equal**, the line connecting points on a graph or map that have equal or corresponding values with regard to certain variables). See p. 75 for *iso-* words.

wordextras

In Greek, *orchestra* originally designated a flat surface used for threshing grain. In Greek drama, *orchestra* came to mean the area where the chorus danced, and later where the chorus danced *and* sang. *Khoros* in Greek meant **dance**, the meaning of which is retained in *choreography*, the arrangement of dance movements. See *halo*, p. 92, for original meaning similar to *orchestra*.

Amigo, Spanish for **friend**, from Latin *amicus*, **friend**, is originally from Latin *amare*, **to love**. *Amiable, amicable,* and *amicus curiae* (**friend of the court**; see p. 29), as well as *enemy* (see p. 96 under **wordanalysis**), are from *amicus*.

Ampersand is a coalescence of **and per se and**, that is, (the sign &) by itself (&). The *ampersand sign* (&) began as the Latin word for **and**: *et*, as in *et cetera*. The letters of the alphabet, the numerals, and the ampersand were printed on early slate boards and recited by the class in unison.

Monument, from Latin *monere*, **to remind**, **warn**, designates that which is set up to keep alive the memory of a person or an event, as a tablet, statue, pillar, building, e.g., Jefferson Memorial, Washington Monument, Lincoln Memorial, Vietnam War Memorial (**The Wall**), Korean War Memorial, and World War II Memorial, all on or near the National Mall in Washington, DC. The Iwo Jima Memorial is located adjacent to Arlington National Cemetery and Fort Myer, as well as the Netherlands Carillons, Arlington, VA. *Monere* is the base of the following words: **mon**ition, **mon**itor, **mon**itory; **mon**ster, **mon**strance, **mon**strosity, **mon**strous; **mon**umental; ad**mon**ish, pre-**mon**ish, ad**mon**ition, pre**mon**ition; de**monstr**ate, re**monstr**ate; sum**mon**. *Muster* is also from *monere*; see p. 95.

Cairn, from Scottish Gaelic *carn*, **an elevation**, is a conical heap of stones built as a monument or landmark. *Cairn* is from Latin *cornu*, **horn**, and ultimately from IE *ker-n*, **horn**, highest part of the body, thus, **tip**, **peak**.

Pyramid, from Greek, is any large structure with a square base and four sloping, triangular sides meeting at the top, as those built by the ancient Egyptians for royal tombs. *The Great Pyramids* designates the three large pyramids in Giza, Egypt, the largest of which is the Pyramid of Khufu.

Ziggurat, from Akkadian *zaqru*, **high**, **massive**, is a *terraced* pyramid of successively receding stories. *Ziggurats* designated the temple towers of ancient Assyrians and Babylonians. *Pyramids* and *ziggurats* have been built not only in Egypt and Assyria, respectively, but also in Mesopotamia, Sumeria, Ireland, England, India, Mexico, China, and Peru, as well as in the ancient African kingdom of Cush.

Common element base: satis

Meaning: full, complete, enough

IE base: *sa-*: **to satisfy**; **German**: *voll*, as in *volle Fahrt*, **at full speed**

Clavis

sate:
to fill full or completely; to satisfy an appetite, desire, craving, to the full; also, to provide with more than enough so as to weary or disgust; **to glut**; *insatiate* (adjective): **not satisfied**; never satisfied, greedy; *insatiable* (adjective), **wanting more**, as *an insatiable desire to learn.*

satiety:
the condition of being **full to satisfaction**, as with food; also, the condition of being gratified beyond the point of satisfaction; **surfeit** (see p. 91). Pronounced: suh TIE uh tee.

satire:
from *lanx satura*, **a full dish**, originally, a composite of fruits and vegetables; hence, **a medley**; now, a literary work filled with vices, follies, stupidities, and abuses that are held up to ridicule, derision, and contempt. For methods of *satire*, see *burlesque, innuendo, invective, irony, parody, sarcasm, travesty* in a literary handbook or the Internet. See p. 162 for *satire* under *tetralogy.*

satisfy:
-fy, from *facere*, **to make**; **to make enough**, to make sufficient; thus, to gratify a need, desire, or expectation of. SYNONYMS: compensate, indemnify, recompense, reimburse, remunerate.

saturate:
to fill up; to cause to be thoroughly soaked, imbued, or penetrated; in *chemistry*, to cause a substance to combine to the **full** extent of the combining capacity with another; to neutralize.

assets:
from Anglo-French *asetz*, from Vulgar Latin *ad satis*; hence, the legal phrase, *aver assets*, **to have enough**. (*Aver* in this phrase is **not** the synonym for *assert*, but is from Old French *aiver*, and further from *haber*, **to have, to hold**.) *Vulgar Latin* designated the everyday speech of the Roman people, from which the Romance languages (French, Romanian, Italian, Portuguese, Spanish) developed.

expletive:
ex-, **out**; **that which fills out**; a word considered as regularly filling the syntactic position of another, as *it* in "*It* is his duty to go," or *there* in "*There* were many people at the exhibition." The actual subject of the foregoing sentence is "people"; restructured: *Many people were at the exhibition.* Grammatically, expletives themselves have no meaning; some grammarians call them simply "sentence starters." Also, a profane exclamation or oath, as a base attempt **to complete** one's meaning. In quoting a person verbatim, newspapers and captioned newscasts often place deleted expletives, or unprintable statements, in brackets: [expletives deleted]. Used as an adjective as well.

implement:
in-, **in**; **to fill up**; as a *noun*, any article or device used or needed in a given activity; tool, instrument, utensil; any thing or person used as a means to some end; as a *verb*, **to carry into effect**; fulfill; accomplish; to provide with implements.

compliment:
and *complement* both **fill**, or **complete**, e.g., *compliments* **fill** another with appreciation, and *complements* complete or bring to perfection, as "The salad was an excellent *complement* to the meal." *Complementary* angles compose, constitute, or complete a right, or 90°, angle. While *complement* means to add to that which is felt to be lacking, *supplement* means merely **to add to**, without any implication of deficiency. See p. 153, **A Writing Tip.**

accomplish:
ac-, intensive and assimilation of *ad-*, **to, toward** + *complete*; **to do**; succeed in doing; to make complete; perfect (as a verb, pronounced pur FECT).

plenary:
Greek *plenus*, **full**; attended by the full body, as *a plenary assembly*, as of the United Nations. SYNONYMS: absolute, complete, replete, unqualified.

sad:
from Old English *saed*, **sated**, **weary**, which evolved from IE *sa-*; *sad* has come to mean "low in spirit; dejected; sorrowful; unhappy."

wordextras

Salaam, Farsi (the modern language of Iran), and Hebrew *shalom* both mean **peace**, and are greetings similar to English *Hello*, Danish *Skoal*, German *guten Tag* (**good Day**), Spanish *buenos días* (**good day**), and Hawaiian *Aloha* (means either **hello** or **goodbye**).

Steward, one meaning of which is the keeper of another's affairs, originally meant **a pig keeper**, from Anglo-Saxon *stig*, **sty** + *weard*, **keeper** (see p. 167). Compare *lord*, **loaf keeper**, p. 25.

Curtail, **to cut short**, **reduce**, **abridge**, is from *curtus*, **short**, which also yields *curtal*, a horse with a docked tail.

```
┌─────────────────────────────────────────────────────────────────────────────┐
│                         Word Cluster No. 87                                    │
│                                                                                │
│    sequacious          sequel            sequela            sequence           │
│    sequentive          sequestrum      consequence          obsequious         │
│  subsequent        inconsequential        second            secondary          │
│                        sect              sectarian         consecution         │
│   consecutive          execute          executioner         executive          │
│    executrix           secundines        persecute          prosecute          │
│                                                                                │
│  Common elements_____Inferred Meaning_____  │
└─────────────────────────────────────────────────────────────────────────────┘
```

Romance Cognates	French	Romanian	Italian	Portuguese	Spanish
	suivre	secventa	seguire	seguir	seguir

Triplets: persecute:prosecute:pursue

Words with disguised Latin roots: ensue, extrinsic, intrinsic, pursue, pursuit, pursuivant, segue, seguidilla (a fast Spanish dance), sequester, sue (originally, **to appeal to**; petition; in law, to petition in court), suer, suit, suite, suitor

Romance word and phrase: *secondo; tout de suite*, **all in succession**; immediately

Latin words and phrases: *secundum; nolle prosequi* (see p. 138)*; non sequitur; et sequens; et sequential data fata secutus*: **following what is decreed by fate**. Virgil; *Nulli secundus*: **second to none**

Placename: El Segundo, California (Spanish for "the second" Standard Oil* refining site in California). The motto of El Segundo is "Second to None." Learn more on El Segundo's website. *Esso, now, Exxon®.

Latin *socius*, from related *sequi*, **to follow**: sociable, social, societal, society; sociocultural, sociogram, socioeconomic, sociolinguistics, sociology, sociometry, sociopath, sociopolitical; associate, consociate, dissociate.

Latin *signum*, sign: sign, signage; signal, signalize; signation, signature, signet, signory; significant, signify; assign, cosign, consign, countersign, design, ensign, resign; designate; assignation, designation, resignation, subsignation; insignia; *segno, dal segno* (D.S.), *locus sigilli* (L.S.); scarlet, seal (one meaning).

---
wordbuilder #57

Greek *kallos*, **beauty**, yields **calli**graphy, **calli**opsis, **calli**pygian (describing beautiful or shapely buttocks); **cali**sthenics (**beautiful strength**); **callo**mania (a condition marked by delusions of personal beauty); and **kal**eidoscope (*eidos*, **shape** + *skopein*, **to see**, **examine**; an optical instrument in which bits of glass, beads, etc. are shown in continually changing symmetrical forms by reflection in two or more mirrors set at angles to each other).

Do not confuse this root with Latin *callus*, **hardened**, **insensitive**, and yielding **callo**sal, **calli**section (vivisection of anesthetized animals), **callo**sity, **callo**sum, **call**us.

---
wordextras

Confiscate, from *com-*, **together** + *fiscus*, **money basket**, **public treasury**, means to seize private property for the public treasury, usually as a penalty; also, to seize by, or as by, authority; appropriate. *Fiscal*, as *fiscal year* and *fiscal responsibility*, also comes from *fiscus*. See p. 197.

Complicate, **to fold together**, from *com-*, **together** + *plicare*, **to fold**, means "to make or become difficult"; in *biology*, folded lengthwise, as some leaves or insects' wings; *plicare* yields the following words: *plicate; duplicate, explicate, implicate; explicit, implicit; duplicity, simplicity; exploit; ploy, deploy, employ; ply, plywood, apply, multiply, reply; appliqué; display* (**to fold out**); plait, pleat; pliable, pliers, plissé (a crinkled finish given to cotton, nylon, etc., by treatment with a caustic soda solution); Synonyms of *display*: exhibit, expose, flaunt, show.

Japanese *sayonara*, **goodbye**, **farewell**, from *sayo*, **that way** + *nara*, **if**, is literally "if it has to be that way."

Kosciusko, MS, TX, named after Tadeusz (Thaddeus) Kosciusko (1746-1817), was a Polish patriot and general; he served in the Colonial army during the American Revolution (1763-1775). After the war, General Kosciusko returned to his native Poland. *Kosciusko*, MS, is the birthplace of Oprah Winfrey, a popular talk show host.

Chancellor, originally, **keeper of the barrier**, **secretary**, is so called from the lattice, or chancel, behind which he worked. From first meaning an official secretary to a nobleman, especially a king, it has come to mean the title of the president or a high executive in some universities. Explore other meanings; explore *chancery* as well.

Common element base: sequi   **Meaning**: to follow

IE base: *sekw-¹*: **to follow**, and yielding Latin *secundus*, **following**, thus yielding words beginning with *sec-* as well.

German: *folgen*, **to follow, succeed, obey, mind**

Clavis

sect:	sometimes thought of as coming from *secare*, **to cut**, as in *bisect*, since a religious denomination is often divided into *sects*; however, this *sect* refers to those who **follow** or constitute a particular group within the established church, e.g., the less-strict Mennonites are a sect of the Amish faith.
secondo:	Italian; in *music*, the **second** part in a duet; *primo*, **prime**, is the main, first, or principal part. Most music terms are Italian, or derived from Italian, since Italy was the center of the Renaissance in music. See p. 134 for *Renaissance*.
secundine:	in *botany*, the **second**, or inner, coat of an ovule; *plural*, **the afterbirth**, the placenta and fetal membranes expelled from the uterus after birth.
secundum:	in Latin, **according to**, as in *secundum usum*, **according to the usage**.
consecutive:	*con-*, **with, together**; **following in order**; without interruption; successive.
non sequitur:	abbreviated *non seq.*; **it does not follow**; in *logic*, a conclusion or inference not supported by the premises or evidence upon which the conclusion is based; in *writing* and *speaking*, a sentence that has no bearing on what was previously said. "His speech was nothing more than a hodgepodge of *non sequiturs*." See more on p. 138, under **Clavis**.
segue:	as a *verb*, **to follow**, or to continue without break to or into the next part; as a *noun*, an immediate transition from one part to another, as in a music score. Pronounced SEG way, or SAY gway.
locus sigilli:	**the place of the seal**, or **the sign**; abbreviated *L.S.* (or, l.s.) on legal documents; often thought to stand for *Legal Signature*, which, in effect, it is. See more on p. 118, under **Clavis**.
dal segno:	Italian; abbreviated *DS*; **from the sign**; a direction in music to return and **repeat from the sign**, a slanted *S* with a diagonal mark connecting its tips.
suit:	in *law*, the act, process, or instance of **suing** in a court of law; **legal prosecution**; **lawsuit**; the **pursuit** of a case; in clothing, furniture, etc., a set, or those items that **follow** or go together.
suite:	a group of attendants or servants; **retinue**; a set of matched pieces of furniture; in *music*, an early form of instrumental composition consisting of a series of dances in the same key; also, a modern instrumental composition in a number of movements; pronounced generally *sweet*, it can also be pronounced *soot*, as is *suit*, previous entry.
pursue:	*persecute*, and *prosecute* are triplets. Old French changed *pro-* to *por-* or *pur-*, and Low Latin *sequire* to *suir*. *Prosequi*, **to prosecute**, thus became French *poursuivre* and English *pursue*. **Pursue**: to follow after in order to overtake; capture; **prosecute**: to follow up or pursue (something) to a conclusion, as *to prosecute a war against terrorists*; **persecute**: to afflict or harass constantly.
pursuivant:	from Old French *poursuir*; ultimately from *prosequi*, **to follow forth**; a follower; attendant. In the British College of Heralds, a *pursuivant* is an officer ranking below a herald. See previous entry. Pronounced: PUR suh vunt, or PUR swi vunt.
sequel:	also, *sequela*; **anything that follows**; subsequent or succeeding; explore *sequela* as a medical term.
sign:	from *signum*, **an identifying mark**, or an object **that follows**; may have originated with *secare*, **to cut**; therefore, **an incised mark**. Related to *seal*, base of *locus sigilli*, above.
assignation:	*as-*, assimilation of *ad-*, **to, toward**; an assigning or being assigned; an appointment to meet, especially one made secretly by lovers; tryst; rendezvous.

A phrase from Roman history: *to cross the Rubicon*, to commit oneself to a definite act or decision, from which there is no turning back. When Caesar crossed the Rubicon in 49 B.C., on his march on Rome, he began a civil war with Pompey (106-48 B.C.), Roman general and triumvir. See p. 102 for phrase *alea jacta est*, **the die is cast**, in reference to crossing the Rubicon.

Word Cluster No. 88

sedan	**sed**ate	**sed**ative	**sed**entary
sediment	super**sede**	**sess**ile	**sess**ion
	a**ssess**	in**sess**orial	ob**sess**ion
po**ssess**	repo**ssess**	a**ssid**uous	di**ssid**ent
in**sid**ious	pre**side**	pre**sid**io	pre**sid**ent
re**side**	re**sid**ue	sub**side**	sub**sid**y
re**sid**ence	re**sid**ual	re**sid**uary	re**sid**uum

Common elements_____Inferred Meaning_____

Romance Cognates	**French** asseoir	**Romanian** sedea	**Italian** sedere	**Portuguese** sentar	**Spanish** sentar

Words with disguised Latin roots: assize; besiege; hostage; see (one meaning, that of *seat*; e.g., Holy See), séance; seat; sewer (a medieval servant of high rank in charge of serving meals and *seating* guests), siege, sizar; size (one meaning); surcease

Placename: Presidio of Monterey, California (a *presidio* is a fortified place or military post)

Law term: *supersedeas*; **Latin phrase**: *duabus sellis sedere*: **to sit in two saddles**; to equivocate, waver

Motto of the University of Texas: *Disciplina praesidium civitatis:* **Instruction is the safeguard of the state.**

NB: *Seder* and *sedition* are not in this family. See p. 208, Item 113, for *sedition* in *itere* family.

Greek cognates, from *hedra*, **chair**: cat**hedra**, cat**hedra**l; ex cat**hedra** (see *ipse dixit*, p. 65), San**hedr**in, ep**hedr**ine, ex**edra**, [di**hedra**l, hexa**hedr**on, penta**hedr**on, poly**hedr**on, tetra**hedr**on] The [bracketed words] are geometric shapes, where the root means **face, side, surface**, or a geometric figure or a crystal with a specified number of surfaces. See p. 207, Item 102.

Explore both *eisteddfod* (Welsh) and *Upanishad* (Sanskrit). See **Clavis** for *eisteddfod*.

wordextras

Candidate, originally meaning **white-robed**, designated those in Roman times who aspired to public office. To signify their purity of intentions, candidates attired themselves in **white togas**. *Cand*idate, *cand*id, *cand*le, *cand*or and *incand*escent are in the same family. See further comments under **Word Cluster No. 1**, p. 1.

Swahili originally designated a Bantu people who were inhabitants of the island of Zanzibar, off the east coast of Africa. *Swahili* comes from Arabic *sawhil*, the plural of *sahil*, **coast** + *-iy*, **belonging to**; thus, a people belonging to the coasts. *Swahili* is also a language, characterized by many Arabic words and used as a lingua franca in East Central Africa and parts of the Democratic Republic of the Congo. See more on *Swahili*, under *jumbo*, p. 197.

CCCP, pronounced es es es ehr, seen most often on the uniforms of former Soviet Union athletes, is Russian for *USSR*. The initials transliterate *Soyuz Sovietskikh Sotsialstichekikh Republikh. Soyuz* translates into English *union*; *Soyuz 19* was the name of the Soviet spacecraft whose crew—while in space—joined, or formed a *union* with, the crew of Apollo 18 in 1975; the joint crews conducted experiments, shared meals, and held a joint news conference.

Sacramento, the capital of California, is Spanish for **sacrament**. There is also Sacramento, Kentucky.

French *embouchure*, from Latin *in-*, **in** + *bucca*, **the cheek**, means **to put into the mouth**, and originally referred to **the mouth of a river**. In *music*, it designates the mouthpiece of a wind instrument, such as the oboe, clarinet, and English horn. In addition, it refers to the method of applying the lips and tongue to the mouthpiece of a wind instrument.

Oriole, the state bird of Maryland, is from Old French *oriol*, and further from Latin *aurum*, **gold**. *Baltimore orioles* have a bright plumage of orange (or yellow) and black, and are known for building intricately woven hanging nests. *Baltimore Orioles* designates a major-league baseball team, often referred to as "the Birds."

Pundit, from Hindi *pandit*, and further from Sanskrit *pandita*, means **a learned person**.

Phrase from a Greek legend: *cutting the Gordian knot*; from a knot tied by King Gordius of Phrygia, which an oracle had revealed would be undone only by the future master of Asia; Alexander the Great, failing to untie it, slashed the knot with his sword; thus, *to cut the Gordian knot* is to find a quick, bold solution to a perplexing problem.

175

Common element base: sedere

Meaning: to sit

IE base: *sed-¹*: **to sit**; **German**: *sitzen*

Clavis

assessor:
as-, assimilation of *ad-*, **to**, **toward**; **to sit to**; originally one who **sat by** as a judge of a fine or property value. Archaic *assize*, originally, **a court session**, comes from the same root.

possess:
from *potis*, **able**; originally, **to sit as master**, **owner**. *Posse*, a deputized force of civilians, is a shortening of *posse comitatus*, **the power of the county**; see **wordextras**, p. 14.

assiduous:
as-, assimilation of *ad-*, **to**, **toward**; describes one who **sits by** a task until it is finished; marked by careful, unremitting attention or persistent application. SYNONYMS: diligent, industrious, sedulous.

insidious:
in-, **in**; **sitting in or on**, **lying in wait for**, as in an ambush or plot; characterized by treachery or slyness; crafty; wily; operating in a slow or not easily apparent manner; more dangerous than seems evident, as *an insidious illness*, notably *cancer*, that which seems dormant, but is poised to strike again.

president:
and *preside*; *pre-*, **before**; **one who sits before**, or **in front of**; originally, **to protect**. *Preside*: to be in the position of authority in an assembly; to serve as chairperson; *president*: one who presides, usually of a company, society, university, club, country, etc.

subsidy:
sub-, **under**; literally, **a sitting under**; hence, originally, reserve troops; consequently, aid, help, support, as *a federal subsidy to farmers*; the verb form is *subsidize*; adjective and noun, *subsidiary*.

dissident:
dis-, **apart**, **away**; **sitting apart**; not agreeing; dissenting, as *a dissident member of the board*, or *a dissident juror*. Also used as a noun, e.g, a dissident person; a dissenter.

sedan:
originally *sedan chair*; now, an automobile with two or four doors and with front and rear seats.

siege:
from *obsidium* (*ob-*, **over**, **before**, **against**; see **Word Cluster No. 70**, p. 139); originally, **sitting before** a town by the enemy; also used figuratively, as *a siege of illness, financial problems,* or *adversity*.

hostage:
from *obsidiatus*, **sitting in the way of**; *host*, *hostage*, and *hostile* are all related to *hospice*, from *hospitium*, **hospitality inn**; lodging; *hospitium* is from *hostis*, **stranger**. History bears out that some countries see strangers as friends to show kindness toward, while others see them as a threat, and therefore taken hostage; hence, the difference between *hostage* and *host*.

cathedral:
Greek *kata-*, **down** + *hedra*, **chair**. The official *chair* of the bishop is located in the *cathedral*, the principal church of a bishop's *see*, or *seat*; thus, *to speak ex cathedra*, **to speak from the chair**, or with authority, or with infallibility. Often used pejoratively, as in "He is so dogmatic, speaking *ex cathedra* on every subject." See **wordbuilder #58**, p. 177.

Sanhedrin:
Greek *san-* from *syn-*, **together** + *hedron*, **sitting**; **a sitting together**; the highest ecclesiastical and judicial council of the ancient Jewish nation, comprising 70 to 72 members; not to be confused with *Septuagint*, the translation of the Hebrew scriptures into Greek by 70 to 72 Palestinian Jews. The translation was completed in 72 days on Pharos, an island within the city of Alexandria, Egypt.

eisteddfod:
Welsh; **a sitting**, **session**; in Wales, a yearly meeting of poets, musicians, etc., at which prizes are given for compositions and performances; a 19th-century revival of an ancient Welsh custom. Pronounced: ay STETH vod.

---

wordextras

Yiddish has provided English with a number of words, including ***bagel, blintz, chutzpah, kibitzer, kosher*** (see p. 181), *lox, nosh, schlemiel, schlep, schmaltz* (see p. 178). Yiddish developed from Middle High German, spoken by East European Jews as well as their descendants in countries outside Eastern Europe; it contains borrowings from Hebrew, Russian, Polish, and English, as well as other languages.

The ***paisley*** pattern from Paisley, a town near Glasgow, Scotland, originally referred to woolen shawls with an intricate multicolored design typically of abstract curving figures resembling fat commas, from the designs on cashmere shawls imported from India.

Swain, from Old Norse *sveinn*, **boy**, **servant**, originally designated **a country**, or **rustic youth**; **a lover** or **suitor**.

Word Cluster No. 89

sine	sine cruce	sinecure	sinecurism
sine die	sine qua non	sine luce	sine nomine
sine prole	sin duda (Spanish)	sine mora	sine nervis

Common element_____ Inferred Meaning _____

Romance Cognates	French	Romanian	Italian	Portuguese	Spanish
	sans	fara (noncognate)	senza	sem	sin

Latin phrases: *Nec tecum possum vivere, nec sine te:* **I can neither live with you nor without you.** Martial
Palma non sine pulvere; Nil sine numine; Nil sine magno labore
Sine cruce, sine luce: **without the Cross, without light**.

French words and phrases: *sans, sans-culotte; sans doute* (**without doubt; doubtless**)*; sans-gêne; sans serif; sans souci; sans égal; sans-raison; sans-pareil; sans peur et sans reproche*, **without fear and without reproach**

Greek *a-, an-*, **negative**; *a-*: abyss, achromatic, agnostic, amoral, apolitical, atheist, atrophy
an-: anaerobe, analgesic, anarchy, anarthria, anecdote, anemia, anergy, anesthesia, anestrus, aneurysm, anorexia, anosmia, anaphrodisiac (that which lessens sexual desire, from *Aphrodite*, Greek goddess of love).

Latin *a-, ab-*, **negative**; *a-*: abate, amanuensis, amusia, aversion, avert; *ab-*: abdicate, abducent, abduct, aberrant, abhor, abject, abjure, ablate, abluent, abnegate, abnormal, abolish, aborigine, abort, abrupt; *abs-*: absent (*esse*, **to be**; thus, **to be away**), abscess, abscise, abscissa, abscond, abstain, abstemious, abstract, abstruse.

NB: Though there are popular stories purporting that *sincere* means **without wax**, that which covered the cracks in pottery, professional etymologists do not support these stories. It is an interesting word to explore, however.

> **Quote**: When I use a word, it means just what I choose it to mean — neither more or less. Humpty Dumpty

wordbuilder #58

Greek *kata-*, **down, away, against, according to**, yields **cat**ion (a positively charged ion); **cat**echesis (**oral instuction**), **cat**echism, **cat**echumen, **cat**egory, **cat**hedral (see **Clavis**, p. 176), **cat**heter, **cat**hexis, **cat**hode, **cat**holic; **cat**abasis (also spelled *katabasis*), **cat**abolism, **cat**achresis, **cat**aclastic, **cat**acomb (see p. 88, **wordextras**), **cat**alog, **cat**alysis, **cat**aplasia, **cat**apult, **cat**arrh, **cat**astasis, **cat**astrophe, **cat**atonia; *catalogue raisonné* (**a reasoned catalog**: a systematic annotated catalog, especially, a critical bibliography). **NB**: *Catharsis* is not in this family; see p. 178.

wordextras

Denizen, from Old French *denzein*, **native inhabitant**, and further from Latin *de intus*, **from within**, can mean **an inhabitant or occupant**; **a frequenter of a particular place**; or an animal, plant, foreign word, etc., that has become naturalized. See more on *denizen*, p. 98.

A game played by the Canadian Indians utilized a stick that to the early French explorers resembled a bishop's staff, a *crosse*. Consequently, a bishop's staff forms the base of Canadian French *lacrosse*, **the staff**. See p. 51.

Serenade, originally from Latin *serenus*, **clear**, is influenced by Italian *sera*, **evening**, from *serus*, **late**. A *serenade* is a vocal or instrumental performance of music outdoors at night, especially by a lover under the window of his sweetheart. *Serene* and *serenity* come from the same source. See more on *serenade*, under *alba* and *alborado*, p. 2.

Proselyte, designating a person who has been converted from one religion to another, or from one belief, sect, party, etc., to another, is from Greek *pros-*, **toward** + *erkesthai*, **to go**.

Santa Fe, capital of New Mexico, is Spanish for **holy faith**.

Semantics is the branch of linguistics concerned with the nature, structure, development and changes of the meaning of speech forms, or with contextual meaning. From *sema-*, **sign**, *semantics* is in the same family as *semaphore*, any apparatus for signaling, as the arrangement of lights, flags, and mechanical arms. See more *sema-* words, p. 36.

177

Common element base: sine   **Meaning**: without

IE base: *sen*-[2]: **apart**, **separated**, yielding *sunder, asunder, sundry*, **miscellaneous**; **various**; **divers**.

Clavis

sinecure:	from *beneficium sine cura*; in *ecclesiastics*, a benefice (a church position) **without a care** (for souls); in general use, a paid position, but with little, or no responsibility; the practice of such is *sinecurism*; the person holding a sinecure is a *sinecurist*. Pronunciation of *benefice*: BEN uh fis.
sine die:	**without a day** being set to reconvene; also, "for an indefinite period," as Congress adjourned *sine die*. Pronunciation: SIGH nee DIE ee. See *adjourn*, p. 104.
sine mora:	**without delay**. See *moratorium*, under *demurrer* (**wordextras**), p. 113.
sine nervis:	**without nerves**; without strength. See *enervate*, p. 16.
sine prole:	**without issue**; in *law*, childless; without offspring; leaving no heirs. Pronounced: SIGH nee PRO leh.
sine qua non:	**without which not**; indispensable; that which is absolutely essential, as the voice of the people is the *sine qua non* to a democracy. Pronounced: SIGH nee kway NAHN, or SIN ay kwah NOHN.
sans-pareil:	French; **without par**; without equal; matchless; see *ne plus ultra,* pp. 153, 198.
sans serif:	French; **without a serif**; a typeface without serifs, or fine lines finishing off the main strokes at the tops and bottoms of letters; also called Gothic. *Helvetica* is a popular *sans serif* typeface.
sans-souci:	French; **without care** or worry; **gay**; **carefree**. *Sans Souci*: the palace built by Frederick the Great, near Potsdam, Germany. See *insouciant*, **wordextras**, p. 20.
Sanka®:	brand name; *san-* + *ka*, phonetic spelling of first two letters of *caffeine*; hence, General Foods' trade name or brand name for decaffeinated coffee, or coffee **without caffeine**.

Palma non sine pulvere: **No palm** (symbol of victory) **without the dust**; no reward without the struggle. *The Epistles of Horace*, 1, 1, 51. *Pulvere* is the base of *pulverize*, **to make as dust**; *pollen* comes from the same verb.

Nil sine numine: **Nothing without the divine will** (or, providence). Motto of the State of Colorado.

Nil sine magno labore: **Nothing without great effort**. Motto of Brooklyn College. This motto is a shortening of *nil aughsine magno vita labore debit mortalibus*. **Life has given nothing to man *without* great effort**. Horace

wordextras

The literal translation of Italian ***fettucine*** is **small ribbons**; ***lasagna***, **cooking pot**; ***linguine***, **small tongues**; ***manicotti***, **small sleeves**; ***penne***, **quills**; ***rotini***, **shapes**; ***spaghetti***, **small cords**; ***vermicelli***, **small worms**.

Schmaltz, previously referred to as a word from Yiddish, is **melted fat**. Originally meaning "animal fat used as food," *schmaltz* has come to mean "excessive sentimentality in art or music." ***Yiddish***, the language of the Jewish people in Eastern Europe and Germany, is from Middle High German *jüdisch deutsch*, **Jewish German**. See more on *Yiddish*, p. 176.

Repair, as a transitive verb, and ***repair***, as an intransitive verb, come from separate backgrounds. As a transitive verb, *repair* comes from *reparare*, **to prepare again**, and means "to mend, restore, remedy, compensate." This *repair* can also function as a noun, as *to make repairs*. As an intransitive verb, *repair* comes from *repatriare*, **to return to one's fatherland**, *as in repatriate*. In actual usage, *repair* means **to betake oneself**; to go, as to a place, as "to *repair* to Florida for the winter months." This *repair* can be used as a noun as well, as "Our *repair* to Florida was delightful."

Notre Dame, **Our Lady** (Mary, mother of Jesus), referred originally to a famous early Gothic cathedral in Paris, built 1163-1257, the full name of which was *Notre Dame de Paris*. The University of Notre Dame, near South Bend, Indiana, is known for its Fightin' Irish football team.

Heroin, a term coined in 1898 by H. Dresner, a German chemist, is so named because of the powerful narcotic drug's euphoric effect, that of "a hero," not be to be confused with *heroine*, the female protagonist (hero) in a story.

Stevedore, Spanish for a *longshoreman*, is from *steeve* (from Latin *stipare*, **to cram**, **pack**) as in *constipation* and *obstipation*, **severe constipation**.

Catharsis, from Greek *kathairein*, **to purify**, originally meant **purgation**, especially of the bowels. ***Cathartic*** is both an adjective and a noun; as an *adjective*, describing a catharsis; as a *noun*, a purgation, laxative, aperient.

Word Cluster No. 90

state(ment)	constitute	constant	stable
stately	constituent	distant	stabile
static	destitute	instant	constable
stator	institute		establish
statue	prostitute	circumstance	
statute	substituent	instance	armistice
statuesque	superstition	substance	interstice
stationary	obstinate	store	solstice
stationery	destine	restore	

assist   desist   exist   existentialism   persist   resist   subsist
transistor

Common elements_____**Inferred Meaning**_____

Romance Cognates	French	Romanian	Italian	Portuguese	Spanish
	état	sta	stare	estar	estar

Doublets: estate:state; stationary:stationery (see **Clavis**)

Words with disguised roots: arrest, contrast, cost, obstacle, obstetrician, oust, ouster, post (one meaning), restaurant, restive, stadholder, stage, stagecoach, stagnant, stall, stalwart (see p. 69), stamen, stamina, stance, stanch, stand, standard, stanchion, stanza, starboard, staunch, stay, stead, steadfast, stet, stud, valet

Romance words and phrases: *coup d'état; étagère* (see p. 1), *ostinato; Gestapo* (partly German*); pièce de résistance*

French phrase: *L'Etat, c'est moi*: **the State, it is I**: saying formerly attributed to Louis XIV.

Latin phrases: *non obstante; status quo; Stabat Mater dolorosa*: **There stood the sorrowful mother**—in reference to the mother of Jesus at his crucifixion. See *Via Dolorosa*, p. 72, under **Clavis**.

Motto of Tulane University: *perstare et praestare*: **To persevere and surpass**.

Explore *existentialism* in philosophy, religion, and literature, as well as in atheism.

Greek cognates: apostasy, catastasis, diastasis, epistasis, ecstasy, metastasis, epistemology, prostate, **stoa**, system.

wordextras

As a transitive verb, Yiddish *schlep* (see p. 176), from German *schleppen*, **to drag**, means **to carry, take, haul, drag**, etc.; as an intransitive verb, **to go or move with effort**; drag oneself. As a *noun*, slang for *an ineffectual person*.

Esquire, from Latin *scutarius*, is **shield bearer**, and in the Middle Ages, was a squire attendant of a knight. From the same base is *scutum*, a large, oblong *shield* used by legionnaires in ancient Rome.

Man is probably from IE *men-*, **to think**. The basic meaning of *man* is **the one who thinks**. IE *men-* produces **ment**al, a**ment**ia, com**ment**, com**ment**ary, re**mind**er; re**min**isce; non compos **ment**is, **not of sound mind**.

Petulant, from Latin *petere*, **to rush at**, **fall**, originally meant **forward**, **immodest**, but now means **pert**, **insolent**; **impatient**, **irritable**, especially over a petty annoyance; peevish. The word describes one who is likely to have little fits of bad temper, or snits. See other words from *petere*, p. 86, under *centrifugal*.

Vallejo, CA, is named after Mariano G. Vallejo (1808-1890), the owner of the site. Pronounced: vuh LAY hoh, or oh.

Monticello, **little mountain**, is the home and burial place of Thomas Jefferson, near Charlottesville, Virginia.

Prevaricate, **to turn aside from or evade the truth**, is from Latin *pre-*, **before** + *varicare*, **to straddle**. Synonyms: equivocate, fabricate, fib, lie. The noun form is *prevarication*.

A Writing Tip: Adjectives in a series are *coordinate* if each adjective modifies the noun separately. Example of *coordinate adjectives*: The British colony of Hong Kong grew up around a *beautiful, sheltered, accessible* port. If *and* can be inserted between the adjectives with no loss of meaning, the adjectives are coordinate. They are *cumulative*, not *coordinate*, if any adjective in the series modifies the total concept that follows it. Example of *cumulative adjectives*: Hong Kong is the *third-largest international financial* center in the world. Inserting *and* between cumulative adjectives would render the sentence senseless. See **A Writing Tip**, p. 18.

Common element base: sistere   **Meaning:** to stand, take a position
IE base: *sta-*: **to stand**, with derivatives meaning **place**, or **a thing that is standing**.
German: *stand* as in *stillgestanden!* **Stand still!** Stand at attention!

Clavis

circumstance: *circum-*, **around**; **a standing around**; a fact or event accompanying another, either incidentally or as an essential condition or determining factor. Explore *circumstantial evidence*; see p. 40.

stationery: like *stationary*, originally described that which **stayed** in one place. *Stationers* set up a permanent shop rather than peddle their wares. It is not known for certain when *stationers* became associated with only paper and office supplies. *Stationery*, noun; *stationary*, adjective.

statuesque: *-esque*, **in the manner of**, or **style of**; of or like a **statue**, especially **tall and well-proportioned**; having a stately grace and beauty. Other *-esque* words include Antonin Dvorák's *Humoresque*, a piano piece; *Arabesque; Lincolnesque; grotesque, picaresque* (see p. 104), *picturesque*.

destitute: from *destituere*, **to forsake, abandon**; **to not have**; **to be without**; lacking the necessities of life; living in complete poverty. SYNONYMS: impecunious, impoverished, indigent, poor.

constituent: *con-*, **with, together**; necessary in forming or making up a whole component; SYNONYMS: element, factor, ingredient. *Constitute, constitution; institute* and *institution* are from the same elements.

desist: *de-*, **away**; **to stand away**. A *cease and desist order* of an administrative agency prohibits a person or business firm from continuing a particular course of conduct or action.

restaur: or *restor*; the legal recourse that insurers have against each other according to the date of their insurance; the recourse of an insurer against the master of a ship if loss occurs through the master's negligence.

restaurant: *re-*, **again** + *store*; where one may be *restored* with nourishment. A restaurant proprietor, or owner, is a *restaurateur*, with alternate spelling *restauranteur*. See *proprietor* and other *propr-* words, p. 96.

solstice: *sol*, **sun**; when **the sun stands still**, i.e., *summer and winter solstices*, the two days a year when the sun, farthest north or south of the equator, has no apparent northward or southward motion, and that occur around June 21 and December 21, the longest and shortest days of the year respectively. See *armistice*, p. 12; *equinox*, p. 76; *halcyon*, p. 92.

stanza: from Vulgar Latin *stantia*, **a stopping place**; originally from Latin *stare*, **to stand**; a group of lines or verses forming one of the divisions of a poem or song. See *quatrain*, p. 162, under **Clavis**.

rheostat: Greek *rhein*, **to flow**; a device that **sets the flow** of electrical current; thus, **a light dimmer device**. See p. 84 for more on *rheostat*. Other words from *rhein*: diar**rhea**, logor**rhea**, menor**rhagia**.

Gestapo: German; shortening of *Ge(heime) Sta(ats) Po(lizei)*; **Secret State Police** of Nazi Germany.

pièce de résistance: **piece with lasting power**; the main course or dish; also, the most valuable object in a collection.

wordextras

Ukulele, from Hawaiian *uku*, **flea** + *lele*, **to jump**, is the **jump of the flea**. The term was first applied to a nimble player of the instrument, then to the instrument itself.

Volley, from Latin *volare*, **to fly**, is seen in *volleyball*, a game in which the intent is to return the ball—to keep the ball *flying*—without it touching the ground. *Volatile* is also from the verb *volare*.

Spinnaker, a large, triangular, baggy headsail used on racing yachts when running before the wind, is so named after *Sphinx*, the name of a yacht that carried the sail.

Surprise, from Old French *soprendre*, means **to take unawares**. See *prehendere*, p. 211, Item 152.

Montpelier, the capital of Vermont, is named after Montpellier, France.

Word from a Greek lawgiver: *Draconian*, **rigorous, severe, cruel**; from *Draco*, an Athenian statesman whose law code (621 B.C.) was proverbially harsh.

Word from a Greek philosopher: *epicurean*, **given to luxury**; from Epicurus who held that the goal of man was the life of calm pleasure. *Epicurean* is capitalized when referring to the philosophy of Epicurus.

Sectional Word Cluster Test

INSTRUCTIONS: For each set of words from Latin and Greek (and sometimes, French, Italian, Spanish, and German), write the common meaning in the blank. In this particular test, there is a Russian word.

Example: **hypo**tenuse, **hypo**thesis, **sub**ject   <u>under</u>

	Presection Answer	Postsection Answer
91. in**sult**, de**sult**ory, re**sil**ient, as**sault**	_____	_____
92. **super**structure, **supr**eme, **sopr**ano, **hyper**bole	_____	_____
93. con**tam**inate, **tang**ent, con**tact**, in**teg**rate	_____	_____
94. **ten**et, **ten**nis, **ten**or, lieu**ten**ant, de**tain**	_____	_____
95. ex**tent**, ex**ten**uating, os**tent**atious, hypo**tenuse**	_____	_____
96. **terr**itory, inter, per**igee**, **geo**synchronous	_____	_____
97. **trans**it, **trans**vestite, **tran**quil, **dia**meter	_____	_____
98. **tri**dent, **tri**vial, **trio**, **troi**ka, **tre**llis, **Trini**dad	_____	_____
99. **ultra**marine, **outré**, **meta**phor, **meta**morphosis	_____	_____
100. contra**vene**, ad**vent**, sou**ven**ir, re**ven**ue, a**ven**ue	_____	_____

_____   _____
Presection Score   Postsection Score

Note: Enter scores for this test and the following ones after completing this section; then, enter them on p. xvii.

Sectional Wordbuilder Test

Throughout the book and as a supplement, there are wordbuilders; these wordbuilders are designed to help you build a family of words from a single root.

	Presection Answer	Postsection Answer

59. What is the meaning of *ceros-, cerat-* as in rhino**ceros**, tri**cerat**ops?

                                               _____   _____

60. What is the meaning of *cereb-* as in **cereb**ellum, **cereb**rate?   _____   _____

                                               _____   _____

                                       Presection Score   Postsection Score

After entering the scores here, enter them on pp. xviii.

```
┌─────────────────────────────────────────────────────────────────────────────┐
│                          Word Cluster No. 91                                  │
│                                                                               │
│  desultory      exult         assault        saltant       saltigrade         │
│  insult         exultance      somersault     saltate       saltimbanco        │
│  result         exultancy                     saltation                        │
│  resultant      exultant        salient        saltire       dessilient        │
│  resultative    exultation      salacious      saltier       transilient       │
│  assail         assailant       salmon         saltica       resilient         │
│  assailment     assailable      sally          saltarello    resilience        │
│                                                                               │
│  Common elements_____Inferred Meaning_____  │
└─────────────────────────────────────────────────────────────────────────────┘
```

Romance Cognates	French	Romanian	Italian	Portuguese	Spanish
	sauter	salta	saltare	saltar	saltar

Latin phrase: *per saltum*, **by a leap**; at a single bound   **Doublets**: assail:assault

French word and phrase: sauté; *cela saute aux yeux*: **that leaps before the eyes**; self-evident

Italian word and phrase: saltimbocca; *arco saltando*: **jumping arch**; rapid staccato in bowing a stringed instrument

NB: *Consult*, coming from *counsel*, is not in this family. **Greek**: halter; see **Clavis**.

```
┌───────────────────────────────────────────────────────────────────┐
│  Quote: What is thinking? In what does it consist? Thinking, in    │
│  substance, is the process of getting the meanings of things.      │
│  Threshing meanings out, refining them in the mind, is done by     │
│  means of the word, spoken and written.                            │
│              Michael Demiashkevich (1891-1938)                     │
└───────────────────────────────────────────────────────────────────┘
```

wordextras

French *bivouac*, from Old High German *biwacht*, **by-watch**, originally designated a night guard to avoid a surprise attack; in present-day military usage, a temporary encampment in the open with only tents or improvised shelter.

Caucus, probably of Virginia Algonquian Indian extraction, originally meant **council**, as recorded by Captain John Smith; the word now refers to a *private council of political party leaders* to decide on matters of policy.

Cede, **to yield**, comes from *cedere*, **to go**, **leave**, which yields words with disparately spelled roots: ac**cede**, con**cede**, inter**cede**, pre**cede**, re**cede**, se**cede**; ante**ced**ent, de**ced**ent, pre**ced**ence; ex**ceed**, pro**ceed**, suc**ceed**; abs**cess**, pro**cess**, suc**cess**; con**cess**ion, ne**cess**ary, re**cess**ive, suc**cess**ive; **cease**, de**cease**; an**ces**tor; and the law term *cease and desist*.

Yiddish *kosher* is originally from Hebrew *kasher*, **fit**, **right**, **proper**; in *slang*, the word still means the same as the original. In Judaism, however, it is applied to that which is clean or fit to eat according to the dietary laws. There are other associated meanings. See p. 176 for other Yiddish words.

Boulder, from Middle English *bulderston*, is further from Swedish *bullersten*, **big stone** (in a stream). There is Boulder, Colorado (after the large stones nearby), as well as Boulder Dam, on the Colorado River.

Duluth, Minnesota, on Lake Superior, is named after Daniel G. du Lhut (or Du Luth), 1636-1710, French explorer.

San Antonio, Texas, is named for Saint Anthony of Padua (Italy). Born in Lisbon, Portugal, in 1195, he died in Verelli, Italy, in 1231. He was known for his remarkable intelligence and for the miracles he wrought. He was called "The Hammerer of the Heretics." The account of his brief life can be found on the Internet.

Butter is from Greek *boutyron* (*bous*, **cow** + *tyros*, **cheese**); thus, **cow cheese**.

Dote, *dotage*, *dotard*, and *dotty* are from Middle English, influenced by Middle Dutch *dotten*, **to be insane**. *Dote* means "to be foolish or weak-minded," especially because of old age; can also mean to be excessively or foolishly fond of, as *to dote on* or *dote upon* (someone); *dotage* refers to *senility*; *dotard* refers to a foolish and doddering old person; *dotty* describes someone who is feeble, unsteady, shaky; also, feeble-minded or crazy.

Ciao, Italian for both **hello** and **goodbye**, is altered from Lombard *schiavo*, **slave**, translated from Austrian *servus*, for "your obedient servant." *Lombardy* is a region of Italy on the border with Switzerland. Pronounced: chou.

Cajun French *andouille* is a highly spiced smoked-pork sausage flavored with garlic. Pronounced: ahn DOO yuh.

Common element base: salire   **Meaning**: to spring, jump, leap
IE base: *sel-*[4]: **to jump**; **German**: *springen*; noun is *Sprung*; **Afrikaans**: *springbok*, **springing buck**.

Clavis

assault: *as-*, assimilation of *ad-*, **to**, **toward**; **to jump forward**; a violent attack, either physical or verbal; in *law*, an unlawful threat or an unsuccessful attempt to do physical harm; also used as verb. See *battery*, p. 16.

assail: see *assault* for the assimilation; **to leap on**; to attack physically and violently, as *to assail a project with vigor and determination*; to have a forceful effect on. *Assail* and *assault* are doublets.

somersault: French; *somer* from Latin *supra-*, **over**; **to jump over**; a complete revolution of the body, jumping heels over head. Figuratively, a complete reversal of opinions, sympathies, attitudes. See p. 183.

insult: *in-*, **in**, **on**; **to leap upon**; to treat or speak to with scorn, insolence, or great disrespect. SYNONYMS: affront, offend, outrage. As a *noun*, an insulting act, remark; in *medicine*, damage or injury to tissues or organs of the body; also, anything that causes damage or injury.

result: *re-*, **back**, **again**; **to leap back**; to happen or issue as a consequence or effect, often used with *from*, as failure *resulting from* not applying oneself. Used as a noun as well. NOUN SYNONYMS: consequence, effect, issue; VERB SYNONYMS: ensue, follow, succeed.

saltire: originally, an X-shaped animal barricade that can be **jumped** over by people; later, the design was used for the St. Andrew's Cross. *Saltire* is also the title of the student handbook of the St. Andrew's Presbyterian College, Laurinburg, NC; also, *saltier*; pronounced the same as *saltire*, that is, SAL ter.

salient: **a projecting point**, as though **jumping** out; in the *military*, the central projecting angle of a bastion; the outward projection of a battle line. As an *adjective*, describing the most important aspects, as *the salient points of a lecture*, or the *salient aspects of the campaign finance reform proposal*.

salacious: *-ious*, an adjective-forming suffix; **fond of leaping**: originally said of male animals; **lustful**; stimulating to the sexual imagination; morbidly appealing to lust. With *-ity*, a noun-forming suffix, the nominal form is *salacity*. Consider also *atrocious*, atroc<u>ity</u>; *clear*, clar<u>ity</u>; *ferocious*, feroc<u>ity</u>; *veracious*, verac<u>ity</u>.

saltigrade: *gradi*, **to step**, **walk**; having legs adapted for **leaping**, such as those of the deer and kangaroo; also, the *Salticidae* family, which includes the jumping spiders. See other *-grade* words, **wordbuilder #54**, p. 145.

salmon: from *salmo salar*, **the leaping fish**. Salmon are *anadromous*, going from salt water to fresh to spawn.

saltimbocca: Italian; **jumps into the mouth**; an Italian dish of veal and ham, rolled, and sautéed in butter.

exultation: *ex-*, **out**; **jumping** or **leaping out**; state of being exceedingly joyful; jubilation; triumph.

desultory: *de-*, **down**; **leaping down**; originally, a *desultor* was a rider in Roman circus games who leaped (or, leapt, lept) from one horse to another; now, passing from one thing to another with no definite aim, as *a desultory conversation*. SYNONYMS: casual, chance, haphazard, incidental, random.

sauté: French; from *sauter*, **to leap**; tossed in a pan; to fry lightly in an open pan.

resilient: *re-*, **back**; **jumping back**; **springing back**; **buoyant**; resuming a prior position or form after being stretched or pressed; the nominal form is *resilience*: the ability to recover quickly from depression, adversity, illness, change, or misfortune.

transilient: *trans-*, **across**, **through**; **leaping across**; passing abruptly or leaping from one thing, condition, etc., to another. Note similarity to meaning of *desultory*, above. The noun is *transilience*.

sally: as a *verb*, **to rush forth suddenly**, as of attacking troops; as a *noun*, **a sudden rushing forth**; any sudden start into activity; quick witticism; bright retort; quip.

halter: Greek *hallesthai*, **to jump**; originally, leaden weights used in *leaping* exercises; in *entomology*, applied to either of the small, clublike balancing organs that are the rudimentary hind wings of *dipterous* insects, such as flies or mosquitoes. *Dipterous*: pertaining to *two-winged insects*. Greek *ptero*: **wing**.

Word from Greek history: *philippic*, **a bitter verbal attack**; from the verbal attacks of Demosthenes against *King Philip II* of Macedonia, an ancient country in the Balkan Peninsula, north of ancient Greece.

superable	superannuated	superb	supernal
supercilious	supererogation	superfamily	superfecundation
superfetation	superfluent	superfluid	superfluous
supergalaxy	superincumbent	superimpose	superintendent
superjacent	superlative	superscribe	superstition
superstructure	supervene	supervise	supernatant
supra	supraglottal	supralapsarian	supraliminal
supramolecular	supranational	supraorbital	suprarenal
surcharge	surcingle	surfeit	surmise
surmount	surname	surplice	surplus
surprise	surreal	surround	surtax
surtout	surveillance	survey	survive

Common elements_____Inferred Meaning_____

Romance Cognates	French	Romanian	Italian	Portuguese	Spanish
	sur	asupra	sopra	sôbre	sobre

Other words appropriate for cluster: superior, superiority, superabound, superabundant, superadd, superscript, supernatural, supernormal, superovulation, superparasite, superpower, supersede, supersession, supersonic; others

Words with disguised Latin roots: sirloin, somersault (*sault*, see p. 181, **Word Cluster No. 91**), soprano, soubrette, sovereign, sum, summit, supremacist, supremacy, supreme, surrender, suzerain (**a feudal lord**; other meanings)

Psychoanalysis term: super ego, that part of the psyche that is critical of the self or ego, enforcing moral standards

Placenames: There is a *Superior* in each of the following states: AZ, CO, ID, IA, MN, NE, WI, WY.
Surplus Canal, UT; Surprise, AZ; Île de la Surprise, New Caledonia; Lac Surprise, Quebec;
Lake Surprise, Australia; Surprise Lake, British Colombia

International lake: Lake Superior (see **Clavis**)

Latin phrases: *Ne sutor supra crepidam judicaret*: **Let not the shoemaker criticize beyond his last**. Pliny
The saying of the painter Apelles to a cobbler who criticized not only the shoes in a picture Apelles had painted, but also the painting generally. The moral: Beware of critiquing subjects in which you are not qualified.
debellare superbos: **to overthrow the proud**. Virgil
ut supra, **as shown or stated above**; *Sursum Corda*, **Lift up your hearts**

Motto of the University of Arizona: *Sursum*: **Upwards**
Motto of the State of Missouri: *Salus populi suprema lex esto*. See p. 167 for translation.

Law phrases: *Superflua non nocent*: **Superfluities do not prejudice**.
Chartarum super fidem, mortuis testibus, ad patriam de necessitudine recurrendum est:
(A dispute) regarding the veracity of deeds, when witnesses are dead, must necessarily be referred to the jury.

Greek cognates: **hyper**acidity, **hyper**acusis, **hyper**baton, **hyper**bola, **hyper**bole, **hyper**cathexis, **hyper**chromia, **hyper**conjugation (see *conjugate*, p. 108, under **Clavis**), **hyper**critical, **hyper**dulia, **hyper**emia, **hyper**glycemia, **hyper**kinesis, **hyper**pyrexia, **hyper**sensitive, **hyper**sonic, **hyper**tension, **hyper**tonic, **hyper**trophy

Definitions of selected words from *hyper*- family
hyperbaton: transposition or inversion of idiomatic word order, e.g., "echoed the hills" for "the hills echoed"
hypercathexis: excessive concentration of desire upon a particular object

wordextra

Mosquito, designating a dipterous (**two-winged**) insect, is a diminutive of both Spanish and Portuguese *mosca*, which itself is from Latin *musca*, **a fly**. The females have skin-piercing antennae (mouthparts), used to suck blood.

A Writing Tip: The phrase *it says,* referring to information in newspapers, magazines, books, and the like, though common in speech, is unacceptable in writing, except in dialogue. **Spoken**: *It says* in the newspaper that Chad is one of the world's poorest countries. **Written**: *The newspaper says* that Chad is one of the world's poorest countries.

Common element base: super-   **Meaning**: above, over, beyond
IE base: *uper-*: **over**, yielding **English** *over*; **Dutch** *orlop*, **overleap**. **German** *über*, as in *übersee*, **overseas**; its opposite, *unter*, as in *Unterseeboot*, **undersea boat**, or **U-boat**, the German submarine used in World War II.

Clavis

supercilious: *cilium*, **eyebrow**; raising the eyebrows in haughtiness or contempt. SYNONYMS: arrogant, disdainful, haughty, imperious, lordly, overbearing, proud. See **wordextras**, p. 144.

superfecundation: *fecund*, **fertile**; successive fertilization of two or more ova from the same ovulation, especially by different males. Compare *superfetation*, a fertilization when a fetus is already present in the uterus. See p. 134 for *fecund*.

Lake Superior: **largest** of the Great Lakes; spans the United States and Canadian border. Having the largest *surface* area of any freshwater lake in the world, it covers an area larger than the state of Maine or almost that of South Carolina. By volume, or capacity, the lake could fill all the other Great Lakes (Huron, Ontario, Michigan, Erie) plus three others the size of Lake Erie. The east to west distance is 350 miles, and north to south, 160 miles. Its shoreline length is 1,826 miles, or the distance between Duluth, MN, and Miami. Only Siberia's Lake Baikal, the deepest lake in the world, and Lake Tanganyika in east-central Africa have larger *volumes* of fresh water.

sum: from *summus*, **highest**, **topmost**; originally, the total of a column of numbers, from the Roman custom of counting upward and placing the *sum* at the top; the aggregation of two or more numbers, magnitudes, quantities, or particulars as determined by the mathematical process of addition. Also used figuratively, e.g., *the sum of our knowledge*; *the sum of our resources*. SYNONYMS: aggregate, amount, total.

surcharge: *sur-* from *super-*; **to overcharge**; **to overload**; **overburden**; as a *verb*, to fill to excess or beyond normal capacity; in *law*, to show an omission, as of a credit (in an account); as a *noun*, an amount added to the usual charge; other uses as both noun and verb.

surround: *sur-* from *super-*; *undare*, **to move or rise in waves**. SYNONYMS: circle, compass, encompass, encircle, gird, girdle, ring. From *undare* are the following: *undulant, abundance, inundate, redundant, redound, abound*. See p. 213, Item 181. Not related to *round*, describing a circle.

surmise: *sur-* from *super-*; with the past participle of French *mettre*, **to put**; from Latin *mittere*, **to send**, to form an idea or opinion from evidence that is neither positive nor conclusive; **to conjecture**; as a *verb*, pronounced sur MIZE; as a noun, SUR mize. *Conjecture*, **to throw together**; can be used as either noun or verb. SYNONYM: guess, as both noun and verb. See more on *surmise*, p. 130.

surplice: *sur-* from *super-*; *pelliceum*, **fur robe**; from *pellis*, **skin**, an outer ecclesiastical vestment.

survey: *sur-* from *super-*; *-vey* from *videre*, **to look**; **to look over**; to inspect for a specific purpose.

soprano: Italian; the **highest** singing voice, or the voice **over** all the others, whether of females or boys before voice-change; at one time, designated the voices of *castrati*, **castrated adult men**.

hyperbola: Greek *ballein*, **to throw**; as with *hyperbole*, **a throwing beyond**; in *geometry*, a *hyperbola* is formed from a conic section, when the angle made by the base of the cone and the intersecting plane is **greater** than the angle formed by a parabola. A figure of speech, *hyperbole* is an exaggeration or an extravagant statement not meant to deceive, as "This bookcase must weigh 16 tons!" or "I am so tired I could literally sleep for a week." See more on *literally* used hyperbolically, p. 116.

Word Cluster No. 93

tact	**contact**	**tang**ent	con**tag**ion
tactful	**contact**ual	**tang**ible	con**tag**ious
tactile	in**tact**	in**tang**ible	con**tam**inate
taction	**tact**less	**tang**ential	con**tig**uous
tactual		co**tang**ent	con**ting**ent

Common elements_____**Inferred Meaning**_____

Romance Cognates	French	Romanian	Italian	Portuguese	Spanish
	toucher	atinge	toccare	tocar	tocar

Words with disguised Latin roots: attain, attainder, attaint, entire, integer, integrable, integral, integrand, integrant, integrate, integration, integrity, disintegrate, reintegrate, task, taste, tasteful, tasteless, distasteful, tax, taxicab

Placenames: Tangent, Oregon; Tangent Point, Alaska (see **Clavis**)

Latin phrase: *noli me tangere* (see **Clavis**)

NB: The following words are *not* in this family: *tactics, taxonomy, taxidermist, eutaxy, hypotaxis, syntax;* neither is *tangerine* nor *continent, pertain*, and *contain*.
Tactics and the *tax-* words come from Greek *tassein*, **to arrange**, as in *syntax* and **taxidermy**.
Tangerine is an orange originally from *Tangiers*, Morocco.
Continent, pertain, and *contain* are in the next family (**Word Cluster No. 94**, p. 187).

Quote: A well-educated gentleman may not know many languages, may have read very few books. But whatever languages he knows, he knows precisely; whatever word he pronounces, he pronounces rightly; above all, he is learned in the peerage of words; knows the words of true descent and ancient blood at a glance from the words of modern *canaille* (see p. 28); remembers all their ancestry, their intermarriage, their distant relationships. John Ruskin, 19th-century English philosopher—*italics* and *page reference* by authors

wordextras

In Anglo-Saxon, ***neighbor*** was *neahgebur*, **nearby boor** (farmer). The cognates of *boor* include Dutch *boer*, Low German *Bur*, and German *Bauer*. See p. 167 to see *neighbor* grouped with other Anglo-Saxon words.

Vermouth, from French *vermout*, and further from German *Wermut*, **wormroot**, is a dry white fortified wine flavored with aromatic herbs; used in cocktails and as an aperitif. *Aperitif, aperture, aperient* are from Latin *aperire*, **to open**.

Cognac, a French brandy, is so named from its being distilled from wine in the area of Cognac, France; loosely, *any* French brandy; more loosely, *any* brandy. ***Brandy*** itself is from Dutch *brandewijn*, **burnt wine**: so called from being distilled.

Bourbon whiskey, named for Bourbon County, Kentucky, where it was originated and where it continues to be produced, is made from a fermented mash of corn, rye, wheat, malted barley, or malted rye grain.

Champagne was originally produced in *Champagne*, a former province in northeastern France.

Deviled, construed as **hot**, as in *deviled eggs* or *deviled crabs*, originated when the British explorers brought back to England very hot, cayenne pepper they had discovered in South America.

Pulaski, VA, is named for Casimir Pulaski (1748-79), a Polish general in the American Revolutionary Army. A brilliant cavalry strategist, he was killed in battle in Savannah, GA. Many other towns in the US are named for him, e.g., in AR, GA, IA, IL, IN, KY, MI, MO, MS, NY, OH, PA, SD, TN, WI, as well as counties, parks, schools, statues.

There are a number of English-Latin word pairs in Modern English, e.g., anger:ire; behead:decapitate; blessing:benediction; bodily:corporal; building:edifice; cat:feline; chew:masticate; choose:select; cleave:divide; clothes:apparel; dog:canine; draw:delineate; dying:moribund; earthly:terrestrial; faithfulness:fidelity; fiery:igneous; forerunner:precursor; friend:companion; friendly:amiable; ghost:specter; heavenly:celestial; hide:conceal; home:residence; kiss:osculate; knave:villain; learned:erudite; lie:prevaricate; near:contiguous; red:vermillion; sky:firmament; spit:expectorate; tongue:language; witchcraft:sorcery. See other such pairs, p. 199.

Common element base: tangere   **Meaning**: to touch
IE base: *tag-*: **to touch**, **handle**; **German**: *berühren*

Clavis

tangent:
touching, or making *contact* at a single point or along a line; touching, but not intersecting. In *geometry* and *trigonometry*, *linea tangens*, the ratio of the ordinate to the abscissa. *To go off on a tangent*: to change abruptly a course or direction. *Tangent Point*, one of the two northernmost points in Alaska, *touches* upon Beaufort Sea. *Nome* is the other northernmost point (see p. 135).

tangential:
of, like, or in the direction of a **tangent**; drawn as a tangent; going off on a tangent; diverging or digressing; merely touching on a subject, not dealing with it at length, as *a tangential reference*.

tangible:
that can be **touched** or can be felt by **touch**; having actual form and substance, as *tangible evidence*, *tangible property*. SYNONYMS: appreciable, palpable, perceptible, sensible.

tact:
If one has *tact*, he or she has the **touch**, or the ability to appreciate the delicacy of the situation and to do or say the kindest or most fitting thing. SYNONYMS: diplomacy, finesse, savoir-faire, subtlety.

tactual:
of the sense touch or the organs of **touch**; causing a sensation of touch; caused by touch.

intact:
in-, **not**; **untouched**; nothing missing, injured, altered, or diminished; remaining uninjured, sound, or whole, as *an intact personality*. The prefix *in-* has other meanings; see p. 95.

entire:
en-, **not**; from Old French *entier*; further from Latin *integer* (see next two entries); same base as *intact*, previous entry. SYNONYMS: complete, whole.

integer:
in-, **not**; **untouched**; therefore, anything complete in itself; **entity**; **whole**. In *mathematics*, a whole number, which may be positive or negative, e.g., +2, +10, or -2, -10; any number not a fraction.

integrate:
from *integer*, previous entry; **to make whole** or **complete** by bringing together parts, or making the parts **touch**; to give or indicate the sum, whole, or total; in *mathematics*, to calculate the integral or integrals of a function or an equation.

contagious:
con-, **with**, **together**; *contagious* (adjective) and *contagion* (noun) both come from *contact*, **to touch together**; *contagious* describes that which can be caught or transmitted by touching, as *a contagious disease*; also used figuratively, as *contagious laughter*, or *contagious yawning*.

contiguous:
con-, **with**, **together**; **touching upon**; in physical contact, *touching* along all or most of one side; next, near, or adjacent, as the *contiguous 48 states*; also, connected in time; uninterrupted, as serving two *contiguous* terms of office. SYNONYMS: adjacent, adjoining, neighboring, tangent.

contingent:
con-, **with**, **together**; originally, **touching**; tangential; that may or may not happen; possible; happening by chance; accidental; fortuitous; as a noun, an accidental or chance happening.

attain:
at-, assimilation of *ad-*, **to**; **to touch**, but meaning **to reach**, **to gain**, **to accomplish**.

taste:
frequentative (denotes repeated action) of *tangere*, **to touch**; to feel, to touch sharply.

tax:
from Middle English *taxen*; from the frequentative of *tangere*; thus, **to touch repeatedly**, **to handle**, so as *to appraise appropriately*.

Noli me tangere: **touch me not**; a warning against touching or meddling; also, the jewelweed (genus Impatiens) of the balsam family; see note on p. 138.

wordextra

Shambles, from Middle English *schamel*, was originally **a bench**, as for displaying fresh meat for sale; next, a place where any meat was sold; then, **a slaughterhouse**, or abattoir (see p. 15 for *abattoir* in its respective family); then, a scene of great slaughter, bloodshed, or carnage; finally, any scene or condition of great destruction or disorder, as *the shambles of a college dormitory room*, or *the shambles of a war scene*. The verb *shamble*: to shuffle or to walk in a lazy or clumsy manner, barely lifting the feet, as though the walker were tethered to a bench.

Word from Greek philosophy: *stoic*, **repressing emotion**. The Stoics, founded by Zeno, held that the wise man should follow virtue alone, obtained through reason, remaining indifferent to the external world and to passion or emotion. Zeno taught from his *stoa*, **porch**; thus, the name of the *Stoicism* school of philosophy. See *Cynics*, p. 28.

Word Cluster No. 94

tenable	tenace	tenacious	tenacity	tenaculum
tenaille	tenance	tenant	tenement	tenet
tennis	tenon	tenor	tenure	tenuto
lieutenant	maintenance	sustenance	appurtenance	untenable
abstention	detention	content(s)		
abstain	appertain	contain	detain	entertain
maintain	obtain	pertain	retain	sustain
abstinence	continence	continent	continue	impertinent
pertinacious	pertinent	retinue	continuum	detinue

Common elements_____Inferred Meaning_____

Romance Cognates	French	Romanian	Italian	Portuguese	Spanish
	tenir	tine	tenere	ter	tener

Words with disguised Latin roots: rein, sostenuto

Motto of the State of Connecticut: *Qui transtulit, sustinet*: **He who transplants, sustains**. See p. 193.

Explore *tenor and vehicle* as the essential elements of a metaphor or simile in a literary handbook. See p. 198.

English word from German: *heldentenor*, a voice of great power and endurance; specifically a tenor especially suited to sing heroic roles in Wagner's operas.

wordextras

Lunatic, from Latin *luna*, **moon**, describes one who is "moon-struck," or **insane**. *Lunatic* can also be used as an adjective, as *one's lunatic ideas*. See p. 53 for *Monday*, or *Moonday*.

Chinese *sampan* was originally *san pan*, **a small boat**, from *san*, **three** + *pan*, **board, plank**. See more on p. 195.

Originally the distance of both arms outstretched (**to embrace, to measure**), *fathom* evolved to mean the length of six feet, used as a measurement for the depth of water or the length of a rope or cable. Also used as a verb: to understand thoroughly; to get to the bottom of, as in "Many people cannot *fathom* the concepts of calculus."

The root of the **arrowroot** was used by American Indians as an antidote to draw poison from arrow wounds.

Natchez, Mississippi, is from a placename of the Natchez Indians, who once lived in SW Mississippi and later in Oklahoma. Natchez, the now-extinct language of this people, was the sole member of its family.

Mulct, basically meaning **to defraud**, is from Latin *multa*, **a fine**. Originally, *mulct* meant to punish by a fine or to deprive of something; now, to extract money, property, from someone, as by fraud or deceit. As a noun, a fine or similar penalty. Pronounced: mulkt.

Pharaoh, the title of the kings of ancient Egypt, is probably from a Coptic word meaning **great house**.

Greek and Latin Words with Root-by-Root Correspondence

There are numerous Greek-Latin word pairs in the English language, that is, words from both languages that have a root-per-root correspondence in meaning. The following are only a few examples: arctic:ursine (pertaining to **bears**); cynical:canine (~ **dogs**); erotic:amorous (~ **sexual love**); eulogy:benediction (**the speaking of good words**); hyperbole:projection (**a throwing forward**); orthogonal:rectangular (~ **straight angles**); periphery:circumference (**the distance around**); polyglot:multilingual (**speaking many tongues**); program:prescription (**a writing before**); sarcophagus:carnivore (**flesh-eating**); symbiotic:convivial (**living together**); synchronous:contemporary (**at the same time**); syntax:composition (**a placing together**);. See English-Latin word pairs, pp. 185, 199.

Scientific medical terms? Not always!

The body is a conglomerate of *blades, drums, hammers, helmets, hinged doors, keys, knobs, pans, pipes, purses, shields, spades, stirrups, swords, trumpets, vinegar bottles, water pitchers,* and *wineskins*. These bodily parts are known in the medical profession as **acetabulum, ampulla, ascites, bursa, clavicle, gladiolus, malleus, patella, salpinx, scapula, spatula, thorax, thyroid, tibia, umbilicus,** and **xiphisternum,** though not necessarily in the order as their less sophisticated, but more colorful counterparts. Stumped? Write danner@occoquanbooks.com for answers.

Common element base: tenere   **Meaning**: to hold
IE base: *ten-*: **to stretch**; compare with next family, which is related; p. 189; **German**: *halten* (see p. 30)

Clavis

tenet: a one-word Latin sentence: **He holds**; hence, a doctrine, principle, or belief generally **held** to be true, especially, a belief shared or **held** by members of an organization, group, or movement.

tennis: Old French *tenez!* **Hold it!** "Receive the ball!" originally, a cry by the server before playing the ball.

tenon: a projecting part cut on the end of a piece of wood for insertion into a corresponding opening or hole (mortise); as a verb, to secure or **hold** a joint; thus, the phrase *mortise and tenon*; *mortise* is from Arabic *murtazza*, **joint**.

tenor: during the Middle Ages, the tenor **held** or carried the melody in 6-part choral music; can be used to indicate a general tendency, as the *tenor* of the President's message was all-out war.

untenable: describing that which *cannot* be **held**, defended, or maintained, as *an untenable argument*, or *position*.

abstinence: *abs-*, **from**; from *abstain*, **to hold from**; to hold oneself back; refrain from, as *to abstain from smoking*. *Abstinence*, a noun, is the act of voluntarily doing without some or all food, drink, or other necessity; can also mean abstaining from alcoholic liquors. *Abstinence* is not etymologically related to *abstemious*, though the meanings are similar. *Abstemious*: *abs-*, **from** + *temetum*, **strong drink**; thus, moderate, especially in eating and drinking; also, characterized by *abstinence*. Confusing?

continent: from the verb *contain*, which itself is from French *contenir*, **to hold**; as a *noun*, originally *terra continens*, **continuous land**; any of the main land areas of the earth conventionally regarded as units. The landmass of Eurasia is regarded as two continents—Europe and Asia—because of their disparate features, peoples, civilizations, etc. The other continents are Africa, Antarctica, Australia, North America, South America. Once a separate continent, India is a subcontinent of Asia. On its northward movement, the continent crashed into China's landmass, creating the Himalayas! See p. 93.

retinue: *re-*, **back**; from the same base as *retain*, **to hold back**; a body of assistants, followers, or servants attending a person of rank or importance; a train of attendants or *retainers*. Pronounced: RET n YOO.

maintain: from *manu tenere*; literally, **to hold in the hand**; the noun is *maintenance*.

pertain: *per-*, **intensive**; **to stretch out**, **reach**; to belong to; to be connected to, or to be associated with; to be a part, accessory, etc., *rights **pertaining** to a landlord*; *responsibilities **pertaining** to parenthood*.

impertinent: *im-*, **not**; **not pertinent**, or **does not pertain**; having no connection with a given matter; **irrelevant**; also, not showing proper respect or manners; **sassy**; **saucy**; **insolent**; **impudent**.

appertain: *ap-*, assimilation of *ad-*, **to**, **toward** + *pertain*; to belong properly as a function, part, etc.; have to do with; relate; pertain. *Give it unto him to whom it appertaineth*. Leviticus 6:5.

appurtenance: from the same base of *appertain*; that which *appertains*; in *law*, an additional, subordinate right or privilege; pluralized, apparatus or equipment; accessories.

lieutenant: French *lieu* (from Latin *locus*), **place**; **one who holds the place** of another. See p. 118 for comments pertaining to *lieutenant* as a military rank, and for *locum tenens*, substitute for a doctor or lawyer.

sostenuto: Italian music term; played at a slower, but *sustained* tempo, with each note held for its full value; as a *noun*, a movement or passage played in this manner.

rein: same as *retain* (under *retinue*, above); **to hold back**; **to harness**. *Reins* guide, control, check, or restrain, as *the reins of government*, or the *reins* used to control a horse.

---

wordextras

MVD, the name of the secret police in the former Soviet Union, is from the initials of *Ministerstro Vnutrennikh Deyl*, or the **Ministry of Internal Affairs**. Its successor was *KGB*, for *Komitet Gosudarstawenoi Bezopasnosti*, **Committee for Government Security**.

Vaseline®, a petroleum jelly manufactured by Chesebrough Ponds, is a combination of German *Was* (pronounced vahs, from *Wasser*, **water**) and Greek *elaion*, **oil**, and the *–ine* suffix. See *Wasser*, p. 110.

Word Cluster No. 95

tend	tendance	tendency	tendentious
tender	tendon	attend	extend
extendible	contend	distend	intend
portend	pretend	superintendent	subtend
tent	tentacle	tenterhooks	attentive
contention	extent	intent	intention
ostentatious	portent	pretentious	distension
tense	tensile	tensimeter	intense
extension	extensive	extensor	pretense
intensify	intensive	ostensible	hypotenuse
tenuity	tenuous	attenuate	extenuating

Common elements_____Inferred Meaning_____

Romance Cognates	French	Romanian	Italian	Portuguese	Spanish
	tendre	intinde	tendere	estender	tender

Word with disguised Latin roots: dance (possibly; see **Clavis**)

Placename: Teniente Origone, Argentina

Latin phrase: *neque semper arcum tendit Apollo*: **Apollo does not always keep his bow bent.** Horace
High tension should be followed by relaxation.

Latin law term: *nolo contendere*; see p. 138.

French terms: *détente; double-entendre; entente cordiale*

Explore *tension* as the unity of a poem. See literary handbook, or search on Google.

Greek cognates: ana**tase**, bronchiec**tasis**, en**tasis**, epi**tasis**, pro**tasis**, telangiec**tasis**, peri**ton**eum, **ten**esmus

wordbuilders #59, 60

Greek *keras*, **horn**, yields **car**at (**small horn**; see p. 133), **car**rot (**shaped like a horn**); **cera**stes (**the horned viper**), cheli**cera**, clado**cer**an, rhino**cer**os (**nose horn**; see p. 135), tri**cera**tops (**three-horn-eye**; thus, a dinosaur with a long horn over each eye, plus a short one over the nose, and similar to the rhinoceros), Dino**ceros**, an extinct genus of huge, horned, ungulate mammals in the Eocene period of North America; Mono**ceros** (**the unicorn**, a constellation).

Greek *cerebrum*, **head**, or **top of head**, thus **brain**, is descended from the same base as *keras*, above. From *cerebrum* are **cereb**ellum, **cerebr**al, and **cerebr**ate, "to use one's brain," **cerebr**um, de**cerebr**ate; cernuous; saveloy.

wordextras

Ten-penny nails derive their name from the practice in 15th-century England of selling nails in lots of 100, with a lot of a certain size costing ten pence or ten denarii (plural of *denarius*). With the first letter of <u>d</u>enarii, this particular size is now referred to as a 10d (or, ten-penny) nail.

Soffit, from the same elements as *suffix* (*suf-*, assimilation of *sub-*, **under** + *figere*, **to fix**), is the horizontal underside of an eave, cornice, etc.; in *architecture*, the intrados of an arch or vault. *Intrados*: **inside the back**; see p. 25.

Laird, the Scottish form of English *lord*, is a landowner, especially a wealthy one. English pronunciation: lerd; Scottish, layrd. See pp. 25, 167 for more on *lord*.

Russian *Izvestia*, **news**, and *Pravda*, **truth**, were the two official Soviet state newspapers. It has been said that *Izvestia* didn't print the *truth*, and *Pravda* didn't print the *news*. Just a little play on words!

Russian *saiga* is a small, stocky antelope with a broad, fleshy snout, native to the steppes of Russia and Siberia. Pronounced SIE guh. *Steppe*: a Russian word for a treeless plain; a savanna; compare *Savannah*, Georgia, p. 111.

TASS, the former Soviet Union news agency, stood for *Telegrafroe Agenstvo Sovetskova Soyuz*, **Telegraph Agency of the Soviet Union.**

Motto of the Commonwealth of Virginia: *Sic temper tyrannis*: **Thus Always to Tyrants.**
Motto of Clark University, Worcester, Massachusetts: *Fiat lux*: **Let there be light.**

Common element base: tendere   **Meaning**: to stretch; thin
Related to previous family *tenere*, **to hold**; extended to mean **to hold and stretch until thin**; therefore, **weak**
IE base: *ten-*: **to stretch**: **Greek**: *teinein*, **to stretch**; **German**: *strecken*

Clavis

tendency: an inclination to move or act in a particular direction or way. SYNONYMS: current, drift, tenor, trend.

tenuous: from *tenuis*, **thin, rare, fine**; having a **thin** or slender form, as a fiber; having a thin consistency; **diluted**; **rarefied**, as air at high altitudes; of little significance; **weak**; **unsubstantial**; **flimsy**; as *a tenuous proposition*, or *tenuous evidence*.

tenuity: the quality or state of being *tenuous*; specifically, **thinness**; **slenderness**; **fineness**; a lack of substance.

tendon: a band or cord of dense, tough, inelastic, white fibrous tissue that connect a muscle with a bone or other part. Even though defined as "inelastic," *tendons* are in fact **stretched** to connect the bones.

portend: *por-* from *per-*, **through**; **to stretch through**; to be an omen or warning of; **foreshadow**; **presage**; to be an indication of; **signify**. *Portent*: that which *portends* an event about to occur, especially an unfortunate one.

pretend: *pre-*, **before**; **to stretch before**; thus, to claim, profess, allege, as *to pretend ignorance of the law*; to claim or profess falsely; **feign, simulate**, as *to pretend anger*; to make believe, as *to pretend to be a spaceman*; other meanings and applications. Related forms: *pretense, pretension, pretentious*. ***Pretentious***: making claims to some distinction; affectedly grand; ostentatious.

détente: French; *dé-*, from Latin *dis-*, **from** + *tender*; **relaxing**, or **unstretching tension**; used especially in relationships between hostile or estranged nations. Pronounced: day TAHNT; also, DAY TAHNT.

ostensible: *os-*, variant of *ob-*, **against**; **to stretch against**; given or appearing as such; **seeming**; **pretended**; **professed**, as "His *ostensible* purpose was philanthropic, but his real goal was selfish aggrandizement." A more meliorative, or positive, meaning is **apparent, conspicuous**, as "the *ostensible* value of increasing one's academic and professional vocabulary." See p. 139 for *ob-* family.

ostentation: from the same elements as *ostensible*, previous entry; **showy display**, as of wealth, knowledge, etc., **pretentiousness**; the adjectival form is *ostentatious*. See *pretentious*, under *pretend*, above.

extenuating: *ex-*, **out**; **making thin**; serving to qualify guilt or blame, as in the phrase *extenuating circumstances*; often used in court by the defense in a plea for clemency.

attenuate: *at-*, assimilation of *ad-*, **to, toward**; **to stretch thin**; to make slender or thin; to dilute or rarefy; in *telecommunications*, to reduce the amplitude or strength of an electrical signal.

tendentious: characterizing a **tendency toward**; advancing or favoring a particular view, as "tendentious writings." SYNONYMS: biased, jaundiced, one-sided, prejudiced, warped.

dance: probably from Old High German, meaning **to stretch out, extend**; however, other authorities indicate that it comes from *de-* + *ante-*, **in front of**; therefore, possibly **to stretch out in front of**. See p. 10, under **Clavis**.

hypotenuse: Greek *hypo-*, **under** + *teinein*, **to stretch**; from phrase *pleura* (**side**) *hypotenusa*, **side subtended**, or **stretched under**; the longest side of a right triangle. If lying on a plane instead of on a slant, the *hypotenuse* would indeed be *under* the right angle; see p. 136. Do not confuse with *hypothesis*, **that which is placed under**, as *a null hypothesis* in research. See p. 117 for more words from *thesis*, e.g., anti**thesis**, epen**thesis**, meta**thesis** (see pp. 117, 198) paren**thesis**, pro**thesis**, pros**thesis**, syn**thesis**.

peritoneum: Greek *peri-*, **around** + *teinein*, **to stretch**; the transparent serous membrane lining the abdominal cavity and reflected inward at various places to cover the visceral, or internal, organs.

epitasis: Greek *epi-*, **upon** + *teinein*, **to stretch**; in classical drama, that part of the play between the *protasis*, or **exposition**, and the *catastrophe* or *denouement*, **the unknotting** (of the plot).

Word from Greek mythology: *Adonis*, **a very handsome young man**. Loved by Aphrodite, goddess of love and beauty, *Adonis* was killed by a wild boar.

Word Cluster No. 96

terra	extraterrestrial	extraterritorial	terreplein
terrace	terrain	Terramycin®	terrane
terraqueous	terrarium	terrazzo	terrene
terrestrial	terricolous	terrier	terrigenous
terrine	parterre	territory	Mediterranean
inter	disinter	interment	subterranean

Common elements_____Inferred Meaning_____

Romance Cognates	French	Romanian	Italian	Portuguese	Spanish
	terre	teren	terra	terra	tierra

Words with disguised Latin roots: fumitory (from *fumus terrae*, **smoke of the earth**; a former medicinal plant), tureen (see **Clavis**), turmeric, verditer (**green of the earth**)

Placenames: Terra Australis Incognita (Australia); Terre Haute, IN; Terrebonne, OR; Terra Alta, WV; Terra Bella, CA; Terra Linda, CA; Bonne Terre, MO; Terraville, SD; Tierra Amarilla, NM; Terrebonne Bay, LA; Mediterranean Sea; Tierra del Fuego, **earth of fire**: southern tip of South America

Latin phrases: *Sit tibi terra levis*; *terra firma* (see **Clavis**)

French phrases: *terre à terre*: **commonplace**; *à fleur de terre; pied-à-terre; pomme de terre; terre verte*

Italian term: *terra cotta*, **baked earth**, unglazed earthenware used for pottery, sculpture, etc.

Motto of Amherst College, Amherst, Massachusetts: *Terras irradient*: **Let them illumine the lands**.

NB: C<u>eme</u>tery, **a sleeping place**, is not in this family, although the letters *ter*, as in *inter*, is a mnemonic for spelling the word correctly. Another memory device is that there are three e's in the word.

Words with Germanic elements: trass (a volcanic rock, powdered and used in making hydraulic cement), thirst

Greek *ge-*, **earth**: **geo**botany, **geo**centric, **geo**chemistry, **geo**chronology, **geo**desic, **geo**desy, **geo**detic, **geo**dynamics, **geo**economics, **geo**gnosy, **geo**graphy, **geo**logy, **geo**magnetic, **geo**mancy, **geo**metric, **geo**metrid, **geo**metry, **geo**morphic, **geo**phagy, **geo**phone, **geo**physics, **geo**phyte, **geo**politics, **geo**potential, **geo**pressured, **geo**science, **geo**stationary, **geo**strophic, **geo**synchronous (**in time with the earth**, as *a geosynchrous satellite*), **geo**syncline, **geo**taxis, **geo**tectonic, **geo**thermal, **geo**tropism; **ge**anticline, **ge**ode, **ge**oid, **ge**orgic; apo**gee**, peri**gee**; epi**geal**, hypo**geal**; hypo**geum**; iso**geo**therm; hydro**geology**, photo**geology**, phyto**geography**, zoo**geography**; apo**geo**tropism.

wordextras

Whether pertaining to helping verbs or designating adjuncts to the local fire department, *auxiliary* is from Latin *auxilium*, **helper**. An auxiliary verb helps convey special shades of meaning; some auxiliary verbs are as follows: can, could; do, did; may, might; shall, should; will, would; must. The dictionary form of *any* verb can combine with *any* auxiliary verb, e.g., *can read, could read; do read, did read; may read, might read; shall read, should read; will read, would read; must read.* See **wordbuilder #19**, p. 41, for more words in this family.

Tweed was originally so called because the fabric was made with a *double thread* known as *twill* in Scottish, and was later associated by mere coincidence with *Tweed*, Scotland, where the fabric was first made.

Satin is the English spelling of *Zaitun*, the medieval name of *Chanchou*, China, where the fabric was first made.

Rebuke, from *re-*, **back** + *buchier*, **to beat**, meaning **to criticize or reprove sharply**, is from Old North French *rebuker*, **to strike**, **chop wood**. Synonyms: censure, chastise, reprimand, scold. *Rebuke* is also used as a noun. As far as can be determined, there are no other English words derived from *buchier*.

Javanese *lahar* designates a landslide or mudflow of volcanic fragments on the flanks of a volcano; also, the deposit produced by such an occurrence.

Sapor, from Latin *sapere*, **to taste**, is that quality in a substance that produces taste or flavor; savor.

In Spanish-speaking regions of the US, *ladrone* is a **robber**, **bandit**, and comes from Latin *latro*, **a hired servant**.

Rotary Club is so named because the members originally *rotated* from one business to another for meetings.

Common element base: terra   **Meaning**: earth; land; originally, dry, arid
IE base: *ters-*: yields *thirst, toast, torrent, torrid*
German *Erde*, the basis of **English** *earth*, from IE *er-²*; yields **Afrikaans** *aardvark,** **earth pig**, and ***aardwolf***. Afrikaans, spoken in areas of South Africa, developed out of the speech of 17th-century Boer settlers from Holland and is still very much like Dutch. *Afrikaans* is also referred to as *die Taal*, Dutch for **the Language**. **Aardvark*, now obsolete, has been replaced by *erdvark*. With a long, sticky tongue, the *erdvark*, also known as *anteater*, feeds mostly on ants and termites.

Clavis

terrarium:	*-arium*, **a place where**, as in *aquarium, planetarium, sanitarium*, is an indoor, transparent enclosure in which to keep small land animals, such as turtles; also, a glass container enclosing a garden of small plants.
terricolous:	*colere*, **to dwell**; **living on or in the ground**, as *terricolous worms*; originally from *terricola*, **earth-dweller**. Other words ending in *-colous*: *arenicolous* (**sand**), *nidicolous* (**nest**; describing those birds, such as wrens and sparrows, that remain in the nest until mature enough to fly; opposed to *nidifugous*; see p. 86), *saxicolous* (**rocks**), *silvicolous* (**forest or woodlands**, as deer), *stercoricolous* (**dung**, as certain insects). Pronounced: ter RIK uh lus, or tuh RIK uh lus.
terra firma:	**firm earth, solid ground**, as in "Though the astronauts were awed by outer space, each of them was glad to set foot again on the *terra firma*." See more words from *firm*, **wordbuilder #30**, p. 83.
Terre Haute:	French; **high earth** (see p. 4); a city situated above the high-water line on the Wabash River in Indiana. The city is *not* the highest point in the state, however. See other words from *alt-*, p. 3.
terra incognita:	literally, **unknown land**; unexplored territory; more figuratively, an unknown or unexplored field of knowledge. The original name of Australia was *Terra Australis Incognita*, or **Unidentified Southern Land**.
inter:	*in-*, **in**, to bury (a person) **in the earth**; *to disinter* is to exhume a corpse, especially for forensic examinations. *Exhume* shares its root with *humus, humble*, and *human*, all of which convey the idea of **earth** or **soil**. See p. 94 for more on *exhume*.
torrid:	Since *terre* originally meant **dry, arid**, as opposed to the ocean's water, the connection to *torrid*, **scorching**, thus, **burning**, is clearer.
tureen:	also, *terrine*; a bowl for serving stews and soups and originally made of **earthenware**.
Sit tibi terra levis:	**May the earth lie lightly on thee**: addressed to the dead; an old epitaph, or tombstone inscription.
apogee:	Greek *apo-*, **from** + *gaia*, **earth**; the point farthest from *Earth* (capitalized when referred to as a planet) in the orbit of the moon or of a man-made satellite; opposed to *perigee*, next entry.
perigee:	Greek *peri-*, **around** + *gaia*, **earth**; the point nearest *Earth* in the orbit of the moon or of a man-made satellite; opposed to *apogee*, previous entry.
geosynchronous:	Greek *syn-*, **with, together** + *chronos*, **time**; **in time with the earth**; a *geosynchronous* satellite maintains a fixed position at about 22,000 miles over the **earth's** equator.

wordextras

Gazeta, from a Venetian dialect, was the name of **a small coin**, the price of a newspaper. Hence, ***gazette*** has become part of the name of many newspapers. ***Picayune***, a small coin of French Louisiana, was also once the price of a newspaper, thus part of the name of New Orleans' daily, *The Times-Picayune*.

Nether means **under, below**; the ***Netherlands***, a small kingdom on the North Sea, is aptly named, because more than two-fifths of the country's land was once claimed by the sea, or by lakes and swamps. The Dutch have reclaimed much of this land with an elaborate system of dikes, windmills, and pumps. There is a saying in the Netherlands: God may have created the universe, but the Dutch created Holland.

A Writing Tip: Use appositives, either nouns or noun phrases, to rename or to explain a nearby noun. Example: Antarctica, *the coldest place on Earth*, is the only continent where no mosquitoes exist. [*the coldest place on Earth*, the appositive, is said "to be in apposition" to *Antarctica*.] Appositives are in the same grammatical form as the noun renamed or explained. In this example, both *place* and *Antarctica* are nouns.

```
┌─────────────────────────────────────────────────────────────────────────────┐
│                          Word Cluster No. 97                                  │
│                                                                               │
│  transact                 transceiver              transcendent              │
│  transcontinental         transcendentalism        transcribe                │
│  transcription            transfer                 transfiguration           │
│  transfinite              transformation           transfusion               │
│  transient                transilluminate          transistor                │
│  transit                  transitive                translate                │
│  transliterate            translucent               translunary              │
│  transmigrate             transmission              transmutation            │
│  transparency             transpicuous             transposition             │
│  transuranic              transvestite             transport                 │
│  transubstantiate         transudation             transverse                │
│                                                                               │
│  Common element_____Inferred Meaning_____│
└─────────────────────────────────────────────────────────────────────────────┘
```

Romance Cognates	French	Romanian	Italian	Portuguese	Spanish
	traverse	traversa	traversa	travessa	través

Words with disguised Latin elements: tradition, traducianism, traitor, tranquil, transept (*septum*, **enclosure**), transom, treason, trench, trespass, trestle, truncate (distant relationship; see *trencherman*, p. 111), traffic

Latin phrases: *Sic transit gloria mundi*: **Thus passes the glory of the world.**

Motto of the State of Connecticut: *Qui transtulit, sustinet*: **He who transplants, sustains.** See p. 187.

Greek *dia-*, **across, through**: diallel, diallage, diapophysis, diarthrosis, dieresis, diestrus, diopter, diuresis; diabase, diabetes, diabetic, diabolic, diachrony, diacritical, diadem, diadromous, diagenesis, diageotropism, diagnose, diagnosis, diagonal, diagram, diakinesis, dialect, dialogue, dialysis, diameter, dianoetic, diapason, diapedesis, diaper, diaphanous (see p. 42), diaphone, diaphoresis, diaphragm (see *midriff*, p. 32), diaphysis, diapositive, diarrhea (see p. 83), Diaspora, diastase, diastem, diastema, diastole, diastrophism, diatessaron, diathermancy, diathesis, diatonic, diatribe, diatropism; deacon.

Greek *meta-*, **along with, after, between, among, other**, regarded as equivalent of *trans-*: meteor, method, Methodist, methodize, methodology, metonym, metonymy (a figure of speech, similar to *synecdoche*, see p. 77); metabasis, metabolism, metacarpal, metacenter, metachromatism, metacriticism, metafiction, metagalaxy, metagenesis, metagnathous, metalanguage, metalinguistics, metamathematics, metamer, metamorphosis, metatfhnephros, metaphase, metaphor, metaphrase, metaphrast, metaphysical, metaplasm, metaprotein, metapsychosis, metasomatism, metastable, metastasis, metatarsus, metathesis (see p. 198), metathorax, metaxylem, metazoan.

NB: *Diamond* is not in this family; see **Clavis**.

```
┌─────────────────────────────────────────────────────────────────┐
│  Quote: How long a time lies in one little word. Shakespeare      │
└─────────────────────────────────────────────────────────────────┘
```

wordextras

The state of **Wyoming** is named after **Wyoming Valley**, a valley of the Susquehanna River, in Pennsylvania: site of a massacre in 1778. The valley was named from German *Wayomick*, a transliteration of Munsee (a Delaware language) *chwewamink*, meaning "large river bottom."

Ombudsman, from Swedish *ombud*, **a deputy**, **representative**, is a public official appointed to investigate citizens' complaints concerning government agencies. The base of *ombudsman* is Latin *ambi-*, **on both sides**, **around**.

A ***gibbous*** moon, from Latin *gibba*, **hump**, is one in which more than half, but not all, the face reflects sunlight to Earth. [*Earth* is capitalized when referred to as a planet, as are Mars, Venus, Mercury, Jupiter, Saturn, Uranus, Neptune, Pluto, as of now! Others yet to be named are being discovered.]

Term from Greek mythology: *Achilles' heel*: **one's vulnerable spot**, from the myth that Achilles was invulnerable except in the heel. His mother dipped him in the River Styx to make him strong and invulnerable; however, she held him by the heel, thus making it the *only* vulnerable part of his body. The *Achilles tendon* connects the back of the heel to the muscles of the calf. It is probably the most vulnerable part of an athlete's body.

Common element base: trans-   **Meaning**: across, through, over, beyond, on the other side
IE base: *tere(e)-²*: with meanings the same as Latin, but also **to pass through, overcome**; yields **English** *nostril*, **nose hole**; and *thrill*. See **Word Cluster No. 99**.

Clavis

transistor:

from **trans**(fer) + (re)**sistor**; a device that **transfers** a current **across** a resistor; term also applied to the transistorized radio. The root *–sist* is from *stare*, **to stand**; see p. 179, **Word Cluster No. 90**.

transcend:

scandere, **to climb**; **to climb beyond**; to go beyond the limits of; **overstep**; **exceed**. ***Transcendent***: in *philosophy*, beyond the limits of possible experience; in *theology*, existing apart from the material universe. Related philosophical and theological terms include *transcendental* and *transcendentalism*. In the United States, *transcendentalism* became not only a philosophy, but also a literary, religious, and social movement. The main leader of the movement was Ralph Waldo Emerson; other influential transcendentalists include Bronson Alcott (father of Louisa May Alcott, author of *Little Women*), Margaret Fuller, Theodore Parker, and Henry David Thoreau, author of *Walden*. Though not members, Nathaniel Hawthorne and Emily Dickinson were influenced by the movement.

transvestite:

vestire, **to clothe**; **one who clothes or dresses across**; one, especially a male, who derives erotic pleasure and emotional gratification from dressing in clothes of the opposite sex.

travesty:

from same elements as *transvestite*; that which is **clothed beyond**; exaggerated imitation with intent to ridicule; a burlesque; in *literature*, a broad and grotesque parody on a lofty and serious work; also, a crude or distorted representation of something, as *a travesty of justice*. See *satire*, p. 172.

transverse:

vertere, **to turn**; **to turn across**; lying, situated, placed across; crossing side to side; **crosswise**; athwart; in *geometry*, designating the axis that passes through the foci (plural of *focus*) of a *hyperbola*, or the part of the axis between the vertices. Can also mean **shortcut**. Opposed to *longitudinal*: running or placed lengthwise. See *hyperbola*, p. 184.

transitive:

from the same roots as *transit*: it from *ire*, **to go**; **going across**; in *grammar*, expressing an action that is thought of as passing over to and taking effect on some person or thing, e.g., in *Gerald kicked the football*, *kicked* is a transitive verb because the *thing* (football) received the action of *kicked*; in *mathematics*, designating a relation having the property that whenever a first element bears a particular relation to a second, that in turn bears this same relation to a third, then the third element bears this relation to the first, or if a = b and b = c, then c = a.

traducianism:

ducere, **to lead**; **that which is brought over**; the theological belief that the soul is inherited along with the body from one's parents; opposed to *creationism* and *infusionism*.

treason:

and *tradition* both are originally from *trans- + dare*, **to give**; therefore, **to give over**. A story handed down or given over is *tradition*, while the handing over of the State to its enemies is Old French *traison*, which became English *treason*. *Traitor*, coming from the same roots, denotes one guilty of *treason*. See more words from *dare*, p. 73; see more on *traitor*, p. 74.

tranquil:

quies, **quiet**; **beyond quietness**. SYNONYMS: calm, even, peaceful, serene, steady, unruffled.

diagonal:

Greek *dia-*, **across** + *gonia*, **angle**; as an *adjective*, connecting two nonadjacent angles or vertices of a polygon or polyhedron, as a straight line; as a *noun*, designates something that is diagonal; also, a set of entries in a square matrix. See other *gonia* words, p. 207, Item 98.

diameter:

Greek *dia-*, **across** + *meterein*, **to measure**; measurement through or across a circle, sphere, cylinder, from one side to the other. In *optics*, the unit of measure of the magnifying power of a lens.

diamond:

from Greek *adamas*, the same base as for *adamant*, **unyielding**. See **wordextras**, p. 114.

nectar:

nec- from Greek *nekros*, **death**; *tar* is possibly from Sanskrit *tarati*, **he overcomes**; thus, *nectar* was originally held to be death-overcoming, conferring immortality. Together with *ambrosia*, nectar constituted sustenance for the gods. See more on *nectar*, p. 131.

Word from Greek mythology: *Cassandra*, **a prophet of doom**; from *Cassandra*, a prophetess cursed by Apollo so that her prophecies, though they were true, were fated never to be believed.

Word Cluster No. 98

triad	trialogue	triangle	triarchy
Triassic	triathlete	triaxial	tribasic
tribune	tricameral	tricentennial	triceps
triceratops	trichotomy	trichroism	tricyclic
tridactyl	trident	trifecta	trifid
trifolium	triforium	trifurcate	trigeminal
triglyph	trigonometry	trillium	trilocular
trilogy	trimerous	trimester	trimeter
trimorphous	trinity	trinomial	trio
triolet	tripartite	triple(t)	tripod
trireme	tritium	triumvirate	trivet
trivial	trivium	tritone	trichromatic
treble	trefoil	trellis	trephine
terce	tercentenary	tercet	terdiurnal
tergeminate	ternary	ternian	tertian
tertiary	terzetto	sesterce	tervalent

Words from both Latin and Greek are placed together since the common element is spelled the same in both languages.

Common elements_____**Inferred Meaning**_____

Romance Cognates	French	Romanian	Italian	Portuguese	Spanish
	trois	trei	tre	três	tres

Words with disguised roots: trammel, travail:travel (see **Doublets**, p. 147), trey, trocar; trepan:trephine (see p. 81)

Placenames: *Trinidad and Tobago* (a two-island nation in the Atlantic off Venezuela). There are a number of municipalities—too numerous to list—throughout the United States with the names of *Trinidad, Trinity, Trio,* and *Tripoli* (**three cities**). *Tres Pinos* (**Three Pines**), CA; *Tres Ritos* (**Three Rites**), NM.

Latin phrase: *tertium quid*: **a third something**, something between two opposites or resulting from the union of two opposing forces; something that is neither mind nor matter.

French phrase: *ménage à trois*: **household of three**, but usually refers to a married couple plus a lover, as living together or having sexual relations.

Explore *American Heritage Dictionary's* Appendix for IE root *trei-* to see the relationship of *tri-* to **test**ament, **test**icle, **test**ify, at**test**, con**test**, de**test**, ob**test**, pro**test**. The basic meaning is "witness."

Explore *terza rima*, a **three-line** stanza form borrowed from the Italian poets. See Robert Browning's "The Statue and the Bust"; also, Percy Shelley's "Ode to the West Wind."

See *King Henry VI* as a **trilogy**; also, Eugene O'Neill's *Mourning Becomes Electra*, in which Aeschylus' theme of fate haunts an American family. Aeschylus (c. 525-456 B.C.), writer of Greek tragedies.

Persian: sitar; **Chinese**: sampan (see **wordextras**, p. 187 for more on *sampan*); **Hindi**: teapoy, Trimurti (see p. 10)

---

wordextras

Academic is from Greek *Akademia*, the estate of *Akademos*, who encouraged Plato and other Athenian philosophers to discuss important issues at his estate, used by the philosophers as a retreat.

Harass, from Old French *harer*, **to set a dog on**, is to trouble, worry, or torment, as with cares, debts, repeated questions, etc. The preferred pronunciation is HAIR ess, but is usually pronounced huh RASS.

Fardel, from Arabic *fardah*, originally meant **bundle**; it has come to mean **burden**. *Who would fardels bear,/To grunt and sweat under a weary life?* Shakespeare. Pronunciation: FARD uhl.

Post, a contraction of *positum*, from Latin *ponere*, **to place**, originally referred to the series of mounted riders or runners stationed at intervals, or posts, for the rapid carrying of mail. See p. 157 for other words from *ponere*.

ZIP code is the acronym for *Zone Improvement Plan*, and was begun in 1963.

Common element base: tri   **Meaning**: three

Both Greek and Latin are from IE *trei-*, **three**. **German**: *drei*; **Russian**: *TPH*, pronounced *tree*; the actual character represented by *H* cannot be represented in English; *troika*: a carriage drawn by three horses

Clavis

trillium:
of the lily family, a plant of various colors that bears a whorl of **three** leaves and a single flower with **three** sepals and **three** petals.

trio:
designates a set or group of **three** persons, things, etc.; also a composition for **three** voices or **three** instruments, as well as the **three** performers of such a composition. In addition, designates the middle, or episodic, section of a minuet, scherzo, march, or of various dance forms, originally written in *three* voices, or parts.

Trinidad:
Spanish for *Trinity*. At Trinidad, there rise from the sea **three** mountains that appeared to Columbus from a distance to be **three** islands; as he sailed nearer, he discovered that instead of **three** islands, there was only one; hence, he named the entity after the Christian concept of the **Holy Trinity**: Father, Son, and Holy Spirit, the **three** manifestations of God. (The suffix *–ity* often corresponds to *–dad* in Spanish, e.g., verity — truth, *verdad*; veracity, *veracidad*; vicinity, *vecindad*.)

triple threat:
an Americanism; a football player who is a skillful runner, passer, and kicker; also, any person who is an expert or is adept in **three** fields, skills, professions.

trivia:
via, **way**; **three ways**; crossroads. *Trivia* probably developed from the small talk that sojourners engaged in at the crossroads; in *biology*, *trivial* is a specific name as opposed to a generic name.

trivium:
from same elements as *trivia*; in medieval universities, the **three** studies (*grammar*, *logic*, *rhetoric*) leading to a Bachelor of Arts degree. See *quadrivium*, p. 162; *liberal arts*, p. 114.

travel:
travel and *travail* are doublets; originally, an instrument of torture using **three stakes**. *Travel* in the early days was often described as *travail* because of <u>torturous</u>, as well as <u>tortuous</u>, roads; underlined words both from *torquere*, **to twist**: *torturous*, twisting, as in pain, or grief; *tortuous*, twisting, winding, and curvy, as *a tortuous mountain highway*; also, not straightforward; deceitful or tricky.

tercet:
a group of **three** lines that rime (or, rhyme); in *music*, a triplet. *Rime* is the preferred spelling by many authorities as being historically correct.

trefoil:
foil from *folium*, **leaf**; any of a number of plants with leaves divided into **three** leaflets, as the clover, tick trefoil, and certain species of lotus; any flower or leaf with **three** lobes; any ornamental figure resembling a **threefold** leaf. See p. 206, Item 90 for more words from *folium*.

trinomial:
Greek *nomos*, **law**; a mathematical expression of **three** terms connected by plus or minus signs; also, the scientific name of a plant or animal taxon, consisting of **three** words designating in respective order, the *genus*, the *species*, and the *subspecies* or *variety*. Also, comprised of *three* terms.

sitar:
from Hindi (through Sanskrit, a cognate of English); originally, a **three-stringed**, but now a *six-* stringed, musical instrument, which also has a number of sympathetic strings.

teapoy:
hybrid of Hindi *tin*, **three** + Persian *pai*, **foot**; a **three-legged** table for serving tea. The spelling of *teapoy* is influenced by its use as a *teacart*. Etymologically, *teapoy* is related to *pajamas*; see p. 151.

wordextras

Anglo-Saxon ***husband*** is from *husbonde*, **housebound**; ***midwife*** means literally **with woman** (see p. 167).

Shreveport, Louisiana, is named for H. M. Shreve (1780-1851), a Mississippi riverboat captain. Shreveport itself is bordered by the Red River, and is in Caddo Parish. Louisiana is the only state to refer to counties as *parishes*.

Harbinger, now "a herald of news," is from Old Norse, where it meant **army shelter**, and referred to an advance team that made food and shelter provisions for the ensuing army. *The robin is a **harbinger** of spring.*

Tuscaloosa, Alabama, home of the University of Alabama, and the Crimson Tide, is Choctaw for the name of a chief *Black Warrior* (*taska*, **warrior** + *lusa*, **black**). *Black Warrior River* flows through Tuscaloosa.

Word from Greek mythology: *cornucopia*; **horn of plenty**, an overflowing supply; from the horn of the goat that suckled Zeus, the chief deity in Greek mythology. See *copious*, **wordextras**, p. 131.

```
┌─────────────────────────────────────────────────────────────────────────────┐
│                          Word Cluster No. 99                                  │
│                                                                               │
│    ultra             ultraism         ultracentrifuge    ultraconservatism    │
│    ultramicroscopic  ultramodern      ultramontane       ultramundane         │
│    ultrashort        ultranationalism ultrasonic         ultrastellar         │
│    ulterior          ultimate         ultramarine        ultraviolet          │
│  penult              penultimate      ultimatum          ultimo               │
│                                                                               │
│  Common Elements_____Inferred Meaning_____ │
└─────────────────────────────────────────────────────────────────────────────┘
```

Romance Cognates	French	Romanian	Italian	Portuguese	Spanish
	outre	ultra	oltre	ultra	ultra

Words with disguised Latin roots: adulterate, adultery, allegiance, alert, El Dorado, else, outrage, utterance (one meaning).

Terms and Places: ultrahigh frequency (UHF); ultima Thule, **farthest Thule**. According to the ancients, referred to the northernmost region of the world, possibly Norway or Iceland. Figuratively, the term signifies any far-off mysterious place, or some unattainable goal. There is *Thule*, Greenland, near the North Geomagnetic Pole.

Romance word and phrase: *outré, à outrance*   **Latin phrases**: *ne plus ultra; ultra vires*

Explore *metaphysical poets* in a literary handbook; also, explore *metaphor* and *simile* as literary devices.

> **Quote**: The vocabulary of science and medicine is the language of Greece and Rome. Lack of knowledge of Greek and Latin roots hampers the mastery of scientific terminology. Dean John Pomfet

wordextras

Lady, from Anglo-Saxon *hlaefdige*, originally meant **loaf-kneader** (see p. 69 under **wordbuilder #28**). Compare with *lord*, p. 25. See other Anglo-Saxon words, p. 167, under *Britain*, **wordextras**.

Daughter is "similarly" spelled in many of the Indo-European languages: German, *Tochter*; Gothic, *dauhtar*; Sanskrit, *duhitár*; and Greek, *thugater*. Some etymologists believe that in Sanskrit, from which *daughter* was derived, *duhitár* meant **one who milks the cows**; others surmise that the original use was Greek.

Fisc, originally, **a basket**, **bag**, then **a treasury**, is a royal or state treasury; an exchequer. Thus, *fiscal*, an adjective, pertains to the public treasury or revenues, as in *fiscal year*, *fiscal responsibility*. See *confiscate*, p. 173.

Jumbo, the name of a large elephant in Barnum's circus, is originally from Swahili *jumbe*, **chief**. Swahili is a *lingua franca*, **common language**, of east-central Africa and parts of the Congo. See more on *Swahili*, p. 175.

The *Diesel* engine is named for Rudolph Diesel (1858-1913), a German inventor. He apparently committed suicide by jumping from the ship while crossing the English Channel. After amassing a fortune, he died penniless.

Word from a person's name: *guillotine*; from Joseph Ignace Guillotin (1738-1814), a French physician. Dr. Guillotin did not invent the decapitation device that bears his name, inasmuch as a similar one had been used for centuries in other countries. However, as a humanitarian, he advised that the weight of the blade be increased and that it be honed razor-sharp, thus insuring a swift and painless death for the thousands beheaded during the French Revolution. Prior to the instrument's modification, partially beheaded victims often lived for many hours—and even days—before finally dying from blood loss and a broken neck. The doctor vehemently protested the attachment of his name to the device; after his death, his children sued to have the name of the device changed. The court's decision was that the children could change their own last name, but that the device would continue to be called the *guillotine*. Note that the doctor's name is *Guillotin*; the device is *guillotine*.

A Writing Tip: *They* requires a specific antecedent in all but the most informal writing. **Spoken**: *They* say on the news that Macon, Georgia, has more ornamental cherry trees than does Washington, DC. **Written**: *It was reported* on the news that Macon, Georgia, has more ornamental cherry trees than does Washington, DC. **Spoken**: They said on the radio that the Baltimore Tunnel would be closed tomorrow for repairs. **Written**: The radio reporter said that the Baltimore Tunnel would be closed tomorrow for repairs.

Common element base: ultra- **Meaning**: over, beyond, on the other side
IE base: *al-*: **beyond**; **German**: *jenseits*, **the other side of**, **beyond**.
Latin *cis-*: **this side of**, or **near side of**, e.g., *cislunar*, as well as *Cismont*, Virginia, near Charlottesville. *Cismont* is "this side of" the Blue Ridge Mountains as one faces them, oriented from the east.

Clavis

ultimo:	from *ultimo mense*, **in the last month**, ablative singular of *ultimus*; **in the preceding month**: an old-fashioned usage, e.g., *yours*, i.e., **your letter**, of the 13th (day) **ultimo** received. Compare with *proximo*. *Ablative*: in grammar, designates removal, deprivation, direction from, source, cause, etc.
ultimate:	superlative of *ulter*, **farther**; thus, **last**; *ultima* designates the last syllable of a word; **ultimate**: beyond which it is impossible to go; **farthest**, most remote or distant; beyond which further analysis, division, etc., cannot be made; **elemental**; **fundamental**; **primary**. From the same root is *ultimatum*, **a final, uncompromising demand**.
penultimate:	*pen-*, **almost**; **almost the end**; **next to the last**, as *the penultimate syllable of a word*; *peninsula*, bordered on three sides by water, is "almost an island," e.g., *the state of Florida*, *Baja* (Lower) *California*, and the *Arabian Peninsula*. There is also *Peninsula*, in northcentral Ohio; in addition, there is *Presque Isle*, Maine. See more on *Presque Isle*, p. 143.
ultramontane:	**beyond the mountains**; originally, in the Roman Catholic Church (RCC), an ecclesiastic in a country north of the Alps; refers to the policy that absolute ecclesiastic authority in the RCC is vested in the Pope; opposed to *Gallicanism*, which favors the restriction of papal control. *Gallicanism* originated among the French RCC clergy.
ultramundane:	*mundus*, **world**; **beyond the world**, or beyond the limits of the solar system.
ultra vires:	*vir*, **man**; **beyond persons**; beyond the legal power of a person or corporation. From *vir* come also *virtue* and *virtuoso*. See p. 102 for more on *virtue*; see p. 213, Item 189 for other words from *vir*.
ne plus ultra:	**no more beyond**; thus, **the ultimate**; especially the finest, best, most perfect, etc.
outré:	French; **beyond** (the bounds of propriety); the basis of *outrage*. Pronounced: oo TRAY.
ulterior:	**beyond** what is seen or expected, as in "Tom waited tables, but his *ulterior* desire was to become an actor"; also used pejoratively, i.e., **concealed intentionally**, so as to deceive, as *an ulterior motive*.
utterance:	though now obsolete, *utterance* is seen in medieval works; **the uttermost end or extremity**; bitter end; death. *Utterance* also means the act of expressing words, whether written or spoken. In *law*, *to utter* is to pass counterfeit money or to forge checks.
metaphor:	*pherein*, **to carry**; **to carry over or beyond**; a figure of speech containing an implied comparison, in which a word or phrase ordinarily and primarily used for one thing is applied to another, e.g., *the curtain of night*, or Shakespeare's *all the world's a stage*. Robert Burns' simile "My love is *like* a red, red rose," can be made into a metaphor by deleting *like*: "My love *is* a red, red rose." Explore *tenor and vehicle* (p. 187) in understanding similes and metaphors; search on Google.
metaphysical:	transliterated from Greek *Ta meta ta phusika*, **the things after the physics**; Aristotle's treatise on *transcendental philosophy*, for example, **followed**, or **went beyond**, his works in physics; also designates the branch of philosophy that systematically investigates the nature of first principles and problems of ultimate reality. Compare *ontology* and *cosmology*. See *transcendentalism*, p. 194.
metaphrase:	*meta-*, **along with** in this word; a translation, especially, a literal, word-for-word translation, as distinguished from *paraphrase*, which rewords a passage for clarity.
metathesis:	*thesis* from *tithenai*, **to place**; **to put over**, **transpose**; transposition or interchange; specifically, the transposition of sounds in a word or between words; by metathesis, *clasp,* for example, developed from Middle English *clapse*; *spoonerisms* are also examples of *metathesis*. See p. 193 for *metathesis*, listed with the *meta-* family. See p. 117 for *spoonerism*. Pronunciation: muh TATH uh sis.

Word from Greek mythology: *aegis*, **protection or sponsorship**; originally, a goatskin, and was the shield borne by Zeus, and later by Athena, the goddess of wisdom, skills, and warfare.

```
┌────────────────────────────────────────────────────────────────────────────┐
│                         Word Cluster No. 100                                  │
│                                                                               │
│    venue            avenue            advene            covenant              │
│  convene          convenient        intervene          parvenu               │
│  provenance         revenant          revenue           souvenir             │
│  subvene          supervene         conventicle        convention            │
│    venture          advent          adventitious         convent             │
│    event          eventuate          inventory          obvention            │
│                                                                               │
│  Common elements_____Inferred Meaning_____    │
└────────────────────────────────────────────────────────────────────────────┘
```

Romance Cognates	French	Romanian	Italian	Portuguese	Spanish
	venir	veni	venire	vir	venir

Romance words and phrases: *bienvenue; abat-vent; ben venuto*

Latin words and phrases: *Optima mors Parca quae venit apta die.* Propertius (c. 50-15 B.C.), Roman poet
The best death is that which comes on the day fixed by Fate.
Post cineres gloria sera venit: **After one is reduced to ashes, fame comes too late.** Martial (40-104 A.D), Roman poet
Quod erat inveniendum (Q.E.I.): **which was to be found**
Amo ut invenio: **I love as I find** (or light upon).
Veni, vedi, vici: Caesar's message to the Roman senate, announcing his victory over Pharnaces, king of Pontus.
Venit summa dies et ineluctabile tempus: **The last day of (Troy) has come and the inevitable hour.** Virgil
invenit; venire facias; Venite

French phrases: *cela viendra*: **that will come some day**; all in good time.
Venez m'aider, **come help me**; shortened to *m'aider*; thus, *Mayday*, used by ships and aircraft in distress.

Explore *invention* or *originality in thought*, as well as *style, diction, imagery*, and *plot* in a literary handbook.

Law terms: venue (the locality in which a cause of action or a crime is committed), change of venue

wordextras

French and Middle English ***coup***, a brilliant and successful action, is from Greek *kolaphos*, **a box on the ear**. The word is also seen in *coup de grâce, coup d'état, coup de foudre, coup de main, coup de theatre, coup d'oeil.*

Enthusiasm, from Greek *enthous* (*en-*, **in** + *theos*, **god**), **possessed by a god**, was originally a supernatural inspiration or possession; it came to mean inspired prophetic or poetic ecstasy; then, intense or eager interest, zeal, fervor. *Theos* is also seen in ***theocracy, theogony, theology, theomorphic, theophany;*** see pp. 42, 59, for other *theo-* words.

Philology, an earlier term for linguistics, has come to mean **love of learning and literature**, and is used mostly to refer to the study of written records, especially literary texts in order to determine their authenticity, meaning, etc. *Philos* is also seen in ***philter*** (a potion thought to arouse sexual love, especially toward a certain person; any magic potion; as a *verb*, to charm or arouse with a philter), ***Philadelphia, philander, philanthropy, philharmonic; philodendron, philogyny, philosophy;*** *acidophile, cryophile, heterophile, hemophile, homophile, oenophile, pedophile, technophile; coprophilia, hemophilia, necrophilia, nemophilia; cryophilic, hydrophilic, lycophilic, psychrophilic.*

Symposium, from Greek *sym-*, **with, together** + *pos*, from *pinein*, **to drink**, originally was **a drinking together**. In ancient Greece and Rome, *symposium* designated a party, usually following a dinner, for drinking and conversations; *symposium* came to designate conversation without restraint; now, a formal meeting at which several specialists deliver short addresses on a designated topic. See other *sym-* words, p. 161.

Prude, backformation of French *prude femme*, **virtuous woman**, is a person who is overly modest or proper in behavior, dress, or speech, especially in a way that annoys others.

Emblements, in *law*, means cultivated growing crops that are produced annually; also, the profits from such crops.

English-Latin word-pairs include the following: loving:amatory; name:appellation; oversee:supervise; scare: terrify; shield:protect; small:diminutive; sparkle:scintillate; starry:stellar; straightway:immediately; sunny:solar; teacher:instructor; thin:emaciated; truth:veracity; unfriendly:inimical; unload:exonerate; unreadable:illegible; uproot:eradicate; walk:ambulate; wholesome:salubrious. See additional English-Latin word-pairs on p. 185. See Latin-Greek word-pairs, p. 187.

199

Common element base: venir

Meaning: to come

IE base: *gwa-, gwen-*: **to come**, as seen in *come* itself; **German**: *kommen*

Clavis

adventure: *ad-*, **to**, **toward**; produces *avenue* and *Advent*, **to come to**, as well. See *Advent*, next entry.

Advent: when capitalized, **Christ's coming to Earth**, either at birth or at His coming again; also, the four Sundays preceding Christmas; in lowercase, nonreligious use, as *the advent of spring*.

souvenir: *sou-*, French for *sub-*, **under**; **that which comes from under**, or more figuratively, that which calls to mind; that which serves as a reminder; a memento, keepsake.

revenue: *re-*, **back**; **that which comes back** or **in**; the *income* of a government from taxation and other sources appropriated for public expenses; a word pair of English *income*. The two are differentiated in that *revenue* applies to government, and *income*, to individuals.

covenant: *co-*, truncation of *com-*, **with**, **together**; **a coming together**, a solemn agreement; in *theology*, God's promises to His people, recorded in both the Old and New Testaments. In *law*, a formal sealed agreement. *Coven*, from the same elements, is a gathering of witches.

convent: and *convene* from *con-*, **with**, **together**; **a coming together**; a community of nuns or, sometimes, monks, living under strict religious vows; also, the building or buildings occupied by such a community. SYNONYMS: abbey, cloister, monastery, nunnery, priory.

adventitious: *ad-*, **to**, **toward**; **coming to**; **accidentally**; in *botany*, occurring in unusual places, as *adventitious leaves or roots*; also, foreign; added extrinsically.

intervene: *inter-*, **between**; to come, be, or lie between; in *law*, to come in as a third party to a suit, to protect one's own interests. Other applications.

parvenu: French; *par-* from *per-*, **through**; **to come through**; thus, **an arriving**, **a reaching**; a person who has suddenly risen above his or her social and economic class without the background or qualifications to appreciate his or her new status; **an upstart**. Pronunciation: PAR vuh NOO.

invent: from *invenire*, **to come upon**; **to find**; thus, **to think up**; devise or fabricate in the mind, as *to invent excuses*; to think out or produce a new device, process, etc.; originate, as by experiment; devise for the first time. Thomas Edison *invented* the light bulb and the phonograph. See *discover*, p. 70.

invention: from same elements as *invent*; in *music*, a short composition, usually for a keyboard instrument, developing a single short motive in 2- or 3-voice counterpoint, especially, any of a group of these by J.S. Bach (1685-1750), a master of contrapuntal composition; also, that which one invents.

inventory: from same bases as *invent*; **a coming upon**; an enumeration. SYNONYMS: catalog, list, register, roll.

eventual: *e-*, elision of *ex-*, **out**; **coming out**, **happening**; happening at the end of, or as a result of, a series of events; **ultimate**; **final**, as the *eventual* outcome of a life of crime is usually incarceration.

venire facias: Latin law term: **to cause to come**, but literally "to make (one) to come"; an order summoning persons to serve as jurors. *Sub poena* (originally, first words of writ; **under penalty**) is an order summoning a person or persons to appear in court to testify.

veni, vidi, vici: Julius Caesar's "I came, I saw, I conquered." An example of the rhetorical device *asyndeton*, a condensed expression. Compare *asyndeton* with *polysyndeton*, the intentional repetition of conjunctions in close succession. See more on *polysyndeton*, p. 154.

Expression from Roman mythology: *Janus-faced*, **two-faced**, **hypocritical**. In Roman mythology, Janus was a two-faced god, with one face in the front of his head and the other at the back. He was the guardian of the portals and the patron of beginnings and endings. He was considered a benevolent god, one who could advise on past failures and counsel on future endeavors. *January*, coming at the beginning of the year, is named after Janus.

Consult a literary dictionary to differentiate the following types of ***dramas***: chronicle plays; comedy; folk drama; heroic drama; masque; melodrama; miracle plays; morality plays; interludes; pantomime and dumb show; problem play; sentimental comedy; tragedy; tragicomedy.

SUPPLEMENTAL WORDBUILDER SECTION

Sectional Wordbuilder Tests
Take this test before and after each section.
It is suggested that you take only ten at a time.
After finishing the entire book, take the posttest on wordbuilders, p. 217.
Enter the score on p. xviii.

What is the meaning of the italicized root in the following words?

		Pretest	Posttest
61.	andr- as in an*andr*ous and *andr*ogynous	_____	_____
62.	angi- as in *angi*osperm and *angi*oplasty	_____	_____
63.	arthr- as in *arthr*algia and *arthr*ocentesis	_____	_____
64.	batho-, bathy- as in *batho*meter and *bathy*sphere	_____	_____
65.	bibl- as in *Bibl*e and *bibl*iography	_____	_____
66.	bryo- as in *bryo*logy and *bryo*phyte	_____	_____
67.	cant- as in *cant*icle and des*cant*	_____	_____
68.	caten- as in *caten*a and con*caten*ate	_____	_____
69.	caus-, caut-, as in *caus*tic and *caut*erize	_____	_____
70.	cent- as in *cent*ury and *cent*urion	_____	_____
71.	cente- as in arthro*cente*sis and entero*cente*sis	_____	_____
72.	chlor- as in *chlor*ine and *chlor*ophyll	_____	_____
73.	chrom- as in a*chrom*atic and *chrom*osome	_____	_____
74.	clud-, clus-, as in in*clud*e and se*clus*ion	_____	_____
75.	cosm- as in *cosm*os and micro*cosm*	_____	_____
76.	crac-, crat-, as in aristo*crac*y and demo*crat*	_____	_____
77.	cred- as in *cred*entials and *cred*o	_____	_____
78.	cryo- as in *cryo*bank and *cryo*biology	_____	_____
79.	crypt- as in *crypt*ic and *crypt*ogram	_____	_____
80.	cuss- as in con*cuss*ion and per*cuss*ion	_____	_____
81.	cycl- as in *Cycl*ops and bi*cycl*e	_____	_____
82.	cyto- as in *cyto*logy and *cyto*plasm	_____	_____
83.	demo- as in *demo*crat and *demo*graphy	_____	_____
84.	dendro- as in *dendro*logy and philo*dendro*n	_____	_____
85.	dogma- as in *dogma* and *dogma*tic	_____	_____
86.	drom- as in *drom*edary and syn*drom*e	_____	_____
87.	dulc- as in *dulc*et and *dulc*imer	_____	_____
88.	ecto- as in *ecto*blast and *ecto*plasm	_____	_____
89.	empt- as in caveat *empt*or and pre*empt*	_____	_____
90.	foli- as in *foli*age, port*foli*o, and ex*foli*ate	_____	_____
91.	fric- as in *fric*tion and af*fric*ate	_____	_____
92.	genu-, gon- as in *genu*flect and *gon*algia	_____	_____
93.	glad- as in *glad*iator and *glad*iolus	_____	_____
94.	glob-, glom- as in hemo*glob*ulin and con*glom*erate	_____	_____
95.	gloss- as in *gloss*ary and *gloss*olalia	_____	_____
96.	gluc-, glyc- as in *gluc*ose and *glyc*erin	_____	_____
97.	gnos-, gnom- as in dia*gnos*tic and physio*gnom*y	_____	_____
98.	gon- as in poly*gon* and trig*on*ometry	_____	_____
99.	grav- as in *grav*id and ag*grav*ate	_____	_____
100.	gymn- as in *gymn*asium and *gymn*osperm	_____	_____

What is the meaning of the italicized root in the following words?   Pretest   Posttest

101. *gyn-* as in <u>gyn</u>ecology and miso<u>gyn</u>ist
102. *hedr-* as in cat<u>hedr</u>al and ex cat<u>hedr</u>a
103. *hem-* as in <u>hem</u>ophiliac and hypoglyc<u>em</u>ia
104. *hetero-* as in <u>hetero</u>geneous and <u>hetero</u>sexual
105. *hom-* as in <u>hom</u>osexual and <u>hom</u>eopathy
106. *hypn-* as in <u>hypn</u>osis and <u>hypn</u>ophobia
107. *hypo-* as in <u>hypo</u>tenuse, <u>hypo</u>crite and <u>hypo</u>glycemia
108. *hyster-* as in <u>hyster</u>ectomy and <u>hyster</u>ia
109. *iatr-* as in psych<u>iatr</u>y and pod<u>iatr</u>y
110. *ichthy-* as in <u>ichthy</u>saurus and <u>ichthy</u>ology

111. *icon-* as in <u>icon</u>oclast and <u>icon</u>ography
112. *infra-* as in <u>infra</u>costal and <u>infra</u>structure
113. *it-* as in <u>it</u>inerary, ad<u>it</u>, ex<u>it</u>, and ob<u>it</u>
114. *juv-* as in <u>juv</u>enile and re<u>juv</u>enate
115. *kilo-* as in <u>kilo</u>watt and <u>kilo</u>cycle
116. *luc-, lum-, lus-* as in <u>luc</u>id, <u>lum</u>inary, and il<u>lus</u>trate
117. *macr-* as in <u>macr</u>odont and <u>macr</u>ocosm
118. *mater-, matri-* as in <u>mater</u>nal and <u>matri</u>arch
119. *med-* as in <u>med</u>ian and <u>med</u>iocrity
120. *misce-* as in <u>misce</u>llaneous and <u>misce</u>genation

121. *mne-* as in <u>mne</u>monics, a<u>mne</u>sia, and a<u>mne</u>sty
122. *mob-, mov-* as in <u>mob</u>ile and re<u>mov</u>e
123. *mono-* as in <u>mono</u>chrome and <u>mono</u>logue
124. *morph-* as in <u>morph</u>eme and meta<u>morph</u>osis
125. *multi-* as in <u>multi</u>tude and <u>multi</u>ply
126. *myo-* as in <u>myo</u>cardium and <u>myo</u>carditis
127. *neo-* as in <u>neo</u>n and <u>Neo</u>lithic
128. *nephr-* as in <u>nephr</u>itis and <u>nephr</u>ology
129. *noc-, nox-* as in <u>noc</u>turnal and equi<u>nox</u>
130. *nom-* as in econo<u>my</u> and autono<u>my</u>

131. *nyct-* as in <u>nyct</u>aphonia and <u>nyct</u>itropism
132. *oo-* as in <u>oo</u>cyst, <u>oo</u>tid and <u>oo</u>cyte
133. *oophoro-* as in <u>oophoro</u>n and <u>oophor</u>algia
134. *orec-, orex-* as in <u>orec</u>tic and an<u>orex</u>ia
135. *ornith-* as in <u>ornith</u>ic and <u>ornith</u>ology
136. *oto-* as in <u>oto</u>scope and <u>oto</u>lith
137. *ov-* as in <u>ov</u>al and <u>ov</u>iduct
138. *oxy-* as in <u>oxy</u>gen, <u>oxy</u>cephaly, and <u>oxy</u>moron
139. *pali-* as in <u>pali</u>ndrome and <u>pali</u>kinesia
140. *para-* as in <u>para</u>graph, <u>para</u>phrase, and <u>para</u>llel

141. *pend-, pens-* as in per<u>pend</u>icular and <u>pens</u>ive
142. *penit-* as in <u>penit</u>ent and <u>penit</u>entiary
143. *petr-* as in <u>petr</u>oleum and <u>petr</u>ify
144. *phon-* as in tele<u>phon</u>e, eu<u>phon</u>y and stereo<u>phon</u>ic
145. *phyll-* as in <u>phyll</u>opod and chloro<u>phyll</u>
146. *phyt-* as in <u>phyt</u>on and <u>phyt</u>ogenesis
147. *plas-* as in <u>plas</u>tic and <u>plas</u>ma
148. *platy-, plac-* as in <u>platy</u>pus and <u>plac</u>enta
149. *pleb-* as in <u>pleb</u>e and <u>pleb</u>iscite
150. *pne-* as in a<u>pne</u>a and dys<u>pne</u>a

What is the meaning of the italicized root in the following words?   Pretest   Posttest

151. *pneumo-* as in *pneumonia* and *pneumocardial*
152. *prehen-* as in *prehensile* and *comprehend*
153. *pter-* as in *helicopter* and *pterodactyl*
154. *pug-* as in *pugnacious* and *pugilist*
155. *punct-, pung-,* as in *punctuation* and *expunge*
156. *quer-, quest-,* as in *query* and *question*
157. *rad-* as in *radish* and *eradicate*
158. *retro-* as in *retroactive* and *retrograde*
159. *rob-* as in *robust* and *corroborate*
160. *rod-* as in *rodent, corrode* and *erode*

161. *rupt-* as in *rupture, corrupt,* and *erupt*
162. *saur-* as in *brontosaurus* and *plesiosaurus*
163. *sclera-* as in *scleritis* and *scleroderma*
164. *scop-, skep-* as in *scope, telescope,* and *skeptic*
165. *scrib-, scrip-* as in *describe* and *inscription*
166. *sen-* as in *senior, senator,* and *señor*
167. *sex-, sen-* as in *sextile* and *senary*
168. *sider-* as in *sidereal* and *consider*
169. *som-* as in *somatic* and *chromosome*
170. *son-* as in *sonar, sonnet* and *consonant*

171. *spec, spis* as in *specify, inspect* and *despise*
172. *spir* as in *conspire* and *transpire*
173. *stell* as in *stellar* and *constellation*
174. *stroph* as in *strophic* and *antistrophe*
175. *struct* as in *structure, construct,* and *instruct*
176. *sub-* as in *subtend, subtract, souvenir, sombrero*
177. *tele-* as in *telephony* and *telegraphy*
178. *tract* as in *tractor, abstract,* and *subtract*
179. *trud, trus* as in *intrude, retrude,* and *intrusion*
180. *umbr* as in *umbrella, penumbra,* and *sombrero*

181. *unda-* as in *abundant, inundate* and *undulate*
182. *uni-* as in *unit, unicycle,* and *universe*
183. *verm-* as in *vermicelli* and *vermillion*
184. *vers-, vert-* as in *version* and *introvert*
185. *via-, voy-* as in *trivial* and *convoy*
186. *vicar-* as in *vicar* and *vicarious*
187. *vid-, vis-* as in *provide* and *improvise*
188. *vinc-, vict-* as in *convince* and *victim*
189. *vir-* as in *virile* and *triumvirate*
190. *vit-* as in *vitamin, vital,* and *vitality*

191. *voc-, vok-* as in *vocation, invoke,* and *revoke*
192. *vol-ve* as in *volume, involve, revolve*
193. *vor-* as in *voracious* and *carnivorous*
194. *xanth-* as in *xanthate* and *xanthoderma*
195. *xeno-* as in *xenogamy* and *xenomania*
196. *xero-* as in *xeroderma* and *xerography*
197. *xiph-* as in *xiphoid* and *xiphersternum*
198. *xylo-* as in *xylophone* and *xylophagous*
199. *zo-* as in *zoo, zoological,* and *zodiac*
200. *zym-* as in *zymosis* and *enzyme*

SUPPLEMENTAL WORDBUILDER SECTION
Exposition

61. Greek *andros*, **man**, **male**, **anther**, **stamen** (pollen-producing organ of certain plants), yields **andr**oid; **andr**oecium; **andr**ogen, **andr**ogenesis, **andr**ogenous, **andr**ogynous, **andr**osterone; an**andr**ia; an**andr**ous, dec**andr**ous, di**andr**ous, dodec**andr**ous, enne**andr**ous, hept**andr**ous, mon**andr**ous (having a single stamen), oct**andr**ous, olig**andr**ous, pent**andr**ous, poly**andr**ous (having many husbands, or many stamens); gyn**andr**omorph. Compare Latin *homo* (see **Word Cluster No. 47**, p. 93); *masc*, as in **masc**uline, e**masc**ulate; *vir*, as in *vir*ile (see **Item 189**). Greek: *anthropos*, as in **anthrop**oid; **anthropo**centric, **anthropo**genesis, **anthropo**graphy, **anthropo**logy, **anthropo**metry, **anthropo**morphic (p. 93), **anthropo**pathy, **anthropo**phagus, **anthropo**sophy; paleo**anthropo**logy, lyc**anthrop**y, mis**anthrop**y (*misos*, **hate**), phil**anthrop**y (*philos*, **love**), zoo**anthrop**y (*zoos*, **animal**)

62. Greek *angos*, **vessel** (extended to mean **blood vessel**), yields **angi**ectomy, **angi**oma; **angi**ogram, **angi**ography, **angi**ology, **angi**oplasty, **angi**osarcoma, **angi**osperm, **angi**otrophic; spor**angi**ferous; the flower hydr**ang**ea (*hydro*, **water**; literally, **water vessel**, from the cuplike shape of the seed pod). In addition to **vessel**, this root can also mean **seed**, something contained within a vessel. Compare Latin *vas*, as in **vas**e, **vas**cular, **vas**ectomy, cardio**vas**cular, **vas** deferens; extra**vas**ate, intra**vas**ation.

63. Greek *arthron*, **joint**, yields **arthr**ous; **arthr**agra, **arthr**algia, **arthr**itis, **arthr**odynia (*arthro + odyne*, **pain**), **arthr**osis; **arthro**cele, **arthro**centesis, **arthro**gram, **arthro**mere, **arthro**pod, **arthro**scope, **arthro**spore; cox**arthr**itis, gon**arthr**itis, hol**arthr**itis, mono**arthr**itis, oligo**arthr**itis, osteo**arthr**itis.

64. Greek *bathys*, **deep**, yields **bath**etic, **bath**os; **batho**lith, **batho**meter, **batho**phobia; **bathy**al, **bathy**bic, **bathy**smal; **bathy**bic, **bathy**cardia, **bathy**gram, **bathy**graph, **bathy**meter, **bathy**metric, **bathy**pelagic, **bathy**phyll, **bathy**pnea, **bathy**scape, **bathy**scaph, **bathy**seism, **bathy**sphere; eury**bath** (an organism that can live in a wide range of water depths; opposed to stenobath) iso**bath**, steno**bath**; a**byss** (literally, **no bottom**; a bottomless gulf; in *theology*, the primeval void or chaos before Creation).

65. Greek *biblios*, **book**, yields **Bible**, **bibli**cal, **bibli**cist, **bibli**otic; **biblio**graphy, **biblio**klept, **biblio**latry, **biblio**logy, **biblio**mancy, **biblio**mania, **biblio**pegy, **biblio**phile, **biblio**pole, **biblio**theca, **biblio**teca (Spanish for **library**). Latin: *liber* (originally, inner bark or rind of a tree, which was written on), as in **libr**ary, **libr**etto, **libr**iform. There is also the unrelated *liber*, **free**, as in **liber**al, **liber**ate, **Liber**ia, **liber**ty (see p. 113). Another unrelated *liber* means **to weigh**, as in de**liber**ate, equi**libr**ate, equi**libr**ium.

66. Greek *bryon*, **moss**, yields **bry**ales, **bry**anthus; **bryo**logy, **bryo**phyllum, **bryo**phyte, **bryo**zoan, **bryo**zoology. Latin *muscus*, from which only *most*, **new wine**, and *mustard* are derived; however, French *mousseron* yields Anglo-Saxon *mushroom*; notice the similarity of pronunciation. For more on *mushroom*, see p. 91.

67. Latin *cantare*, **to sing**, yields **can**orous; **cant**, **cant**abile, **cant**alina, **cant**ata (see p. 44 under **sonata**), **cant**atrice, **cant**icle, **cant**o; des**cant**, in**cant**ation, re**cant**; ac**cent**, ac**cent**ual, ac**cent**uate, con**cent**, in**cent**ive (that which sets the tune; inciting); **chant**, en**chant**; *cantus firmus*, canzone (also, canzona—a lyric poem of Provençal or early Italian troubadours); charm; oscine (a suborder of birds).

68. Latin *catena*, **chain**, yields **catena** (plural, catenae), **caten**ary (both noun and adjective), **caten**ate, **caten**ating (forming part of a chain or complex of symptoms), **caten**ation, **caten**oid, **caten**ulate; con**caten**ate; chain; chignon (a knot or coil of hair worn at the back of the neck). Explore *concatenation* as a writing technique, linking sentences within a paragraph.

69. Greek *caust, cauter*, from *kaiein*, **to burn**, yields **caust**ic; **caus**algia; en**caust**ic (from which is derived *ink*; see **wordextras**, p. 108), holo**caust**, hypo**caust**; **cauter**ization, **cauter**ize, **cauter**y; cryo**cauter**y; calm (see p. 106, under *siesta*). Latin: *calor*, as in *calor*ie; see **Word Cluster No. 12**, p. 23.

70. Latin *centum*, **100**, yields **cent**, **cent**ury, **cent**urion, **cent**ile; **cent**enary, **cent**enarian, **cent**ennial (see **Word Cluster No. 4**, p. 7), **cent**avo; **centi**grade, **centi**gram, **centi**newton, **centi**pede; **cent**uple; per**cent**. Do not confuse this root with *Centaur*, which, in Greek mythology, was a race of monsters with a man's head, trunk, and arms, and a horse's body and legs; thus *centaury*, a plant in which it was said that the centaur Chiron discovered medicinal properties. Greek: *hecto*, as in **hecato**mb (with *bous*, **cow**, the slaughter of 100 cattle at one time as a sacrifice to the gods); **hect**are; **hecto**cotylus, **hecto**gram, **hecto**graph, **hecto**liter, **hecto**meter. See p. 58, top of page for more *cent-* words.

71. Greek *kentesis*, **puncture**, yields **centesis**, amnio**centesis**, arthro**centesis**, cephalo**centesis**, entero-**centesis**, pneumono**centesis**. Latin *pungere*, **to pierce**, yields **pung**ent, ex**pung**e; **punct**ate, **punct**ilio (from which is derived *pun* (see p. 89), **punct**ilious (see p. 146), **punct**ual, **punct**ure, **punct**uate, com**punct**ion. See Item 155 for more *punct-* words.

72. Greek *chloros*, **pale green**, yields **chlor**al (even though colorless), **chlor**amine (NH₂Cl), **chlor**ate, **chlor**dane, **chlor**ella, **chlor**ic, **chlor**ine; **chlor**oma, **chlor**osis; **chlor**oform, **chlor**ophyll, **chlor**ophyte, **chlor**ophane, **chlor**oplast; **Chlor**ide, AZ.

73. Greek *chroma*, **color** (of the skin), yields **chrom**ate, **chrom**atic, **chrom**atics (the scientific study of color in reference to hues and saturation), **chrom**atic scale (a musical scale made up of 13 successive half-tones to the octave; compare *diatonic scale*), **chrom**atin, **chrom**ium (Cr), **chrom**ous; **chromo**-center, **chromo**gen, **chromo**mere, **chromo**nema, **chromo**phil, **chromo**phore, **chromo**plast, **chromo**protein, **chromo**some (see **Clavis**, p. 50), **chromo**sphere, **chromo**therapy; **chrom**atography, **chrom**atolysis; auto**chrome**, auxo**chrome**, Koda**chrome**®, mono**chrome**, Pan**chrom**atic®, phyto-**chrome**, poly**chrome**; a**chrom**atic, poly**chrom**atic; possibly **Chroma**, NJ; **Chromo**, CO.

74. Latin *claudere*, **to close**, yields the verb-noun-adjective sequences: con**clud**e, con**clus**ion, con**clus**ive; ex**clud**e, ex**clus**ion, ex**clus**ive; in**clud**e, in**clus**ion, in**clus**ive; oc**clud**e, oc**clus**ion, oc**clus**ive; pre**clud**e, pre**clus**ion, pre**clus**ive; se**clud**e, se**clus**ion, se**clus**ive; and the noun-noun-adjective sequence: re**clus**e, re**clus**ion, re**clus**ive; **claus**al, **claus**e, **claus**tral; **claustro**phobia; cloister, cloisonné, cloture; e**clos**ion; mal**occlus**ion; sluice (see p. 28); mare clausum; Greek **cleisto**gamy (see **wordbuilder #23**, p. 44).

75. Greek *cosmos*, **world**, yields **cosm**esis, **cosm**etic, **cosm**etician, **cosm**ic, **cosm**os; **cosm**etologist (hair dresser/beautician), **cosm**etology, **cosm**ogony, **cosm**ography, **cosm**ology, **cosm**onaut, **cosm**opolitan; macro**cosm**, micro**cosm**; **Cosmos**, MN; **Cosmo**polis, WA (see p. 65). Latin *mundus*, as in **mund**ane, ante**mund**ane, extra**mund**ane, infra**mund**ane, inter**mund**ane, post**mund**ane, pre**mund**ane, super-**mund**ane, trans**mund**ane, ultra**mund**ane; demimonde, demimondaine.

76. Greek *kratos*, **rule**, **strength**, **power**, yields aristo**crat** (*crat* can be replaced with *cracy* in each of the following words; thus *aristocracy*): auto**crat**, demo**crat**, iso**crat**, physio**crat**, pluto**crat**, theo**crat**. See *plutocracy*, p. 32, **wordextras**. Latin *rect* as in cor**rect**, di**rect**. See **Word Cluster No. 82**, p. 163.

77. Latin *credere*, **to believe**, **trust**, yields **cred**ence, **cred**enda, **cred**ent, **cred**ential, **cred**enza, **cred**ible, **cred**it, **cred**itable, **cred**itor; **cred**o; **cred**ulity, **cred**ulous; ac**cred**it, disac**cred**it, dis**cred**it, micro-**cred**it; in**cred**ible, in**cred**ulity, in**cred**ulous; mis**cre**ant, re**cre**ant; **cre**ed; grant. See pp. 48, 79.

78. Greek *kryos*, **cold**, yields **cry**stal; **cry**onic; **cryo**bank, **cryo**biology, **cryo**cautery, **cryo**genics, **cryo**globulin, **cryo**hydrate, **cryo**meter, **cryo**phile, **cryo**phyte, **cryo**scope, **cryo**therapy.

79. Greek *kryptein*, **to hide**, yields **crypt**, **crypt**ic, **crypt**esthesia, **crypt**onym, **crypt**orchidism (see *orchid*, p. 86); **crypto**biosis, **crypto**clastic, **crypto**gamous, **crypto**genic, **crypto**gram, **crypto**graphy, **crypto**logy; Apo**crypha**; de**crypt**, en**crypt**; in**crypt**ic, pro**crypt**ic. Latin *condere*: abs**cond**, re**cond**ite.

80. Latin *quatere*, **to shake**, **strike**, yields con**cuss**ion, dis**cuss**ion, per**cuss**ion, reper**cuss**ion; in**cus**e, as well as in**cus**, a bone in the ear, shaped like an anvil (that which is struck); re**cus**e; re**cus**ant; the verb **cashier**: to dismiss from a position as though shaken from it (see p. 73, under **wordextras**); cascara, cask, scotch, rescue (to shake out of).

81. Greek *kyklos*, **circle**, yields **cycl**amate, **cycl**e, **cycl**one; **cycl**oid (*oidos*, **form**), **Cycl**ops (*ops*, **eye**), **cycl**orama, **cycl**osis; **cyclo**branchiate, **cyclo**meter, **cyclo**plegia, **cyclo**stome, **cyclo**thymia (*thym*, **mind**; therefore, a form of manic-depressive psychosis characterized by alternating periods of activity and excitement and periods of inactivity or depression); auto**cycle**, bi**cycle**, bio**cycle**, epi**cycle**, hemi**cycle**, motor**cycle**, peri**cycle**, tri**cycle**, uni**cycle**; en**cycl**ical, en**cyclo**pedia, Ku **Klux** Klan; Cyclone Park, MT.

82. Greek *kytos*, **hollow**, or "hollow vessel," but meaning **cell**, yields **cyt**on, **cyt**ula; **cyto**biology, **cyto**biotaxis, **cyto**blast, **cyto**cerastic, **cyto**chemistry, **cyto**chrome, **cyto**cidal, **cyto**clastic, **cyto**cyst, **cyto**genesis, **cyto**kinesis, **cyto**logy, **cyto**lysis, **cyto**phagy, **cyto**plasm, **cyto**plast, **cyto**sine, **cyto**taxonomy, **cyto**toxic, **cyto**zoic, hema**cyto**meter; amphi**cyt**ic. See *angos*, Item 62.

83. Greek *demos*, **the people**, yields **dem**iurge (not to be confused with *demi-*, **half**), **dem**otic; **dem**agogue (*agein*, **to lead**), **demo**cracy, **demo**cratic, **demo**graphics, **demo**graphy; en**dem**ic, epi**dem**ic, pan**dem**ic; **Demo**polis (literally, **People City**), AL (see p. 6). Latin *populus*, as in **popul**ace, **popul**ar, **popul**ation, **popul**ous; *pueblo* (Spanish for **town**). See p. 62, top of page.

84. Greek *dendron*, **t r e e**, yields **dendr**ite, **dendr**ous; **dendr**oid; **dendr**iform; **dendro**chronology, **dendro**latry, **dendro**logy, **dendro**phagous, **dendro**philia, **dendro**phobia, **dendro**toxin; philo**dendron** (see p. 28) rhodo**dendron** (see p. 89), epi**dendr**um; **Dendron**, VA. Latin: *arbor*, as in **arbor**, **arbor**eal, **arbor**eous, **arbor**escent, **arbor**etum, **arbor**ization; **Arbor** Day; **arbor** vitae.

85. Greek *dokein*, **to seem, to think true**, yields **dogma**; **dogma**tic, **dogma**tics, **dogma**tize; **dox**ology; hetero**dox**, ortho**dox**, para**dox**; **doctr**ine, in**doctr**inate; **docu**ment, **docu**mentary. Latin *verus*, **true**, as in **veri**dical, **veri**fy, **veri**similar, **veri**similitude, **veri**sm, **veri**smo, **veri**ty. Spanish: *verdad*, **veri**ty: truth.

86. Greek *dromein*, **to run**, yields **drome**dary, **dromo**maniac; aero**drome**, hippo**drome**, lampa**drome**, loxo**drome**, palin**drome** (see p. 107), pro**drome**, syn**drome** (literally, **a running together**); anti**dromic**, palin**dromic**; amphi**dromous**, ana**dromous**, cata**dromous**, dia**dromous**, hetero**dromous**, homo-**dromous**, oceano**dromous**, pro**dromous**. Latin *currere*, **to run**; see **wordbuilder #1**, p. 1.

87. Latin *dulcis*, **sweet**, yields **dulc**et; **dulc**ify, **dulc**imer; **dolce**, **douce**ur, *billet-doux* (sweet letters, or love letters); *dolce far niente* (**it is sweet doing nothing**: pleasant idleness or inactivity), *dolce vita*; **dulci**ana (organ stop with a sweet, mellow tone like that of a stringed instrument); Dulce, NM. Don Quixote's ladylove: Dulcinea. Greek *glykeros*, as in **glyc**erin and hypo**glyc**emia. See Item 96.

88. Greek *ektos*, **outside, external**, yields **ect**organism, **ect**ostosis; **ecto**biology, **ecto**blast, **ecto**cardia, **ecto**-colon, **ecto**commensal, **ecto**cornea, **ecto**cranial, **ecto**crine, **ecto**cyst, **ecto**derm, **ecto**enzyme, **ecto**genous, **ecto**gony, **ecto**mere, **ecto**morph, **ecto**nuclear, **ecto**parasite, **ecto**plasm, **ecto**proct, **ecto**sarc, **ecto**sphere, **ecto**thermal, **ecto**thrix, **ecto**toxin, **ecto**trophic, **ecto**zoon. No clear-cut Latin equivalent; however, in some cases, *ex-* approximates the meaning of *ektos*. Compare Greek *exo-*, p. 14.

89. Latin *emere*, **to buy**, as well as **to take**, yields ad**empt**ion (adeem), co**empt**ion, ex**empl**ar, ex**empl**ary, ex**empl**um; ex**empl**ify, ex**empt** (ex**empt**ion), per**empt**ory, pre**empt**, pre**empt**ive, red**empt**ion (redeem, redeemer, irredeemable); diriment (in the RCC, an obstacle invalidating an attempted marriage), example, premium, prompt, ransom, sample, sampler, vintage, impromptu, irredentist (from Italian *irredentista Italia*, **unredeemed Italy**, a political term; see p. 11); *caveat emptor*, **let the buyer beware**.

90. Latin *folium*, **leaf**, yields **foli**aceous, **foli**age, **foli**ate, **foli**c (as folic acid), **foli**o, **foli**olate, **foli**um; **foli**ferous, **foli**icolous, **foli**iform (*double i* correct in the two previous words); bi**foli**ate, brevi**foli**ate, de-**foli**ate, ex**foli**ate, port**folio** (see p. 156, used in *port* family), quinque**foli**olate, uni**foli**olate; tri**folium**; **foil** (one meaning), cinqu**foil**, counter**foil**, milfoil, quatre**foil**, tre**foil**; feuilleton, mille-feuille. Greek *phyllos*, as in *chlorophyll*. See Item 145.

91. Latin *fricare*, **to rub**, yields **fric**ative, **fric**tion; af**fric**ate, denti**fric**e; af**fric**tion, anti**fric**tion; fray, frayed, frazzle, friable (easily crumbled or crushed into powder); from Gaulish: debris; French brisance (the shattering effect of the sudden release of energy).

92. Greek *genu*, *gon*, **knee**, yields **genu**flect (see **wordbuilder #26**, p. 57), **gen**iculate, **gon**algia. See Greek *gon*, **angle**, Item 98.

93. Latin *gladius*, **sword**, yields **gladi**ate, **gladi**ator, **gladi**atorial, **gladi**olus (both the flower and the bone); glaive (archaic for *a sword*). See Greek *xiphos*, Item 197.

94. Latin *globus*, *glomus*, **ball, sphere**, yields **glob**e, **glob**ular, **glob**ulin; con**glob**ate, hemo**glob**ulin; Globe, AZ; **glom**erate, **glom**erule; ag**glom**erate, con**glom**erate. See **wordbuilder #43**, p. 111, for *spher-* words.

95. Greek *glossa*, **tongue**, yields **gloss** (one meaning), **gloss**a, **gloss**ary; **gloss**agra, **gloss**algia, **gloss**ectomy, **gloss**itis; **gladi**ator **gloss**ography, **gloss**olalia; iso**gloss**; hypo**gloss**al, odonto**gloss**um, pachy**gloss**ia; **glott**al, **glott**is; di**glot**, mono**glot**, poly**glot**; epi**glott**is, pro**glott**id; Glossa, Greece. Latin *lingua*, as in **ling**o, **ling**ua, **ling**ual, **ling**uine (see p. 178), **ling**uistic(s), **ling**ulate; **ling**uiform; bi**lingual**, col**lingual**, mono**lingual**, multi**lingual**, quadri**lingual**, pre**lingual**, retro**lingual**, sub**lingual**, uni**lingual**.

96. Greek *gleukos*, *glykeros*, **sweet**, yields **gluc**onate; **gluc**agon, **gluc**ose; **gluco**side; **glyc**erine, **glyc**erol; **glyco**gen, **glyco**genesis, **glyco**lysis, **glyco**side; hyper**glyc**emia, hypo**glyc**emia (see Item 103 for meaning of the suffix *–emia*). Latin *dulcis*; see Item 87, above.

97. Greek *gnosis*, *gnome*, **knowledge, knowing**, yields **gnosis**, **Gnos**tic, **Gnos**ticism; a**gnos**ia, a**gnos**tic, dia**gnose** (diagnostic), pro**gnos**is (prognostic); geo**gnos**y, pharmaco**gnos**y; **gnome**, **gnom**ic, **gnom**on; **gnomo**logic; patho**gnom**y, physio**gnom**y. Latin *scire*, **to know**, from which are derived **sci**ence, **sci**licet, **sci**olism; ad**sci**titious, con**sci**ence, con**sci**ous, ne**sci**ence, omni**sci**ent, plebi**sci**te, pre**sci**ent; nice. Also, Latin co**gni**tion, co**gni**tive, preco**gni**tion; inco**gni**to; reco**gni**ze; reconnaissance, reconnoiter.

98. Greek *gonia*, **corner**, **angle** [bent like the knee; see Item 92], yields **goni**on; **goni**ometer, **goni**opuncture; deca**gon**, ennea**gon**, hepta**gon**, hexa**gon**, octa**gon**, ortho**gon**, penta**gon**, peri**gon**, poly**gon**, quindeca**gon**, tetra**gon**, trimetro**gon**; dia**gon**al, iso**gon**al, ortho**gon**al; tri**gon**ometry (the measurement of three angles, or in Latin, *a triangle*); a**gon**ic, iso**gon**ic; tri**gon**ous. See p. 134 for **gon**ad, **gon**ophore.

99. Latin *gravis*, **heavy**, yields **grav**e (meaning *serious*), **grav**id, **grav**ida (a pregnant woman, e.g., gravida I for first pregnancy, gravida II for second pregnancy, etc.), **grav**idism, **grav**iditas, **grav**itate, **grav**iton, **grav**ity; **grav**imeter, **grav**idocardiac; ag**grav**ate, ag**grav**ation; hyper**gravity**, hypo**gravity**, micro**gravity**, super**gravity**; grief, grieve. NB: *Gravy* may be from *granum*, **grain** (see p. 89). Greek *baros*; see p. 44, **Word Cluster No. 24**).

100. Greek *gymnos*, **naked**, **nude**, **stripped**, yields **gymn**asium (originally, a place to exercise in the nude), **gymn**ast, **gymn**astics; **gymn**asiarch; **gymn**odont; **gymn**oblast, **gymn**ocarpium, **gymn**ocolon (irrigation of colon), **gymn**ocyte, **gymn**ophilia, **gymn**ophobia (morbid aversion to the sight of a naked body), **gymn**oscopic (inclined to or concerned with viewing the naked body), **gymn**osophist (see p. 50 under phrase *mens sana. . .*), **gymn**osperm, **gymn**ospore. Latin *nudus*, **nude**; **nudi**branch, de**nude**.

101. Greek *gyne*, **woman**, **female**, yields **gyn**aeceum; **gyn**andromorph, **gyn**androus, **gyn**archy, **gyn**oecium; **gyne**phobia; **gyne**cocracy, **gyne**cology, **gyne**comania, **gyne**comastia; **gyn**ogenesis, **gyn**opathic, **gyn**ophobia, **gyn**ophore; tricho**gyne**; andro**gyn**ous, epi**gyn**ous, hetero**gyn**ous, hypo**gyn**ous, mono**gyn**ous, peri**gyn**ous, poly**gyn**ous; miso**gyny**, mono**gyny**, philo**gyny**, poly**gyny**.

102. Greek *hedra*, **seat**, **chair**, yields cat**hedra**, cat**hedra**l (*kata-*, **down**; where the bishop sits down, the cathedral being the largest church in the see); also means **side**: di**hedral**, hemi**hedral**, rhombo**hedral**, tetarto**hedral**, tetra**hedral**; chilia**hedron**, deca**hedron**, hexa**hedron**, octo**hedron**, penta**hedron**, poly**hedron**, rhombo**hedron**, tetra**hedron** (see p. 175), triocto**hedron**; ex cat**hedra** (to speak from the chair; thus, infallible, or seemingly so; see *ipse dixit*, p. 65), San**hedr**in (see p. 176).

103. Greek *hema-*, *hemato-*, *hemo-*, are from *haima*, **blood**, and yields **hem**al; **hem**angioma; **hemat**al, **hemat**ic, **hemat**in; **hemat**oma, **hemat**uria; **hemat**oblast, **hemat**ocrit, **hemat**ogenous, **hemo**globin, **hemo**lysis, **hemo**philia, **hemo**ptysis, **hemo**rrhage; *-em-* is the elided form, as in an**emia**, anox**emia**, hyper**emia**, hyperglyc**emia**, hypocalc**emia**, hypoglyc**emia**, isch**emia**, leuk**emia**, pachy**hemia**, py**emia**, tox**emia** (*emia* indicates a diseased, or abnormal, condition of the blood). Many others; search onelook.

104. Greek *heteros*, **other**, yields **heter**esthesia, **heter**odont, **heter**oecious, **heter**onym; **heter**odox, **hetero**blastic, **hetero**centric, **hetero**cercal, **hetero**chromatic, **hetero**chronia, **hetero**chtonous, **hetero**cladic, **hetero**clite, **hetero**gamete, **hetero**geneous, **hetero**sexual, **hetero**sphere; many others. Another Greek root with the same basic meaning is *allo*; see p. 5; see also Latin *alter*, p. 7.

105. Greek *homos*, **like**, **same**, **similar**, yields **homo**ecious, **homo**nym; **homo**centric, **homo**cercal, **homo**chromatic, **homo**cladic, **homo**eroticism, **homo**gamete, **homo**gamy, **homo**geneous, **homo**genize, **homo**lateral, **homo**logous, **homo**phone, **homo**sexual (see p. 94, top of page); **homeo**pathy; **homoio**podal; ano**mal**y. Latin: *similis*, as in **simile**, **simil**ar, **simil**arity, **simil**itude, **simul**taneous; fac**simile**; as**simil**ate, dis**simil**ate, veri**simil**itude; as**sem**ble (assembly; see p. 66); en**sem**ble; seem, some.

106. Greek *hypnos*, **sleep**, yields *Hypnos* (god of sleep) **hypn**agogic, **hypn**osis (hypnotic), **hypno**analysis, **hypno**bate, **hypno**genesis, **hypno**logy, **hypno**phobia, **hypno**scope, **hypno**therapy; post**hypn**otic. Latin: *dormire*, see wordbuilder #34, p. 87; also Latin *somnus*, as in **somn**olent, *Somnus* (god of sleep), **somn**ambulant (see p. 6), **somn**iferous, **somn**iloquy, **Somn**inex®, **somn**iphobia; in**somn**ia.

107. Greek *hypo-*, **under**, **less than**, yields **hypo**blast, **hypo**capnia, **hypo**chondriac, **hypo**crite, **hypo**dermic, **hypo**geal, **hypo**glossal, **hypo**glycemia, **hypo**mania, **hypo**taxis, **hypo**tenuse, **hypo**thesis; **hyph**en (hyphenate); many others. See p. 183 for *hyper-*, the opposite of *hypo-*. Latin *sub-*, as in **sub**ject, **sub**marine, **sub**tract (see Item 176); also *infra-*, as in **infra**structure (see Item 112).

108. Greek *hyster* [**uterus** (Latin); **womb** (Anglo-Saxon)] yields **hyster**ia (see p. 92, **wordextras**), **hyster**ical (often used figuratively), **hyster**algia, **hyster**ectomy, **hyster**oid; **hyster**ocele. There are numerous other examples of this root in a medical dictionary. *Hysteresis*, pertaining to **later**, **behind**, a physics term, is *not* related to this root.

109. Greek *iatros*, **physician** (*iasthai*, **to heal**), yields **iatr**ic (referring to medicine, the medical profession, or physicians), **iatr**ical; **iatr**ochemistry, **iatr**ogenic, **iatr**aliptics, **iatr**ology; geri**atr**ics (the branch of medicine that deals with the diseases and problems of old age), pedi**atr**ics; pod**iatr**y, psych**iatr**y.

110. Greek *ichthy*, **fish**, yields **ichthy**oid, **ichthy**osis; **ichthy**ology, **ichthy**ophagous (fish-eating, as *an ichthyophagous bird*), **ichthy**ornis. Latin *piscis*, as in **Pisces**, **pisc**ary, **pisc**ation, **pisc**atorial, **pisc**ine; **pisc**atology; **pisci**cide, **pisci**culture, **pisci**form, **pisci**vorous; por**pois**e (see p. 154). Spanish: **pes**cado.

111. Greek *icon*, **image, symbol**, yields **icon**, **icon**ic; **icono**centric, **icono**clasm, **icono**clast (*klaein*, **to break**, in latter two words), **icono**dule, **icono**graphy, **icono**latry, **icono**logy, **icono**mania, **icono**philia, **icono**scope, **icono**stasis; orth**icon**. Do not confuse this root with a similarly spelled one, as in **icosa**hedron [a polyhedron having 20 sides; see *hedra*, Item 102].

112. Latin *infra-*, **under**, yields **infra**-axillary, **infra**branchial, **infra**bulge, **infra**cardiac, **infra**clavicular, **infra**cortical, **infra**costal, **infra**dian, **infra**lapsarian (a theological term), **infra**mammary, **infra**natural, **infra**occlusion, **infra**pubic, **infra**red, **infra**sonic, **infra**structure, **infra**territorial, *ut infra*, *infra dig* (see *dainty*, p. 87). Compare Latin *sub-*, as in **sub**tract (see Item 176); Greek *hypo-*, as in **hypo**crite, **hypo**dermic, **hypo**tenuse, **hypo**thesis; see Item 107.

113. Latin *itere*, **to go**, yields **it**inerary, **it**inerant; ad**it**, ex**it**, circu**it**, intro**it** (see p. 100), ob**it**, preter**it**, trans**it**; co**it**us, concom**it**ant, in**it**ial, in**it**iate, ob**it**uary; amb**it**ion, co**it**ion, sed**it**ion, preter**it**ion, sed**it**ion, trans**it**ion; sub**it**o, trans**it**ive; amb**ient**, trans**ient**; errant, issue, perish, sudden; ab initio; coitus interruptus; obiter dictum. Compare *ambulare*, as in **amb**le, **amb**ulance; see **Word Cluster No. 3**, p. 5.

114. Latin *juvenis*, **young**, yields **juven**al, **juven**escent, **juven**ile (juvenile delinquency; juvenile plants; juvenile cell), **juven**ilia, **juven**ility; re**juven**ate; **junior**, **junior**ity. Greek: *hebe*, as in **Hebe**, the goddess of youth), **hebe**tic; **hebi**atrics (same as *ephebiatrics*); **hebe**philia (sexual attraction to teenagers by adults), **hebe**phobia, **hebe**phrenia; ep**hebe**, ep**hebus**. See *neos*, **young**, Item 127.

115. Greek *kilo*, **1,000**, yields **kilo**bar, **kilo**calorie, **kilo**cycle, **kilo**gram, **kilo**hertz, **kilo**liter, **kilo**meter, **kilo**parsec, **kilo**ton, **kilo**volt, **kilo**watt; chiliad. There are a number of Latin American cities with the name Kilómetro. Compare Latin *mil*, as in **mil**, **mil**e (see p. 51, **wordextras**), **mil**eage, **mill**age; **mill**enary, **mill**ennium, **mill**esimal, **mill**ion; **mil**foil; **milli**meter, **milli**pede; post**mill**ennial, pre**mill**ennial.

116. Latin *lumen*, *lux*, **light**, *lucere*, **to shine**, yield **lumen**; **lumin**aire, **lumin**ance, **lumin**ary, **lumin**escence, **lumin**osity; **lumin**iferous; il**lumin**e; **luc**id, trans**luc**ent, e**luc**idate, pel**luc**id; **lust**er, **lust**rate, **lust**ring, **lust**rous, **lust**rum, il**lust**rate; **lux**, abbreviated l$_x$ (the International System of Units for a unit of illumination); **Lux**, MS; **Lux**® (the soap bar). Greek *photo*, see p. 41. These roots are related to **luna**, **moon**, which yields **luna**r, **luna**rian, **luna**te, **luna**tic, **luna**tion. See *lunatic*, **wordextras**, p. 187.

117. Greek *makros*, **long, elongated**, but has come also to mean **large**, yields **macr**on; **macr**odont, **macr**osis, **macr**uran; **macro**benthos, **macro**biotics, **macro**blast, **macro**cardia, **macro**cephaly, **macro**climate, **macro**cosm, **macro**cyst, **macro**gamete, **macro**molecule, **macro**nucleus, **macro**nutrient, **macro**phage, **macro**phallus, **macro**plasia, **macro**pterous, **macro**scopic, **macro**somia; amphi**macer** (see p. 6), meager, see p. 113. There are many other words with this root in a medical dictionary. See *mikro*, **small**, p. 127.

118. Latin *mater*, **mother**, yields **mater**nal, *alma mater* (literally, **nourishing mother**), **mater**nity; **matri**culate, **matri**mony; **matri**arch, **matri**cide, **matri**lineal, **matri**local (see p. 118), **matri**x, **matr**on.

119. Latin *medius*, **middle**, yields **med**ian, **med**ium (pl., **med**ia), **med**iate; **medi**ocre (literally, **middle of the peak**; neither good nor bad), **medi**ocrity; **Medi**terranean (see p. 63); inter**medi**ate, im**medi**ate; **mezz**anine, **mezzo**-soprano, moiety. Greek *meso*, as in **meso**derm, **meso**morphic, **Meso**potamia (in the middle of, or between, the rivers—the Tigris and Euphrates), **meso**sphere, **meso**trophic.

120. Latin *miscere*, **to mix**, yields **mix**, **mix**ture; **mixo**gamous; ad**mix**ture, inter**mix**; amphi**mix**is, com**mix**ure; **misc**ellaneous, **misc**ible, **misc**egenation; im**misc**ible, pro**misc**uous; **mast**iff, **mêl**ée, **medd**le, **med**ley, **mél**ange, **ming**le; com**ming**le, inter**ming**le; **mest**izo, **mest**iso, **mul**atto, **mul**e, **must**ang (see p. 69).

121. Greek *mnem* (*mnasthai*, **to remember**) yields **mnem**onics; a**mnes**ia, a**mnes**ty, par**amnes**ia, ana**mnes**is; auto**mat**ic. Latin *memor*, **mindful**, yields **memor**y, **memor**able, **memor**andum, com**memor**ate.

122. Latin *movere*, **to move**, yields **move**, **move**ment; com**move**, re**move**; **mob** (from *mobile vulgus*, **movable crowd**), **Mobil**®, **mob**ile, **mob**ilize; auto**mob**ile, im**mob**ile; **mot**if, **mot**ile, **mot**ion, **mot**ivate, **mot**ive, **mot**ivity, **motor**, **motor**ize; de**mote**, e**mote**, pro**mote**, re**mote**; com**mot**ion, de**mot**ion, e**mot**ion, pro**mot**ion; auto**mot**ive, e**mot**ive, loco**mot**ive, thermo**mot**ive, as well as **mom**ent, **mom**entarily, **mom**entary, **mom**entum; mu**t**iny; French: é**meute** (an uprising). Mobile, Alabama, is most likely an American Indian name. There is also Mobile, Arizona (derivation unknown).

123. Greek *monos*, **single**, **alone**, **one**, yields **mon**achal, **mon**ad, **mon**astery, **mon**ocle (*mono-* + *oculus*, **eye**), **mono**acid, **mono**chord, **mono**chrome, **mono**coque (as of an automobile or airplane), **mono**cracy, **mono**cycle (unicycle), **mono**dactyl, **mono**ecious (or, monecious), **mono**gamy, **mono**genesis, **mono**gram, **mono**graph, **mono**gyny, **mono**latry, **mono**lith, **mono**logue, **mono**mial (*mono-* + *nomos*); minster (a church or cathedral on monastery grounds; not related to minister; see p. 21); **monk**, **monk**ery; Monolith, CA. Latin *uni-*, as in **uni**corn, **uni**cycle, **uni**son; **unit**, **unit**e (see Item 182); **uni**valve, **uni**valent, **uni**verse; Unicorn, MD; Unity, ME. Also *solus*, as in **soli**tary, **soli**tude, **soli**loquy; solo.

124. Greek *morphe*, **form**, yields **morph**, **morph**eme, **morph**emics, **morph**ic, **morph**ing; **morph**allaxis, **morph**osis; **morpho**genesis, **morpho**logy, **morpho**phonemics; a**morph**, allo**morph**, ana**morph**, bio**morph**, di**morph**, ecto**morph**, endo**morph**, homeo**morph**, iso**morph**, lago**morph**, meso**morph**, myo**morph**, para**morph**, peri**morph**, poly**morph**, pseudo**morph**, tri**morph**, xero**morph**, zygo**morph**; bi**morph**emic; anthropo**morph**ic, ecto**morph**ic, holo**morph**ic; patho**morph**ism; geo**morph**ology; anthro**morph**osis, meta**morph**osis; a**morph**ous (s e e p . 6 3 , **wordextras**), p o l y**morph**ous, z y g o-**morph**ous; gynandro**morph**y. See p. 69, **wordbuilder #28** for *fic-*, *fig-*, the Latin equivalents.

125. Latin *multi-*, **many**, yields **multi**tude, **multi**tudinous; **multi**atom, **multi**axial, **multi**causal, **multi**cellular, **multi**ceps, **multi**cultural, **multi**ethnic, **multi**farious, **multi**fid, **multi**lingual, **multi**media, **multi**parous, **multi**partite, **multi**ped, **multi**ple, **multi**ply. Compare Greek *myria*, as in **myriad**, **myria**podiasis. See Greek *poly-* (see p. 153); see *pluri-*, **Word Cluster No. 77**, p. 153.

126. Greek *mys*, **muscle**, yields **my**algia, **my**atonia, **my**atrophy, **my**odynia, **my**oma; **myo**bradia, **myo**carditis, **myo**cardium, **myo**clonus (pronounced my OCK lih nus), **myo**cardiograph, **myo**carditis, **myo**dermal, **myo**graph, **myo**tone. Latin: *mus*, as in *muscle*, *mussel*, means *mouse*; see pp. 20, 32, 85.

127. Greek *neos*, **young**, **new**, yields **neon**; Neocene, **neo**classicism, **neo**gala (see **wordbuilder #31**, p. 85), **neo**genesis, Neolithic, **neo**logism, **neo**nate, **neo**natology (see **Clavis**, p. 134), **neo**pathy, **neo**phrenia, **neo**phyte (see Item 146), **neo**plasm. Latin *novus*, as in **no**vation, **nov**el, **nov**elty, **no**vitiate, inno**vate**, reno**vate**; nouveau, nouvelle; Spanish: nuevo. See *juvenis*, **young**, Item 114.

128. Greek *nephros*, **kidney**, yields **nephr**idium, **nephr**ite, **nephr**on; **nephr**algia, **nephr**ectomy, **nephr**itis, **nephr**oma (see **wordbuilder #17**, p. 28, for *-oma*), **nephr**osis; **nephr**ology, **nephr**otomy. Latin *ren-*, as in **ren**al; **ren**iform, **ren**ipelvic, **ren**iportal; ad**ren**alin; supra**ren**al; **reins** (one meaning).

129. Latin *nox*, **night**, yields equi**nox**; **noct**ule, **noct**urn, **noct**urne, **noct**urnal, **noct**ambulate (same as *somnambulate*), **noct**uria (also called *nycturia*); trinoctial. See Item 131 for corresponding Greek root.

130. Greek *nomos*, **law**, **order**, yields **nom**arch; **n o m**othetic; metro**nome**; anthropo**nomy**, astro**nomy**, auto**nomy**, eco**nomy**, taxo**nomy** (see under *nomen novum*, p. 136); anti**nome**, astro**nomer**, bino**mial** (see p. 135), Deutero**nomy** (see **Clavis**, p. 58, under *Decalogue*), **numis**matics; **num**mular.

131. Greek *nyx*, **night**, yields **nyct**ea (a genus of birds consisting of the snowy owl), **nyct**erine, **nyct**uria (also called *nocturia*), **nyct**algia (pain that occurs in sleep only), **nyct**alopia (**night blindness**), **nyct**aphonia (loss of voice during the night); **nycti**tropism; **nycto**hemeral, **nycto**philia, **nycto**phobia. The genus *Nycteris* designates the bat, because of its nocturnal activity. See Item 129 for Latin root.

132. Greek *oion*, **egg**, yields **oo**tid; **oo**cyesis, **oo**cyst, **oo**cyte, **oo**gamous, **oo**genesis, **oo**gonium, **oo**kinesis, **oo**lite (a tiny, spherical or ellipsoid particle with concentric layers, found in sea waters), **oo**logy (the branch o f ornithology that studies birds' eggs), **oo**mycete, **oo**phore, **oo**phyte, **oo**plasm, **oo**sperm, **oo**sphere, **oo**spore, **oo**theca. NB: *Oolong*, from Chinese *wu lung*, **black dragon**, a particular tea, and *oomiak,* or *umiak*, an Eskimo boat, are not in this family. See Item 137, for Latin equivalent.

133. Greek *oophoron* (*oion*, **egg** + *pherein*, **to bear**; thus, **bearing eggs**) yields **oophor**algia, **oophor**ectomy, **oophor**itis; **oophoro**cytosis, **oophoro**pexy, **oophor**rhagia (*oophor* + *rrhagia*, **overflowing**).

134. Greek *oregein*, **to reach for**, thus, **appetite**, yields **orec**tic, **orex**is; **orexi**mania; ano**rexia**, cyno**rexia**, hyper**orexia**, lyco**rexia**, para**orexia**, xeno**rexia** (see Item 195).

135. Greek *ornis*, **bird**, yields **ornis**; **orni**scopy (*ornis* + *skopein*, **to watch**); **ornith**ic, **ornith**oid, **ornith**osis; **ornitho**fauna, **ornitho**logy, **ornitho**mancy (divination by watching the flight of birds); **ornith**opter (a heavier-than-air airplane deriving its chief support and propulsion from flapping wings), **ornitho**scopy (wild-bird watching). Latin *avis*, as in **avi**an, **avi**ary, **avi**ator; **avi**culture, **avi**onics, and rara **avis** (literally, **rare bird**, an unusual or extraordinary person or thing; rarity); also *auspices, auspicious* (interesting relationship).

136. Greek *ous*, **ear**, yields ot**o**dynia (*odyne*, **pain**), ot**e**ctomy, ot**i**tis; ot**o**antritis, ot**o**cyst, ot**o**genic, ot**o**genous, ot**o**rhinolaryngology ot**o**laryngology, ot**o**lith, ot**o**logy, ot**o**mycosis, ot**o**sclerosis; par**o**tid, par**o**titis.

137. Latin *ovum*, **egg**, yields **ov**al (in the shape of an egg), **ov**ary, **ov**ate; **ov**oid; **ov**ular, **ov**ulate, **ov**ulation, **ov**ule; **ov**ariectomy; **ov**iduct, **ov**iferous, **ov**iform, **ov**iposit, **ov**isac; **ov**otestis, **ov**oviviparous; ob**ov**ate, sub**ov**ate; ob**ov**oid; syn**ov**ia, asyn**ov**ia; *ab ovo*, literally, **from the egg**; from the beginning. Oval, PA; Ovalo, TX. See Item 132 for Greek equivalent. **NB:** *Ovation* is not from this root.

138. Greek *oxys*, **sharp**, **pointed**, **acute**, **acid**, yields **ox**ide, **ox**ime; **ox**acilin, **ox**alate, **ox**alic acid, **ox**alis, **ox**azine; amphi**ox**us, par**ox**ysm (see *ejaculate*, p. 102), per**ox**ide; **oxy**cephaly, **oxy**gen, **oxy**moron (see p. 102), **oxy**tocic. Latin: *acere*, as in **acer**bic, **acid**, **acumen**, **acute**; ex**acer**bate; **acri**monious, **acri**mony.

139. Greek *palin*, **again**, **back**, **backward**, yields **palin**drome (see p. 107), **palin**dromic rheumatism, **palin**esthesia, **palin**genesis, **palin**graphia, **palin**ode, **palin**opsia, **palin**phrasia, **palin**urus (literally, **back tail**, an Old World spiny lobster), **pali**kinesia. Latin: *retro-*, Item 158.

140. Greek *para-*, **beside**, yields **par**agogue, **par**agon (*akone*, **whetstone**), **par**allax (*allassein*, **to change**), **par**allel (*allelos*, **one another**), **par**allelepiped, **par**allelism, **par**allelogram, **par**egoric (see p. 88), **par**enthesis, **par**esis, **par**helion, **par**ody, **par**onomasia, **par**onymous, **par**otid, **par**otitis, **par**oxysm; **para**biosis, **para**ble (*ballein*, **to throw**; see p. 62, top of page), **para**bola, **para**digm, **para**dox, **para**genesis, **para**graph, **para**legal, **para**leipsis, **para**logism, **para**lysis, **para**mecium, **para**meter, **para**military, **para**mnesia, **para**morphism, **para**mount, **para**noia, **para**phrase, **para**physis, **para**praxis, **para**psychology, **para**site (see p. 61, **wordextras**), **para**synthesis, **para**taxis, **para**zoan.

141. Latin *pendere*, **to hang**, **weigh**, yields **pend**ant, **pend**ing, **pend**ulum, **pend**ulous; ap**pend**, com**pend**, de**pend**, ex**pend**, im**pend**, per**pend**, pro**pend**, sti**pend**, sus**pend**, vili**pend**; de**pend**ent, com**pend**ium; **pens**ion, **pens**ive; dis**pens**e, ex**pens**e, pre**pens**e, pro**pens**e; com**pens**ation, dis**pens**ary; pro**pens**ity (see p. 151 under **wordextras**); sus**pens**ion, ex**pens**ive; ante**pend**ium, per**pend**icular (see p. 136, **wordextras**), ap**pend**ix, ex**pend**iture; **poise**, equi**poise** (see p. 76, **Clavis**); **ponder**, **ponder**osa (pine), **ponder**ous; penthouse; spend, spontaneous; speiss. **NB:** *Despond* and *despondent* are not in this family, but from *spondere*, **to promise**. Other words from this family include **spond**ee; **spons**or, corre**spond**, re**spond**; re**spons**ible, irre**spons**ible, re**spons**ive, tran**spond**er; **spous**e, e**spous**e; riposte.

142. Latin *paenitere*, **to repent**, yields **pen**ance; **pen**itence, **pen**itent, **pen**itential, **pen**itentiary (influenced by *poena*, **penalty**, **fine**); im**pen**itent; re**pen**t, re**pen**tance, re**pen**tant; **pine** (one meaning), re**pine**.

143. Latin (originally, Greek) *petra*, **rock**, yields **petro**l, **petro**latum, **petro**leum (Greek *oleum*, **oil**, in the three foregoing words); **petro**chemistry, **petro**glyph, **petro**graphy, **petro**logy, **petro**sal; **petr**el (a bird that appears to walk on water, in the manner of Peter, a disciple of Jesus), **petr**ous; **petri**fy; salt-peter; parsley; Peter; Petros, TN; Petrolia (CA, TX; Ontario); Petrified National Forest. Also, Latin *lapis*, as in **lapis**; **lapid**ary, **lapid**ate (to stone to death); di**lapid**ate. Greek *lithos* (see **wordbuilder #53**, p. 139).

144. Greek *phone*, **sound**, yields **phon**ate, **phon**eme, **phon**etic, **phon**etist, **phon**ics; **phono**graph, **phono**logy, **phono**meter, **phono**scope; anti**phon** (see *anthem*, below); allo**phone**, homo**phone**, idio**phone**, iso**phone**, mega**phone**, micro**phone**, saxo**phone**, tele**phone**, xylo**phone**; anti**phony**, eu**phony**; a**phonia**, dys**phonia**, eu**phonia**, hyper**phonia**; eu**phon**ious, eu**phon**ium; stereo**phonic** (*stereos*, **solid**); anthem (*anti-* + *phone*; see p. 9). See Latin *son-* (Item 170), as in *sonnet*, *sonorant*.

145. Greek *phyllon*, **leaf**, yields **phyll**idium, **phyllo** (or, filo), **phyllo**de, **phyll**oid, **phyll**ome; **phyllo**clade, **phyllo**phagous, **phyllo**pod, **phyllo**taxy, **phyllo**xera; cata**phyll**, chloro**phyll**, clado**phyll**, meso**phyll**, sporo**phyll**, xantho**phyll**; a**phyllous**, deca**phyllous**, di**phyllous**, endo**phyllous**, epi**phyllous**, exo**phyllous**, hetero**phyllous**, homo**phyllous**, iso**phyllous**, malaco**phyllous**, micro**phyllous**, mono**phyllous**, poly**phyllous**, quadri**phyllous**, tri**phyllous**. Latin: *folium* (see Item 90).

146. Greek *phyton*, **plant**, yields **phyt**elephas; **phyt**ivorous; **phyto**chrome, **phyto**genesis, **phyto**geography, **phyto**graphy, **phyto**lite, **phyto**pathology, **phyto**phagous, **phyto**toxic; cryo**phyte**, micro**phyte**, neo**phyte**, xero**phyte**; holo**phyt**ic. A medical term is *osteophyte*, a small pathological bony outgrowth.

147. Greek *plassein*, **to form**, yields **plasm**a, **plasm**id, **plasm**odium; **plast**er, **plast**ic, **plast**id; ana**plasty**, dys**plast**; ecto**plasm**, meta**plasm**, proto**plasm**; hypo**plasia**; cranio**plasty**, hetero**plasty**; piaster. Latin: *figura*, from *fingere*, **to form**; see **wordbuilder #28**, p. 69; also, Greek *morphe*, Item 124.

148. Greek *platys*, **broad**, **flat**, yields **plate**, **platter**, **plat**itude; **place**, **place**nta; **platy**cephalic, **platy**helminth, **platy**podia (flat-footed), **platy**pus, **platy**rrhine; piazza, plaza; Spanish *playa*, **beach**.

149. Latin *plebs*, **the common people** [of Rome], yields **pleb**, **plebs**, **plebe** (first-year cadet at United States Military Academy), **pleb**eian (also spelled *plebian*), **pleb**icular; **plebi**scitary, **plebi**scite, **plebi**scitum.

150. Greek *pnein*, **to breathe**, yields **pneo**dynamics, **pneo**gram, **pneo**meter, **pneo**scope; a**pnea**, ana**pnea**, bathy**pnea**, brady**pnea**, dys**pnea**, eu**pnea**, hyper**pnea**, hypo**pnea**, oligo**pnea**, ortho**pnea**, platy**pnea**, poly**pnea**, tachy**pnea**, trepo**pnea**; ana**pnoic**. Latin *spirare*, as in per**spire**, re**spire**. See Item 172.

151. Greek *pneuma*, **air**, **spirit**; *pneumono-*, **lung**, **air**, **respiration**, yield **pneuma**, **pneuma**tic, **pneumon**ia, **pneumon**ic; **pneumon**itis; **pneumo**cardial, **pneumo**cele, **pneumo**centesis; search onelook for others.

152. Latin *prehendere*, **to seize**, **hold**, **take**, yields **prehens**ible, **prehens**ile, **prehens**ion; ap**prehend**, com**prehend**, re**prehend**; ap**prehens**ive, com**prehens**ive, re**prehens**ive; ap**prise**, com**prise**, enter**prise**, re**prise**, sur**prise**; mis**prision**; **pris**on; a**pprent**ice; entre**preneur**. Enterprise (in various States; see p. 97). See **Word Cluster No. 15**, p. 29, for words from *capere*, **to hold**, **seize**, **take**: **cap**tion, **cap**tive.

153. Greek *pteron*, **wing**, **feather**, yields **ptero**dactyl, **ptero**pod; **ptero**saur; acci**pter**, caly**pter**, chiro**pter** (see p. 126), helico**pter**, ornitho**pter**; a**pteral**, peri**pteral**, hemi**pteral**; a**pterous**, brachy**pterous**, di**pterous**, hemi**pterous**, hetero**pterous**, hymeno**pterous**, macro**pterous**, ortho**pterous**, tetra**pterous**; **pter**ygium, **pter**ygoid bone; ptarmigan. This root can also mean **winglike**, therefore, *fins*, as of a fish.

154. Latin *pugnare*, **to fight**, yields **pug**ilism, **pug**ilist; **pugn**acious; ex**pugn**, im**pugn**, op**pugn**, re**pugn**; ex**pugnable**, im**pugnable**, inex**pugnable**; re**pugn**ance; op**pugnant**, re**pugnant**; im**pugn**ation; im**pugner**, op**pugner**; poniard (a dagger; as a *verb*, to stab with a poniard).

155. Latin *pungere*, **to prick**, yields **pun** (see p. 89), **punct**ate, **punct**ilio, **punct**ilious (see p. 146), **punct**ual, **punct**uation, **punct**ulate, **punct**ure; com**punction**, ex**punction**, inter**punction**; com**punct**ious; acu**puncture**, aqua**puncture**, igni**puncture**, micro**puncture**, sono**puncture**, vaso**puncture**, veni**puncture**; ex**punge**; contrapuntal; counterpane; **point**, ap**point**, counter**point** (the adjectival form is *contrapuntal*), ap**point**ment; pivot, poignant, pounce, counterpane; Punta Gorda, FL; Grosse Pointe, MI.

156. Latin *quaerere*, **to ask**, **inquire**, **seek**, yields **quer**ist, **quer**y, con**quer**; **quest**, **quest**ion, **quest**ionable, **quest**ionless, **quest**ionnaire; ac**quest**, con**quest**, in**quest**, re**quest**; ac**quisi**tion, dis**quisi**tion, in**quisi**tion, requisition; ex**quisite**, per**quisite**, prere**quisite**, re**quisite**; con**quista**dor (see p. 163); in**quisi**tive; in**quisi**tor, in**quisi**torial; ac**quire**, in**quire**, re**quire**; in**quir**y; quarrel (one meaning).

157. Latin *radix*, **root**, yields **radic**al, **radic**alism, **radic**and, **radic**le, **radi**sh, **radi**x, e**radic**ate, de**raci**nate. Greek *rhiz*, as in **rhiz**oid, **rhiz**ome; **rhizo**bium, **rhizo**carpous, **rhizo**cephalan, **rhizo**ctonia, **rhizo**genic, **rhizo**morphous, **rhizo**phagous, **rhizo**pod, **rhizo**sphere, **rhizo**tomy; glycyr**rhiza** (also called *licorice*).

158. Latin *retro*, **backward** (from *re- back* + *-tro*, as in *intro-*) yields **retro**active, **retro**cede, **retro**fit, **retro**flex, **retro**grade (see p. 145, **wordbuilder #54**, for *grad-* words), **retro**gress, **retro**lental, **retro**rocket, **retro**spect, **retro**version; rear, arrears; reredos; derrière. See Greek *palin*, Item 139.

159. Latin *robustus*, **oaken**, **hard**, **strong**, yields **rob**le, **rob**orant, **rob**ust, **rob**ustious; cor**rob**orant, cor**rob**orate; rambunctious (probably an alteration of *robustus*).

160. Latin *rodere*, **to gnaw**, **scrape**, **scratch**, yields **rod**ent; cor**rod**e (corrosion, corrosive), e**rod**e (erose, erosion, erosive); rostrum (interesting relationship).

161. Latin *rumpere*, **to break**, yields **rupt**ure; ab**rupt**, bank**rupt**, cor**rupt**, dis**rupt**, e**rupt**, inter**rupt**, ir**rupt**. Another Latin root is *fract* as in **fract**ure, in**fract**ion, re**fract**ion; fragile (see wordbuilder #37, p. 91).

162. Greek *sauros*, **lizard**, yields **saur**ian, **saur**ischian; **sauro**pod; dino**saur**, elasmo**saur**, hadro**saur**, ptero**saur**; allo**saurus**, bronto**saurus**, ichthy**saurus**, plesio**saurus**, stego**saurus**, tyranno**saurus**.

163. Greek *scleros*, **hard**, or **hardening**, yields **scler**a, **scler**itis, **scler**otic; **sclero**derma, **sclero**meter; arterio**scler**osis. Latin *dur*, as in **dur**able, **Dur**on®, en**dure**, **dura** mater; **dour** (see wordextras, p. 166).

164. Greek *skopein*, **to examine**, yields **scope**, Epi**scop**al, cryo**scop**y, horo**scope**, kaleido**scope**, micro**scope**, peri**scope**, tele**scope**; bishop; skeptic, skeptical. Latin *vis* as in **vis**ion, **vis**or (see Item 187).

165. Latin *scribere*, **to write**, yields **scrib**al, **scribe**; a**scribe**, circum**scribe** de**scribe**, in**scribe**, pre**scribe**, pro**scribe**, sub**scribe**, super**scribe**, tran**scribe**; a**scrib**able, circum**scrib**able, inde**scrib**able; a**scription**, circum**scription**, con**scription**, de**scription**, in**scription**, pre**scription**, pro**scription**, re**scription**, sub**scription**, super**scription**, tran**scription**; **script**, **scrip**sit, **script**orium, **script**ure; con**script**, re**script**; manu**script**, nonde**script**, post**script** (P.S.); scribble; serif; shrive. Greek *graphein*, as in **graph**, **graph**ite, calli**graph**y, para**graph** (see p. 103, wordextras, under *grammar*).

166. Latin *senex*, **old**, yields **sen**ate, **sen**ator, **sen**atorial, **sen**ectitude, **sen**escent, **sen**eschal, **sen**ile, **sen**ility; **senior**, **senior**ity; **sen**opia; **seign**ior, **seign**iorage; sir, sire, surly (earlier, *sirly*, **masterful, imperious**). Spanish: señor, **señora**, señorita; French: mon**sieur**; Italian: mon**seign**or.

167. Latin *sex*, **six**, yields **sext**, **sext**ant, **sext**et, **sext**ile, **sext**illion; **sexto**decimo, **sext**uple; **sen**ary; **se**mester (literally, **six months**; see p. 143), siesta (originally, *sexta hora*, **sixth hour** after sunrise; see p. 106).

168. Latin *siderus* (genitive, *sideris*), **star**, yields **sider**eal; **sidero**stat (a more common term is *heliostat*) con**sider** (see p. 23), con**sider**able, con**sider**ate (incon**sider**ate, uncon**sider**ed), de**sider**ate, de**sider**ative, de**sider**atum; de**sir**able, de**sire**, de**sir**ous. Do not confuse with Greek *sider*, **iron**, as in **sider**ite, **sider**osis, **sider**urgy, **sidero**blast, **sidero**cyte, **sidero**derma, **sidero**phile.

169. Greek *soma* (genitive, *somatos*), **body**, yields **soma** (the *body*, as distinguished from the *mind*), **soma**tic; **somat**algia (*algos*, **pain**); **somato**genic, **somato**logy, **somato**plasm, **somato**pleure, **somato**psychic, **somato**scopy, **somato**sexual, **somato**statin, **somato**type; acro**some**, apo**some**, chromo**some**, desmo**some**, hyalo**some**, hydro**some**, lipo**some**, mono**some**, nucleo**some**, schisto**some**; phyllo**soma**; psycho**soma**tic (see p. 50); ana**som**ia; hetero**somat**ous. Latin *corpus*, as i n **corp**oral, **corp**ulent, **corp**oration; in**corp**orate; esprit de corps. See other *corpus* words, **Word Cluster No. 25**, p. 49.

170. Latin *sonare*, **to sound**, yields **son**ance, **son**ant, **son**ar, **son**ata, **son**atina, **son**de, **son**e, **son**ic, **son**net (see **wordextras**, p. 44), **sono**rant, **sono**rity, **sono**rous; **sono**buoy, **sono**gram, **sono**meter; as**son**ance, con**son**ance, re**son**ance; ab**son**ant, as**son**ant, con**son**ant, dis**son**ant, re**son**ant; re**son**ate; Pana**sonic**®, sub**sonic**, super**sonic**, tran**sonic**, ultra**sonic**; uni**son**; sound; swan; Sonnette, MT; French *son et lumière* (**sound and light**). See Greek *phone*, as in **phone**me, tele**phone**; Item 144.

171. Latin *specere*, **to see**, yields **spec**ial (e**spec**ial), **spec**ies, **spec**imen, **spec**ious, **spec**tacle, **spec**tacles (eyeglasses), **spec**tator, **spec**trum, **spec**ulate; a**spect**, circum**spect**, ex**pect** (elided because of s-sound of prefix *ex-*), in**spect**, pro**spect**, re**spect**, su**spect**; in**spec**tion, intro**spec**tion, retro**spec**tion; per**spec**tive; con**spic**uous; de**spise** (de**spic**able), **spite**, re**spite**; su**spic**ion; soup**çon** (see p. 138, **wordextras** for *suspicion* and *soupçon*); spy, e**spy**, e**spi**al; e**spi**onage. Pro**spect** (KY, ME, OH, OR, PA, TN). Another Latin equivalent: *videre* (Item 187); also, Greek *scope,* Item 164.

172. Latin *spirare*, **to breathe**, yields **spir**acle, **spir**acular, **spir**ant; **spirit**, **spirit**ed, **spirit**ism, **spirit**ual, **spirit**uous; d i**spirit**, di**spirit**ed, in**spirit**; a**spire**, con**spire**, ex**pire**, in**spire**, per**spire**, re**spire**, su**spire**, tran**spire**; a**spir**ation, e x**pir**ation, in**spir**ation, per**spir**ation, re**spir**ation, tran**spir**ation; French: **spirit**uel, esprit de corps (see p. 50). Greek *pneum*, as in **pneum**onia. See Items 150, 151.

173. Latin *stella*, **star**, yields **stell**ar, **stell**ate, **stell**iform, **stell**ular; **stell**iferous, **stell**iform; con**stell**ate, con**stell**ation; circum**stell**ar, inter**stell**ar, sub**stell**ar, ultra**stell**ar; Stella, NE. Another Latin element for star is *sider*, as in **sider**eal, con**sider**; see Item 168. From *ster-*, **star**, the same IE root as *stella,* is Greek *aster*, as in **aster**isk, **aster**oid; **astro**dome, **astro**naut, **astro**sphere. See **Clavis**, p. 70 under *disaster.*

174. Greek *strophein*, **to turn, twist**, yields **strophe**, **stroph**ic; ana**strophe**, anti**strophe**, apo**strophe**, cata**strophe**, epi**strophe**, hypo**strophe**, mono**strophe**; ex**strophy**; **strepto**mycin. A Latin equivalent: *vertere* (Item 184). A Latin element more closely meaning *twist* is *torque* as in **torque** itself; **tort**urous, **tort**uous (see p. 196 under *travel*); na**sturt**ium (see **wordextras**, p. 46).

175. Latin *struere*, **to pile up, arrange, build**, yields **struct**ure; con**struct**, in**struct**, ob**struct**; con**struct**ion, de**struct**ion, in**struct**ion, ob**struct**ion; de**struct**ible; con**struct**ive; in**struct**or; infra**struct**ure, micro**struct**ure, re**struct**ure, sub**struct**ure, super**struct**ure; de**stroy**; in**stru**ment, in**stru**mental; indu**str**y (indu**str**ial, indu**str**ious); con**stru**e (miscon**stru**e); **strat**agem, **strat**osphere; straw, strew, street.

176. Latin *sub-*, **under**, yields **sub**acid, **sub**acute, **sub**altern, **sub**alternate, **sub**aqueous, **sub**audition, **sub**clavian, **sub**conscious, **sub**costal, **sub**culture, **sub**cutaneous, **sub**divide, **sub**dominant, **sub**due, **sub**fusc, **sub**genus, **sub**glacial, **sub**grade, **sub**ito, **sub**ject, **sub**jugate, **sub**marine, **sub**merge, **sub**merse, **sub**mit, **sub**ordinate, **sub**poena, **sub**reption (**sur**reptitious; see p. 43, **wordextras**), **sub**scribe, **sub**sequent, **sub**side, **sub**sidiary, **sub**sidy, **sub**sist, **sub**soil, **sub**tend, **sub**stratum, **sub**sumption; sombrero (Spanish for **hat**; literally, **under the shade**; see Item 180), souvenir (literally, **to come from under**; see p. 200). Latin *infra-*, Item 112, for **infra**red, **infra**structure.

177. Greek *tele-*, **far, from afar**, yields **tel**encephalon (*encephalon*, **brain**), **tel**esthesia, **tel**pher; **tele**cast, **tele**communication, **tele**genic, **tele**gony, **tele**gram, **tele**graph, **tele**graphy, **tele**kinesis, **tele**meter, **tele**pathy, **tele**phone, **tele**phony, **tele**scope; **tele**vision; Telegraph, Texas. See *teleo,* p. 81.

178. Latin *trahere*, **to draw**, **pull**, yields **tract**, **tract**able, **tract**ate, **tract**ile, **tract**ion, **tract**or; abs**tract** (abstracted, abstraction, abstractive), at**tract** (attraction, attractive), con**tract** (contraction, contractive), de**tract** (detraction), dis**tract** (distracted, distraction, distractive), ex**tract** (extraction) pro**tract**, pro**tract**or, re**tract** (retraction, retractive), sub**tract** (subtraction, subtractive); con**tract**able, in**tract**able, re**tract**able; pro**tract**ile, re**tract**ile; sub**trah**end; por**tray** (portrayal), trace, tracer; trail, trailer, train, trait (distrait, portrait), trawl; treat, treatise, treatment, treaty; entreat, entreaty, mistreat, retreat, distraught.

179. Latin *trudere*, **to thrust**, **push**, yields de**trude**, ex**trude**, in**trude**, ob**trude**, pro**trude**, re**trude**; abs**truse**; de**trusion**, ex**trusion** (extrusive), in**trusion** (intrusive), ob**trusion** (obtrusive), pro**trusion** (protrusive), pro**trus**ile; threat; thrust. See p. 140, under *obtrude*; see p. 35 for *abstruse*.

180. Latin *umbra*, **shade**, yields **umbra**, **umbra**ge, **umbra**geous, **umbr**ella (Italian: **small shade**); **umb**el; **umbri**ferous; ad**umbr**al, ad**umbr**ate, pen**umbra**; sub**umbr**ella; somber; sombrero (Spanish: **under the shade**; a large wide-brimmed hat; see Item 176).

181. Latin *unda*, **wave**, yields **und**ine, **und**ulant, **und**ulate, **und**ulation; ab**und**ance; ab**und**ant, in**und**ant; in**und**ate; red**und**ant, superab**und**ant; abound, redound, superabound, surround; sound—one meaning.

182. Latin *uni-*, **one**, yields **uni**on, **uni**que, **uni**t, **Uni**tarian, **uni**tary, **uni**te, **uni**tize, **uni**ty; **un**animous; **uni**axial, **uni**body, **uni**cameral (see p. 26), **uni**capsular, **uni**cellular, **uni**ceps, **uni**clinal, **uni**corn, **uni**cornate, **uni**costate, **uni**cycle, **uni**dimensional, **uni**foliate, **uni**form, **uni**fy (unifiable), **uni**jugate, **uni**lateral, **uni**linear, **uni**lingual, **uni**locular, **uni**parous, **uni**personal, **uni**petalous, **uni**planar, **uni**polar, **uni**potent, **uni**ramous, **uni**sex, **uni**son, **uni**valent, **uni**valve, **uni**versal, **uni**verse, **uni**versity, **uni**vocal; coad**un**ate; tri**une**; re**uni**fy; dis**uni**on, re**uni**on; dis**uni**te (disunity), re**uni**te; inch, onion (see **wordextras**, p. 119); Unity, OR; Unityville, PA. Greek *mono-* (Item 123).

183. Latin *vermis*, **worm**, yields **vermi**cular, **vermi**culate; **vermi**n, **vermi**nation, **vermi**nous; **vermi**cide, **vermi**form, **vermi**fuge, **vermi**phobia; **vermi**celli (Italian; literally, **small worms**); **verm**eil, **vermi**lion (the color of red worms); **verm**outh (see **wordextras**, p. 185); Vermi̱lion, OH; Vermi̱llion (KS, SD). Greek *helminth*, as in **helminth**iasis, platy**helminth** (flatworm).

184. Latin *vertere*, **to turn**, yields **vert**ex, **verte**bra (pl., vertebrae), **vert**ical, **vert**icil, **vert**icillate, **vert**igo; a**vert**, ad**vert**, ante**vert**, con**vert**, contro**vert**, di**vert**, e**vert**, extro**vert**, in**vert**, intro**vert**, ob**vert**, per**vert**, re**vert**, sub**vert**; **vers**ant, **vers**atile, **verse** (versed), **vers**icle, **vers**ion, **vers**us; anniver**sar**y; ad**verse**, di**verse**, per**verse**, re**verse**, uni**verse**; uni**vers**ity; ad**vers**ary, contro**vers**y, di**vers**, di**vers**ity, di**vers**ionary; ad**vert**ise, inad**vert**ent; ante**version**, con**version**, di**version**, per**version**, retro**version**, sub**version**; **vort**ex. A Greek equivalent is *strophein*; see Item 174.

185. Latin *via*, **a way**, yields **via**duct, **via**ticum; de**via**te, ob**via**te; de**vi**ous, ob**vi**ous, per**vi**ous (impervious), pre**vi**ous, tri**vi**al; con**vey** (conveyance); quadri**vi**um (see p. 161), tri**vi**um; **voy**age; con**voy**, en**voy** (has two different meanings); in**voi**ce. Greek *hodos*, as in **od**ometer; exodus (see **wordbuilder #42**, p. 109).

186. Latin *vic* (from IE *weik-*, **to bend**, **change**), **turn**, **alteration**, **substitute**, yields **vic**ar (see p. 51), **vic**arage, **vic**arial, **vic**ariate, **vic**arious (see p. 51), **vic**issitude; **vis**count, **vic**e-president, **vic**e versa (see Item 184 for *vertere* words, e.g., **vert**ical, sub**vert**; **verse**, **vers**icle, **vers**ion).

187. Latin *videre*, **to see**, **look**, yields **vid**eo; **vis**a, **vis**age (envisage), **vis**ible (invisible), **vis**ion (envision), **vist**a; ad**vise**, impro**vise**, pre**vise**, re**vise**, super**vise**; **voy**eur, clair**voy**ance; ad**vice**; p**rovide**; e**nvy**; e**vid**ent; in**vid**ious; **view** (interview, preview, review); sur**vey**. Greek *skopein* (see Item 164).

188. Latin *vincere*, **to conquer**, yields **vinc**ible, **vind**icable, **vind**icate, **vind**ictive; con**vince**, e**vince**; con**vinc**ing, in**vinc**ible; a**venge**, re**venge**; **vict**im, **vict**or, **vict**orious, **vict**ory; con**vict**, e**vict**; vanquish.

189. Latin *vir*, **man**, yields **vir**ile, **vir**tual, **vir**tue, **vir**tuosity, **vir**tuoso; decem**vir**, duum**vir**, trium**vir**. Another Latin root meaning *man* is *homo* as in **hom**icide, see Item 61; in that item, note equivalent Greek roots: *andro-*, *anthropo-*.

190. Latin *vita*, **life**, yields **vita**, **vita**l, **vita**ls, **vita**lity, **Vita**lis® (a hair tonic), **vita**min; **viva**cious, **viv**id; re**vive**, sur**vive**; re**viv**al, con**viv**ial; **vi**able (inviable); victual(s). See *bio-*, **life**, **wordbuilder #25**, p. 51.

191. Latin *vocare*, **to call**, yields **voc**able, **voc**abulary, **voc**ation, **voc**ational, **voc**ative; a**voc**ation, con**voc**ation, e**voc**ation, in**voc**ation, re**voc**ation, pro**voc**ation; e**voc**ative; con**voke**, e**voke**, in**voke**, pro**voke**, re**voke**. A related meaning is **voice**, as in **voc**al, equi**voc**al, uni**voc**al; **voice**, **vow**el (the adjectival form is *vocalic*); **voc**iferate; abat-**voix** (see **Clavis**, p. 16); **vouch** (avouch), **vow** (avow).

192. Latin *volvere*, **to roll**, yields **vol**uble; **volume** (originally, **a roll of parchment**), **volum**inous; **volum**eter (*volume + meter*); **volute**, **volut**ion; circum**volute**, e**volute**, in**volute**, ob**volute**, re**volute**, super**volute**; circum**volve**, con**volve**, de**volve**, e**volve**, in**volve**, inter**volve**, re**volve**; con**volut**ion, de**volut**ion, e**volut**ion, in**volut**ion, ob**volut**ion, re**volut**ion; cavort, vault, vaulted, vaulting; vulva. Do not confuse this element with *volo*, **I wish**, from *velle*, **to be willing**, as in **vol**ition, **vol**untary, **vol**unteer; **vol**uptuous.

193. Latin *vorare*, **to eat**, **devour**, yields **vor**acious, **vor**acity, **vor**ago, **vor**ant (heraldry term); carni**vore**, detriti**vore**, frugi**vore**, herbi**vore**, insecti**vore**, muci**vore**, nectari**vore**, omni**vore**, pollini**vore**, verbi-**vore**; algi**vorous**, amphi**vorous**, api**vorous**, arachni**vorous**, bacci**vorous**, calci**vorous**, carni**vorous**, equi**vorous**, frugi**vorous**, fuci**vorous** (eating fucus or seaweeds), fungi**vorous**, gramini**vorous**, grani**vorous**, herbi**vorous**, insecti**vorous**, lacti**vorous**, omni**vorous**, pisci**vorous**; de**vour**; gorge; also, *gorgeous*, although the etymology is convoluted. See *phag-*, **wordbuilder #51**, p. 128.

194. Greek *xanthos*, **yellow**, yields **xanth**ate, **xanth**ein, **xanth**ic, **xanth**ous; **xantho**cephalus (the **yellow**-headed blackbird), **xantho**chroid, **xantho**derma, **xantho**genic, **xantho**phore, **xantho**phyll. Latin *flavus*, as in **flav**escent, **flav**in; ribo**flav**in. (**NB**: *Flavor* is not related to this root.) See Amarillo, Texas (p. 125).

195. Greek *xenos*, **stranger**, **foreign**, yields **xen**ia, **xen**on (symbol Xe); **xen**orexia (an appetite disorder leading to the repeated swallowings of foreign bodies not ordinarily digested; see Item 134); **xeno**biotic, **xeno**blast, **xeno**cryst, **xeno**gamy, **xeno**genesis, **xeno**graft, **xeno**lith, **xeno**mania, **xeno**philia, **xeno**-phobia, **xeno**phonia; a**xen**ic, anti**xen**ic, holo**xen**ic, mono**xen**ic, pyro**xen**ic.

196. Greek *xeros*, **dry**, yields **xer**ic; **xer**arch, **xer**opthalmia, **xer**osis (**xer**otic); **xero**chilia (dryness of the lips), **xero**cyte, **xero**derma, **xero**dermosteosis (*derm*, **skin** + *osteo*, **bone** + *osis*, **condition**), **xero**graphy, **xero**phagy, **xero**philous, **xero**phyte (**xero**phytic), **xero**sere, **xero**thermic; **Xerox**® (company that makes dry copiers); phyllo**xer**a; eli**xir** (a powder for drying wounds); serene (serenity).

197. Greek *xiphos*, **sword**, yields **xiph**idium; **xiph**oid, **xiph**odon; **xipho**costal, **xipho**phyllous, **xipho**-sternum, **xipho**suran. See Item 93, for Latin *gladius*, **sword**, as in **glad**iator, **glad**iolus.

198. Greek *xylon*, **wood**, yields **xyl**an, **xyl**em, **xyl**ene, **xyl**ose; **xylo**graphy, **xylo**phagous (wood-eating, as certain mollusks), **xylo**phone, **xylo**tomous, **xylo**tomy; meta**xyl**em, proto**xyl**em.

199. Greek *zoion*, **animal**, yields **zo**diac, **zo**ea, **zo**ism, **zoo**, **zoo**id; **zoo**flagellate, **zoo**gamete, **zoo**genic, **zoo**-geography, **zoo**graphy, **zoo**latry, **zoo**logy, **zoo**metry, **zoo**morphic, **zoo**morphism, **zoo**nosis, **zoo**parasite, **zoo**phagous, **zoo**philia, **zoo**phobia, **zoo**phyte, **zoo**plankton, **zoo**sporangium, **zoo**spore, **zoo**sterol, **zoo**tomy; **zoid**ogamous; a**zoa**, ecto**zoa**, endo**zoa**, ento**zoa**, epi**zoa**, meso**zoa**, meta**zoa**, micro**zoa**, mono**zoa**, poly**zoa**, proto**zoa**; bryo**zoa**, hydro**zoa**, malaco**zoa** (*malacos*, **soft**, as in *mollusk* and *mollify*) oo**zoa**, proto**zoa**, spermato**zoa**, sporo**zoa**; a**zo**te, a**zo**temia; Ceno**zoic**, holo**zoic**, Meso**zoic**, cyto**zoic**; ento**zoon**, epi**zoon**, hemato**zoon**, spermato**zoon**; en**zo**otic, epi**zo**otic. Latin *anima*, as in **anim**al, **anim**ated, un**anim**ous; see **wordbuilder #10**, p. 22.

200. Greek *zyme*, **to leaven**, **ferment**, yields **zym**ase, **zym**e, **zym**oid, **zym**osis (**zym**otic), **zym**urgy; **zym**ogen, **zymo**genesis, **zymo**genic, **zymo**logy, **zymo**lysis, **zymo**meter, **zymo**nema, **zymo**plastic, **zymo**scope, **zymo**sthenic; en**zym**e, en**zym**ology; lyso**zym**e.

201. Greek *idios*, **one's own**, yields **idio**cy, **idio**m, **idio**matic; **idio**t, **idio**tic; **idio**blast, **idio**chromatic, **idio**cratic, **idio**gamist, **idio**graphic, **idio**lalia, **idio**latry, **idio**lect, **idio**morphic, **idio**pathic, **idio**plasm, **idio**syncrasy; idiot savant. See p. 96 for *propio-* words, e.g., **prop**erty, **prop**rietor, **prop**riety.

202. Latin and Greek *pro-*, **before**, **forward**, **forth**, **substituting for**, yields **pro**active, **pro**blem, **pro**blematic, **pro**boscis, **pro**cambium, **pro**carp, **pro**cathedral, **pro**cedure, **pro**ceed, **pro**cess, **pro**claim, **pro**clama-tion, **pro**clitic, **pro**clivity, **pro**consul, **pro**crastinate, **pro**creant, **pro**create, **pro**cumbent (see p. 54), **pro**curator, **pro**cure, **pro**drome, **pro**duce, **pro**duct, **pro**fane, **pro**fess, **pro**fessor, **pro**ficient, **pro**file, **pro**fit, **pro**fligate, **pro**fluent, **pro**found, **pro**fundity, **pro**fuse, **pro**genitor, **pro**geny, **pro**gnathous, **pro**gnosis, **pro**gnosticate, **pro**gram, **pro**gress, **pro**hibit, **pro**ject, **pro**lapse, **pro**late, **pro**legomenon, **pro**lepsis, **pro**lific (base of *alere*, **to nourish** + *facere*, **to make**), **pro**lix, **pro**locutor, **pro**logue, **pro**long, **pro**menade, **p r o**miscuous, **pro**mise, **pro**missory, **pro**montory, **pro**mote, **pro**mulgate (see p. 30, **wordextras**), **pro**noun, **pro**nounce, **pro**pagate, **pro**pel, **pro**pensity, **pro**phecy, **pro**phesy, **pro**phet, **pro**-phylactic, **pro**pitiate, **pro**ponent, **pro**portion, **pro**pose, **pro**pound, **pro**scenium, **pro**scribe, **pro**secute, **pro**spect, **pro**sper, **pro**state, **pro**stitute, **pro**strate, **pro**tect, **pro**test, **pro**tract, **pro**vide, **pro**vision; **pro**digal, **pro**digy; **pro**ffer; **pro**verb, **pro**vocation, **pro**voke; **por**trait, **por**tray; reci**pro**cate.

APPENDIX A—WORD CLUSTER POSTTEST

INSTRUCTIONS: For each set of words, write the common meaning in the blank.

1. albumin, albino, leukemia, edelweiss _____
2. altimeter, contralto, acrophobia, oboe _____
3. preamble, somnambulist, amble, ambition _____
4. superannuated, annus mirabilis, annuity _____
5. penny ante, antediluvian, antecedent _____
6. armistice, armadillo, gendarme, Luftwaffe _____
7. audit, oyez, ausculate, obey _____
8. combat, debate, abattoir, abatement _____
9. cui bono?, debonair, benefit, euphony, eulogy _____
10. bivalve, biscuit, balance, dilemma, bifid _____

11. abbreviate, brevier, abridge, breviped _____
12. calorie, calenture, nonchalant, chowder _____
13. bicameral, unicameral, incamera, chamber _____
14. canine, Canis Major, cynic, cynodon _____
15. caption, forceps, emancipate, capsize _____
16. per capita, biceps, decapitate, kerchief _____
17. carnivorous, carnation, pancreas, sarcophagus _____
18. centrifugal, geocentric, androcenter, centroid _____
19. decadent, cascade, deciduous, recidivist _____
20. circumference, research, perimeter, circadian _____

21. clarinet, clarify, declarative _____
22. conclave, enclave, clavicle, exclave _____
23. contrapuntal, counterpoint, antidote _____
24. cordial, concordance, cardiac, pericardium _____
25. corpulent, corporation, chromosome _____
26. crucify, excruciating, Vera Cruz, cruise _____
27. cubicle, cubit, incubus, incumbent, succumb _____
28. culprit, culpable, culpability, exculpate _____
29. decapod, decathlon, dime, Decapolis, dean _____
30. deist, theist, theocracy, divine, adiós _____

31. eudemon, demonologic, pandemonium _____
32. dandelion, dentiloquy, orthodontist, mastodon _____
33. dictionary, edict, verdict, benediction _____
34. diary, circadian, sine die, carpe diem _____
35. disease, discriminate, dessert, dimension _____
36. condolement, indolent, hangnail, analgesic _____
37. donation, pardon, surrender, rendezvous _____
38. equilateral, equinox, egalitarian, Ecuador _____
39. fable, infantry, infant, prophet, dysphasia _____
40. affidavit, confide, confidant, confident _____

41. define, finance, finitude, infinite, finite _____
42. influenza, influence, flume, influx, fluent _____
43. vermifuge, centrifugal, refugee, fugitive _____
44. congregation, egregious, agoraphobia _____
45. habeas corpus, rehabilitate, prohibit _____
46. heredity, heir, inherit, heritage _____
47. Ecce homo, ad hominem, Homo sapiens, homicide _____
48. in absentia, in esse, in loco parentis _____
49. interaction, intercede, interstate _____
50. intravenous, intrinsic, entrails, entre nous _____

51. projectile, eject, projector, jetty, parable _____
52. journal, adjourn, bonjour, sojourn _____
53. judicial, judgment, justice, hoosegow _____
54. conjugate, conjunction, junta, syzygy _____
55. lava, lavatory, ablution, antediluvian _____
56. elevator, alleviate, lever, legerdemain _____
57. liberate, Liberia, liberal, libertarian _____
58. illiteracy, literal, literate, transliterate _____
59. allocate, lieutenant, thesis, hypothesis _____
60. colloquy, elocution, ventriloquist, soliloquy _____

61. magnum, magnum opus, Magna Carta _____
62. dismal, malicious, malady, dyslexia, dysentery _____
63. manuscript, manufacture, chiropractor, surgeon _____
64. minus, minuet, administration, minestrone _____
65. transmit, committee, admission, missionary _____
66. mortality, immortal, "Thanatopsis," euthanasia _____
67. international, natal, nativity, congenital _____
68. nomenclature, nominate, anonymous, synonym _____
69. umpire, nolo contendere, persona non grata _____
70. obese, obsequious, obliterate, occlude _____

71. binoculars, inoculate, synopsis, "Thanatopsis" _____
72. omnivorous, panacea, omnipotent, pancreas _____
73. oratory, peroration, adore, inexorable _____
74. pacific, Pacific Ocean, pacifier, pacifist _____
75. partner, partition, participle, parse _____
76. pedestal, impedence, octopus, decapoda _____
77. plural, ne plus ultra, pluperfect, nonplused _____
78. portable, transport, rapport, circumference _____
79. posterior, postlude, post script (P.S.) _____
80. primeval, principle, principal, primogeniture _____

81. quatrain, quadrate, quartet, carillon, cadre _____
82. correct, regimen, direction, orthodontics _____
83. salary, salami, sauce, sausage, silt, halogen _____
84. salute, salutation, salubrious, Gesundheit _____
85. sanctuary, sacred, execrate, consecrate _____
86. satire, satisfy, polyunsaturated, plethora _____
87. second, sequence, subsequent, pursue, suite _____
88. session, supersede, subsidize, cathedral _____
89. sinecure, sans-souci, sin duda _____
90. transistor, armistice, stationery, thesis _____

91. insult, desultory, resilient, assault _____
92. superstructure, supreme, soprano, hyperbole _____
93. contaminate, tangent, contact, integrate _____
94. tenet, tenor, lieutenant, detain, tennis _____
95. extent, extenuating, ostentatious, hypotenuse _____
96. territory, inter, perigee, geosynchronous _____
97. transit, transvestite, tranquil, diameter _____
98. trident, trivial, trio, troika, trellis _____
99. ultramarine, outré, metaphor, metamorphosis _____
100. contravene, advent, souvenir, revenue, avenue _____

Total Posttest Score_____
Place this score on p. xvii.

APPENDIX B—WORDBUILDERS POSTTEST

You are now ready to see how well you mastered the wordbuilders.

INSTRUCTIONS: Place the meaning of each of the roots in the blanks; then check the answers in Appendix D.

1.	cur-	___	42.	ode-	___
2.	allo-	___	43.	spher-	___
3.	pachy-	___	44.	ster-	___
4.	alter-	___	45.	glypt-	___
5.	clam-	___	46.	myel-	___
6.	exo-	___	47.	mut-	___
7.	vest-	___	48.	-mere	___
8.	dactyl-	___	49.	derm-	___
9.	ana-	___	50.	lect-	___
10.	anima-	___	51.	phag-	___
11.	chron-	___	52.	rhin-	___
12.	-tom-	___	53.	lith	___
13.	anth-	___	54.	grad-	___
14.	dors-	___	55.	caco-	___
15.	duc-	___	56.	sym-	___
16.	-itis	___	57.	calli-	___
17.	-oma	___	58.	cata-	___
18.	blast-	___	59.	cerat-	___
19.	aug-	___	60.	cerebr-	___
20.	auto-	___	61.	andr-	___
21.	endo-	___	62.	angi-	___
22.	erg-	___	63.	arthr-	___
23.	gam-	___	64.	bathy-	___
24.	bar-	___	65.	biblio-	___
25.	bio-	___	66.	bryo-	___
26.	flect-	___	67.	cant-	___
27.	fac-	___	68.	caten-	___
28.	fig-	___	69.	caus-	___
29.	eco-	___	70.	cent-	___
30.	firm-	___	71.	cente-	___
31.	galact-	___	72.	chlor-	___
32.	lact-	___	73.	chrom-	___
33.	cine-	___	74.	clud-	___
34.	dorm-	___	75.	cosm-	___
35.	frater-	___	76.	crat-	___
36.	gran-	___	77.	cred-	___
37.	fract-	___	78.	cry-	___
38.	carp-	___	79.	crypt-	___
39.	brady-	___	80.	cuss-	___
40.	gastr-	___	81.	cycl-	___
41.	hydr-	___	82.	cyto-	___

83.	demo- _____		129.	nox- _____
84.	dendro- _____		130.	nom- _____
85.	dogma- _____		131.	nyc- _____
86.	drom- _____		132.	oo- _____
87.	dulc- _____		133.	oophor- _____
88.	ecto- _____		134.	orex- _____
89.	emp- _____		135.	orni- _____
90.	foli- _____		136.	oto- _____
91.	fric- _____		137.	ovum- _____
92.	genu- _____		138.	oxy- _____
93.	glad- _____		139.	palin- _____
94.	glob- _____		140.	para- _____
95.	gloss- _____		141.	pend- _____
96.	glyc- _____		142.	penit- _____
97.	gnos- _____		143.	petro- _____
98.	gon- _____		144.	phon- _____
99.	grav- _____		145.	phyll- _____
100.	gymn- _____		146.	phyt- _____
101.	gyn- _____		147.	plas- _____
102.	hedr- _____		148.	platy- _____
103.	hemo- _____		149.	pleb- _____
104.	hetero- _____		150.	pne- _____
105.	homo- _____		151.	pneu- _____
106.	hypn- _____		152.	prehen- _____
107.	hypo- _____		153.	pter- _____
108.	hyster- _____		154.	pug- _____
109.	iatr- _____		155.	pung- _____
110.	ichthy- _____		156.	quest- _____
111.	icon- _____		157.	rad- _____
112.	infra- _____		158.	retro- _____
113.	it- _____		159.	rob- _____
114.	juv- _____		160.	rod- _____
115.	kilo- _____		161.	rupt- _____
116.	luc- _____		162.	saur- _____
117.	macro- _____		163.	scler- _____
118.	mater- _____		164.	scop- _____
119.	med- _____		165.	scrib- _____
120.	misc- _____		166.	sen- _____
121.	mnem- _____		167.	sex- _____
122.	mob- _____		168.	sider- _____
123.	mono- _____		169.	soma- _____
124.	morph- _____		170.	son _____
125.	multi- _____		171.	spec _____
126.	myo- _____		172.	spir _____
127.	neo- _____		173.	stell- _____
128.	nephr- _____		174.	stroph- _____

175.	struct-	_____	188.	vinc-	_____
176.	sub-	_____	189.	vir-	_____
177.	tele-	_____	190.	vit-	_____
178.	tract-	_____	191.	voc -	_____
179.	trud-	_____	192.	volv-	_____
180.	umbra-	_____	193.	vor-	_____
181.	unda-	_____	194.	xanth-	_____
182.	uni-	_____	195.	xeno-	_____
183.	verm-	_____	196.	xero-	_____
184.	vert-	_____	197.	xiph-	_____
185.	via-	_____	198.	xylo-	_____
186.	vic-	_____	199.	zo-	_____
187.	vid-	_____	200.	zym-	_____

After checking answers in Appendix D, place score on p. xviii.

APPENDIX C — WORD CLUSTER ANSWERS

Only short answers are given; see text for additional answers or explanatory notes.

1.	white, gleaming		43.	to flee
2.	high, height		44.	flock, herd
3.	to walk, go		45.	to have, to hold
4.	year		46.	heir
5.	before		47.	man
6.	shield, protection		48.	in (preposition, adverb)
7.	to hear, listen		49.	between
8.	to strike		50.	within
9.	good, well		51.	to throw
10.	two		52.	day
11.	short		53.	to judge
12.	heat, warmth		54.	to join
13.	room, chamber		55.	to wash, flood
14.	dog		56.	to raise, lift up
15.	to catch, seize		57.	to free
16.	head		58.	letter
17.	meat, flesh		59.	to place
18.	center, point		60.	to speak
19.	to fall, die		61.	great
20.	around		62.	bad
21.	clear		63.	hand
22.	key		64.	small, less
23.	against		65.	to send
24.	heart		66.	death
25.	body		67.	birth
26.	cross		68.	name
27.	to lie down		69.	negative
28.	guilt, blame		70.	against
29.	ten		71.	eye
30.	God, god		72.	all
31.	devil, demon		73.	to speak; also, mouth
32.	tooth		74.	peace, peaceful
33.	to say, speak; also, words		75.	part, portion
34.	day		76.	foot
35.	negative		77.	more, additional
36.	pain, sorrow		78.	to bear, to carry
37.	to give		79.	after
38.	equal		80.	first
39.	to speak		81.	four
40.	to trust, believe		82.	straight
41.	boundary, end		83.	salt
42.	to flow		84.	health

85. holy; to bless
86. full, complete
87. to follow
88. to sit; in Greek, chair
89. without
90. to stand
91. to jump
92. over, above, beyond
93. to touch
94. to hold
95. to stretch
96. earth
97. across
98. three
99. beyond
100. to come

APPENDIX D—WORDBUILDER ANSWERS

1. run
2. other
3. thick
4. other
5. shout, cry out
6. out, outside
7. dress, clothing
8. finger
9. again, other
10. life, spirit
11. time
12. cut
13. flower
14. back (of body)
15. to lead
16. inflammation of
17. swelling, tumor
18. sprout, shoot
19. increase
20. self
21. inside, within
22. work
23. marriage
24. weight, heavy
25. life
26. bend
27. make, do
28. to form, fashion
29. home
30. solid
31. milk
32. milk
33. movement
34. sleep
35. brother
36. seed, grain
37. break
38. fruit
39. slow
40. stomach
41. water
42. road, way
43. ball, globe
44. solid
45. carving
46. marrow
47. change
48. part
49. skin
50. choose
51. eat
52. nose
53. stone
54. step
55. bad, poor, harsh
56. with, together
57. beautiful
58. down, away, against
59. horn
60. brain
61. man
62. vessel, pod
63. joint (of body)
64. deep
65. book
66. moss
67. sing
68. link (of fence)
69. heat, burn
70. 100
71. puncture
72. green
73. color
74. close
75. world, universe
76. rule (of government)
77. believe, trust
78. cold
79. secret
80. strike against
81. circle
82. cell
83. people
84. tree
85. belief
86. run
87. sweet
88. outside
89. buy, purchase
90. leaf
91. rub against
92. knee
93. sword
94. ball, sphere
95. tongue, language
96. sweet
97. knowledge
98. angle
99. heavy
100. nude, naked
101. woman
102. chair, also, side
103. blood
104. other
105. same
106. sleep
107. under, below
108. uterus, womb
109. healing
110. fish
111. idol, image
112. under
113. to go
114. young
115. 1,000
116. light
117. big, large
118. mother
119. middle
120. mixture
121. memory
122. move
123. one, alone
124. shape, form
125. many
126. muscle
127. new
128. kidney
129. night
130. law
131. night
132. egg
133. egg-bearing
134. appetite
135. bird
136. ear
137. egg
138. sharp
139. backwards
140. alongside
141. hanging
142. punish
143. rock
144. sound
145. leaf
146. plant growth
147. to form
148. flat, broad
149. the common people
150. breathe
151. air, spirit
152. to grasp, seize
153. wing
154. fight with fists
155. point
156. ask, seek
157. scrape
158. backwards
159. strong
160. eat, gnaw
161. break
162. lizard
163. harden
164. see, look
165. write
166. old
167. six
168. star
169. body of person
170. sound
171. seek, look
172. breathe
173. star
174. turn, twist
175. build

176. under,
     below
177. from afar
178. draw, pull,
     drag
179. to thrust
180. shade
181. wave
182. one
183. worm
184. turn
185. way, road
186. substitute,
     change
187. see, look
188. conquer
189. man
190. life
191. call
192. roll
193. eat
194. yellow
195. stranger
196. dry
197. sword
198. wood
199. animal
200. ferment

Appendix E
Latin and Greek Equivalents for Common English Words

English meaning	Latin element	Greek element	Examples
across	trans-	dia-, meta-	transport, transfer; diagonal, diagnosis; metamorphosis
again	re-	ana-	repute, return; anadromous, analysis
against	ob-, contra-	anti-	obstruct, contradict; antonym, antidote
air	aer-	aero-, pneum-	aerate, aerial; aerobatics; pneumatic
all	omni-	pan-	omnivorous; pantheon
alone	soli-	mono-	solitude, soliloquy; monologue, monophobia
angle	angl-	gon-	rectangle, triangle; pentagon, polygon
animal (life)	anima-	zo-	animal, animated; zoography, zoology
around	circum-	peri-, cycl-	circumcise, circumference; perimeter, bicycle
around, both	ambi-	amphi-	ambidextrous; amphitheater
away	ab-, abs-, de-, re-	apo-	aberration, absent, depart, repudiate; apothecary, apostrophe
back, backwards	retro-	palin-	retroactive, retrogress; palindrome, palingraphia
bad, wrong	mal-	caco-, dys-	dismal, malicious; cacophony, dysentery
ball, globe	glob-, glom-	spher-	globular, conglomerate; spheroid, hemisphere
beauty	bell-	calli-	belle, embellish; calisthenics, calligraphy
beyond	super-	hyper-	superlative, supernal; hyperbole, hypertension
bird	avi-	ornith-	aviary, aviate; ornithology, ornithopter
birth	nat-	gen-	natal; genesis
blood	sang-	hemo-	sangria, sanguine; hemoglobin, hemophiliac
body	corp-	soma-	corpulent; chromosome
bone	oss-	oste-	ossein, ossicle; osteitis, osteocyte
book	libr-	biblio-, teuch-	library; bibliography, Pentateuch
bottom, deep	fund-	bathy-	fundamental; bathysphere
brain	cereb-	encephal-	cerebral; encephalitis
break (verb)	frac-, rupt-	clast-	fracture, rupture, erupt; anaclastic, iconoclast
breast	mamm-	masto-	mammal, mammary; mastitis, mastodon
breathe	spir-	pneum-	spirit, aspire, conspire; pneumonia, apnea

225

broad, wide	plac-	eury-, platy-	placoderm; euryphagous, aneurysm, platypus
call	voc-	cles-, clet-	vocation, avocation, evocation; ecclesia, paraclete
cancer	canc-	carcin-	cancer, cancroid; carcinogen, carcinoma
chest	pect-	stheth-	pectoral, expectorate; stethacoustic, stethoscope
circle	circ-	cycl-	circulate, circumference; cyclic, cyclone, bicycle
city	urb-	poli-, -polis	urban, suburb; police, cosmopolitan, metropolis
cold	frig-	cryo-, psychro-	frigid, refrigerate; cryobiology, psychroalgia
color	color-	chromo-	Colorado, discolor; chromatic, chromosome
corner	angl-	canth-, gon-	angle, triangle; epicanthus, decant, diagonal
cure, heal	cur-	-acea, iatr-	curator, cure; panacea, pediatrics, psychiatry
cut	sect-	tom-	bisect; atom
day	dia-	hemera-	diary; ephemeral
death	mort-	necr-	mortal; necrotomy
deep	fund-	bathy-	fundamental; bathysphere
dog	can-	cyn-	canine; cynical
down	de-	cata-	decline, depend; catalog, cathedral
drink	bib-, pot-	pos-	imbibe, potable; symposium
dry	sic-	xero-	siccative, dessicate; xeroderma, xerography, Xerox®
ear	aur-	oto-	aural, binaural; otocyst, otoscope
earth	terr-	geo-	territory; geography
eat	vor-	phag-	voracious, carnivore; phagocyte, euryphagous
egg	ov-	oo-	oval, ovary, ovum; oocyst, ootheca
empty	vac-	cen-	vacuous, evacuate; cenophobia, cenotaph
equal	equi-	iso-	equivalent; isobar
eye	ocul-	ophthm-	oculist; ophthmology
feather (related to *wing*)	penn-, plum-	pter-	pinnate, penniform, plumage; chiropter, helicopter
first	prim-	proto-	primary, primate; protocol, prototype
fish	pisc-	ichthy-	piscine, piscatology; ichthyology, ichthyophagous
five	cinq-, quin-	penta-	cinquefoil, quincunx; pentagon
flesh, meat	carni-	crea-	carnivorous; pancreas
flock	greg-	agora-	gregarious; agoraphobia
flow	flu-	rheo-	fluent; rheostat, diarrhea

flower	flor-	antho-	florid, Florida, effloresce; anthology, chrysanthemum
foot	ped-	pod-	pedestrian; podiatrist
form	fic-, fig-, form-	morph-, plas-	fiction, figure, formal, format; morpheme, plastic
four	quadr-, quat-	tetra-	quadrangle, quatrain; tetrachord, tetrahedron
fruit	fruct-	carp-	fructose, fructivorous; carpology, epicarp
full	plen-, plet-; sat-	pleth-	plenitude, replete, satisfy; plethora, isopleth
give	don-	dos-, dot-	donate; dose, antidote
globe	glob-, glom-	spher-	globule, hemoglobin; spheroid, hemisphere
go	ced-, it-	bat-	recede, itinerary; acrobat
God, god	dei-	theo-	deity; theology
good	bene-, bon-	eu-	benefit; eulogy
great	grand-, magn-	mega-	grandiloquent, grandiose, magnify; megaphone
green	verd-	chloro-	verdant; chlorophyll
guard	cust-, guard-, ward-	phylac-	custody, guardian, warden; phylactery, prophylactic
hair	capill-	trich-	capillary; trichinosis
hand	man-	chir-	manual, manufacture; chiropractor, chiropter
hard	dur-	scler-	durable, endure; schlerois, schleroderma
hate	od-	miso-	odious; misogamy
head	cap-	cephal-	capital; microcephalic
hear	aud-	acous-	audition; acoustics
heart	cord-	card-	accord, concordance; cardiologoy, carditis
heat	cal-	therm-	calorie; thermometer
heaven	celes-	uran-	celestial; uranography
heavy	grav-	baro-, bary-	gravity, aggravate; barometer, barysphere
hide (verb)	cond-	crypt-	abscond, recondite; cryptogram, encrypt
high, height	alt-, alti-	acro-	altitude; acrophobia
hollow, cell	cav-	cyt-	cavern; cytoblast
holy	sacr-, sanct-	hiero-	sacred, sanctify; hierocracy, hieroglyphics
horse	cav-, equ-	hippo-	cavalry, equestrian, equine; hippodrome, hippopotamus
hundred	cent-	hecto-	centurion, century; hectogram, hectometer
image	imag-	icon-	imaginary, imagine; icon, iconoclasm, iconolatry
inflammation	-itis	phlog-	bursitis; phlogistic
into, within	eso-	intro-	esoteric, esoneural; introduce, introject
join	jug-	zygo-	jugular, conjugate; zygodactyls. zygospore

kidney	ren-	nephr-	renal, adrenalin; nephritis, nephrotomy
knowledge	sci-	gnos-	science, conscience; diagnosis, prognosis
large	ampl-	macro-	ample, amplitude; macrodont, macrocephaly
lead (verb)	duc-	agog-	ductile, educate, educe; pedagogue, synagogue
leaf	foli-	phyll-	foliage, portfolio; phylloid, chlorophyll
life	anim-, vit-, viv-	bio-	animate, vital, revive; biology
light	luc-, lum-, lun-	photo-	lucid, luminesce, lunar; photograph, photosynthesis
line, thread	fil-, lin-	sticho-	filament, delineate; acrostic, hemistich
lip	lab-	chilo-	labial, labionasal; chiloma, chiloplasty
long	long-	macro-	longitude, elongate; macron, macrodont
love	am-	ero-, philo-	amatory, amorous; erogenous, philanthropy
man	hom-, masc-, vir-	anthropo-	homicide, masculine, virile, virtue; anthropology
many	multi-, plur-	poly-	multiple, plural; polyglot
marriage	marit-, nub-, nup-	gam-	marital, nubile, nuptial; bigamy, exogamy
memory	mem-	mne-	memory, remember; mnemonic, amnesia, amnesty
middle	med-	meso-	median, intermediate; mesomorphic, Mesopotomia
milk	lact-	galact-	lactate; galactagogue
mind	ment-	phren-, psych-	mental; phrenology, psychology
moon	lun-	seleno-	lunar, lunatic; selenography, selenology
more	extra-	hyper-	extracurricular; hypertension
mouth	or-	stoma-	oral; stomach
move	mob-, mot-	kine-	mobile, motile; kinetics
muscle (mouse)	mus-	myo-	muscle, muscular; myatrophy, myodynia
name	nom-	onomato-, -onym	nominal, nominate; onomatopoeia, antonym, synonym
navel	umbil-	omphal-	umbilicus; omphalos, omphalectomy
new	nov-	neo-	novel, renovate; neonate, neophyte
night	noc-, nox-	nyct-	nocturnal, equinox; nyctitropism, nycturia
nine	nov-	ennea-	November, novena; ennead
nourish	nurs-, nurt-	troph-	nurse, nourish; trophoblast, trophoplasm

nude, naked	nudi-	gymn-	nude, nudibranch; gymnasium, gymnophobia
old	sen-	ger-, presby-	senior, senator, señor; geriatrics, presbyacusis
one, single	uni-	mono-	unit, universe; monastery, monogram
one's own	propr-	idio-	property, proprietor; idiom, idioblast, idiosyncrasy
other	alter-	allo-, hetero-	alternate; allogamy, heterogamy, heterosexual
over	super-	epi-	superlative, superintendent; epidermis, epigram, eponym
pain	dol-	alg-, odyn-	condole, indolent; neuralgia, arthrodynia
people	popul-, pleb-, vulg-	demo-	population, populous; plebe, vulgar, promulgate; democracy, demography
place	loc-, sit-	theca-, thes-; topo-	location, situation; apothecary, hypothesis; topic, topography
puncture	punct-, pung-	cente-	punctilious, pungent; centesis, arthrocentesis
remember	mem-	mne-	memory, remember; mnemonic, amnesia, amnesty
rock	lapid-	petr-	lapidary, delapidate; petrel, petroleum
root	rad-	rhiz-	radical, eradicate; rhizoid, rhizopod
rule (verb)	rect-	crat-	direct; autocrat, democrat
run	curr-, curs-	drom-	current, cursive; dromedary, anadromous
salt	sal-	hal-	salami, salary; halophile, halophyte
same	sim-	homo-	similar, simultaneous; homogenize, homophone
see	vid-, vis-	scop-	video, vision; scope, telescope
seed	semin-	gon-	seminary, disseminate; gonad
self	ipse, sui-	auto-	ipse dixit, suicide; autograph, automobile
seven	sept-	hepta-	September, septet; heptad, heptagon
sharp	acu-	oxy-	acumen, acute; oxygen, oxymoron
short	brev-	brach-y	brevity; amphibrach
sing	cant-	od-	canticle, descant; ode, odeum, palinode
sit, seat	sed-, sess-	hedra-	sedative, session; cathedral, polyhedron
skin	cut-	derm-	cuticle, subcutaneous; dermatology, hypodermic
sleep	dorm-, somn-	hypn-	dormitory, somnolent, insomnia; hypnosis

slow	tard-	brady-	tardy, retardant; bradyacusia, bradyphagia
small	min-	micr-	minute; microscope
solid	rob-, sol-	stere-	robust, corroborate, solid; stereophonic, stereotype
sound	son-	phono-	sonogram, unison; phonograph, euphonious
speak	fess-, loq-	log-, phras-	confess, loquacious; dialogue, phraseology, paraphrase
split	fiss-	schiz-	fissure; schizophrenia
stand	stat-, stic-, stit-	stas-	statue, armistice, constitute; apostasy, ecstasy
star	sider-, stell	aster-	sidereal, consider, stellar; asteroid, astronaut
step	grad-	bat-	gradual, degradation; acrobat
stomach	ventr-	gastr-	ventral; gastritis
stone	lap-, petri-	litho-	lapidary, dilapidate, petrel, petrify; lithography, monolith
straight	rect-, reg-	ortho-	rectangle, correct, regular orthodox, orthopedics
stretch	tend-, tens-	-tasis	contend, intend, tension; epitasis, protasis
strong, strength	firm-, fort-	sthen-	firmament, confirm; forte, fortitude; asthenic, calisthenics
sweet	dulc-	glyc-	dulcet, dulcify; glycerine, hypoglycemia
sword	glad-	xipho-	gladiator, gladiolus; xiphoid, xiphophyllous
tail	caud-, cerc-, pen-	uro-	caudate, cercal, penicillin, penis; urochord
ten	dec-	deca-	decade; decagon
testicle, witness	test-	orchid-	testicle, testament; orchidectomy, orchiditis
thick	dens-	pachy-	density, condense; pachycephalic, pachyderm
thousand	mil-	kilo-	mile, millennium; kilocycle, kilometer
throw	ject-	ball-, bol-	project, reject; ballistic, hyperbole
time	temp-	chrono-	tempo, contemporary; chronograph, ananchronism
tongue	lingu-	gloss-, glot-	lingual, linguine; glossary, polyglot
tooth	dent-	odonto-	dental; orthodontics
tree	arb-	dendro-	arbor, arboreal; dendrology, philodendron
true (to think)	ver-	doc-, dog-	verity, verify; doctrine, dogma
turn	vers-, vert-	stroph-	verse, vertical; antistrophe, apostrophe
two	bi-	di-	bicycle; dilemma
under	sub-, infra-	hypo-	subtract, infrastructure; hypotenuse, hypothesis

vein	ven-	phleb-	intravenous; phlebotomy
vessel	vas-	angi-	vase, vascular; angiogram, hydrangea
water	aqua-, rig-	hydr-	aquatic, aquamarine, irrigate; hydrangea, hydraulic
way	via-	odo-	viaduct, obvious, trivia; odometer, exodus
white	alb-	leuk-	albumin; leukemia
wing	ali-	pter-	aliform; helicopter
with, together	com-, con-	sym-, syn-	committee, contest; sympathy, synchronous
within	intra-, intro-	endo-	intramural, introduce; endocardium, endodontics
woman, female	fem-	gyne-	female, feminine; gynecology, monogyny
womb	uter-	hyster-	uterus, intrauterine; hysteria, hysterectomy
world	mund-	cosmo-	mundane; cosmology
worm	verm-	helminth-	vermicelli, vermin; helminthiasis, platyhelminth
wound	vuln-	trauma-	vulnerable; traumatic
write	scrib-, scrip-	gram-, graph-	describe, scripture; diagram calligraphy, paragraph
wrong, bad	mal-	dys-	malform; dysentery
yellow	flav-	xanth-	flavescent, riboflavin; xanthogenic, xanthophyll
young	jun-, juven-	hebe-	junior, juvenile; hebephilia, hebiatrics

LIST OF WORKS MOST FREQUENTLY CONSULTED

Abrams, M. H., *A Glossary of Literary Terms*, Third Edition. New York: Holt, Rinehart and Winston, 1971.

Alexander, Henry, *The Story of Our Language*. Garden City, New York: Dolphin Books (Doubleday & Company, Inc.), 1962.

American Heritage Dictionary of the English Language, The. Boston: Houghton Mifflin Company, 1975.

Arlotto, Anthony, *Introduction to Historical Linguistics*. Boston: Houghton Mifflin Company, 1972.

Ayers, Donald M., *English Words from Latin and Greek Elements*. Tucson: The University of Arizona Press, 1965.

Bartlett, John, *Familiar Quotations*. Boston: Little, Brown and Company, 1980.

Beiser, Arthur, *Applied Physics*, Third Edition. New York: McGraw-Hill, Inc., 1995

Black, Henry Campbell, *Black's Law Dictionary*. St. Paul: West Publishing Co., 1979.

Borror, Donald J., *Dictionary of Word Roots and Combining Forms*. Palo Alto: Mayfield Publishing Company, 1960.

Brusaw, Charles T. et al., *Handbook of Technical Writing*, Second Edition. New York: St. Martin's Press, 1982.

Burris, Eli E., *Latin and Greek in Current Use*, Second Edition. Englewood Cliffs, NJ: Prentice-Hall, Inc. 1949.

Bynon, Theodora, *Historical Linguistics*. Cambridge: Cambridge University Press, 1977.

Castillo, Carlos, *Spanish Dictionary*. Chicago: The University of Chicago Press, 1948.

Ciardi, John, *A Browser's Dictionary*. New York: Harper & Row, Publishers, 1980.

_____, *Good Words to You*. New York: Harper & Row, Publishers, 1987.

Colwell, C. Carter, *A Student's Guide to Literature*. New York: Washington Square Press, 1968.

Davis, Nancy B., *Basic Vocabulary Skills*. New York: McGraw-Hill Book Company, 1969.

Durant, Will, *The Story of Philosophy*. New York: Washington Square Press, 1961.

Freeman, Morton S., *The Story Behind the Word*. Philadelphia: ISI (Institute for Scientific Information) Press, 1985.

Funk, Peter, "It Pays to Increase Your Word Power," *Reader's Digest* monthly columns.

Funk, Wilfred, *Word Origins and Their Romantic Stories*. New York: Bell Publishing Company, 1978.

Grant, Michael, *Greek and Latin Authors, 800 B.C–A.D. 1000*. New York: The H. W. Wilson Co., 1980.

Greene, Amsel, *Word Clues, The Vocabulary Builder*. New York: Harper & Row, Publishers, Inc., 1984.

Hacker, Diane, A Writer's Reference, Fifth Edition. Boston/New York: Bedford/St. Martin's, 2003.

Hart, Archibald, *Twelve Ways to Build a Vocabulary*. New York: Barnes & Noble, Inc., 1967.

_____, *The Latin Key to Better English*. New York: E. P. Hutton & Company, 1942.

_____, *The Growing Vocabulary, Fun and Adventure with Words*. New York: E. P. Dutton & Company, 1947.

Harvard Dictionary of Music, Willi Apel, Ed. Cambridge: Harvard University Press, 1944.

Hendrickson, Robert, *Human Words*. Philadelphia: Clinton Book Company, 1972.

Hill, Robert H., *A Dictionary of Difficult Words*. New York: The New American Library, Inc., 1979.

Interesting Origins of English Words. Springfield, Massachusetts: G. & C. Merriam Company, 1961.

Jespersen, Otto, *Growth and Structure of the English Language*. New York: The Free Press, 1968.

Johnson, Edwin Lee, *Latin Words of Common English*. New York: D.C. Heath and Company, 1931.

Laird, Charlton, *The Miracle of Language*. Greenwich, Connecticut: Fawcett Publications, 1953.

Lederer, Richard, *The Miracle of Language*. New York: Pocket Books, 1991.

Leggett, Glenn, et al., *Prentice-Hall Handbook for Writers*, 7th Edition. Englewood Cliffs, New Jersey: Prentice-Hall, 1978.

Lewis, Norman, *Better English, Revised Edition*. New York: Dell Publishing Co., Inc., 1956.

Lord, Robert, *Comparative Linguistics*. London: The English Universities Press, Ltd., 1966.

Luschning, C.A.E., et al., *Etyma: An Introduction to Vocabulary-Building from Latin and Greek*. Lanham, Maryland: University Press of America, 1982.

Maleska, Eugene T., *A Pleasure in Words*. New York: Simon and Schuster, 1981.

Mawson, C. O. Sylvester, *Dictionary of Foreign Terms*, Second Edition. New York: Barnes & Noble Books, 1975.

Morris, William and Mary, *Dictionary of Word and Phrase Origins*. New York: Harper & Row, Publishers, 1962.

New Cassell's German Dictionary, The. New York: Funk & Wagnalls, 1962.

Nurnberg, Maxwell, et al., *All about Words*. New York: The New American Library, 1968.

Page, Kogan, *Le Mot Juste: A Dictionary of Classical & Foreign Words & Phrases*. New York: Vintage Books (Random House), 1980.

Partridge, Eric, Origins: *A Short Etymological Dictionary of Modern English*. New York: The Macmillan Company, 1961.

Pei, Mario, *The Story of the English Language*. New York: Simon and Schuster, 1967.

Price, A. Rae, *Developing Your Vocabulary*. Dubuque, Iowa: Wm. C. Brown Company Publishers, 1973.

Random House Dictionary of the English Language, The, College Edition. New York: Random House, 1968.

Robertson, Stuart, et al., *The Development of Modern English*, Second Edition. Englewood Cliffs, New Jersey: Prentice-Hall, Inc., 1954.

Roget's International Thesaurus. New York: Thomas Y. Crowell Company, 1946.

Roget's II: The New Thesaurus. Boston: Houghton Mifflin Company, 1980.

Sabin, Frances E., *Classical Myths That Live Today*. New York: Silver Burdett Company, 1940.

Schur, Norman, *1,000 Most Important Words*. New York: Ballantine Books, 1982.

Shaw, Harry, *Spell It Right!* New York: Barnes & Noble, Inc., 1961.

Skillin, Marjorie E., et al., *Words into Type*. Englewood Cliffs, New Jersey: Prentice-Hall, Inc., 1974.

Smith, Robert W. L., *Dictionary of English Word Roots*. Totowa, New Jersey: Littlefield, Adams & Co., 1966.

Taber's Cyclopedic Medical Dictionary, Edition 14. Philadelphia: F. A. Davis Company, 1981.

Thrall, William Flint, et al., *A Handbook to Literature*. Indianapolis: The Odyssey Press, 1960.

Tulleja, Tad, *Namesakes*. New York: McGraw-Hill Book Company, 1987.

Urdang, Lawrence, *Picturesque Expressions*. Detroit: Gale Research Company, 1980.

Webster's New World Dictionary of the American Language, Fourth College Edition. New York, 1999.

Webster's Third New International Dictionary of the English Language, Unabridged. Springfield, Massachusetts: G. & C. Merriam Company, Publishers, 1976.

Williams, Joseph M., *Origins of the English Language*: A Social and Linguistic History. New York: The Free Press, 1975.

INDEX OF SPECIAL WORD GROUPS

GENERAL INDEX

amend, 55
American Indian Words
  Adirondack, 36
  Alabama, 109
  Arizona, 92
  Baton Rouge, LA, 149
  Biloxi, MS, 62
  caucus, 181
  chinquapin, 135
  chipmunk, 47
  Equinunc, PA, 75
  Erie, PA, 149
  hickory, 47
  menhaden, 47
  Miami, FL, 146
  Michigan, 146
  Mississippi River, 127
  moose, 47
  Natchez, MS, 187
  Okefenokee, 43
  Oklahoma, 103
  pecan, 135
  Pensacola, FL, 111
  persimmon, 135
  poncho, 8
  powwow, 48
  raccoon, 48
  Schenectady, NY, 125
  skunk, 48
  Spokane, WA, 34
  Tallahassee, FL, 90
  tepee, 48
  Texas, 121
  tomahawk, 47
  Tombigbee River, AL, 146
  Tuscaloosa, AL, 196
  wapiti, 47
  Wyoming, 193
Amherst College, Motto of, 191
ami- (**friend**) words, 171
amicable:friendly, 31
amigo, 171
Amite, VA, 96
amnesia, amnesty, 74, 208
amorous, 187
amorphia, 209
amortize, 131
ampere (amp), 59
ampersand, 171
amphi- (**around**) words, 5, 39
amphiblastula, 34
amphibole, 39, 101
amphibrach, 6, 39
amphimacer, 6, 208

amphimixis, 5, 39, 208
amphitheater, 39
ampulla, 187
amputate, 5
an- (**negative**) words, 177
ana- (**again**) words, 22
anachorism, 92
anachronism, 22 (twice)
anadromous, 22, 206
anakatadidymus, 22
analgesia, 72, 177
analogous, 119
anamnesis, 22, 208
ananaphylaxis, 22
anandria, 204
anapest, 22, 169
anaphora, 22, 155
anaplasty, 22, 210
anapnea, 211
anasomia, 212
anastomosis, 145
anastrophe, 22, 212
anathema, 22, 118
anatomy, 22, 23
ancestor, 9, 181
Anchorage, AK, 136
ancient, 9
andante, 5
andouille, 181
andro- (**man**) words, 204
androgenous, 133, 204
androgynous, 204, 207
android, 204
anecdote, 74, 177
anemia, 1, 207
anesthesia, 14, 177
ang- (**pain**) words, 72
anger:ire, 185
angi- (**vessel**) words, 204
angioblast, 34, 204
Anglo-Saxon (Old English) words
  aern (**house**), 166
  Angleland (**England**), 167
  angnaegl (**hangnail**), 72
  antefin (**anthem**), 10
  bana (**murderer**), 141
  beleogan (**to belie**), 162
  bricg (**bridge**), 22
  brustian (**browse**), 43
  brothor (**brother**), 167
  cene (**keen**), 158
  cwealm (**qualm**), 24
  cwellan (**to kill; to quell**), 166
  cwencan (**to quench**), 166

cwethan (**to say**), 92
deore (**dear; high-priced**), 131
endleofan (**eleven**), 20
færthing (**farthing**), 161
feoh (**fee: cattle**), 98
feond (**fiend: the one hating**), 100
feower (**four**), 162
freond (**friend**), 114
furlang (**furlong**) 167
gainsay, 31, 46, 132
gar (**spear**), 119
geloma (**utensil, tool**), 92
glad (**glade**), 47
grisan (**to shudder with fear:
  grisly**), 157
haerfest (**harvest**), 155
heofon (**heaven**), 26
hlæfdige (**loaf-kneader: lady**), 167
hlafordic (**lordly**), 165
hlafwærd (**loaf-ward: lord**), 167
hleapan (**to leap**), 21
hrif (**belly**), 50
husbonde (**housebound:
  husband**), 196
kith (**sprig**), 50
leac (**leek**), 119
leggen (**to lie flat; ledger**), 9
lengten (**to lengthen**), 168
mitwif (**midwife**), 167
monandaeg (**Monday**), 53
mydhrif (**midriff**), 32
mynster (**minster: church**), 21
myrge (**merry**), 22
neahgebur (**neighbor**), 167, 185
nog (**beer, ale**), 114
pitha (**pith**), 67
saed (**sad**), 172
soth (**sooth: truth**), 151
statholwyrthe (**stalwart**), 69
stig (**sty**), 172
stiweard (**sty-ward: steward**), 167
taecan (**to teach**), 66
teoth (**tenth**), 58
thræll (**thrall**), 83
thymel (**thimble**), 110
treow (**true, faith**), 60, 80
twalif (**twelve**), 20
wærleogan (**warlock**), 108, 167
weardian (**to ward, guard**), 112
wik (**village**), 112
Woden, 113
wordhoard, 48
wulf (**wolf**), 22
anima- (**life, soul**) words, 22

Animals, or Words Pertaining to
aardvark, 192
alligator, 27
altricial, 57
amble, ambulatorial, 6
amphibian, 5, 39
amphibiotic, 5, 39
amphipod, 39, 151
anadromous, 22, 206
anserine, 73
antlers, 10, 141
aquiline, 73
arachnivorous, 73
armadillo, armature, 12
arrect, 164
asinine, 73
Augensprossen, 10, 141
bantam, 44
behemoth, 12
bellwether, 24
borzoi, 56
bovine, 73
brachiation, 6
brevicaudate, brevipennate,
  brevirostrate, 21
cacomistle, 156
callisection, 173
camerata, 26
canine, caprine, 73
carnassial, 34
carnivorous, 34, 73, 214
cerastes, 189
cattle, 32
chamois, 108
cheetah, 53
Chihuahua, 38
chipmunk, 47
chiropter, 126
clamatorial, 13
corgi, 27
corvine, 73
cuirass, 33
curtal, 172
cynophilist, 28
decoy, 6
denizen, 177
destrier, 12
digitigrade, 145
dinoceros, 189
dinosaur, 211
diurnal, 104
dromedary, 107
elephant, 5
epibenthos, 140

epizoic, 139
epizoon, epizootic, 214
equine, 73
estray, 66
ewe, 137
fang, 148
feline, 73
Fido, 58
gelding, 67
gemsbok, 108
goose, geese, 45
grizzly, 157
halcyon, 92
herbivorous, 73, 214
hippopotamus, 5, 12
hircine, 73
holotype, 167
jaguar, 36
jumbo, 197
kennel, 28
Lhasa apso, 146
mammoth, 56
mastiff, 208
mastodont, 64
mongoose, 45, 53
moose, 47
moult, 28
mule, 208
mushing dog, 69
mustang, 69, 208
nidifugous, 86
octopus, 62
omnivorous, 144
oology, 209
ophidian, 1
orangutan, 2
oriole, 175
orthograde, 145, 163
ossifrage (osprey), 91
ossivorous, 73
ovine, 73, 137
pachyderm, 5, 117
pavonine, 73
petrel, 210
pheasant, 8
phoenix (mythological), 160
plantigrade, 145
platypus, 152, 210
polecat, 95
polygyny, 153, 207
porpoise, 154
prehensile, 211
primate, 160
proboscis, 214

pronograde, 145
pterodactyl, 21, 211
pteropod, 152, 211
punctate, 89
quail, 13
quarter horse, 162
raccoon, 47
reins, 188
remuda, 113
retractable, 213
rhinoceros, 5, 135, 189
saiga, 189
salacious, salmon, 182
saltigrade, 145, 182
saltire, 182
skunk, 47
springbok, 182
squirrel, 103
taurine, 73
terrarium, 192
triceratops, 189, 195
ursine, 73
veterinarian, 31
vulpine, 73
wapiti, 47
xanthocephalus, 213
Zehnender, 57
animosity, 22
ann- (**year**) words, 7
annals, 8
Annapolis, MD, 65
anniversary, 7, 213
anno Domini, 7
annoy, 1, 96, 133
anodyne, 71
anomaly, 71, 207
anonymous, 135
anorexia, 177, 209
antagonist, 9, 45, 58
ante- (**before**) words, 9
ante meridiem, 9, 67
ante mortem, 9, 131
antebellum, 9
antediluvian, 9, 109
antejuramentum, 9, 105
antenatal, 9, 133
anteocular (see *antlers*), 10
antependium, 9, 210
anteversion, 10, 213
anthem, 9, 25, 77
anther, 25
antho- (**flower**) words, 25
anthropo- (**man**) words, 36, 93, 204
anthropocentric, 36, 204

anthropoid, 64, 204
anthropomorphic, 36, 93, 204
anthropophagi, 94, 204
anti- (against) words, 9, 45
anticipate, 9, 29
anticlimax, 45
antidote, 9, 45, 73
antinomy, 45, 209
antipasto, 10
antiphony, 9, 45, 210
Antisthenes, 27
antistrophe, 9, 212
antithesis, 45, 117, 190
antlers, 10, 141
antonomasia, 45, 135
antonym, 45, 135
apartheid, 150
aperçu, 1
aperture, 129
aphasia, 77
aphelion, 36, 71, 157
aphorism, 132, 157

Aphorisms, Examples of (see also
   Exalted Aphorisms)
   bird in the hand, 19
   burnt child, 3
   cake, having; eating it, 119
   changing horses, 17
   crooked stick, 137
   foolish fish, 33
   geese, swans, 107
   great cry, little wool, 112
   lead a horse to water, 117
   pilot in a calm sea, 117
   ride a free horse, 117
   sailing in an eggshell, 117
   seven captains, 97
   small fish, empty dish, 123
   sticks and stones, 126
   too many cooks, 97
   wise men and fools, 118
aphyllous, 210
aplanatic, 132
aplomb, 105
apnea, 211
apo- (away) words, 157
apocalypse, 157
Apocrypha, 157, 205
apodosis, 157
apogamy, 4, 44, 157
apogee, 157, 192
apogeotropism, 191
apologue, apology, 120, 157
apophysis, 78, 157

aposiopesis, 158
apostasy, 157, 179
apostle, 130, 157
apostrophe, 158, 212
apothecary, 117, 157
apothem, 157
apotheosis, 59, 157
apparel:clothes, 185
appease, 148
appellation:name, 199
appendectomy, 23
appendicitis, 26
appertain, 188
appetite, 86
applaud, 16
appoggiatura, 151
appoint, 211
apport, 155
appreciate, 145
apprehend, apprentice, apprise, 211
appurtenance, 188
apricot, 56, 127

Arabic Words
   admiral, 41, 115
   albacore, 1, 66, 115
   albatross, 2, 66, 115
   alcohol, 66
   alcove, 66
   alfalfa, 47
   algebra, 66, 115
   Alhambra, 66
   amber, 47
   ameer, 125
   azimuth, 47
   cotton, 47
   drub, 41
   emir, 125
   Hegira, 8
   magazine, 60, 115
   mattress, 47, 82, 115
   monsoon, 9
   mortise and tenon, 188
   nabob, 3
   nadir, 53, 115
   Ramadan, 167
   safari, 115, 147
   saffron, 47
   Sahara, 115, 147
   spinach, 115
   sugar, 47
   Swahili, 175
   syrup, 47
   talisman, 82
   zenith, 49, 115

zero, 47
arbor- (tree) words, 206
arcane, 38
Arcanum, OH, 38
archegonium, 134
Architectural Terms
   abattoir, 16, 186
   abat-voix, 16, 213
   acrolith, 3
   Acropolis, 4
   adobe, 47, 163
   agora, 87
   alcove, 47, 66
   ambulacrum, ambulatory, 6
   amphiprostyle, 5, 58
   amphistylar, 5
   amphitheater, 39
   anteroom, 9
   architrave, 58
   auditorium, 14
   baroque, 142
   berm, 129
   boiserie, 103
   bungalow, 53
   cairn, 171
   candelabrum, 1
   cantilever, 127
   capital, capitol, 32
   cathedral, 176, 207
   chancel, 173
   chimney, 26, 61
   clerestory, 42
   cloister, 44, 205
   coliseum, 40
   column, 135
   concourse, 1
   condominium, 147
   contraflexure, 46
   corridor, 1
   cromlech, 50, 123
   decastyle, 58
   dolmen, 50, 123
   dormer, 87
   dungeon, 33
   Eiffel Tower, 15
   epistyle, 58
   façade, 131
   fascia, 5
   Ferris wheel, 26
   gentrify, 159
   gymnasium, 50, 207
   ha-ha, 59
   hypostyle, 58
   intrados, 25, 99, 189

cytozoic, 214

da capo, 31
dacha, 74
dactyl- (**finger**) words, 21
dactyl, 21, 169
dahlia, 78
daisy, 67, 141
damsel, 125
dance, 10, 190
Dances; Dance Terms
   antistrophe, 9, 212
   ball, ballet, 101
   beguine, 54
   canary, 28
   choreography, 171
   courante, 1
   dance, 10, 190
   do-si-do, 25
   jeté, 101
   leotard, 155
   minuet, 128
   orchestra, 171
   polka, polonaise, 165
   port de bras, 156
   sequidilla, 173
   shindig, 130
   suite, 174
   tarantella, 166
   trio, 196
dandelion, 64
danger, 35
Das Kapital, 31
date, dative, 74
daub, 2
daughter, 197
deacon, 193
dean, 58
dearth, 131
débat, 15
debauch, 88
debenture, 90
debonair, 18
debt, 90
debut, 46
dec-, deca- (**ten**) words, 57
decadent, 38
decalescent, 23
Decalogue, 58, 119
Decameron, 58
decamp, 142
decapitate:behead, 185
Decapolis, 58, 65
decathlon, 58

decay, 37
deceit, deceive, 29
decelerate, 71
December, 58, 165
decemvir, 58
deception, 29
deci- (**tenth**) words, 57
decibel, 58
deciduous, 37
decimate, 58
declaim, 13
declarative, declare, 42
decoupage, 38
decumbent, 54
decussate, 6, 58
define, 82
defoliate, 206
defray, 91
defy, 80
degrade, degree, degression, 145
dei- (**god, God**) words, 59
deictic, 65
deific, 59
deism, 60
dejected, 101
Delaware, University of, Motto of, 101
delicatessen, 3
delineate:draw, 185
delirium, 109
deliver, 113
deluge, 110
demagogue, 205
demand, 125
demise, 130
demitasse, 143
demiurge, 43, 205
demo- (**people**) words, 62, 205
demon- (**demon, devil**) words, 61
demoniac, demonolatry, 62
demonstrate, 171
Demopolis, AL, 6, 205
demote, 208
demurrer, 113
dendro- (**tree**) words, 206
denim, 97
denizen, 98, 177
denomination, 135
dent- (**tooth**) words, 63
dent corn, 64
dentifrice, 63, 206
dentiloquy, 63, 119
dentoid, 64
dentro (Spanish), 99

Denver, University of, Motto of, 99
deo- (**god, God**) words, 59
Deo Volente, MS, 59
deodand, 73
depend, 210
deport, 155
deprecate, depreciate, 145
deracinate, 211
derm- (**skin**) words, 117
descant, 70, 204
describe, 211
desecrate, 170
desegregation, 87
desiderative, desire, 212
desist, 180
despise, 212
dessert, 70
destitute, 180
destroy, destruction, 212
desultory, 182
detain, 187
détente, 190
detrude, 213
deuce, 19
deus ex machina, 59
deuterogamy, 4, 44
Deuteronomy, 58, 209
deviate, devious, 213
devolve, 214
Dewer, Sir James, 24
dexter, 12
di- (**two**) words, 19
di-, dis- (**negative**) words, 69
dia- (**across**) words, 42, 193
diachron, 22, 193
diagnose, 193, 206
diagonal, 194, 207
dialysis, 193
diameter, diamond, 194
diapason, 144, 193
diaphanous, 42, 193
Diaries (67)
   Burney, Fanny
   Byrd, John
   Evelyn, John
   Fox, George
   Knight, Sarah K.
   Pepys, Samuel
   Sewell, Samuel
   Swift, Jonathan
   Wesley, John
   Whitelock, Bulstrode
diarrhea, 83, 193
diary, 68

terrarium, 192
terrestrial:earthly, 185
terricolous, 192
terrify:scare, 199
tessera, 161
test- (**witness**) words, 195
testicle, 86
tête-bêche, 19
tetra- (**four**) words, 161
tetrahedron, 161, 175, 207
tetralogy, 162
Texas, University of, Motto of, 175
thanat- (**death**) words, 131
"Thanatopsis," 131
theo- (**God**) words, 59, 199
theocracy, 59, 205
theodicy, 65
Theology Terms (see Religion and Theology Terms)
theophany, 42
therm- (**heat**) words, 23
Thermos®, 24
thermostat, 179
thesaurus, 60, 77
-thesis (**a placing**) words, 117, 190
thesis, theses, 9
thin, 190
thin:emaciated, 199
thorax, 187
Thoreau, Henry David, 194
thyroid, 187
tiffany, 41
tig- (**to touch**) words, 185
timorous, 91
Timothy, 59
tin- (**to hold**) words, 187
tinsel, 30
Titles of Persons
  admiral, 41, 115
  ameer, 125
  colonel, 41
  dean, 58
  doyen, 57
  duchess, duke, 25
  emeer, 125
  Führer, 155
  Il Duce, 25
  jumbo, 197
  lieutenant, 118
  mahatma, 122, 131, 148
  mahout, 131
  marquis, 96
  pharaoh, 187
  principal, 159

rajah, 81
rani, 81
sahib, 53
sergeant, 135
swami, 53
viscount, 213
tmesis, 81
Tochter, 150
tom- (**to cut**) words, 23
tomahawk, 47
tomato, 115
tome, 23
tongue:language, 185
tonsillitis, 26
torrid, 192
town, 26
tract- (**to pull**, **draw**) words, 213
tractate, tractable, tractile, tractor, 213
trade winds, 59
tradition, traducianism, 194
tragedy, 20
traitor, 74, 194
trajectory, 101, 193
tranquil, 194
trans- (**across**) words, 193
transcend, 194
transient, transit, 193, 208
transilient, 182
transitive, transistor, 194
translate, 155, 193
transmission, 129, 193
transmutation, 113, 193
transom, 193
transport, 156, 193
transubstantiation, 34, 193
transverse, 194
transvestite, 15, 194
trapezium, 161
travail:travel, 196
travesty, treason, 194
trefoil, 196
trellis, 195
trep- (**to tremble**) words, 86
trespass, 193
tri- (**three**) words, 195
tribrach, 22
tribune, 195
triceps, 20, 195
tricinium, 19
triglyph, 111, 195
trigonometry, 195, 207
triliteral, 116
trillium, 196

Trinity:Trinidad, 196
trio, 196
trit- (**to rub**) words, 24
trivial, 196, 213
trochaic, 169
trop- (**to turn**) words, 5, 163
troph- (**to nourish, feed**) words, 127
trud- (**to thrust**) words, 213
truth:veracity, 199
tumor, 28
turban, 46
tureen, 192
turmeric, 191
twain, 20
tweed, 191
twelve, 20
tycoon, 35, 43
tympani, 79
typhoon, 35
tyrannosaurus, 211

ubiquitous, 100
ukulele, 180
ul- (**tail**) words [see *adulate*], 44
ulterior, ultimate, ultimo, 198
ultra- (**beyond**) words, 197
ultramontane, ultramundane, 198
umbilical, 187
umbra- (**shade**) words, 213
umbrella, 213
umlaut, 6
umpire, 138, 149
unagi, 35
unanimous, 22, 213, 214
unassuming, 93
unda- (**a wave**) words, 184, 213
unfriendly:inimical, 199
uni- (**one**) words, 213
unicameral, 20, 26, 213
unijugate, 107, 213
unique, 2
unjust, 106
unload:exonerate, 199
unreadable:illegible, 199
untenable, 188
Upanishad, 175
uproot:eradicate, 199
uterus, 92
utopia, 4
utterance, 198
uxoricide, 38, 114
uxorious, 114

vagabond, 23
vagina, 31, 86

retreat, 57
retrogress, 211
retrude, 213
ridicule, 48
sabotage, 18
sack (**to loot**), 55
sacrifice, 170
sally, 182
salute, 168
salvage, 168
sate, saturate, 172
scrutinize, 146
search, 40
secede, 181
segregate, 88
segue, 174
shamble, 186
shampoo, 184
sluice, 28
snoop, 25
sojourn, 104
speculate, 212
succeed, 181
succor, 1
surcharge, 184
surge, 164
surmise, 130, 184
surprise, 180
surround, 184
surtax, 94
survey, 184
tarnish, 76
transcend, 194
transliterate, 116
transmogrify, 71
transport, 156
transverse, 194
umpire, 138
vandalize, 55
vanquish, vindictive, 213
vitiate, 72
vituperate, 137
verdict, 66
verdure, 69
veri- (**true**) words, 206
verm- (**worm**) words, 213
vermicelli, 178, 213
vermillion:red, 185
Vermont, University of, Motto of, 51
vermouth, 185
vers-, vert- (**to turn**) words, 213
vest- (**to clothe**) words, 15
vestige, 146

veto, 114
vey-, via- (**a way**) words, 213
via (in *a writing tip*), 3
via dolorosa, 71
viaduct, 25, 213
viaticum, 29, 213
vic- (**change, substitute**) words, 213
vic-, vict- (**to conquer**) words, 213
vid- (**to see**) words, 18, 213
Vietnam, 41
vigil- (**to watch**) words, 61
vignette, 90
villain:knave, 185
-ville (**placename suffix**), 121
vinc- (**to conquer**) words, 213
vindauga, 141
vinegar, 50
vintage, 206
vir- (**man**) words, 102, 213
Virginia, State of, Motto of, 189
virtual, 102, 213
vis- (**to see**) words, 18, 213
vit- (**life**) words, 213
vitri- (**glass**) words, 125
vituperate, 137
viv- (**life**) words, 213
voc- (**to call**) words, 213
vodka, 77
voice, 213
vol- (**to be willing**) words, 214
volition, 214
volleyball, 180
volt, 59
volunteer, 214
volv- (**to turn**) words, 214
vor- (**to eat**) words, 144, 214
voracious, 144
-vorous (**of eating**) words, 73, 214
voy- (**a way**) words, 213
voyage, 29, 213
voyeur, 213
vulg- (**common people**) words, 30

walk:ambulate, 199
Walpole, Horace (collected letters of), 115
Wanderjahr, 7
Weapons, and Words Relating to
bayonet, 11
boomerang, 147
foible, 11
forte, 31
glaive, 206
howitzer, 101

poniard, 211
projectile, 102
saber, 31
scutum, 179
shrapnel, 153
tomahawk, 47
wappenschawing, 11
Weather Words
anticyclone, 45
col, 106
cyclone, hurricane, 93
monsoon, 9
tornado, 69
trade winds, 59
Wednesday, 53
Weihnachten, 169
werfen, 101
Wesley, John (diary of), 67
West Virginia, State of, Motto of, 113
whiskey, 77
Whitelock, Bulstrode (diary of), 67
wholesome:salubrious, 199
-wick (**placename suffix**), 121
Wilde, Oscar, 157
window, 10, 142
wisteria, 78
witchcraft:sorcery, 185
Woolman, John (journal of), 103
wordanalysis (*enemy* and *inimical*) 96
wordbuilders
acu- (**sharp**), 210
allo- (**other**), 5
alt-, alter- (**other**), 7
ana- (**again**), 22
andr- (**man**), 204
angi- (**vessel**), 204
anima- (**life, spirit**), 22
antho- (**flower**), 25
arthr- (**joint**), 204
auct-, aug- (**to increase**), 41
auto- (**self**), 41
aux- (**to increase**), 41
avi- (**bird**), 209
baro- (**weight**), 44
bathy- (**deep**), 204
biblio- (**book**), 204
bio- (**life**), 51
blast- (**bud, shoot**), 34
brady- (**slow**), 94
bryo- (**moss**), 204
caco- (**bad, abnormal**), 156
calli- (**beautiful**), 173

Au (**chemical symbol**), 39
August, 165
austere, 85
Austin, TX, 145
autophobia, 159
auxiliary, 191
avarice, 88
avocado, 27
avuncular, 149
axel, 71
axis, 9
azalea, 46
azimuth, 47
azure, 46
bacterium, 2
bagel, 176
bail, bailiff, bailiwick, 112
Baja California, 9
baksheesh, 46
banal, 45
bandanna, 85
bandit, 83
bane, 141
bangle, 53
banshee, 54
bantam, 44
barber, 13
Bar Mitzvah, 57, 165
barn, 166
baroque, 142
barrister, 113
barter, 43
BASIC (**computer language**), 33
BASIC English, 33
Bath Mitzvah, 57, 165
Baton Rouge, LA, 149
baud, 60
bayonet, 11
bazaar, 22
beaucoup, 103
beguine, 54
Beijing, 61
belfry, 141
belie, 162
bellwether, 24
bemuse, 91
Benelux countries, 81
bequeath, bequest, 92
berceuse, 59
berm, 129
Bernoulli, 60
Bessemer, AL, 79
bête noire, 30
bikini, 5

Biloxi, MS, 62
bishop, 119
Bismarck, ND, 139
bit (**computer term**), 60
bivouac, 181
bizarre, 22
blatant, 103
blight, 104
blintz, 176
blithe, 27
Boca Raton, FL, 122
Boise, ID, 103
bond paper, 64
boneset, 68
bonsai, 43
boomerang, 147
boondocks, 1
booty, 9
borsch, 56
borzoi, 56
bouillabaisse, 105
boulder; Boulder, CO, 181
bourbon, 185
bovine, 73
brat (Russian), 12
bric-a-brac, 3
broach, 105
brobdingnagian, 144
brogan, brogue, 165
brother, 12
browse, 43
brusque, 25
budget, 76
buenos dias, 172
Buffalo, NY, 146
bungalow, 53
bureau, 7
-burg (placename suffix), 159
burgeon, 107
bursa, 187
bursitis, 63
butler, 91
butte, 151
butter, 181
cabal, 47
caboose, 61
café, 47
cairn, 171
cajole, 111
California, 123
callow, 109
calm, 106, 204
candidate, 175
canine, 73

canorous, 85
cantilever, 127
canvas, canvass, 33
caprine, 73
carat, 133
caravan, 46, 166
caret, 132
cashier, 73
cashmere, 53
castigate, castrate, 7
catacomb, 88
catafalque, 55
catamaran, 87
cater, 17
catharsis, 178
caucus, 181
cavil, 17
CCCP, 175
cede, 181
celerity, 71
celibate, 112
Celsius, 54
cereal, 13
cermet, 49
chagrin, 98
chalcography, 168
chambray, 97
champagne, 185
chancellor, 173
charisma, 87
charity, 127
chasm, 113
chaste, chasten, chastity, 7
chasuble, 159
chaussure, 147
check, 46
checkmate, 46
cheddar, 6
cheetah, 53
Chef Menteur, 149
chess, 46
chicory, 47
chignon, 37
Chihuahua, 38
chiliarch, chiliasm, 167
chimney, 61
chinquapin, 135
chintz, 53
chipmunk, 47
chit, 53
chocolate, 115
chopsticks, 101
chortle, 152
chronic, 61

chutzpah, 176
ciao, 181
cicatrix, 139
Cincinnati, OH, 53
clavicle, 187
clemency, 114
clique, 137
cloak, 11
cockroach, 55
coffee, 47
cognac, 185
cohere, 36
col, 106
coleslaw, 100
coliseum, 40
colonel, 41
colossal, 40
complacent, 29
complain, 167
complicate, 173
compose, comprise, 119
condominium, 147
confiscate, 173
congress, 30
conquistador, 163
consider, 23
consummate, 25
contrite, contrition, 24
contrive, 120
contumacious, 64
conurbation, 64
cookie, 61
coolie, 53
copious, 131
copra, 53
cotton, 47
coulee, 27
coup, 199
covet, 10
crag, 61
cravat, 148
creosote, 137
Crescent City [New Orleans, LA], 33
crew, 45
crisis, 9
crisscross, 41
criterion, 7
croissant, 33
cromlech, 123
croupier, 63
crude, crudités, 99
Cu (chemical symbol), 39
cul-de-sac, 140

culminate, 135
cummerbund, 53
cunning, 95
cupidity, 10
curriculum, 9
curry, 53
curtail, 172
dactyl, 169
dainty, 87
damask, 97
damsel, 125
danger, 35
daughter, 197
daunt, 2
dearth, 131
debauch, 88
debut, 46
decamp, 142
decant, 43
decoy, 6
delicatessen, 3
delirium, 109
delphinium, 21
demigod, demijohn, demitasse, 143
democracy, 6
demurrer, 113
denim, 97
denizen, 177
deprecate, 144
dernier cri, 166
Des Moines, IA, 147
desire, 23
detonate, 69
Detroit, MI, 152
deviled, 185
dexter, 12
Diesel, 197
digitalis, 110
dilapidated, 25
dimeter, 169
dinghy, 53
disabuse, 115
disembogue, 127
disgust, 29, 105
disoblige, 77
disparage, 55
disseminate, 114
divan, 46
doctor, 61
dolabriform, 51
dollar, 80
dotage, dotard, dote, 181
dour, 166, 211

dreadnought, 137
drub, 41
Dudelsack, 112
duel, 20
duffel, 67
Duluth, MN, 181, 184
dungaree, 53, 97
dungeon, 33
easel, 152
ebullient, 74
ecclesia, 73
ecru, 99
eerie, 87
eggnog, 115
Eiffel Tower, 15
elbow, 71
eleemosynary, 73
elicit, 145
elite, 57
ell, 71
elope, 21
El Paso, TX, 146
El Sobrante, CA, 125
embarrass, 60
emblements, 199
embouchure, 175
embrocate, 9
emeritus, 27
emolument, 51
emulate, 149
encyclopedia, 151
enervate, 16
England, 91, 167
English horn, 95
enigma, 148
ennui, 133
ensiform, 3
enthusiasm, 199
epaulet, 26
Episcopal, 119, 211
equine, 73
era, 133
Erie, PA, 149
ersatz, 35
Escalator®, 54
Eskimo, 107
espionage, 18
esquire, 179
essay, 68
estray, 56
et al., 104
étagère, 1
etiquette, 75
eugenics, 64

innuendo, 12
insinuate, 165
insouciant, 20
instigate, 106
insulin, 24
interloper, 21
intimidate, 91
intoxicate, 47
intrepid, 149
investigator, 146
inveterate, 31
invidious, 62
ipse dixit, 65
irascible, irate, 29
irredentist, 11
isinglass, 25
isthmus, 81
Izvestia, 189
jaguar, 36
jai alai, 164
jalousie, 154
janizary, 3
Japan, 83
jasmine, 46
je ne sais quoi, 16
jipijapa, 59
jocose, jocular, jocund, 114
jodhpurs, 153
joke, 114
joust, 155
juggernaut, 149
July, 165
jumbo, 197
jungle, 53
K (chemical symbol), 39
kamikaze, 43
karate, 115
kayak, 107
keen, 158
ketchup, 56
khaki, 46, 68
kibitzer, 176
kimono, 156
kindergarten, 25
knapsack, 153
Kosciusko, MS, 173
kosher, 176, 181
Kremlin, 122
kudzu, 43
labyrinth, 157
lachrymose, 110
laconic, 75
lacrosse, 177
lacuna, 52

ladrone, 191
lady, 197
lagniappe, 11
lahar, 191
laird, 189
laissez faire, 45
lasagna, 178
laser, 161
lassitude, 94
launch, 152, 153
lb., 149
Lebensraum, 23
ledger, 9
legend, 159
leitmotif, 11
lemon, 46
lens, 10
Lent, 167, 168
Lhasa apso, 146
lien, 49
lilac, 46
Lilliputian, 144
Lincoln, NE, 153
linguine, 178
Linzer torte, 28
Little Rock, AR, 53
livid, 84
locus, 81
lollygag, 125
longshoreman, 49
loot, 53
lord, 25
Lord's Prayer, The, 63
lordling, lordly, 165
Los Angeles, CA, 125
louver, 154
lox, 176
lucrative, 128
ludicrous, 89
lugubrious, 135
lumbricalis, 143
lunatic, 187, 208
lurid, 145
machete, 2
Madeira Islands, 73
maelstrom, 79
magazine, 60, 115
magnet, 77
mahout, 131
mai tai, 56
mammoth, 56
man, 179
manicotti, 178
marathon, 168

maraud, 29
marigold, 46
mascot, 86
maser, 161
mattress, 82, 115
Mayday, 45
meager, 113
measly, 82
Mediterranean, 63
Mein Kampf, 83
Memphis, TN, 161
menhaden, 47
menhir, 50
menial, 49
Mensa Society, 67
mesa, 67
mestizo, 69
Miami, FL, 146
miasma, 85
mica, 25
Michigan, 146
midriff, 32
midwife, 196
mien, 66
miércoles, 53
migraine, 23
mile, 51
milliner, 57
minacious, 161
minster, 21
mirabile dictu, 58
misadventure, 130
misandry, 61
miscellaneous, 69
mischief, 130
misogyny, 61
Missouri, 101
modem, 87
Modesto, CA, 147
modicum, 124
mogul, 46, 53
mojo, 11
Monday, 53, 113
mongoose, 45
monsoon, 9
Montana, 161
Montevideo, 29
Monticello, 179
Montpelier, VT, 180
Montreal, Canada, 93
monument, 171
moo goo gai pan, 148
moose, 47
Mormon, 131

specious, 124
spinach, 115
spinster, 104
Spokane, WA, 34
spondaic, 169
spurious, 19
squalid, squalor, 116
squirrel, 103
staccato, 155
stadium, 51
Stalag, 27
stalwart, 69
starboard, 62
stevedore, 178
steward, 172
stigma, 114
stipend, 168
Stonehenge, 125
story (of building), 99
stubborn, 95
stymie, 121
suave, 67
subito, 67
sub rosa, 87
sugar, 47
suitor, 125
supercilious, 144, 184
surfeit, 91
surprise, 180
surrey, 95
surtax, 94
sushi, 141
suspicion, 138
sutler, 85
svelte, 51
Swahili, 175
swain, 176
symposium, 199
synecdoche, 77
synthesis, 9
syrup, 47
Tabasco, 38
tabernacle, 167
table d'hôte, 5
tabula rasa, 86
taffeta, 46
Taj Mahal, 27
talisman, 134
Tallahassee, FL, 90
tantamount, 33
tarentella, 166
target, 31
tarmac, 134
tarnish, 76

TASS, 189
tatter, 83
taurine, 73
tawdry, 19
ten-penny nails, 189
tepee, 47
tequila, 101
Texas, 121
thesaurus, 60, 77
thesis, 9
thimble, 112
thrall, 83
ticket, 75
timid, timorous, 91
tinsel, 30
tmesis, 81
toddy, 53
tomahawk, 47
tomato, 115
tornado, 69
tort, tortfeasor, 128
torte, 28
town, 26
trade winds, 59
tragedy, 20
transmogrify, 71
trencherman, 111
trepidation, 86
trimeter, trochaic, 169
turban, 46
Tuscaloosa, AL, 196
tweed, 191
tycoon, 35
tympani, 79
typhoon, 35
ubiquitous, 100
ukulele, 180
umbilicus, 187
unagi, 35
Urdu, 167
ursine, 73
usher, 146
uxorious, 114
vacuum, 17
vagina, 31
valiant, 141
vamoose, 141
vandal, 55
vanilla, 31
Vaseline®, 110, 188
veal, 165
vellum, 165
vendetta, 153
Venezuela, 93

veranda, 43
verbiage, 130
verdure, 69
vermicelli, 178
Vermont, 109
vermouth, 185
vestige, 146
vicar, 51
vichyssoise, 25
Vietnam, 41
vignette, 90
villain, villien, 82
-ville (placename suffix), 121
vindicate, 66, 213
vinegar, 50
virago, 21
Virgin Islands, 7
virtual, 102
virulent, 86
vitiate, 72
vitriol, 125
vituperate, 137
vodka, 77
volley, 180
volt, 59
votary, 130
voyage, 29
vulpine, 73
W (chemical symbol), 39
wapiti, 47
wappenschawing, 11
ward, warden, 112
warlock, 108, 167
Wednesday, 53, 113
werewolf, 22
whisk, 56
whiskey, 77
-wich (placename suffix), 121
wife, 196
wordhoard, 48
Wunderkind, 114
Wyoming, 193
yacht, 87
zenith, 49, 115
zero, 47
ziggurat, 171
ZIP code, 195
wordhoard, 48
Word Pairs
  almighty:omnipotent, 31
  amicable:friendly, 31
  anger:ire, 185
  arctic:ursine, 187
  behead:decapitate, 185

ABOUT THE AUTHORS

Horace G. Danner is from Clio, in South Alabama. Fascination with words and how they developed has been his lifelong passion. He received a BA in Social Sciences from University of the Philippines, Quezon City, and holds a Ph.D. in Education from American University, Washington, DC. He teaches a number of writing courses for University of Maryland University College, Adelphi, MD.

He is a retired Chief Master Sergeant of the United States Air Force.

Dr. Danner has published his memoirs, *Out of the Cotton Fields: and into the Classroom*.

Roger Noël, a native of Belgium, grew up speaking French and Walloon. He received a Ph.D. in French Language and Literature from Washington University, St. Louis, MO. Proficient in Dutch, English, German, Italian, Latin, and Greek, Dr. Noël is chairperson of the Department of Modern Foreign Languages, Georgia College and State University, Milledgeville, GA.

Both authors have collaborated on *The English Tree of Roots: And Words from Around the World*, and *A Thesaurus of Medical Word Roots*, both available from Occoquan Books at www.occoquanbooks.com.